The Collected Works
of
Saint John of the Cross

CHRIST CRUCIFIED
A DRAWING BY ST. JOHN OF THE CROSS

The Collected Works

of

Saint John of the Cross

REVISED EDITION

Translated by
Kieran Kavanaugh, O.C.D.
and
Otilio Rodriguez, O.C.D.

With Revisions and Introductions by
Kieran Kavanaugh, O.C.D.

ICS Publications
Institute of Carmelite Studies
Washington, D.C.

Institute of Carmelite Studies

ICS Publications
2131 Lincoln Road NE
Washington, D.C. 20002-1199

Library of Congress Cataloguing in Publication Data

John of the Cross, Saint, 1542-1591
    [Works. English. 1991]
    The collected works of St. John of the Cross/
translated by Kieran Kavanaugh and Otilio Rodriguez;
with introductions by Kieran Kavanaugh. – Rev. ed.
          p.   cm.
    Translation of: Obras de San Juan de la Cruz
    Includes bibliographical references and index.
    ISBN: 0-935216-15-4 (hard.)
    ISBN: 0-935216-14-6 (pbk)
    1. Mysticism—Catholic Church 2. Catholic
    Church—Doctrines.
I. Title II. Title: Collected works of Saint John of the Cross.
BX890.J623313   1991
230'.2—dc20   90-26713
                                       CIP

CONTENTS

THE DARK NIGHT

THE SPIRITUAL CANTICLE

THE LIVING FLAME OF LOVE

SPECIAL COUNSELS

LETTERS

GLOSSARY AND INDICES

FOREWORD

The Collected Works of St. John of the Cross first appeared, in a one volume edition, in 1964. Since then numerous reprintings have been made in both hardback and paperback. In 1979, our publishers printed a second edition that added an index and two brief, previously unknown letters.

During the years that our English translation has been in print, major advances in sanjuanist scholarship have occurred, and new popular critical editions of John's works have come out. Now, at the fourth centenary celebration of the death of St. John of the Cross in 1591, seems the appropriate time to provide further enlightenment for his readers by incorporating the recent research into a revised English translation.

To begin with, I have followed the practice in the new Spanish editions of changing the order in which John's works appear. Editors are now reminding readers of the benefit of reading the poems first and letting the symbolism speak, before going on to the treatises and commentaries. John never intended his readers to restrict themselves to his commentaries, although certainly his explanations are of inestimable value; they greatly expand our horizons. Also, in the new Spanish editions, the *Sayings of Light and Love* precede the larger works. Before undertaking the latter, John gave spiritual guidance in writing through brief, compact counsels that were like dense summaries of his oral teaching. These maxims overflow with spiritual wisdom and whet the appetite for more; they prepare the way for his major works.

With the passing of years, I began thinking that it would be more beneficial to the reader if some of the information in the introductions were in footnotes at the appropriate place. Doing so in this edition gave me an opportunity to include new information about doctrine and sources and some helpful cross-references. Also, in the back of the book is a glossary of terms that gives the reader further explanations and references to some of John of the Cross's terminology.

Since our book first appeared, a number of new English translations of the Bible have come into general use. Their editors use the normal English spelling of Bible names in preference to that based on the Latin Vulgate. I have used this more common spelling and, when necessary, have adjusted the scriptural references. Especially in the psalms, the numbering in the Latin Vulgate differs from that of the Hebrew Scriptures, which the new translations follow. St. John of the Cross read and quoted Scripture from the Latin Vulgate and then made his own—at times quite free—translations into Spanish. Occasionally his biblical passages seem to be far from the reading offered in present-day versions. In such cases the reader may find something closer to John's by consulting a Rheims-Douay version.

A particularly sensitive problem today is the question of discrimination in language. At present there is little agreement about the best way to deal with many of the difficulties this poses. Since any piece of writing is a product of a particular time and culture, the views expressed in it and the language in which they are expressed reflect a cultural conditioning, often quite different from contemporary ideas and concerns. I have preserved John's traditional and biblical ways of speaking about God and Christ, which often have a profound theological import, and his use of masculine nouns and pronouns. But writers of English, more and more, shun the use of the masculine singular pronoun for the generic. Fidelity to John's thought poses no dilemma in this regard; writing in Spanish, he did not use the masculine for the generic since he expresses the pronoun by inflecting the verb and without specifying gender. In various ways, I have avoided the masculine generic by recasting the sentence. Besides some other stylistic changes, I revised passages that were not as clear as they might have been or where by being more literal I could bring out nuances lost in a freer rendering.

In preparing this revised edition I made continual use of two particularly valuable Spanish editions of the works of St. John of the Cross: *San Juan de la Cruz: Obras Completas,* eds. José Vicente Rodriguez and Federico Ruiz Salvador (Madrid: Editorial de Espiritualidad, 1980); and *San Juan de la Cruz: Obras Completas,* ed., Eulogio Pacho (Burgos: Editorial Monte Carmelo, 1982). These editions are so special because of their introductions, notes, and revisions of the text. I owe a debt of gratitude to these editors.

Thanks are due to David Malkovsky, Sr. Joseph Marie of the Trinity, H.T. and Jude Langsam for their work on the indexing and production of this volume. In addition, I owe many thanks to my colleagues in the Institute of Carmelite Studies, especially Fr. Steven Payne, O.C.D., who offered some excellent suggestions, and Fr. Regis Jordan, O.C.D., who, by attending to many time-consuming details, enabled me to concentrate on the revision itself. I regret that Fr. Otilio Rodriguez's health did not allow him to work with me on this. My hope is that this revised volume will continue to inspire and enlighten students and devotees of the teachings of St. John of the Cross, the Church's Mystical Doctor.

Kieran Kavanaugh, O.C.D.
Carmelite Monastery
Boston, Massachusetts

Abbreviations in references: A=Ascent of Mount Carmel; N=Dark Night; C=Spiritual Canticle; F=Living Flame; P=Poetry; S=Sayings of Light and Love; Pr=Precautions; L=Letters. The levels of division of a work (book, chapter, paragraph number; or stanza, paragraph number) are separated by periods; successions of references on the same level are separated by commas; hyphens separate continuing numbers.

GENERAL INTRODUCTION

BIOGRAPHICAL SKETCH

The Early Years

On an unknown day, the month uncertain, in 1542, Juan de Yepes was born in a small town called Fontiveros. It lay on rocky and barren land in the central plateau of Old Castile midway between Madrid and Salamanca. With a population of about 5,000, the town included some small weaving shops. Juan's father, Gonzalo de Yepes, who belonged to a wealthy family of silk merchants in Toledo, had stopped in Fontiveros on a business journey to Medina del Campo, and there met Catalina Alvarez, a weaver of poor and humble background. Despite the difference in their status, the two fell in love and married in 1529. Shocked and disturbed by what they considered shameful—a marriage to a girl of low position—the merchant family disinherited Gonzalo. Deprived of financial security, he had to adapt to the drudgery of the poor, which in his case meant the lowly trade of weaving. Under these trying circumstances, both Gonzalo and Catalina had to find strength in their mutual friendship and intimacy.

The couple had three sons: Francisco, Luis, and the youngest, Juan (later to be known as St. John of the Cross). But John was little more than two years old when his father died, worn out from the terrible suffering of a long illness. Reduced to penury, the young widow—afflicted but courageous—set out with hope on a tiring journey to visit the wealthy members of her husband's family, to beg assistance in her dire need. Rejected by them, she had to manage as best she could on her own in Fontiveros. During this time John's brother Luis died, perhaps as a result of insufficient nourishment. Catalina then felt constrained to try elsewhere, abandoning her little home and moving to Arévalo, where things were hardly an improvement, and finally to Medina del Campo, the bustling market center of Castile, where she resumed her work of weaving.

Here John entered a school for poor children where he received an elementary education, principally of Christian doctrine, and had the opportunity to become an apprentice in some trade or profession. The school resembled an orphananange where the children received food,

9

clothing, and lodging. At this time, the priest who was the director of the school chose John to serve as an acolyte at La Magdalena, a nearby monastery of Augustinian nuns. While on duty, the young boy assisted in the sacristy for four hours in the morning, and in the afternoons whenever the superior, the chaplain, or the sacristan needed him. As for the apprenticeships—in carpentry, tailoring, sculpturing, and paint-ing—John showed no enthusiasm. Rather, his gentleness and patience led to the discovery of his gift for compassion toward the sick. Don Alonso Alvarez, administrator of the hospital in Medina for poor people with the plague or other contagious diseases, took an interest in John and enlisted his services as nurse and alms-collector.

Don Alonso also provided John with the opportunity for further study. At age 17, the bright young lad enrolled at the Jesuit school, where lectures in grammar, rhetoric, Latin, and Greek were the rule. The future poet came in contact with Latin and Spanish classics, a contact that was anything but superficial, since the Jesuits insisted on high standards and an abundance of exercises, reading, and composition. Becoming ac-quainted with classical imagery, the gifted pupil learned about literary technique and opened himself to the world around him. These years of hospital work and study, tasks that called for responsibility and diligence, complemented John's early experiences of poverty.

Carmelite Vocation

When John finished his studies, Don Alonso offered him a secure future: ordination to the priesthood and the post of chaplain at the hospital. In turn, the young man could have then assisted his mother and brother out of their poverty, a goal toward which he must have felt the strongest urgings. The Jesuits, who appreciated his intellectual gifts and piety, also made their overtures. But surprisingly, in 1563, at age 21, John entered the Carmelite novitiate recently founded in Medina. What prompted this unexpected decision was probably Carmel's contempla-tive spirit and its devotion to Mary, the mother of God.

Receiving the name Fray (Brother) John of St. Matthias, he passed his novitiate year, we can suppose, studying the Carmelite Rule and the order's ancient spirituality. In *The Book of the First Monks,* a medieval Carmelite work on the spirit of the order that John must have pondered over during his novitiate, the following teaching stands out:

> The goal of this life is twofold. One part we acquire, with the
> help of divine grace, through our efforts and virtuous works.
> This is to offer God a pure heart, free from all stain of actual sin.
> We do this when we are perfect and in Cherith, that is, hidden

in that charity of which the Wise Man says: "Charity covers all sins" [Prov. 10:12]. God desired Elijah to advance thus far when he said to him: "Hide yourself by the brook Cherith" [1 Kgs. 17:3-4]. The other part of the goal of this life is granted us as the free gift of God: namely, to taste somewhat in the heart and to experience in the soul, not only after death but even in this mortal life, the intensity of the divine presence and the sweetness of the glory of heaven. This is to drink of the torrent of the love of God. God promised it to Elijah in the words: "You shall drink from the brook." It is in view of this double end that the monk ought to give himself to the eremitic and prophetic life.

It must have been toward the end of 1564 that John of St. Matthias, after his novitiate year, arrived in Salamanca for studies in philosophy and theology. The sight of the university town with its churches and cathedrals, palaces and lordly estates undoubtedly thrilled him. In its period of greatest splendor, the university of Salamanca boasted professors of high prestige, large numbers of students from all parts of Spain, an emphasis on biblical and theological studies, and a variety of schools of thought. It ranked with the great universities of Bologna, Paris, and Oxford. There you would find Fray Luis de León, who taught theology in the chair of Durando; Mancio de Corpus Christi, a worthy successor of Vitoria and of Melchor Cano, who held the chair of Prime, the most important in the university; the Augustinian Juan de Guevara, who gave the afternoon lecture and whose explanations were called miraculous; Gregorio Gallo, in place of Domingo Soto, who took over the chair of Sacred Scripture; and Cristóbal Vela, who gave lectures on Scotus.

John's name appears on the matriculation records in the school of arts for three years. Knowledge has reached us about the courses that were offered there and the names of the eminent men who held professorships. Master Enrique Hernández, the author of a treatise on philosophy, taught the classes in natural philosophy; Francisco Navarro held the chair of ethics; Hernando Aguilera, who had worked out an astrolabe, reigned in the chair of astronomy; Francisco Sanchez taught grammar and even today is considered an authority on this subject; Master Martin de Peralta explained the *Summulas* (an introduction to logic); and Juan de Ubredo held the chair of music.

The statutes of the university prescribed the works of Aristotle for the arts course, but this merely meant that a text from the Philosopher was to be read at the beginning of the lecture; the professor could then go on to interpret it with full liberty, if not leave it aside entirely. It is not known, though, which classes John actually followed in the arts course.

In the school year 1567-68, John registered in theology. Again, no record tells of the courses he took. He would probably have assisted at the

Prime lecture, which went on for an hour and a half, beginning early in the morning. At this lecture, the Dominican Mancio de Corpus Christi explained the *Summa theologiae* of St. Thomas Aquinas. He followed the method and style of the Dominican school initiated by Vitoria and Cano. It comprised a return to the sources (Sacred Scripture, the Fathers of the Church, and Aquinas) along with a concern for dealing with new themes and contemporary questions. This theology was expressed in sober and direct language. Whether John might have attended Gaspar Grajal's lectures in Sacred Scripture is a matter for speculation. At the time there was a lively struggle within the university over the interpretation of Scripture. The "scholastics," tenacious partisans of fidelity to the biblical tradition of the preceding centuries, opposed the "scripturists," who sought the literal sense of Scripture through development of scientific methods and the study of languages. Grajal was prominent among the "scripturists" and later, because of his ideas, was sent to prison for a time by the Inquisition.

Besides studies at the university, the Carmelite students, like all religious, had to study at home the doctors belonging to their own order, especially John Baconthorp (c. 1290-1348)—a grandnephew of Roger Bacon—who had taught at the University of Cambridge.

We are told that Fray John was remarkable for his "outstanding talent" and application, testimony bolstered by his appointment as prefect of studies while still a student. With this office went the obligation to teach class daily, defend public theses, and resolve objections that were raised.

But for some reason the brilliant young Carmelite was dissatisfied. Was it with the academic atmosphere where the pursuit of knowledge too easily turned into a pursuit of self-exaltation, a quest for titles, chairs, promotions, and awards? Was John beginning to discern there a stubborn attachment to familiar systems of thought, and a reluctance to admit the ultimate inadequacy of all speculations? Was this what he had sought in making his vows? In any case, his horizons lay elsewhere; he found his attention turning frequently to the purely contemplative Carthusians. Though John enjoyed his studies, the contemplative life that had originally attracted him to Carmel was now struggling for first place.

The Teresian Ideal

In 1567, at the time of this vocational crisis, Fray John was ordained a priest and came to Medina to sing his first Mass. There, in the early part of autumn, the fateful meeting with Madre Teresa de Jesús took place. In the city for the foundation of a second community of nuns who would make profession of the Carmelite life according to the new contemplative style that she had developed in Avila, the determined Madre was now weighing the possibility of extending this mode of life to the friars. Having been told of John's exceptional qualities, she arranged for an interview with him. She was 52 at the time; he was 25. Hearing about his aspirations toward more solitude and prayer and about his thought of transferring to the Carthusians, she pointed out to him that he could find all he was seeking without leaving "Our Lady's order," and with her characteristic zeal and friendliness she spoke to him animatedly of her plan to adapt this new way of life for friars. Fray John listened, he felt inspired, caught the enthusiasm, and beheld a new future opening before him. He promised to join Teresa, but on one condition—that he would not have long to wait. Teresa rejoiced over the eagerness of her young recruit and his unwillingness to delay, he who was later to write a treatise on how to reach union with God quickly.

The following year, in August, she set off with a small group from Medina to Valladolid, where she intended to make another foundation; and traveling with them to learn more about this new Carmelite life was Fray John, now finished with his studies.

Teresa's ideal of founding small communities, in contrast to her former monastery of the Incarnation at Avila where as many as 180 nuns lived, had its background in a larger movement of reform that had spread through sixteenth-century Spain. Certain common characteristics marked the spirit of this Spanish reform: the return to one's origins, primitive rules, and founders; a life lived in community with practices of poverty, fasting, silence, and enclosure; and, as the most important part, the life of prayer. People used different terms to designate the new communities that had these traits: reformed, observant, recollect, discalced, hermit, contemplative. The name "discalced" became the popular one in referring to Teresa's nuns and friars because of their practice of wearing sandals rather than shoes.

These efforts at reforming religious life began in the fifteenth century in response to the upheavals in religious life caused by the Black Death. The early attempts carried an anti-intellectual strain, placing emphasis on affectivity, external ceremonies, devotions, and community vocal prayer. But long hours of community vocal prayer day after day became tedious and mechanical. The only noticeable fruit was the desire for something different, more time for interior prayer. As a matter of fact, a new practice called "recollection," whose followers were called "recogidos," developed in many Franciscan houses. This spirituality made union with God through love its most important concern, seeking nourishment in Scripture and classic spiritual works. These latter works— by authors such as Augustine, Gregory the Great, Bernard, and Bonaventure—appeared in print at the time from newly established presses.

The Franciscan friar Francisco de Osuna elaborated this spirituality in *The Third Spiritual Alphabet,* a book that inspired Teresa and initiated her into the way of interior prayer. Osuna taught that to advance spiritually you must practice recollection in imitation of Jesus Christ, who went alone into the desert to pray secretly. By this recollection, also called mental prayer, Osuna explained, you withdraw from people and noise and enter within yourself.

But the mystical graces God began to give Teresa (despite her waverings and after she persevered for many years through countless struggles to devote two hours to mental prayer each day) taught her more than all her books. Only with Jesus Christ could she enter the inner castle through prayer; there he became increasingly present as she advanced toward the inmost dwelling place. Presence to Christ was what made prayer for Teresa, in the beginning stages, in the middle, and in the highest as well. "Never leave Christ in whom the human and divine are joined, and who is always one's companion," she warned the theologians who began to come to her to learn about contemplation. "He is the one through whom all blessings come. He is always looking at you; can you not turn the eyes of your soul to look at him?"

Her communities, too, had no meaning without Jesus Christ in the center. They were to be small communities; only 12 nuns at first, gathered around Christ as his friends. No class distinctions! These class divisions characterized women's cloisters in those times, ruled by the nobility, as was the case at the Incarnation. In Jesus Christ all were to be equal, Teresa insisted, and the superior the first to take her turn sweeping the floor.

By this time the Madre had written two books of her own: one for her spiritual directors, her *Life,* in which she carefully analyzed all the stages of prayer and explained many of the mystical graces given her by God, bearing testimony that His Majesty never tires of giving; the other for her nuns, *The Way of Perfection,* in which she laid out the kind of life and prayer they were to live together, not only for their own sanctification but for the Church whose troubles distressed her as much as the thought of Christ's own sufferings. For Teresa the sufferings of the Church were the sufferings of Christ.

How much there was, then, for John of St. Matthias to learn from this humble, simple, awesome nun. Teresa, for her part, marvelled as she got to know the small friar better. "Though he is small in stature, I believe that he is great in God's eyes," she wrote at the time. John was speaking so knowingly and brilliantly about the wonders of God and the mysteries of the divine goodness that the group began to refer to him as "God's archives."

There were also differences between the Madre and her first friar, and she admits to having become vexed with him at times. She had wanted learned men for her new communities of friars so that they might be good guides not only through experience of the same style of life but through their learning. Having suffered much from the vincible ignorance of her confessors, Teresa was keen to spare her daughters anything similar. John, at the time, tended to stress the limitations of learning. Teresa thought an expert was a person with a degree who knew a lot about something; John didn't seem to think anybody knew much about anything—an expert was someone who knew the mistakes that could be made and how to avoid them. Fearing that austerities and penances might frighten university students away from her new friars, Teresa insisted on a balanced life in which the Christian virtues such as charity, detachment, and humility would receive far more favor than austerities. Austerities in those times were closely associated with sanctity, and John, though recognizing Teresa's claims, leaned toward austerities, which reforming friars also liked to think of as the manly path. Later, in his writings, John too was to treat austerities with a certain skepticism, pointing out how, along with so many other good things, they can end up wrecking the spiritual life. Teresa thought that Christian joy ought to permeate her communities; the nuns took time for recreation together each day, and sang and wrote poetry for one another. There was no reason for them to be somber. "Be affable, agreeable, and pleasing to persons with whom you deal," Teresa warmly counseled, "so that all will love your conversation and desire your manner of living and acting." John needed time to get used to this.

Recitation of the Divine Office was much simpler in Teresa's communities than it had been at the Incarnation. This allowed an hour in the morning and an hour in the evening for mental prayer. Like the early hermits on Mount Carmel, the nuns lived their day mostly in silence and solitude, alone in their cells, engaging in the manual labor of spinning to help support themselves. But Teresa's friars' daily routine would differ because she wanted them to engage in study and preaching and the ministry of the sacraments.

As in her writings, then, during these days from mid-August to October, Teresa energetically fulfilled her role as teacher, although she confessed she felt that Fray John was so good she could have learned more from him than he from her. On finishing his brief "novitiate" under the Madre's guidance, John of St. Matthias left Valladolid with a new Teresian ardor to start work on converting into a monastery the little farmhouse Teresa acquired for her first friars. It was situated in a lonely spot called Duruelo, midway between Avila and Salamanca. By the end of November Fray John had transformed the small house with its porch, main room, alcove, garret, and tiny kitchen into the first monastery for discalced Carmelite friars. On November 28, 1568, with a young deacon and Fray Antonio de Heredia (who had been prior in Medina), in the presence of the provincial, Fray John of St. Matthias embraced the new life, promising to live without mitigation according to the ancient Carmelite Rule. At that time he changed his name to John of the Cross.

The following spring the provincial appointed Fray Antonio prior and Fray John novice master, and in the autumn two novices arrived. The house then became too small, so the community moved to the nearby town of Mancera de Abajo in June 1570. In this year John also traveled to Pastrana to help organize another novitiate, and within a year moved to Alcalá de Henares to set up a house of studies for the new friars near the famous university of Alcalá. He became its first rector, guiding the students in their studies and spiritual development. Right from the beginning, then, John dedicated himself to a task of immediate urgency, spiritual direction. With his Bible, his experience, and his penetrating grasp of both philosophy and theology, he began to ponder spiritual growth, observing the ways of human beings, discerning the ways of God.

His work now had to expand. Teresa, who had recently been sent by the visitator, Pedro Fernández, to take up duties as prioress at the Incarnation in Avila, received permission to enlist the help of Fray John of the Cross as confessor and skilled spiritual director for the large number of nuns there. It was a community weighed down with many economic and social problems. Fernández, a Dominican, was acting as visitator to the Carmelites in Castile by order of Pope Pius V, who entrusted their reform to Dominican friars. Another Dominican, Francisco Vargas, was responsible for the Carmelites in Andalusia. These visitators had ample powers. They could move religious from house to house and province to province, assist superiors in their offices, and depute other superiors from either the Dominicans or the Carmelites. They were entitled to perform all acts necessary for the "visitation, correction, and reform of both head and members of all houses of friars and nuns." A deep mutual respect and easy working relationship developed between the tactful and diplomatic Fernández and Teresa.

Toward the end of May 1572, John of the Cross arrived in Avila and entered the feminine religious world, a world that was to become his special field of spiritual ministry. This ministry included guiding Teresa herself. From her he received as much as he gave in those years of profound and open conversation, a conversation that once on Trinity Sunday so soared that the two not only went into ecstasy but were seen elevated from the ground.

On November 18, 1572, while John was her director, Teresa unexpectedly received the grace of spiritual marriage. She was now in the seventh and final dwelling place of her spiritual journey; there in the center room of the interior castle she came to know the highest state of intimacy with God.

The experience of those years, when from so privileged a position the confessor could see God's work in Teresa, left more of a trace in John's later writings than one might first suppose. With the exception of the Bible, Teresa provided a source more enlightening than all of the books Fray John had studied. And she herself did not hold back from extolling the gifts of her director, referring to him in a letter as a "divine and heavenly man" and affirming that she had found no spiritual director like him in all Castile. There they were in Avila, Teresa and John; so much alike, so very different, destined in their writings to complement each other.

John's spiritual direction ministry also extended into the city, to a wide range of people, including well-known sinners. He tried to find time for everyone, even the children of the poor. Remembering his own childhood, he gathered these children and taught them to read and write.

Conflicts of Jurisdiction

King Philip II was himself curiously involved in the reform of religious orders and this led to a chain of misunderstandings, to a dark night for the small friar. Fernández had exercised his authority prudently and in harmony with the Carmelite provincial of Castile. In the south, proceeding independently, Francisco Vargas requested the discalced friars to make foundations in Sevilla, Granada, and La Peñuela (all in Andalusia), an action contrary to the prior general's explicit orders against the expansion of the discalced friars into that region. At a chapter of the order convened in Piacenza (Italy) in May 1575, the Carmelite order came to some strong decisions about all that they had heard was taking place in Spain, particularly in Andalusia. Unfortunately the two provincials from Castile and Andalusia, who might have been able to cast some light on the events, were absent. So the ordinances stipulated that those who had been made superiors "against the obedience due superiors within the order itself, or who had accepted offices or lived in monasteries or places prohibited by the same superiors should be removed, with the aid of the secular arm if necessary." Those resisting would be considered disobedient, rebellious, and contumacious, and were to be severely punished. Jerónimo Tostado was appointed the order's visitator to Spain, with full powers to carry out the decrees of the chapter.

In a papal brief in August of the previous year, at the request of the Carmelite order Gregory XIII had declared an end to the Dominican visitation and had ordained that from then on the Carmelites should be visited by the prior general and his delegates, leaving in effect what had been established by the visitators. But the king was not pleased. Why hadn't this matter been presented to him first for his royal *placet?* In due time the papal nuncio Nicolás Ormaneto, working closely with the king, received assurance that as nuncio he still had powers to visit and reform religious orders. Ormaneto appointed Jerónimo Gracián (a learned priest from the university of Alcalá who had entered the discalced Carmelites and became a close collaborator with Teresa in many of her business affairs) as the new visitator to the Carmelites in Andalusia.

After Teresa's term as prioress at the Incarnation ended, John was ordered by the nuncio to remain at the Incarnation because (it seems) of the excellent work he was doing there. In view of the chapter of Piacenza, John realized that his presence was a cause of tension and sought a change. In fact, he was arrested by the Carmelites of the observance in January 1576, but then released through the nuncio's intervention. Whatever the reason, he remained on, and when Ormaneto, the nuncio, died in June 1577, John was without a defender and his presence in Avila was increasingly resented by those who held that it contradicted the ordinances of Piacenza.

It wasn't long before something was done. On the night of December 2, 1577, a group of Carmelites, lay people, and men-at-arms broke into the chaplain's quarters, seized Fray John, and took him away. By a secret journey, with orders from Tostado, they carted him off, handcuffed and often blindfolded, to the monastery in Toledo, the order's finest in Castile, where nearly 85 friars lived. The acts of the chapter in Piacenza were read aloud to John by which he stood accused of being rebellious and contumacious. He would have to submit, or undergo severe punishment. But the accused friar reasoned that the chapter acts did not apply to him because he was at the Incarnation by order of legitimate authority, and he certainly was not obliged to renounce the way of life he had embraced along with Teresa. The punishment he received was imprisonment, according to the constitutions.

His accusers locked him first in the monastery prison, but at the end of two months, for fear of an escape, they moved him to another spot, a room narrow and dark, without air or light except for whatever filtered through a small slit high up in the wall. The room was six feet wide and ten feet long. There John remained alone, without anything but his breviary, through the terribly cold winter months and the suffocating heat of summer. Added to all this were the floggings, fasting on bread and water, wearing the same bedraggled clothes month after month without being washed—and the lice. Teresa wrote to the king and pleaded that for the love of God he order Fray John set free at once.

In the midst of this deprivation, Fray John was seeking relief by composing poetry in his mind, leaving to posterity some of the greatest lyric stanzas in Spanish literature—among them a major portion of *The Spiritual Canticle*. These verses suggest that in that cramped prison, stripped of all earthly comfort, he was touched with some rays of divine light. The cramped conditions faded, the friar's awareness expanded. "My beloved, the mountains." Here too, in the dark emptiness, a spiritual synthesis began to flower. "Faith and love will lead you along a path unknown to you, to the place where God is hidden." Everything else gone, no one could divest him of these, and they gave him God.

Taking advantage of a new jailer who was kinder and more lenient, John managed to get paper and ink so as to write down his poems. He also had the opportunity, during a daily reprieve from his cell, to familiarize himself with the monastery surroundings. Then, one hot night in August, after being held prisoner for nine months, emaciated and close to death, John chose life and undertook a dangerous escape he had plotted during the short periods out of his cell. He had discovered a window that looked down on the Tajo river, and underneath the window was the top of a wall. But, of course, there was a lock on his prison door. He solved that problem by loosening the screws of the lock while his jailer was absent. When the friars seemed to be asleep and the house all still, he pushed hard on the door of his prison and the lock came loose. This enabled him to leave his prison and find his way in the dark to the window. By means of a kind of rope made out of strips torn from two old bed covers and attached to a lamp hook, he escaped through the window onto the top of the wall. The wall encircled the monastery and its garden, so he walked around the top of it until he came to what he thought was the street side. There he jumped from the wall, only to find himself in another bad predicament. He had landed inside the courtyard of the Franciscan nuns of the Conception monastery that was adjacent to that of the Carmelites. Fortunately, in one corner of the nuns' garden he found that the stones in the wall could be used as steps, allowing him to climb over the wall to the city street and to his freedom. Some claimed his escape was miraculous. At any rate he was able to find refuge first with Teresa's nuns in Toledo and then, through their intervention, at the nearby hospital of Santa Cruz, where he was cared for secretly.

The new nuncio, Felipe Sega, not at all like his predecessor, showed displeasure with Teresa, and especially her friars, who already numbered more than 300 members. With Tostado's help he explored ways to bring about some kind of order. In October 1578, nearly desperate, the discalced friars convened a chapter in Almodóvar del Campo, southwest of Toledo, despite doubts about its legality. They merely wanted, they claimed, to execute what they had agreed on in a previous chapter called by Gracián in 1576, while Ormaneto was still alive. The fugitive Fray John of the Cross was appointed vicar of El Calvario, a monastery situated in a mountainous solitude near Beas in Andalusia. Here he would be safer against any attempts to recapture him.

When Sega learned of the chapter at Almodóvar he declared it null and void, angrily sent Gracián and others to prison, and placed the discalced friars and nuns under the authority of the provincial of the observant Carmelites. But the king had already set up a maneuver to dampen Sega's ardor: a commission to study the accusations against the discalced. In April 1579 the commission reached its decision, appointing Angel de Salazar, a former provincial of the observant Carmelites, in charge of Teresa's friars and nuns. Teresa rejoiced in the appointment, and Gracián praised Salazar as a gentle and discreet man whose main concern was to console the afflicted and promote peace.

Poet and Spiritual Father

John must have felt consolation and peace when a year and a few months previous to this he arrived to take up his office at El Calvario, a place of spectacular beauty far away from the jurisdictional conflicts and threats. He never cared to go over the past and talk about his imprisonment. He bore no animosity; he neither complained nor boasted about what he had endured. Now more than ever he could listen to nature through his senses; the flowers, the whistling breezes, the night, the dawn, the rushing streams, all spoke to him. God was present everywhere.

But in less than a year he had to move to the city again, this time to the university town of Baeza to serve as rector of the new college for the Teresian friars in the south. Unable to compete with places like Salamanca or Alcalá, the univesrsity of Baeza did enjoy a certain prestige and was making important contributions to Scripture studies. While rector of the Carmelite college (1579-82), John guided his own students in their studies, becoming acquainted as well with the professors at the university. Records reveal that they frequently consulted and had long conversations with him about the Bible.

In these years after his escape, John took up once more the ministry of spiritual direction, not only of the friars but also of the nuns. He made frequent journeys through the mountains to Beas, a typical little Andalusian town with small whitewashed houses, grilles in front of large windows, and balconies full of flowering plants. The town is important in John's life, for here he met Ana de Jesús, the prioress, who did not at first recognize his depth and spirituality. In a letter to Ana, responding to her complaint about having no spiritual director, Teresa made clear her thoughts about Fray John of the Cross:

> I'm really surprised, daughter, at your complaining so un-
> reasonably, when you have Father Fray John of the Cross with
> you, who is a divine, heavenly man. I can tell you, daughter, that
> since he went away I have found no one like him in all Castile,
> nor anyone who inspires people with so much fervor on the way

to heaven. You would not believe how lonely his absence makes me feel. You should reflect that you have a great treasure in that holy man, and all those in the monastery should see him and open their souls to him, when they will see what great good they get and will find themselves to have made great progress in spirituality and perfection, for our Lord has given him a special grace for this [December 1578].

She went on to extol his holiness, kindness, experience, and learning. Soon Ana de Jesús and her nuns affirmed Teresa's words through their own experience. John shared his poems with them, and began the work of commentary through his talks to them on his *Spiritual Canticle*.

While the saintly friar served as rector at Baeza, his discalced brethren, through the intervention of the king, obtained juridical independence. In 1580 the Holy See allowed them to erect an autonomous province, but under the higher jurisdiction of the general of the order. Complete independence did not come until 1593, after the deaths of both Teresa and John, when Pope Clement VIII accorded the discalced Carmelites the same rights and privileges as other religious orders.

In 1582, Fray John was elected prior of a monastery adjacent to the site of the Alhambra, with an outstanding view of the Sierra Nevada and overlooking the enchanting city of Granada with its exotic traces of Moorish culture in evidence everywhere. Here, in addition to leading the community, John designed and worked on a new aqueduct and a new monastery building that became a model for the discalced. At the same time, his ministry of spiritual direction—not only to the friars and nuns but also to the clergy and lay people who came knocking at the monastery door seeking help—set in motion his work as a writer, and he began to compose his classic works of spirituality.

In 1585, at a chapter in Lisbon, John was elected vicar provincial of Andalusia. This office obliged him to travel frequently. He had to attend all the houses of friars and nuns in Andalusia, visiting each formally at least once a year. He founded seven new monasteries. All this brought him to Córdoba, Málaga, Caravaca, Jaén, and other renowned cities in the south of Spain.

Final Years

In the summer of 1588, John was elected third councillor to the vicar general for the discalced, Father Nicolás Doria, and had to return to Segovia in Castile, where in this capacity he was also prior. At his new site, one with a splendid view of Segovia and the surrounding area, he spent a good portion of his time again in manual labor, designing an addition to the monastery, quarrying stone for it, and working on its construction. He no longer wrote, but spent more time in prayer, going off to a cave on the property where he could view the countryside and have solitude for his deep contemplation. He had brought his latest work, *The Living Flame of Love*, to an unexpectedly swift close, confessing that he did not want to explain any further about the breathing of the Holy Spirit in the soul, "for I am aware of being incapable of so doing, and were I to try, it might seem less than it is."

Never one to shun those who came for help, John continued his ministry of spiritual direction; the business matters of the order's government were always claiming attention as well. In fact, these latter sparked another conflict, this time among the discalced themselves. The clash began when Nicolás Doria called an extraordinary chapter in June 1590 for the purpose of undertaking two controversial moves. First he wanted to abandon jurisdiction over the nuns, a reprisal against Madre Ana de Jesús who opposed his plans; Doria had hoped both to make changes in Teresa's constitutions and to govern the nuns through a body of councillors rather than through one friar appointed to the task. Second, he proposed the expulsion of Teresa's close collaborator, Father Jerónimo Gracián, from the discalced Carmelites. Fray John spoke in opposition to both moves. In the chapter the following year, different councillors were elected to assist Doria, and John remained without an office, a fact that was more a problem for others than for himself. When the news got about, some began raising strong protests. But John looked at things differently, as he so often did, and expressed his mind in a letter to the prioress in Segovia:

> Do not let what is happening to me, daughter, cause you any grief, for it does not cause me any. What greatly grieves me is that one who is not at fault is blamed. Men do not do these things, but God, who knows what is suitable for us and arranges things for our own good. Think nothing else but that God ordains all, and where there is no love, put love, and you will draw out love [July 6, 1591].

Doria, in what seemed a rebuff, sent John of the Cross back into Andalusia, to an isolated monastery called La Peñuela, a solitude like Duruelo or El Calvario. However, John was to stay there only in preparation for a mission to Mexico where he was to lead a group of 12 friars. He was happy in the solitude, but some ugly maneuverings began to disturb the peace of his friends, whom he had helped as spiritual director, and shattered the impressive silence of La Peñuela. Fray Diego Evangelista, with bitter resentment against his former superior, was going about threatening and intimidating, trying to gather information against the spiritual friar so as to have him expelled from the discalced. Fray Diego never had time to proceed far with his designs.

In mid-September John began to suffer a slight fever caused by an inflammation of the leg. Thinking it nothing serious, he paid little attention, but when it persisted he was forced to make the journey to Ubeda for the medical assistance that was unavailable at La Peñuela. Given the choice between Baeza and Ubeda, he chose Ubeda, "for at Baeza they know me very well, and in Ubeda nobody knows me." It was the last journey of his life.

The prior of the monastery at Ubeda, Fray Francisco Crisóstomo, did not welcome the sick man. Learned and famous as a preacher, Fray Crisóstomo had his weaknesses, among them a tendency to be mean and rigid. A sick friar was a nuisance and an expense as far as he was concerned, and he showed his vexation; nor did he care for people who were supposedly holy.

John's sickness grew worse. His leg was already ulcerated, and the disease, erysipelas, spread to his back where a new fist-sized tumor formed. On December 13, Fray John of the Cross, knowing that time was running short, called for the prior and begged pardon for all the trouble he had caused. This profoundly changed the prior, who himself then begged forgiveness and left the cell in tears, totally transformed. According to witnesses Fray Francisco Crisóstomo later died in the odor of sanctity.

That same night, when the friars began to recite the prayers for the dying, Fray John of the Cross begged, "No, read some verses from the Song of Songs," and then exclaimed, "Oh, what precious pearls!" At midnight, without agony, without struggle, he died, repeating the words of the psalmist: "Into your hands, O Lord, I commend my spirit." The favors he had asked for in his last years he had now received: not to die as a superior, to die in a place where he was unknown, and to die after having suffered much.

A Portrait of the Saint

These main events in the short life of St. John of the Cross do not leave us with the full picture of his character and personal spirituality. His early first-hand acquaintance with deprivation, the later misunderstandings and imprisonment, the final persecution that he suffered, all might more easily have brought forth a bitter cynic; instead, the result was a man purified and enlightened. Events outwardly sad but inwardly transforming bore fruits in charity toward others and deep compassion for the sufferer. Together with these came a rare, clear vision of the beauty of God's creation and an intimacy with the Blessed Trinity that John found somewhat describable only through comparisons to the life of glory.

But first, regarding the physical appearance of Fray John of the Cross, he was a small man, measuring four feet, eleven inches. Whenever St. Teresa referred to him she seemed almost obliged to use the diminutive. In describing his imprisonment, she writes: "For the whole nine months he was in a small prison where, little as he is, there was not enough room for him to move." He was also thin, but his lean, oval face and his broad forehead, receding into baldness, gave him a venerable appearance. His nose was slightly aquiline, his eyes dark and large. Rounding off this figure of Fray John was his old, rough, brown habit and a white cloak so coarse it seemed made of goat hair.

Marked by the poverty he suffered as a child and even as a friar, he found it hard to ignore others in the distress of material need. With his penitents he did not limit himself to seeking their spiritual good, but he looked for ways to help them when they were in want. Sometimes he gave them alms from the meager funds of the monastery, or sometimes he begged alms for them from other devout people. Noticing once that a priest who came to him for confession was wearing a worn-out cassock, he asked some benefactors for money to buy the priest a new one. He grieved over the poverty of many of the nuns at the Incarnation who didn't have the material resources enjoyed by those from well-to-do families.

One day, entering the convent for his ministry, he saw a nun sweeping the floor barefooted, and doing so not out of penance but because she had no shoes. Immediately he trudged up to the city and asked some charitable persons for money, which he in turn gave to the nun so she could buy shoes for herself. Then there was the year 1584, a year of barrenness and hunger in Andalusia. As prior in Granada John did everything he could to help with either food or money all the needy who came to the monastery gate. Those of higher lineage he helped secretly because, even though in want, they were ashamed to beg openly.

Finding the poor wherever he journeyed, he also found the sick. He began to understand intimately the affliction of the latter during his hospital work as a youth in Medina. Taking pains to show the most delicate sympathy for the sick, he knew how to care for them, comfort them, and give them hope. He would not allow the question of money to interfere with his desire to give his sick friars the best possible care. He once asked a doctor if there were any remedy for a lay brother who was undergoing extraordinary suffering. The doctor answered that the only medicine he knew was very expensive and would do no more than relieve the suffering somewhat. Despite the penury of the community John sent for the medicine and administered it to the sick brother himself, and did so happily. On arriving at a monastery he always made it a point first to greet the sick after his visit to the Blessed Sacrament.

Quick to perceive sadness or depression in another and eager to comfort the downcast, he could appreciate humor. Surprisingly, witnesses have told of his gift for humor and the enjoyment he got from making others laugh. They looked forward to having him present.

As prior he accepted the responsibility of having to call others to account, but he was intent on not discouraging anyone. His opinion was that people "become pusillanimous in undertaking works of great virtue when they are treated harshly by superiors." Nor did he think he had the answers to all problems. His practice was to consult others in the community, a method of government that helped to create an atmosphere of serenity. Being a saint does not free one from the capacity for making mistakes, nor does being a superior, and John once remarked of himself at the end of his life: "When I recall the foolish mistakes I made as superior, I blush."

Human needs are not only material and psychological; there are distinctive spiritual needs as well. In his oral teaching John used to point out that the more you love God the more you desire that all people love and honor him and as the desire grows you work harder toward that end, both in prayer and in all other possible works. His preferred work was spiritual direction, whereby he could help to free individuals from their moral and spiritual illnesses.

In this endeavor he did not spare himself, so special was his awareness of our exalted destiny. From university professor to humble, unlettered shepherds' wives, people of all classes felt the allure of his confessional. The ease the humble lay sister, Catalina de la Cruz, experienced in his presence is evident in the kind of question she once asked him: "Why when I go to the garden do the frogs jump in the water?" Quickly seizing an opportunity to draw out a spiritual lesson, John replied that it was because they felt safe in the depth of the pool and "that is what you must do, flee from creatures and hide yourself in God." Sinners also found their way to him without fear. "The holier a confessor," he used to say, "the less fear one should have of him."

In his spiritual direction of others John focused on communion with God in faith, hope, and love, called by some the "theological life." This life is both active and passive and encompasses everything, from the first steps in Christian living to the highest reaches of the mystical journey. In an age that found severe austerities a fascinating and necessary part of spiritual pursuit, his ascetical teaching pointed to faith, hope, and love as the way to sanctity in the following of Christ.

But his deepest concern was for those who were suffering in their spiritual life. The needs of souls struggling with inner trials stirred him to write *The Ascent of Mount Carmel* and *The Dark Night*. If his intense portrayal of the afflictions of the dark night can prove frightening to some, his desire in so presenting them was to include everyone by describing these sufferings in their extreme form. He wanted everyone to find comfort in the thought that however severe it may be, purification is still the work of God's gentle hand, clearing away the debris of attachment and making room for the divine light. Pain for him was not a misfortune but a value when suffered with and for Christ.

Nothing about John's life indicates that he thought he should have a specialist's priorities in the use of his time. He participated in all the different tasks necessary to keep a community running. We find him in the choir, the confessional, the kitchen, weeding the garden, decorating the altars, making architectural plans, joining in construction work, visiting the sick and, of course, writing. Hard physical labor, small and delicate though he was, seemed to attract him. Was it his way of protesting the thought of the Illuminists who held that the servants of God should not undertake manual labor? At both Granada and Segovia, when these monasteries were being built, he joined the workmen in quarrying stone for the construction. At Beas, when free from counseling the nuns he would do chores for them, setting up partitions, laying bricks, and scrubbing floors.

He observed how creatures can enslave and darken and torment. But the deceptive delights of those who are attached to creatures cannot compare with the joy of people who are detached from them. Beholding in creation a trace of the divine beauty, power, and loving wisdom, John could not easily resist the enchantment of nature. Because he missed the lyric country solitude of El Calvario after founding the student college in Baeza, he acquired some property in the country, making it possible for him and the young Carmelites to escape from the bustling city. He would take the friars out to the mountains, sometimes for the sake of relaxation, "to prevent their wanting to leave the monastery from spending too much time in it," as he once remarked; sometimes, so that each might pass the day alone there "in solitary prayer." At Segovia he had his favorite grotto, hollowed out by nature, high up on the back bluff overlooking a marvelous stretch of sky, river, and landscape. He grew to love this silent grotto and spent all the time he could spare there.

John's letters exhibit the warmth with which he usually communed with others. But his brother Francisco seems to have given him special happiness. He used to introduce Francisco by saying, "May I introduce you to my brother, who is the treasure I value most in the world." St. Teresa, also, it should go without saying, awakened in him particular admiration, so much so that he carried her portrait about with him.

Accompanying the outward, evangelical simplicity of his manner was a soul on fire, like Teresa's. Of his intimacy with God he once admitted in Granada: "God communicates the mystery of the Trinity to this sinner in such a way that if His Majesty did not strengthen my weakness by a special help, it would be impossible for me to live." Overwhelmed with awareness of God's goodness, he was frequently heard to exclaim, "Oh, what a good God we have!" Requiring little sleep, he spent much of the night in prayer, sometimes kneeling at the altar steps before the Blessed Sacrament; at other times he knelt beneath the trees in the garden, and sometimes at the window of his cell, from which he could look out at the heavens and all the countryside. In the latter years of his brief life, his absorption in God could become so profound that he experienced difficulty in attending to ordinary affairs, secretly having to hit his knuckles against the wall so as not to lose the trend of conversation.

His experience of God was always rooted in the life of the Church, nourished by the sacraments and the liturgy. Witnesses of his life spoke of the devotion with which he celebrated Mass. A center of his contemplation, Mass often proved to be an occasion for special graces. During the celebration he could become so lost in God that he had no consciousness of his surroundings. His greatest suffering during the imprisonment in Toledo was being deprived of the Eucharist. The Blessed Sacrament was "all his glory, all his happiness, and for him far surpassed all the things of the earth." The one privilege he accepted when major superior in Segovia was the cell closest to the Blessed Sacrament.

The liturgical feasts and seasons meant more than an external commemoration; they were the occasion of an interior transformation in the spirit of the mystery being celebrated. On the day before Christmas he used to organize with the friars a kind of paraliturgical procession to recall how Mary and Joseph went in search of lodging for the divine Infant. At Christmas time above all he felt his heart pulsate with love for the Child Jesus. One Christmas, seeing a statue of the Infant lying on a cushion, he cried out, "Lord, if love is to slay me, the hour has now come." Another Christmas, taken with love, he took the statue of the Infant in his arms and began to dance with enraptured joy.

His countenance, in fact, corresponded with the Church's liturgy. Once during Holy Week he suffered so intensely from the Passion of Christ that he found it impossible to leave the monastery to hear the nuns' confessions. Among his favorite feasts, besides those of the Blessed Trinity and Corpus Christi, were the feasts of the Blessed Virgin. In his prison cell, on the Vigil of the Assumption, after nine months of severe privation, he was asked what he was thinking of. He replied, "I was thinking that tomorrow is the feast of our Lady and that it would give me great joy to say Mass." The sight of an image of the Mother of God brought love and brightness to his soul. Once, on seeing an image of our Lady while he was preaching to the nuns in Caravaca, he could not conceal his love for her and exclaimed: "How happy I would be to live alone in a desert with that image."

The Bible, the book he cherished most of all, helped him to enter into intimacy with the three Persons of the Trinity. He loved to withdraw to hidden parts of the monastery with his Bible. While he was in Lisbon, the other friars urged him to come with them to visit a famed stigmatic of that city, but he refused; drawn by the ocean, he remained on the shore reading his Bible while the others went off to observe the curious phenomenon.

From his Bible and his nearness to God, John knew that loving confidence in Providence was the appropriate response to life's worries and anxieties. He observed that when God, like a loving mother, wants to carry us, we kick and cry and insist on walking by ourselves, and get nowhere. Some thought that since he was prior of a poor monastery he should show more concern about material needs. They would have liked him to worry. But his habit of seeing the hand of God in all things contributed, in fact, to an air of peace and calm.

This was his way, too, in persecution. He saw the hand of God there and urged others not to speak uncharitably of his persecutors, but to think "only that God ordains all." He wrote that trust in God should be so great that even if the whole world were to collapse one should not become disturbed. Enduring things with equanimity reaps many blessings, he said, and helps a person in the middle of adversity to make an appropriate judgment and find the right option. This total trust in God gave him peace in his final illness. Being reminded of all he had suffered, he replied with these remarkable words: "Padre, this is not the time to be thinking of that; it is by the merits of the blood of our Lord Jesus Christ that I hope to be saved."

BIOGRAPHICAL CHRONOLOGY

1529   Marriage in Fontiveros of Gonzalo de Yepes and Catalina
            Alvarez, John's parents.
1530   Francisco, the first son, is born.
1532-40   Luis, the second son, is born; year uncertain.
1542   John (Juan de Yepes) is born; month and day uncertain.
1545   Don Gonzalo dies.
1545-46   Doña Catalina travels to Toledo with her three children in
            search of help from her husband's family. A brother-in-
            law takes Francisco, who suffers a year of abusive treat
            ment by his aunt. Doña Catalina returns, rejected, to
            Fontiveros with her other boys.
1547   Luis dies.
1548-51   The family moves to Arévalo. Here Francisco marries Ana
            Izquierdo.
1551   The family moves to Medina del Campo.
1551-58   John attends the Catechism school. Tries apprenticeships at

various trades. Serves as acolyte at La Magdalena.

1556   St. Ignatius Loyola dies. Charles V (d. 1559) abdicates. Philip II becomes king.

1559-63   John studies humanities and perhaps philosophy with the Jesuits. He also works at humble tasks for the hospital in Medina.

1562   St. Teresa establishes the reform at St. Joseph's in Avila.

1563   The Council of Trent closes.

John enters the novitiate of the Carmelites at Santa Ana in Medina and makes profession the following year.

1564-68   He attends the University of Salamanca: three years in the arts program and one year in theology.

1567   Early months: the Carmelite General, Juan Bautista Rossi (Rubeo), visits Castile, authorizes Teresa to found discalced Carmelite monasteries of friars and nuns outside Avila.

1567   April: John is named prefect of students by the provincial chapter held in Avila.

July: ordained a priest in Salamanca.

August: sings his first Mass in Medina.

September-October: First meeting with St. Teresa, who wins John over to her cause.

1568   John finishes his theological course at Salamanca and agrees to take part in the first house of discalced Carmelite friars.

August: he journeys with Teresa to Valladolid and remains there several months to learn the Teresian way of life.

October: moves to Duruelo to adapt the house to a monastery.

November 28: inauguration of the discalced friars' first house in Duruelo; John is appointed subprior and novice master.

1569   Lent: St. Teresa visits Duruelo.

1570   June: Duruelo turns out to be unhealthy. The community moves to Mancera de Abajo. At the end of the year John visits Pastrana to bring unity in the criteria for formation.

1571   January: he accompanies Teresa to Alba de Tormes for her foundation of nuns there.

He becomes rector of the university college of Alcalá de Henares. A new visit to Pastrana.

1572   May: in Avila, at Teresa's request, Fray John of the Cross becomes the vicar and confessor at the monastery of the Incarnation. He remains there with brief interruptions until 1577.

1574	March: he accompanies Teresa on the foundation in Segovia and returns at the end of April.
1575	Goes to Medina to discern the spirit of a discalced nun.
	May: the general chapter of the order at Piacenza (Italy) decrees reabsorption of the discalced Carmelites into the order.
1576	January: the first arrest of Fray John and his companion by the Carmelites of the Observance. The two are released through the intervention of the nuncio.
	September 9: the discalced Carmelites meet in Almodóvar del Campo. Fray John attends. Gracián presides.
	Christmas: John participates in the "Satirical Critique" proposed and judged by Teresa, on the theme "Seek yourself in Me."
1577	June 2: St. Teresa begins to write *The Interior Castle* in Toledo. The nuncio Ormaneto dies. His successor does not favor the discalced Carmelites.
	December 2: John is abducted in Avila; between the 4th and the 8th he is brought to Toledo, where he remains for nine months in the monastery prison.
1578	August: during the octave after the Assumption, between 2 and 3 a.m., he escapes from prison. He takes with him a notebook containing various poems and remains hidden for a time in Toledo.
	October: on his way to Andalusia he attends the secret chapter of discalced Carmelites at Almodóvar. Elected vicar of El Calvario (Sierra del Segura, Jaén).
	November: John arrives at El Calvario and takes up his office.
1579	Fruitful activity among the nuns at Beas. "The Sketch of the Mount," many of the "Sayings of Light and Love," some undeveloped commentary on stanzas from *The Spiritual Canticle* and *The Dark Night.*
	April-May: he makes frequent trips to Baeza to plan the foundation of a new college there.
	June: John founds the university college in Baeza and becomes the rector.
1580	John's mother, Doña Catalina, dies in Medina.
	John visits Caravaca at Teresa's request.
	June 22: a brief from Gregory XIII decrees a separation between the calced and discalced Carmelites.
	John is given a gift of property at Castellar de Santisteban as a place for relaxation and prayer.
1581	March: attends the chapter at Alcalá where the brief of separation is implemented. Padre Gracián is named

provincial; John, third definitor.

June: John travels to Caravaca.

November: John travels to Avila with the intention of bringing St. Teresa to Granada to make a foundation of nuns there. On returning without Teresa, he passes through Beas to take Ana de Jesús with him as foundress in Granada.

1582   January: continues on the journey to Granada. They arrive on the 20th. Doña Ana de Peñalosa enters into the plans for the foundation.

John becomes prior of Los Mártires in Granada, where he writes most of his commentaries and various poems.

April 8: five discalced Carmelite friars destined for the missions in the Congo set sail from Lisbon.

October 4: St. Teresa dies in Alba de Tormes.

1583   May: John attends a chapter in Almodóvar. He is confirmed in his office as prior in Granada.

1585   February: John travels to Málaga for the nuns' foundation.

May: attends the provincial chapter in Lisbon. He is elected second definitor.

June-July: he returns from Lisbon by way of Sevilla, and then goes to Málaga.

July-August: further travels to various communities.

October: in Pastrana for the continuation of the chapter that began in Lisbon. The new provincial, Padre Doria, had to return first from Italy. John is appointed vicar provincial of Andalusia, with his residence in Granada.

1586   February: he travels to Caravaca.

May: in Córdoba for a new foundation there.

June: in Sevilla for the move of the discalced Carmelite nuns. He draws up papers for the foundation of friars at the Marian shrine in Guadalcázar. He journeys to Ecija, Guadalcázar, and Córdoba.

July: he goes to Málaga.

August-September: attends a meeting of definitors in Madrid. He brings Ana de Jesús with him for a foundation of nuns in Madrid. The definitory decrees the publication of Teresa's works and substitution of the Roman liturgy for that of the Holy Sepulcher, which the Carmelites had been using.

October: makes a foundation of friars in Manchuela (Jaén).

November: travels once more to Málaga.

December: travels to Caravaca where he makes a foundation of friars. Travels to Bujalance to make plans for a foundation.

1587   January: plans for the foundation in Bujalance fail.

February: a quick trip to Madrid at the request of the provincial, Nicolás Doria.

March: travels to Caravaca to intervene in a litigation between the nuns and the Jesuits. He then moves on to Baeza. On the 8th, he is at the Marian shrine of Fuensanta (Jaén), which was entrusted to the discalced Carmelites.

April: travels to Valladolid to take part in the provincial chapter. His duties as vicar provincial cease. He is elected prior of Granada once more.

1588   June: Doria convokes an extraordinary chapter in Madrid. John (a definitor on a committee for procedure) is elected first councillor (among six) in the new form of government called the *consulta*. He will reside in Segovia. During the absence of the vicar general (Doria), John will act as the major definitor and president of the *consulta*. He is also prior of the house.

Some discalced Carmelites embark with the "Invincible Armada."

1589-90   As prior in Segovia, he makes important improvements on the property and undertakes building the new monastery. Doña Ana de Peñalosa is the benefactress.

1590   June: an extraordinary chapter is held in Madrid. Serious disagreements surface. John does not support Doria's plans for dealing with Gracián or with some nuns who were disenchanted with the idea of the *consulta*.

1591   June 1: on the eve of Pentecost, the chapter begins in Madrid. Doria is reelected. John has no office, is willing to go to Mexico.

July-August: he moves to the solitude of La Peñuela in Andalusia.

September: suffers from fevers and gangrenous sores on his foot. He transfers to Ubeda for medical care.

November 27: the vicar provincial, Fr. Antonio de Jesús, arrives in Ubeda.

December 7-8: John's condition worsens.

December 11: he requests Viaticum.

December 13: he bids farewell and begs the prior's pardon for any disturbances he may have caused and an old habit for his burial. He receives the Last Rites and alludes frequently to the hour of his death. When the clock strikes midnight (December 14) and the monastery bell rings for Matins, he goes, as he had foretold, "to sing Matins in heaven."

1593	May: his remains are transferred to Segovia. Perhaps alluded to by Cervantes (*Don Quixote*, 1. 19).
1618	The first edition of John of the Cross's works (Alcalá), without *The Spiritual Canticle.*
1622	The first French edition of *The Spiritual Canticle* (Paris).
1627	The first Spanish edition of *The Spiritual Canticle* (Brussels).
1630	The first edition of the complete works in Spanish, prepared by Jerónimo de San José (Madrid).
1675	January 22: Clement X beatifies John of the Cross.
1726	December 27: Benedict XIII canonizes him.
1874	The Royal Academy of the Spanish Language includes John of the Cross in its official catalogue of writers who can serve as authorities in the use of words and phrases in the Castilian tongue.
1926	August 24: Pius XI declares St. John of the Cross a Doctor of the universal Church.
	His body is moved to the present tomb in Segovia designed by Félix Granda.
1952	The Spanish Ministry of National Education names John of the Cross the patron of Spanish poets.

THE WRITINGS

The works of St. John of the Cross do not compare in quantity and thematic variety with the writings of other great Doctors of the Church. As a poet, first of all, John presented the rich content of his mystical experience in lyric poetry, and by this has contributed a sublime treasure to Spanish literature. In addition, he has left us four major prose works: *The Ascent of Mount Carmel; The Dark Night; The Spiritual Canticle;* and *The Living Flame of Love.* The only other writings left are relatively few letters and various maxims and counsels. Written during the last 14 years of his life, after his intellectual and spiritual growth had come to full flower, his extant works show a doctrinal synthesis of the spiritual life that was substantially complete in his mind once he began to write. No essential change of thought occurs in his teaching; there is no "earlier John" to contrast with the "later John." The themes he dwells on also remain constant: union with God, its trinitarian origins and final outcome in glory; Jesus Christ, Word and Beloved; faith, as both the content of the mystery and the obscure way to union; love, the going out from self to live in the other; the active and passive development of the theological life;

the communication of God in silent prayer; the appetites, a dynamic of sin and destruction.

In the field of Spanish literature, John of the Cross has won a prominent place for his poetry. As for his prose style, he writes in different modes. Sometimes he explains through common symbols, at other times in biblical language, or again through the conceptual terms of the scholastic theologian; sometimes the style is very much his own creation. But it is not apparent that he took pains to polish his prose. His sentences can get complicated, repetitious, and cluttered. Not infrequently, however, the inspiration of his poetry overflows into his prose, offering passages of literary power, originality, and beauty.

With the exception of *The Sayings of Light and Love* and some letters whose autographs have been conserved, John of the Cross's original manuscripts have been lost. His writings come to us in numerous codices that hand on more or less faithful copies. Thus we have a critical problem concerning the original reading and the selection of the codex that seems most faithful to the original. The particular introductions to each work will point out the codex considered most trustworthy by specialists; this copy will then be followed in the translation.

Here is an overview of the authentic works and their actual or approximate places and dates of composition:

Toledo Prison (1578)

The Spiritual Canticle (poem, 31 stanzas)
For I Know Well the Spring (poem)
The Romances: On the Gospel text "In principio erat Verbum" (poem)
On the psalm "Super flumina Babylonis" (poem)

Calvario-Beas-Baeza (1578-81)

The Dark Night (poem, 1578 or 1579)
The Sketch of the Mount
The Sayings of Light and Love
The Precautions
Counsels to a Religious
The Ascent of Mount Carmel (treatise, 1581-85)
Additions to The Spiritual Canticle (poem); other poems (1580-84)

Granada (1582-88)

The Spiritual Canticle (commentary in a first redaction, 1584)
The Dark Night (commentary, 1584-85)
Last poems in Granada (1585)
The Living Flame of Love (commentary in a first redaction, 1585-86)
The Spiritual Canticle (commentary in a second redaction, 1585-86)

La Peñuela (1591)
The Living Flame of Love (commentary in a second redaction)

Sources

In his writings, John seized the opportunity to communicate with his readers as a mystic, poet, teacher, and ardent lover of God. For the sake of instructing, he draws on his knowledge of theology, psychology, and spiritual direction. Beginning with the symbols of his poetry, he then leads the reader to his conceptual system with its own language and applications.

As for sources, in John's time the past provided not merely source material but authority. The Church acknowledged certain writers as authoritative. Scripture, above all, settled matters. A biblical passage was considered an authority from Scripture, and was often referred to as such by John. The modern concern with accurate texts and critical scholarship was not then in force; it seems John often quoted from memory or from medieval compilations. Some of the nonscriptural works he quotes are now known as spurious. The point is that instead of historical scholarship, textual accuracy, and a cautious mind with regard to the received wisdom, John's world set high store by a tradition handed down through the centuries and mediated through sometimes corrupt texts.

In both structure and outline of thought, John's writings display the influences of Aquinas and the scholastics. Certain elements of the mysticism reflect Augustine and Neoplatonism. Some images and stages suggest both the German and Rhineland mystics and the themes, problems, and language of the earlier Spanish mystics. A susceptibility to sensual impressions and symbols characteristic of Spanish poetry in this period is obvious; there may also be symbolic and linguistic influences from Islam. But however much we speculate on all this, the only book that can be properly called a fount of John's experience and writings is the Bible.

For John, the Bible served as a living and unfailing wellspring. Its waters pervade the entire being of this mystical thinker, poet, and writer. The Bible was his hymnal, his meditation book, a book for travel, for contemplation, and for writing. Scriptural quotations throughout his works show how deeply he had assimilated the Divine Word, but he never keeps to a single exegetical style; and the reader might find this disconcerting.

Three principal ways to benefit from the biblical text attracted John. First, the Bible offered him an excellent expression of his own spiritual experience. Second, he found in the Bible a confirmation of his theological argument. Finally, he enjoyed and followed the contemporary practice of using scriptural passages in an accommodated sense.

John discovered a close alliance between biblical history and his own personal history, an identification of ancient experiences with actual ones. Reading the Bible as a Christian, in a Christocentric light, he recognized his own life reflected and described there. He noted that here and now the grace and truth of the biblical word was being accomplished. The disorder of the appetites could be compared with the idolatrous love of ancient Israel. Job, the psalmist, and Jeremiah suffered and put to song the dark night of the spirit. The quest for union repeated the steps of the *Song of Songs.*

In special ways, he identified with persons of the Bible: with Moses, David, Job, the psalmist, Jeremiah, Paul, and John. He was drawn to the personal, concrete experiences presented there, inclining toward individuals whose vocation and attitudes were well defined and who had expressed their experiences in the first person. Not content with merely quoting the doctrines and deeds of these people, he turned his attention to their experiences in relation to God. He recounted and sang of his own joys, sufferings, and experiences of God's mercies and favors by disguising them in the words of the prophet, the psalmist, or St. Paul.

All the while, the living and collective consciousness of the whole Church is present. In John's teaching, God will not bring clarification and confirmation of the truth to the heart of one who is alone. Such a one would remain weak and cold in regard to the truth. As he went out from himself and passed through the spiritual night, John entered more and more into the substance of the Church, into God's self-manifestation in time. He found no difficulty in relying on the judgment of the Church in matters relating to the expression of his experience and teaching. Church life, doctrine, and prayer supplied the context in which he read and used Scripture.

John also recognized that we cannot understand the truth of Christ without the Holy Spirit. He does not say that the Holy Spirit "spoke" to us, but that he "speaks" to us in the Scriptures, leading us to the complete truth. If we can never fully understand the secret truths and diverse meanings of God's words, these words will, nevertheless, in a certain manner grow with those who read them in the Spirit.

That John was a mystic in no way prejudiced his work as a spiritual director or theologian. A central purpose of his was to transmit the content of his mystical experience. Such experience favored theological reflection because the mystic enjoys a particularly enlightened perception of the mysteries of God, of divine action, and of the life of grace in individuals. From a pastoral viewpoint as well, the mystic knows the goal, and is in a better position to delineate the way and evaluate the means.

Enlightened by his own experience and the experience of others, sometimes—notably in the case of the great St. Teresa herself—as rich and deep as his own, he entered as theologian the most difficult and unexplored regions. He sought to take the revealed mysteries that had been analyzed by theologians and create a doctrinal synthesis that would bring unity and cohesion to all the converging realities of the process of divinization. But in his work as a theologian John also, in veiled ways, sought to transmit something of his own intimate experience of God's mystery so as to awaken a similar experience in his readers. He presented the mystery so others might come close and be totally transformed by it: "One speaks badly of the intimate depths of the spirit if one does not do so with a deeply recollected soul."

NOTE ON THE DRAWING OF CHRIST ON THE CROSS

One day during the years when Fray John of the Cross was chaplain at the monastery of the Incarnation in Avila, probably between 1574 and 1577, he was praying in a loft overlooking the sanctuary. Suddenly he received a vision. Taking a pen he sketched on a small piece of paper what he had beheld.

The sketch is of Christ crucified, hanging in space, turned toward his people, and seen from a new perspective. The cross is erect. The body, lifeless and contorted, with the head bent over, hangs forward so that the arms are held only by the nails. Christ is seen from above, from the view of the Father. He is more worm than man, weighed down by the sins of human beings, leaning toward the world for which he died.

John, who was to write so many cautions against visions and images, later gave the pen sketch to one of his devout penitents at the Incarnation, Ana María de Jesús. She guarded it until the time of her death in 1618, when she gave it to María Pinel who was later to become prioress.

In 1641, at the time of Madre María's death, the drawing was placed in a small monstrance, elliptical in shape, where it was conserved until 1968. It was then sent for study and restoration to the Central Institute in Madrid for the conservation and restoration of works of art. Now restored and provided with a new reliquary, it is once more available for all to see at the Incarnation in Avila.

The French Carmelite biographer of St. John of the Cross, Bruno de Jésus-Marie, in 1945 and 1950 discussed the drawing with two renowned Spanish painters of the twentieth century, José María Sert and Salvador Dalí.

The former turned the drawing sideways and interpreted the work to represent the cross leaning forward like a crucifix pressed to the lips of a dying man. Christ is seen then as dragging away from it, his arms stretched almost to the breaking point, his head bent. However, careful study of the drawing has since demonstrated that John's crucified Christ is in a vertical position.

Dalí, in turn, was inspired to do a painting from a similar perspective, "The Christ of St. John of the Cross." In Dalí's painting, in contrast to John's original drawing, the crucified body reminds one more of a Greek god than of the suffering servant.

René Huyghe, once Conservator-in-Chief of the paintings in the Museum of the Louvre, wrote concerning the Spanish Carmelite's drawing:

> Saint John of the Cross escapes right out of those visual habits by which all artists form a part of their period. He knows nothing of the rules and limitations of contemporary vision; he is not dependent on the manner of seeing current in his century; he is dependent on nothing but the object of his contemplation....The vertical perspective—bold, almost violent, emphasized by light and shade—in which he caught his Christ on the cross cannot be matched in contemporary art; in the context of that art it is hardly imaginable.

The Poetry

INTRODUCTION TO THE POETRY

St. John of the Cross has won universal recognition for his poetry. But some 300 years went by before this recognition was achieved. Dámaso Alonso in his noted study of the poetry of St. John of the Cross calls him a wonderful literary artist and the loftiest poet of Spain. Menéndez Pelayo had already pointed out the heavenly character of John's poetry, noting that it didn't seem to be of this world. Other critical studies have demonstrated that this poetry is more than a simple overflow of mystical experience; it is an artistic creation of the highest craftsmanship as well. Nonetheless, the divine tone that pervades John's work of art undeniably owes its presence also to the mystical experience.

While John was a student in Medina del Campo he learned about poetry and practiced composing his own poems. Nothing from those early exercises has come down to us. The first indications of his poetic work reach us through St. Teresa. Discovering in poetry a means for celebrating liturgical feasts and other special occasions, she introduced into her Carmels the practice of writing verses. In addition, like a greeting card, poems represented for her a simple way of sending a special word to another. A recently discovered letter written to her brother Lorenzo in January 1577, while John was confessor at the monastery of the Incarnation, shows that Teresa's first friar also participated in this practice of celebrating through poetry. Teresa, sending her brother a little poem written by John, tells Lorenzo that she finds it delightful. John gradually came to realize that these symbolic expressions of poetry could also provide an excellent introduction into the intimate knowledge of the mystery of God.

The largest block of poetry comes to us from John's days in the dark prison of Toledo. This comprises the *Romances* on the Trinity and on the psalm "Super flumina Babylonis, "For I know well the spring," and the first 31 stanzas of *The Spiritual Canticle*. Whether any of the other poems predate his imprisonment is a matter for speculation. Possibly "I entered into unknowing" and "I live but not in myself" were written during John's years in Avila. The rest of the poetry was written after the imprisonment.

Always turning to the Bible as a tool for expressing his own experience, John does not surprise us by the way his exalted poetry resonates Scripture. This inspired word is always a primary source for him. Alongside the Bible one notes the literary surroundings of the time. Boscán and Garcilaso were two poets John mentioned and apparently esteemed. Nor did he shrink from working with some of the popular verses of his day. He adds *a lo divino,* that is, with a spiritual meaning, to the title of some of his poems. These are usually compositions taken from the secular world and reworked to give them a religious interpretation. A good example of this is "A lone young shepherd," a secular poem that, through some carefully made changes, John turned into a delicate work of literary art.

Lyric poetry, strictly speaking, was meant to be sung, not recited. Singing was popular in Carmelite monasteries. The nuns and friars sang to celebrate liturgical feasts and also for simple recreation. Deeply sensitive to singing, John could be profoundly moved by melodious voices coming from the street, or by a nun singing of the pains of divine love faintly from behind the convent grille. His companions testify that he frequently sang, especially on long journeys through the countryside. He sang psalms, hymns to our Lady, and other songs with melodies he had made up himself. The happiness of being out in the country induced him to burst into song. The nuns could not help putting his poems to music. We know that Teresa herself listened with delight and joined her nuns in singing the poems of Fray John of the Cross.

His commentaries on his three outstanding poems help us discern the theological and spiritual riches in the other poems that received no commentary. In some of his poetry John contemplates the great Christian mysteries; in the rest he speaks of his spiritual experiences, which also bear a doctrinal content.

The particular introductions to the commentaries on *The Spiritual Canticle, The Dark Night,* and *The Living Flame of Love* will deal with those three, the most resplendent of John's poems. A brief word about the others is in order.

I entered into unknowing. This poem sings about a mystical understanding of God that far transcends all human knowledge. But paradoxically, in this lofty understanding God is revealed as ever transcendent, infinitely distant from all human understanding, so that the more one understands the less it seems one understands.

I live, but not in myself. This poem has the same refrain as one of Teresa's. The soul sees separation from God on this earth as a kind of dying and longs to die in order to live and enjoy her true life completely.

I went out seeking love. The prey in this poem is the loved one. The poet sings of how through faith, love, humility, and hope one flies high enough to catch the prey.

A lone young shepherd. Recasting a popular pastoral love song and giving it a religious meaning, John interprets the Incarnation, life, and death of Christ from the perspective of love. The delicacy in tone and development have a stunning effect. Love is rejected and forgotten; it weeps, it seeks, it goes great distances; it finally suffers a lonely death.

For I know well the spring. Using the symbol of a flowing spring, this poem deals with God's intimate life. The poet knows this divine life in the darkness of faith, the night of faith remaining throughout the poem. But aspects of the flowing spring unfold as one proceeds: It is hidden, the source of creation, beauty, and light; its streams are threefold; we can drink from its waters in the bread of the Eucharist.

The Romances. As poetry, these romances do not match the literary quality of the other poems. We find in them, however, the great themes of John's theological and spiritual thought. The view extends from the preparatory beginnings of salvation history to the Incarnation of Christ. In groups of two they present the story in descending levels: 1-2, Trinitarian life and predestination; 3-4, creation as a plan and then its realization; 5-6, the hope of humanity in general and then of some persons in particular; 7-8, the Incarnation as a plan and then its historical realization; 9, the birth, in which the Word takes on our humanity.

On the psalm "By the waters of Babylon." In this poem John adds his own creative touches to psalm 137. It invites a twofold interpretation: composed in prison, it may refer to John's isolation there from his brothers and friends; or it may refer to the ongoing experience of the "moaning" that refers to hope and that accompanies this earthly life.

Without support yet with support. The poet sings of the happiness that comes from life in God, detachment, and a love that grows in dark faith.

Not for all of beauty. The mystical experience of God causes a kind of love-sickness that makes it impossible for the soul to find happiness anywhere but in God alone, who on this earth is known always in faith.

Christmas Refrain. This fragment probably comes from a longer hymn John composed for the friars to sing during the Advent processions preparatory for Christmas.

The Sum of Perfection. A small summary of John's teaching.

The basic codices followed for the poetry are *Sanlúcar de Barrameda* and *Jaén.*

1.
CANTICO ESPIRITUAL
(Primera redacción: CA)

1.
THE SPIRITUAL CANTICLE
(First redaction: CA)

Canciones entre el alma y el Esposo

Songs between the soul and the Bridegroom

Esposa
1. ¿Adonde te escondiste,
Amado, y me dejaste con gemido?
Como el ciervo huiste,
habiéndome herido;
salí tras ti clamando, y eras ido.

Bride
1. Where have you hidden,
Beloved, and left me moaning?
You fled like the stag
after wounding me;
I went out calling you, but you
    were gone.

2. Pastores los que fuerdes
allá por las majadas al otero,
si por ventura vierdes
aquel que yo más quiero,
decilde que adolezco, peno y
    muero.

2. Shepherds, you who go
up through the sheepfolds to the
    hill,
if by chance you see
him I love most,
tell him I am sick, I suffer, and I die.

3. Buscando mis amores,
iré por esos montes y riberas;
ni cogeré las flores,
ni temeré las fieras,
y pasaré los fuertes y fronteras.

3. Seeking my love
I will head for the mountains and
    for watersides;
I will not gather flowers,
nor fear wild beasts;
I will go beyond strong men and
    frontiers.

4. ¡Oh bosques y espesuras,
plantadas por la mano del Amado!
¡Oh prado de verduras,
de flores esmaltado,
decid si por vosotros ha pasado!

4. O woods and thickets
planted by the hand of my Beloved!
O green meadow,
coated, bright, with flowers,
tell me, has he passed by you?

5. Mil gracias derramando
pasó por estos sotos con presura,
e, yéndolos mirando,
con sola su figura,
vestidos los dejó de hermosura.

5. Pouring out a thousand graces,
he passed these groves in haste;
and having looked at them,
with his image alone,
clothed them in beauty.

6. ¡Ay, quién podrá sanarme!
¡Acaba de entregarte ya de vero;
no quieras enviarme
de hoy más ya mensajero
que no saben decirme lo que quiero!

7. Y todos cuantos vagan
de ti me van mil gracia refiriendo,
y todos más me llagan,
y déjeme muriendo
un no sé qué quedan balbuciendo.

8. Mas ¿como perseveras,
¡oh vida!, no viviendo donde vives,
y haciendo porque mueras
las flechas que recibes
de lo que del Amado en ti concibes?

9. ¿Por qué, pues has llagado
aqueste corazón, no le sanaste?
Y, pues me le has robado,
¿por qué así le dejaste,
y no tomas el robo que robaste?

10. ¡Apaga mis enojos,
pues que ninguno basta a deshacellos,
y véante mis ojos,
pues eres lumbre dellos,
y sólo para ti quiero tenellos!

6. Ah, who has the power to heal me?
Now wholly surrender yourself!
Do not send me
any more messengers;
they cannot tell me what I must hear.

7. All who are free
tell me a thousand graceful things of you;
all wound me more
and leave me dying
of, ah, I-don't-know-what behind their stammering.

8. How do you endure
O life, not living where you live,
and being brought near death
by the arrows you receive
from that which you conceive of your Beloved?

9. Why, since you wounded
this heart, don't you heal it?
And why, since you stole it from me,
do you leave it so,
and fail to carry off what you have stolen?

10. Extinguish these miseries,
since no one else can stamp them out;
and may my eyes behold you,
because you are their light,
and I would open them to you alone.[1]

---

1. In the second redaction and other versions, a new stanza was added here: Descubre tu presencia,/ y máteme tu vista y hermosura;/ mira que la dolencia/ de amor, que no se cura/ sino con la presencia y la figura. Reveal your presence/ and may the vision of your beauty be my death/ for the sickness of love/ is not cured/ except by your very presence and image.

11. ¡Oh cristalina fuente,
si en esos tus semblantes plateados
formases de repente
los ojos deseados
que tengo en mis entrañas di
   bujados!

11. O spring like crystal!
If only, on your silvered-over faces,
you would suddenly form
the eyes I have desired,
that I bear sketched deep within
   my heart.

12. ¡Apártalos, Amado,
que voy de vuelo!

12. Withdraw them, Beloved,
I am taking flight!

Esposo
—Vuélvate, paloma,
que el ciervo vulnerado
por el otero asoma
al aire de tu vuelo, y fresco toma!

Bridegroom
—Return, dove,
the wounded stag
is in sight on the hill,
cooled by the breeze of your flight.

La esposa
13. Mi Amado, las montañas,
los valles solitarios nemorosos,
las ínsulas extrañas,
los ríos sonorosos,
el silbo de los aires amorosos,

The Bride
13. My Beloved, the mountains,
and lonely wooded valleys,
strange islands,
and resounding rivers,
the whistling of love-stirring
   breezes,

14. la noche sosegada
en par de los levantes de la aurora,
la música callada,
la soledad sonora,
la cena que recrea y enamora.

14. the tranquil night
at the time of the rising dawn,
silent music,
sounding solitude,
the supper that refreshes, and
   deepens love.

15. Nuestro lecho florido,
de cuevas de leones enlazado,
en púrpura tendido,
de paz edificado,
de mil escudos de oro coronado.

15. Our bed is in flower,
bound round with linking dens of
   lions,
hung with purple,
built up in peace,
and crowned with a thousand
   shields of gold.

16. A zaga de tu huella
las jóvenes discurren al camino,
al toque de centella,
al adobado vino,
emisiones de bálsamo divino.

16. Following your footprints
maidens run along the way;
the touch of a spark,
the spiced wine,
cause flowings in them from the
   balsam of God.

17. En la interior bodega
de mi Amado bebí, y cuando salía
por toda aquesta vega,
ya cosa no sabía;
y el ganado perdí que antes seguía.

17. In the inner wine cellar
I drank of my Beloved, and, when
  I went abroad
through all this valley,
I no longer knew anything,
and lost the herd that I was
  following.

18. Allí me dio su pecho,
allí me enseñó ciencia muy
  sabrosa;
y yo le di de hecho
a mí, sin dejar cosa;
allí le prometí de ser su esposa.

18. There he gave me his breast;
there he taught me a sweet and
  living knowledge;
and I gave myself to him,
keeping nothing back;
there I promised to be his bride.

19. Mi alma se ha empleado,
y todo mi caudal en su servicio;
ya no guardo ganado,
ni ya tengo otro oficio,
que ya sólo en amar es mi ejercicio.

19. Now I occupy my soul
and all my energy in his service;
I no longer tend the herd,
nor have I any other work
now that my every act is love.

20. Pues ya si en el ejido
de hoy más no fuere vista ni
  hallada,
diréis que me ha perdido;
que, andando enamorada,
me hice perdidiza y fui ganada.

20. If, then, I am no longer
seen or found on the common,
you will say that I am lost;
that, stricken by love,
I lost myself, and was found.

21. De flores y esmeraldas,
en las frescas mañanas escogidas,
haremos las guirnaldas
en tu amor florecidas
y en un cabello mío entretejidas.

21. With flowers and emeralds
chosen on cool mornings
we shall weave garlands
flowering in your love,
and bound with one hair of mine.

22. En solo aquel cabello
que en mi cuello volar
  consideraste,
mirástele en mi cuello,
y en él preso quedaste,
y en uno de mis ojos te llagaste.

22. You considered
that one hair fluttering at my neck;
you gazed at it upon my neck
and it captivated you;
and one of my eyes wounded you.

23. Cuando tú me mirabas
su gracia en mí tus ojos imprimían;

23. When you looked at me
your eyes imprinted your grace in
  me;

por eso me adamabas,
y en eso merecían
los míos adorar lo que en ti vían.

24. No quieras despreciarme,
que, si color moreno en mí
   hallaste,
ya bien puedes mirarme
después que me miraste,
que gracia y hermosura en mí
   dejaste.

25. Cogednos las raposas,
que está ya florecida nuestra viña,
en tanto que de rosas
hacemos una piña,
y no parezca nadie en la montiña.

26. Detente, cierzo muerto;
ven, austro, que recuerdas los
   amores,
aspira por mi huerto,
y corran sus olores,
y pacerá el Amado entre las flores.

Esposo
27. Entrado se ha la esposa
en el ameno huerto deseado,
y a su sabor reposa,
el cuello reclinado
sobre los dulces brazos del Amado.

28. Debajo del manzano,
allí conmigo fuiste desposada;
allí te di la mano
y fuiste reparada
donde tu madre fuera violada.

29. A las aves ligeras,
leones, ciervos, gamos saltadores,
montes, valles, riberas,
aguas, aires, ardores,
y miedos de las noches veladores:

for this you loved me ardently;
and thus my eyes deserved
to adore what they beheld in you.

24. Do not despise me;
for if, before, you found me dark,
now truly you can look at me
since you have looked
and left in me grace and beauty.

25. Catch us the foxes,
for our vineyard is now in flower,
while we fashion a cone of roses
intricate as the pine's;
and let no one appear on the hill.

26. Be still, deadening north wind;
south wind come, you that waken
   love,
breathe through my garden,
let its fragrance flow,
and the Beloved will feed amid the
   flowers.

Bridegroom
27. The bride has entered
the sweet garden of her desire,
and she rests in delight,
laying her neck
on the gentle arms of her Beloved.

28. Beneath the apple tree:
there I took you for my own,
there I offered you my hand,
and restored you,
where your mother was corrupted.

29. Swift-winged birds,
lions, stags, and leaping roes,
mountains, lowlands, and river
   banks,
waters, winds, and ardors,
watching fears of night:

30. Por las amenas liras
y canto de serenas os conjuro
que cesen vuestras iras,
y no toquéis al muro,
porque la esposa duerma más
  seguro.

30. By the pleasant lyres
and the siren's song, I conjure you
to cease your anger
and not touch the wall,
that the bride may sleep in deeper
  peace.

Esposa
31. ¡Oh ninfas de Judea!
en tanto que en las flores y rosales
el ámbar perfumea,
morá en los arrabales,
y no queráis tocar nuestros
  umbrales.

Bride
31. You girls of Judea,
while among flowers and roses
the amber spreads its perfume,
stay away, there on the outskirts:
do not so much as seek to touch
  our thresholds.

32. Escóndete, Carillo,
y mira con tu haz a las montañas,
y no quieras decillo;
mas mira las compañas
de la que va por ínsulas extrañas.

32. Hide yourself, my love;
turn your face toward the
  mountains,
and do not speak;
but look at those companions
going with her through strange
  islands.

Esposo
33. La blanca palomica
al arca con el ramo se ha tornado;
y ya la tortolica
al socio deseado
en las riberas verdes ha hallado.

Bridegroom
33. The small white dove
has returned to the ark with an
  olive branch;
and now the turtledove
has found its longed-for mate
by the green river banks.

34. En soledad vivía,
y en soldedad ha puesto ya su nido,
y en soledad la guía
a solas su querido,
también en soledad de amor
  herido.

34. She lived in solitude,
and now in solitude has built her
  nest;
and in solitude he guides her,
he alone, who also bears
in solitude the wound of love.

Esposa
35. Gocémonos, Amado,
y vámonos a ver en tu hermosura
al monte y al collado
do mana el agua pura;
entremos más adentro en la
  espesura,

Bride
35. Let us rejoice, Beloved,
and let us go forth to behold
  ourselves in your beauty,
to the mountain and to the hill,
to where the pure water flows,
and further, deep into the thicket.

36. y luego a las subidas
cavernas de la piedra nos iremos,
que están bien escondidas,
y allí nos entraremos,
y el mosto de granadas
   gustaremos.

36. And then we will go on
to the high caverns in the rock
which are so well concealed;
there we shall enter
and taste the fresh juice of the
   pomegranates.

37. Allí me mostrarías
aquello que mi alma pretendía,
y luego me darías
allí, tú, ¡vida mía!
aquello que me diste el otro día:

37. There you will show me
what my soul has been seeking,
and then you will give me,
you, my life, will give me there
what you gave me on that other
   day:

38. el aspirar del aire,
el canto de la dulce filomena,
el soto y su donaire,
en la noche serena,
con llama que consume y no da
   pena.

38. the breathing of the air,
the song of the sweet nightingale;
the grove and its living beauty
in the serene night,
with a flame that is consuming
   and painless.

39. Que nadie lo miraba;
Aminadab tampoco parecía
y el cerco sosegaba
y la caballería
a vista de las aguas descendía.

39. No one looked at her,
nor did Aminadab appear;
the siege was still;
and the cavalry,
at the sight of the waters,
   descended.

2.
NOCHE OSCURA

2.
THE DARK NIGHT

Canciones de el alma que se goza
de haber llegado al alto estado de
la perfección, que es la unión con
Dios, por el camino de la negación
espiritual.

Songs of the soul that rejoices in
having reached the high state of
perfection, which is union with
God, by the path of spiritual negation.

1. En una noche oscura,
con ansias, en amores inflamada,
¡oh dichosa ventura!
salí sin ser notada
estando ya mi casa sosegada.

1. One dark night,
fired with love's urgent longings
—ah, the sheer grace!—
I went out unseen,
my house being now all stilled.

2. A oscuras y segura,
por la secreta escala disfrazada,
¡oh dichosa ventura!
a oscuras y en celada,
estando ya mi casa sosegada.

3. En la noche dichosa,
en secreto, que nadie me veía,
ni yo miraba cosa,
sin otra luz y quía
sino la que en el corazón ardía.

4. Aquésta me guiaba
más cierto que la luz del
   mediodía,
adónde me esperaba
quien yo bien me sabía,
en parte donde nadie parecía.

5.¡Oh noche que guiaste!
¡Oh noche amable más que el
   alborada!
¡Oh noche que juntaste
Amado con amada,
amada en el Amado transformada!

6. En mi pecho florido,
que entero para él solo se
   guardaba,
allí quedó dormido,
y yo le regalaba,
y el ventalle de cedros aire daba.

7. El aire de la almena,
cuando yo sus cabellos esparcía,
con su mano serena
en mi cuello hería
y todos mis sentidos suspendía.

2. In darkness, and secure,
by the secret ladder, disguised,
—ah, the sheer grace!—
in darkness and concealment,
my house being now all stilled.

3. On that glad night
in secret, for no one saw me,
nor did I look at anything
with no other light or guide
than the one that burned in my
   heart.

4. This guided me
more surely than the light of noon
to where he was awaiting me
—him I knew so well—
there in a place where no one
   appeared.

5. O guiding night!
O night more lovely than the dawn!
O night that has united
the Lover with his beloved,
transforming the beloved in her
   Lover.

6. Upon my flowering breast,
which I kept wholly for him alone,
there he lay sleeping,
and I caressing him
there in a breeze from the fanning
   cedars.

7. When the breeze blew from the
   turret,
as I parted his hair,
it wounded my neck
with its gentle hand,
suspending all my senses.

8. Quedéme y olvidéme,
el rostro recliné sobre el Amado,
cesó todo y dejéme,
dejando me cuidado
entre las azucenas olvidado.

8. I abandoned and forgot myself,
laying my face on my Beloved;
all things ceased; I went out from
  myself,
leaving my cares
forgotten among the lilies.

3.
LLAMA DE AMOR VIVA

3.
THE LIVING FLAME OF LOVE

Canciones del alma en la intima
communicación de unión de amor
de Dios.

Songs of the soul in the intimate
communication of loving union
with God.

1. ¡Oh llama de amor viva,
que tiernamente hieres
de mi alma en el más profundo
  centro!
Pues ya no eres esquiva,
acaba ya, si quieres;
¡rompe la tela de este dulce
  encuentro!

1. O living flame of love
that tenderly wounds my soul
in its deepest center! Since
now you are not oppressive,
now consummate! if it be your
  will:
tear through the veil of this
  sweet encounter!

2. ¡Oh cauterio suave!
¡Oh regalada llaga!
¡Oh mano blanda! ¡Oh toque
  delicado,
que a vida eterna sabe,
y toda deuda paga!
Matando, muerte en vida la has
  trocado.

2. O sweet cautery,
O delightful wound!
O gentle hand! O delicate touch
that tastes of eternal life
and pays every debt!
In killing you changed death to
  life.

3. ¡Oh lamparas de fuego,
en cuyos resplandores
las profundas cavernas del
  sentido,
que estaba oscuro y ciego,
con extraños primores
calor y luz dan junto a su
  Querido!

3. O lamps of fire!
in whose splendors
the deep caverns of feeling,
once obscure and blind,
now give forth, so rarely, so
  exquisitely,
both warmth and light to their
  Beloved.

4. ¡Cuán manso y amoroso
recuerdas en mi seno,
donde secretamente solo moras,
y en tu aspirar sabroso,
de bien y gloria lleno,
cuán delicadamente me
   enamoras!

4. How gently and lovingly
you wake in my heart,
where in secret you dwell alone;
and in your sweet breathing,
filled with good and glory,
how tenderly you swell my heart
   with love.

4.
Coplas del mismo hechas sobre un éxtasis de harta contemplación.

4.
Stanzas concerning an ecstasy experienced in high contemplation.

Entréme donde no supe,
y quedéme no sabiendo,
toda ciencia trascendiendo.

I entered into unknowing,
and there I remained unknowing
transcending all knowledge.

1. Yo no supe dónde estaba,
pero, cuando allí me vi,
sin saber dónde me estaba,
grandes cosas entendí;
no diré lo que sentí,
que me quedé no sabiendo,
toda ciencia trascendiendo.

1. I entered into unknowing,
yet when I saw myself there,
without knowing where I was,
I understood great things;
I will not say what I felt
for I remained in unknowing
transcending all knowledge.

2. De paz y de piedad
era la ciencia perfecta,
en profunda soledad
entendida, vía recta;
era cosa tan secreta,
que me quedé balbuciendo,
toda ciencia trascendiendo.

2. That perfect knowledge
was of peace and holiness
held at no remove
in profound solitude;
it was something so secret
that I was left stammering,
transcending all knowledge.

3. Estaba tan embebido,
tan absorto y ajenado,
que se quedó mi sentido
de todo sentir privado,
y el espíritu dotado
de un entender no entendiendo,
toda ciencia trascendiendo.

3. I was so 'whelmed,
so absorbed and withdrawn,
that my senses were left
deprived of all their sensing,
and my spirit was given
an understanding while not
   understanding,
transcending all knowledge.

4. El que allí llega de vero
de sí mismo desfallece;

4. He who truly arrives there
cuts free from himself;

cuanto sabía primero
mucho bajo le parece,
y su ciencia tanto crece,
que se queda no sabiendo,
toda ciencia trascendiendo.

5. Cuanto más alto se sube,
tanto menos se entendía,
que es la tenebrosa nube
que a la noche esclarecía:
por eso quien la sabía
queda siempre no sabiendo,
toda ciencia trascendiendo.

6. Este saber no sabiendo
es de tan alto poder,
que los sabios arguyendo
jamás le pueden vencer;
que no llega su saber
a no entender entendiendo,
toda ciencia trascendiendo.

7. Y es de tan alta excelencia
aqueste sumo saber,
que no hay facultad ni ciencia
que le puedan emprender
quien se supiere vencer
con un no saber sabiendo,
irá siempre trascendiendo.

8. Y, si lo queréis oír,
consiste esta suma ciencia
en un subido sentir
de la divinal esencia;
es obra de su clemencia
hacer quedar no entendiendo,
toda ciencia trascendiendo.

all that he knew before
now seems worthless,
and his knowledge so soars
that he is left in unknowing
transcending all knowledge.

5. The higher he ascends
the less he understands,
because the cloud is dark
which lit up the night;
whoever knows this
remains always in unknowing
transcending all knowledge.

6. This knowledge in unknowing
is so overwhelming
that wise men disputing
can never overthrow it,
for their knowledge does not
   reach
to the understanding of not
   understanding,
transcending all knowledge.

7. And this supreme knowledge
   is so exalted
that no power of man or learning
can grasp it;
he who masters himself
will, with knowledge in
   unknowing,
always be transcending.

8. And if you should want to
   hear:
this highest knowledge lies
in the loftiest sense
of the essence of God;
this is a work of his mercy,
to leave one without
   understanding,
transcending all knowledge.

5.

Coplas del alma que pena por ver a Dios.

Vivo sin vivir en mí
y de tal manera espero,
que muero porque no muero.

1. En mí yo no vivo ya,
y sin Dios vivir no puedo;
pues sin él y sin mí quedo,
este vivir ¿qué será?
Mil muertes se me hará,
pues mi misma vida espero,
muriendo porque no muero.

2. Esta vida que yo vivo
es privación de vivir;
y así, es continuo morir
hasta que viva contigo.
Oye, mi Dios, lo que digo:
que esta vida no la quiero,
que muero porque no muero.

3. Estando ausente de ti
¿qué vida puedo tener,
sino muerte padecer
la mayor que nunca vi?
Lástima tengo de mí,
pues de suerte persevero,
que muero porque no muero.

4. El pez que del agua sale
aun de alivio no carece,
que en la muerte que padece
al fin la muerte le vale.
¿Qué muerte habrá que se
    iguale
a mi vivir lastimero,
pues si más vivo más muero?

5. Cuando me pienso aliviar
de verte en el Sacramento,

5.

Stanzas of the soul that suffers with longing to see God.

I live, but not in myself,
and I have such hope
that I die because I do not die.

1. I no longer live within myself
and I cannot live without God,
for having neither him nor
    myself
what will life be?
It will be a thousand deaths,
longing for my true life
and dying because I do not die.

2. This life that I live
is no life at all,
and so I die continually
until I live with you;
hear me, my God:
I do not desire this life,
I am dying because I do not die.

3. When I am away from you
what life can I have
except to endure
the bitterest death known?
I pity myself,
for I go on and on living,
dying because I do not die.

4. A fish that leaves the water
    has this relief:
the dying it endures
ends at last in death.
What death can equal my
    pitiable life?
For the longer I live, the more
    drawn out is my dying.

5. When I try to find relief
seeing you in the Sacrament,

háceme más sentimiento	I find this greater sorrow:
el no te poder gozar;	I cannot enjoy you wholly.
todo es para más penar	All things are affliction
por no verte como quiero,	since I do not see you as I desire,
y muero porque no muero.	*and I die because I do not die.*

6. Y si me gozo, Señor,	6. And if I rejoice, Lord,
con esperanza de verte,	in the hope of seeing you,
en ver que puedo perderte	yet seeing I can lose you
se me dobla mi dolor;	doubles my sorrow.
viviendo en tanto pavor	Living in such fear
y esperando como espero,	and hoping as I hope,
muérome porque no muero.	*I die because I do not die.*

7. ¡Sácame de aquesta muerte,	7. Lift me from this death,
mi Dios, y dame la vida;	my God, and give me life;
no me tengas impedida	do not hold me bound
en este lazo tan fuerte;	with these bonds so strong;
mira que peno por verte,	see how I long to see you;
y mi mal es tan entero,	my wretchedness is so complete
que muero porque no muero!	*that I die because I do not die.*

8. Lloraré me muerte ya	8. I will cry out for death
y lamentaré mi vida,	and mourn my living
en tanto que detenida	while I am held here
por mis pecados está.	for my sins.
¡Oh mi Dios!, ¿cuándo será	O my God, when will it be
cuando yo diga de vero:	that I can truly say:
vivo ya porque no muero?	*now I live because I do not die?*

6.

Otras del mismo a lo divino.

6.

Stanzas given a spiritual meaning.

Tras de un amoroso lance,	*I went out seeking love,*
y no de esperanza falto,	*and with unfaltering hope*
volé tan alto, tan alto,	*I flew so high, so high,*
que le di a la caza alcance.	*that I overtook the prey.*

1. Para que yo alcance diese	1. That I might take the prey
a aqueste lance divino,	of this adventuring in God
tanto volar me convino	I had to fly so high
que de vista me perdiese;	that I was lost from sight;
y, con todo, en este trance	and though in this adventure
en el vuelo quedé falto;	I faltered in my flight,

mas el amor fue tan alto,
que le di a la caza alcance.

yet love had already flown so high
that I took the prey.

2. Cuanto más alto subía
deslumbróseme la vista,
y la más fuerte conquista
en oscuro se hacía;
mas, por ser de amor el lance,
di un ciego y oscuro salto,
y fui tan alto, tan alto,
que le di a la caza alcance.

2. When I ascended higher
my vision was dazzled,
and the most difficult conquest
came about in darkness;
but since I was seeking love
the leap I made was blind and
    dark,
and I rose so high, so high,
that I took the prey.

3. Cuanto más alto llegaba
de este lance tan subido,
tanto más bajo y rendido
y abatido me hallaba;
dije: ¡No habrá quien alcance!;
y abatíme tanto, tanto,
que fui tan alto, tan alto,
que le di a la caza alcance.

3. The higher I ascended
in this seeking so lofty
the lower and more subdued
and abased I became.
I said: No one can overtake it!
And sank, ah, so low,
that I was so high, so high,
that I took the prey.

4. Por una extraña manera
mil vuelos pasé de un vuelo,
porque esperanza del cielo
tanto alcanza cuanto espera;
esperé solo este lance,
y en esperar no fui falto,
pues fui tan alto, tan alto,
que le di a la caza alcance.

4. In a wonderful way
my one flight surpassed a
    thousand,
for the hope of heaven
attains as much as it hopes for;
this seeking is my only hope,
and in hoping, I made no
    mistake,
because I flew so high, so high,
that I took the prey.

7.
**Otras canciones a lo divino de
Cristo y el alma.**

7.
**Stanzas applied spiritually to
Christ and the soul.**

1. Un pastorcico solo está
    penado,
ajeno de placer y de contento,
y en su pastora puesto el
    pensamiento,
y el pecho del amor muy lastimado.

1. A lone young shepherd lived
    in pain
withdrawn from pleasure and
    contentment,
his thoughts fixed on a
    shepherd-girl
his heart an open wound with love.

2. No llora por haberle amor
  llagado,
que no le pena verse así afligido,
aunque en el corazón está
  herido;
mas llora por pensar que está
  olvidado.

3. Que sólo de pensar que está
  olvidado
de su bella pastora, con gran
  pena
se deja maltratar in tierra ajena,
el pecho del amor muy lastimado.

4. Y dice el pastorcico: ¡Ay,
  desdichado
de aquel que de mi amor ha
  hecho ausencia
y no quiere gozar la mi presencia,
*y el pecho por su amor muy
  lastimado.*

5. Y a cabo de un gran rato se ha
  encumbrado
sobre un árbol, do abrió sus
  brazos bellos,
y muerto se ha quedado asido
  dellos,
el pecho del amor muy lastimado.

2. He weeps, but not from the
  wound of love,
there is no pain in such affliction,
even though the heart is pierced;
he weeps in knowing he's been
  forgotten.

3. That one thought: his shining
  one
has forgotten him, is such great
  pain
that he bows to brutal handling
  in a foreign land,
his heart an open wound with love.

4. The shepherd says: I pity the
  one
who draws herself back from my
  love,
and does not seek the joy of my
  presence,
*though my heart is an open wound
  with love for her.*

5. After a long time he climbed a
  tree,
and spread his shining arms,
and hung by them, and died,
his heart an open wound with love.

8.
Cantar del alma que se huelga de conocer a Dios por fe.

*Que bien sé yo la fonte que mana y
corre, aunque es de noche.*

1. Aquella eterna fonte está
  escondida,

8.
Song of the soul that rejoices in knowing God through faith.

*For I know well the spring that flows
  and runs,
although it is night.*

1. That eternal spring is hidden,

que bien sé yo do tiene su
  manida,
aunque es de noche.

2. Su origen no lo sé, pues no le
  tiene,
mas sé que todo origen de ella
  viene,
aunque es de noch.

3. Sé que no puede ser cosa tan
  bella,
y que cielos y tierra beben de
  ella,
aunque es de noche.

4. Bien sé que suelo en ella no se
  halla,
y que ninguno puede vadealla,
aunque es de noche.

5. Su claridad nunca es
  oscurecida,
y sé que toda luz de ella es venida,
aunque es de noche.

6. Sé ser tan caudalosos sus
  corrientes,
que infiernos, cielos riegan y las
  gentes,
aunque es de noche.

7. El corriente que nace de esta
  fuente
bien sé que es tan capaz y
  omnipotente,
aunque es de noche.

8. El corriente que de estas dos
  procede
sé que ninguna de ellas le
  precede,
aunque es de noche.

for I know well where it has its
  rise,
although it is night.

2. I do not know its origin, nor
  has it one,
but I know that every origin has
  come from it,
although it is night.

3. I know that nothing else is so
  beautiful,
and that the heavens and the
  earth drink there,
although it is night.

4. I know well that it is bottomless
and no one is able to cross it,
although it is night.

5. Its clarity is never darkened,
and I know that every light has
  come from it,
although it is night.

6. I know that its streams are so
  brimming
they water the lands of hell, the
  heavens, and earth,
although it is night.

7. I know well the stream that
  flows from this spring
is mighty in compass and power,
although it is night.

8. I know the stream proceeding
  from these two,
that neither of them in fact
  precedes it,
although it is night.

9. Aquesta eterna fonte está
    escondida
en este vivo pan por darnos vida,
aunque es de noche.

9. This eternal spring is hidden
in this living bread for our life's
    sake,
although it is night.

10. Aquí se está llamando a las
    criaturas,
y de esta agua se hartan, aunque
    a oscuras,
porque es de noche.

10. It is here calling out to
    creatures;
and they satisfy their thirst,
    although in darkness,
because it is night.

11. Aquesta viva fuente que
    deseo,
en este pan de vida yo la veo,
aunque es de noche.

11. This living spring that I long
    for,
I see in this bread of life,
although it is night.

9.
ROMANCES

9.
ROMANCES

1. Romance sobre el Evangelio "In principio erat Verbum," acerca de la Santisima Trinidad.

1. Romance on the Gospel text "In principio erat Verbum," regarding the Blessed Trinity.

En el principio moraba
el Verbo, y en Dios vivía,
en quien su felicidad
infinita poseía.
El mismo Verbo Dios era,
que el principio se decía;
él moraba en el principio,
y principio no tenía.
El era el mismo principio,
por eso de él carecía.
El Verbo se llama Hijo,
que del principio nacía;
hale siempre concebido
y siempre le concebía;
dale siempre su sustancia,
y siempre se la tenía.
Y así la gloria del Hijo
es la que en el Padre había,
y toda su gloria el Padre
en el Hijo poseía.

In the beginning the Word
was; he lived in God
and possessed in him
his infinite happiness.
That same Word was God,
who is the Beginning;
he was in the beginning
and had no beginning.
He was himself the Beginning
and therefore had no beginning.
The Word is called Son;
he was born of the Beginning
who had always conceived him,
giving of his substance always,
yet always possessing it.
And thus the glory of the Son
was the Father's glory,
and the Father possessed
all his glory in the Son.

Como amado en el amante	As the lover in the beloved
uno en otro residía,	each lived in the other,
y aquese amor que los une	and the Love that unites them
en lo mismo convenía	is one with them,
con el uno y con el otro	their equal, excellent as
en igualdad y valía.	the One and the Other:
Tres Personas y un amado	Three Persons, and one Beloved
entre todos tres había,	among all three.
y un amor en todas ellas	One love in them all
y un amante las hacía,	makes of them one Lover,
y el amante es el amado	and the Lover is the Beloved
en que cada cual vivía;	in whom each one lives.
que el ser que los tres posseen	For the being that the three
cada cual le poseía,	possess
y cada cual de ellos ama	each of them possesses,
a la que este ser tenía.	and each of them loves
Este ser es cada una,	him who bears this being.
y éste solo las unía	Each one is this being,
en un inefable nudo	which alone unites them,
que decir no se sabía;	binding them deeply,
por lo cual era infinito	one beyond words.
el amor que las unía,	Thus it is a boundless Love that
porque un solo amor tres tienen,	unites them,
que su esencia se decía;	for the three have one love
que el amor cuanto más uno,	which is their essence;
tanto más amor hacía.	and the more love is one
	the more it is love.

2. De la comunicación de las tres Personas.	*2. On the communication among the Three Persons.*

En aquel amor inmenso	In that immense love
que de los dos procedía,	proceeding from the two
palabras de gran regalo	the Father spoke words
el Padre al Hijo decía,	of great affection to the Son,
de tan profundo deleite,	words of such profound delight
que nadie las entendía;	that no one understood them;
sólo el Hijo lo gozaba,	they were meant for the Son,
que es a quien pertenecía.	and he alone rejoiced in them.
Pero aquello que se entiende,	What he heard
de esta manera decía:	was this:
"Nada me contenta, Hijo,	"My Son, only your
fuera de tu compañía;	company contents me,
y si algo me contenta,	and when something pleases me

en ti mismo lo quería.
El que a ti más se parece
a mí más satisfacía,
y el que en nada te semeja
en mí nada hallaría.
En ti solo me he agradado,
¡oh vida de vida mía!
Eres lumbre de mi lumbre,
eres mi sabiduría,
figura de mi sustancia,
en quien bien me complacía.
Al que a ti te amare, Hijo,
a mi mismo le daría,
y el amor que yo en ti tengo
ese mismo en él pondría,
en razón de haber amado
a quien yo tanto quería."

3. De la creación.

"Una esposa que te ame,
mi Hijo, darte quería,
que por tu valor merezca
tener nuestra compañía
y comer pan a una mesa,
del mismo que yo comía,
porque conozca los bienes
que en tal hijo yo tenía,
y se congracie conmigo
de tu gracia y lozanía."
    "Mucho lo agradezco, Padre,
—el Hijo le respondía—;
a la esposa que me dieres
yo mi claridad daría,
para que por ella vea
cuánto mi Padre valía,
y cómo el ser que poseo
de su ser le recibía.
Reclinarla he yo en mi brazo,
y en tu amor se abrasaría,
y con eterno deleite
tu bondad sublimaría."

I love that thing in you;
whoever resembles you most
satisfies me most,
and whoever is like you in
    nothing
will find nothing in me.
I am pleased with you alone,
O life of my life!
You are the light of my light,
you are my wisdom,
the image of my substance
in whom I am well pleased.
My Son, I will give myself
to him who loves you
and I will love him
with the same love I have for you,
because he has loved
you whom I love so."

3. On creation.

"My Son, I wish to give you
a bride who will love you.
Because of you she will deserve
to share our company,
and eat at our table,
the same bread I eat,
that she may know the good
I have in such a Son;
and rejoice with me
in your grace and fullness."
    "I am very grateful,"
the Son answered;
"I will show my brightness
to the bride you give me,
so that by it she may see
how great my Father is,
and how I have received
my being from your being.
I will hold her in my arms
and she will burn with your love,
and with eternal delight
she will exalt your goodness."

4. Prosigue

"Hágase, pues"—dijo el
    Padre—,
,que tu amor lo merecía";
y en este dicho que dijo,
el mundo criado había
palacio para la esposa
hecho en gran sabiduría;
el cual en dos aposentos,
alto y bajo, dividía.
El bajo de diferencias
infinitas componía;
mas el alto hermoseaba
de admirable pedrería,
porque conozca la esposa
el Esposo que tenía.
En el alto colocaba
la angélica jerarquía;
pero la natura humana
en el bajo la ponía,
por ser en su compostura
algo de menor valía.
Y aunque el ser y los lugares
de esta suerte los partía,
pero todos son un cuerpo
de la esposa que decía;
que el amor de un mismo Esposo
una esposa los hacía.
Los de arriba poseían
el Esposo en alegría;
los de abajo, en esperanza
de fe que les infundía,
diciéndoles que algún tiempo
él los engrandecería
y que aquella su bajeza
él se la levantaría
de manera que ninguno
ya la vituperaría;
porque en todo semejante
él a ellos se haría
y se vendría con ellos,
y con ellos moraría;
y que Dios sería hombre,

4. Continues

"Let it be done, then," said the
    Father,
for your love has deserved it.
And by these words
the world was created,
a palace for the bride
made with great wisdom
and divided into rooms,
one above, the other below.
The lower was furnished
with infinite variety,
while the higher was made
    beautiful
with marvelous jewels,
that the bride might know
the Bridegroom she had.
The orders of angels
were placed in the higher,
but humanity was given
the lower place,
for it was, in its being,
a lesser thing.
And though beings and places
were divided in this way,
yet all form one,
who is called the bride;
for love of the same Bridegroom
made one bride of them.
Those higher ones possessed
the Bridegroom in gladness;
the lower in hope, founded
on the faith that he infused in
    them,
telling them that one day
he would exalt them,
and that he would lift them
up from their lowness
so that no one
could mock it any more;
for he would make himself
wholly like them,
and he would come to them

y que el hombre Dios sería,	and dwell with them;
y trataría con ellos,	and God would be man
comería y bebería;	and man would be God,
y que con ellos contino	and he would walk with them
él mismo se quedaría,	and eat and drink with them;
hasta que se consumase	and he himself would be
este siglo que corría,	with them continually
cuando se gozaran juntos	until the consummation
en eterna melodía;	of this world,
porque él era la cabeza	when, joined, they would rejoice
de la esposa que tenía,	in eternal song;
a la cual todos los miembros	for he was the Head
de los justos juntaría,	of this bride of his
que son cuerpo de la esposa,	to whom all the members
a la cual él tomaría	of the just would be joined,
en sus brazos tiernamente,	who form the body of the bride.
y allí su amor la daría;	He would take her
y que, así juntos en uno,	tenderly in his arms
al Padre la llevaría,	and there give her his love;
donde del mismo deleite	and when they were thus one,
que Dios goza, gozaría;	he would lift her to the Father
que, como el Padre y el Hijo,	where God's very joy
y el que de ellos procedía	would be her joy.
el uno vive en el otro,	For as the Father and the Son
así la esposa sería,	and he who proceeds from them
que, dentro de Dios absorta,	live in one another,
vida de Dios viviría.	so it would be with the bride;
	for, taken wholly into God,
	she will live the life of God.

5. Prosigue	*5. Continues*
Con esta buena esperanza	By this bright hope
que de arriba les venía,	which came to them from above,
el tedio de sus trabajos	their wearying labors
más leve se les hacía;	were lightened;
pero la esperanza larga	but the drawn-out waiting
y el deseo que crecía	and their growing desire
de gozarse con su Esposo	to rejoice with their Bridegroom
contino les afligía;	wore on them continually.
por lo cual con oraciones,	So, with prayers
con suspiros y agonía,	and sighs and suffering,
con lágrimas y gemidos	with tears and moanings
le rogaban noche y día	they asked night and day

que ya se determinase
a les dar su compañía.
Unos decían: "¡O si fuese
en mi tiempo el alegría!"
Otros: "¡Acaba, Señor;
al que has de enviar, envía!"
Otros: "¡Oh si ya rompieses
esos cielos, y vería
con mis ojos que bajases,
y mi llanto cesaría!"
"¡Regad, nubes de lo alto,
que la tierra lo pedía
y ábrase ya la tierra,
que espinas nos producía,
y produzca aquella flor
con que ella florecería!"
Otros decían: "¡Oh dichoso
el que en tal tiempo sería,
que merezca ver a Dios
con los ojos que tenía,
y tratarle con sus manos,
y andar en su compañía,
y gozar de los misterios
que entonces ordenaría!"

that now he would determine
to grant them his company.
Some said: "If only
this joy would come in my time!"
Others: "Come, Lord,
send him whom you will send!"
And others: "Oh, if only these
heavens
would break, and with my own
eyes
I could see him descending;
then I would stop my crying out."
"Oh, clouds, rain down from
your height,
earth needs you,
and let the earth open,
which has borne us thorns;
let it bring forth that flower
that would be its flowering."
Others said: "What gladness
for him who is living then,
who will be able to see God
with his own eyes,
and touch him with his hand
and walk with him
and enjoy the mysteries
which he will then ordain."

6. Prosigue

En aquestos y otros ruegos
gran tiempo pasado había;
pero en los postreros años
el fervor mucho crecía,
cuando el viejo Simeón
en deseo se encendía,
rogando a Dios que quisiese
dejalle ver este día.
Y así, el Espíritu Santo
al buen viejo respondía:
Que le daba su palabra
que la muerte no vería
hasta que la vida viese
que de arriba descendía,

6. Continues

In these and other prayers
a long time had passed;
but in the later years
their fervor swelled and grew
when the aged Simeon
burned with longing,
and begged God that he
might see this day.
And so the Holy Spirit
answering the good old man
gave him his word
that he would not see death
until he saw Life
descending from the heights,

y que él en sus mismas manos
al mismo Dios tomaría,
y le tendría en sus brazos
y consigo abrazaría.

until he took God himself
into his own hands
and holding him in his arms,
pressed him to himself.

7. Prosigue la Encarnación

7. The Incarnation

Ya que el tiempo era llegado
en que hacerse convenía
el rescate de la esposa,
que en duro yugo servía
debajo de aquella ley
que Moisés dado le había,
el Padre con amor tierno
de esta manera decía:
"Ya ves, Hijo, que a tu esposa
a tu imagen hecho había,
y en lo que a ti se parece
contigo bien convenía;
pero difiere en la carne
que en tu simple ser no había.
En los amores perfectos
esta ley se requería:
que se haga semejante
el amante a quien quería;
que la mayor semejanza
más deleite contenía;
el cual, sin duda, en tu esposa
grandemente crecería
si te viere semejante
en la carne que tenía."
"Mi voluntad es la tuya
—el Hijo le respondía—
y la gloria que yo tengo
es tu voluntad ser mía,
y a mí me conviene, Padre,
lo que tu Alteza decía,
porque por esta manera
tu bondad más se vería;
veráse tu gran potencia,
justicia y sabiduría;
irélo a decir al mundo
y noticia le daría
de tu belleza y dulzura

Now that the time had come
when it would be good
to ransom the bride
serving under the hard yoke
of that law
which Moses had given her,
the Father, with tender love,
spoke in this way:
"Now you see, Son, that your
    bride
was made in your image,
and so far as she is like you
she will suit you well;
yet she is different, in her flesh,
which your simple being does
    not have.
In perfect love
this law holds:
that the lover become
like the one he loves;
for the greater their likeness
the greater their delight.
Surely your bride's delight
would greatly increase
were she to see you like her,
in her own flesh."
"My will is yours,"
the Son replied,
"and my glory is
that your will be mine.
This is fitting, Father,
what you, the Most High, say;
for in this way
your goodness will be more
    evident,
your great power will be seen
and your justice and wisdom.

y de tu soberanía.
Iré a buscar a mi esposa,
y sobre mí tomaría
sus fatigas y trabajos,
en que tanto padecía;
y porque ella vida tenga,
yo por ella moriría,
y sacándola del lago
a ti te la volvería."

I will go and tell the world,
spreading the word
of your beauty and sweetness
and of your sovereignty.
I will go seek my bride
and take upon myself
her weariness and labors
in which she suffers so;
and that she may have life,
I will die for her,
and lifting her out of that deep,
I will restore her to you."

8. Prosigue

8. Continues

Entónces llamó a un arcángel
que san Gabriel se decía,
y enviólo a una doncella
que se llamaba María,
de cuyo consentimiento
el misterio se hacía;
en la cual la Trinidad
de carne al Verbo vestía;
y aunque tres hacen la obra,
en el uno se hacía;
y quedó el Verbo encarnado
en el vientre de María.
Y el que tenía sólo Padre,
ya también Madre tenía,
aunque no como cualquiera
que de varón concebía,
que de las entrañas de ella
él su carne recibía;
por lo cual Hijo de Dios
y del hombre se decía.

Then he called
the archangel Gabriel
and sent him to
the virgin Mary,
at whose consent
the mystery was wrought,
in whom the Trinity
clothed the Word with flesh.
and though Three work this,
it is wrought in the One;
and the Word lived incarnate
in the womb of Mary.
And he who had only a Father
now had a Mother too,
but she was not like others
who conceive by man.
From her own flesh
he received his flesh,
so he is called
Son of God and of man.

9. Del Nacimiento

9. The Birth

Ya que era llegado el tiempo
en que de nacer había,
así como desposado
de su tálamo salía
abrazado con su esposa,
que en sus brazos la traía,

When the time had come
for him to be born,
he went forth like the
    bridegroom
from his bridal chamber,
embracing his bride,

al cual la graciosa Madre
en un pesebre ponía,
entre unos animales
que a la sazón allí había.
Los hombres decían cantares,
los ángeles melodía,
festejando el desposorio
que entre tales dos había.
Pero Dios en el pesebre
allí lloraba y gemía,
que eran joyas que la esposa
al desposorio traía.
Y la Madre estaba en pasmo
de que tal trueque veía:
el llanto del hombre en Dios,
y en el hombre la alegría,
lo cual del uno y del otro
tan ajeno ser solía.

holding her in his arms,
whom the gracious Mother
laid in a manger
among some animals
that were there at that time.
Men sang songs
and angels melodies
celebrating the marriage
of Two such as these.
But God there in the manger
cried and moaned;
and these tears were jewels
the bride brought to the
   wedding.
The Mother gazed in sheer
   wonder
on such an exchange:
in God, man's weeping,
and in man, gladness,
to the one and the other
things usually so strange.

Finis

Finis

10.
Romance sobre el salmo "Super flumina Babilonis" [Ps. 137].

10.
A romance on the psalm "By the waters of Babylon" [Ps. 137].

Encima de las corrientes
que en Babilonia hallaba,
allí me senté llorando,
allí la tierra regaba,
acordándome de ti,
¡oh Sión!, a quien amaba.
Era dulce tu memoria,
y con ella más lloraba.
Dejé los trajes de fiesta,
los de trabajo tomaba,
y colgué en los verdes sauces
la música que llevaba,
poneiéndola en esperanza
de aquello que en ti esperaba.
Allí me hirió el amor,

By the rivers
of Babylon
I sat down weeping,
there on the ground.
And remembering you,
O Zion, whom I loved,
in that sweet memory
I wept even more.
I took off my feastday clothes
and put on my working ones;
I hung on the green willows
all the joy I had in song,
putting it aside for that
which I hoped for in you.
There love wounded me

y el corazón me sacaba.	and took away my heart.
Díjele que me matase,	I begged love to kill me
pues de tal suerte llagaba;	since it had so wounded me;
yo me metía en su fuego,	I threw myself in its fire
sabiendo que me abrasaba,	knowing it burned,
disculpando al avecica	excusing now the young bird
que en el fuego se acababa.	that would die in the fire.
Estábame en mí muriendo,	I was dying in myself,
y en ti sólo respiraba,	breathing in you alone.
en mí por ti me moría,	I died within myself for you
y por ti resucitaba,	and for you I revived,
que la memoria de ti	because the memory of you
daba vida y la quitaba.	gave life and took it away.
Gozábanse los extraños	The strangers among whom
entre quien cautivo estaba;	I was captive rejoiced;
preguntábanme cantares	they asked me to sing
de lo que en Sión cantaba:	what I sang in Zion:
—Canta de Sión un himno,	Sing us a song from Zion,
veamos cómo sonaba.	let's hear how it sounds.
—Decid, ¿como en tierra ajena,	I said: How can I sing,
donde por Sión lloraba,	in a strange land where I weep
cantaré yo la alegría	for Zion, sing of the happiness
que en Sión se me quedaba?	that I had there?
Echaríala en olvido	I would be forgetting her
si en la ajena me gozaba.	if I rejoiced in a strange land.
Con mi paladar se junte	May the tongue I speak with
la lengua con que hablaba,	cling to my palate
si de ti yo me olvidare,	if I forget you
en la tierra do moraba.	in this land where I am.
¡Sión, por los verdes ramos	Zion, by the green branches
que Babilonia me daba,	Babylon holds out to me,
de mí se olvide mi diestra,	may my right hand be forgotten
que es lo que en ti más amaba,	(that I so loved when home in you)
si de ti no me acordare,	if I do not remember you,
en lo que más me gozaba,	my greatest joy,
y si yo tuviere fiesta	or celebrate one feastday,
y sin ti la festejaba!	or feast at all without you.
¡Oh hija de Babilonia,	O Daughter of Babylon,
misera y desventurada!	miserable and wretched!
Bienaventurado era	Blessed is he
aquel en quien confiaba,	in whom I have trusted,
que te ha de dar el castigo	for he will punish you
que de tu mano llevaba,	as you have me;
y juntará sus pequeños,	

y a mí, porque en ti lloraba,
a la piedra, que era Cristo,
por el cual yo te dejaba.

and he will gather his little ones
and me, who wept because of
    you,
at the rock who is Christ
for whom I abandoned you.

11.
Glosa "a lo divino."

11.
A gloss (with spiritual meaning).

Sin arrimo y con arrimo,
sin luz y a oscuras viviendo,
todo my voy consumiendo.

Without support yet with support,
living without light, in darkness,
I am wholly being consumed.

1. Mi alma está desasida
de toda cosa criada,
y sobre sí levantada,
y en una sabrosa vida
sólo en su Dios arrimada.
Por eso ya se dirá
la cosa que más estimo,
que mi alma se ve ya
sin arrimo y con arrimo.

1. My soul is disentangled
from every created thing
and lifted above itself
in a life of gladness
supported only in God.
So now it can be said
that I most value this:
My soul now sees itself
without support yet with support.

2. Y, aunque tinieblas padezco
en esta vida mortal,
no es tan crecido mi mal,
porque, si de luz carezco,
tengo vida celestial;
porque el amor de tal vida,
cuando más ciego va siendo,
que tiene al alma rendida,
sin luz y a oscuras viviendo.

2. And though I suffer darknesses
in this mortal life,
that is not so hard a thing;
for even if I have no light
I have the life of heaven.
For the blinder love is
the more it gives such life,
holding the soul surrendered,
living without light in darkness.

3. Hace tal obra el amor
después que le conocí,
que, si hay bien o mal en mí,
todo lo hace de un sabor,
y al alma transforma en sí;
y así, en su llama sabrosa,
la cual en mí estoy sintiendo,
apriesa, sin quedar cosa,
todo me voy consumiendo.

3. After I have known it
love works so in me
that whether things go well or
    badly
love turns them to one sweetness
transforming the soul in itself.
And so in its delighting flame
which I am feeling within me,
swiftly, with nothing spared,
I am wholly being consumed.

12.
Glosa "a lo divino."

12.
A gloss (with a spiritual meaning).

Por toda la hermosura
nunca yo me perderé,
sino por un no sé qué
que se alcanza por ventura.

Not for all of beauty
will I ever lose myself,
but for I-don't-know-what
which is so gladly gained.

1. Sabor de bien que es finito,
lo más que puede llegar
es cansar el apetito
y estragar el paladar;
y así, por toda dulzura
nunca yo me perderé,
sino por un no sé qué
que se halla por ventura.

1. Delight in the world's good
   things
at the very most
can only tire the appetite
and spoil the palate;
and so, not for all of sweetness
will I ever lose myself,
but for I-don't-know-what
which is so gladly found.

2. El corazón generoso
nunca cura de parar
donde se puede pasar,
sino en más dificultoso;
nada le causa hartura,
y sube tanto su fe,
que gusta de un no sé qué
que se halla por ventura.

2. The generous heart
never delays with easy things
but eagerly goes on
to things more difficult.
Nothing satisfies it,
and its faith ascends so high
that it tastes I-don't-know-what
which is so gladly found.

3. El que de amor adolece,
del divino ser tocado,
tiene el gusto tan trocado
que a los gustos desfallece;
como el que con calentura
fastidia el manjar que ve,
y apetece un no sé qué
que se halla por ventura.

3. He who is sick with love,
whom God himself has touched,
finds his tastes so changed
that they fall away
like a fevered man's
who loathes any food he sees
and desires I-don't know-what
which is so gladly found.

4. No os maravilléis de aquesto,
que el gusto se quede tal,
porque es la causa del mal
ajena de todo el resto;
y así toda criatura
enajenada se ve
y gusta de un no sé gué
que se halla por ventura.

4. Do not wonder
that the taste should be left like
   this,
for the cause of this sickness
differs from all others;
and so he is withdrawn
from all creatures,
and tastes I-don't-know-what
which is so gladly found.

5. Que estando la voluntad
de Divinidad tocada,
no puede quedar pagada
sino con Divinidad;
mas, por ser tal su hermosura
que sólo se ve por fe,
gústala en un no sé qué
que se halla por ventura.

5. For when once the will
is touched by God himself,
it cannot find contentment
except in the Divinity;
but since his Beauty is open
to faith alone, the will
tastes him in I-don't-know-what
which is so gladly found.

6. Pues, de tal enamorado,
decidme si habréis dolor,
pues que no tiene sabor
entre todo lo criado;
solo, sin forma y figura,
sin hallar arrimo y pie,
gustando allá un no sé qué
que se halla por ventura.

6. Tell me, then, would you pity
a person so in love,
who takes no delight
in all creation;
alone, mind empty of form and
   figure,
finding no support or foothold,
he tastes there I-don't-know-what
which is so gladly found.

7. No penséis que el interior,
que es de mucha más valía,
halla gozo y alegría
en lo que acá da sabor;
mas sobre toda hermosura,
y lo que es y será y fue,
gusta de allá un no sé qué
que se halla por ventura.

7. Do not think that he who lives
the so-precious inner life
finds joy and gladness
in the sweetness of the earth;
but there beyond all beauty
and what is and will be and was,
he tastes I-don't-know-what
which is so gladly found.

8. Más emplea su cuidado,
quien se quiere aventajar.
en lo que está por ganar
que en lo que tiene ganado;
y así, para más altura,
yo siempre me inclinaré
sobre todo a un no sé qué
que se halla por ventura.

8. Whoever seeks to advance
takes much more care
in what he has yet to gain
than in what he has already
   gained;
and so I will always tend
toward greater heights;
beyond all things, to I-don't-know-
   what
which is so gladly found.

9. Por lo que por el sentido
puede acá comprehenderse
y todo lo que entenderse,

9. I will never lose myself
for that which the senses
can take in here,

aunque sea muy subido,
ni por gracia y hermosura
yo nunca me perderé,
sino por un no sé qué
que se halla por ventura.

nor for all the mind can hold,
no matter how lofty,
nor for grace or beauty,
but only for I-don't-know-what
which is so gladly found.

13.
Letrilla Navideña

Del Verbo divino
la Virgen preñada
viene de camino:
¡si le dais posada!

13.
Christmas Refrain

The Virgin, weighed
with the Word of God,
comes down the road:
if only you'll shelter her.

14.
Suma de la perfección

Olvido de lo criado,
memoria del Criador,
atención a lo interior,
y estarse amando al Amado.

14.
The Sum of Perfection

Forgetfulness of created things,
remembrance of the Creator,
attention turned toward inward
    things,
and loving the Beloved.

15.
CANTICO ESPIRITUAL
(CB)

Canciones entre el alma y el Esposo

Esposa
1. ¿Adonde te escondiste,
Amado, y me dejaste con
    gemido?
Como el ciervo huiste,
habiéndome herido;
salí tras ti clamando, y eras ido.

2. Pastores los que fuerdes
allá por las majadas al otero,
si por ventura vierdes

15.
THE SPIRITUAL CANTICLE
(CB)

Songs between the soul and the Bride-groom

Bride
1. Where have you hidden,
Beloved, and left me moaning?
You fled like the stag
after wounding me;
I went out calling you, but you
    were gone.

2. Shepherds, you who go
up through the sheepfolds to the
    hill,

aquel que yo más quiero,
decilde que adolezco, peno y
    muero.

3. Buscando mis amores,
iré por esos montes y riberas;
ni cogeré las flores,
ni temeré las fieras,
y pasaré los fuertes y fronteras.

4. ¡Oh bosques y espesuras,
plantadas por la mano del
    Amado!
¡Oh prado de verduras,
de flores esmaltado,
decid si por vosotros ha pasado!

5. Mil gracias derramando
pasó por estos sotos con presura,
y, yéndolos mirando,
con sola su figura,
vestidos los dejó de hermosura.

6. ¡Ay, quién podrá sanarme!
¡Acaba de entregarte ya de vero;
no quieras enviarme
de hoy más ya mensajero
que no saben decirme lo que
    quiero!

7. Y todos cuantos vagan
de ti me van mil gracia
    refiriendo,
y todos más me llagan,
y déjeme muriendo
un no sé qué quedan
    balbuciendo.

if by chance you see
him I love most,
tell him I am sick, I suffer,
    and I die.

3. Seeking my love
I will head for the mountains
    and for watersides;
I will not gather flowers,
nor fear wild beasts;
I will go beyond strong men and
    frontiers.

4. O woods and thickets
planted by the hand of my
    Beloved!
O green meadow,
coated, bright, with flowers,
tell me, has he passed by you?

5. Pouring out a thousand graces,
he passed these groves in haste;
and having looked at them,
with his image alone,
clothed them in beauty.

6. Ah, who has the power to heal
    me?
Now wholly surrender yourself!
Do not send me
any more messengers;
they cannot tell me what I must
    hear.

7. All who are free
tell me a thousand graceful
    things of you;
all wound me more
and leave me dying
of, ah, I-don't-know-what behind
    their stammering.

8. Mas ¿como perseveras,
¡oh vida!, no viviendo donde
vives,
y haciendo porque mueras
las flechas que recibes
de lo que del Amado en ti
concibes?

8. How do you endure
O life, not living where you live,
and being brought near death
by the arrows you receive
from that which you conceive of
your Beloved?

9. ¿Por qué, pues has llagado
aqueste corazón, no le sanaste?
Y, pues me le has robado,
¿por qué así le dejaste,
y no tomas el robo que robaste?

9. Why, since you wounded
this heart, don't you heal it?
And why, since you stole it from
me,
do you leave it so,
and fail to carry off what you
have stolen?

10. ¡Apaga mis enojos,
pues que ninguno basta a
deshacellos,
y véante mis ojos,
pues eres lumbre dellos,
y sólo para ti quiero tenellos!

10. Extinguish these miseries,
since no one else can stamp
them out;
and may my eyes behold you,
because you are their light,
and I would open them to you
alone.

11. Descubre tu presencia
y máteme tu vista y hermosura
mira que la dolencia
de amor, que no se cura
sino con la presencia y la figura.

11. Reveal your presence,
and may the vision of your
beauty be my death;
for the sickness of love
is not cured
except by your very presence
and image.

12. ¡Oh cristalina fuente,
si en esos tus semblantes
plateados
formases de repente
los ojos deseados
que tengo en mis entrañas
dibujados!

12. O spring like crystal!
If only, on your silvered-over
faces,
you would suddenly form
the eyes I have desired,
which I bear sketched deep
within my heart.

13. ¡Apártalos, Amado,
que voy de vuelo!

13. Withdraw them, Beloved,
I am taking flight!

Esposo
—Vuélvate, paloma,
que el ciervo vulnerado
por el otero asoma
al aire de tu vuelo, y fresco toma!

Bridegroom
—Return, dove,
the wounded stag
is in sight on the hill,
cooled by the breeze of your
    flight.

Esposa
14. Mi Amado, las montañas,
los valles solitarios nemorosos,
las ínsulas extrañas,
los ríos sonorosos,
el silbo de los aires amorosos,

The Bride
14. My Beloved, the mountains,
and lonely wooded valleys,
strange islands,
and resounding rivers,
the whistling of love-stirring
    breezes,

15. la noche sosegada
en par de los levantes de la
    aurora,
la música callada,
la soledad sonora,
la cena que recrea y enamora.

15. the tranquil night
at the time of the rising dawn,
silent music,
sounding solitude,
the supper that refreshes and
    deepens love.

16. Cazadnos las raposas,
que está ya florecida nuestra viña,
en tanto que de rosas
hacemos una piña,
y no parezca nadie en la
    montiña.

16. Catch us the foxes,
for our vineyard is now in flower,
while we fashion a cone of roses
intricate as the pine's;
and let no one appear on the hill.

17. Detente, cierzo muerto;
ven, austro, que recuerdas los
    amores,
aspira por mi huerto,
y corran sus olores,
y pacerá el Amado entre las
    flores.

17. Be still, deadening north
    wind; south wind, come, you
    that waken love,
breathe through my garden,
let its fragrance flow,
and the Beloved will feed amid
    the flowers.

18. ¡Oh ninfas de Judea!
en tanto que en las flores y
    rosales
el ámbar perfumea,
morá en los arrabales,
y no queráis tocar nuestros
    umbrales.

18. You girls of Judea,
while among flowers and roses
the amber spreads its perfume,
stay away, there on the outskirts:
do not so much as seek to touch
    our thresholds.

19. Escóndete, Carillo,
y mira con tu haz a las montañas,
y no quieras decillo;
mas mira las compañas
de la que va por ínsulas extrañas.

19. Hide yourself, my love;
turn your face toward the
    mountains,
and do not speak;
but look at those companions
going with her through strange
    islands.

Esposo
20. A las aves ligeras,
leones, ciervos, gamos saltadores,
montes, valles, riberas,
aguas, aires, ardores,
y miedos de las noches
    veladores:

Bridegroom
20. Swift-winged birds,
lions, stags, and leaping roes,
mountains, lowlands, and river
    banks,
waters, winds, and ardors,
watching fears of night:

21. por las amenas liras
y canto de serenas os conjuro
que cesen vuestras iras,
y no toquéis al muro,
porque la esposa duerma más
    seguro.

21. By the pleasant lyres
and the siren's song, I conjure
    you
to cease your anger
and not touch the wall,
that the bride may sleep in
    deeper peace.

22. Entrado se ha la esposa
en el ameno huerto deseado,
y a su sabor reposa,
el cuello reclinado
sobre los dulces brazos del
    Amado.

22. The bride has entered
the sweet garden of her desire,
and she rests in delight,
laying her neck
on the gentle arms of her
    Beloved.

23. Debajo del manzano,
allí conmigo fuiste desposada;
allí te di la mano
y fuiste reparada
donde tu madre fuera violada.

23. Beneath the apple tree:
there I took you for my own,
there I offered you my hand,
and restored you,
where your mother was
    corrupted.

Esposa
24. Nuestro lecho florido,
de cuevas de leones enlazado,

Bride
24. Our bed is in flower,
bound round with linking dens
    of lions,

en púrpura tendido,
de paz edificado,
de mil escudos de oro coronado.

hung with purple,
built up in peace,
and crowned with a thousand
shields of gold.

25. A zaga de tu huella
las jóvenes discurren al camino,
al toque de centella,
al adobado vino,
emisiones de bálsamo divino.

25. Following your footprints
maidens run along the way;
the touch of a spark,
the spiced wine,
cause flowings in them from the
balsam of God.

26. En la interior bodega
de mi Amado bebí, y cuando
salía
por toda aquesta vega,
ya cosa no sabía;
y el ganado perdí que antes
seguía.

26. In the inner wine cellar
I drank of my Beloved, and,
when I went abroad
through all this valley,
I no longer knew anything,
and lost the herd that I was
following.

27. Allí me dio su pecho,
allí me enseñó ciencia muy
sabrosa;
y yo le di de hecho
a mí, sin dejar cosa;
allí le prometí de ser su esposa.

27. There he gave me his breast;
there he taught me a sweet and
living knowledge;
and I gave myself to him,
keeping nothing back;
there I promised to be his bride.

28. Mi alma se ha empleado,
y todo mi caudal en su servicio;
ya no guardo ganado,
ni ya tengo otro oficio,
que ya sólo en amar es mi
ejercicio.

28. Now I occupy my soul
and all my energy in his service;
I no longer tend the herd,
nor have I any other work
now that my every act is love.

29. Pues ya si en el ejido
de hoy más no fuere vista ni
hallada,
diréis que me ha perdido;
que, andando enamorada,
me hice perdidiza y fui ganada.

29. If, then, I am no longer
seen or found on the common,
you will say that I am lost;
that, stricken by love,
I lost myself, and was found.

30. De flores y esmeraldas,
en las frescas mañanas escogidas,

30. With flowers and emeralds
chosen on cool mornings

haremos las guirnaldas
en tu amor florecidas
y en un cabello mío entretejidas.

we shall weave garlands
flowering in your love,
and bound with one hair of
    mine.

31. En solo aquel cabello
que en mi cuello volar
    consideraste,
mirástele en mi cuello,
y en él preso quedaste,
y en uno de mis ojos te llagaste.

31. You considered
that one hair fluttering at my
    neck;
you gazed at it upon my neck
and it captivated you;
and one of my eyes wounded you.

32. Cuando tú me mirabas
su gracia en mí tus ojos
    imprimían;
por eso me adamabas,
y en eso merecían
los míos adorar lo que en ti vían.

32. When you looked at me
your eyes imprinted your grace
    in me;
for this you loved me ardently;
and thus my eyes deserved
to adore what they beheld in you.

33. No quieras despreciarme,
que, si color moreno en mí
    hallaste,
ya bien puedes mirarme
después que me miraste,
que gracia y hermosura en mí
    dejaste.

33. Do not despise me;
for if, before, you found me dark,
now truly you can look at me
since you have looked
and left in me grace and beauty.

Esposo
34. La blanca palomica
al arca con el ramo se ha
    tornado;
y ya la tortolica
al socio deseado
en las riberas verdes ha hallado.

Bridegroom
34. The small white dove
has returned to the ark with an
    olive branch;
and now the turtledove
has found its longed-for mate
by the green river banks.

35. En soledad vivía,
y en soldedad ha puesto ya su
    nido,
y en soledad la guía
a solas su querido,
también en soledad de amor
    herido.

35. She lived in solitude,
and now in solitude has built her
    nest;
and in solitude he guides her,
he alone, who also bears
in solitude the wound of love.

Esposa	*Bride*
36. Gocémonos, Amado,	36. Let us rejoice, Beloved,
y vámonos a ver en tu	and let us go forth to behold
hermosura	ourselves in your beauty,
al monte y al collado	to the mountain and to the hill,
do mana el agua pura;	to where the pure water flows,
entremos más adentro en la	and further, deep into the
espesura,	thicket.
37. Y luego a las subidas	37. And then we will go on
cavernas de la piedra nos iremos,	to the high caverns in the rock
que están bien escondidas,	that are so well concealed;
y allí nos entraremos,	there we shall enter
y el mosto de granadas	and taste the fresh juice of the
gustaremos.	pomegranates.
38. Allí me mostrarías	38. There you will show me
aquello que mi alma pretendía,	what my soul has been seeking,
y luego me darías	and then you will give me,
allí, tú, ¡vida mía!	you, my life, will give me there
aquello que me diste el otro día:	what you gave me on that other
	day:
39. El aspirar del aire,	39. the breathing of the air,
el canto de la dulce filomena,	the song of the sweet nightingale;
el soto y su donaire,	the grove and its living beauty
en la noche serena,	in the serene night,
con llama que consume y no da	with a flame that is consuming
pena.	and painless.
40. Que nadie lo miraba;	40. No one looked at her,
Aminadab tampoco parecía	nor did Aminadab appear;
y el cerco sosegaba	the siege was still;
y la caballería	and the cavalry,
a vista de las aguas descendía.	at the sight of the waters,
	descended.

The Sayings
of
Light and Love

INTRODUCTION TO

THE SAYINGS OF LIGHT AND LOVE

In the style of the apothegms of the Desert Fathers, John of the Cross's teaching first comes in these hard, clean, unsentimental sayings that overflow with spiritual wisdom. They give to their recipients treasures that must first be unlocked; as maxims they were to be repeated and mulled over.

While he was spiritual director in Avila, before he had undertaken any of his larger treatises, John jotted down many thoughts and counsels for the guidance of those whom he directed, probably similar to the ones expressed in the later collections. None of those earlier sayings has come down to us, but we know from witnesses that this practice was characteristic of the Carmelite confessor at that time.

After John's imprisonment in Toledo, when he took up spiritual direction again, this time in Andalusia, he returned once more to the practice of condensing his thought into concise spiritual counsels for his penitents. They could keep them for inspiration, so as to be stirred in the Lord's service and love. Sometimes these sayings were directed to the particular needs of an individual; at other times they were destined more for a group of persons. The number of sayings that circulated must have been large, but comparatively few have come down to us, and they come through different collections.

The most distinguished collection is contained in an autograph manuscript, the largest autograph we have from John. Restored in 1976 and reproduced in a facsimile edition, the manuscript is preserved in the church Santa María la Mayor in Andújar (Jaén). In his prologue to this collection, John calls his maxims "sayings of light and love."

The title, *Sayings of Light and Love,* comes then from John's own words, and provides a good general designation for the other collections as well. Footnotes will indicate where one collection ends and another begins and the source from which each comes.

Sometimes, rather than being counsels destined for others, these sayings have an autobiographical coloring, as for example in the celebrated *Prayer of a Soul Taken with Love.* Here John in a profound experience of spiritual poverty becomes aware that God has pardoned him and given him everything in Jesus Christ; love then carries him off in a lyric outburst.

Though these sayings do not follow in any systematic order, we do find in them the important themes that the Carmelite friar developed at length in his major works. What he there expounds in detail, he here compresses into dense aphorisms.

Much difficulty lies in deciding whether many of the maxims attributed to John actually did come from his pen, or disciples culled them from his sermons and conferences, or if they are simply spurious. Omitting the counsels of Madre Magdalena because they are repetitions of those given in chapter 13 of the first book of the *The Ascent of Mount Carmel*, we include here only those sayings that editors have considered trustworthy.

1

SAYINGS OF LIGHT AND LOVE

Prologue

O my God and my delight, for your love I have also desired to give my soul to composing these sayings of light and love concerning you. Since, although I can express them in words, I do not have the works and virtues they imply (which is what pleases you, O my Lord, more than the words and wisdom they contain), may others, perhaps stirred by them, go forward in your service and love—in which I am wanting. I will thereby find consolation, that these sayings be an occasion for your finding in others the things that I lack.

Lord, you love discretion, you love light, you love love; these three you love above the other operations of the soul. Hence these will be sayings of discretion for the wayfarer, of light for the way, and of love in the wayfaring. May there be nothing of worldly rhetoric in them or the long-winded and dry eloquence of weak and artificial human wisdom, which never pleases you. Let us speak to the heart words bathed in sweetness and love that do indeed please you, removing obstacles and stumbling blocks from the paths of many souls who unknowingly trip and unconsciously walk in the path of error—poor souls who think they are right in what concerns the following of your beloved Son, our Lord Jesus Christ, in becoming like him, imitating his life, actions, and virtues, and the form of his nakedness and purity of spirit. Father of mercies, come to our aid, for without you, Lord, we can do nothing.

1. The Lord has always revealed to mortals the treasures of his wisdom and his spirit, but now that the face of evil bares itself more and more, so does the Lord bare his treasures more.

2. O Lord, my God, who will seek you with simple and pure love, and not find that you are all one can desire, for you show yourself first and go out to meet those who seek you?

3. Though the path is plain and smooth for people of good will, those who walk it will not travel far, and will do so only with difficulty if they do not have good feet, courage, and tenacity of spirit.

4. It is better to be burdened and in company with the strong than to be unburdened and with the weak. When you are burdened you are

close to God, your strength, who abides with the afflicted. When you are relieved of the burden you are close to yourself, your own weakness; for virtue and strength of soul grow and are confirmed in the trials of patience.

5. Whoever wants to stand alone without the support of a master and guide will be like the tree that stands alone in a field without a proprietor. No matter how much the tree bears, passers-by will pick the fruit before it ripens.

6. A tree that is cultivated and guarded through the care of its owner produces its fruit at the expected time.

7. The virtuous soul that is alone and without a master is like a lone burning coal; it will grow colder rather than hotter.

8. Those who fall alone remain alone in their fall, and they value their soul little since they entrust it to themselves alone.

9. If you do not fear falling alone, do you presume that you will rise up alone? Consider how much more can be accomplished by two together than by one alone.

10. Whoever falls while heavily laden will find it difficult to rise under the burden.

11. The blind person who falls will not be able to get up alone; the blind person who does get up alone will go off on the wrong road.

12. God desires the smallest degree of purity of conscience in you more than all the works you can perform.

13. God desires the least degree of obedience and submissiveness more than all those services you think of rendering him.

14. God values in you the inclination to dryness and suffering for love of him more than all the consolations, spiritual visions, and meditations you could possibly have.

15. Deny your desires and you will find what your heart longs for. For how do you know if any desire of yours is according to God?

16. O sweetest love of God, so little known, whoever has found this rich mine is at rest!

17. Since a double measure of bitterness must follow the doing of your own will, do not do it even though you remain in single bitterness.

18. The soul that carries within itself the least appetite for worldly things bears more unseemliness and impurity in its journey to God than if it were troubled by all the hideous and annoying temptations and darknesses describable; for, so long as it does not consent to these temptations, a soul thus tried can approach God confidently, by doing the will of His Majesty, who proclaims: *Come to me, all you who labor and are heavily burdened, and I will refresh you* [Mt. 11:28].

19. The soul that in aridity and trial submits to the dictates of reason is more pleasing to God than one that does everything with consolation, yet fails in this submission.

20. God is more pleased by one work, however small, done secretly,

without desire that it be known, than a thousand done with the desire that people know of them. Those who work for God with purest love not only care nothing about whether others see their works, but do not even seek that God himself know of them. Such persons would not cease to render God the same services, with the same joy and purity of love, even if God were never to know of these.

21. The pure and whole work done for God in a pure heart merits a whole kingdom for its owner.

22. A bird caught in birdlime has a twofold task: It must free itself and cleanse itself. And by satisfying their appetites, people suffer in a twofold way: They must detach themselves and, after being detached, clean themselves of what has clung to them.

23. Those who do not allow their appetites to carry them away will soar in their spirit as swiftly as the bird that lacks no feathers.

24. The fly that clings to honey hinders its flight, and the soul that allows itself attachment to spiritual sweetness hinders its own liberty and contemplation.

25. Withdraw from creatures if you desire to preserve, clear and simple in your soul, the image of God. Empty your spirit and withdraw far from them and you will walk in divine lights, for God is not like creatures.

Prayer of a Soul Taken with Love

26. Lord God, my Beloved, if you still remember my sins in such a way that you do not do what I beg of you, do your will concerning them, my God, which is what I most desire, and exercise your goodness and mercy, and you will be known through them. And if you are waiting for my good works so as to hear my prayer through their means, grant them to me, and work them for me, and the sufferings you desire to accept, and let it be done. But if you are not waiting for my works, what is it that makes you wait, my most clement Lord? Why do you delay? For if, after all, I am to receive the grace and mercy that I entreat of you in your Son, take my mite, since you desire it, and grant me this blessing, since you also desire that.

Who can free themselves from lowly manners and limitations if you do not lift them to yourself, my God, in purity of love? How will human beings begotten and nurtured in lowliness rise up to you, Lord, if you do not raise them with your hand that made them?

You will not take from me, my God, what you once gave me in your only Son, Jesus Christ, in whom you gave me all I desire. Hence I rejoice that if I wait for you, you will not delay.

With what procrastinations do you wait, since from this very moment you can love God in your heart?

27. Mine are the heavens and mine is the earth. Mine are the nations,

the just are mine, and mine the sinners. The angels are mine, and the Mother of God, and all things are mine; and God himself is mine and for me, because Christ is mine and all for me. What do you ask, then, and seek, my soul? Yours is all of this, and all is for you. Do not engage yourself in something less or pay heed to the crumbs that fall from your Father's table. Go forth and exult in your Glory! Hide yourself in it and rejoice, and you will obtain the supplications of your heart.

28. The very pure spirit does not bother about the regard of others or human respect, but communes inwardly with God, alone and in solitude as to all forms, and with delightful tranquility, for the knowledge of God is received in divine silence.

29. A soul enkindled with love is a gentle, meek, humble, and patient soul.

30. A soul that is hard because of self-love grows harder.

31. O good Jesus, if you do not soften it, it will ever continue in its natural hardness.

32. If you lose an opportunity you will be like one who lets the bird fly away; you will never get it back.

33. I didn't know you, my Lord, because I still desired to know and relish things.

34. Well and good if all things change, Lord God, provided we are rooted in you.

35. One human thought alone is worth more than the entire world, hence God alone is worthy of it.

36. For the insensible, what you do not feel; for the sensible, the senses; and for the spirit of God, thought.

37. Reflect that your guardian angel does not always move your desire for an action, but he does always enlighten your reason. Hence, in order to practice virtue do not wait until you feel like it, for your reason and intellect are sufficient.

38. When fixed on something else, one's appetite leaves no room for the angel to move it.

39. My spirit has become dry because it forgets to feed on you.

40. What you most seek and desire you will not find by this way of yours, nor through high contemplation, but in much humility and submission of heart.

41. Do not tire yourself, for you will not enter into the savor and sweetness of spirit if you do not apply yourself to the mortification of all this that you desire.

42. Reflect that the most delicate flower loses its fragrance and withers fastest; therefore guard yourself against seeking to walk in a spirit of delight, for you will not be constant. Choose rather for yourself a robust spirit, detached from everything, and you will discover abundant peace and sweetness, for delicious and durable fruit is gathered in a cold and dry climate.

43. Bear in mind that your flesh is weak and that no worldly thing can comfort or strengthen your spirit, for what is born of the world is world and what is born of the flesh is flesh. The good spirit is born only of the Spirit of God, who communicates himself neither through the world nor through the flesh.

44. Be attentive to your reason in order to do what it tells you concerning the way to God. It will be more valuable before your God than all the works you perform without this attentiveness and all the spiritual delights you seek.

45. Blessed are they who, setting aside their own pleasure and inclination, consider things according to reason and justice before doing them.

46. If you make use of your reason, you are like one who eats substantial food; but if you are moved by the satisfaction of your will, you are like one who eats insipid fruit.

47. Lord, you return gladly and lovingly to lift up the one who offends you, but I do not turn to raise and honor the one who annoys me.

48. O mighty Lord, if a spark from the empire of your justice effects so much in the mortal ruler who governs the nations, what will your all-powerful justice do with the righteous and the sinner?

49. If you purify your soul of attachments and desires, you will understand things spiritually. If you deny your appetite for them, you will enjoy their truth, understanding what is certain in them.

50. O Lord, my God, you are no stranger to those who do not estrange themselves from you. How do they say that it is you who absent yourself?

51. That person has truly mastered all things who is not moved to joy by the satisfaction they afford or saddened by their insipidness.

52. If you wish to attain holy recollection, you will do so not by receiving but by denying.

53. Going everywhere, my God, with you, everywhere things will happen as I desire for you.

54. Souls will be unable to reach perfection who do not strive to be content with having nothing, in such fashion that their natural and spiritual desire is satisfied with emptiness; for this is necessary in order to reach the highest tranquility and peace of spirit. Hence the love of God in the pure and simple soul is almost continually in act.

55. Since God is inaccessible, be careful not to concern yourself with all that your faculties can comprehend and your senses feel, so that you do not become satisfied with less and lose the lightness of soul suitable for going to him.

56. The soul that journeys to God, but does not shake off its cares and quiet its appetites, is like one who drags a cart uphill.

57. It is not God's will that a soul be disturbed by anything or suffer trials, for if one suffers trials in the adversities of the world it is because of a weakness in virtue. The perfect soul rejoices in what afflicts the

imperfect one.

58. This way of life contains very little business and bustling, and demands mortification of the will more than knowledge. The less one takes of things and pleasures the farther one advances along this way.

59. Think not that pleasing God lies so much in doing a great deal as in doing it with good will, without possessiveness and human respect.

60. When evening comes, you will be examined in love. Learn to love as God desires to be loved and abandon your own ways of acting.

61. See that you do not interfere in the affairs of others, nor even allow them to pass through your memory; for perhaps you will be unable to accomplish your own task.

62. Because the virtues you have in mind do not shine in your neighbor, do not think that your neighbor will not be precious in God's sight for reasons that you have not in mind.

63. Human beings know neither how to rejoice properly nor how to grieve properly, for they do not understand the distance between good and evil.

64. See that you are not suddenly saddened by the adversities of this world, for you do not know the good they bring, being ordained in the judgments of God for the everlasting joy of the elect.

65. Do not rejoice in temporal prosperity, since you do not know if it gives you assurance of eternal life.

66. In tribulation, immediately draw near to God with trust, and you will receive strength, enlightenment, and instruction.

67. In joys and pleasures, immediately draw near to God in fear and truth, and you will be neither deceived nor involved in vanity.

68. Take God for your bridegroom and friend, and walk with him continually; and you will not sin and will learn to love, and the things you must do will work out prosperously for you.

69. You will without labor subject the nations and bring things to serve you if you forget them and yourself as well.

70. Abide in peace, banish cares, take no account of all that happens, and you will serve God according to his good pleasure, and rest in him.

71. Consider that God reigns only in the peaceful and disinterested soul.

72. Although you perform many works, if you do not deny your will and submit yourself, losing all solicitude about yourself and your affairs, you will not make progress.

73. What does it profit you to give God one thing if he asks of you another? Consider what it is God wants, and then do it. You will as a result satisfy your heart better than with something toward which you yourself are inclined.

74. How is it you dare to relax so fearlessly, since you must appear before God to render an account of the least word and thought?

75. Reflect that *many are called but few are chosen* [Mt. 22:14] and that,

if you are not careful, your perdition is more certain than your salvation, especially since the path to eternal life is so constricted [Mt. 7:14].

76. Do not rejoice vainly, for you know how many sins you have committed and you do not know how you stand before God; but have fear together with confidence.

77. Since, when the hour of reckoning comes, you will be sorry for not having used this time in the service of God, why do you not arrange and use it now as you would wish to have done were you dying?

78. If you desire that devotion be born in your spirit and that the love of God and the desire for divine things increase, cleanse your soul of every desire, attachment, and ambition in such a way that you have no concern about anything. Just as a sick person is immediately aware of good health once the bad humor has been thrown off and a desire to eat is felt, so will you recover your health, in God, if you cure yourself as was said. Without doing this, you will not advance no matter how much you do.

79. If you desire to discover peace and consolation for your soul and to serve God truly, do not find your satisfaction in what you have left behind, because in that which now concerns you you may be as impeded as you were before, or even more. But leave as well all these other things and attend to one thing alone that brings all these with it (namely, holy solitude, together with prayer and spiritual and divine reading), and persevere there in forgetfulness of all things. For if these things are not incumbent on you, you will be more pleasing to God in knowing how to guard and perfect yourself than by gaining all other things together; *what profit would there be for one to gain the whole world and suffer the loss of one's soul?* [Mt. 16:26].[1]

2

80. Bridle your tongue and your thoughts very much, direct your affection habitually toward God, and your spirit will be divinely enkindled.

81. Feed not your spirit on anything but God. Cast off concern about things, and bear peace and recollection in your heart.

82. Keep spiritually tranquil in a loving attentiveness to God, and when it is necessary to speak, let it be with the same calm and peace.

83. Preserve a habitual remembrance of eternal life, recalling that those who hold themselves the lowest and poorest and least of all will

---

1. The autograph manuscript ends here abruptly. The following sayings are the *Maxims on Love* gathered by the Discalced Carmelite nuns in Beas. A manuscript copy is preserved in the Silverian archives in Burgos.

enjoy the highest dominion and glory in God.

84. Rejoice habitually in God, who is your salvation [Lk. 1:47], and reflect that it is good to suffer in any way for him who is good.

85. Reflect how necessary it is to be enemies of self and to walk to perfection by the path of holy rigor, and understand that every word spoken without the order of obedience is laid to your account by God.

86. Have an intimate desire that His Majesty grant you what he knows you lack for his honor.

87. Crucified inwardly and outwardly with Christ, you will live in this life with fullness and satisfaction of soul, and possess your soul in patience [Lk. 21:19].

88. Preserve a loving attentiveness to God with no desire to feel or understand any particular thing concerning him.

89. Keep habitual confidence in God, esteeming in yourself and in your Sisters those things that God most values, which are spiritual goods.

90. Enter within yourself and work in the presence of your Bridegroom, who is ever present loving you.

91. Be hostile to admitting into your soul things that of themselves have no spiritual substance, lest they make you lose your liking for devotion and recollection.

92. Let Christ crucified be enough for you, and with him suffer and take your rest, and hence annihilate yourself in all inward and outward things.

93. Endeavor always that things be not for you, nor you for them, but forgetful of all, abide in recollection with your Bridegroom.

94. Have great love for trials and think of them as but a small way of pleasing your Bridegroom, who did not hesitate to die for you.

95. Bear fortitude in your heart against all things that move you to that which is not God, and be a friend of the Passion of Christ.

96. Be interiorly detached from all things and do not seek pleasure in any temporal thing, and your soul will concentrate on goods you do not know.

97. The soul that walks in love neither tires others nor grows tired.

98. The poor one who is naked will be clothed; and the soul that is naked of desires and whims, God will clothe with his purity, pleasure, and will.

99. There are souls that wallow in the mire like animals, and there are others that soar like birds, which purify and cleanse themselves in the air.

100. The Father spoke one Word, which was his Son, and this Word he speaks always in eternal silence, and in silence must it be heard by the soul.

101. We must adjust our trials to ourselves, and not ourselves to our trials.

102. He who seeks not the cross of Christ seeks not the glory of Christ.

103. To be taken with love for a soul, God does not look on its

greatness, but on the greatness of its humility.

104. "Whoever is ashamed to confess me before others, I shall be ashamed to confess before My Father," says the Lord [Mt. 10:33].

105. Frequent combing gives the hair more luster and makes it easier to comb; a soul that frequently examines its thoughts, words, and deeds, which are its hair, doing all things for the love of God, will have lustrous hair. Then the Bridegroom will look on the neck of the bride and thereby be captivated; and will be wounded by one of her eyes, that is, by the purity of intention she has in all she does. If in combing hair one wants it to have luster, one begins from the crown. All our works must begin from the crown (the love of God) if we wish them to be pure and lustrous.[2]

106. Heaven is stable and is not subject to generation; and souls of a heavenly nature are stable and not subject to the engendering of desires or of anything else, for in their way they resemble God who does not move forever.

107. Eat not in forbidden pastures (those of this life), because *blessed are they who hunger and thirst for justice, for they will be satisfied* [Mt. 5:6]. What God seeks, he being himself God by nature, is to make us gods through participation, just as fire converts all things into fire.

108. All the goodness we possess is lent to us, and God considers it his own work. God and his work is God.

109. Wisdom enters through love, silence, and mortification. It is great wisdom to know how to be silent and to look at neither the remarks, nor the deeds, nor the lives of others.

110. All for me and nothing for you.

111. All for you and nothing for me.

112. Allow yourself to be taught, allow yourself to receive orders, allow yourself to be subjected and despised, and you will be perfect.

113. Any appetite causes five kinds of harm in the soul: first, disquiet; second, turbidity; third, defilement; fourth, weakness; fifth, obscurity.[3]

114. Perfection does not lie in the virtues that the soul knows it has, but in the virtues that our Lord sees in it. This is a closed book; hence one has no reason for presumption, but must remain prostrate on the ground with respect to self.

115. Love consists not in feeling great things but in having great detachment and in suffering for the Beloved.

116. The entire world is not worthy of a human being's thought, for this belongs to God alone; any thought, therefore, not centered on God is stolen from him.

117. Not all the faculties and senses have to be employed in things, but only those that are required; as for the others, leave them unoccupied for God.

---

2. Cf. C. 31. 5-6.
3. Cf. A. 1. 6-10.

118. Ignoring the imperfections of others, preserving silence and a continual communion with God will eradicate great imperfections from the soul and make it the possessor of great virtues.

119. There are three signs of inner recollection: first, a lack of satisfaction in passing things; second, a liking for solitude and silence, and an attentiveness to all that is more perfect; third, the considerations, meditations and acts that formerly helped the soul now hinder it, and it brings to prayer no other support than faith, hope, and love.[4]

120. If a soul has more patience in suffering and more forbearance in going without satisfaction, the sign is there of its being more proficient in virtue.

121. The traits of the solitary bird are five: first, it seeks the highest place; second, it withstands no company; third, it holds its beak in the air; fourth, it has no definite color; fifth, it sings sweetly. These traits must be possessed by the contemplative soul. It must rise above passing things, paying no more heed to them than if they did not exist. It must likewise be so fond of silence and solitude that it does not tolerate the company of another creature. It must hold its beak in the air of the Holy Spirit, responding to his inspirations, that by so doing it may become worthy of his company. It must have no definite color, desiring to do nothing definite other than the will of God. It must sing sweetly in the contemplation and love of its Bridegroom.[5]

122. Habitual voluntary imperfections that are never completely overcome not only hinder the divine union, but also the attainment of perfection. Such imperfections are: the habit of being very talkative; a small unconquered attachment, such as to a person, to clothing, to a cell, a book, or to the way food is prepared, and to other conversations and little satisfactions in tasting things, in knowing, and hearing, and the like.[6]

3

123. If you wish to glory in yourself, but do not wish to appear ignorant and foolish, discard the things that are not yours and you will have glory in what remains. But certainly if you discard all that is not yours, nothing will be left, since you must not glory in anything if you do not want to fall into vanity. But let us descend now especially to those graces, the gifts that make people pleasing in God's sight. It is certain that you must not glory in these gifts, for you do not even know if you possess

---

4. For more on these signs of contemplation, cf. A. 2. 13-14; N. 1. 9.
5. Cf. C. 15. 24
6. Cf. A. 1. 11. 3-4. The following maxims are from the edition of Gerona, published in 1650.

them.

124. Oh, how sweet your presence will be to me, you who are the supreme good! I must draw near you in silence and uncover your feet that you may be pleased to unite me to you in marriage [Ru. 3:7], and I will not rest until I rejoice in your arms. Now I ask you, Lord, not to abandon me at any time in my recollection, for I am a squanderer of my soul.

125. Detached from exterior things, dispossessed of interior things, disappropriated of the things of God—neither will prosperity detain you nor adversity hinder you.

126. The devil fears a soul united to God as he does God himself.[7]

127. The purest suffering produces the purest understanding.[8]

128. The soul that desires God to surrender himself to it entirely must surrender itself entirely to him without keeping anything for itself.

129. The soul that has reached the union of love does not even experience the first motions of sin.

130. Old friends of God scarcely ever fail him, for they stand above all that can make them fail.[9]

131. My Beloved, all that is rugged and toilsome I desire for myself, and all that is sweet and delightful I desire for you.[10]

132. What we need most in order to make progress is to be silent before this great God with our appetite and with our tongue, for the language he best hears is silent love.

133. The submission of a servant is necessary in seeking God. In outward things light helps to prevent one from falling; but in the things of God just the opposite is true: It is better for the soul not to see if it is to be more secure.

134. More is gained in one hour from God's good things than in a whole lifetime from your own.

135. Love to be unknown both by yourself and by others. Never look at the good or evil of others.

136. Walk in solitude with God; act according to the just measure; hide the blessings of God.

137. To lose always and let everyone else win is a trait of valiant souls, generous spirits, and unselfish hearts; it is their manner to give rather than receive even to the extent of giving themselves. They consider it a heavy burden to possess themselves, and it pleases them more to be possessed by others and withdrawn from themselves, since we belong more to that infinite Good than we do to ourselves.

138. It is seriously wrong to have more regard for God's blessings than for God himself: prayer and detachment.

---

7. Cf. C. 24. 4.
8. Cf. C. 36. 12. .
9. Cf. C. 25. 9-11.
10. Cf. C. 28. 10.

139. Look at that infinite knowledge and that hidden secret. What peace, what love, what silence is in that divine bosom! How lofty the science God teaches there, which is what we call the anagogical acts that so enkindle the heart.

140. The secret of one's conscience is considerably harmed and damaged as often as its fruits are manifested to others, for then one receives as reward the fruit of fleeting fame.

141. Speak little and do not meddle in matters about which you are not asked.

142. Strive always to keep God present and to preserve within yourself the purity he teaches you.

143. Do not excuse yourself or refuse to be corrected by all; listen to every reproof with a serene countenance; think that God utters it.

144. Live as though only God and yourself were in this world, so that your heart may not be detained by anything human.

145. Consider it the mercy of God that someone occasionally speaks a good word to you, for you deserve none.

146. Never allow yourself to pour out your heart, even though it be but for the space of a Creed.

147. Never listen to talk about the weaknesses of others, and if someone complains of another, you can tell her humbly to say nothing of it to you.

148. Do not complain about anyone, or ask for anything; and if it is necessary for you to ask, let it be with few words.

149. Do not refuse work even though it seems that you cannot do it. Let all find compassion in you.

150. Do not contradict; by no means speak words that are not pure.

151. Let your speech be such that no one may be offended, and let it concern things that would not cause you regret were all to know of them.

152. Do not refuse anything you possess, even though you may need it.

153. Be silent concerning what God may have given you and recall that saying of the bride: *My secret for myself* [Is. 24:16].

154. Strive to preserve your heart in peace; let no event of this world disturb it; reflect that all must come to an end.

155. Take neither great nor little notice of who is with you or against you, and try always to please God. Ask him that his will be done in you. Love him intensely, as he deserves to be loved.

156. Twelve stars for reaching the highest perfection: love of God, love of neighbor, obedience, chastity, poverty, attendance at choir, penance, humility, mortification, prayer, silence, peace.

157. Never take others for your example in the tasks you have to perform, however holy they may be, for the devil will set their imperfec-

tions before you. But imitate Christ, who is supremely perfect and supremely holy, and you will never err.

158. Seek in reading and you will find in meditation; knock in prayer and it will be opened to you in contemplation.[11]

4

159. The further you withdraw from earthly things the closer you approach heavenly things and the more you find in God.

160. Whoever knows how to die in all will have life in all.

161. Abandon evil, do good, and seek peace [Ps. 34:14].

162. Anyone who complains or grumbles is not perfect, nor even a good Christian.

163. The humble are those who hide in their own nothingness and know how to abandon themselves to God.

164. The meek are those who know how to suffer their neighbor and themselves.

165. If you desire to be perfect, sell your will, give it to the poor in spirit, come to Christ in meekness and humility, and follow him to Calvary and the sepulcher.

166. Those who trust in themselves are worse than the devil.

167. Those who do not love their neighbor abhor God.

168. Anyone who does things lukewarmly is close to falling.

169. Whoever flees prayer flees all that is good.

170. Conquering the tongue is better than fasting on bread and water.

171. Suffering for God is better than working miracles.

172. Oh, what blessings we will enjoy in the vision of the Most Blessed Trinity!

173. Do not be suspicious of your brother, for you will lose purity of heart.

174. As for trials, the more the better.

175. What does anyone know who doesn't know how to suffer for Christ?

---

11. This saying comes from the Carthusian Guigo II's *Scala paradisi*, ch. 2, in Migne, PL 40. 998. The counsels that follow come from an old manuscript belonging to the Carmelite nuns in Antequera. A copy is conserved in the National Library of Madrid.

The Ascent

of

Mount Carmel

INTRODUCTION TO

THE ASCENT OF MOUNT CARMEL

Three components make up the *Ascent of Mount Carmel:* the sketch of the mount of perfection; the poem *The Dark Night;* and the treatise on them. Closely linked to this treatise is the work entitled *The Dark Night,* which deals with the passive nights and is a commentary on the poem, as will be explained in the particular introduction to that work.

The Sketch of the Mount

John of the Cross made many copies of his drawing, called either "The Mount of Perfection" or "Mount Carmel," first for the Carmelite nuns in Beas and later for his own friars in Baeza and Granada. In addition to the copies he made for these religious, he also, according to his explicit testimony, placed one at the beginning of the *Ascent* to serve as a summary of the doctrine contained in the treatise. According to Magdalena del Espíritu Santo, a nun at Beas, he gave each Sister a copy to keep in her breviary, but later added and changed some things. None of the autograph drawings has been found; but reproduced in this translation is a faithful and authenticated replica of an autograph that was preserved in the monastery of Nuestra Señora de las Nieves in Málaga. With this, we are certain of having "The Mount of Perfection" as sketched by its author and made for "my daughter Magdalena," the nun just mentioned.

Later editors of John's works, unimpressed by the rough primitive appearance of his sketches, had their own more elaborate drawings made, but did not always take care to preserve the pure doctrine. The drawing itself served as a pedagogical tool by which John's disciples could keep before their eyes a summary of the teaching that he developed at length in the treatise, which provides us with the best means for understanding the sketch.

The Poem

Written by John while, it seems, the lacerating affliction of his imprisonment still lingered, the stanzas of the poem resonate with the symbol "night," or dark night. The figure evokes John's natural experiences of night; the biblical and patristic tradition that notes the darkness in which God communicates with mortals; and the poet's own experience of darkness and abandonment in Toledo, representative of sensory and spiritual purification.

Consisting of eight stanzas, each having five verses, the poem speaks first of an escape at night (1-2); then of the wonders of that night as a guide and means (3-5); and finally of the actual communion with the beloved realized in that night (6-8).

The Treatise

The sketch of the mount of perfection shows a noticeably narrow path that ascends to a circular expanse of freedom and fruitfulness where only the honor and glory of God dwell. The path or way to this summit is a path called *nada.* A reading of *The Ascent of Mount Carmel* gradually reveals more about this path. It is also a "dark night," or the theological life, which is the way of the theological virtues. Finally, it becomes clear that the path is the narrow gate and constricted road that leads to life, which Jesus spoke of in St. Matthew's Gospel; it is Jesus who is the way.

In the opening pages of the *Ascent,* John of the Cross indicates the nature of his work, declaring his intention to explain how one reaches the "high state of perfection." This initial assertion plainly marks the practical character of his book. It is a work that explains the path one must follow in order to reach perfection, or "union with God" (to use John's preferred expression). Yet the book amounts to far more than a collection of workable rules and techniques. In addition to setting down rules, the *Ascent* analyzes the principles supporting them. It provides a systematic presentation of both the theory and the practical norms governing the development of the spiritual life; it is a work of spiritual theology.

John wrote this work after he had sung about his happiness in having escaped and reached union with his Beloved by night, having climbed through active and passive purifications to the peak of the mountain. He had arrived, and from the very height itself he views that path, which ascends to the top without deviation. He can look back with a clarity of vision unobtainable by those who are on the way. His excellent view from the summit prompted him to write; he felt compelled to encourage spiritual persons along the journey.

What specifically were John's concerns in writing? He felt a sadness at seeing many who failed to advance because of what he calls darknesses and trials. They do not go through the darkness because they do not want to, or they do not accept all that this entails, or they misunderstand, or they lack suitable guides. Their guides do not comfort and encourage them but too often increase their trials and add gloom to the darkness. John wants to encourage, to comfort; what he has learned and must explain is that God alone brings one to the summit, and so one ought to know how to adapt to the Lord's method of procedure. Joys, afflictions, hopes, and sorrows accompany the journey with God, but can also come from not adapting, from resisting God. One must know which are which, discerning the signs of God's work; and one must know how to journey. Here John gives substantial and solid doctrine, as he says, so that one can move along correctly without hampering God's work—that is, in poverty of spirit.

In Book One, chapter two of the *Ascent,* John explains that there are three reasons for calling the path to the height of Mount Carmel a "dark night." These stem from the three factors philosophers find in all change: the *term from which,* the *mean,* and the *term to which.* In other words, a person must pass from an initial state of disorder, along the way of faith, to God, the goal of every human being. From all of this John deduces that the entire way to union with God can be called a dark night because, just as in darkness there is a privation of light, this way demands privation. Individuals must set out by depriving themselves of the gratification of their disordered appetites; journey in faith, deprived of light; and thereby reach God whose brightest light is total darkness to us in this life. This needs explaining, and that is what he promises to do in his work: explain the three reasons for calling the journey to union with God a dark night.

This promise comes as a surprise, for he had already presented a seemingly different plan in chapter one. There he speaks of the necessity of passing through two principal kinds of night, which he also refers to as purgations or purifications. These nights are purifications of the two principal dimensions of the human person: the senses and the spirit. They are wrought in a double manner: actively, through a person's own efforts; and passively, through God's work. John informs his readers that he will deal with the active night of purification of the sensory part in the first section of his work, with the active night of the spiritual part in the second and third, and with the passive night in the fourth section.

To determine how or whether these two plans fit together in the work

itself, the reader has to pay close attention to what John actually does as
he proceeds.

Book One

A perusal of the first book of the *Ascent* reveals that its main theme is
depriving oneself of the gratification of the appetites. John explains why
doing so is a night and the necessity for such a night if one is to reach
union with God. In arguing for this necessity, he offers the reader
reflections garnered from Scripture as well as from philosophical and
theological principles. He then presents a radical and vivid description
of the human condition of a person in sin, turned, converted toward creatures and away from God. The appetites, in the way John uses the term,
turn one away from God and wreak havoc. They "torment, weary, blind,
defile, weaken a person," and, worst of all, "deprive one of the Lord's
Spirit."

The seriousness of the harm will depend on the matter involved.
John's reflections arise from his own experience of light, his conversion
to God, from the right ordering of the appetites, and from the virtues,
which produce effects of peace, comfort, light, purity, and strength,
effects opposite those of the vices. Of course, he understands that,
however hard he may try to describe the sad condition of sinners, or even
of the imperfect, they probably will not see what he sees; and he knows
that even those who have set out on their way to God do not easily
acknowledge the seriousness of their smaller disorders. Nonetheless, his
effort to convince is clearly present.

Not until he gets well into this first section does John clarify what he
means in speaking of the appetites as a hindrance to union. He is not
referring to all the appetites that contribute to human experience apart
from the will, but only to those that are voluntary (or willful) and
inordinate, not directed at least in some way toward giving honor and
glory to God. Even among these he is particularly concerned with the
habitual appetites, since a sporadic act would not amount to a hindrance
to union.

The principle that creatures in themselves are good and do not thwart
union receives John's full support; the inordinate willful appetites for
creatures are the problem, especially when habitual. Only Christian love
can set these appetites in order. When individuals place all activity under
the rule of this love, they will then not search simply for personal satisfaction in the use of things but ardently seek only God's glory and honor.
This love, necessary for the vanquishing of the disordered appetites, is

enkindled by Christ, who becomes also the perfect model since love produces likeness in the lover. In chapter 13 John finally gives some counsels on the method of entering the active night of the senses. The method is abridged: Study the life of Jesus Christ and imitate him; out of love for him renounce and remain empty of any sensory satisfaction that is not purely for the honor and glory of God. "In his life he had no other gratification, nor desired any other, than the fulfillment of his Father's will, which he called his meat and food." The other counsels are but elaborations on these.

Book One of the *Ascent,* then, deals with the point of departure (the need to deprive oneself of the gratification of the inordinate appetites) and also with the active night of the senses. These two themes are not identical, but neither are they exclusive of each other.

Books Two and Three

The nature of the road of faith along which one advances toward God is the second reason for naming the path to divine union a dark night. One aspect of faith, its obscurity, prompted John of the Cross to term the whole life of faith a dark night. He so stresses the darkness that it sometimes seems that faith does away with all knowledge. In thus turning our attention to the obscurity of faith, he wishes to impress on our minds that the intellect cannot through its own power either acquire the knowledge that faith affords or fully understand the content of faith once it has been revealed.

In speaking of the journey in faith, John understands faith in its broadest sense, which includes hope and love. Through faith one moves, advances, journeys on a path to union with God. This faith has many aspects, some relating to its objective dimension, others to its subjective one. From the perspective of the subject, it is dark. From the perspective of its object, it is light.

The central moment in the entire presentation of the journey in faith comes in chapter 22 of Book Two. Illumining all that precedes it and all that follows, this chapter explains that Christ is the entire content of the Father's revelation, God's definitive Word that leaves nothing else to be revealed. "If I have already told you all things in my Word, my Son, and if I have no other word, what answer or revelation can I now make that would surpass this?"

Faith, then, is personal. The revelation given to us is that Christ is our brother, companion, and master, our savior, beloved, and bridegroom; he is a light that both blinds and illumines the human person (or as John says, "by blinding it illumines"). As a result the encounter in faith with the master, the beloved bridegroom, is an obscure one; especially with those who bring to prayer no other support than faith, hope, and love, who are inclined to move away from discursive acts and exercises, from ideas and images, and abide in God's presence with a general loving attention. In faith we are responding to one who awakens love, Christ, the Father's Beloved Son in whom every good is given to us.

If the object, indeed, is personal, the attitude on the part of the subject to what is being communicated in faith will also be personal, one of listening, responding, attentiveness, and generous surrender. In this kind of recollection, in faith, "the proximate means to union," individuals dispose themselves so that "little by little the divine calm and peace with a wondrous sublime knowledge of God, enveloped in divine love, will be infused into their souls." God's self-communication in the form of contemplation, or loving knowledge given to the spirit, is here more abundant since it need no longer restrict itself to images and ideas. In faith, both the attraction to God and the dark sense of his presence grow stronger.

Though the content of faith is always the same, it is not always received in the same way. There is no end to the variety of shadings, the ways in which the truths may be illumined for individuals. But the journey toward union follows the kind of progress we find in human knowing: from the senses to the imagination, to discursive thinking, to intuition or contemplation.

The content of faith includes the law of Christ and the human and visible means he established in the Church and her ministers. Faith touches on the whole of life and draws the believer to embrace its values and demands, stirs one to seek assurance and confirmation in the community of the Church. Journeying by faith, one also chooses to remain within the boundaries of the ordinary and to refrain from searching for the divine in the extraordinary phenomena of visions, revelations, locutions, or spiritual feelings. In this respect, one learns to esteem reason and the common search in the quest for a solution to life's problems; God draws near to those who come together in an endeavor to know truth.

To spell out this journey in faith, John introduces a further structure and breaks the theme into treatises on the dynamics of the three theological virtues, each purifying its respective faculty as the person advances. In response to Christ's call for spiritual nakedness, poverty, selflessness, and purity (which here refer more or less to the same reality), John presents a method to empty and purify the faculties of all that is not God. "Those who want to reach union with God should advance neither by understanding nor by the support of their own experience nor by feeling or imagination." Since God always transcends any image, idea, or feeling (even of God), none of these can be our goal. Throughout much of Books Two and Three, then, John analyzes in detail how "the intellect must be perfected in the darkness of faith, the memory in the emptiness of hope, and the will in the nakedness and absence of every affection."

As with the senses, the honor and glory of God is the norm in the use of the spiritual faculties. As these faculties are purified, the senses are further purified. Indeed, we find more in Books Two and Three about the active purification of the senses than in Book One.

Through the theological life, the life of faith, hope, and love, a person uproots every habitual disorder and becomes one with God. In their inner dynamism these virtues grow by purifying, and purify by growing. To the extent that they unite a soul with God, they empty it of what is not God; and to the extent that they empty it of what is not God, they unite it with God. As they grow there is a movement in prayer from sense to spirit, from ideas about Christ to an inner, more personal relationship, an interiorization and simplification in the way of communing and being with him. In their activity they constitute the journey in faith. John, in fact, thinks of them as forms of God's self-communication: transcendent truth, generous love, possession. In our lives, they are capable of incorporating all kinds of means and, at the same time, of making these means relative, propelling us to communion with the living God, distinct from all means.

Analyzing these many factors, John found himself going into apparently unending divisions of his material; he wasn't getting to the subject matter that mainly concerned him: the passive purification or night. Far into his treatise on the active purification, aware that he had expounded the essentials of his thought on the matter, he abandoned *The Ascent of Mount Carmel* without completing it.

The work, as it stands, may be divided this way:

Book One:

The meaning of "night" in the first verse of the poem; the divisions of the night (chapters 1-3).
The necessity of passing through the night:
    from philosophy and theology (chapter 4),
    from Scripture (chapter 5),
    from harm caused by voluntary inordinate appetites (chapters 6-
    12).
Counsels for entering the night of the senses.
Commentary on the rest of the first stanza of the poem: love and
    freedom.

Book Two:

Commentary on the second stanza from the perspective of the journey
in faith (chapters 1-2).
Why the journey is called a night (chapters 3-4).
The nature of union (chapter 5).
The journey of faith as a purification of the intellect, memory, and will
through faith, hope, and love (chapter 6).
The Scriptural basis for this purification (chapter 7).
Faith, the proximate means to union for the intellect (chapters 8-9).
Classification of the intellectual apprehensions (chapter 10).
Apprehensions coming through the senses:
    external, supernatural (chapter 11),
    internal, natural (chapter 12);
    signs of contemplation (chapters 13-15),
    internal, supernatural (chapter 16).
The way of faith in God's method of dealing with his creatures
    (chapters 17-22).
Apprehensions received directly by the intellect: visions, revelations,
    locutions, and spiritual feelings (chapters 23-32).

Book Three:

Purification of the memory through hope and of the will through love.
The three kinds of apprehensions of which hope purifies the memory:
    natural (chapters 2-6);
    supernatural imaginative (chapters 7-13);
    spiritual (chapter 14).
General rules for governing the memory (chapter 15).
The inordinate emotions or passions of which love purifies the will
    (chapter 16):
    joy and the basic rule for directing it to God (chapter 17) in
        temporal (chapters 18-20),
        natural (chapters 21-23),
        sensory (chapters 24-26),
        moral (chapters 27-29),
        supernatural (chapters 30-32), and
        spiritual goods (chapters 33-34):
            motivating (chapters 35-44),
            provocative (chapter 45).

Since John of the Cross's autograph versions have been lost, editors must turn to copies judged most reliable. The copy of *The Ascent of Mount Carmel* that provides the most trustworthy reading is the codex of *Alcaudete* conserved in the Silverian archives in Burgos. The handwriting of the copy belongs to Juan Evangelista, John's confessor, secretary, and close companion. Another acceptable copy of the *Ascent* that is often used when *Alcaudete* is deficient is the codex of *Alba*, which is conserved in the archives of the discalced Carmelite friars in Alba de Tormes.

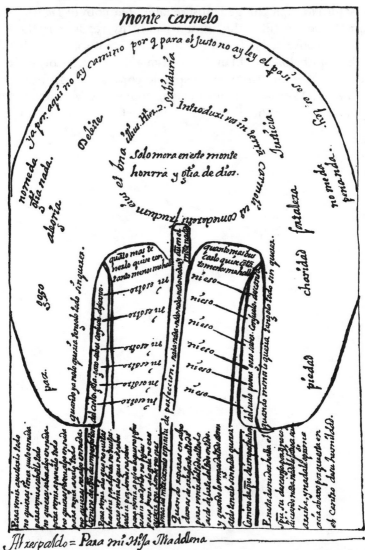

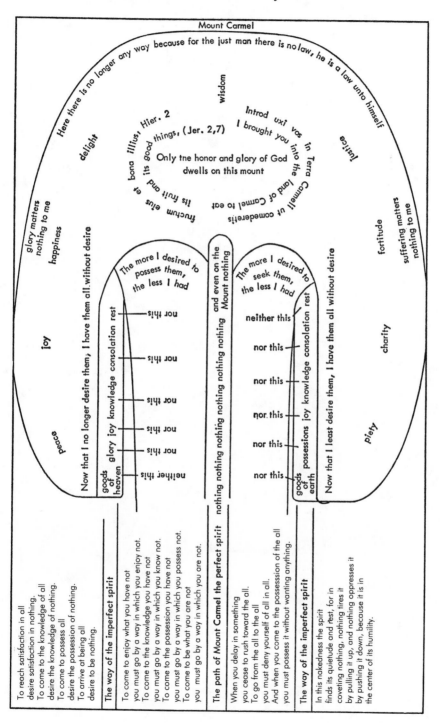

Mount Carmel

Here there is no longer any way because for the just man there is no law, he is a law unto himself

wisdom

delight

Introd uxi vos in Terra Camelli
I brought you into the land of Carmel to eat

justice

bona Illius, Hier. 2

its good things, (Jer. 2,7)

Only tne honor and glory of God dwells on this mount

fructum elus et its fruit and

fructum elus ut comederetis

glory matters nothing to me

happiness

fortitude

suffering matters nothing to me

The more I desired to possess them, the less I had

and even on the Mount nothing

The more I desired to seek them, the less I had

joy

neither this

peace

goods of heaven — glory joy knowledge consolation rest

nor this

nor this

nor this

nor this

nor this

nor this

charity

neither this

nothing nothing nothing nothing nothing Mount nothing

The path of Mount Carmel the perfect spirit

nor this

nor this

nor this

nor this

nor this

goods of earth — possessions joy knowledge consolation rest

piety

Now that I no longer desire them, I have them all without desire

Now that I least desire them, I have them all without desire

To reach satisfaction in all
desire satisfaction in nothing.
To come to the knowledge of all
desire the knowledge of nothing.
To come to possess all
desire the possession of nothing.
To arrive at being all
desire to be nothing.

The way of the imperfect spirit

To come to enjoy what you have not
you must go by a way in which you enjoy not.
To come to the knowledge you have not
you must go by a way in which you know not.
To come to the possession you have not
you must go by a way in which you possess not.
To come to be what you are not
you must go by a way in which you are not.

The path of Mount Carmel the perfect spirit

When you delay in something
you cease to rush toward the all.
To go from the all to the all
you must deny yourself of all in all.
And when you come to the possesssion of the all
you must possess it without wanting anything.

The way of the imperfect spirit

In this nakedness the spirit
finds its quietude and rest, for in
coveting nothing, nothing tires it
by pulling it up, and nothing oppresses it
by pushing it down, because it is in
the center of its humility.

THE ASCENT OF MOUNT CARMEL

This treatise explains how to reach divine union quickly. It presents instruction and doctrine valuable for beginners and proficients alike that they may learn how to unburden themselves of all earthly things, avoid spiritual obstacles, and live in that complete nakedness and freedom of spirit necessary for divine union. It was composed by Padre Fray John of the Cross, Discalced Carmelite.

THEME

The following stanzas include all the doctrine I intend to discuss in this book, *The Ascent of Mount Carmel.* They describe the way that leads to the summit of the mount—that high state of perfection we here call union of a soul with God. Since these stanzas will serve as a basis for all I shall say, I want to cite them here in full that the reader may see in them a summary of the doctrine to be expounded. Yet I will quote each stanza again before its explanation and give the verses separately if the subject so requires.

STANZAS

A song of the soul's happiness in having passed through the dark night of faith, in nakedness and purgation, to union with its Beloved.

> 1. One dark night,
> fired with love's urgent longings
> —ah, the sheer grace!—
> I went out unseen,
> my house being now all stilled.

> 2. In darkness and secure,
> by the secret ladder, disguised,
> —ah, the sheer grace!—
> in darkness and concealment,
> my house being now all stilled.

3. On that glad night,
in secret, for no one saw me,
nor did I look at anything,
with no other light or guide
than the one that burned in my heart.

4. This guided me
more surely than the light of noon
to where he was awaiting me
—him I knew so well—
there in a place where no one appeared.

5. O guiding night!
O night more lovely than the dawn!
O night that has united
the Lover with his beloved,
transforming the beloved in her Lover.

6. Upon my flowering breast
which I kept wholly for him alone,
there he lay sleeping,
and I caressing him
there in a breeze from the fanning cedars.

7. When the breeze blew from the turret,
as I parted his hair,
it wounded my neck
with its gentle hand,
suspending all my senses.

8. I abandoned and forgot myself,
laying my face on my Beloved;
all things ceased; I went out from myself,
leaving my cares
forgotten among the lilies.

PROLOGUE

1. A deeper enlightenment and wider experience than mine is necessary to explain the dark night through which a soul journeys toward that divine light of perfect union with God that is achieved, insofar as possible in this life, through love. The darknesses and trials, spiritual and temporal, that fortunate souls ordinarily undergo on their way to the high state

of perfection are so numerous and profound that human science cannot understand them adequately. Nor does experience of them equip one to explain them. Only those who suffer them will know what this experience is like, but they won't be able to describe it.

2. In discussing this dark night, therefore, I will not rely on experience or science, for these can fail and deceive us. Although I will not neglect whatever possible use I can make of them, my help in all that, with God's favor, I shall say, will be Sacred Scripture, at least in the most important matters, or those that are difficult to understand. Taking Scripture as our guide we do not err, since the Holy Spirit speaks to us through it. Should I misunderstand or be mistaken on some point, whether I deduce it from Scripture or not, I will not be intending to deviate from the true meaning of Sacred Scripture or from the doctrine of our Holy Mother the Catholic Church. Should there be some mistake, I submit entirely to the Church, or even to anyone who judges more competently about the matter than I.

3. I am not undertaking this arduous task because of any particular confidence in my own abilities. Rather, I am confident that the Lord will help me explain this matter because it is extremely necessary to so many souls. Even though these souls have begun to walk along the road of virtue, and our Lord desires to place them in the dark night that they may move on to the divine union, they do not advance. The reason for this may be that sometimes they do not want to enter the dark night or allow themselves to be placed in it, or that sometimes they misunderstand themselves and are without suitable and alert directors who will show them the way to the summit. God gives many souls the talent and grace for advancing, and should they desire to make the effort they would arrive at this high state. And so it is sad to see them continue in their lowly method of communion with God because they do not want or know how to advance, or because they receive no direction on breaking away from the methods of beginners. Even if our Lord finally comes to their aid to the extent of making them advance without these helps, they reach the summit much later, expend more effort, and gain less merit, because they do not willingly adapt themselves to God's work of placing them on the pure and reliable road leading to union. Although God does lead them—since he can do so without their cooperation—they do not accept his guidance. In resisting God who is conducting them, they make little progress and fail in merit because they do not apply their wills; as a result they must endure greater suffering. Some souls, instead of abandoning themselves to God and cooperating with him, hamper him by their indiscreet activity or their resistance. They resemble children who kick and cry and struggle to walk by themselves when their mothers want to

carry them; in walking by themselves they make no headway, or if they do, it is at a child's pace.

4. With God's help, then, we will propose doctrine and counsel for beginners and proficients that they may understand or at least know how to practice abandonment to God's guidance when He wants them to advance.[1]

Some spiritual fathers are likely to be a hindrance and harm rather than a help to these souls that journey on this road. Such directors have neither understanding nor experience of these ways. They are like the builders of the tower of Babel [Gn. 11:1-9]. When these builders were supposed to provide the proper materials for the project, they brought entirely different supplies because they failed to understand the language. And thus nothing was accomplished. Hence, it is arduous and difficult for a soul in these periods of the spiritual life when it cannot understand itself or find anyone else who understands it.

It will happen to individuals that while they are being conducted by God along a sublime path of dark contemplation and aridity, in which they feel lost and filled with darknesses, trials, conflicts, and temptations, they will meet someone who, in the style of Job's comforters [Jb. 4:8-11], will proclaim that all of this is due to melancholia, depression, or temperament, or to some hidden wickedness, and that as a result God has forsaken them. Therefore the usual verdict is that these individuals must have lived an evil life since such trials afflict them.

5. Other directors will tell them that they are falling back since they find no satisfaction or consolation as they previously did in the things of God. Such talk only doubles the trial of a poor soul. It will happen that the soul's greatest suffering will be caused by the knowledge of its own miseries. That it is full of evil and sin is as clear as day to it, and even clearer, for, as we shall say further on, God is the author of this enlightenment in the night of contemplation. And when this soul finds someone who agrees with what it feels (that these trials are all its own fault), its suffering and distress grow without bounds. And this suffering usually becomes worse than death. Such a confessor is not satisfied with this but, in judging these trials to be the result of sin, he urges souls who endure them to go over their past and make many general confessions— which is another crucifixion. The director does not understand that now

---

1. Throughout his work John refers to the traditional division of the spiritual life into three stages: beginners, proficients, and the perfect. Here he speaks only of beginners and proficients because the perfect will have already reached the summit. Elsewhere, he uses another basically equivalent division, that of the three ways: purgative, illuminative, and unitive.

perhaps is not the time for such activity. Indeed, it is a period for leaving these persons alone in the purgation God is working in them, a time to give comfort and encouragement that they may desire to endure this suffering as long as God wills, for until then no remedy—whatever the soul does, or the confessor says—is adequate.

6. With divine help we will discuss all this: how individuals should behave; what method the confessor should use in dealing with them; signs to recognize this purification of the soul that we call the dark night; whether it is the purification of the senses or of the spirit; and how we can discern whether this affliction is caused by melancholia or some other deficiency of sense or spirit.

Some souls—or their confessors—may think that God is leading them along this road of the dark night of spiritual purgation, but perhaps this will not be so. What they suffer will be due to one of these deficiencies. Likewise, many individuals think they are not praying when, indeed, their prayer is deep. Others place high value on their prayer while it amounts to little more than nothing.

7. Some people—and it is sad to see them—work and tire themselves greatly, and yet go backward; they look for progress in what brings no progress but instead hinders them. Others, in peace and tranquility, continue to advance well. Some others let themselves be encumbered by the very consolations and favors God bestows on them for the sake of their advancing, and they advance not at all.

We will also discuss many other experiences of those who walk along this road: joys, afflictions, hopes, and sorrows—some of these originating from the spirit of perfection, others from the spirit of imperfection. Our goal will be to explain, with God's help, all these points so that those who read this book will in some way discover the road they are walking along, and the one they ought to follow if they want to reach the summit of this mount.

8. Readers should not be surprised if this doctrine on the dark night— through which a soul advances toward God—appears somewhat obscure. This, I believe, will be the case as they begin to read, but as they read on they will understand it better since the latter parts will explain the former. Then, if they read this work a second time, the matter will seem clearer and the doctrine sounder.

But if some people still find difficulty in understanding this doctrine, it will be due to my deficient knowledge and awkward style, for the doctrine itself is good and very necessary. But I am inclined to believe that, even if it were presented with greater accuracy and polish, only a few would find profit in it, because we are not writing on moral and pleasing topics addressed to the kind of spiritual people who like to approach God along sweet and satisfying paths. We are presenting a substantial and solid doctrine for all those who desire to reach this nakedness of spirit.

9. My main intention is not to address everyone, but only some of the persons of our holy order of the primitive observance of Mount Carmel, both friars and nuns, whom God favors by putting on the path leading up this mount, since they are the ones who asked me to write this work. Because they are already detached to a great extent from the temporal things of this world, they will more easily grasp this doctrine on nakedness of spirit.

BOOK ONE

CHAPTER 1

Some remarks about the two different nights through which spiritual persons pass in both the lower and higher parts of their nature. A commentary on the first stanza.

[First Stanza]

One dark night,
fired with love's urgent longings
—ah, the sheer grace!—
I went out unseen,
my house being now all stilled.

1. The soul sings in this first stanza of its good luck and the grace it had in departing from its inordinate sensory appetites and imperfections.[1] To understand this departure one should know that a soul must ordinarily pass through two principal kinds of night—which spiritual persons call purgations or purifications of the soul—in order to reach the state of perfection. Here we will term these purgations nights because in both of them the soul journeys in darkness as though by night.

---

1. In John's usage the term "appetite" (unless otherwise stated) refers to an inordinate longing or craving, an impulse that is not rightly ordered to a moral or spiritual good. It involves more than the simple inclination referred to in scholastic philosophy.

2. The first night or purgation, to which this stanza refers and which will be discussed in the first section of this book, concerns the sensory part of the soul. The second night, to which the second stanza refers, concerns the spiritual part. We will deal with this second night, insofar as it is active, in the second and third sections of the book. In the fourth section we will discuss the night insofar as it is passive.[2]

3. This first night is the lot of beginners, at the time God commences to introduce them into the state of contemplation. It is a night in which their spirit also participates, as we will explain in due time. The second night or purification takes place in those who are already proficients, at the time God desires to lead them into the state of divine union. This purgation, of course, is more obscure, dark, and dreadful, as we will subsequently point out.

Commentary on the Stanza

4. In this stanza the soul desires to declare in summary fashion that it departed on a dark night, attracted by God and enkindled with love for him alone. This dark night is a privation and purgation of all sensible appetites for the external things of the world, the delights of the flesh, and the gratifications of the will. All this deprivation is wrought in the purgation of sense. That is why the poem proclaims that the soul departed when its house was stilled, for the appetites of the sensory part were stilled and asleep in the soul, and the soul was stilled in them. One is not freed from the sufferings and anguish of the confining appetites until they are tempered and put to sleep. So it was a sheer grace, the soul declares, to have gone out unseen without encumbrance from the appetites of the flesh, or from anything else. It was also fortunate the departure took place at night; that is, that God took from the soul all these things through a privation that was a night to it.

5. It was a sheer grace to be placed by God in this night that occasioned so much good. The soul would not have succeeded in entering it, because souls are unable alone to empty themselves of all their appetites in order to reach God.

6. Summarily, then, we have an explanation of the first stanza. Now we

---

2. In the general division of the work, the sections become books. The fourth section refers to the entire work of the Dark Night; the first three sections, to the three books of the Ascent. John does not remain entirely faithful to this projected division.

will expound on it verse by verse and explain whatever pertains to our subject. We will follow the method mentioned in the prologue: first cite each stanza and comment on it; then, the individual verses.[3]

CHAPTER 2

The nature of the dark night through which a soul journeys to divine union.

One dark night

1. We can offer three reasons for calling this journey toward union with God a night.

The first has to do with the point of departure, because individuals must deprive themselves of their appetites for worldly possessions. This denial and privation is like a night for all one's senses.

The second reason refers to the means or the road along which a person travels to this union. Now this road is faith, and for the intellect faith is also like a dark night.

The third reason pertains to the point of arrival, namely God. And God is also a dark night to the soul in this life. These three nights pass through a soul, or better, the soul passes through them in order to reach union with God.

2. They are represented in the Book of Tobias [Tb. 6:18-22], where we read that the angel ordered the young Tobias to wait three nights before any union with his bride.

On the first night he was to burn the fish heart in the fire. That heart signified the human heart that is attached to worldly things. To undertake the journey to God the heart must be burned with the fire of divine love and purified of all creatures. Such a purgation puts the devil to flight, for he has power over people through their attachment to temporal and bodily things.

3. Tobias, on the second night, as the angel told him, was to be admitted into the society of the holy patriarchs, the fathers of the faith. After passing through the first night (the privation of all sensible objects), a person enters the second night by living in faith alone; not in a faith that is exclusive of charity but a faith that excludes other intellectual knowledge, as we shall explain later, for faith does not fall into the province of the senses.

---

3. This method was not mentioned in the prologue but in the theme. Actually, in the *Ascent* John does not follow through on this promise.

4. The angel told Tobias that on the third night he would obtain the blessing, which is God. God, by means of faith, which is the second night, communicates himself so secretly and intimately that he becomes another night for the soul. This communication of God is a night much darker than those other two nights, as we will soon point out. When this third night (God's communication to the spirit, which usually occurs in extreme darkness of soul) has passed, a union with the bride, who is the Wisdom of God, then follows. Tobias was also told by the angel that, after the third night had come to an end, he would be joined to his bride in the fear of the Lord. Now when the fear of God is perfect, love is also perfect, which means that the transformation of the soul in God through love is accomplished.

5. In actuality these three nights comprise only one night, a night divided into three parts like natural night. The first part, the night of the senses, resembles early evening, that time of twilight when things begin to fade from sight. The second part, faith, is completely dark, like midnight. The third part, representing God, is like the very early dawn just before the break of day. To provide further enlightenment about all this, we will discuss each of these causes of night separately.[1]

CHAPTER 3

The first cause of this night—the privation of the appetite in all things. The reason for the use of the expression "night."

1. We are using the expression "night" to signify a deprival of the gratification of the soul's appetites in all things. Just as night is nothing but the privation of light and, consequently, of all objects visible by means of the light—darkness and emptiness, then, for the faculty of sight—the mortification of the appetites can be called a night for the soul. To deprive oneself of the gratification of the appetites in all things is like

---

1. The three reasons for calling the journey a night, the three nights of Tobias, and the one night with three parts deal with the symbol somewhat differently and thus show incongruities if compared. Here John basically presents a three-part division different from the four-part division of the previous chapter. He deduces this new division from the three reasons for calling the spiritual journey a night. As he goes on he tries to adjust these different divisions. Sometimes the threefold prevails, at other times the fourfold. This is the point at which the work moves from being a commentary on the poem to being a treatise on the spiritual journey.

living in darkness and in a void.[1] The eye feeds on its objects by means of light in such a way that when the light is extinguished the eye no longer sees them. Similarly do people by means of their appetites feed and pasture on worldly things that gratify their faculties. When the appetites are extinguished—or mortified—one no longer feeds on the pleasure of these things, but lives in a void and in darkness with respect to the appetites.

2. Let us draw an example from each of the faculties. By depriving itself of its appetites for the delights of hearing, a soul lives in darkness and emptiness in this sense faculty. And by depriving itself of the pleasure of seeing things, it lives in darkness and poverty in the faculty of sight. By denying itself the fragrances pleasing to the sense of smell, a soul abides in emptiness and darkness in this sense faculty. Then too by denying the palate the pleasures of delicious foods, it is also in the void and in darkness in the sense of taste. Finally, by mortifying itself of all the delights and satisfactions of the sense of touch, a soul likewise dwells in darkness and in a void in this faculty. The conclusion is that any individuals who may have denied and rejected the gratification that all things afford them, by mortifying their appetite for them, live as though in the night—in darkness, which is nothing else than a void within them of all things.

3. The cause of this darkness is attributable to the fact that—as the scholastic philosophers say—the soul is like a *tabula rasa* [a clean slate] when God infuses it into the body. Without the knowledge it receives through its senses it would be ignorant, because no knowledge is communicated to it naturally from any other source. Accordingly, the presence of the soul in the body resembles the presence of a prisoner in a dark dungeon who knows no more than what he manages to behold through the windows of his prison and has nowhere else to turn if nothing is seen through them. For the soul possesses no other natural means of perceiving what is communicated to it than the senses (the windows of its prison).

4. We can easily affirm that if a soul denies whatever is perceptible through the senses, it lives in darkness and in a void since light can enter

---

1. The denial has to do with a gratification of the appetites. The symbol of darkness may lead one to think in terms of knowing, of the light of intellectual vision, an aristotelian-scholastic analogy. But here John is focusing on the affective level. What gives one the feeling of life is the satisfaction things provide, not the material perception of them. Without such satisfaction, whether the object is present or not, on the affective level the person may feel emptiness or depression.

by no other natural means than these five senses. Now it is true that the sensory perceptions of hearing, sight, smell, taste, and touch are unavoidable; yet they will no more hinder a soul—if it denies them—than if they were not experienced. It is true also that those desiring to keep their eyes closed will live in darkness just like the blind. David says on this subject: *Pauper sum ego, et in laboribus a juventute mea.* (I am poor and in labors from my youth) [Ps. 88:15]. Even though he was manifestly rich, he says he was poor because his will was not fixed on riches; and he thereby lived as though really poor. On the other hand, had he been actually poor, without his will being so, there would have been no true poverty, because the appetite of his soul would have been rich and full.

Hence, we call this nakedness a night for the soul, for we are not discussing the mere lack of things; this lack will not divest the soul if it craves for all these objects. We are dealing with the denudation of the soul's appetites and gratifications. This is what leaves it free and empty of all things, even though it possesses them. Since the things of the world cannot enter the soul, they are not in themselves an encumbrance or harm to it; rather, it is the will and appetite dwelling within that cause the damage when set on these things.[2]

5. This first kind of night refers to the sensory part of the soul, and it is one of the two nights mentioned above through which a person must pass to reach union with God. It is time to explain how fitting it is that the soul leave its house and journey through this dark night toward union with God.

CHAPTER 4

The necessity of truly passing through this dark night of sense (the mortification of the appetites) in order to journey to union with God.

1. The necessity to pass through this dark night (the mortification of the appetites and denial of pleasure in all things) to attain divine union with God arises from the fact that all of a person's attachments to creatures are pure darkness in God's sight. Clothed in these affections, people are incapable of the enlightenment and dominating fullness of God's pure and simple light; first they must reject them. There can be no concordance between light and darkness; as St. John says: *Tenebrae eam no comprehenderunt* (The darkness could not receive the light) [Jn. 1:5].

2. The reason, as we learn in philosophy, is that two contraries cannot

---

2. This clarification is essential to the understanding of John's teaching throughout the present work.

coexist in the same subject.[1] Darkness, an attachment to creatures, and light, which is God, are contraries and bear no likeness toward each other, as St. Paul teaches in his letter to the Corinthians: *Quae conventio lucis ad tenebras?* (What conformity is there between light and darkness?) [2 Cor. 6:14] Consequently, the light of divine union cannot be established in the soul until these affections are eradicated.

3. For a better proof of this, it ought to be kept in mind that an attachment to a creature makes a person equal to that creature; the stronger the attachment, the closer is the likeness to the creature and the greater the equality, for love effects a likeness between the lover and the loved. As a result David said of those who set their hearts on their idols: *Similes illis fiant qui faciunt ea, et omnes qui confidunt in eis* (Let all who set their hearts on them become like them) [Ps. 115:8]. Anyone who loves a creature, then, is as low as that creature and in some way even lower because love not only equates but even subjects the lover to the loved creature.[2]

By the mere fact that a soul loves something, it becomes incapable of pure union and transformation in God; for the lowness of the creature is far less capable of the height of the Creator than is darkness of light.

All creatures of heaven and earth are nothing when compared to God, as Jeremiah points out: *Aspexi terram, et ecce vacua erat et nihil; et caelos, et non erat lux in eis* (I looked at the earth, and it was empty and nothing; and at the heavens, and I saw they had no light) [Jer. 4:23]. By saying that he saw an empty earth, he meant that all its creatures were nothing and that the earth too was nothing. In stating that he looked up to the heavens and beheld no light, he meant that all the heavenly luminaries were pure darkness in comparison to God. All creatures considered in this way are nothing, and a person's attachments to them are less than nothing since these attachments are an impediment to and deprive the soul of transformation in God—just as darkness is nothing and less than nothing since it is a privation of light. One who is in darkness does not comprehend the light, so neither will a person attached to creatures be able to comprehend God. Until a soul is purged of its attachments it will be unable to possess God, neither here below through the pure transformation of love nor in heaven through the beatific vision. For the sake of greater clarity we will be more specific.

---

1. This principle, basic to John's thought, comes from Aristotle *On sensation* 8.
2. This fundamental idea in John's teaching, that love effects a likeness between the lover and the loved, has its roots in the classic Greek and Roman poets and philosophers. Though John insists so much on the divine transcendence, a likeness or equality between God and humans can still be effected, not on the ontological but on the affective plane. God when he loves humans makes them his equals in love. Cf. C. 38, 3-4.

4. We just asserted that all the being of creatures compared to the infinite being of God is nothing and that, therefore, anyone attached to creatures is nothing in the sight of God, and even less than nothing because love causes equality and likeness and even brings the lover lower than the loved object. In no way, then, is such a person capable of union with the infinite being of God. There is no likeness between what is not and what is. To be particular, here are some examples.

All the beauty of creatures compared to the infinite beauty of God is the height of ugliness. As Solomon says in Proverbs: *Fallax gratia, et vana est pulchritudo* (Comeliness is deceiving and beauty vain) [Prv. 31:30]. So a person attached to the beauty of any creature is extremely ugly in God's sight. A soul so unsightly is incapable of transformation into the beauty that is God because ugliness does not attain to beauty.

All the grace and elegance of creatures compared to God's grace is utter coarseness and crudity. That is why a person captivated by this grace and elegance of creatures becomes highly coarse and crude in God's sight. Someone like this is incapable of the infinite grace and beauty of God because of the extreme difference between the coarse and the infinitely elegant.

Compared to the infinite goodness of God, all the goodness of the creatures of the world can be called wickedness. Nothing is good save God only [Lk. 18:19]. Those who set their hearts on the good things of the world become extremely wicked in the sight of God. Since wickedness does not comprehend goodness, such persons will be incapable of union with God, who is supreme goodness.

All the world's wisdom and human ability compared to the infinite wisdom of God is pure and utter ignorance, as St. Paul writes to the Corinthians: *Sapientia hujus mundi stultitia est apud Deum* (The wisdom of this world is foolishness in God's sight) [1 Cor. 3:19].

5. Those, therefore, who value their knowledge and ability as a means of reaching union with the wisdom of God are highly ignorant in God's sight and will be left behind, far away from this wisdom. Ignorance does not grasp what wisdom is. St. Paul says that such wisdom is foolishness to God, for in God's sight those who think they have some wisdom are very ignorant. The Apostle says of them in writing to the Romans: *Dicentes enim se esse sapientes, stulti facti sunt* (Taking themselves for wise, they became fools) [Rom. 1:22].

Only those who set aside their own knowledge and walk in God's service like unlearned children receive wisdom from God. This is the wisdom about which St. Paul taught the Corinthians: *Si quis videtur inter vos sapiens esse in hoc saeculo, stultus fiat ut sit sapiens. Sapientia enim hujus mundi stultitia est apud Deum* (If anyone among you thinks he is wise, let him become ignorant so as to be wise. For the wisdom of this world is foolishness with God) [1 Cor. 3:18-19]. Accordingly, to reach union with the wisdom of God a person must advance by unknowing rather than by knowing.

6. All the sovereignty and freedom of the world compared to the freedom and sovereignty of the Spirit of God is utter slavery, anguish, and captivity. Those, then, who are attached to prelacies or to other such dignities and to freedom of their appetites will be considered and treated by God as base slaves and captives, not as offspring. And this because of their not wanting to accept his holy teaching in which he instructs us that *Whoever wants to be the greater will be the least, and whoever wants to be the least will be the greater* [Lk. 22:26]. Thus they will be unable to reach the royal freedom of spirit attained in divine union, for freedom has nothing to do with slavery. And freedom cannot abide in a heart dominated by desires, in a slave's heart. It abides in a liberated heart, in a child's heart. This is why Sarah told her husband Abraham to cast out the bondwoman and her son, declaring that the bondwoman's son should not be an heir together with the free son [Gn. 21:10].

7. All the delights and satisfactions of the will in the things of the world compared to all the delight that is God are intense suffering, torment, and bitterness. Those who link their hearts to these delights, then, deserve in God's eyes intense suffering, torment, and bitterness. They will not be capable of attaining the delights of the embrace of union with God, since they merit suffering and bitterness.

All the wealth and glory of creation compared to the wealth that is God is utter poverty and misery in the Lord's sight. The person who loves and possesses these things is completely poor and miserable before God and will be unable to attain the richness and glory of transformation in God; the miserable and poor is very far from the supremely rich and glorious.

8. Divine Wisdom, with pity for these souls that become ugly, abject, miserable, and poor because of their love for worldly things, which in their opinion are rich and beautiful, exclaims in Proverbs: *O viri, ad vos clamito, et vox mea ad filios hominum. Intelligite, parvuli, astutiam, et insipientes, animadverte. Audite quia de rebus magnis locutura sum.* And further on: *Mecum sunt divitiae et gloria, opes superbae et justitia. Melior est fructus meus auro et lapide pretioso, et genimina mea argento electo. In viis justitiae ambulo, in medio semitarum judicii, ut ditem diligentes me, et thesauros eorum repleam.* The meaning of this passage is: O people, I cry to you, my voice is directed to the children of this earth. Be attentive, little ones, to cunning and sagacity; and you ignorant, be careful. Listen, because I want to speak of great things. Riches and glory are mine, high riches and justice. The fruit you will find in me is better than gold and precious stones; and my

generations (what will be engendered of me in your souls) are better than choice silver. I walk along the ways of justice, in the midst of the paths of judgment, to enrich those who love me and to fill their treasures completely [Prv. 8:4-6, 18-21].

Divine Wisdom speaks, here, to all those who are attached to the things of the world. She calls them little ones because they become as little as the things they love. She tells them, accordingly, to be cunning and careful, that she is dealing with great things, not small things, as they are; and that the riches and glory they love are with her and in her, not where they think; and that lofty riches and justice are present in her. Although in their opinion the things of this world are riches, she tells them to bear in mind that her riches are more precious, that the fruit found in them will be better than gold and precious stones, and that what she begets in souls has greater value than cherished silver, which signifies every kind of affection possible in this life.

CHAPTER 5

Continuation of the same matter. Proofs from passages and figures of Sacred Scripture for the necessity of journeying to God through this dark night, the mortification of the appetites.

1. We have some idea, from what was said, of the distance that lies between what creatures are in themselves and what God is in himself, and, since love produces equality and likeness, of how souls attached to any of these creatures are just as distant from God. With a clear realization of this distance, St. Augustine addressed God in the *Soliloquies: Miserable man that I am, when will my pusillanimity and imperfection be able to conform with your righteousness? You indeed are good, and I evil; You are merciful, and I unmerciful; You are holy, and I miserable; You are just, and I unjust; You are light, and I blindness; You are life, and I death; You are medicine, and I sickness; You are supreme truth; and I utter vanity.*[1] These are the words of the saint.

2. People, indeed, are ignorant who think it is possible to reach this high state of union with God without first emptying their appetite of all the natural and supernatural things that can be a hindrance to them, as we will explain further on. For there is an extreme distance between such appetites and that which is given in this state, which is nothing less than transformation in God. Instructing us about this way, our Lord stated according to St. Luke: *Qui non renuntiat omnibus quae possidet, non potest*

---

1. This text is from the pseudo-Augustinian work, *Liber soliloquiorum animae ad Deum*, ch. 2, in Migne, PL 40. 866.

meus esse discipulus (Whoever does not renounce all that the will possesses cannot be my disciple) [Lk. 14:33]. This statement is clear, for the doctrine the Son of Man came to teach is contempt for all things so we may receive the gift of God's Spirit. As long as people fail to rid themselves of these possessions, they are incapable of receiving God's Spirit in pure transformation.

3. We have a figure of this in Exodus [Ex. 16] where we read that God did not give the children of Israel the heavenly manna until they exhausted the flour brought from Egypt. The meaning here is that first a total renunciation is needed, for this bread of angels is disagreeable to the palate of anyone who wants to taste human food. Persons feeding on other strange tastes not only become incapable of the divine Spirit, but even greatly anger the divine Majesty because in their aspirations for spiritual food they are not satisfied with God alone, but mix with these aspirations a desire and affection for other things. This is likewise apparent in the same book of Sacred Scripture [Ex. 16:8-13] where it states that the people, discontented with that simple food, requested and craved meat, and seriously angered our Lord because of their desire to commingle a food so base and coarse with one so high and simple that, even though simple, contained the savor and substance of all foods. Consequently, while morsels of manna were yet in their mouths, the wrath of God descended on them (as David also says: *Ira Dei descendit super eos* [Ps. 78:31]), spouting fire from heaven and reducing thousands of them to ashes [Nm. 11:1]. For God thought it shameful for them to crave other food while he was giving them heavenly food.

4. Oh, if spiritual persons knew how much spiritual good and abundance they lose by not attempting to raise their appetites above childish things, and if they knew to what extent, by not desiring the taste of these trifles, they would discover in this simple spiritual food the savor of all things! The Israelites did not perceive the taste of every other food that was contained in the manna, because their appetite was not centered on this manna alone. They were unsuccessful in deriving from the manna all the taste and strength they were looking for, not because the manna didn't have these but because of their craving for other foods. Similarly, those who love something together with God undoubtedly make little of God, for they weigh in the balance with God an object far distant from God, as we have said.

5. It is well known from experience that when the will is attached to an object, it esteems that object higher than any other, even though another, not as pleasing, may deserve higher admiration. And if people desire pleasure from two objects, they are necessarily offensive to the more deserving because through their desire for both they equate the

two. Since nothing equals God, those who love and are attached to something along with God offend him exceedingly. If this is true, what would happen if they loved something more than God?

6. This was also indicated when God ordered Moses to climb to the top of the mountain. He did this that Moses might be able to speak to him. He commanded Moses not only to ascend alone and leave the children of Israel below, but to rule against even the pasturing of beasts on the mountainside [Ex. 34:3]. The meaning is that those who ascend this mount of perfection to converse with God must not only renounce all things by leaving them at the bottom, but also restrict their appetites (the beasts) from pasturing on the mountainside, on things that are not purely God. For in God, or in the state of perfection, all appetites cease.

The road and ascent to God, then, necessarily demands a habitual effort to renounce and mortify the appetites; the sooner this mortification is achieved, the sooner the soul reaches the top. But until the appetites are eliminated, one will not arrive no matter how much virtue is practiced. For one will be failing to acquire perfect virtue, which lies in keeping the soul empty, naked, and purified of every appetite.

We also have a striking figure of this in Genesis. When the patriarch Jacob desired to ascend Mount Bethel to build an altar to offer sacrifice to God, he first ordered his people to do three things: destroy all strange gods; purify themselves; and change their garments [Gn. 35:2].

7. Those desiring to climb to the summit of the mount in order to become an altar for the offering of a sacrifice of pure love and praise and reverence to God must first accomplish these three tasks perfectly. First, *(1)* they must cast out strange gods, all alien affections and attachments. *(2)* Second, by denying these appetites and repenting of them—through the dark night of the senses—they must purify themselves of the residue. *(3)* Third, in order to reach the top of this high mount, their garments must be changed. By means of the first two works, God will substitute new garments for the old. The soul will be clothed in a new understanding of God in God (through removal of the old understanding) and in a new love of God in God, once the will is stripped of all the old cravings and satisfactions. And God will vest the soul with new knowledge when the other old ideas and images are cast aside [Col. 3:9]. He causes all that is of the old self, the abilities of one's natural being, to cease, and he attires all the faculties with new supernatural abilities. As a result, one's activities, once human, now become divine. This is achieved in the state of union when the soul, in which God alone dwells, has no other function than that of an altar on which God is adored in praise and love.

God commanded that the altar of the Ark of the Covenant be empty and hollow [Ex. 27:8] to remind the soul how void of all things God wishes it to be if it is to serve as a worthy dwelling for His Majesty. It was forbidden that the altar have any strange fire, or that its own go out; so much so that when Nadab and Abihu, the sons of the high priest Aaron, offered strange fire on our Lord's altar God became angry and slew them there in front of the altar [Lv. 10:1-2]. The lesson we derive here is that one's love for God must never fail or be mixed with alien loves if one wants to be a worthy altar of sacrifice.

8. God allows nothing else to dwell together with him. We read, consequently, in the First Book of Kings that when the Philistines put the Ark of the Covenant in a temple with their idol, the idol was hurled to the ground at the dawn of each day and broken into pieces [1 Sm. 5:2-4]. The only appetite God permits and wants in his dwelling place is the desire for the perfect fulfillment of his law and the carrying of the cross of Christ. Scripture teaches that God ordered nothing else to be placed in the Ark where the manna was than the Law and the rod of Moses (signifying the cross) [Dt. 31: 6; Nm. 17:10]. Those who have no other goal than the perfect observance of the Lord's law and the carrying of the cross of Christ will be true arks, and they will bear within themselves the real manna, which is God, when they possess perfectly, without anything else, this law and this rod.

CHAPTER 6

The harm, privative as well as positive, that appetites cause in the soul.

1. For the sake of a clearer and fuller understanding of our assertions, it will be beneficial to explain here how these appetites cause harm in two principal ways within those in whom they dwell: They deprive them of God's Spirit; and they weary, torment, darken, defile, and weaken them. Jeremiah mentions this in Chapter 2: *Duo mala fecit populus meus: dereliquerunt fontem aquae vivae, et foderunt sibi cisternas dissipatas, quae continere non valent aquas* (They have forsaken me, the fountain of living water, and dug for themselves leaking cisterns that hold no water) [Jer. 2:13]. Any inordinate act of the appetite causes both this privative and positive damage.

To begin with, it is clear in speaking of the privative harm that a person by mere attachment to a created thing is less capable of God; and this, in the measure that the appetite has entity in the soul. For two contraries cannot coexist in the same subject, as the philosophers say, and as we also mentioned in Chapter 4.[1] Since love of God and attachment to creatures

---

1. In nos. 2-3. Cf. Aristotle, *On generation and decay* 1. 3 and *On the soul* 3. 4; Aquinas, *Summa theologiae*, 1. 19. 9; 1. 118. 2. ad 2; 1-2. 113. 6. ad 2.

are contraries, they cannot coexist in the same will. What has creature to do with Creator, sensory with spiritual, visible with invisible, temporal with eternal, heavenly food that is pure and spiritual with food that is entirely sensory, the nakedness of Christ with attachment to something?

2. In natural generation a new form cannot be introduced into a subject without expulsion of the form already there, which is an impediment to the new form because of the existing contrariety. Similarly, insofar as a person is subject to a sensory spirit, an entirely spiritual one cannot enter. This is why our Lord said through St. Matthew: *Non est bonum sumere panem filiorum et mittere canibus* (It is unbecoming to take the children's bread and give it to the dogs) [Mt. 15:26]. Also in another part he says through the same evangelist: *Nolite sanctum dare canibus* (Do not give what is holy to the dogs) [Mt. 7:6]. All those who dispose themselves for the pure reception of God's Spirit through the denial of their appetites for creatures, our Lord compares to the children of God. And all those who desire to feed their appetites on creatures, he compares to the dogs. It is the privilege of children to eat at table with their father and from his dish, which is to share in his Spirit; but the dogs must eat the crumbs that fall from the table [Mt. 15: 26-27].

3. Our lesson here is that all creatures are like crumbs that have fallen from God's table. Those who go about feeding on creatures, then, are rightly designated as dogs and are deprived of the children's bread because they refuse to rise from the crumbs of creatures to the uncreated Spirit of their Father. This is precisely why they wander about hungry as dogs. The crumbs serve more to whet their appetite than to satisfy their hunger. David says of them: *Famem patientur ut canes, et circuibunt civitatem. Si vero no fuerint saturati, et murmurabunt* (They will suffer hunger like dogs, and wander around the city. And if they are not filled, they will murmur) [Ps. 59:14-15]. This is the characteristic of those with appetites; they are always dissatisfied and bitter, like someone who is hungry.

What, then, has the hunger caused by creatures in common with the fullness caused by the Spirit of God? This uncreated fullness cannot enter a soul until this other hunger caused by the desires is expelled. Since hunger and fullness are contraries they cannot coexist in the same person.

4. It will be evident from our explanation that God accomplishes more in cleansing and purging people of these contraries than he does in creating them from nothing. These impediments of contrary attachments and appetites are more opposed and resistant to God than nothingness, for nothingness does not resist.

Since we have already said a good deal about this first kind of harm (resistance to God's Spirit) caused by the appetites, our comments here should be sufficient.

5. Let us now deal with the second effect, the numerous kinds of impairment wrought in the soul. For the appetites weary, torment, darken, defile, and weaken it. We shall discuss these five effects separately.

6. As for the first, it is plain that the appetites are wearisome and tiring. They resemble little children, restless and hard to please, always whining to their mother for this thing or that, and never satisfied. Just as anyone who digs covetously for a treasure grows tired and exhausted, so does anyone who strives to satisfy the appetites' demands become wearied and fatigued. And even if a soul does finally fill them, it is still always weary because it is never satisfied. For, after all, one digs leaking cisterns that cannot contain the water that slakes thirst. As Isaiah says: *Lassus adhuc sitit, et anima ejus vacua est,* which means: He is yet faint with thirst and his soul is empty [Is. 29:8].

A soul with desires wearies itself, because it is like someone with a fever whose thirst increases by the minute, and who feels ill until the fever leaves. It is said in the Book of Job: *Cum satiatus fuerit, arctabitur, aestuabit, et omnis dolor irruet super eum* (When he has satisfied his appetite, he will be more burdened and oppressed; the heat of appetite will have increased and every sorrow will fall upon him) [Jb. 20:22].

The appetites are wearisome and tiring because they agitate and disturb one just as wind disturbs water. And they so upset the soul that they do not let it rest in any place or thing. Isaiah declares of such a soul: *Cor impii quasi mare fervens* (The heart of the wicked is like a stormy sea) [Is. 57:20]. And anyone who does not conquer the appetites is wicked.

People seeking the satisfaction of their desires grow tired, because they are like the famished who open their mouths to satisfy themselves with air. But they find that instead of being filled the mouth dries up more since air is not one's proper food. With this in mind Jeremiah says: *In desiderio animae suae attraxit ventum amoris sui* (In the appetite of his will he drew in the air of his attachment) [Jer. 2:24]. To comment on the dryness in which the soul is left, he immediately adds the advice: *Prohibe pedem tuum a nuditate, et guttur tuum a siti.* This means: Hold back your foot (that is, your mind) from nakedness, and your throat from thirst (that is, your will from satisfying its desire, which only causes greater thirst) [Jer. 2:25].

Just as a lover is wearied and depressed when on a longed-for day his opportunity is frustrated, so is the soul wearied and tired by all its appetites and their fulfillment, because the fulfillment only causes more hunger and emptiness. An appetite, as they say, is like a fire that blazes up when wood is thrown on it, but necessarily dies out when the wood is consumed.

7. In regard to the appetites, things are even worse. The fire dwindles as the wood is consumed, but the intensity of the appetite does not diminish when the appetite is satisfied, even though the object is gone. Instead of waning like the fire after the wood is burned, the appetite faints with fatigue because its hunger has increased and its food diminished. Isaiah refers to this: *Declinabit ad dexteram, et esuriet; et comedet ad sinistram, et non saturabitur* (He will turn to the right and be hungry, and eat toward the left and not be filled) [Is. 9:20]. When those who do not mortify their appetites turn to the right, they of course see the abundance of the sweet spirit that is the lot of those who are at the right hand of God but is not granted to them. When they eat at the left (satisfy their appetite with some creature), they of course grow discontented because, in turning from what alone satisfies, they feed on what augments their hunger. It is clear, then, that the appetites weary and fatigue a person.

CHAPTER 7

How the appetites torment a person. Proofs through comparisons and passages from Sacred Scripture.

1. Torment and affliction is the second kind of damage the appetites cause in an individual. The affliction they engender is similar to the torture of the rack, where a person has no relief until freed from the torment of being bound by these cords. David says of this torture: *Funes peccatorum circumplexi sunt me* (The cords of my sins—my appetites—have tightened around me) [Ps. 119:61].

A soul is tormented and afflicted when it reclines on its appetites just as is someone lying naked on thorns and nails. Like thorns, the appetites wound and hurt, stick to a person and cause pain. David says of them: *Circumdederunt me sicut apes, et exarserunt sicut ignis in spinis.* (They circled around me like bees, stung me, and burned me like fire among thorns) [Ps. 118:12]. For among the appetites, which are the thorns, the fire of anguish and torment increases.

Just as a peasant, covetous of the desired harvest, goads and torments the ox that pulls the plow, so concupiscence, in order to attain the object of its longing, afflicts the one who lives under the yoke of the appetites. This is evident in Delilah's desire to know where Samson acquired such strength. Scripture states that the desire was such a fatigue and torment to her that she fainted away and almost died: *Defecit anima ejus, et ad mortem usque lassata est* [Jgs. 16:15-16].[1]

2. The appetite torments in the measure of its intensity. Thus there is

---

1. "His soul fainted and was wearied even unto death."

as much torment as there is appetite, and the more numerous the appetites that possess a soul the greater in number are its torments. In the person possessed by appetites we find fulfilled even in this life what is said of Babylon in the Apocalypse: *Quantum glorificavit se, et in deliciis fuit, tantum date illi tormentum et luctum* (In the measure of her desire for self-exaltation and fulfillment of her appetites, give her torment and anguish) [Rv. 18:7].

Those who let their appetites take hold of them suffer torture and affliction like an enemy held prisoner. The Book of Judges contains a figure of this in the passage that narrates how the enemies captured mighty Samson, who was once the free, strong judge of Israel, and weakened him, pulled out his eyes, and chained him to grind at the millstone where he was grievously tortured and tormented [Jgs. 16:21]. This same thing happens to a person in whom the enemy appetites reside and triumph. First these appetites weaken and blind, as we shall point out below, then they afflict and torment by chaining that person to the mill of concupiscence, for they are the chains by which a soul is bound.

3. God, then, with compassion for all those who through such labor and cost to themselves strive to satisfy the thirst and hunger of their appetites for creatures, proclaims through Isaiah: *Omnes sitientes, venite ad aquas; et qui no habetis argentum, properate, emite, et comedite: venite, emite absque argento vinum et lac. Quare appenditis argentum non in panibus, et laborem vestrum non in saturitate?* [Is. 55:1-2]. This is interpreted: Come to the waters, all you who experience the thirst of your appetites; and you who have not the silver of your own will and desires, make haste; buy from me and eat; come and buy wine and milk (peace and spiritual sweetness) from me without the silver of your own will, without paying with labor as you do for the satisfaction of your appetites. Why do you offer the silver of your will for what is not bread (the bread of the divine Spirit) and waste the efforts of your appetites on what cannot satisfy them? Come, listen to me, and you will have the food you desire, and your soul will delight in abundance.

4. This coming to abundance is a going away from all the pleasures derived through creatures, because the creature torments while the Spirit of God refreshes. Accordingly, God calls us through St. Matthew: *Venite ad me, omnes qui laboratis et oneratis estis, et ego reficiam vos, et invenietis requiem animabus vestris,* as though he were to say: All you going about tormented, afflicted, and weighed down by your cares and appetites, depart from them, come to me and I will refresh you; and you will find the rest for your souls that the desires take away from you [Mt. 11:28-29]. They are indeed a heavy burden, because David says of them: *Sicut onus grave gravatae sunt super me* [Ps. 37:5].[2]

CHAPTER 8

The appetites darken and blind a person.

1. The third kind of harm the appetites bring upon a person is blindness and darkness. Vapors make the air murky and are a hindrance to the bright sunshine; a cloudy mirror does not clearly reflect a person's countenance; so too muddy water reflects only a hazy image of one's features. In just this way a person's intellect, clouded by the appetites, becomes dark and impedes the sun of either natural reason or God's supernatural wisdom from shining within and completely illumining it. As a result David says when speaking of this: *Comprehenderunt me iniquitates meae, et non potui ut viderem* (My iniquities surrounded me and I was unable to see) [Ps. 40:12].

2. And because of the darkening of the intellect, the will becomes weak and the memory dull and disordered in its proper operation. Since these faculties depend on the intellect in their operations, they are manifestly disordered and troubled when the intellect is hindered. Thus David says: *Anima mea turbata est valde* (My soul is exceedingly troubled) [Ps. 6:4]. This is like saying the faculties of my soul are disordered. For, as we said, the intellect (as the murky air in relation to the sun's light) is incapable of receiving the illumination of God's wisdom; and the will is incapable of embracing God within itself in pure love (just as the mirror clouded with steam has not the capacity to clearly reflect the countenance before it); and the memory obscured by the darkness of appetite has still less capacity for receiving serenely the impression of God's image (as muddy water cannot clearly reflect the features of one who looks in it).

3. The appetite blinds and darkens the soul because the appetite as such is blind. It is blind because, of itself, it has no intellect. Reason always acts as a blind person's guide for the appetite.[1] Consequently, as often as people are led by their appetites, they are blinded, just as we might say that when a blind person guides someone who has good eyesight both are blind. The logical outcome is what our Lord proclaims in St. Matthew: *Si caecus caeco ducatum praestet, ambo in foveam cadunt.* (If one blind person leads another, both will fall into the ditch) [Mt. 15:14].

A moth is not helped much by its eyes because, blinded in its desire for the beauty of light, it will fly directly into a bonfire. Those who feed on their appetites are like a fish dazzled by a light that so darkens it that the

---

2. "As a heavy burden they weigh upon me."

1. Here John, speaking of the purification of the spiritual faculties, makes us aware of how in this first book he is dealing with more than the purification of the senses.

fisherman's snares cannot be seen. David describes this blindness well: *Supercecidit ignis, et non viderunt solem* (Fire, that gives off heat and dazzles by its light, came upon them) [Ps. 58: 8-9]. The appetites cause this in the soul: They enkindle concupiscence and overwhelm the intellect so that it cannot see its light. The reason is that a new light set directly in front of the visual faculty blinds this faculty so that it fails to see the light farther away. And since the appetite is so close to individuals as to be actually within them, they are impeded by this interior light, feed upon it, and are unable to see the clear light of the intellect; nor will they see it until they extinguish this blinding light of their appetite.

4. The ignorance of some is extremely lamentable; they burden themselves with extraordinary penances and many other exercises, thinking these are sufficient to attain union with divine Wisdom. But such practices are insufficient if these souls do not diligently strive to deny their appetites. If they would attempt to devote only half of that energy to the renunciation of their desires, they would profit more in a month than in years with all these other exercises. As the tilling of soil is necessary for its fruitfulness—untilled soil produces only weeds—mortification of the appetites is necessary for one's spiritual fruitfulness. I venture to say that without this mortification all that is done for the sake of advancement in perfection and in knowledge of God and of oneself is no more profitable than seed sown on uncultivated ground. Accordingly, darkness and coarseness will always be with a soul until its appetites are extinguished. The appetites are like a cataract on the eye or specks of dust in it; until removed they obstruct vision.

5. David, observing the blindness of such people, how impeded their souls are from seeing truth clearly, and the extent of God's anger with them warns: *Priusquam intelligerent spinae vestrae rhamnum: sicut viventes, sic in ira absorbet eos,* as though to say: Before your thorns (that is, your appetites) understand, God will absorb them in his wrath as he would the living [Ps. 58:9]. Before the appetites living in the soul come to an understanding of God, he will absorb them in this life, or in the next, by chastisement and correction, that is, through purgation. David says God will absorb them in wrath, because the suffering caused by the mortification of the appetites is a chastisement for the havoc they produce in the soul.

6. Oh, if people but knew what a treasure of divine light this blindness caused by their affections and appetites takes from them and the number of misfortunes and evils these appetites occasion each day when left unmortified! Individuals must not so rely on their good intelligence or the gifts received from God as to think that even though they have attachments or appetites these will not blind, darken, and cause them to grow

gradually worse. Who would have thought that a man as perfect in the wisdom and gifts of God as Solomon could have sunk into such blindness and torpor of will, when he was already old, as to construct altars to count- less idols and then worship them himself? Yet this was caused by nothing else than his affection for women and his neglect to deny the appetites and delights of his heart [1 Kgs. 3:12-13; 11:1-4]. He says in Ecclesiastes that he did not deny his heart what it asked of him [Eccl. 2:10]. Although in the beginning he was truly restrained, this rush after his desires and the failure to deny them, gradually blinded and darkened his intellect so that finally the powerful light of God's wisdom was extinguished. Conse- quently, in his old age, Solomon abandoned God.

7. If the unmortified appetites could do this in a man who possessed such lofty knowledge of the distance between good and evil, what terrible damage can they cause in us who are ignorant. For as God said to Jonah about the people of Nineveh: *We do not know the difference between our right hand and our left* [Jon. 4:11]. At every step we mistake evil for good and good for evil. This is peculiar to our nature. But what will happen if appetite is added to our natural darkness? Nothing else than what Isaiah says: *Palpavimus sicut caeci parietem et quasi absque oculis attrectavimus: impegimus meridie quasi in tenebris* [Is. 59:10]. The prophet is speaking with those who love to pursue their appetites, as though to say: We have felt our way along the wall as though blind, we have groped as if without eyes, and our blindness has reached the point that we stumble along in broad daylight as though walking in the dark. For this is a characteristic of those who are blinded by their appetites; when they are in the midst of the truth and of what is suitable for them, they no more see it than if they were in the dark.

CHAPTER 9

The appetites defile the soul. Proofs through comparisons and passages from Sacred Scripture.

1. The fourth way the appetites harm the soul is by defiling and staining it. The Book of Ecclesiasticus teaches: *Qui tetigerit picem, inquina- bitur ab ea* (the one who touches pitch will be defiled by it) [Ecclus. 13:1]. And a person handles pitch by satisfying the will's appetite for some creature. It is noteworthy that the Wise Man compares creatures to pitch, for the difference between the excellence of the soul and the best in creatures is greater than that between pure gold, or a bright diamond, and pitch. The gold, or the diamond, when placed on hot pitch becomes more stained and unsightly as the heat melting the pitch increases. Similarly, those who are fired by their appetite for some creature are

stained and blackened by that creature because of the heat of their desire.

There is as much difference between the soul and other corporeal creatures as there is between a transparent liquid and the filthiest mire. This liquid would be polluted if mud were mixed with it; so too attachment to a creature defiles a soul, because this attachment makes it similar to the creature. Strokes of soot would ruin a perfect and extraordinarily beautiful portrait, so too inordinate appetites defile and dirty the soul, in itself a perfect and extremely beautiful image of God.

2. Jeremiah, weeping over the ravages of unsightliness these inordinate appetites cause in a soul, first lists the soul's beauty and then its ugliness: *Candidiores sunt nazarei ejus nive, nitidiores lacte, rubicundiores ebore antiquo, saphiro pulchriores. Denigrata est super carbones facies eorum, et non sunt cogniti in plateis* (Its hair—that is, of the soul—is whiter than snow, more resplendent than milk, ruddier than ancient ivory, more beautiful than sapphire stone. Its surface became blacker than coal and went unrecognized in the public squares) [Lam. 4:7-8]. The hair refers to the soul's affections and thoughts; when ordered to the end intended by God—which is God himself—it is whiter than snow, clearer than milk, ruddier than ancient ivory, and more beautiful than sapphire. These four objects of comparison indicate every kind of beauty and excellence in corporeal creatures; yet the beauty and excellence of the soul's operations, which are signified by the Nazarites or hair, are, he says, greater. If these operations of the soul are inordinate and occupied in an end not intended by God—that is, in creatures—their surface, says Jeremiah, will become blacker than coal.

3. Inordinate appetites for the things of the world do all this damage to the beauty of the soul, and even more. So great is the harm that if we try to express how ugly and dirty is the imprint the appetites leave in the soul we find nothing comparable to it—neither a place full of cobwebs and lizards nor the unsightliness of a dead body nor the filthiest thing imaginable in this life.

Although it is true that the disordered soul possesses in its natural being the perfection that God bestowed when creating it, nevertheless in its rational being it is ugly, abominable, dirty, dark, and full of all the evils here described, and many more besides. One inordinate appetite alone, as we will explain,[1] suffices to make a soul so captive, dirty, and unsightly that until the appetite is purified the soul is incapable of conformity with God in union. This is true even though there may be no matter for mortal sin in the appetite. What then will be the ugliness of a soul entirely

---

1. In chapters 11 and 12 of this book.

disordered in its passions and surrendered to its appetites? How far it will be from God and his purity!

4. The variety of filth caused in the soul is both inexplicable and unintelligible! For were it comprehensible and explainable it would be surprising and also distressing to see how in the measure of its quantity and quality each appetite leaves a deposit of filth and an unsightly mark in the soul. It would be a surprise and a pity to observe how only one inordinate act can in its own way occasion innumerable kinds and various degrees of filth. The well-ordered soul of the just in a single perfect act possesses countless rich gifts and beautiful virtues. Each of these gifts and virtues is different and pleasing in its own way according to the multitude and diversity of the affections the soul has had for God. Similarly, in an inordinate soul the deposit of filth and degradation is as miserable and has the same variety as the variety of its appetites for creatures.

5. We have an excellent figure of these varied appetites in Ezekiel. It is written that God showed this prophet all kinds of crawling reptiles and all the abomination of unclean animals painted on the interior walls of the temple. God then said to Ezekiel: *Son of man, have you not seen indeed the abominations that each of these accomplishes in the secrecy of his chamber?* And when God commanded the prophet to enter further and behold greater abominations, Ezekiel says he saw women seated there and weeping for Adonis, the god of love. Being commanded by God to penetrate still further for the sight of even greater abominations, he says he beheld there 25 old men whose backs were turned on the temple [Ez. 8:10-16].

6. The many reptiles and unclean animals painted on the walls of the first room in the temple represent intellectual thoughts of abject earthly things and of all creatures. These creatures are painted just as they are in the temple of the soul if it allows its intellect, the first chamber, to be encumbered with them.

The women further within, in the second chamber, weeping for the god Adonis, represent the appetites residing in the second faculty of the soul, which is the will. These appetites weep as it were by coveting what the will is attached to; that is, they covet the reptiles painted in the intellect.

The men in the third room are a representation of the images of creatures that the third part of the soul, the memory, preserves and focuses on. The passage states that these men turned their backs on the temple, for when the soul is wholly joined with an earthly object by embracing it with these three faculties, we can say that soul has turned its back on the temple of God. And the temple of God represents the soul's right reason, which admits nothing of creatures.

7. What we have said is sufficient at present for some understanding of the unsightly disorder of the soul caused by its appetites. We would never finish if we tried to discuss in particular the lesser degree of ugliness, and its variety, that imperfections cause in the soul, or the still greater degree, and its variety, produced by venial sins, or the degree of total ugliness caused by mortally sinful appetites. The variety of the total ugliness corresponds to the extensive diversity of all three degrees. Not even the angelic intellect could have an adequate understanding of all this unsightliness. The point I am making and desire to make is that any appetite, even one that is just slightly imperfect, stains and defiles the soul.

CHAPTER 10

The appetites weaken a soul and make it lukewarm in the practice of virtue.

1. Weakness and tepidity is the fifth kind of harm the appetites produce in a person. The appetites sap the strength needed for perseverance in the practice of virtue. Because the force of the desire is divided, the appetite becomes weaker than if it were completely fixed on one object. The more objects there are dividing an appetite, the weaker this appetite becomes for each. This is why the philosophers say that virtue when united is stronger than when scattered. It is therefore clear that if the appetite of the will pours itself out on something other than virtue, it grows weaker in the practice of virtue. A person whose will is divided among trifles is like water that, leaking out at the bottom, will not rise higher and is therefore useless. This is why the patriarch Jacob compared his son Reuben, who had given rein to his appetites in a certain sin, to spilled water: *You are poured out like water, grow not* [Gn. 49:4]. This was like saying: Because according to the appetites you are poured out like water, you will not grow in virtue.

Hot water quickly loses its heat if left uncovered, and aromatic spices when unwrapped eventually lose the strength and pungency of their scent. So the soul that is not recollected in one appetite alone, the desire for God, loses heat and strength in the practice of virtue. Clearly understanding this, David said to God: *Fortitudinem meam ad te custodiam* (I will keep my strength for you) [Ps. 59:9]. I will do this by concentrating the strength of my appetites on you alone.

2. The appetites weaken a person's virtue because they are like shoots burgeoning about a tree, sapping its strength, and causing it to be fruitless. The Lord says of such people: *Vae praegnantibus et nutrientibus in illis diebus!* (Woe to them who will be with child in those days, and to them

who will be nursing!) [Mt. 24:19]. Being with child and nursing refer to the growth of the appetites that, if not cut off, will weaken the soul in virtue. Their growth will be costly, like the growth of sprouts around the tree. Our Lord consequently advises us: *Let your loins be girt* [Lk. 12:35]. The loins here indicate the appetites. They are indeed like leeches, always sucking blood from one's veins. This is what the Wise Man calls them: *The daughters* (the appetites) *are leeches always calling: give! give!* [Prv. 30:15].

3. Manifestly, then, the appetites do not bring any good to a person. Rather they rob one of what one already has. And if one does not mortify them, they will not cease until they accomplish what the offspring of vipers are said to do within the mother: While growing within her they eat away at her entrails and finally kill her, remaining alive at her expense. So the unmortified appetites result in killing the soul in its relationship with God, and thus, because it did not put them to death first, they alone live in it. This is why it says in the Book of Ecclesiasticus: *Aufer a me Domine ventris concupiscentias et concubitus concupiscentiae ne apprehendant me* [Ecclus. 23:6].[1]

4. Even though they do not go to this extent, it is sad to consider the condition of the poor soul in whom they dwell. How unhappy it is with itself, how cold toward its neighbors, how sluggish and slothful in the things of God! No illness makes walking as burdensome, or eating as distasteful, as do the appetites for creatures render the practice of virtue burdensome and saddening to a person. Ordinarily, the reason many people do not have diligence and eagerness for the acquisition of virtue is that their appetites and affections are not fixed purely on God.

CHAPTER 11

Proofs of how freedom from all appetites, even the smallest, is necessary to attain divine union.

1. The reader has apparently desired for quite a while to ask if the total mortification of all the appetites, large and small, is a requirement to attain this high state of perfection, or if it is sufficient to mortify just some of them and leave the others, at least those that seem trifling. For it seems it would be an arduous task for individuals to attain such purity and nakedness that they would have no attachment to anything.

---

1. "Take away from me, O Lord, lustful cravings; let not the desires of the flesh lay hold of me."

2. First, I respond that it is true that the appetites are not all equally detrimental, nor are all equally a hindrance to the soul. I am speaking of the voluntary appetites because the natural ones are little or no hindrance at all to the attainment of union, provided they do not receive one's consent or pass beyond the first movements, those stirrings in which the rational will does not take part either before or after. To eradicate the natural appetites, that is, to mortify them entirely, is impossible in this life. Even though they are not entirely mortified, as I say, they are not such a hindrance as to prevent one from attaining divine union. A soul can easily experience them in its sensitive nature and yet be free of them in the rational part of its being. It will happen sometimes that while a person is experiencing an intense union of will in the prayer of quiet these appetites will be actually dwelling in the sensory part. Yet the superior part of the soul, which is in prayer, will be paying no attention to them.[1]

But all the other voluntary appetites, whether they be the most serious that involve mortal sin, or less grave in that they concern venial sin, or whether they be the least serious of all in that they only involve imperfections, must be mortified. A person must be liberated of them all, however slight they be, in order to arrive at this complete union. The reason is that in the state of divine union a person's will is so completely transformed into God's will that it excludes everything contrary to God's will, and in all and through all is motivated by the will of God.

3. Here we have the reason for stating that two wills become one. And this one will is God's will, which also becomes the soul's. If a person were to desire an imperfection unwanted by God, this one will of God would be undone because of the desire for what God does not will.

Clearly, for a soul to reach union with God through its will and love, it must first be freed from every appetite, however slight. That is, one must not give consent of the will advertently and knowingly to an imperfection, and one must have the power and freedom to be able, upon advertence, to refuse this consent.

I say "knowingly" because one will fall into imperfections, venial sins, and the above-mentioned natural appetites without having advertence or knowledge or control in the matter. It is written of these semivoluntary and inadvertent sins that the just will fall seven times a day and rise up again [Prv. 24:16]. But any one of the voluntary appetites that are advertent venial sins, even if trifling, if not conquered is sufficient to impede union, as I have said. I am referring here to habitual appetites because certain scattered acts of different desires are not such a hin-

1. This teaching by John and other spiritual writers was misinterpreted and misused in the doctrines that were denounced as quietist. With regard to John's doctrine on imperfections, natural first movements, and sins, cf. C. 18; 20-21; N. 1. 4. 1-5; N. 2. 1. 2; 16. 3.

drance to union when the habitual appetites are mortified. However, the soul must be liberated of these acts too, since they also proceed from habitual imperfection. Yet some habitual voluntary imperfections that are never completely conquered are an impediment not only to divine union but to spiritual progress as well.

4. Some examples of these habitual imperfections are: the common habit of being very talkative; a small attachment one never really desires to conquer, for example, to a person, to clothing, to a book or a cell, or to the way food is prepared, and to other trifling conversations and little satisfactions in tasting, knowing, and hearing things, and so on. Any of these habitual imperfections to which there is attachment is as harmful to progress in virtue as the daily commission of many other imperfections and sporadic venial sins that do not result from a bad habit. These latter will not hinder a person as much as will the attachment to something. As long as this attachment remains, it is impossible to make progress in perfection, even though the imperfection may be very small.[2]

It makes little difference whether a bird is tied by a thin thread or by a cord. Even if it is tied by thread, the bird will be held bound just as surely as if it were tied by cord; that is, it will be impeded from flying as long as it does not break the thread. Admittedly the thread is easier to break, but no matter how easily this may be done, the bird will not fly away without first doing so. This is the lot of those who are attached to something: No matter how much virtue they have they will not reach the freedom of the divine union.

An individual's appetite and attachment resemble the remora, which, if successful in clinging to a ship, will hold it back and prevent it from reaching port, or even from sailing, even though this fish is exceptionally small. It is regrettable, then, to behold some souls, laden as rich vessels with wealth, deeds, spiritual exercises, virtues, and favors from God, who never advance because they lack the courage to make a complete break with some little satisfaction, attachment, or affection (which are all about the same) and thereby never reach the port of perfection. This requires no more than a sudden flap of one's wings in order to tear the thread of attachment, or to get rid of the clinging remora.

5. It is a matter for deep sorrow that, while God has bestowed on them the power to break other stronger cords of attachment to sins and vanities, they fail to attain so much good because they do not become detached from some childish thing that God has asked them to conquer out of love for him and that amounts to no more than a thread or hair. What is worse, not only do they fail to advance, but they turn back because of their small attachment, losing what they gained on their journey at the

---

2. Cf. C. 26. 18; 20. 8, for some examples of corresponding doctrine.

cost of so much time and effort. Everyone knows that not to go forward on this road is to turn back, and not to gain ground is to lose. This is what our Lord wanted to teach when he said: *The one who is not with me is against me, and the one who does not gather with me scatters* [Mt. 12:30].

If one small crack in a pitcher goes unrepaired, the damage will be enough to cause all the liquid to leak out. The Book of Ecclesiasticus gives clear teaching of this when it says: *One who despises small things will fall little by little* [Ecclus. 19:1]. For as it teaches elsewhere: *A great fire is occasioned by a tiny spark* [Ecclus. 11:32]. Accordingly, one imperfection leads to another, and these to still more. You will scarcely ever find a person negligent in the conquering of one appetite who will not have many others flowing from the identical weakness and imperfection caused by this one appetite. Such persons, consequently, are ever faltering along the road. We have witnessed many persons, whom God was favoring with much progress in detachment and freedom, fall from happiness and stability in their spiritual exercises and end up losing everything merely because they began to indulge in some slight attachment to conversation and friendship under the appearance of good. For by this attachment they gradually emptied themselves of both holy solitude and the spirit and joy of God. All this happened because they did not put a stop to their initial satisfaction and sensitive pleasure, and preserve themselves for God in solitude.[3]

6. The attainment of our goal demands that we never stop on this road, which means we must continually get rid of our wants rather than indulging them. For if we do not get rid of them all completely, we will not wholly reach our goal. A log of wood cannot be transformed into the fire if even a single degree of heat is lacking to its preparation for this.[4] The soul, similarly, will not be transformed in God even if it has only one imperfection. As we shall explain in speaking of the night of faith, a person has only one will and if that is encumbered or occupied by anything, the person will not possess the freedom, solitude, and purity requisite for divine transformation.

7. We have a figure of this in the Book of Judges. It narrates that the angel announced to the children of Israel that because they had not completely destroyed their enemies but made a pact with some of them, these enemies would be left in their midst to be an occasion of their fall and perdition [Jgs. 2:1-3]. God does precisely this with some souls. He has

---

3. On the blessings the state of solitude brings once freedom from the appetites is attained, see C. 35; N. 2. 14; 23-24.

4. The log of wood in the fire is a basic image John turns to throughout his works to illustrate the process of transformation in God. Cf. A. 2. 8. 2; N. 2. 10. 1-9; 11. 1; F. prol. 3; 1. 3-4, 19-25, 33.

withdrawn them from the world, slain the giants, which are their sins, and destroyed the multitude of their enemies (the occasions of sin encountered in the world) solely so that they can enter with greater freedom into the promised land of divine union. Nevertheless, in spite of all this, they fraternize and make pacts with the insignificant people—their imperfections—by not mortifying them completely. And God in his anger allows them to go from bad to worse in their appetites.

8. We find another figure of this in the Book of Joshua. There we read that God commanded Joshua, who was about to enter into possession of the promised land, to destroy everything in the city of Jericho without leaving anything alive, neither men nor women, young nor old, nor any animals. God ordered him not to covet or seize any of the booty [Jos. 6:18-19, 21]. The lesson here is that all objects living in the soul—whether they be many or few, large or small—must die in order that the soul enter divine union, and it must bear no desire for them but remain detached as though they were nonexistent to it, and it to them. St. Paul teaches this clearly in Corinthians: *What I tell you, brothers, is that the time is short; what remains and suits you is that those with wives should act as though they had none, and those who weep for the things of this world as though they were not weeping, and those who rejoice as though not rejoicing, and the buyers as though they did not possess, and the users of the world should behave as though they made no use of it* [1 Cor. 7:29-31]. In this text the Apostle teaches us how detached our souls must be from all things in order to go to God.

CHAPTER 12

The answer to another question. An explanation of the kinds of appetites that can bring this harm on a soul.

1. We could explain this night of sense at greater length by mentioning everything relevant to the kind of damage the appetites cause, for they injure not merely in the ways described but in many others as well. What we have explained, however, is sufficient for our purpose. It has probably been understood how the mortification of the appetites can be called night and how suitable it is for people to enter this night in their approach to God. The only point that remains before we treat, in conclusion, the method of entering this night is to settle a doubt that may occur to the reader concerning this matter.[1]

---

1. Until now John has been demonstrating that the mortification of the appetites is a night, a general condition necessary for reaching union, and consequently has been dealing with a broader topic than the night of the senses.

2. First, can any appetite produce and cause the two evils mentioned above, namely: the privative, which removes God's grace from the soul; and the positive, which causes the five principal kinds of harm we explained?

Second, is any appetite, however slight or of whatever kind, enough to produce all these types of harm together, or does each cause only a particular kind, in that one may produce torment, another weariness, another darkness, and so on?

3. To the first query, I answer that relevant to the privative evil, the loss of grace, only the voluntary appetites involving a matter of mortal sin can cause this completely, for they deprive the soul of grace in this life and of glory, the possession of God, in the next.

To the second, my answer is that all these positive evils are together occasioned in the soul by each of these appetites. This is true whether the appetites concern mortal sin, venial sin, or imperfection. We call these evils positive, though in a certain fashion they are privative, because they correspond to a conversion to the creature, just as the privative evils correspond to the aversion from God.

Yet there is this difference: The appetites for mortal sin produce total blindness, torment, filth, weakness, and so on; the others do not cause these kinds of harm to a complete and absolute degree. For they do not deprive the soul of grace—a privation that would give them full possession, since the death of grace means life for the appetites. But these smaller appetites do cause this damage in a lesser degree according to the loss of grace they occasion. The extent of the torment, blindness, and defilement corresponds to the weakening of grace brought on by the appetites.

4. It is noteworthy, however, that, though each appetite causes all these kinds of positive harm, it will cause one kind principally and directly, and the others indirectly. For though it is true that a sensual appetite breeds all these kinds of evil, it principally and properly speaking defiles the soul and body. And an appetite of avarice produces them all too, yet principally and directly it causes afflictions. One of vainglory similarly causes them all, yet principally and directly it darkens and blinds. And whereas an appetite of gluttony begets all the evils, it chiefly produces lukewarmness in virtue. And so on with the others.

5. The reason any act of a voluntary appetite produces all these evils together is that it directly opposes the acts of virtue that produce the contrary effects. An act of virtue produces and fosters in the soul mildness, peace, comfort, light, purity, and strength, just as an inordinate appetite brings about torment, fatigue, weariness, blindness, and weak-

ness. Through the practice of one virtue all the virtues grow, and similarly, through an increase of one vice, all the vices and their effects grow.

These evils do not unmask themselves at the moment the appetite is being satisfied, since the pleasure of the moment is an obstacle to this. Yet sooner or later the harmful effects will certainly be felt. A good illustration of this is found in the Apocalypse. An angel commanded St. John to eat the book, which was sweet to the mouth but bitter in the stomach [Rv. 10:9]. When satisfied the appetite seems sweet and pleasant, but eventually the bitter effect is felt. This truth will certainly be clear to those who allow themselves to be carried away by their appetites. I realize, however, that there are some so blind and unaware that they do not experience this bitter effect. Since they do not walk in God, they do not perceive what keeps them from him.

6. I am not speaking here of the other natural, involuntary appetites, or of thoughts that do not pass beyond the first movements, or of other temptations in which there is no consent. These things do not give rise to any of the evils previously mentioned. Though the passion and disturbance they momentarily cause make it seem that one is being defiled and blinded, such is not the case; rather, they occasion the opposite good effects. Insofar as one resists them, one wins strength, purity, comfort, and many blessings, as our Lord told St. Paul: *Virtue is made perfect in weakness* [2 Cor. 12:9].[2]

But the voluntary appetites bring on all these evils, and even more. That is why the chief concern of spiritual masters with their disciples is the immediate mortification of every appetite. The directors should make them remain empty of what they desire so as to liberate them from so much misery.

CHAPTER 13

The manner and method of entering this night of sense.

1. Some counsels are in order now that the individual may both know the way of entering this night and be able to do so. It should be understood, consequently, that a person ordinarily enters this night of sense in two ways: active and passive.

The active way, which will be the subject of the following counsels,

---

2. An important observation. The struggle against an appetite can cause suffering because one is resisting a strong and deep-rooted tendency. The suffering is not an indication of something harmful but good. Cf. A. 3. 28. 8.

comprises what one can do and does by oneself to enter this night.

The passive way is that in which one does nothing, but God accomplishes the work in the soul while the soul acts as the recipient. This will be the subject of the fourth book, where we will discuss beginners. Since with God's help I will give many counsels regarding the numerous imperfections beginners ordinarily possess on this road, I will not take the time to offer many here. Nor is this the proper place to give them, since here we are dealing only with the reasons for calling this journey a night, and with the nature and divisions of this night.[1]

Nevertheless, if we do not offer some immediate remedy or counsel for exercising oneself in this night of the appetites, this part would seem very short and of little help. Therefore I want to set down the following abridged method. And I will do the same at the end of my discussion of each of the next two parts (or reasons for the use of the term "night") which, with God's help, will follow.

2. Though these counsels for the conquering of the appetites are brief and few in number, I believe they are as profitable and efficacious as they are concise. A person who sincerely wants to practice them will need no others since all the others are included in these.[2]

3. First, have habitual desire to imitate Christ in all your deeds by bringing your life into conformity with his. You must then study his life in order to know how to imitate him and behave in all events as he would.

4. Second, in order to be successful in this imitation, renounce and remain empty of any sensory satisfaction that is not purely for the honor and glory of God. Do this out of love for Jesus Christ. In his life he had no other gratification, nor desired any other, than the fulfillment of his Father's will, which he called his meat and food [Jn. 4:34].

For example, if you are offered the satisfaction of hearing things that have no relation to the service and glory of God, do not desire this pleasure or the hearing of these things. When you have an opportunity for the gratification of looking upon objects that will not help you love

---

1. For the first time he refers to an active and passive purification in regard to the night of the senses. In this chapter he will deal briefly with the active night of the senses, leaving the treatment of the passive night of the senses for later, in a "fourth book" where he will go into more detail. In reality, in the unfinished *Ascent* John never reached the proposed fourth book. But in the first book of the *Dark Night* we find the material that he promises to deal with in the fourth book.

2. The practices of denial that follow cannot be performed coldly but suppose a twofold theological basis: the love of Christ and the acceptance of his teachings. John deals with the purification of the senses also in Books Two and Three of the *Ascent,* and especially when speaking of the purification of the will.

God more, do not desire this gratification or sight. And if in speaking there is a similar opportunity, act in the same way. And so on with all the senses insofar as you can duly avoid such satisfaction. If you cannot escape the experience of this satisfaction, it will be sufficient to have no desire for it.

By this method you should endeavor, then, to leave the senses as though in darkness, mortified and empty of that satisfaction. With such vigilance you will gain a great deal in a short time.

5. Many blessings flow when the four natural passions (joy, hope, fear, and sorrow) are in harmony and at peace. The following maxims contain a complete method for mortifying and pacifying them. If put into practice these maxims will give rise to abundant merit and great virtues.

6. Endeavor to be inclined always:

> not to the easiest, but to the most difficult;
> not to the most delightful, but to the most distasteful;
> not to the most gratifying, but to the less pleasant;
> not to what means rest for you, but to hard work;
> not to the consoling, but to the unconsoling;
> not to the most, but to the least;
> not to the highest and most precious, but to the lowest and most despised;
> not to wanting something, but to wanting nothing.

Do not go about looking for the best of temporal things, but for the worst, and, for Christ, desire to enter into complete nakedness, emptiness, and poverty in everything in the world.[3]

7. You should embrace these practices earnestly and try to overcome the repugnance of your will toward them. If you sincerely put them into practice with order and discretion, you will discover in them great delight and consolation.

8. These counsels if truly carried out are sufficient for entry into the night of senses. But, to ensure that we give abundant enough counsel, here is another exercise that teaches mortification of concupiscence of the flesh, concupiscence of the eyes, and pride of life, which, as St. John says, reign in the world and give rise to all the other appetites [1 Jn. 2:16].

---

3. By the introductory words, "endeavor to be inclined," he reveals that he is speaking of a habit of mind. Through the love of Christ and this inner attitude, one will find the freedom and power necessary to do the Father's will, whatever it may be. Cf. A. 2. 7. 7.

9. <u>First</u>, try to act with contempt for yourself and desire that all others do likewise.

<u>Second</u>, endeavor to speak in contempt of yourself and desire all others to do so.

<u>Third</u>, try to think lowly and contemptuously of yourself and desire that all others do the same.

10. As a conclusion to these counsels and rules it would be appropriate to repeat the verses in *The Ascent of the Mount* [the drawing at the beginning of the book], which are instructions for climbing to the summit, the high state of union. Although in the drawing we admittedly refer to the spiritual and interior aspect, we also deal with the spirit of imperfection existent in the sensory and exterior part of the soul, as is evident by the two ways, one on each side of that path that leads to perfection. Consequently these verses will here bear reference to the sensory part. Afterward, in the second division of this night, they may be interpreted in relationship to the spiritual part.[4]

11. The verses are:

> To reach satisfaction in all
> desire satisfaction in nothing.
> To come to possess all
> desire the possession of nothing.
> To arrive at being all
> desire to be nothing.
> To come to the knowledge of all
> desire the knowledge of nothing.

> To come to enjoy what you have not
> you must go by a way in which you enjoy not.
> To come to the knowledge you have not
> you must go by a way in which you know not.
> To come to the possession you have not
> you must go by a way in which you possess not.
> To come to be what you are not
> you must go by a way in which you are not.

---

4. The sketch of the mount has four parts: 1) The summit, abounding in virtues and gifts; 2) The middle path in which the word "nothing" is repeated seven times; 3) The ways of the imperfect spirits on each side with their short-lived goods; 4) The verses at the bottom of the mount teaching the way to climb the mount. This teaching is applicable throughout the journey. Cf. A. 3. 15. 1; A. 2. 7. 3; 8. 7.

A Method to Avoid Impeding the All

12. When you delay in something
you cease to rush toward the all.
For to go from the all to the all
you must deny yourself of all in all.
And when you come to the possession of the all
you must possess it without wanting anything.
Because if you desire to have something in all
your treasure in God is not purely your all.

13. In this nakedness the spirit finds its quietude and rest. For in coveting nothing, nothing tires it by pulling it up and nothing oppresses it by pushing it down, because it is in the center of its humility. When it covets something, by this very fact it tires itself.

CHAPTER 14

An explanation of verse 2 of the first stanza.

fired with love's urgent longings

1. Now that we have explained the first verse of this stanza, which treats of the night of sense, and have discussed the nature of this night, the reason for calling it night, and the method of actively entering it, we should, in due order, continue with an explanation of the admirable properties and effects contained in the remaining verses of this stanza. I will explain these verses, as promised in the prologue, by merely touching on them, and then proceed to Book Two, a treatise on the remaining, or spiritual, part of this night.[1]

2. The soul, then, states that "fired with love's urgent longings" it passed through this night of sense to union with the Beloved. A love of pleasure, and attachment to it, usually fires the will toward the enjoyment of things that give pleasure. A more intense enkindling of another, better love (love of the soul's Bridegroom) is necessary for the vanquishing of the appetites and the denial of this pleasure. By finding satisfaction and strength in this love, it will have the courage and constancy to readily deny all other appetites. The love of its Bridegroom is not the only requisite for

---

1. John returns to take up the commentary on the poem as promised not in the prologue but in the theme. Though he does so hastily, he still seems to think he can join a commentary on the poem with the treatise that is in process.

conquering the strength of the sensitive appetites; an enkindling with urgent longings of love is also necessary. For the sensory appetites are moved and attracted toward sensory objects with such cravings that if the spiritual part of the soul is not fired with other, more urgent longings for spiritual things, the soul will be able neither to overcome the yoke of nature nor to enter the night of sense; nor will it have the courage to live in the darkness of all things by denying its appetites for them.[2]

3. This is not the appropriate section for a description—nor would this be possible—of the nature of these longings of love or of the numerous ways they occur at the outset of the journey to union. Neither is it the place for a discussion of the diligence and ingenuity of persons in departing from their house (self-will) into the night of the mortification of their senses, or of how easy, sweet, and delightful these longings for their Bridegroom make all the trials and dangers of this night seem. It is better to experience all of this and meditate on it than to write of it. We will proceed, consequently, to the next chapter and explain the remaining verses.

CHAPTER 15

An exposition of the remaining verses of the first stanza.

—Ah, the sheer grace!—
I went out unseen,
my house being now all stilled.

1. The soul uses as a metaphor the wretched state of captivity. It is a sheer grace to be released from this prison without hindrance from the jailers.[1] The soul through original sin is a captive in the mortal body, subject to passions and natural appetites; when liberated from this bondage and submission, it considers its escape, in which it is unnoticed, unimpeded, and unapprehended by its passions and appetites, a sheer grace.

2. To achieve this liberation it was advantageous for the soul to depart in the dark night, that is, in the privation of all satisfactions and in the

---

2. John has not explained when one should enter the night. Here it becomes quite clear that one begins to enter not with denial but with theological love. Cf. C. 3; 29. 10.

1. John undoubtedly has in mind his own prison experience in Toledo and his escape at night. Cf. N. 2. 14. 1.

mortification of all appetites, as we mentioned. "My house being now all stilled" means that the house of all the appetites, the sensitive part of the soul, is now stilled, and the desires conquered and lulled to sleep. Until slumber comes to the appetites through the mortification of sensuality, and until this very sensuality is stilled in such a way that the appetites do not war against the spirit, the soul will not go out to genuine freedom, to the enjoyment of union with its Beloved.

The End of the First Book

BOOK TWO

This book is a treatise on faith, the proximate means of ascent to union with God. It consequently considers the second part of this night, the night of spirit to which the following stanza refers.

CHAPTER 1

The Second Stanza

In darkness and secure,
by the secret ladder, disguised,
—ah, the sheer grace!—
in darkness and concealment,
my house being now all stilled.

1. This second stanza tells in song of the sheer grace that was the soul's in divesting the spirit of all imperfections and appetites for spiritual possessions. The good fortune is far greater here because of the greater hardship involved in quieting the house that is one's spiritual nature and entering this interior darkness (the spiritual nakedness of all sensory and immaterial things), leaning on pure faith alone, in an ascent by it to God.

The secret ladder represents faith, because all the rungs or articles of faith are secret to and hidden from both the senses and the intellect. Accordingly the soul lived in darkness, without any light from the senses and intellect, and went out beyond every natural and rational boundary to climb the divine ladder of faith that leads up to and penetrates the deep things of God [1 Cor. 2:10].

The soul declares that it was disguised because in the ascent through faith its garments, apparel, and capacities were changed from natural to divine. On account of this disguise, neither temporal nor rational things nor the devil recognized or detained it. None of these can do harm to the one who walks in faith.

The soul's advance, moreover, was so concealed, hidden, and withdrawn from all the wiles of the devil that it indeed involved darkness and concealment. That is, the soul was hidden from the devil, to whom the light of faith is worse than darkness. We can say as a result that a person who walks in faith walks concealed and hidden from the devil; this will be more evident as we proceed.

2. The soul, consequently, affirms that it departed "in darkness, and

154

secure." For anyone fortunate enough to possess the ability to journey in the obscurity of faith, as do the blind with their guide, and depart from all natural phantasms and intellectual reasonings, walks securely.

The soul also asserts that it departed in this spiritual night because its house was now all stilled. That is, the spiritual and rational part of the soul was stilled, because once the soul attains union with God, the natural faculties and the impulses and anxieties of the spiritual part remain at rest. The poem does not proclaim that the soul went out with urgent longings, as it does of the first night of sense. To enter the night of sense and denude itself of sensible things, the soul needed the longings of sensitive love. But all that is required for complete pacification of the spiritual house is the negation through pure faith of all the spiritual faculties and gratifications and appetites. This achieved, the soul will be joined with the Beloved in a union of simplicity and purity and love and likeness.

3. It is noteworthy that the first stanza of the poem, in speaking of the senses, asserts that the soul departed on a dark night, and this second stanza, in speaking of the spirit, says that the soul went out in darkness. The obscurity of the spirit is far more intense, just as "in darkness" indicates thicker obscurity than "dark night." For however dark a night may be, some objects are still visible, but in total darkness nothing at all can be seen. In the night of sense there is yet some light, because the intellect and reason remain and suffer no blindness. But this spiritual night, which is faith, removes everything, both in the intellect and in the senses. As a result the soul declares in this stanza that it departed in darkness and secure, which it did not assert in the former. For the less a soul works with its own abilities, the more securely it proceeds because its progress in faith is greater.

This darkness of faith will be the subject matter of Book Two, and we shall discuss it at length. The devout reader, consequently, must proceed thoughtfully, because our explanation will be most important for persons of genuine spirituality. Though these truths are somewhat obscure, they so shed light on one another that I believe they will all be clearly understood.

CHAPTER 2

Faith, the second cause or part of this night. Two proofs of why it is darker than the first and third parts.

1. Faith, the second part of this night, is our next subject for discussion. Faith is that admirable means of advancing to God, our goal. And God,

we said, is also for the soul naturally a part, or the third cause, of this night.[1]

Faith, the means, is comparable to midnight. We can affirm, then, that it is darker for a person than the first part of the night and, in a certain way, darker than the third. The first part, pertinent to the senses, resembles twilight, the time sensible objects begin to fade from sight. Accordingly, it is not a time so far removed from all light as is midnight.

The third part, that period before dawn, approximates the light of day. The darkness is not like that of midnight, since in this third period of the night we approach the illumination of day. And this daylight we compare to God. Although naturally speaking God is indeed as dark a night to the soul as is faith, it can be affirmed that he is less dark. For when these three parts of the night—which are night to the soul from a natural viewpoint—have passed, God supernaturally illumines the soul with the ray of his divine light. This light is the principle of the perfect union that follows after the third night.

2. The first night pertains to the lower, sensory part of human nature and is consequently more external. As a result the second night is darker. The second, darker night of faith belongs to the rational, superior part; it is darker and more interior because it deprives this part of its rational light, or better, blinds it. Accordingly, it is indeed comparable to midnight, the innermost and darkest period of night.

3. We must prove, now, how this second part, faith, is night to the spirit just as the first part is to the senses. Then we will also discuss the factors in opposition to this night and how a person actively prepares to enter it. In its proper place we shall speak of passivity, that is, of God's work—without the soul—in effecting this night. I plan to discuss this matter in the third book.[2]

---

1. Cf. A. 1. 2; C. 15. 23. John now undertakes his treatise on faith and abandons the poem, which never again appears in the *Ascent,* and his project of commenting on it.

2. Here John turns to the other, fourfold outline he has in mind, the night of the senses and of the spirit, active and passive. But instead of saying he will treat of passivity in the fourth book as he did previously (cf. A. 1. 1. 2), he refers to the third book, where the matter is not treated. Here he is probably thinking of his work in terms of three books: active night of the senses; active night of the spirit; and passive night. He in fact treats of the passive night, since the *Ascent* remains unfinished, in the *Dark Night.*

CHAPTER 3

Arguments, passages, and figures from Scripture in proof that faith is a dark night for the soul.

1. Faith, the theologians say, is a certain and obscure habit of soul.[1] It is an obscure habit because it brings us to believe divinely revealed truths that transcend every natural light and infinitely exceed all human understanding. As a result the excessive light of faith bestowed on a soul is darkness for it; a brighter light will eclipse and suppress a dimmer one. The sun so obscures all other lights that they do not seem to be lights at all when it is shining, and instead of affording vision to the eyes, it overwhelms, blinds, and deprives them of vision since its light is excessive and unproportioned to the visual faculty. Similarly, the light of faith in its abundance suppresses and overwhelms that of the intellect. For the intellect, by its own power, extends only to natural knowledge, though it has the potency to be raised to a supernatural act whenever our Lord wishes.

2. The intellect knows only in the natural way, that is, by means of the senses. If one is to know in this natural way, the phantasms and species of objects will have to be present either in themselves or in their likenesses; otherwise one will be incapable of knowing naturally. As the scholastic philosophers say: *Ab ojecto et potentia paritur notitia* (Knowledge arises in the soul from both the faculty and the object at hand).[2] If we were told of objects we had never known or seen resemblances of, we would in the end have no more knowledge than before.

For example, if we were informed that on a certain island there was an animal whose like or kind we had never seen, we would then have no more idea or image of that animal in our mind than previously, no matter how much we were told.

Another clearer example will shed more light on this subject: If those born blind were told about the nature of the colors white or yellow, they would understand absolutely nothing no matter how much instruction they received. Since they never saw these colors nor others like them, they would not have the means to form a judgment about them. Only the names of these colors would be grasped since the names are perceptible

---

1. Cf. Aquinas, *Summa Theologiae* 2-2. 1-4; 6. 1; *Contra Gentiles* 3. 40; and *De Veritate* 14. 1. Here John's interest is in highlighting only a certain aspect of faith, how it contrasts with the light of reason. For another description with a different stress see C. 15.

2. This philosophical axiom has its roots in Aristotle, *On the Soul* 1. 2; 3. 8.

through hearing; but never their form or image, because these colors were never seen by those born blind.[3]

3. Such is faith to the soul; it informs us of matters we have never seen or known, either in themselves or in their likenesses. In fact, nothing like them exists. The light of natural knowledge does not show us the object of faith, since this object is unproportioned to any of the senses. Yet we come to know it through hearing, by believing what faith teaches us, blinding our natural light and bringing it into submission. St. Paul states: *Fides ex auditu* [Rom. 10:17]. This amounts to saying that faith is not a knowledge derived from the senses but an assent of the soul to what enters through hearing.

4. Faith, moreover, far exceeds what these examples teach us. Not only does it fail to produce knowledge and science but, as we said,[4] it deprives and blinds people of any other knowledge by which they may judge it. Other knowledge is acquired by the light of the intellect, but not the knowledge of faith. Faith nullifies the light of the intellect; and if this light is not darkened, the knowledge of faith is lost. Accordingly, Isaiah said: *Si no credideritis, non intelligetis* (If you do not believe, you will not understand) [Is. 7:9].

Faith, manifestly, is a dark night for souls, but in this way it gives them light. The more darkness it brings on them, the more light it sheds. For by blinding, it illumines them, according to those words of Isaiah that if you do not believe you will not understand; that is, you will not have light [Is. 7:9].

Faith was foreshadowed in that cloud that separated the children of Israel, just before their entry into the Red Sea, from the Egyptians [Ex. 14:19-20]. Scripture says of the cloud: *Erat nubes tenebrosa et illuminans noctem* (The cloud was dark and illuminated the night) [Ex. 14:20].

5. How wonderful it was: A cloud, dark in itself, could illumine the night! This was related to illustrate how faith, a dark and obscure cloud to souls (also a night in that it blinds and deprives them of their natural light), illumines and pours light into their darkness by means of its own darkness. This is fitting so that the disciple may be like the master.

A person in darkness does not receive adequate enlightenment save

---

3. John also uses these examples to explain contemplation, a reality he identifies with faith. Cf. N. 2. 17. 3.

4. In no. 2; also in A. 2. 2. 2. He refers to faith in its twofold dimension: the content unattainable by reason and the unconditional adherence of the human mind. Faith is a night for a person insofar as it eliminates reasons or natural lights as motivations in its spiritual operation.

by another darkness, according to David's teaching: *Dies diei eructat verbum et nox nocti indicat scientiam* (The day brims over and breathes speech to the day, and the night manifests knowledge to the night) [Ps. 19:3]. Expressed more clearly, this means: The day, which is God (in bliss where it is day), communicates and pronounces the Word, his Son, to the angels and blessed souls, who are now day; and this he does that they may have knowledge and enjoyment of him. And the night, which is the faith, present in the Church Militant where it is still night, manifests knowledge to the Church and, consequently, to every soul. This knowledge is night to souls because they do not yet possess the clear beatific wisdom, and because faith blinds them as to their own natural light.

6. Our deduction is that since faith is a dark night, it illumines the soul that is in darkness. We verify, then, David's assertion on this matter: *Et nox illuminatio in deliciis meis* (Night will be my illumination in the midst of my delights) [Ps. 139:12]. This amounts to saying: The night of faith will be my guide in the delights of my pure contemplation and union with God. By this passage David clearly informs us of the darkness demanded on this road if a soul is to receive light.

CHAPTER 4

A general discussion of how the soul with respect to its own efforts must remain in darkness so as to be well guided by faith to supreme contemplation.

1. I believe you are learning how faith is a dark night for the soul and how the soul as well must be dark—or in darkness as to its own light—that it may allow itself to be guided by faith to this high goal of union. But for knowledge of how to do this, a somewhat more detailed explanation of the darkness required for entering this abyss of faith will be beneficial. In this chapter I will deal with this darkness in a general way. Further on I will explain, with God's help, more in particular about the behavior necessary for obviating error in faith and any encumbrance to its guidance.

2. I affirm, then, that if people take faith as a good guide to this state, not only must they live in darkness in the sensory and lower part of their nature (concerning creatures and temporal things), which we have already discussed, but they must also darken and blind themselves in that part of their nature that bears relation to God and spiritual things. This latter part, which we are now discussing, is the rational and higher part of their nature. Attaining supernatural transformation manifestly demands a darkening of the soul and an elevation above all the sensory and

rational parts of nature, for the word "supernatural" indicates that which is above nature; nature, consequently, remains beneath.

Since this transformation and union is something that does not fall within the reach of the senses and of human capability, the soul must perfectly and voluntarily empty itself—I mean in its affection and will—of all the earthly and heavenly things it can grasp. It must do this insofar as it can. As for God, who will stop him from accomplishing his desires in the soul that is resigned, annihilated, and despoiled?

But people must empty themselves of all, insofar as they can, so that however many supernatural communications they receive, they will continually live as though denuded of them and in darkness. Like the blind, they must lean on dark faith, accept it for their guide and light, and rest on nothing of what they understand, taste, feel, or imagine. All these perceptions are darkness that will lead them astray. Faith lies beyond all this understanding, taste, feeling, and imagining. If they do not blind themselves in these things and abide in total darkness, they will not reach what is greater: the teaching of faith.

3. Those who are not yet entirely blind will not allow a good guide to lead them. Still able to perceive a little, they think that the road they see is the best, for they are unable to see other and better ones. And because these individuals themselves are the ones giving the orders, they will consequently lead astray their young guide who has better vision. Similarly, if the soul in traveling this road leans on any elements of its own knowledge or of its experience or knowledge of God, it will easily go astray or be detained because it did not desire to abide in complete blindness, in the faith that is its guide. However impressive may be one's knowledge or experience of God, that knowledge or experience will have no resemblance to God and amount to very little.

4. St. Paul also meant this in his assertion: *Accedentem ad Deum oportet credere quod est* (Whoever would approach union with God should believe in His existence) [Heb. 11:6]. This is like saying: Those who want to reach union with God should advance neither by understanding, nor by the support of their own experience, nor by feeling or imagination, but by belief in God's being. For God's being cannot be grasped by the intellect, appetite, imagination, or any other sense; nor can it be known in this life. The most that can be felt and tasted of God in this life is infinitely distant from God and the pure possession of him. Isaiah and St. Paul affirm: *Nec oculus videt, nec auris audivit, nec in cor hominis ascendit quae praeparavit Deus iis qui diligunt illum* (No eye has ever seen, nor ear heard, nor has the human heart or thought ever grasped what God has prepared for those who love him) [Is. 64:4; 1 Cor. 2:9].

Now souls in this life may be seeking to unite themselves perfectly through grace with what they will be united to in the next through glory (with what St. Paul says eye has not seen, nor ear heard, nor the human, fleshly heart grasped). But, manifestly, the perfect union in this life through grace and love demands that they live in darkness to all the objects of sight, hearing, and imagination, and to everything comprehensible to the heart, which signifies the soul.

Those are decidedly hindered, then, from attainment of this high state of union with God who are attached to any understanding, feeling, imagining, opinion, desire, or way of their own, or to any other of their works or affairs, and know not how to detach and denude themselves of these impediments. Their goal, as we said, transcends all of this, even the loftiest object that can be known or experienced. Consequently they must pass beyond everything to unknowing.

5. As regards this road to union, entering on the road means leaving one's own road; or better, moving on to the goal. And turning from one's own mode implies entry into what has no mode, that is, God. Individuals who reach this state no longer have any modes or methods, still less are they attached to them, nor can they be. I am referring to modes of understanding, tasting, and feeling. Within themselves, though, they possess all methods, like one who though having nothing yet possesses all things [2 Cor. 6:10]. By being courageous enough to pass beyond the interior and exterior limits of their own nature, they enter into supernatural bounds—bounds that have no mode, yet in substance possess all modes. To reach these supernatural bounds, souls must depart from their natural bounds—and leave self far off in respect to both bounds—in order to mount from a low state to the highest.

6. Passing beyond all that is naturally and spiritually intelligible or comprehensible, souls ought to desire with all their might to attain what in this life could never be known or enter the human heart. And parting company with all they can or do taste and feel, temporally and spiritually, they must ardently long to acquire what surpasses all taste and feeling. To be empty and free for the achievement of this, they should by no means seize on what they receive spiritually or sensitively (as we shall explain in our particular discussion of this matter), but consider it of little import. The higher the rank and esteem they give to all this knowledge, experience, and imagining (whether spiritual or not), the more they subtract from the Supreme Good and the more they delay in their journey toward him. And the less they esteem what they can possess—however estimable it may be relative to the Supreme Good—the more they value and prize him, and, consequently, the closer they come to him. In this way, in obscurity, souls approach union swiftly by means of faith, which is also dark. And in this way faith gives them wondrous light. Obviously, if they should

desire to see, they would be in darkness as regards God more quickly than anyone who looks to see the blinding brightness of the sun.

7. By blinding one's faculties along this road, one will see light, as the Savior proclaims in the Gospel: *In judicium veni in hunc mundum: ut qui non vident videant, et qui vident caeci fiant* (I have come into this world for judgment, that they who see not, may see, and that they who see may become blind) [Jn. 9:39]. In reference to the spiritual road, these words should be understood literally, that is: Those who both live in darkness and blind themselves to all their natural lights will have supernatural vision, and those who want to lean on some light of their own will become blind and be held back on this road leading to union.

8. That we may continue with less confusion, I believe it will be necessary in the following chapter to explain this reality we call union with God. Since an understanding of the nature of union will shed more light on the subsequent doctrine, I think this is the suitable place for a discussion of it. Although our thread of thought will be interrupted, we will not be digressing, because an explanation of this union will serve to illustrate the matter we are treating. The following chapter will be like a parenthesis within the same enthymeme, since in this second night we plan to treat of the relationship of the three faculties of the soul to the three theological virtues.

CHAPTER 5

Explanation of the nature of union with God. An illustration.

1. In our previous discussion, we have already given some indication of the meaning of the phrase "union of the soul with God." Thus our teaching here about the nature of this union will be more understandable.

It is not my intention now to discuss the divisions and parts of this union. Indeed, I would never finish were I to begin explaining the union of the intellect, or that of the will or the memory, or trying to expound the nature of the transitory and the permanent union in each of these faculties, or the significance of the total, the transitory, or the permanent union wrought in these three faculties together. We will discuss all this frequently in the course of our treatise. But such an exposition is unnecessary for an understanding of what we now wish to state about these different unions. A better explanation of them will be given in sections dealing with the subject, and then we shall have a concrete example to go with the actual teaching. In those sections the reader will note and understand the union being discussed and will form a better judgment of it.

2. Here I intend to discuss only this total and permanent union in the substance and faculties of the soul. And I shall be speaking of the obscure habit of union, for we will explain later, with God's help, how a permanent actual union of the faculties in this life is impossible; such a union can only be transitory.[1]

3. To understand the nature of this union, one should first know that God sustains every soul and dwells in it substantially, even though it may be that of the greatest sinner in the world. This union between God and creatures always exists. By it he conserves their being so that if the union should end they would immediately be annihilated and cease to exist. Consequently, in discussing union with God we are not discussing the substantial union that always exists, but the soul's union with and transformation in God that does not always exist, except when there is likeness of love. We will call it the union of likeness; and the former, the essential or substantial union. The union of likeness is supernatural; the other, natural. The supernatural union exists when God's will and the soul's are in conformity, so that nothing in the one is repugnant to the other. When the soul rids itself completely of what is repugnant and unconformed to the divine will, it rests transformed in God through love.

4. Ridding oneself of what is repugnant to God's will should be understood not only of one's acts but of one's habits as well. Not only must actual voluntary imperfections cease, but habitual imperfections must be annihilated too.

No creature, none of its actions and abilities, can reach or encompass God's nature. Consequently, a soul must strip itself of everything pertaining to creatures and of its actions and abilities (of its understanding, satisfaction, and feeling), so that when everything unlike and unconformed to God is cast out, it may receive the likeness of God. And the soul will receive this likeness because nothing contrary to the will of God will be left in it. Thus it will be transformed in God.

It is true that God is ever present in the soul, as we said, and thereby bestows and preserves its natural being by his sustaining presence. Yet he does not always communicate supernatural being to it. He communicates supernatural being only through love and grace, which not all souls possess. And those who do, do not possess them in the same degree. Some have attained higher degrees of love, others remain in lower degrees. To

---

1. The chief distinctions of the union are: permanent and transitory; in the substance and in the faculties; habitual and actual. For examples see C. 26. 5-11; F. 1. 3-4; 4. 14-16. This chapter is fundamental to the entire work because the whole process of purification flows from the nature of the union.

the soul that is more advanced in love, more conformed to the divine will, God communicates himself more. A person who has reached complete conformity and likeness of will has attained total supernatural union and transformation in God.

Manifestly, then, the more that individuals through attachment and habit are clothed with their own abilities and with creatures, the less disposed they are for this union. For they do not afford God full opportunity to transform their souls into the supernatural. As a result, individuals have nothing more to do than to strip their souls of these natural contraries and dissimilarities so that God, who is naturally communicating himself to them through nature, may do so supernaturally through grace.

5. This is what St. John meant when he said: *Qui non ex sanguinibus, neque ex voluntate carnis, neque ex voluntate viri, sed ex Deo nati sunt* [Jn. 1:13], which can be interpreted: He gives power for becoming the children of God (for being transformed in God) only to those who are not born of blood (combinations of the natural humors), or of the will of the flesh (the free will included in one's natural aptitude and capacity), or even less of the human will (which includes every mode and manner by which the intellect judges and understands). To none of these has he conferred the power of becoming the children of God; only to those who are born of God (those who, in their rebirth through grace and death to everything of the old self [Eph. 4:22], rise above themselves to the supernatural and receive from God this rebirth and relationship as his children, which transcends everything imaginable).

St. John affirms elsewhere: *Nisi quis renatus fuerit ex aqua et spiritu Sancto non potest videre regnum Dei* (The one who is not reborn in the Holy Spirit will be unable to see the kingdom of God, which is the state of perfection) [Jn. 3:5]. To be reborn in the Holy Spirit during this life is to become most like God in purity, without any mixture of imperfection. Accordingly, pure transformation can be effected—although not essentially—through the participation of union.

6. Here is an example that will provide a better understanding of this explanation. A ray of sunlight shining on a smudgy window is unable to illumine that window completely and transform it into its own light. It could do this if the window were cleaned and polished. The less the film and stain are wiped away, the less the window will be illumined; and the cleaner the window is, the brighter will be its illumination. The extent of illumination is not dependent on the ray of sunlight but on the window. If the window is totally clean and pure, the sunlight will so transform and illumine it that to all appearances the window will be identical with the ray of sunlight and shine just as the sun's ray. Although obviously the nature of the window is distinct from that of the sun's ray (even if the two

seem identical), we can assert that the window is the ray or light of the sun by participation. The soul on which the divine light of God's being is ever shining, or better, in which it is ever dwelling by nature, is like this window, as we have affirmed.

7. A soul makes room for God by wiping away all the smudges and smears of creatures, by uniting its will perfectly to God's; for to love is to labor to divest and deprive oneself for God of all that is not God. When this is done the soul will be illumined by and transformed in God. And God will so communicate his supernatural being to the soul that it will appear to be God himself and will possess what God himself possesses.

When God grants this supernatural favor to the soul, so great a union is caused that all the things of both God and the soul become one in participant transformation, and the soul appears to be God more than a soul. Indeed, it is God by participation. Yet truly, its being (even though transformed) is naturally as distinct from God's as it was before, just as the window, although illumined by the ray, has being distinct from the ray's.

8. Consequently, we understand with greater clarity that the preparation for this union, as we said,[2] is not an understanding by the soul, nor the taste, feeling, or imagining of God or of any other object, but purity and love, the stripping off and perfect renunciation of all such experiences for God alone. Also we clearly see how perfect transformation is impossible without perfect purity, and how the illumination of the soul and its union with God correspond to the measure of its purity. The illumination will not be perfect until the soul is entirely cleansed, clear, and perfect.

9. The following example will also shed light on the nature of this union. Let us imagine a perfect painting with many finely wrought details and delicate, subtle adornments, including some so delicate and subtle that they are not wholly discernible. Now one whose sense of sight is not too clear and refined will discover less detail and delicacy in the painting; one whose vision is somewhat purer will discover more details and perfections; and another with yet clearer vision will find still more perfection; finally, the one who possesses the clearest faculty will discern the greatest number of excellent qualities and perfections. There is so much to behold in the painting that no matter how much one sees in it, still more remains unseen.

10. We can make the same application to souls in their relationship with God in this illumination and transformation. Although individuals

---

2. In the previous chapter, especially in no. 4.

may have truly reached union, this union will be proportioned to their lesser or greater capacity, for not all souls attain an identical degree of union. This depends on what the Lord wishes to grant each one. Here we have a resemblance to the saints' vision of God in heaven: Some see more, others less, but all see him and are happy because, whatever their capacity, it is fully satisfied.

11. In this life we may encounter individuals who are in the state of perfection and enjoy equal peace and tranquility, and the capacity of each will be satisfied, yet one may be many degrees higher than the other. Those who do not reach purity in the measure of their capacity never reach true peace and satisfaction; they have not attained in their faculties the nakedness and emptiness that are required for the simple union.

CHAPTER 6

The theological virtues perfect the faculties of the soul and produce emptiness and darkness in them.

1. We must discuss the method of leading the three faculties (intellect, memory, and will) into this spiritual night, the means to divine union. But we must first explain how the theological virtues, faith, hope, and charity (related to these faculties as their proper supernatural objects), through which the soul is united with God, cause the same emptiness and darkness in their respective faculties: faith in the intellect, hope in the memory, and charity in the will. Then we shall explain how in order to journey to God the intellect must be perfected in the darkness of faith, the memory in the emptiness of hope, and the will in the nakedness and absence of every affection.

As a result it will be seen how necessary it is for the soul, if it is to walk securely, to journey through this dark night with the support of these three virtues. They darken and empty it of all things. As we said,[1] the soul is not united with God in this life through understanding, or through enjoyment, or through imagination, or through any other sense; but only faith, hope, and charity (according to the intellect, memory, and will) can unite the soul with God in this life.

2. These virtues, as we said, void the faculties: Faith causes darkness and a void of understanding in the intellect, hope begets an emptiness of possessions in the memory, and charity produces the nakedness and emptiness of affection and joy in all that is not God.

Faith, we saw, affirms what cannot be understood by the intellect. St.

---

1. A. 2. 4.

Paul refers to it *ad Hebraeos* in this way: *Fides est sperandarum substantia rerum, argumentum non apparentium* [Heb. 11:1]. In relation to our discussion here, this means that faith is the substance of things to be hoped for and that these things are not manifest to the intellect, even though its consent to them is firm and certain. If they were manifest, there would be no faith. For though faith brings certitude to the intellect, it does not produce clarity, but only darkness.

3. Hope, also, undoubtedly puts the memory in darkness and emptiness as regards all earthly and heavenly objects. Hope always pertains to the unpossessed object. If something were possessed there could no longer be hope for it. St. Paul says *ad Romanos: Spes quae videtur, non est spes; nam quod videt quis, quid sperat?* (Hope that is seen is not hope, for how does a person hope for what is seen—that is, what is possessed?) [Rom. 8:24]. As a result this virtue also occasions emptiness, since it is concerned with unpossessed things and not with the possessed object.

4. Charity, too, causes a void in the will regarding all things since it obliges us to love God above everything. We have to withdraw our affection from all in order to center it wholly upon God. Christ says through St. Luke: *Qui non renuntiat omnibus quae possidet, not potest meus esse discipulus* (Whoever does not renounce all that the will possesses cannot be my disciple) [Lk. 14:33]. Consequently, these three virtues place a soul in darkness and emptiness in respect to all things.

5. That parable our Redeemer told in the 11th chapter of St. Luke is noteworthy here [Lk. 11:5]. He related that one friend went to another at midnight to ask for three loaves (which signify these three virtues). And he asserted that the friend asked for them at midnight to indicate that the soul must acquire these three virtues by a darkness in its faculties regarding all things, and must perfect itself in these virtues by means of this night.

In the sixth chapter of Isaiah we read that the prophet saw a seraph at each side of God, and that they each had six wings: with two wings they covered their feet, which signified the blinding and quenching of the affections of the will for God; with two they covered their faces, which signified the darkness of the intellect in God's presence; and with the two remaining wings they flew, so as to indicate the flight of hope toward things that are not possessed, an elevation above everything outside of God that can be possessed, earthly or heavenly [Is. 6:2].[2]

---

2. Here we have two classic examples of John's frequent use of the Bible in an accommodated sense. He freely adapts the text in order to illustrate the theme being dealt with and does not intend to use it as a proof of some truth or as an expression of his own intimate experience.

6. We must lead the faculties of the soul, then, to these three virtues and inform each faculty with one of them by stripping and darkening it of everything that is not conformable to these virtues. Doing this refers to the spiritual night that we above called active,[3] because one does what lies in one's own power to enter this night. As we outlined for the sensory night a method of emptying the sense faculties, with regard to the appetite, of their visible objects so that the soul might leave the point of departure for the mean, which is faith, so for this spiritual night we will present, with divine help, a way to empty and purify the spiritual faculties of all that is not God. By this method these faculties can abide in the darkness of these three virtues, which are the means and preparation, as we said, for the soul's union with God.

7. This method provides complete security against the cunning of the devil and the power of self-love in all its ramifications. Usually self-love subtly deceives and hinders the journey of spiritual persons along this road, because they do not know how to denude and govern themselves by means of these three virtues. They never succeed, therefore, in finding the substance and purity of spiritual good; neither do they journey by as straight and short a road as they might.

8. Remember that I am now especially addressing those who have begun to enter the state of contemplation; with regard to beginners this journey should be discussed in somewhat more detail. We will do this with God's help in the second book when we deal with the characteristics of beginners.[4]

CHAPTER 7

The extreme narrowness of the path leading to eternal life. The denudation and freedom required of those who tread it. The nakedness of the intellect.

1. I would need greater knowledge and spirituality than I possess to treat of the denudation and purity of the three faculties of the soul. For I desire to give clear instructions to spiritual persons on the narrowness

---

3. In A. 1. 1. 2; cf. also A. 1. 13. 1.
4. Those who "have begun to enter the state of contemplation" are in John's terminology proficients. He has them especially in mind in this treatment of the purification of the spiritual faculties. He promises to go into more detail about beginners in what he here calls the second part, elsewhere referred to as the fourth part (cf. A. 1. 1. 2) or the third part (cf. A. 2. 2. 3). This projected teaching about beginners is actually found in the *Dark Night*, 1. 1-7.

of the way leading to life—that narrowness of which our Savior spoke—
so that convinced of this they will not marvel at the emptiness and
nakedness in which we must leave the faculties of the soul in this night.

2. We ought to note carefully our Savior's words in St. Matthew's
Gospel, chapter seven, about this road: *Quam angusta porta et arcta via est
quae ducit ad vitam! Et pauci sunt qui inveniunt eam* (How narrow is the gate
and constricting the way that leads to life! And few there are who find it)
[Mt. 7:14]. We should note particularly in this passage the exaggeration
and hyperbole conveyed by the word *quam*. This is like saying: Indeed the
gate is very narrow, more so than you think.

We must also note that first he says the gate is narrow to teach that
entrance through this gate of Christ (the beginning of the journey)
involves a divestment and narrowing of the will in relation to all sensible
and temporal objects by loving God more than all of them. This task
belongs to the night of sense, as we have said.[1]

3. Next he asserts that the way (that is, of perfection) is constricting in
order to teach that the journey along this way involves not only entering
through the narrow gate, a void of sense objects, but also constricting
oneself through dispossession and the removal of obstacles in matters
relating to the spiritual part of the soul.

We can apply, then, what Christ says about the narrow gate to the
sensitive part of the human person, and what he says about the constricting way to the spiritual or rational part. Since he proclaims that few find
it, we ought to note the cause: Few there are with the knowledge and
desire to enter into this supreme nakedness and emptiness of spirit. As
this path on the high mount of perfection is narrow and steep, it demands
travelers who are neither weighed down by the lower part of their nature
nor burdened in the higher part. This is a venture in which God alone is
sought and gained; thus only God ought to be sought and gained.

4. Obviously one's journey must not merely exclude the hindrance of
creatures but also embody a dispossession and annihilation in the
spiritual part of one's nature. Our Lord, for our instruction and guidance
along this road, imparted that wonderful teaching—I think it is possible
to affirm that the more necessary the doctrine the less it is practiced by
spiritual persons—that I will quote fully and explain in its genuine and
spiritual sense because of its importance and relevance to our subject. He

---

1. See A. 1. 13. The need for denial in the life of the theological virtues forms a
part of both the following of Christ as response to his word (nos. 1-8) and the
sharing in the mystery of his death on the cross as response to his deed (nos. 9-
12).

states in the eighth chapter of St. Mark: *Si quis vult me sequi, deneget semetipsum et tollat crucem suam et sequatur me. Qui enim voluerit animam suam salvam facere, perdet eam; qui autem perdiderit animam suam propter me ... salvam faciet eam* (If anyone wishes to follow my way, let him deny himself, take up his cross and follow me. For whoever would save his soul will lose it, but whoever loses it for me will gain it) [Mk. 8:34-35].

5. Oh, who can make this counsel of our Savior on self-denial understandable, and practicable, and attractive, that spiritual persons might become aware of the difference between the method many of them think is good and the one that ought to be used in traveling this road! They are of the opinion that any kind of withdrawal from the world, or reformation of life, suffices. Some are content with a certain degree of virtue, perseverance in prayer, and mortification, but never achieve the nakedness, poverty, selflessness, or spiritual purity (which are all the same) about which the Lord counsels us here. For they still feed and clothe their natural selves with spiritual feelings and consolations instead of divesting and denying themselves of these for God's sake. They think denial of self in worldly matters is sufficient without annihilation and purification in the spiritual domain. It happens that, when some of this solid, perfect food (the annihilation of all sweetness in God—the pure spiritual cross and nakedness of Christ's poverty of spirit) is offered them in dryness, distaste, and trial, they run from it as from death and wander about in search only of sweetness and delightful communications from God. Such an attitude is not the hallmark of self-denial and nakedness of spirit but the indication of a spiritual sweet tooth. Through this kind of conduct they become, spiritually speaking, enemies of the cross of Christ [Phil. 3:18].

A genuine spirit seeks rather the distasteful in God than the delectable, leans more toward suffering than toward consolation, more toward going without everything for God than toward possession, and toward dryness and affliction than toward sweet consolation. It knows that this is the significance of following Christ and denying self, that the other method is perhaps a seeking of self in God—something entirely contrary to love. Seeking oneself in God is the same as looking for the caresses and consolations of God. Seeking God in oneself entails not only the desire to do without these consolations for God's sake, but also the inclination to choose for love of Christ all that is most distasteful whether in God or in the world; and this is what loving God means.

6. Oh, who can explain the extent of the denial our Lord wishes of us! This negation must be similar to a temporal, natural, and spiritual death in all things; that is, with regard to the esteem the will has for them. It is in the will that all negation takes place. Our Savior referred to this when

he declared: *Whoever wishes to save his life will lose it* (Those who want to possess something, or seek it for self, will lose it); *and whoever loses his soul for my sake will gain it* [Mt. 16:25; Lk. 9:24]. This latter means: Those who renounce for Christ all that their wills can both desire and enjoy by choosing what bears closer resemblance to the cross—which in St. John our Lord terms hating one's own soul [Jn. 12:25]—these same will gain it.

His Majesty taught this to those two disciples who came to ask him for places at his right and left. Without responding to their request for glory, he offered them the chalice he was about to drink as something safer and more precious on this earth than enjoyment [Mt. 20:22].

7. This chalice means death to one's natural self through denudation and annihilation. By this means one is able to walk along the narrow path in the sensitive part of the soul, as we said,[2] and in the spiritual part (as we will now say), in one's understanding, joy, and feeling. Accordingly, a person can attain to dispossession in both parts of the soul. Not only this, but even in the spirit one will be unhindered in one's journey on the narrow road. For on this road there is room only for self-denial (as our Savior asserts) and the cross. The cross is a supporting staff and greatly lightens and eases the journey.

Our Lord proclaimed through St. Matthew: *My yoke is sweet and my burden light* [Mt. 11:30], the burden being the cross. If individuals resolutely submit to the carrying of the cross, if they decidedly want to find and endure trial in all things for God, they will discover in all of them great relief and sweetness. This will be so because they will be traveling the road denuded of all and with no desire for anything. If they aim after the possession of something, from God or elsewhere, their journey will not be one of nakedness and detachment from all things, and consequently there will be no room for them on this narrow path nor will they be able to climb it.

8. I should like to persuade spiritual persons that the road leading to God does not entail a multiplicity of considerations, methods, manners, and experiences—though in their own way these may be a requirement for beginners—but demands only the one thing necessary: true self-denial, exterior and interior, through surrender of self both to suffering for Christ and to annihilation in all things. In the exercise of this self-denial everything else, and even more, is discovered and accomplished. If one fails in this exercise, the root and sum total of all the virtues, the other methods would amount to no more than going around in circles without getting anywhere, even were one to enjoy considerations and communications as lofty as those of the angels.

2. In A. 1. 13-14; A. 2. 6. 4.

A person makes progress only by imitating Christ, who is the Way, the Truth, and the Life. No one goes to the Father but through him, as he states himself in St. John [Jn. 14:6]. Elsewhere he says: *I am the door; anyone who enters by me shall be saved* [Jn. 10:9]. Accordingly, I would not consider any spirituality worthwhile that wants to walk in sweetness and ease and run from the imitation of Christ.

9. Because I have said that Christ is the way and that this way is a death to our natural selves in the sensory and spiritual parts of the soul, I would like to demonstrate how this death is patterned on Christ's, for he is our model and light.

10. First, during his life he certainly died spiritually to the sensitive part, and at his death he died naturally. He proclaimed during his life that he had no place whereon to lay his head [Mt. 8:20]. And at his death he had less.

11. Second, at the moment of his death he was certainly annihilated in his soul, without any consolation or relief, since the Father had left him that way in innermost aridity in the lower part. He was thereby compelled to cry out: *My God, My God, why have you forsaken me?* [Mt. 27:46]. This was the most extreme abandonment, sensitively, that he had suffered in his life. And by it he accomplished the most marvelous work of his whole life, surpassing all the works and deeds and miracles that he had ever performed on earth or in heaven. That is, he brought about the reconciliation and union of the human race with God through grace. The Lord achieved this, as I say, at the moment in which he was most annihilated in all things: in his reputation before people, since in watching him die they mocked him instead of esteeming him; in his human nature, by dying; and in spiritual help and consolation from his Father, for he was forsaken by his Father at that time, annihilated and reduced to nothing, so as to pay the debt fully and bring people to union with God. David says of him: *Ad nihilum redactus sum et nescivi* [Ps. 73:22], that those who are truly spiritual might understand the mystery of the door and way (which is Christ) leading to union with God, and that they might realize that their union with God and the greatness of the work they accomplish will be measured by their annihilation of themselves for God in the sensory and spiritual parts of their souls. When they are reduced to nothing, the highest degree of humility, the spiritual union between their souls and God will be an accomplished fact. This union is the most noble and sublime state attainable in this life. The journey, then, does not consist in consolations, delights, and spiritual feelings, but in the living death of the cross, sensory and spiritual, exterior and interior.

12. I will not enlarge on this, though I would like to continue discussing the matter because from my observations Christ is little known by those who consider themselves his friends. For we see them going about seeking in him their own consolations and satisfactions, loving themselves very much, but not loving him very much by seeking his bitter trials and deaths.

I am referring to those who believe themselves his friends, not to those who live withdrawn and far away from him, people of extensive learning and high repute, and many others living elsewhere in the world, anxious about their pretensions and rank. These people, we can affirm, do not know Christ. However prosperous the end of their lives may seem, it will be in fact most bitter to them. On judgment day they will be spoken of, for they are the ones to whom we should first speak this word of God [Acts 13:46]. Because of their learning and higher state, they are the ones whom God intended as the target for this doctrine.

13. Let us address the intellects of spiritual people, particularly of those whom God has favored with the state of contemplation, for as I asserted,[3] I am now speaking especially to these people. We will discuss the direction of self to God through faith and the purification of what is contrary to faith, so that by constricting itself the soul may enter on the narrow path of obscure contemplation.

CHAPTER 8

No creature or knowledge comprehensible to the intellect can serve it as a proximate means for divine union with God.

1. Before dealing with faith, the proper and adequate means of union with God, we should prove how nothing created or imagined can serve the intellect as a proper means for union with God, and how all that can be grasped by the intellect would serve as an obstacle rather than a means if a person were to become attached to it.

This chapter will contain a general proof of this; afterward we will discuss in particular all the knowledge that the intellect can receive through the interior or exterior senses. We will also deal with the difficulty and harm occasioned by these exterior and interior ideas, for because of them the intellect does not advance with the support of faith, which is the proper means.

---

3. In A. 2. 6. 8. Throughout the *Ascent* and *Dark Night* he treats of faith, dark night, and contemplation as the same reality.

2. Let it be recalled, then, that according to a philosophical axiom all means must be proportionate to their end.[1] That is, they must manifest a certain accord with and likeness to the end so that through them the desired end may be attained.

Here is an example: Those who want to reach a city must necessarily take the road, the means, that leads to the city. Another example: If fire is to be united with a log of wood, it is necessary for heat, the means, to prepare the log first, through so many degrees of heat, with a certain likeness and proportion to the fire. Now if anyone wanted to prepare the log by a means other than the proper one, which is fire, a means such as air, water, or earth, there would be no possibility of union between the log and the fire, just as it would be impossible to reach the city without taking the proper road that connects with it. If the intellect, then, is to reach union with God in this life, insofar as is possible, it must take the means that bears a proximate likeness to God and unites with him.

3. It is noteworthy that among all creatures, both superior and inferior, none bears a likeness to God's being or unites proximately with him. Although truly, as theologians say, all creatures carry with them a certain relation to God and a trace of him (greater or less according to the perfection of their being), yet God has no relation or essential likeness to them.[2] Rather the difference that lies between his divine being and their being is infinite. Consequently, intellectual comprehension of God through heavenly or earthly creatures is impossible; there is no proportion of likeness.

David proclaims in reference to heavenly creatures: *There is none among the gods like you, O Lord!* [Ps. 86:8], calling the angels and saints gods. And elsewhere he declares: *O God, your way is in the holy place, what great God is there like our God?* [Ps. 77:13]. This was equivalent to saying that the way of approach to you, O God, is a holy way, namely, purity of faith. For what god can be great enough (that is, what angel so elevated in being, or saint in glory) to serve as an adequate and sufficient approach to you?

David also proclaims of earthly and heavenly things: *The Lord is high up and looks at low things, and the high things he knows from afar* [Ps. 138:6]. In other words: High in his own being, he looks at the being of objects here below as exceedingly low in comparison with his high being; and the high things, the heavenly creatures, he knows to be far distant from his own being. Thus no creature can serve the intellect as a proportionate means to the attainment of God.

---

1. See, e.g., Aristotle, *Metaphysics* 2. 1; Aquinas, *Summa theologiae* 1-2. 96. 1; 1-2. 102. 1; 1-2. 114. 2.
2. See Aquinas, *Summa theologiae* 1. 4. 3. Cf. also A. 1. 4-5

4. Nothing in this life that could be imagined or received and understood by the intellect can be a proximate means of union with God. In our natural way of knowing, the intellect can grasp an object only through the forms and phantasms of things perceived by the bodily senses. Since, as we said,[3] these things cannot serve as a means, the intellect cannot profit from its natural knowing.

If we speak of supernatural knowing, insofar as one can in this life, we must say that the intellect of its ordinary power, while in the prison of this body, is neither capable of nor prepared for the reception of the clear knowledge of God. Such knowledge does not belong to our earthly state; either one must die or go without this knowledge.

God told Moses, who had asked for this clear knowledge, that no one would be able to see him: *No one shall see me and remain alive* [Ex. 33:20]. St. John says: *No one has ever seen God or anything like him* [Jn. 1:18]. And St. Paul with Isaiah says: *Eye has not seen, nor ear heard, nor has it entered the human heart* [1 Cor. 2:9; Is. 64:4]. This is why Moses, as affirmed in the Acts of the Apostles, did not dare to look at the bush while God was present. He knew that his intellect was powerless to consider God in an appropriate way, a way that conformed to what he felt about him [Acts 7: 30-32]. It is told of our Father Elijah[4] that on the mount he covered his face (blinded his intellect) in the presence of God [1Kgs. 19:11-13]. He did this because, in his lowliness, he did not dare to gaze on something so lofty, and he clearly realized that anything he might behold or understand particularly would be far distant from God and most unlike him.

5. In this mortal life no supernatural knowledge or apprehension can serve as a proximate means for high union with God through love. Everything the intellect can understand, the will enjoy, and the imagination picture is most unlike and disproportioned to God, as we have said.[5]

Isaiah brought this out admirably in a noteworthy passage: *To what have you been able to liken God? Or what image will you fashion like to him? Will the ironsmith by chance be able to cast a statue? Or will the goldsmith be able to mold*

---

3. In nos. 1-2. Throughout his work John follows the Aristotelian-scholastic theory that knowledge comes through the senses by way of abstraction. An understanding of this theory is helpful in interpreting John, but the substance of his teaching is not dependent on any particular system of thought.

4. In the 16th century the Carmelites accepted the tradition, expressed in 1281 in their oldest constitutions, that from the time of the prophets Elijah and Elisha, holy Fathers of both the Old and New Testaments dwelt in solitude near the fount of Elijah on Mount Carmel to contemplate divine things. In referring to Elijah as "our Father," John follows the custom among Carmelites to speak of Elijah as our "leader" and "Father." Cf. A. 2. 20. 2; 24. 3; A. 3. 42. 5; C. 14. 14-15.

5. In no. 3.

him out of gold, or the silversmith with plates of silver? [Is. 40:18-19].

The ironsmith signifies the intellect whose work is to form the concept by removing the iron of sensible species and phantasms. The goldsmith signifies the will, which is capable of receiving the figure and form of delight caused by the gold of love. The silversmith, who was unable to fashion him from plates of silver, signifies both the memory and the imagination. The concepts and images that these powers mold and construct can easily be likened to plates of silver. It is as if Isaiah had said that the intellect will be unable through its ideas to understand anything like God, the will unable to experience a delight and sweetness resembling him, and the memory unable to place in the imagination remembrances and images representing him.

Manifestly, then, none of these ideas can serve the intellect as a proximate means leading to God. In order to draw nearer the divine ray, the intellect must advance by unknowing rather than by the desire to know, and by blinding itself and remaining in darkness rather than by opening its eyes.

6. Contemplation, consequently, by which the intellect has a higher knowledge of God, is called mystical theology, meaning the secret wisdom of God. For this wisdom is secret to the very intellect that receives it. St. Dionysius on this account refers to contemplation as a ray of darkness.[6] The prophet Baruch declares of this wisdom: *There is no one who knows her way or can think of her paths* [Bar. 3:23]. To reach union with God the intellect must obviously blind itself to all the paths along which it can travel. Aristotle teaches that just as the sun is total darkness to the eyes of a bat, so the brightest light in God is total darkness to our intellect. And he teaches in addition that the loftier and clearer the things of God are in themselves, the more unknown and obscure they are to us.[7] The Apostle also affirms this teaching, saying that what is highest in God is least known by humans [Rom. 11:33].

7. We would never finish if we continued to quote authorities and present arguments as proof that there is no ladder among all created, knowable things by which the intellect can reach this high Lord. Rather, it should be known that if the intellect desired to use all or any of these objects as a proximate means to this union, it would be encumbered by them. Not only this, but they would become an occasion of many errors and delusions in the ascent of this mount.

---

6. See Pseudo-Dionysius *The Mystical Theology* 1. 1.
7. Aristotle *Metaphysics* 2. 1.

CHAPTER 9

Faith is the proximate and proportionate means to the intellect for the attainment of the divine union of love. Proofs from passages and figures of Sacred Scripture.

1. We can gather from what has been said that to be prepared for this divine union the intellect must be cleansed and emptied of everything relating to sense, divested and liberated of everything clearly intelligible, inwardly pacified and silenced, and supported by faith alone, which is the only proximate and proportionate means to union with God. For the likeness between faith and God is so close that no other difference exists than that between believing in God and seeing him. Just as God is infinite, faith proposes him to us as infinite. Just as there are three Persons in one God, it presents him to us in this way. And just as God is darkness to our intellect, so faith dazzles and blinds us. Only by means of faith, in divine light exceeding all understanding, does God manifest himself to the soul. The greater one's faith the closer is one's union with God.

St. Paul indicated this in the passage cited above: *The one who would be united with God must believe* [Heb. 11:6]. This means that people must walk by faith in their journey to God. The intellect must be blind and dark and abide in faith alone, because it is joined with God under this cloud. And as David proclaims, God is hidden under the cloud: *He set darkness under his feet. And he rose above the cherubim and flew on the wings of the wind. He made darkness and the dark water his hiding place* [Ps. 18:10-11].

2. This darkness under God's feet and of his hiding place and the dark water of his dwelling denote the obscurity of faith in which he is enclosed. The verse stating that he rose above the cherubim and flew on the wings of the wind alludes to how God soars above all understanding. The cherubim refer to those who understand or contemplate; the wings of the wind signify the subtle ideas and lofty concepts of the spirit. Above these is his being, which no one can reach through human effort.

3. In Scripture we read figuratively of this that when Solomon had completed the temple, God descended in darkness and filled it so that the children of Israel were unable to see. Solomon then said: *The Lord has promised to dwell in darkness* [1Kgs. 8:12]. God was also covered with darkness when he appeared to Moses on the mount [Ex. 24:16]. And as often as God communicated at length with someone, he appeared in darkness. This is evident in the Book of Job, where Scripture asserts that God spoke to Job from the dark air [Jb. 38:1; 40:1].

All of this darkness signifies the obscurity of faith with which the divinity is clothed while communicating itself to the soul. This darkness will be dispelled when, as St. Paul states, that which is in part (this darkness of faith) is taken away, and that which is perfect (the divine light) comes [1 Cor. 13:10]. We also find a fairly good figure of this obscurity of faith in the scriptural narration about the militia of Gideon. According to that account, all the soldiers held lamps in their hands, yet did not see the light because the lamps were hidden in darkness within earthenware jars. But when these jars were broken, the light appeared [Jgs. 7:16-20]. Faith, represented by those clay jars, contains the divine light. When faith reaches its end and is shattered by the ending and breaking of this mortal life, the glory and light of the divinity, the content of faith, will at once appear.

4. Clearly, then, union with God in this life, and direct communication with him, demands that we be united with the darkness in which, as Solomon said [1Kgs. 8:12], God promised to dwell, and that we approach the dark air in which God was pleased to reveal his secrets to Job. Individuals must take in darkness the earthenware jars of Gideon and hold in their hands (the works of their wills) the lamp (the union of love, though in the darkness of faith), so that when the clay jar of this life, which is all that impedes the light of faith, is broken, they may see God face to face in glory.

5. We must discuss now in particular all the concepts and apprehensions of the intellect, the hindrance and harm that can be suffered along this road of faith, and the conduct that is proper for the soul. We do this so that the soul may profit from both sensory and spiritual apprehensions rather than undergo harm.

CHAPTER 10

A division of all apprehensions and ideas comprehensible to the intellect.

1. To discuss in particular both the advantage and the harm that intellectual concepts and apprehensions cause to the soul's faith, which is the means to divine union, we need to set up a division of all the natural and supernatural apprehensions of the intellect. Later, then, in a more logical order we shall be able to guide the intellect through them into the night and darkness of faith. Our division will be as concise as possible.

2. It is noteworthy that the intellect can get ideas and concepts in two ways, naturally and supernaturally. Natural knowledge includes everything the intellect can understand by way of the bodily senses or through reflection. Supernatural knowledge comprises everything imparted to the intellect in a way transcending the intellect's natural ability and capacity.

3. This supernatural knowledge is subdivided into corporeal and spiritual. The corporeal is made up of two kinds: knowledge received from the exterior bodily senses, and knowledge received from the interior bodily senses, including all that the imagination can apprehend, form, or fashion.

4. The spiritual is also made up of two kinds: One is distinct and particular knowledge; the other, vague, dark, and general knowledge. The particular knowledge includes four kinds of distinct apprehensions communicated to the spirit without the means of the bodily senses: visions, revelations, locutions, and spiritual feelings.

The dark and general knowledge (contemplation, which is imparted in faith) is of one kind only. We have to lead the soul to this contemplation by guiding it through all these other apprehensions and divesting it of them, beginning with the first.

CHAPTER 11

The impediment and harm caused by intellectual apprehensions arising from objects supernaturally represented to the exterior senses. The proper conduct of the soul in their regard.

1. The first kind of knowledge referred to in the preceding chapter is that which originates naturally. Since we already discussed this kind of knowledge in the first book where we guided the soul through the night of sense, we will have nothing to say of it here. There we presented appropriate doctrine about this knowledge.[1]

Our discussion in this chapter will deal only with the supernatural knowledge that reaches the intellect by way of the exterior bodily senses (sight, hearing, smell, taste, and touch). Through these senses, spiritual persons can, and usually do, perceive supernatural representations and objects.

As for sight, they are wont to have visions of images and persons from the other life: of saints, of the good and bad angels, and of unusual lights and splendors.

Through hearing they apprehend certain extraordinary words, sometimes from the vision, and at other times without seeing the one who speaks.

---

1. In reality the doctrine developed there up to chapter 12 is general and valid for any kind of knowledge or appetite. The important point here is the distinction between natural and supernatural knowledge coming through the senses. For John the supernatural refers to what cannot be acquired through our natural abilities.

With the sense of smell they sometimes notice sensibly the sweetest fragrances without knowledge of their origin.

Also it happens with regard to taste that they experience very exquisite savors. And concerning touch they feel extreme delight, at times so intense that all the bones and marrow rejoice, flourish, and bathe in it. This delight is usually termed spiritual unction because in pure souls it passes from the spirit to the senses. The experience is common with spiritual persons. It is an overflow from the affection and devotion of the sensible spirit, which individuals receive in their own way.

2. It must be known that even though these apprehensions can come to the bodily senses from God, one must never rely on them or accept them. A person should rather flee from them completely and have no desire to examine whether they be good or bad. The more exterior and corporeal these things are, the less certain is their divine origin. God's self-communication is more commonly and appropriately given to the spirit, in which there is greater security and profit for the soul, than to the senses, where ordinarily there is extreme danger and room for deception. Thinking that spiritual things are identical with what is felt, the bodily sense usually sets itself up as arbiter and judge over them. But spiritual things are as different from what is sensed as is the body from the soul and sensibility from reason. The bodily sense is as ignorant of spiritual matters as a beast is of rational matters, and even more.

3. Individuals who esteem these apprehensions are in serious error and extreme danger of being deceived. Or at least they will hinder their spiritual growth because, as we mentioned,[2] these corporeal perceptions bear no proportion to what is spiritual. Such manifestations ought always to be considered as more surely from the devil than from God, for the devil possesses greater leeway in influencing the exterior and corporeal part of human nature. He can deceive the soul more readily through this action than through a more interior and spiritual kind.

4. The more exterior these corporeal objects and forms, the less profitable they are to the interior and spiritual part of the soul. This is due to the extreme distance and the lack of proportion between the corporeal and the spiritual. Even though some spirituality results from these corporeal communications—which is always the case when they are from God—it is far less than when the communications are more spiritual and interior. As a result they are a ready occasion for the breeding of error, presumption, and vanity in the soul. Palpable, tangible, and material as they are, they strongly affect the senses so that in one's judgment they

---

2. In chaps. 8-9.

seem more worthwhile on account of their being more sensible. A person, then, forsaking faith, will follow after these communications, believing that their light is the guide and means to the goal, which is union with God. But the more importance one gives to these communications the further one strays from faith, the way and means.

5. Furthermore, persons receiving these apprehensions often develop secretly a special opinion of themselves—that now they are important in God's eyes. Such a view is contrary to humility.

The devil too is adept at suggesting to individuals a secret self-satisfaction that becomes truly obvious at times. He often purveys objects to the senses, presenting to the sense of sight images of saints and most beautiful lights, and to the hearing, dissembled words, and to the sense of smell, fragrant odors; in the mouth, sweetness, and in the sense of touch, delight. He does all of this so that by enticing persons through these sensory objects he may induce them into many evils.

Such representations and feelings, consequently, must always be rejected. Even though some may be from God, this rejection is no affront to him. Nor will one, by rejecting and not wanting them, fail to receive the effect and fruit God wishes to produce through them.

6. The reason is that if the corporeal vision or feeling in the senses has a divine origin it produces its effect in the spirit at the very moment of its perception, without allowing any deliberation about wanting or not wanting it. This is likewise so with the more interior communications. Since God grants these favors without the individual's own ability and effort, he causes the desired effect of these favors without this ability and effort since he produces the effect passively in the spirit. The good effect, accordingly, does not depend on one's wanting or not wanting the communication. Were fire to come into immediate contact with a person's flesh, that person's desire not to get burned would hardly be helpful, for the fire produces its effect necessarily. So too with good visions and sensible communications. Even if a person doesn't want them, they produce their effect, and first and foremost in the soul rather than in the body.

Also, those from the devil, even though the soul does not desire them, cause in the spirit agitation, or dryness, or vanity, or presumption. Yet diabolical communications are not as efficacious in doing harm as God's communications are in doing good. For the diabolical communications can only arouse the first movements without being able to move the will any further if it is unwilling to be moved. The unrest caused by them will not last long, unless the individual's lack of courage and caution becomes the occasion for the unrest to continue.

The communications from God, however, penetrate the soul, move the will to love, and leave their effect within. The soul, even if it wants to, can no more resist their effect than can a window withstand the sunlight shining on it.

7. A soul should never dare to want to accept these communications, even though, as I say, they are from God. If it does, six kinds of harm will result.

First, faith will gradually diminish, for sensible experiences greatly detract from it. Faith, as we said,[3] transcends all sense. By not closing the eyes of the soul to all these sensory apprehensions, a person strays from the means to union with God.

Second, if left unrejected these sensory things are an impediment to the spirit because they detain the soul and prevent the spirit from soaring to the invisible. This is one of the reasons our Lord told the disciples that it was fitting for him to go so that the Holy Spirit might come [Jn. 16:7]. And so that Mary Magdalene would ground herself in faith, he refused to allow her to touch his feet after his resurrection [Jn. 20:17].

Third, the soul begins to develop a possessive attitude toward these communications and fails to continue on its journey to genuine renunciation and nakedness of spirit.

Fourth, individuals gradually lose the effect of these communications and the interior spirituality they produce because the individuals set their eyes on the sensible aspect, which is the least part of the communications. As a consequence these persons do not receive so copiously the spirituality caused by them. This spirituality is preserved and more deeply impressed in the soul if the sensible element, which is far different from pure spirituality, is denied.

Fifth, individuals gradually lose God's favors because they receive these favors as something belonging to themselves and do not profit well by them. Taking them as one's own and failing to profit by them is the same as desiring to receive them. God does not bestow them so that the recipient may desire to receive them, for a person must never absolutely believe that they are from God.

Sixth, in desiring to accept them one opens the door to the devil. The devil can then deceive one by other communications expertly feigned and disguised as genuine. In the words of the Apostle, he can transform himself into an angel of light [2 Cor. 11:14]. We shall discuss this matter, with God's help, in the third book, in the chapter on spiritual gluttony.[4]

---

3. See chap. 3.
4. Here he is thinking of his work in terms of a threefold division: active night of the senses, active night of the spirit and passive night. He in fact deals with this material not in the third book of the *Ascent,* which treats of the purification of the memory and will, but in the *Night* 1. 6. .

8. Regardless of the cause of these apprehensions, it is always good for people to reject them with closed eyes. If they fail to do so, they will make room for diabolical representations. And when the devil is given such a free hand, his representations multiply while God's representations gradually cease, so that eventually all these apprehensions will come from the devil and none at all from God. This has happened with many incautious and uninstructed people who in their sureness concerning the reception of these communications met with real difficulty in returning to God through purity of faith. Many have been unable to return because of the deep roots the devil has taken in them. Consequently, it is expedient to be closed to these communications and to deny them all, for in this way diabolical errors coming from the bad apprehensions are eliminated, the hindrance to faith occasioned by the good communications is avoided, and the spirit gathers the fruit.

If these communications are allowed to enter, God will gradually withdraw them. By considering them one's own, one fails to receive the due profit. The devil then inserts and increases his communications, since he finds an opening for them. So too, on the other hand, when a humble and dispossessed soul renounces and opposes these representations, God will augment his favors and give better ones. He will set this soul over many things as in the case of the servant who was faithful in a few things [Mt. 25:21].

9. If individuals remain both faithful and retiring in the midst of these favors, the Lord will not cease raising them degree by degree until they reach divine union and transformation. Our Lord proves and elevates the soul by first bestowing graces that are exterior, lowly, and proportioned to the small capacity of sense. If the person reacts well by taking these first morsels with moderation for strength and nourishment, God will bestow a more abundant and higher quality of food. If individuals are victorious over the devil in the first degree, they will pass on to the second; and if so in the second, they will go to the third; and likewise through all the seven mansions (the seven degrees of love) until the Bridegroom puts them in the wine cellar of perfect charity [Sg. 2:4].

10. Happy the person who knows how to carry on the fight against the beast of the Apocalypse and its seven heads that are in opposition to these seven degrees of love [Rv. 12:3; 13:1]. With each of its heads the beast wars against one of these degrees, and by doing so it wages battle with the soul in each of these mansions. And in every mansion the soul is exercising the love of God and winning another degree. Those who fight faithfully and conquer in each mansion will doubtless merit advancing from degree to degree and from mansion to mansion unto the ultimate where the seven heads of the beast against which the furious war is fought will have been

cut off. This war is so violent that St. John says the beast was permitted to fight against the saints, and was victorious in each of these degrees of love by using arms and abundant munitions [Rv. 13:7].

It is most regrettable that many, on entering this battle against the beast, are even incapable of severing the first head through denial of the sensible objects of the world. Some make the effort and cut it off, but then fail to sever the second, which consists of the sensory visions we are discussing. What is most lamentable is that after some have cut off not only the first and second but the third also (in regard to the interior senses, by passing out of the state of meditation and advancing further), at the moment of their entrance into purity of spirit they are conquered by this spiritual beast that revives and rises up against them even unto the first head. In their fall the last state becomes worse than the first since the beast takes with it seven other spirits worse than itself [Lk. 11:26].

11. Spiritual persons ought to deny all apprehensions and the temporal delights of the exterior senses if they desire to cut off the first and second heads of the beast and thereby enter the first room of love and the second of living faith. They should not want to grasp for sensory communications or weigh themselves down with these, since doing so is what most derogates from faith.

12. Manifestly, these sensory visions and apprehensions cannot serve as a means for union since they bear no proportion to God. This was one of the reasons for Christ's not wanting Mary Magdalene or St. Thomas to touch him [Jn. 20:17, 27-29]. The devil is most pleased when he sees that people desire to accept revelations and are inclined toward them. For then he has an excellent opportunity to inject errors and disparage faith as much as possible. As I have declared,[5] people desiring these apprehensions become coarse in their faith and even expose themselves to many temptations and follies.

13. I have treated of these exterior apprehensions somewhat at length to shed more light in preparation for our discussion of the other apprehensions. There is so much to say, however, on this subject that I doubt whether I would ever finish. And I think I was too brief in only explaining that a person should be careful never to accept them—unless in some rare case and with extremely competent advice, and then without any desire for them. But I think what I said is sufficient.

---

5. See no. 7.

CHAPTER 12

The nature of natural imaginative apprehensions. Proofs that they are inadequate means for the attainment of union with God. The harm caused from attachment to them.

1. Before discussing the imaginative visions, which are usually imparted supernaturally to the interior sense (imaginative power and phantasy), a discussion of the natural apprehensions of this interior corporeal sense is appropriate. As a result we can proceed with order, progressing from the lesser to the greater and from the more exterior to the more interior until reaching the intimate recollection in which the soul is united with God. We have been following this very order: First we discussed divesting the exterior senses of their natural apprehensions, and, consequently, of the natural strength of the appetites. This we did in the first book when we spoke of the night of sense. Then, in the preceding chapter, we began to divest these senses of the supernatural exterior apprehensions so as to lead the soul into the night of the spirit.

2. The first point to consider in this second book concerns the interior corporeal sense (the imaginative power and phantasy). We must also empty this sense of every imaginative form and apprehension that can be naturally grasped by it and demonstrate the impossibility of union with God before the activity relating to these apprehensions ceases. Such apprehensions are incapable of being the proper and proximate means of this union.

3. We are speaking of two interior bodily senses: imagination and phantasy. They are of service to each other in due order because one is discursive with images and the other forms them. For our discussion there will be no need to differentiate between them. This should be remembered if we do not mention them both explicitly.[1]

All that these senses, then, can receive and construct are termed imaginations and phantasms. These are forms represented to the interior senses through material images and figures.

---

1. In speaking of the interior senses and their functions, John fluctuates in his terminology. According to the more widespread scholastic theory, the internal senses consisted of the common sense, the imagination, the estimative sense, and the sense memory (cf. Aquinas, *Summa theologiae* 1. 78. 4). For his purposes, John deals mainly with the sense memory and the imagination. Though he speaks of the imagination and the phantasy as two distinct internal senses, they are so related in their operations that for practical reasons he treats of them as one.

There are two kinds: supernatural and natural. The supernatural are represented passively without the work of the senses. These we call supernatural imaginative visions; we will discuss them afterward. The natural are those the soul can actively construct by its own power through forms, figures, and images.

Meditation is the work of these two faculties since it is a discursive act built on forms, figures, and images, imagined and fashioned by these senses. For example: imagining Christ crucified or at the pillar or in some other scene; or God seated on a throne with resplendent majesty; or imagining and considering glory as a beautiful light, and so on; or, in similar fashion, any other human or divine object imaginable.

The soul will have to empty itself of these images and leave this sense in darkness if it is to reach divine union. For these images, just as the corporeal objects of the exterior senses, cannot be an adequate, proximate means to God.[2]

4. The reason for this is that the imagination cannot fashion or imagine anything beyond what it has experienced through the exterior senses, that is, seen with the eyes, heard with the ears, and so on. At the most it can compose resemblances of these objects that are seen, heard, or felt. But such imitations do not reach a greater being or even as much being as that of the objects of the external senses. Even though individuals may imagine palaces of pearls and mountains of gold—for they have seen gold and pearls—all that is imagined will indeed be less than the essence of a little gold or a pearl. And this is true, even though in the imagination there is a larger quantity and more excellent structure. Since created things, as has been said, have no proportion to God's being, all imaginings fashioned from the likenesses of creatures are incapable of serving as proximate means toward union with God. Rather, as we said,[3] they serve for much less.

5. Those who imagine God through some of these figures (as an

---

2. Having in mind in this section a contemplative simplification of prayer (cf. A. 2. 6. 8), John stresses communion in loving faith more than discursive reflection. These passages do not advise one to turn away from Jesus Christ but insist on the simple gaze of faith and personal communion rather than on imaginative representation. John's teaching is in harmony with St. Teresa of Avila's. Strongly asserting that one must never turn from the humanity of Christ, she nonetheless admits that it is common for contemplative souls to be unable to engage in discursive thought about the mysteries of Christ's life. Communing with the Person, however, "dwelling on his mysteries with a simple gaze," is another matter and "will not impede the most sublime prayer" (cf. *Interior Castle* VI. 7. 6-7, 11-12; *Way of Perfection* 34. 11).

3. In A. 2. 8. 4, 7.

imposing fire or as brightness, or through any other forms) and think that he is somewhat like them are very far from him. These considerations, forms, and methods of meditation are necessary to beginners that the soul may be enamored and fed through the senses, as we shall point out later.[4] They are suitable as the remote means to union with God, which souls must ordinarily use to attain their goal and the abode of spiritual repose. Yet these means must not be so used that one always employs them and never advances, for then one would never achieve the goal, which is unlike the remote means and unproportioned to it—just as none of the steps on a flight of stairs has any resemblance to the goal at the top toward which they are the means. If in climbing them we do not leave each one behind until there are no more, or if we want to stay on one of them, we would never reach the level and peaceful room at the top.

Consequently, a person who wants to arrive at union with the Supreme Repose and Good in this life must climb all the steps, which are considerations, forms, and concepts, and leave them behind, since they are dissimilar and unproportioned to the goal toward which they lead. And this goal is God. Accordingly, St. Paul teaches in the Acts of the Apostles: *Non debemus aestimare auro vel argento, aut lapidi sculpturae artis, et cogitationis hominis divinum esse simile* (We should not consider or esteem the divinity to be like gold or silver, or stone sculptured by the artist, or like anything a person can fashion with the imagination) [Acts 17:29].

6. Many spiritual persons, after having exercised themselves in approaching God through images, forms, and meditations suitable for beginners, err greatly if they do not determine, dare, or know how to detach themselves from these palpable methods to which they are accustomed. For God then wishes to lead them to more spiritual, interior, and invisible graces by removing the gratification derived from discursive meditation. They still try to hold on to these methods, desiring to travel the road of consideration and meditation, using images as before. They think they must always act in this way. Striving hard to meditate, they draw out little satisfaction or none at all. Rather, aridity, fatigue, and restlessness of soul increase in the measure they strive through meditation for that former sweetness, now unobtainable. They will no longer taste that sensible food, as we said, but rather will enjoy another food, more delicate, interior, and spiritual. Not by working with the imagination will they acquire this spiritual nourishment but by pacifying the soul, by leaving it to its more spiritual quiet and repose.

The more spiritual they are, the more they discontinue trying to make particular acts with their faculties, for they become more engrossed in

---

4. In A. 2. 17.

one general, pure act. Once the faculties reach the end of their journey, they cease to work, just as we cease to walk when we reach the end of our journey. If everything consisted in going, one would never arrive; and if everywhere we found means, when and where could we enjoy the end and goal?

7. It is sad to see many disturb their soul when it desires to abide in this calm and repose of interior quietude, where it is filled with God's peace and refreshment. Desiring to make it retrace its steps and turn back from the goal in which it now reposes, they draw their soul out to more exterior activity, to considerations, which are the means. They do this with strong repugnance and reluctance in the soul. The soul wants to remain in that peace, which it does not understand, as in its rightful place. People suffer if, after laboring to reach their place of rest, they are forced to return to their labors.

Since these individuals do not understand the mystery of this new experience, they imagine themselves to be idle and doing nothing. Thus in their struggle with considerations and discursive meditations they disturb their quietude. They become filled with aridity and trial because of efforts to get satisfaction by means no longer apt. We can say that the more intense their efforts, the less will be their gain. The more they persist at meditation, the worse their state becomes because they drag the soul further away from spiritual peace. They resemble one who abandons the greater for the lesser, turns back on a road already covered and wants to redo what is already done.

8. The proper advice for these individuals is that they must learn to abide in that quietude with a loving attentiveness to God and pay no heed to the imagination and its work. At this stage, as was said, the faculties are at rest and do not work actively but passively, by receiving what God is effecting in them. If at times the soul puts the faculties to work, it should not use excessive efforts or studied reasonings , but it should proceed with gentleness of love, moved more by God than by its own abilities, as we will explain later.[5]

This explanation should be sufficient at present for those who want to make progress. They will understand the appropriateness and necessity of detaching oneself at the required time and season from all these methods, ways, and uses of the imagination.

9. To explain just when this practice must be employed, we will describe in the following chapter some signs that spiritual persons must

---

5. He does not fulfill here his promise to explain this loving attentiveness, but cf. *Flame* 3. 32-35.

notice in themselves. These signs will indicate that the time and season has come when they can freely make use of that loving attentiveness and discontinue their journey along the way of reasoning and imagination.

CHAPTER 13

The signs for recognizing in spiritual persons when they should discontinue discursive meditation and pass on to the state of contemplation.

1. To avoid obscurity in this doctrine it will be opportune to point out in this chapter when one ought to discontinue discursive meditation (work through images, forms, and figures) so that the practice will not be abandoned sooner or later than required by the spirit. At the proper time one should abandon this imaginative meditation so that the journey to God may not be hindered, but, so that there is no regression, one should not abandon it before the due time. For though the apprehensions of these faculties are not a proximate means to union for proficients, they are a remote means for beginners. By these sensitive means beginners dispose their spirit and habituate it to spiritual things, and at the same time they void their senses of all other base, temporal, secular, and natural forms and images.

Hence we will delineate some signs and indications by which one can judge whether it is the opportune time for the spiritual person to discontinue meditation.

2. The first is the realization that one cannot make discursive meditation or receive satisfaction from it as before. Dryness is now the outcome of fixing the senses on subjects that formerly provided satisfaction. However, as long as one can make discursive meditation and draw out satisfaction, one must not abandon this method. Meditation must be discontinued only when the soul is placed in that peace and quietude to be spoken of in the third sign.

3. The second sign is an awareness of a disinclination to fix the imagination or sense faculties on other particular objects, exterior or interior. I am not affirming that the imagination will cease to come and go—even in deep recollection it usually wanders freely—but that the person does not want to fix it purposely on extraneous things.[1]

4. The third and surest sign is that a person likes to remain alone in

---

1. St. Teresa also speaks of this difficulty with the wandering imagination during contemplation. Cf. *Interior Castle* IV. 1. 8-9; *Life* 17. 7.

loving awareness of God, without particular considerations, in interior peace and quiet and repose, and without the acts and exercises (at least discursive, those in which one progresses from point to point) of the intellect, memory and will. Such a one prefers to remain only in the general loving awareness and knowledge we mentioned, without any particular knowledge or understanding.

5. To leave safely the state of meditation and sense and enter that of contemplation and spirit, spiritual persons must observe within themselves at least these three signs together.[2]

6. It is insufficient to possess the first without the second. It could be that the inability to imagine and meditate derives from one's dissipation and lack of diligence. The second sign, disinclination and absence of desire to think about extraneous things, must be present. When this inability to concentrate the imagination and sense faculties on the things of God proceeds from dissipation and tepidity, there is yearning to dwell on other things and an inclination to give up meditation.

Neither is the realization of the first and second sign sufficient if the third sign is not observed with them. When one is incapable of making discursive meditation on the things of God and disinclined to consider subjects extraneous to God, the cause could be melancholia or some other kind of humor[3] in the heart or brain capable of producing a certain stupefaction and suspension of the sense faculties. This anomaly would be the explanation for want of thought or of desire and inclination for thought. It would foster in a person the desire to remain in the delightful ravishing. Because of this danger, the third sign, the loving knowledge and awareness in peace, and so on, is necessary.

7. Actually, at the beginning of this state the loving knowledge is almost unnoticeable. There are two reasons for this: First, the loving knowledge initially is likely to be extremely subtle and delicate, almost imperceptible; second, a person who is habituated to the exercise of meditation, which is wholly sensible, hardly perceives or feels this new insensible, purely spiritual experience. This is especially so when through failure to understand it one does not permit oneself to rest in it but strives after the other, more sensory experience. Although the interior peace is more abundant, the individual allows no room to experience and enjoy it. But

---

2. These signs may be compared with those in *Night* 1. 9. Contemplation, as the general loving knowledge of God, is the decisive element in this new situation.
3. In medieval physiology a humor was one of the four fluids entering into the constitution of the body and determining by their relative proportions a person's health and temperament.

the more habituated persons become to this calm, the more their experience of this general loving knowledge of God will increase. This knowledge is more enjoyable than all other things because without the soul's labor it affords peace, rest, savor, and delight.

8. For greater clarity we will expound in the following chapter some reasons showing the necessity for these three signs in order to journey on the road of spirit.

CHAPTER 14

Proves the appropriateness of these three signs and explains why their presence is necessary for one to advance.

1. As for the first sign, it should be known that there are two reasons almost comprised in one for requiring spiritual persons to give up the imaginative way, or sensory meditation, when they are unable to meditate or derive satisfaction from it, and enter the way of the spirit, which is the contemplative way.

First, because these persons have been granted all the spiritual good obtainable through discursive meditation on the things of God. An indication of this is their inability to make discursive meditation as before or derive from it any new satisfaction or pleasure. For previously they had not yet arrived at the spirituality that was in store for them.

Ordinarily, as often as individuals receive some profitable grace, they experience—at least spiritually—gratification in the means through which the grace is obtained. If this is not received, there will rarely be profit; neither will they find in the cause of that former gratification the support and satisfaction they did before when they received grace through that means. This agrees with what the philosophers hold: *Quod sapit, nutrit* (What is savory nourishes and fattens).[1] Hence holy Job asks: *Numquid poterit comedi insulsum, quod non est sale conditum?* (Could one perchance eat the unsavory that is not seasoned with salt?) [Jb. 6:6]. Here we have the cause of the person's inability to consider and meditate as before: the lack of savor and benefit derived by the spirit from this exercise.

2. The second reason is that these persons have now acquired, substantially and habitually, the spirit of meditation. It should be known that the purpose of discursive meditation on divine subjects is the acquisition of some knowledge and love of God. Each time individuals

---

1. Cf. Aristotle *On the soul* 3. 28.

procure through meditation some of this knowledge and love they do so by an act. Many acts, in no matter what area, will engender a habit. Similarly, through many particular acts of this loving knowledge a person reaches the point at which a habit is formed in the soul. God, too, is wont to effect this habit in many souls, placing them in contemplation without these acts as means, or at least without many of them.

What the soul, therefore, was gradually acquiring through the labor of meditation on particular ideas has now, as we said, been converted into habitual and substantial, general loving knowledge. This knowledge is neither distinct nor particular, as was the previous knowledge. Accordingly the moment prayer begins, the soul, as one with a store of water, drinks peaceably without the labor and the need to fetch the water through the channels of past considerations, forms, and figures. The moment it recollects itself in the presence of God it enters into an act of general, loving, peaceful, and tranquil knowledge, drinking wisdom and love and delight.

3. This is why people experience difficulty and displeasure when, despite their being in this calm, they meet others who want to make them meditate and work with particular concepts. Their experience resembles that of a suckling child who finds that the breast is taken away just when it is beginning to taste the milk that was gathered there for it. As a result it is forced to renew its efforts of grasping and squeezing. Or their experience is like that of a person who, while enjoying the substance of the fruit, once the rind is peeled is forced to stop and begin again to remove the rind from the fruit even though the fruit has already been peeled. In such an instance the person would fail to find the rind and cease enjoying the substance of the fruit that is at hand. Or this is like turning away from a captured prey to go hunting for another.

4. Many behave similarly at the beginning of this state. They think that the whole matter consists in understanding particular ideas and in reasoning through images and forms (the rind of the spirit). Since they do not encounter these images in that loving, substantial quietude where nothing is understood particularly and in which they like to rest, they believe they are wasting time and straying from the right road; and they turn back to search for the rind of images and reasoning. They are unsuccessful in their search because the rind has already been removed. There is no enjoyment of the substance nor ability to meditate, and they become disturbed with the thought of backsliding and going astray. They are indeed getting lost, but not in the way they imagine, for they are losing the exercise of their own senses and first mode of experience. This loss indicates that they are approaching the spirit being imparted to them, in which the less they understand the further they penetrate into the night

of the spirit—the subject of this book. They must pass through this night to a union with God beyond all knowing.

5. There is little to be said about the second sign, for it is obvious that these persons at this time necessarily find worldly images dissatisfying. Even those that concern God, which are more conformable to their state, fail to satisfy them, as we explained. Nevertheless, as we mentioned above,[2] the imagination usually wanders back and forth during this recollection. But these individuals do not desire or find delight in this; rather, they are troubled about it because of the disturbance it brings to that gratifying peace.

6. Nor do I believe it is necessary to indicate here why the third sign (the loving general knowledge or awareness of God) is a requirement for discontinuing meditation. Some doctrine has already been expounded about this sign in our explanation of the first one, and afterward in the proper place we will have a special discussion of this when dealing with the general, obscure knowledge. This matter will be taken up after our treatise on the distinct, intellectual apprehensions. We will, however, state one reason that manifests how this loving general knowledge and awareness of God in the soul is required before discontinuing discursive meditation.

Were individuals not to have this knowledge or attentiveness to God, they would, as a consequence, be neither doing anything nor receiving anything. Having left the discursive meditation of the sensitive faculties and still lacking contemplation (the general knowledge in which the spiritual faculties—memory, intellect, and will—are actuated and united in this passive, prepared knowledge), they would have no activity whatsoever relative to God. For a person can neither conceive nor receive knowledge already prepared save through either the sensitive or spiritual faculties. With the sensory faculties, as we affirmed, one can make discursive meditation, seek out and form knowledge from the objects; and with the spiritual faculties one can enjoy the knowledge received without any further activity of the senses.

7. The difference between the functions of these two groups of faculties resembles that existing between toil and the enjoyment of the fruits of this toil; between the drudgery of the journey and the rest and quiet gladdening at its end; or again, between cooking a meal and eating without effort what has already been cooked and prepared; it is like the difference between receiving a gift and profiting by it. If the sensitive faculties are idle as to their work of discursive meditation, and the spiritual faculties as to the contemplation and knowledge received and

---

2. In A. 2. 13. 3.

formed in them, there is no basis for asserting that the soul is occupied. This knowledge is necessary, then, in order to leave the way of discursive meditation.

8. It is noteworthy that this general knowledge is at times so recondite and delicate (especially when purer, simpler, and more perfect), spiritual and interior that the soul does not perceive or feel it even though the soul is employed with it. This is especially so when, as we affirmed,[3] this knowledge is clearer, simpler and more perfect. And then this knowledge is still less perceptible when it shines on a purer soul, one freer from the particular ideas and concepts apprehensible by the senses or intellect. Since one lacks the feelings of the sensitive part of the soul, by not possessing these particular ideas and concepts that the senses and intellect are accustomed to act on, one does not perceive this knowledge.

For this reason the purer, simpler, and more perfect the general knowledge is, the darker it seems to be and the less the intellect perceives. On the other hand, the less pure and simple the knowledge is in itself, although it enlightens the intellect, the clearer and more important it appears to the individual, since it is clothed, wrapped, or commingled with some intelligible forms apprehensible to the intellect or the senses.

9. The following example is a clear illustration of this. In observing a ray of sunlight stream through the window, we notice that the more it is pervaded with particles of dust, the clearer and more palpable and sensible it appears to the senses. Yet obviously the sun ray in itself is less pure, clear, simple, and perfect in that it is full of so many specks of dust. We also notice that when it is more purified of these specks of dust it seems more obscure and impalpable to the material eye. And the purer it is, the more obscure and inapprehensible it seems to be. If the ray of sunlight should be entirely cleansed and purified of all dust particles, even the most minute, it would appear totally obscure and incomprehensible to the eye since visible things, the object of the sense of sight, would be absent. Thus the eye would find no images on which to rest, because light is not the proper object of sight but only the means by which visible things are seen. If there is nothing visible off which the ray of light can reflect, nothing will be seen. If the ray, then, were to enter through one window and go out another without striking any quantitative object, it would be invisible. Yet the ray of sunlight would be purer and cleaner than when it is more manifestly perceived because it is filled with visible objects.

10. The spiritual light has a similar relationship to the intellect, the eye

---

3. In A. 2. 13. 7.

of the soul. This supernatural general knowledge and light shines so purely and simply in the intellect and is so divested and freed of all intelligible forms (the objects of the intellect) that it is imperceptible to the soul. This knowledge, when purer, is even at times the cause of darkness because it dispossesses the intellect of its customary lights, forms, and phantasies and effects a noticeable darkness.

When this divine light does not strike so forcibly, individuals apprehend neither darkness, nor light, nor anything at all from heavenly or earthly sources. Thus they sometimes remain in deep oblivion and afterward will not realize where they were, or what occurred, or how the time passed. As a result it can and does happen that a person will spend many hours in this oblivion, yet on returning to self think that only a moment or no time at all has passed.

11. The purity and simplicity of the knowledge is the cause of this oblivion. While occupying a person's soul it renders that soul simple, pure, and clear of all the apprehensions and forms through which the senses and memory were acting when conscious of time. And thus it leaves the soul in oblivion and unaware of time.

Although, as we asserted, the prayer lasts a long while, it seems of short duration to these souls since they have been united with pure knowledge, which is independent of time. This is the short prayer that, it is said, pierces the heavens [Ecclus. 35:17]. It is short because it is not in time, and it pierces the heavens because the soul is united with heavenly knowledge. When these persons return to themselves they observe the effects this knowledge produced in them without their having been aware of it. These effects are: an elevation of the mind to heavenly knowledge and a withdrawal and abstraction from all objects, forms, and figures and from the remembrance of them.

David declares that such was his experience on returning to himself after this oblivion: *Vigilavi, et factus sum sicut passer solitarius in tecto* (I became conscious and discovered that I was like the solitary sparrow on the housetop) [Ps. 102:8]. By solitary he refers to the withdrawal and abstraction from all things; by the housetop, to the mind elevated on high. The soul remains, in consequence, as though ignorant of all things since it only knows God without knowing how it knows him. For this reason the bride in the Song of Songs, when she states that she went down to him, numbers unknowing among the effects this sleep and oblivion produced in her, saying: *Nescivi* (I knew not) [Sg. 6:12].[4]

As we mentioned,[5] it seems to individuals when occupied with this

---

4. This doctrine on the perception of pure knowledge derives from Aquinas, *Summa theologiae* 1. 85. 4 ad 3; 1-2. 53. 3 ad 3; 1-2. 113. 7 ad 5; *De veritate* 8. 14 ad 12.

5. In no. 4.

knowledge that they are idle because they are not working with their senses or faculties. Nevertheless they must believe that they are not wasting time, for even though the harmonious interaction of their sensory and spiritual faculties ceases, the intellect is occupied with knowledge in the way we explained.[6] This is why, also, in the Song of Songs, the wise bride responded to one of her doubts: *Ego dormio et cor meum vigilat* [Sg. 5:2]. This was like saying: Though I sleep, according to what I am naturally, by ceasing to work, my heart watches, supernaturally elevated to supernatural knowledge.

12. But one should not think this knowledge, if it is to be all we said it was, will necessarily cause oblivion. This forgetfulness occurs only when the knowledge abstracts the soul from the exercise of all the natural and spiritual faculties. Because such knowledge does not always occupy the entire soul, this forgetfulness is less frequent. The knowledge we are discussing only requires abstraction of the intellect from all particular knowledge, be it of temporal or spiritual things, and an unwillingness to think on these things, as we have said.[7] For then we have a sign that the soul is occupied.

This sign is necessary for recognizing this knowledge when it is communicated only to the intellect. For that is what happens when it is sometimes imperceptible to the soul. When, however, there is also a communication to the will, as there almost always is, people will not fail to understand more or less their being occupied with this knowledge if they want to discern the matter. For they will be aware of the delight of love, without particular knowledge of what they love. As a result they will call it a general loving knowledge.

This communication, consequently, is called a general loving knowledge, for just as it is imparted obscurely to the intellect, so too a vague delight and love are given to the will without any distinct knowing of what is loved.

13. This explanation is sufficient at present to understand the need for this knowledge before leaving the way of discursive meditation and for the assurance that, despite its apparent idleness, the soul is well employed if these three signs are noticeable. It is also sufficient for an understanding of how the representation of this light in a more comprehensible and palpable way is not a sign of its greater purity, sublimity, and clarity, as was demonstrated[8] through the example of the ray of sunlight permeated with dust particles and thereby perceptible to the eye. Evidently, as

---

6. In the preceding nos. 8-10.
7. In nos. 5-7.
8. In no. 9.

Aristotle and the theologians assert, the higher and more sublime the divine light, the darker it is to our intellect.[9]

14. A great deal can be said about this divine knowledge, both as to its nature and the effects it produces in the soul. We are reserving this discussion for its proper place.[10] There was no reason for such a lengthy treatment of it here, except that we did not want to leave this doctrine any more obscure than it is. Certainly, I admit, it is very obscure. To the fact that this knowledge is a subject seldom dealt with in this style, in word or in writing, since in itself it is extraordinary and obscure, can be added that of my unpolished style and lack of knowledge. Doubtful of my ability to explain it, I am often aware of exceeding the limits required by that part of the doctrine with which I am dealing. I confess that I sometimes do so intentionally because what is not understandable with one reason may become so by others. Also I think that such a procedure will give more clarification to later explanations.

15. In conclusion, I think a question concerning the duration of this knowledge should be answered. I will do so briefly in the following chapter.

CHAPTER 15

Proficients, at the beginning of their entry into this general knowledge of contemplation, must at times practice discursive meditation and work with the natural faculties.

1. A question may arise about our teaching. Are proficients (those whom God begins to place in this supernatural knowledge of contemplation), because they are beginning to experience contemplation, never again to practice discursive meditation and work with natural forms?

In answer to this, we did not mean that those beginning to have this general loving knowledge should never again try to meditate. In the beginning of this state the habit of contemplation is not so perfect that one can at will enter into this act, neither is one so remote from discursive meditation as to be always incapable of it. One can at times in a natural way meditate discursively as before and discover something new in this. Indeed, at the outset, on judging through the signs mentioned above that

---

9. See Aristotle *Metaphysics* 2. 1. 1. Cf. A. 2. 8. 6.
10. He never takes up the subject directly as planned, although in various places he refers to the matter in passing, especially in the *Dark Night*. Cf. no. 6 of this chapter.

the soul is not occupied in repose and knowledge, individuals will need to make use of meditation. This need will continue until they acquire the habit of contemplation to a certain perfect degree. The indication of this will be that every time they intend to meditate they immediately notice this knowledge and peace as well as their own lack of power or desire to meditate, as we said.[1] Until reaching this stage (of those already proficient in contemplation), people will sometimes meditate and sometimes be in contemplation.

2. They will often find themselves in this loving or peaceful awareness without having first engaged in any active work (regarding particular acts) with their faculties; they will not be working actively but only receiving. But on the other hand they will frequently find it necessary to aid themselves gently and moderately with meditation in order to enter this state.

But once they have been placed in it, as we already pointed out, they do not work with the faculties. It is more exact to say that then the work is done in the soul and the knowledge and delight are already produced, than that the soul does anything besides attentively loving God and refraining from the desire to feel or see anything. In this loving awareness the soul receives God's self-communication passively, just as people receive light passively without doing anything else but keeping their eyes open. This reception of the light infused supernaturally into the soul is passive knowing. It is affirmed that these individuals do nothing, not because they fail to understand but because they understand with no effort other than receiving what is bestowed. This is what happens when God bestows illuminations and inspirations, although here the person freely receives this general obscure knowledge.

3. One should not commingle other, more palpable lights of forms, concepts, or figures of meditative discourse if one wants to receive this divine light in greater simplicity and abundance, for none of these tangible lights are like that serene, limpid light. If individuals were to desire to consider and understand particular things, however spiritual these things may be, they would hinder the general, limpid, and simple light of the spirit. They would be interfering by their cloudy thoughts. When an obstruction is placed in front of the eye, you are impeded from seeing the light and the view before you.

4. What clearly follows is that when individuals have finished purifying and voiding themselves of all forms and apprehensible images, they will abide in this pure and simple light and be perfectly transformed in it. This light is never lacking to the soul, but because of creature forms and

---

1. In chapters 14 and 15.

veils that weigh on it and cover it, the light is never infused. If individuals would eliminate these impediments and veils and live in pure nakedness and poverty of spirit, as we will explain later, their soul in its simplicity and purity would then be immediately transformed into simple and pure Wisdom, the Son of God. As soon as natural things are driven out of the enamored soul, the divine are naturally and supernaturally infused since there can be no void in nature.[2]

5. When spiritual persons cannot meditate, they should learn to remain in God's presence with a loving attention and a tranquil intellect, even though they seem to themselves to be idle. For little by little and very soon the divine calm and peace with a wondrous, sublime knowledge of God, enveloped in divine love, will be infused into their souls. They should not interfere with forms or discursive meditations and imaginings. Otherwise the soul will be disquieted and drawn out of its peaceful contentment to distaste and repugnance. And if, as we said, scruples about their inactivity arise, they should remember that pacification of the soul (making it calm and peaceful, inactive and desireless) is no small accomplishment. This, indeed, is what our Lord asks of us through David: *Vacate et videte quoniam ego sum Deus* [Ps. 46:11]. This would be like saying: Learn to be empty of all things—interiorly and exteriorly—and you will behold that I am God.[3]

CHAPTER 16

The imaginative apprehensions represented supernaturally to the phantasy are incapable of serving as a proximate means to union with God.

1. After our having discussed the natural apprehensions that the phantasy and imagination receive and work with through discursive meditation, it is appropriate that we discuss the supernatural apprehensions that are called imaginative visions. These visions pertain to the phantasy just as natural apprehensions do because they belong to the category of image, form, and figure.

2. You should know that by this term "imaginative vision" we are

---

2. The basis for this is theological, not physical. God in his love "is very ready to comfort and satisfy the soul in her needs and afflictions when she neither has nor desires consolations and satisfaction outside him. The soul who possesses nothing that might withhold her from God cannot remain long without a visit from the Beloved." C. 10. 6.

3. In John's teaching, then, the active purification consists mainly in the personal task of disposing oneself for divine action through "poverty of spirit"; the passive purification is above all the effect of this divine action in the soul.

referring to everything supernaturally represented to the imagination under the category of image, form, figure, and species. All the apprehensions and species represented naturally to the soul through the five bodily senses and impressed upon it can be represented to it supernaturally without the intervention of the exterior senses.

This interior sense, the phantasy, together with the memory, is for the intellect the archives or receptacle in which all the intelligible forms and images are received. Like a mirror, this faculty contains them within itself, whether they come to it from the five bodily senses or supernaturally. It in turn presents them to the intellect, and there the intellect considers and makes a judgment about them. Not only is the phantasy capable of this, but it can even compose and imagine other objects resembling those known.

3. It is noteworthy that as the five exterior senses send the images and species of their objects to these interior senses, so God and the devil can supernaturally represent to these faculties—without the exterior senses—the same images and species; indeed, much more beautiful and perfect ones. God often represents many things to individuals through these images, and teaches them great wisdom, as is obvious throughout Scripture. For example: Isaiah beheld God in his glory under the form of smoke covering the temple and under the form of the seraphim covering their faces and feet with their wings [Is. 6:2-4]; Jeremiah saw the rod keeping watch [Jer. 1:11]; and Daniel, a multitude of visions [Dan. 7:10]; and so on.

The devil, too, attempts with his seemingly good visions to deceive a person. An example of this is found in the Book of Kings, where we read that he deceived all of Ahab's prophets by representing to their imaginations the horns with which, he claimed, Ahab was to destroy the Assyrians. This was a lie [1 Kgs. 22:11-12, 21-22]. And then there are the visions Pilate's wife had about not condemning Christ [Mt. 27:19]; and many others.

It is understandable, therefore, how in this mirror of the proficient's phantasy these imaginative visions are received more frequently than are the corporeal visions in the exterior senses. As far as image and species are concerned these visions do not differ from those coming through the exterior senses. But as for their perfection and the effect produced, there is a great difference, for since they are supernatural and more interior they are more subtle and effective in the soul. Yet this does not mean that some of the exterior corporeal visions may not be more effective, since after all God gives his communications as he pleases. But we are dealing with these visions insofar as they are in themselves more spiritual.

4. The devil ordinarily comes with his wiles, natural or supernatural, to this sense, the imagination and phantasy, for it is the gate and entry to

the soul. Here the intellect comes as though to a seaport or market to buy and sell provisions. As a result, God—and the devil too—comes here with the jewels of images and supernatural forms to offer them to the intellect. Yet God does not depend on this means alone for instructing the soul. He dwells in it substantially and can impart knowledge to it by himself or by other means.

5. There is no reason to delay in giving signs for the discernment of good visions from bad ones, nor in enumerating the various kinds. My sole intention here is to instruct the intellect about them so that it may not be hindered and impeded from union with divine wisdom by the good ones, nor deceived by the false ones.

6. I say, then, that since these imaginative apprehensions, visions, and other forms or species are presented through some image or particular idea, individuals should neither feed upon nor encumber themselves with them. And this is true whether these visions be false and diabolical or if they be recognized as authentic and from God. Neither should people desire to accept them or keep them. Thus these persons can remain detached, divested, pure, simple, and without any mode or method as the union demands.

7. The reason is that in being apprehended these forms are always represented, as we said,[1] in some limited mode or manner. But God's wisdom, to which the intellect must be united, has neither mode nor manner, neither does it have limits nor does it pertain to distinct and particular knowledge, because it is totally pure and simple. That the two extremes, the soul and divine Wisdom, may be united, they will have to come to accord by means of a certain likeness. As a result the soul must also be pure and simple, unlimited and unattached to any particular knowledge, and unmodified by the boundaries of form, species, and image. Since God cannot be encompassed by any image, form, or particular knowledge, in order to be united with him the soul should not be limited by any particular form or knowledge.

8. The Holy Spirit in Deuteronomy clearly manifests that God has no form or likeness: *Vocem verborum ejus audistis, et formam penitus non vidistis* (You heard the voice of his words, and you saw absolutely no form in God) [Dt. 4:12]. But he affirms that darkness, the cloud, and obscurity (that vague, dark knowledge, we mentioned,[2] in which the soul is united to

---

1. In nos. 1-3.
2. In chaps. 14-16. Union with God through this "vague, dark knowledge" is not the state of union the soul is aspiring to but a means that leads to that state.

God) were present. Then further on he adds: *Non vidistis aliquam similitudinem in die qua locutus est vobis Dominus in Horeb de medio ignis* (You did not see God in any image that day on Mount Horeb when he spoke with you from the midst of the fire) [Dt. 4:15].

9. The Holy Spirit also asserts in the Book of Numbers that the soul cannot reach God's height, insofar as is possible in this life, by means of any forms or figures. For God reproves Aaron and Miriam for murmuring against their brother Moses and thus lets them know the high state of union and friendship in which he had placed Moses: *Si quis inter vos fuerit propheta Domini, in visiones apparebo ei, vel per somnium loquar ad illum. At non talis servus meus Moyses, qui in omni domo mea fidelissimus est: ore enim ad os loquor ei, palam, et non per aenigmata, et figuras Dominum videt* (If there is any prophet of the Lord among you, I will appear to him in some vision or form, or speak with him in his dreams. But no one is like my servant Moses, the most faithful one in all my house, and I speak with him mouth to mouth, and he does not see God through comparisons, likenesses, and figures) [Nm. 12:6-8].

Manifestly, in this high state of union God does not communicate himself to the soul—nor is this possible—through the disguise of any imaginative vision, likeness, or figure, but mouth to mouth: the pure and naked essence of God (the mouth of God in love) with the pure and naked essence of the soul (the mouth of the soul in the love of God).

10. To reach this essential union of love of God, a person must be careful not to lean upon imaginative visions, forms, figures, or particular ideas, since they cannot serve as a proportionate and proximate means for such an effect; they would be a hindrance instead. As a result a person should renounce them and endeavor to avoid them. The only reason to admit and value them would be the profit and good effect the genuine ones bring to the soul. But admitting them is unnecessary to obtain this good effect; for the sake of progress, rather, one should always deny them.

As with the exterior corporeal visions, the good these imaginative visions can communicate to the soul is either knowledge, or love, or sweetness. But in order for them to do this it is not necessary for a person to have the desire to accept them. As we pointed out,[3] at the very moment they are present in the imagination they are also in the soul and infuse knowledge and love, or sweetness, or whatever God wants them to cause.

They are present to the imagination and the soul together, but their effects may not be simultaneous. They produce their main effect in the soul passively, without its being able to hinder this, even though it may

---

3. In chap. 11. 6.

desire to do so. It was similarly powerless to know how to acquire the effect—although it did know how to become disposed. As a window is unable to hinder the ray of sunlight shining upon it and is disposed through its cleanness to be illumined passively without active effort, so too, however much individuals may want to reject these visions they cannot but receive the influences and communications of those figures. A negative will, humbly and lovingly resigned, cannot resist the supernatural infusions. Only imperfection and impurity of soul hinder these communications, just as stains on a window impede the bright sunlight.

11. Obviously, in the measure that individuals divest themselves of willful attachments to the apprehensions of those stain-like figures, forms, and images—the wrappings of spiritual communications—these persons will prepare themselves for the goods and communications that are caused by them. Leaving aside all those apprehensions, which are like curtains and veils covering the spiritual goods they contain, the individuals will receive these goods in greater abundance, clarity, freedom of spirit, and simplicity. If the soul desires to feed upon them, the spirit and senses will be so occupied that a free and simple communication of spirituality will be impossible. For, obviously, if it is occupied with the rind, the intellect will have no freedom to receive those spiritual communications.

Should individuals desire to admit and pay attention to these apprehensions, they would be setting up an encumbrance and remaining content with the least important—the form, image, and particular knowledge, which is the only kind of knowledge they can get from these visions. For people are unable to apprehend or understand the more important factor, the spirituality infused in the soul; neither do they know the way they receive this spirituality nor how they may speak about it, since it is purely spiritual. According to their own way of knowing, the only knowledge they can have about these visions concerns the less important element, the forms apprehended through the senses. I affirm, consequently, that the unintelligible or unimaginable element in these visions is communicated passively, exclusive of any effort of the soul to understand. A person would not even know how to go about making this effort.

12. The eyes of the soul, then, should be ever withdrawn from distinct, visible, and intelligible apprehensions. Such elements are pertinent to sense and provide no security or foundation for faith. Its eyes should be fixed on the invisible, on what belongs not to sense but to spirit, and on what, as it is not contained in a sensible figure, brings the soul to union with God in faith, the proper means, as was said.[4] These visions will be

---

4. Especially in chaps. 2-4.

substantially advantageous to the soul insofar as faith is concerned if it
knows clearly how to reject their sensible and intelligible aspect and
make good use of the purpose for which God gives them. As we pointed
out,[5] God does not bestow corporeal visions so that a person will desire
and become attached to them.

13. A question, though, may arise concerning this subject: If it is true
that God in giving supernatural visions does not want one thereby to
desire, lean upon, or pay attention to them, why does he give them at all?
Through them a person can fall into numerous dangers and errors, or at
least encounter the many impediments to further progress described
here. Furthermore, why would God do this if he can communicate to the
soul substantially and spiritually what he bestows upon it through the
sensible communication of these visions and forms?

14. We will explain our answer to this question in the following
chapter. There we will present for spiritual persons and their teachers
doctrine that, in my opinion, is both important and necessary. We will
expound God's method and purpose in bestowing these visions. As a
result of their ignorance about visions, many are unenlightened on how
to behave and how to guide themselves or others through them to union.
They think that, because of their awareness of the genuineness and
divine origin of these visions, it is good to admit and trust them. They do
not reflect that, as with worldly goods, failure to deny them can be a
hindrance, and cause attachment and possessiveness concerning them.
They consider it beneficial to admit some visions as true and reject others
as false. In this way they subject themselves and other souls to the
considerable labor and danger of discerning the truth or falsity of these
visions. God does not impose this task upon them, nor does he desire the
exposure of simple and unlearned people to this dangerous endeavor,
for these persons have faith, a sound and safe doctrine, the means by
which they are to journey.

15. One cannot advance in faith without closing one's eyes to everything pertaining to the senses and to clear, particular knowledge.
Though St. Peter was truly certain of his vision of Christ's glory in the
transfiguration, yet after relating the fact in his second canonical epistle
[2 Pt. 1:16-18] he did not want anyone to take this as the chief testimony
for certitude. But leading them on to faith he declared: *Et habemus
firmiorem propheticum sermonem: cui benefacitis attendentes, quasi lucernae
lucenti in caliginoso loco, donec dies elucescat* (We have a more certain
testimony than this vision of Tabor: the sayings and words of the prophets

---

5. In no. 3 and chaps. 11 and 12.

bearing testimony to Christ which you must make good use of, as a candle shining in a dark place). [2 Pt. 1:19]

Reflecting on this comparison, we discover the doctrine we are teaching here. Telling us to behold the faith spoken of by the prophets as we would a candle shining in a dark place, he asserts that we should live in darkness, with our eyes closed to all other lights, and that in this darkness faith alone—which is dark also—should be the light we use. If we want to employ these other bright lights of distinct knowledge, we cease to make use of faith, the dark light, and we cease to be enlightened in the dark place mentioned by St. Peter. This place (the intellect—the holder on which the candle of faith is placed) must remain in darkness until the day, in the next life, when the clear vision of God dawns upon the soul; and in this life, until the daybreak of transformation in and union with God, the goal of a person's journey.

CHAPTER 17

An answer to the proposed question. God's procedure and purpose in communicating spiritual goods by means of the senses.

1. A great deal may be said about God's intention (the elevation of a soul from its low state to divine union) and method of procedure in bestowing these goods. All spiritual books deal with these points, and in our explanation we will also consider them.[1] Accordingly, in this chapter I will do no more than offer a sufficient solution to our question, which is: Since there is so much danger and hindrance to progress in these supernatural visions, as we said,[2] why does God, who is all wise and in favor of removing obstacles and snares, communicate them?

2. An answer to this requires the establishment of three fundamental principles. The first comes from St. Paul's Epistle to the Romans: *Quae autem sunt, a Deo ordinata sunt* (The works that are done are well-ordered by God) [Rom. 13:1].

The second comes from the Holy Spirit in the Book of Wisdom: *Disponit omnia suaviter.* This is similar to stating: The Wisdom of God,

---

1. This is a key chapter that can serve as a guide in the interpretation of John's whole work. He gives the rationale behind his teaching on knowledge received both through the senses (chaps. 11-16) and directly by the intellect (chaps. 23-32). He explains the principles by which God leads individuals, with their collaboration, and shows how the passive element is present right from the beginning of the spiritual life.
2. In ch. 16. 13.

though she touches from one end to the other (from one extreme to the other), disposes all things gently [Wis. 8:1].

The third comes from the theologians who say: *Omnia movet secundum modum eorum* (God moves each thing according to its mode).

3. In order that God lift the soul from the extreme of its low state to the other extreme of the high state of divine union, he must obviously, in view of these fundamental principles, do so with order, gently, and according to the mode of the soul. Since the order followed in the process of knowing involves the forms and images of created things, and since knowledge is acquired through the senses, God, to achieve his work gently and to lift the soul to supreme knowledge, must begin by touching the low state and extreme of the senses. And from there he must gradually bring the soul after its own manner to the other end, spiritual wisdom, which is incomprehensible to the senses. Thus, naturally or supernaturally, he brings people to his supreme spirit by first instructing them through discursive meditation and through forms, images, and sensible means, according to their own manner of coming to understand.

4. This is the reason God gives a person visions, forms, images, and other sensitive and spiritual knowledge—not because he does not desire to give spiritual wisdom immediately, in the first act. He would do this if the two extremes (human and divine, sense and spirit) could through the ordinary process be united by only one act, and if he could exclude the many preparatory acts that are so connected in gentle and orderly fashion that, as is the case with natural agents, each is the foundation and preparation for the next. The first preparative acts serve the second; the second serve the third, and so on. Therefore God perfects people gradually, according to their human nature, and proceeds from the lowest and most exterior to the highest and most interior.

He first perfects the corporeal senses, moving one to make use of natural exterior objects that are good, such as hearing sermons and Masses, seeing holy objects, mortifying the palate at meals, and disciplining the sense of touch through penance and holy rigor.

When these senses are somewhat disposed, he is wont to perfect them more by granting some supernatural favors and gifts to confirm them further in good. These supernatural communications are, for example, corporeal visions of saints or holy things, very sweet odors, locutions, and extreme delight in the sense of touch. The senses are greatly confirmed in virtue through these communications and the appetites withdrawn from evil objects.

Besides this, the interior bodily senses with which we are dealing, such as the imagination and phantasy, are gradually perfected and accustomed to good through considerations, meditations, and holy reasonings; and through all this the spirit is instructed.

When through this natural exercise these interior senses are prepared, God is wont to enlighten and spiritualize them further with some supernatural imaginative visions from which the spirit profits notably at the same time, as we affirmed. This natural and supernatural exercise of the interior sense gradually reforms and refines the spirit.

This is God's method to bring a soul step by step to the innermost good, although it may not always be necessary for him to keep so mathematically to this order, for sometimes God bestows one kind of communication without the other, or a less interior one by means of a more interior one, or both together. The process depends on what God judges expedient for the soul, or on how he wants to grant it favors. But his ordinary procedure conforms with our explanation.

5. By this method, then, God instructs people and makes them spiritual. He begins by communicating spirituality to them, in accord with their littleness or small capacity, through elements that are exterior, palpable, and accommodated to sense. He does this so that by means of the rind of those sensible things, in themselves good, the spirit, making progress in particular acts and receiving morsels of spiritual communication, may form a habit in spiritual things and reach the actual substance of spirit foreign to all sense. Individuals obtain this only little by little, after their own manner, and by means of the senses to which they have always been attached.

In the measure that souls approach spirit in their dealings with God, they divest and empty themselves of the ways of the senses, of discursive and imaginative meditation. When they have completely attained spiritual communion with God they will be void of all sensory apprehensions concerning God. The more an object approaches one extreme, the further it retreats from the other; on complete attainment of one extreme it will be wholly separated from the other. There is a frequently quoted spiritual axiom that runs: *Gustato spiritu, desipit omnis caro* (Once the taste and savor of the spirit is experienced, everything carnal is insipid). The ways of the flesh (which refer to the use of the senses in spiritual things) afford neither profit nor delight. This is obvious. If something is spiritual it is incomprehensible to the senses; but if the senses can grasp it, it is no longer purely spiritual. The more knowledge the senses and natural apprehensions have about it, the less spiritual and supernatural it will be, as we explained above.[3]

6. As a result the perfect spirit pays no attention to the senses. It neither receives anything through them, nor uses them principally, nor judges

---

3. In nos. 3 and 5.

them to be requisite in its relationship with God, as it did before its spiritual growth.

A passage from St. Paul's epistle to the Corinthians bears this meaning: *Cum essem parvulus, loquebar ut parvulus, sapiebam ut parvulus, cogitabam ut parvulus. Quando autem factus sum vir, evacuavi quae erant parvuli* (When I was a child, I spoke as a child, I knew as a child, I thought as a child. But when I became a man, I put away childish things) [1 Cor. 13:11].

We have already explained how sensible things and the knowledge the spirit can abstract from them are the work of a child. Those who are always attached to them, and never become detached, will never stop being like a little child, or speaking of God as a child, or knowing and thinking of God as a child. In their attachment to the rind of sense (the child), they will never reach the substance of spirit (the perfect person). For the sake of their own spiritual growth, therefore, persons should not admit these revelations, even though God is the author of them, just as a child must be weaned in order to accustom its palate to a hardier and more substantial diet.

7. Is it necessary, you ask, for the soul while it is a child to accept these sensible things and then set them aside when grown, just as an infant must be nourished at the breast until, when it has grown older, it can be weaned?

I reply in regard to discursive meditation, in which individuals begin their quest for God, that it is true that they must not turn away from the breast of the senses for their nourishment until they arrive at the time and season suitable for so doing—that is, when God brings the soul to a more spiritual converse, to contemplation, of which we spoke in chapter 13 of this book.

But when there is a question of imaginative visions or other supernatural communications apprehensible by the senses and independent of one's free will, I affirm that at whatever time or season they occur (in the state of perfection or one less perfect) individuals must have no desire to admit them even though they come from God. And this for two reasons:

First, because God, as we said,[4] produces his effect in the soul without its being able to hinder this, although it can impede the vision—which often happens. Consequently, the effect to be communicated becomes more substantial even though it is given differently. As we said, people cannot hinder the goods God desires to impart, nor in fact do they do so except by some imperfection or possessiveness. And there is no imperfection or possessiveness if they renounce these apprehensions with humility and misgivings.

Second, by so doing individuals free themselves from the task and

---

4. In ch. 16. 11-14.

danger of discerning the true visions from the false ones and deciding whether their visions come from an angel of light or of darkness. Such an effort is profitless, a waste of time, a hindrance to the soul, an occasion of many imperfections as well as of spiritual stagnancy since a person is not then employed with the more important things and disencumbered of the trifles of particular apprehensions and knowledge. This was mentioned regarding the corporeal visions, and it will be asserted further on in respect to imaginative visions.

8. One can be sure that if our Lord did not have to lead a soul according to its own manner of being, he would never communicate the abundance of his Spirit through these aqueducts of forms, figures, and particular knowledge by which he sustains the soul with crumbs. This is why David said: *Mittit crystallum suam sicut bucellas,* which is as much as to say, he sent his wisdom to souls in morsels [Ps. 147:17]. It is regrettable that a soul, having as it were an infinite capacity, should be fed, because of its limited spirituality and sensory incapacity, with morsels for the senses.

St. Paul, too, when writing to the Corinthians grieved over this littleness and limited preparation for the reception of spirituality: "When I came to you, brethren, I could not speak as to spiritual persons, but only as to carnal, because you were unable to receive it, nor can you now." *Tamquam parvulis in Christo lac potum vobis dedi, non escam* (As to infants in Christ I gave you milk to drink and not solid food to eat) [1 Cor. 3:1-2].

9. In conclusion, individuals must not fix the eyes of their souls on that rind of the figure and object supernaturally accorded to the exterior senses, such as locutions and words to the sense of hearing; visions of saints and beautifully resplendent lights to the sense of sight; fragrance to the sense of smell; delicious and sweet tastes to the palate; and other delights, usually derived from the spirit, to the sense of touch, as is more commonly the case with spiritual persons. Neither must they place their eyes on interior imaginative visions. They must instead renounce all these things.

They must fix the eyes of their souls only on the valuable spirituality these experiences cause, and endeavor to preserve it by putting into practice and properly carrying out whatever is for the service of God, and pay no attention to those representations, nor desire any sensible gratification.

With this attitude, individuals take from these apprehensions only what God wants them to take, that is, the spirit of devotion, since God gives these sense experiences for no other principal reason. And they reject the sensory element, which would not have been imparted had they possessed the capacity to receive spirituality without the apprehensions and exercises of the senses.

CHAPTER 18

The harm caused by some spiritual masters in not giving souls adequate guidance with regard to the visions mentioned. An explanation of how both can be misled even by visions that have a divine origin.

1. We are unable to be as brief on this subject of visions as we would like because of the amount of material to be covered. Although we have presented the substance of a suitable explanation of what spiritual persons should do about these visions and how their masters should guide and deal with them, yet it will not be superfluous to particularize a little more on this doctrine and shed some light on the harm that can arise. Even if the visions are from God, spiritual persons and their masters can suffer harm if they are very credulous about them.

2. The reason motivating me to enlarge somewhat on this subject is the want of discretion that I have noticed—from what I can understand—in some spiritual masters. Trusting these supernatural apprehensions, counting them to be authentic and of divine origin, these directors together with their penitents have gone astray and become bewildered, realizing in themselves the words of our Savior: *Si caecus caeco ducatum praestet, ambo in foveam cadunt* (If one blind person leads another, both fall into the pit) [Mt. 15:14]. He does not say they will fall, but that they do fall. It is not necessary to wait until they fall into error in order for them to fall. The mere fact that the one blind person dares to be guided by the other is already an error; and thus the first, though less serious, fall is taken.

The method of some directors is sufficient to encumber souls receiving these visions, or even to lead them astray. They do not guide them along the paths of humility, and they give them a free hand in this matter, which causes a want of the true spirit of faith. Neither do these directors ground their disciples in faith, for they frequently make these visions a topic of conversation. Consequently, the individuals get the idea that their directors are setting store by their visions, and as a result they do the same and stay attached to them, instead of being built up in faith, detached, emptied, and divested of apprehensions so as to soar to the heights of dark faith.

All this arises from the attitude and language the individuals observe in their directors in these matters. This is so true that—I know not how—these persons with immeasurable ease, and an inability to do otherwise, beget a high esteem for these visions—even to the point of withdrawing their eyes from the abyss of faith.

3. The reason souls become so readily engrossed in visions must be the sensible aspect toward which humans have a natural bent. And since individuals are already attracted and disposed through their apprehensions of those distinct and sensible things, it is enough for them to see in their director, or any other person, some esteem for these visions, and they will acquire the same. Not only this but their desire for these visions is also stimulated, and they feed upon them and become more inclined and attached to them without being aware of it.

Numerous imperfections consequently arise, because these individuals lose humility, at least. They think their visions are significant, that they possess something profitable, and that God is giving them prominence. They go about feeling pleased and somewhat satisfied with themselves, which is against humility. Although these persons are unaware of it, the devil then secretly augments this feeling and begins to suggest thoughts about others: whether others receive these visions or not, or if their visions are authentic or not. Such thoughts are contrary to holy simplicity and spiritual solitude.

4. Let us bring to a close for now our discussion of these kinds of harm and of how there is no growth in faith unless souls turn from these visions. There are other, more subtle kinds of harm, more hateful in God's eyes, that may not be as noticeable as these, but that do result from this attitude. The source of these other kinds of harm lies in a failure to walk wholly on the road of nakedness. We will discuss all this when we treat of spiritual gluttony and the other six vices. Then, God willing, we will expound many points about these subtle and delicate stains that, because the director does not guide souls along the way of denudation, adhere to the spirit.[1]

5. Let us now say something about the attitude of some confessors who give their penitents poor instructions. Assuredly, I wish I knew how to speak of this because I think it is difficult to explain how the spirit of the disciple is secretly fashioned after that of the spiritual father. This subject involves such prolixity that it is wearisome to me, for it seems one factor cannot be explained without explaining another, since in these spiritual matters things are interrelated.

6. But to cover the matter sufficiently here, I might point out that it seems to me—and indeed it is so—that if the spiritual father has such a bent toward revelations that they produce in his soul some effect,

---

1. In John's plan there was to be a section in this work that would deal with the capital vices (cf. A. 2. 11. 7). In fact, he never got to treat of them in the *Ascent* but does so in the *Night;* see N. 1. 1-7.

pleasure, or complete satisfaction, he cannot avoid—even though un-aware—affecting his disciples with this attitude and pleasure if they are not more advanced than he. And even if they are more advanced, the director can do serious harm by continuing to give direction. From the inclination the spiritual father has toward these visions and the gratifica-tion he finds in them there rises a certain esteem for them, and unless he is on his guard he will manifest indications of this to the persons he is directing. And if those persons have the same inclination, there cannot be between them, as far as I can see, anything but a communication of esteem for these matters.

7. To be less demanding, let us speak of the confessor who, inclined or not toward these visions, does not use the necessary care to disencum-ber and divest his disciple of desire for them, but rather makes the vision the topic of conversation and the main theme of his spiritual colloquies giving instruction on the signs for the discernment of good visions from bad ones.

Although knowledge of these signs is worthwhile, there is no reason to burden the soul with this labor, solicitude, and danger; by refusing to pay attention to these visions, one escapes all this effort of discernment and does what one ought. But these confessors do not stop here. Observing that their disciples receive these manifestations from God, they ask them to request of him a revelation about some matter pertaining to them-selves or to others, and the foolish souls do so in the belief that this method of gaining knowledge is lawful. Merely because God, in the way or for the motive he wishes, grants a supernatural revelation, they think it is licit to desire that he grant it and they even petition him to do so.

8. If in response to their request God reveals the matter to them, they become more self-confident, thinking that God is pleased with their petition and desires it, whereas in reality he is displeased with such an entreaty and does not desire it. They often act or believe in accordance with the answer or revelation, for since they are attached to this manner of dealing with God, their will becomes adapted to these revelations and firmly rooted in them. They find natural satisfaction in them and fit them naturally into their own way of thinking. They often err exceedingly, and are then taken aback when something turns out differently than they had expected. Then doubts come to the fore concerning the divine origin of these revelations since events do not come to pass as they were led to believe.

They presupposed two things: First, that the revelations were from God since from the beginning they firmly adhered to them. Yet that adherence was probably due to their natural inclination toward them, as we asserted. Second, that since the revelations were from God, events would occur according to what they themselves understood or thought about these revelations.

9. This belief was a gross delusion, for God's revelations or locutions do not always turn out according to people's understanding of them or according to what seems to be the meaning of the words. One should neither find assurance in them nor believe them blindly, even though one knows they are God's revelations, responses, or words. Though they may in themselves be certain and true, they are not always so in their causes or in our way of understanding them. We will prove this in the next chapter. We will also prove that, even though God answers questions supernaturally, he is not pleased to do so, but is even sometimes angered.[2]

CHAPTER 19

Even though visions and locutions from God are true, we can be misled by them. Proofs from Sacred Scripture.

1. We mentioned two reasons why, although, God's visions and locutions are true and certain in themselves, they are not always so for us. The first reason is that our manner of understanding them is defective, and the second is that their basic causes are sometimes variable. We will give proof for both with scriptural texts.

Clearly, in regard to the first, not all revelations turn out according to what we understand by the words. The cause is that, since God is immense and profound, he usually includes in his prophecies, locutions, and revelations other ways, concepts, and ideas remarkably different from the meaning we generally find in them. And the surer and more truthful these latter are, the less they seem so to us.

We see this at every step in Sacred Scripture. With a number of ancients, many of God's prophecies and locutions did not turn out as had been expected, because they understood them in their own way, in another very literal manner. This is apparent in the following texts.

2. In Genesis, God told Abraham when he had brought him into the land of the Canaanites: *Tibi dabo terram hanc* (I will give you this land) [Gn. 15:7]. And since God had promised this frequently, Abraham, already old and still receiving the promise, questioned God: *Domine unde scire possum quod possesurus sum eam?* (Lord, how, or by what sign, am I to know that I will possess it?) [Gn. 15:8]. Then God revealed to him that he was

---

2. He proves the first in chs. 19-20, and the second in ch. 21.

not going to possess it at all but that his offspring would after 400 years [Gn. 15:13]. Thus Abraham finally understood the promise, which in itself was true because, in bestowing the land on his offspring out of love for him, God gave it to him. Consequently Abraham was misled in his understanding of the prophecy. If he had acted according to his understanding he would have erred decidedly since the possession of this land was not to come about during his life. And those who saw him die without having received the promise of the prophecy, after having heard that God was going to grant the land to him, would have been baffled and left with the notion that the prophecy was false.

3. While Abraham's grandson Jacob was on his journey to Egypt at the time Joseph, his son, had ordered him to come because of the famine in Canaan, God appeared to Jacob and said: *Jacob, Jacob, noli timere, descende in Aegyptum, quia in gentem magnam faciam te ibi. Ego descendam tecum illuc, et inde adducam te revertentem* (Jacob, do not fear, go down to Egypt and I will go with you; and when you depart from there, I will lead you out and be your guide) [Gn. 46:1-4].

These words were not fulfilled according to what we would understand from the way they sounded, for we know that saintly old Jacob died in Egypt and never returned from there alive [Gn 49:32]. But the prophecy was to be fulfilled in his offspring whom God, acting himself as guide along the way, delivered from Egypt years later. Manifestly, then, anyone knowing of God's promise to Jacob would have thought that Jacob, who through God's favor and command had entered Egypt in person and alive, would unquestionably make his exit alive and in person, since God had promised this and the help to achieve it. Such a one would have been misled, and filled with wonder over Jacob's death in Egypt because God would not have thereby fulfilled his promise as expected. Although God's promise in itself was true, there could have been much delusion concerning it.

4. In the Book of Judges we also read that when all the tribes of Israel united for war to punish Benjamin's tribe for a certain iniquity, they were positive of victory because God had appointed them a captain of war. So certain were they that, when defeat came and 22,000 of their men were slain, they were amazed and baffled before God and they wept the entire day, ignorant of the cause of their downfall, for they had understood that victory would be theirs.

And when they asked God if they should return to battle, he told them to return. Convinced that now victory was theirs, they set out with remarkable daring, and they were defeated the second time with a loss of 18,000 men. As a result they were extremely bewildered. They did not know what to do, because God had commanded them to wage war and yet they were always vanquished, but especially because they surpassed their enemy in number and strength: 400,000 to 25,700.

They were deluded in their interpretation of God's words, which in themselves were not deceptive. He did not say they would conquer but that they should fight, for in these defeats God wished to punish a certain neglect and presumption of theirs and thus humble them. But when finally he replied that victory would be theirs, it was, though not without much strategy and hardship on their part [Jgs. 20:11-48].

5. In this and many other ways souls are misled by understanding God's locutions and revelations according to the letter, according to the outer rind. As has been explained, God's chief objective in conferring these revelations is to express and impart the spirit that is enclosed within the outer rind. This spirit is difficult to understand, much richer and more plentiful, very extraordinary and far beyond the boundaries of the letter.

Anyone bound to the letter, locution, form, or figure apprehensible in the vision cannot avoid serious error and will later become confused for having been led according to the senses and not having made room for the spirit stripped of the letter. *Littera, enim, occidit, spiritus autem vivificat* (The letter kills and the spirit gives life) [2 Cor. 3:6]. The soul should renounce, then, the literal sense in these cases, and live in the darkness of faith, for faith is the spirit that is incomprehensible to the senses.

6. Because many of the children of Israel understood the words of the prophets very much according to the letter and because these prophecies did not turn out as expected, they began to disregard and distrust them. Hence a saying was born, becoming almost a proverb among them, by which they scoffed at the prophets. Isaiah complains of this in the following passage: *Quem docebit Dominus scientiam? Et quem intelligere faciet auditum? Ablactatos a lacte, avulsos ab uberibus. Quia manda remanda, manda remanda, expecta, reexpecta, expecta, reexpecta; modicum ibi, modicum ibi. In loquela enim labii, et lingua altera loquetur ad populum istum* (Whom will God instruct? And to whom will he explain his word and prophecy? Only to those who are weaned and fresh from their mother's breast. For everyone is saying—concerning the prophets—promise and promise again, wait and wait some more, wait and wait some more, a word with you here, a word with you there. For with words from his lips, but in another tongue, he will speak to this people) [Is. 28:9-11].

In this passage Isaiah clearly demonstrates the mockery these people made of the prophets and the derision repeated in the proverb, "wait and wait some more." He indicates that the prophecies were never fulfilled because the people were bound to the letter (the milk of infants) and to the senses (the breasts), which run contrary to the knowledge of the spirit. Because of this he says: *To whom shall he teach the wisdom of his prophecies? And to whom shall he explain his doctrine,* if not to those who are already *weaned from the milk* of the letter *and the breasts* of the senses? And because these people are not so weaned, they understand only according to the milk of the rind and letter, or according to the breasts of the senses, for they exclaim: *promise and promise again, wait and wait some more,* and so on. God must speak doctrine to them from his own mouth, and not theirs, and in a tongue other than theirs.

7. We must not consider a prophecy from the perspective of our perception and language, for God's language is another one, according to the spirit, very different from what we understand, and difficult. This is so true that even Jeremiah, a prophet himself, observing that the ideas in God's words were so different from the meaning people would ordinarily find in them, seems to be beguiled and defends the people: *Heu, heu, heu, Domine Deus, ergone decipisti populum istum et Jerusalem, dicens: Pax erit vobis, et ecce pervenit gladius usque ad animam?* (Alas, alas, alas, Lord God, have you perchance deceived this people and Jerusalem, saying: Peace will come to you; and behold the sword reaches even to the soul?) [Jer. 4:10].

The reason for the misunderstanding was that the promised peace was to be effected between God and humans through the Messiah who was to be sent to them, whereas they took the words to mean temporal peace. Consequently, when wars and trials came upon them, it seemed God was deceiving them because everything was turning out contrary to their expectations. Thus they proclaimed as Jeremiah also did: *Expectavimus pacem, et non est bonum* (We had hoped for peace, and there is no blessing of peace) [Jer. 8:15]. Guiding themselves, then, by the literal sense it was impossible for them to avoid deception.

Who will not be perplexed and misled if bound to the letter of all David's prophecies about Christ in the 71st psalm? *Et dominabitur a mari usque ad mare; et a flumine usque ad terminos orbis terrarum* (He shall reign from sea to sea; and from the river unto the ends of the earth) [Ps. 71:8]; and also, *Liberabit pauperem a potente, et pauperem cui non erat adjutor* (He will liberate the poor one from the power of the mighty, and the poor one who has no helper) [Ps. 71:12]. For afterward, Christ is born in an humble state, lives in poverty, and dies in misery; and not only did he fail to reign temporally upon the earth, but he was subject to a lowly people until he died under Pontius Pilate's rule. He did not merely fail to liberate his poor disciples from the hands of the temporally powerful, but allowed them to be persecuted and slain for his name's sake.

8. These prophecies about Christ should have been understood in their spiritual sense, in which they were most true. Since Christ was God he was Lord not solely of the earth but of heaven too. And not merely was he to redeem the poor, who were to be his followers, and free them from

the power of the devil (the mighty one against whom they had no helper), but he was also to make them heirs of the kingdom of heaven.

In prophesying about Christ and his followers, God was speaking of the more important factors (the eternal kingdom and eternal freedom), and in their interpretation of these words the people dwelt on matters of slight importance (temporal dominion and temporal freedom) to which God pays little heed, since in his eyes freedom and a temporal dominion are neither freedom nor a kingdom.

Blinded by the baseness of the letter and ignorant of the spirit and truth behind it, they killed their Lord and God, as St. Paul exclaimed: *Qui enim habitabant Jerusalem, et principes ejus hunc ignorantes, et voces propheta-rum, quae per omne Sabbatum leguntur, judicantes impleverunt* (The inhabitants of Jerusalem, and its rulers, ignorant of who he was, and misunderstanding the sayings of the prophets recited each Sabbath, after judging him, put him to death) [Acts 13:27].

9. This difficulty in giving a suitable interpretation to God's words reached such a point that even Christ's very disciples, who went about with him, were deceived. For example: those two who after his death were journeying to the town of Emmaus, sad and distrustful, saying: *Nos autem sperabamus quod ipse esset redempturus Israel* (We were expecting that he would redeem Israel) [Lk. 24:21]. They also were of the opinion that his would be a temporal liberation and reign. But Christ our Redeemer, appearing to them, reproved them for being foolish, dull, and slow of heart to believe the things foretold by the prophets [Lk. 24:25].

Even when he was about to ascend into heaven, some still maintained that dullness and queried of him: *Domine, si in tempore hoc restitues regnum Israel* (Lord, let us know if at this time you will restore the kingdom of Israel) [Acts 1:6].

The Holy Spirit causes many things to be said in which he has a meaning different from that understood by humans. This is seen by what he brought Caiaphas to say of Christ: *It is better that one man die than that the whole nation perish* [Jn. 11:50]. Caiaphas did not say these words on his own, and he expressed and understood them in one way while the Holy Spirit did so in another.

10. Evidently, then, even though the words and revelations are from God we cannot find assurance in them, since in our understanding of them we can easily be deluded, and very much so. They embody an abyss and depth of spirit, and to want to limit them to our interpretation and to what our senses can apprehend is like wanting to grasp a handful of air that will escape the hand entirely, leaving only a particle of dust.

11. Thus, the spiritual master should try to see to it that his disciples

are not detained by the desire to pay heed to supernatural apprehensions (which are no more than small particles of spirit and the only thing the disciples will be left with), and he should turn them away from all visions and locutions and teach them to remain in freedom and the darkness of faith, in which liberty and abundance of spirit are received and, consequently, the wisdom and understanding proper to God's words.

It is impossible for someone unspiritual to judge and understand the things of God correctly; and one is not spiritual if one judges them according to the senses. And thus even though these things are clothed in what is of the senses, they are not understood. This is what St. Paul really asserts: *Animalis autem homo non percipit ea quae sunt spiritus Dei; stultitia enim est illi, et non potest intelligere, quia de spiritualibus examinatur. Spiritualis autem judicat omnia* (The animal person fails to perceive the things that are of the spirit of God, for they are foolishness to him, and he is unable to understand them because they are spiritual. Yet the spiritual person judges all things) [1 Cor. 2:14-15]. "The animal person" refers to those who use only the senses; "the spiritual person" to those who are neither bound to nor guided by the senses. It is therefore rash to dare communicate with God by means of supernatural, sensory apprehensions, or to allow anyone to do so.

12. For the sake of greater clarity here are some examples: Suppose God says to a saintly man who is deeply afflicted because of persecution by his enemies: "I will free you from your enemies." This prophecy could be true; nonetheless the man's enemies will prevail and kill him. Anyone who had given these words a temporal interpretation would have been deceived because God had been speaking of the true and principal freedom and victory—salvation, in which the soul is free and victorious over all its enemies much more truly and loftily than if liberated from them here below. This prophecy had greater truth and richness than was understandable through an interpretation that related the freedom to this life. By his words, God always refers to the more important and profitable meaning, whereas humans will refer the words to a less important sense, in their own way and for their own purpose, and thus be deceived.

We see this in David's messianic prophecy: *Reges eos in virga ferrea, et tamquam vas figuli confringes eos* (You shall rule all nations with an iron rod, and dash them to pieces like a vessel of clay) [Ps. 2:9]. In this prophecy God referred to the principal and perfect dominion, which is the eternal one that did come to pass; not to the least important, temporal dominion, which did not come to pass during Christ's entire life on earth.

13. Here is another example: A soul has intense desires to be a martyr. God answers, "You shall be a martyr" and bestows deep interior consolation and confidence in the truth of this promise. Regardless of the

promise, this person in the end does not die a martyr; yet the promise will have been true. Why, then, was there no fulfillment of the promise? Because it will be fulfilled in its chief, essential meaning: the bestowal of the essential love and reward of a martyr. God truly grants the soul what it formally desired and what he promised it because the formal desire of the soul was not a manner of death but the service of God through martyrdom and the exercise of a martyr's love for him. Death through martyrdom in itself is of no value without this love, and God bestows martyrdom's love and reward perfectly by other means. Even though the soul does not die a martyr, it is profoundly satisfied since God has fulfilled its desire.

When these aspirations and other similar ones born of love are unfulfilled in the way one imagined and understood them, they are fulfilled in another, far better way, and render more honor to God than was thought of in making the request. David proclaims: *Desiderium pauperum exaudivit Dominus* (The Lord has granted the poor their desire) [Ps. 10:17]. And in Proverbs, divine Wisdom affirms: *Desiderium suum justis dabitur* (The desire of the just shall be answered) [Prv. 10:24]. Since numerous saints desired various particular favors from God yet did not receive them in this life, it is a matter of faith that since their desire was just and good it was granted them perfectly in heaven. Consequently, if God promises them in this life, "Your desire shall be fulfilled," it shall be, even though it may be done in a way different from what they had in mind.

14. God's words and visions in this and other ways may be true and certain, yet they can mislead us if we do not know how to understand them in a lofty manner and principally according to the purpose and the meaning God has in giving them. The safest and most suitable method of procedure is to oblige souls to flee prudently from these supernatural things, and to accustom them, as we pointed out,[1] to purity of spirit in dark faith—the means toward union.

CHAPTER 20

Proofs from Sacred Scripture of how God's words, although always true, are not always certain. The certainty of them depends on the causes of the pronouncements.

1. We must prove now the second reason[1] God's visions and locutions, although always true in themselves, are not always certain for us. This

---

1. In no. 5; see also ch. 9. 1.
1. Cf. ch. 18. 9; 19. 1.

uncertainty is due to the causes on which they are founded.

God's affirmations are frequently founded upon creatures and their effects, which are liable to change and failure; consequently, words based on these creatures can also change and fail. If one factor upon which another is dependent fails, the other fails too. For example, if God were to say that in a year he would send a plague upon a kingdom because of an offense committed against him there, and if the offense were to cease or change, the punishment could be withheld. Yet the warning would have been true since it was based on the actual fault, and if the fault were to have continued the threatened punishment would have been executed.

2. This happened in the city of Nineveh when God proclaimed: *Adhuc quadraginta diebus et Ninive subvertetur* (Forty days from now Nineveh will be razed) [Jon. 3:4]. This did not happen because the cause of the threat, their sins, ceased because of the penance that was done [Jon. 3:5-10]. But if they had not done penance the warning would have been carried out. We also read in the Third Book of Kings that when King Ahab had committed a very serious sin, God, through our holy father Elijah, sent him a message threatening severe punishment on his person, his house, and his kingdom [1 Kgs. 21:17-22]. And because Ahab rent his garments with grief, put on a hair shirt, fasted, slept in sackcloth, and went about sad and humbled, God once more sent this prophet to him with these words: *Quia igitur humiliatus est mei causa, non inducam malum in diebus ejus, sed in diebus filii sui* (Insofar as Ahab has humbled himself for love of me I will not in his days send the evil I spoke of, but in those of his son) [1 Kgs. 21:27-29]. Evidently, then, because Ahab changed his conduct and disposition, God also altered his sentence.

3. We can thus deduce for our purpose here that, although God may have revealed or affirmed something to a person (whether it be good or bad, concern this person or another), it can change, becoming greater or less, vary, or be taken away entirely according to a change or variation in this person's tendencies or in the cause on which it is based. Thus the event may not turn out as expected, and frequently no one but God knows why. God usually affirms, teaches, and promises many things, not so there will be an immediate understanding of them, but so that afterward at the proper time, or when the effect is produced, one may receive light about them.

Christ acted this way with his disciples. He told them many parables and maxims the wisdom of which they did not understand until the time for preaching had come, when the Holy Spirit descended on them. The Holy Spirit was to explain to them, as Christ affirmed, all that he had taught them during his life [Jn. 14:26]. St. John, speaking of Christ's entrance into Jerusalem, states: *Haec non cognoverunt discipuli ejus primum: sed quando glorificatus est Jesus, tunc recordati sunt quia haec erant scripta de eo²* [Jn. 12:16]. As a result many particular works of God can come to pass in a soul that neither the soul nor its director can understand until the opportune time.

4. In the First Book of Kings we also read that God, angered because Eli the priest of Israel failed to punish his sons for their sins, sent Samuel to him with, among other messages, the following one: *Loquens locutus sum, ut domus tua, et domus patris tui, ministraret in conspectu meo, usque in sempiternum. Verumtamen absit hoc a me* (Certainly I have said before that your house and the house of your father will continually minister to me in the priesthood and in my presence forever. Yet this proposal is very far from me; I shall not bring it about) [1 Sm. 2:30]. Since the ministry of the priesthood is based on rendering honor and glory to God, God promised it to Eli's father forever. When Eli lacked zeal for the honor of God because, as God himself complained, he gave more honor to his sons than to God, dissimulating their sins so as not to reprove them, the promise also failed [1 Sm. 3:13]. It would have been kept forever if their good service and zeal had been enduring.

We should not think, therefore, that because revelations and locutions come from God—especially if they are dependent on human, changeable causes—they will infallibly and literally come to pass.

5. Although God knows when these locutions and revelations are dependent on human causes, he does not always manifest it, but in his communication of the locution or revelation he will remain silent about the condition. Such was the case when he told the Ninevites definitely that they would be destroyed after 40 days [Jon. 3:4]. At other times he declares, as he did to Rehoboam: *If you keep my commandments as my servant David did, I will also be with you as I was with him, and I will build you a house as I did my servant David* [1 Kgs. 11:38].

Whether God discloses the conditional element or not, individuals cannot find assurance in their own interpretation, because they are incapable of comprehending the secret truths and the diverse meanings contained in God's sayings. God is above the heavens and speaks from the depths of eternity; we on this earth are blind and understand only the ways of the flesh and of time. This, I believe, is why the Wise Man said: *God is above the heavens and you upon the earth; therefore do not be prolix or careless in speech* [Eccl. 5:1].

---

2. "These things his disciples did not at first understand. But when Jesus was glorified, then they remembered that these things were written about him."

6. You will perchance ask: If we are not to understand or get involved with these locutions and revelations, why does God communicate them?

I have already mentioned that by order of him who spoke, everything will be understood at the opportune time; and he whom God wills shall understand clearly, so it was fitting, since God does nothing without cause and truth. But, believe me, people cannot completely grasp the meaning of God's locutions and deeds; nor, without much error and confusion, can they determine this meaning by what appears to be so.

The prophets, entrusted with the word of God, were well aware of this. Prophecy for them was a severe trial because, as we affirmed, the people observed that a good portion of the prophecy did not come about in accord with the letter of what was said to them. As a result the people laughed at the prophets and made much fun of them. It reached such a point that Jeremiah exclaimed: *They mock me all day long, everyone scoffs at and despises me because for a long time now I have cried out against iniquity and promised them destruction, and the Lord's word has become a reproach to me and a mockery all the time. And I said: I do not have to remember him or speak any more in his name* [Jer. 20:7-9].

Although the holy prophet spoke with resignation and in the semblance of a weak man unable to suffer the changing ways of God, he herein teaches us the difference between the fulfillment of the divine locutions and the common meaning given the words. The prophets were considered seducers, and they endured such suffering because of their prophecies that Jeremiah also proclaims in another place: *Formido et laqueus facta est nobis vaticinatio et contritio* (Prophecy has become for us fear, snares, and contradiction of spirit) [Lam. 3:47].

7. When sent by God as the preacher of the destruction of Nineveh, Jonah fled because of his knowledge of the diverse meanings and causes behind God's locutions [Jon. 1:1-3]. Lest the people should make fun of him when his prophecy was unfulfilled, he fled from prophesying and waited outside the city for the entire 40 days to see if his prophecy would be fulfilled [Jon. 4:5]. Since it was not, he became extremely afflicted— to such an extent that he said to God: *Obsecro, Domine, numquid non hoc est verbum meum, cum adhuc essem in terra mea? Propter hoc praeoccupavi, ut fugerem in Tharsis* (I beseech You, Lord, was not this perhaps what I said when in my country? On this account I was contradictory and fled into Tharsis) [Jon. 4:2]. And the saint became angry and petitioned God to take away his life [Jon. 4:1,3].

8. Why, then, should we be surprised if God's locutions and revelations do not materialize as expected? Suppose God affirms or represents to an individual some promise (good or bad, pertaining to that person or to another). If this promise is based on certain causes (devotion or service

rendered to God, or offense committed against him at that time, by that person or another) and these causes remain, the promise will be accomplished. But since it is uncertain how long these causes will continue, the fulfillment of the promise is uncertain too. One should seek assurance, therefore, not in one's understanding but in faith.

CHAPTER 21

God's displeasure at requests for revelations and locutions, even though he sometimes answers them. Proofs of how he is frequently angered in spite of his condescension and response.

1. Some spiritual persons, as we said,[1] convince themselves that their curiosity to know certain things through supernatural means is good. They think this conduct is good and pleasing to God because he responds to their urgent request. Yet the truth is that, regardless of his reply, such behavior is neither good nor pleasing to God. Rather he is displeased; not only displeased but frequently angered and deeply offended.

The reason is that no creature may licitly go beyond the boundaries naturally ordained by God for its governance. He has fixed natural and rational limits by which humans are to be ruled. A desire to transcend them, hence, is unlawful, and to desire to investigate and arrive at knowledge in a supernatural way is to go beyond the natural limits. It is unlawful, consequently, and God who is offended by everything illicit is displeased.

King Ahab knew this well. For although Isaiah told him to ask in God's name for some sign, he was unwilling to do so: *Non petam, et non tentabo Dominum* (I will not ask for such a thing, nor shall I tempt God) [Is. 7:12]. For to tempt God is to desire communication with him in extraordinary ways, supernatural ways.

2. You will say: If it is true that God is displeased, why does he sometimes answer? I reply: Sometimes the devil answers; but when God answers, he does so because of the weakness of the individual who desires to advance in that way. Such persons could become sad and turn back, or imagine that God is unhappy with them, and become over-whelmed. Or there may be other motives known to God, prompted by the weaknesses of these persons. And, as a result, God sees the appropriateness of condescending with such an answer.

God also does this in the singularly sensory communion that many weak and tender souls have with him, as was mentioned above.[2] But he

---

1. In ch. 18. 7-9.
2. In ch. 18. 8.

does not act thus because he is desirous or pleased that communication with him be carried on in such a manner. Rather, he gives according to each one's mode, as we have said.[3] He is like a fountain from which people draw as much water as the jug they carry will hold. Sometimes he lets them draw water through these extraordinary spouts, but it does not follow that the desire to draw water in this way is lawful, for it belongs only to God to bestow water in this manner, when, how, and to whomever he wills, and for whatever reason he desires, and without any right on the part of the soul. Accordingly, as we asserted, he sometimes condescends to the petition of certain individuals, for they are good and simple, and he does not want to let their petition go unanswered lest they become sad. But the fact that he answers them does not mean he is pleased with this practice.

3. Here is an example to better illustrate this truth. A father of a family provides at table many different kinds of food, some better than others. One of his children will ask for a dish not of the better food, but of the first that meets the eye, and the child will do so because it knows how to eat this kind of food better than the other. Now when the father observes that his child refuses to eat the food offered to it and wants and likes only that first dish, he gives it to his child sadly so that it will not go without its meal and be unhappy.

This is the way God acted with the children of Israel when they asked him for a king. He gave them one regretfully because their having one was not good for them. Thus he said to Samuel: *Audi vocem populi in omnibus quae loquuntur tibi: non enim te abjecerunt, sed me* (I heard the voice of this people and granted them the king they requested, for they have not rejected you but have rejected me, that I might not reign over them) [1 Sm. 8:7]. God accordingly condescends to some souls, granting what is not the best for them, because they are ignorant of how to journey by any other way. Some souls obtain sensible or spiritual sweetness from God because they are incapable of eating the stronger and more solid food of the trials of the cross of his Son. He would desire them to take the cross more than any other thing.

4. I consider a desire to know things through supernatural means far worse than a desire for spiritual gratifications in the sensitive part of the soul. I fail to see how a person who tries to get knowledge in this supernatural way—as well as the one who commands this or gives consent—can help but sin, at least venially, no matter how excellent the motives or advanced in perfection that person may be. There is no necessity for any of this kind of knowledge since one can get sufficient

---

3. In ch. 17.

guidance from natural reason and from the law and doctrine of the Gospel. There is no difficulty or necessity that cannot be solved or remedied by these means, which are very pleasing to God and profitable to souls.

We should make such use of reason and the law of the Gospel that, even though—whether we desire it or not—some supernatural truths are told to us, we accept only what is in harmony with reason and the Gospel law. And then we should receive this truth, not because it is privately revealed to us, but because it is reasonable, and we should brush aside all feelings about the revelation. We ought, in fact, to consider and examine the reasonableness of the truth when it is revealed even more than when it is not, since in order to delude souls the devil says much that is true, conformed to reason, and will come to pass.

5. In all our necessities, trials, and difficulties, no better or safer aid exists for us than prayer and hope that God will provide for us by the means he desires. Scripture counsels this where we read that King Jehosaphat, deeply afflicted and surrounded by his enemies [2 Chron. 20:1-4], began to pray to God: *Cum ignoramus quod facere debeamus, hoc solum habemus residui, ut oculos nostros dirigamus ad te* (When means are lacking and reason cannot find a way of providing for our necessities, we have only to raise our eyes to you that you may provide in the manner most pleasing to you) [2 Chron. 20:12].

6. Even though God sometimes responds to these requests, he is angered. This was explained, yet some proofs from Scripture will be helpful.

In the First Book of Kings we read that while King Saul was requesting a locution from the prophet Samuel, who was already dead, this prophet appeared; yet God was angered, because Samuel immediately reproved Saul for having made such a plea: *Quare inquietasti me, ut suscitarer?* (Why have you disturbed me by making me revive?) [1 Sam. 28:15].

We are also well aware that, though God answered the children of Israel by providing the requested flesh meat, he was nonetheless seriously angered. According to the Pentateuch and David's account he immediately sent fire from heaven as a chastisement: *Adhuc escae eorum erant in ore ipsorum et ira Dei descendit super eos* (While the morsels were yet in their mouths, the anger of God descended upon them) [Ps. 78:30-31; Nm. 11:18-33].

We read, too, in the Book of Numbers that because the prophet Balaam went to the Midianites at the beckon of King Balak, God was extremely provoked with him. Although God told Balaam to go, because he had wanted to go and asked God, an angel carrying a sword appeared to him while he was on his way, desirous of killing him, and saying: *Perversa est via tua mihique contraria* (Your way is perverse and contrary to me). Because of this perversity the angel desired to kill Balaam [Nm. 22:15-33].

7. God, though angered, condescends in this and many other ways to the desires of souls. Scripture provides many testimonies and examples of this, but it is unnecessary to cite them since the matter is so clear.

I only say that the desire to communicate with God in this way is extremely dangerous—more so than I can say. The person attached to such ways will go far astray and often become greatly bewildered. Anyone who has esteemed them will understand through experience what I mean.

Besides the hardship of avoiding any error that might result from God's locutions and visions, there is also the fact that among locutions and visions there are usually many that come from the devil. For he commonly deals with the soul in the same manner as God does, imparting communications so similar to God's that, disguised among the flock like the wolf in sheep's clothing, his meddling may be hardly discernible [Mt. 7:15]. Since he says many things that are true and reasonable and turn out as predicted, people can be easily misled, thinking that the revelation must be from God since what was predicted truly comes about. These people do not realize how easy it is for someone with clear natural light to know many past or future events through their causes. Since the devil possesses this light so vividly, he can most easily deduce a particular effect from a specific cause. Yet the effect does not always materialize according to his deduction, since all causes depend upon God's will.

8. Here is an example: The devil perceives that when the earth, air, and sun have reached a certain interrelationship, they will necessarily at that time become corrupted and thereby cause a pestilence. He is also cognizant of the areas in which the pestilence will be grave and those in which it will be mild. The example, then, is that of a pestilence known in its causes. Is it a wonder, then, that the devil's prediction about a pestilence, due within six months or a year, comes true? Yet it is a prophecy of the devil. Similarly, observing that the cavities of the earth are being filled with air, he can foresee earthquakes and predict that at a particular time there will be an earthquake. This is natural knowledge for which an intellect free of the passions is sufficient, as Boethius teaches: *Si vis claro lumine cernere verum, gaudia, pelle, timorem, spemque fugato, nec dolor adsit* (If you want to know truths with natural clarity, cast aside joy, fear, hope, and sorrow).[4]

---

4. See *The Consolation of Philosophy* 1. 7.

9. Supernatural events can also be known in their causes, since divine Providence responds most certainly and justly to what the good or bad causes arising from the children of the earth demand. One can know naturally that a particular person or city, or some other factor, will reach such a point that God in his providence and justice must respond in conformity with the punishment or reward that the cause warrants. With this knowledge one can say: at this particular time God will certainly give this, or do that, or that some other event will ensue.

The holy Judith made Holofernes aware of this when, in order to persuade him that the children of Israel would be destroyed without fail, she first related their numerous sins and evil conduct, and then added: *Et quoniam haec faciunt, certum est quod in perditionem dabuntur* (Because they do these things, it is certain they will be destroyed) [Jdt. 11:7-12]. This represents knowledge of the punishment through its causes. It is like saying: Surely such sins must occasion certain punishments from the most just God. And divine Wisdom says: *Per quae quis peccat, per haec et torquetur* (Each one is punished in, or through, that by which the sin is committed) [Wis. 11:17].

10. The devil can know this not only in a natural way but also from having observed God do similar things, and he can consequently predict something and be right.

The holy Tobias also knew through its cause the coming chastisement of the city of Nineveh. He warned his son: *Behold, son, when your mother and I are dead depart from this land because it will no longer remain. Video enim quia iniquitas ejus finem dabit ei* (I see that its very evil will be the cause of its punishment, the end and destruction of everything) [Tb. 14:12-13]. Tobias and the devil were able to come to this knowledge not merely through the wickedness of the city but through experience, in observing that the Ninevites committed the sins that occasioned the destruction of both the world by the flood and the Sodomites by fire [Gn. 6:12-13; 13:13; 19:24]. Tobias, however, also knew this through divine inspiration.

11. The devil can learn and foretell that Peter's life will naturally last only a certain number of years. And he can determine many other events through such various ways that we would never finish recounting them all, nor could we even begin to explain many because of their intricacy and the devil's craftiness in inserting lies. One cannot be liberated from him without fleeing from all revelations, visions, and supernatural communications.

God is rightly angered with anyone who admits them, for he sees the rashness of exposing oneself to this danger, presumption, curiosity, and pride, to the root and foundation of vainglory, to contempt for the things of God, and to the beginning of the numerous evils into which many fall.

God becomes so angry with these individuals that he purposely allows them to go astray, experience delusion, suffer spiritual darkness, and abandon the established ways of life, by delivering themselves over to their vanities and fancies. Isaiah affirms: *Dominus miscuit in medio ejus spiritum vertiginis* [Is. 19:14]. This is like saying: The Lord has mingled in their midst the spirit of dissension and confusion, which in plain words means the spirit of misunderstanding. Isaiah manifestly says this in accord with our teaching because he refers to those who are striving for supernatural knowledge of future events. As a result he asserts that God mingled in their midst a spirit of misconstruing everything, not because God desired this or really gave them this spirit of error, but because they were desirous of knowing what was naturally unattainable. Provoked by this, God allowed them to go astray and gave no enlightenment concerning this matter in which he did not want them to meddle. Thus Isaiah proclaims that by way of privation God commingled in their midst that spirit of dissension. Accordingly, God is the cause of that harm; that is, the privative cause, which consists in his withdrawing his light and favor to such an extent that they necessarily fall into error.

12. In this way God permits the devil to blind and delude many who merit this by their sins and audacities. The devil is able and successful to the extent that others believe what he says and consider him a good spirit. So firm is their belief that it is impossible for anyone who tries to persuade them of the diabolic origin. For with God's permission they have already been affected by the spirit of misunderstanding. We read that this happened to the prophets of King Ahab whom God allowed to be deluded by the lying spirit. He permitted the devil to lie, saying: *Decipies, et praevalebis; egredere, et fac ita* (You shall prevail with your lie and deceive them; go out and do it thus) [1 Kgs. 22:22]. The devil deceived the prophets and king so successfully that they were unwilling to believe the prophet Micaiah who spoke the truth, which was very much the opposite of what the others had prophesied. That God allowed them to be blinded is the explanation of their unbelief, for in their attachment they wanted events to happen and God to answer according to their own desires and appetites. This was the surest means and preparation for God to abandon them to blindness and deception.

13. Ezekiel prophesied about this in God's name. He censured the curious one who in vanity of spirit desires knowledge in a divine way: *When this man asks the prophet to inquire of me for him, I myself, the Lord, shall answer, and I will set my angry countenance upon that man. And when the prophet shall err in his reply, Ego Dominus decepi prophetam illum* (I the Lord have deceived that prophet) [Ez. 14:7-9]. This signifies that God does not concur with his help to prevent that man's deception; such is the meaning of the

words: I, the Lord, angered, will myself answer (withdraw my grace and favor from such a man). Deception necessarily follows when one is forsaken by God. The devil then intervenes, answering in harmony with that person's desire and pleasure; and since the devil's replies and communications are pleasing and satisfactory, that man will let himself become seriously deluded.

14. We have seemingly wandered somewhat from the matter proposed in the title of this chapter: proofs that although God answers he sometimes is unhappy about it. Nonetheless, if everything we mentioned is thoroughly considered, it will contribute to the proof of our assertion. For in all this it is seen that God is displeased with the desire for these visions because he permits souls to be deceived in so many ways.

CHAPTER 22

Resolving a doubt about why in the law of grace it is not permitted to question God through supernatural means as it was in the old law. Proof from St. Paul.

1. Questions keep springing up so that we are unable to make the rapid progress we would like. Since we raise them, we necessarily have the obligation to answer them so the truth of the doctrine will remain clear and vigorous. These questions have this advantage that, although they slow up our progress, they are still an aid to greater clarity and to further explanations about our subject. Such is the case with this question.[1]

2. In the last chapter we affirmed that it was not God's will that souls desire supernatural communication of distinct knowledge from visions and locutions, and so on. On the other hand, in the testimonies from Scripture, we saw that this kind of communication with God was lawful and made use of in the old law. Not only was this licit, but God commanded it. When the people did not comply, God reproved them. An example of this is seen in Isaiah when the children of Israel desired to descend into Egypt without first asking God; and he thus reprehended them: *Et os meum non interrogastis* (You did not first ask from my mouth what was suitable) [Is. 30:2]. We also read in Joshua that when the children of Israel were deceived by the Gibeonites, the Holy Spirit reminded them of this fault: *Susceperunt ergo de cibariis eorum, et os Domini non interrogaverunt* (They took their food without consulting the mouth of the Lord) [Jos. 9:2-14].

We observe in Sacred Scripture that Moses, King David, and the kings

---

1. This chapter is basic to the understanding of John's thought, and especially his Christology.

of Israel, in their wars and necessities, and the priests and ancients always questioned God, and that he replied and spoke to them without becoming angry. And they had done well if they questioned him, but if they failed to do so they were at fault. This is true. Why, then, in the new law of grace is it different than it was previously?

3. In answer to this, the chief reason in the old law that the inquiries made of God were licit, and the prophets and priests appropriately desired visions and revelations from him, was that at that time faith was not yet perfectly grounded, nor was the Gospel law established. It was necessary for them to question God, and for him to respond sometimes by words, sometimes through visions and revelations, now in figures and likenesses, now through many other kinds of signs. All his answers, locutions, and revelations concerned mysteries of our faith or matters touching on or leading up to it. Since the truths of faith are not derived from other humans but from the mouth of God (for he speaks them through his own mouth), it was required of them to seek an answer from the mouth of God. He therefore reproved them because in their affairs they did not seek counsel from his mouth, that he might answer and direct them toward the unknown and as yet unfounded faith.

But in this era of grace, now that the faith is established through Christ and the Gospel law made manifest, there is no reason for inquiring of him in this way, or expecting him to answer as before. In giving us his Son, his only Word (for he possesses no other), he spoke everything to us at once in this sole Word—and he has no more to say.

4. This is the meaning of that passage where St. Paul tries to persuade the Hebrews to turn from communion with God through the old ways of the Mosaic law and instead fix their eyes on Christ: *Multifariam multisque modis olim Deus loquens patribus in prophetis: novissime autem diebus istis locutus est nobis in Filio* (That which God formerly spoke to our fathers through the prophets in many ways and manners, now, finally, in these days he has spoken to us all at once in his Son) [Heb. 1:1-2]. The Apostle indicates that God has become as it were mute, with no more to say, because what he spoke before to the prophets in parts, he has now spoken all at once by giving us the All, who is his Son.

5. Those who now desire to question God or receive some vision or revelation are guilty not only of foolish behavior but also of offending him by not fixing their eyes entirely on Christ and by living with the desire for some other novelty.

God could answer as follows: If I have already told you all things in my Word, my Son, and if I have no other word, what answer or revelation can I now make that would surpass this? Fasten your eyes on him alone because in him I have spoken and revealed all and in him you will discover even more than you ask for and desire. You are making an appeal for locutions and revelations that are incomplete, but if you turn your eyes to him you will find them complete. For he is my entire locution and response, vision and revelation, which I have already spoken, answered, manifested, and revealed to you by giving him to you as a brother, companion, master, ransom, and reward.[2] On that day when I descended on him with my Spirit on Mount Tabor proclaiming: *Hic est filius meus dilectus in quo mihi bene complacui, ipsum audite* (This is my beloved Son in whom I am well pleased, hear him) [Mt. 17:5], I gave up these methods of answering and teaching and presented them to him. Hear him because I have no more faith to reveal or truths to manifest. If I spoke before, it was to promise Christ. If they questioned me, their inquiries were related to their petitions and longings for Christ in whom they were to obtain every good, as is now explained in all the doctrine of the evangelists and apostles. But now those who might ask me in that way and desire that I speak and reveal something to them would somehow be requesting Christ again and more faith, yet they would be failing in faith because it has already been given in Christ. Accordingly, they would offend my beloved Son deeply because they would not merely be failing him in faith, but obliging him to become incarnate and undergo his life and death again. You will not find anything to ask or desire of me through revelations and visions. Behold him well, for in him you will uncover all of these already made and given, and many more.

6. If you desire me to answer with a word of comfort, behold my Son subject to me and to others out of love for me, and afflicted, and you will see how much he answers you. If you desire me to declare some secret truths or events to you, fix your eyes only on him and you will discern hidden in him the most secret mysteries, and wisdom, and wonders of God, as my Apostle proclaims: *In quo sunt omnes thesauri sapientiae et scientiae Dei absconditi* (In the Son of God are hidden all the treasures of the wisdom and knowledge of God) [Col. 2:3]. These treasures of wisdom and knowledge will be for you far more sublime, delightful, and advantageous than what you want to know.[3] The Apostle, therefore, gloried, affirming that he had acted as though he knew no other than Jesus Christ and him crucified [1 Cor. 2:2]. And if you should seek other divine or corporeal visions and revelations, behold him, become human, and you

---

2. This seems to be inspired by stanza 4 of Aquinas's liturgical hymn *Verbum supernum* for the feast of Corpus Christi: *Se nascens dedit socium* (companion)/ *convescens in edulium/se moriens in pretium* (ransom)/*se regnans dat in praemium*(reward). John adds brother and master to these.
3. For a beautiful commentary on this same text, cf. C. 37. 4.

will find more than you imagine. For the Apostle also says: *In ipso habitat omnis plenitudo Divinitatis corporealiter* (In Christ all the fullness of the divinity dwells bodily) [Col. 2:9].

7. One should not, then, inquire of God in this manner, nor is it necessary for God to speak any more. Since he has finished revealing the faith through Christ, there is no more faith to reveal, nor will there ever be. Anyone wanting to get something in a supernatural way, as we stated,[4] would as it were be accusing God of not having given us in his Son all that is required. Although in having these desires one presupposes the faith and believes in it, still, that curiosity displays a lack of faith. Hence there is no reason to hope for doctrine or anything else through supernatural means.

When Christ dying on the cross exclaimed: *Consummatum est* (It is consummated) [Jn. 19:30], he consummated not these ways alone, but all the other ceremonies and rites of the old law. Thus we must be guided humanly and visibly in all by the law of Christ, who is human, and that of his Church and of his ministers. This is the way to remedy our spiritual ignorances and weaknesses. Here we shall find abundant medicine for them all. Any departure from this road is not only curiosity but extraordinary boldness. One should not believe anything coming in a supernatural way, but believe only the teaching of Christ who is human, as I say, and of his ministers who are human. So true is this that St. Paul insists: *Quod si angelus de coelo evangelizaverit, praeterquam quod evangelizavimus vobis, anathema sit* (If an angel from heaven should preach to you any Gospel other than that which we humans have preached, let him be accursed and excommunicated) [Gal. 1:8].

8. Since it is true that one must ever adhere to Christ's teaching, and that everything unconformed to it is nothing and worthy of disbelief, anyone who desires to commune with God after the manner of old law is walking in vain.

We see even more how true this is when we recall that it was not lawful at that time for just anyone to question God; nor did God give an answer to just anyone, but only to the priests and prophets from whom the multitude were to learn the law and doctrine. Those eager to know something from God did not ask themselves but through a prophet or priest. If David sometimes asked himself, it was because he was a prophet. But even then he did not do so without being clothed in priestly vestments, as is evident in the First Book of Kings when he said to Ahimelech the priest: *Applica ad me Ephod* [1 Sm. 23:9]. The ephod was the most dignified of the priest's vestments, and David wore it for

---

4. In ch. 21. 11-14.

consultation with God. At other times he consulted God through the prophet Nathan or through other prophets. And through the mouth of these prophets and priests the people were to believe that God spoke to them, not through their own opinion.

9. What God said at that time did not have the authority or force to induce complete belief unless approved by the priests and prophets. God is so pleased that the rule and direction of humans be through other humans and that a person be governed by natural reason that he definitely does not want us to bestow entire credence on his supernatural communications, or be confirmed in their strength and security, until they pass through this human channel of the mouth of another human person. As often as he reveals something to individuals, he confers on them a kind of inclination to manifest this to the appropriate person. Until people do this they usually go without complete satisfaction, for they have not received this knowledge from another human like themselves.

In Judges we see that this happened to the captain Gideon. Though God had often told him that he would be conqueror of the Midianites, Gideon nonetheless remained doubtful and cowardly since God left him in that weakness until he had heard through the mouth of other humans what God had revealed to him. Since God saw that Gideon was weak, God declared: Rise up and go down to the camp; ...*et cum audieris quid loquantur, tunc confortabuntur manus tuae, et securior ad hostium castra descendes* (when you hear what the men are saying there, you shall get strength from what I have told you, and you will descend more securely to the enemy host) [Jgs. 7:9-11]. And it happened that when Gideon heard of a Midianite's dream about the future victory, he was deeply strengthened; and full of gladness he prepared for the battle [Jgs. 7:13-15]. Evidently, then, God did not want Gideon to receive assurance through supernatural means alone, for until Gideon had certitude through natural means, God did not bestow on him a feeling of security.

10. And still more wondrous is what happened in a similar instance to Moses. Even though God had commanded him with many persuasive arguments to go and bring about the liberation of the children of Israel, and had confirmed these arguments with signs from the rod that was changed into a serpent and from the leprous hand [Ex. 4:2-4, 6-10], he was so weak and doubtful about this mission that, in spite of God's anger [Ex. 4:14], he did not possess the courage to give strong credence to the mission until heartened by God through his brother Aaron: *Aaron frater tuus Levites, scio quod eloquens sit: Ecce ipse egredietur in occursum tuum, vidensque te, laetabitur corde. Loquere ad eum, et pone verba mea in ore ejus, et ego ero in ore tuo, et in ore illius* (I know that your brother Aaron is an

eloquent man: Behold, he will go to meet you and at sight of you sincerely rejoice. Speak and tell him all my words, and I will be in your mouth and in his so that each of you will receive certitude through the mouth of the other) [Ex. 4:14-15].

11. At these words Moses was immediately encouraged in the hope of the comfort he was to obtain from his brother's counsel [Ex. 4:18]. This is the trait of humble people: They do not dare deal with God independently, nor can they be completely satisfied without human counsel and direction. God wants this, for to declare and strengthen truth on the basis of natural reason, he draws near those who come together in an endeavor to know it. He indicated this by asserting that he would be in the mouth of both Aaron and Moses when they were together for consultation.

This is why he also affirmed in the Gospel: *Ubi fuerint duo vel tres congregati in nomine meo, ibi sum ego in medio eorum* (Where two or three are gathered to consider what is for the greater honor and glory of my name, there I am in the midst of them—that is, clarifying and confirming truths in their hearts) [Mt. 18:20]. It is noteworthy that he did not say: Where there is one alone, there I am; rather, he said: Where there are at least two. Thus God announces that he does not want the soul to believe only by itself the communications it thinks are of divine origin, or for anyone to be assured or confirmed in them without the Church or her ministers. God will not bring clarification and confirmation of the truth to the heart of one who is alone. Such a person would remain weak and cold in regard to truth.

12. This is what Ecclesiastes extols: *Vae soli, quia cum ceciderit, non habet sublevantem se. Si dormierint duo, favebuntur mutuo: Unus quomodo calefiet? et si quispiam praevaluerit contra unum, duo resistent ei* [Eccl. 4:10-12]. This means: Woe to those who are alone, for when they fall they have no one to lift them up. If two sleep together, the one shall give warmth (the warmth of God who is in their midst) to the other; how shall one alone be warm? How shall one alone stop being cold in the things of God? And if one prevails and overcomes the other (that is, if the devil prevails and overcomes anyone who may desire to remain alone in the things of God), two together will resist the devil. And these are the disciple and the master who come together to know the truth and practice it. Until consulting another, one will usually experience only tepidity and weakness in the truth, no matter how much may have been heard from God. This is so true that even after St. Paul had been preaching the Gospel, which he heard not from humans but from God [Gal. 1:12] for a long time, he could not resist going and conferring about it with St. Peter and the apostles: *ne forte in vanum currerem aut cucurrissem* (lest he should run or might have run in vain) [Gal. 2:2]. He did not feel secure until he had

received assurance from other people. This, then, seems remarkable, O Paul! Could not he who revealed the Gospel to you also give security from any error you might make in preaching its truth?

13. This text clearly teaches that there is no assurance in God's revelations save through the means we are describing. Even though individuals have certitude that the revelation is of divine origin—as St. Paul had of his Gospel, since he had already begun to preach it—they can still err in regard to the object of the revelation or its circumstances. Even though God reveals one factor, he does not always manifest the other. Often he will reveal something without telling how to accomplish it. He usually does not effect or reveal to people what can be arrived at through human effort or counsel, even though he may frequently and affably commune with them. St. Paul understood this clearly since, as we are saying, he went to confer about the Gospel in spite of his knowledge that it was divinely revealed.

This is evident, too, in Exodus. Even though God conversed familiarly with Moses, he never gave him that salutary counsel that Moses received from his father-in-law Jethro: that he select other judges as helpers so the people would not be waiting from morning till night [Ex. 18:13-23]. God approved this advice. But he did not give it, because human reason and judgment were sufficient means for solving this problem. Usually God does not manifest such matters through visions, revelations, and locutions, because he is ever desirous that insofar as possible people take advantage of their own reasoning powers. All matters must be regulated by reason save those of faith, which though not contrary to reason transcend it.

14. People should not imagine that just because God and the saints converse amiably with them on many subjects, they will be told their particular faults, for they can come to the knowledge of these through other means. Hence there is no motive for assurance, for we read in the Acts of the Apostles what happened to St. Peter. Though he was a prince of the Church and received immediate instruction from God, he was mistaken about a certain ceremony practiced among the Gentiles. And God was so silent that St. Paul reproved Peter: *Cum vidissem, quod non recte ad veritatem Evangelii ambularent, dixi coram omnibus: Si tu judaeus cum sis, gentiliter vivis, quomodo gentes cogis judaizare?* (As I noticed that the disciples were not walking rightly according to the truth of the Gospel, I said to Peter in front of them all: If you being a Jew, as you are, live as a Gentile, why do you force the Gentiles to live as the Jews?) [Gal. 2:14]. God did not himself inform St. Peter of this fault, because that simulation was rationally discernible.

15. On judgment day God will punish the faults and sins of many with whom he communed familiarly here below and to whom he imparted much light and power, for they neglected their obligations and trusted in their converse with him and the power he bestowed on them. As Christ declares in the Gospel, they will then be surprised and plead: *Domine, Domine, nonne in nomine tuo prophetavimus et in nomine tuo daemonia ejecimus, et in nomine tuo virtutes multas fecimus?* (Lord, Lord, did we not speak in your name the prophecies you spoke to us, and did we not cast out devils in your name and perform many miracles and prodigies?) [Mt. 7:22]. And the Lord states that his reply will be: *Et tunc confitebor illis, quia numquam novi vos: discedite a me omnes qui operamini iniquitatem* (Depart from me, workers of iniquity, for I have never known you) [Mt. 7:23].

Among the workers of iniquity were the prophet Balaam and others like him. Although God spoke with them and bestowed favors on them, they were sinners [Num. 22-24]. But the Lord will also in due proportion, because of their faults and neglects, reprove his friends and chosen ones with whom he conversed familiarly here on earth. It was unnecessary for God himself to inform them of these faults, since he had already done so through the natural law and the reasoning powers he had bestowed on them.

16. I deduce in concluding this part that whatever is received through supernatural means (in whatever manner) should immediately be told clearly, integrally, and simply to one's spiritual master. It may appear that there is no reason for a manifestation to one's spiritual director, or that doing so would be a waste of time since, as we pointed out,[5] one is safe by not wanting these communications, by rejecting and paying no attention to them. This seems especially so in this matter of visions or revelations or other supernatural communications, since either they are clear or it matters little if they are not. Yet it is always necessary to manifest the entire communication even though there is no apparent reason for so doing. This requirement is based on three reasons:

First, the effect, light, strength, and security of many divine communications are not completely confirmed in a soul, as we stated,[6] until it discusses them with one whom God has destined to be spiritual judge over it, who has power to bind, loose, approve, and reprove. We have established this principle through the texts cited above, and through experience we see it verified each day. We witness humble recipients of these experiences obtain new satisfaction, strength, light, and security after consulting about them with the proper person. This is so true that

5. In reference to the different kinds of knowledge dealt with in the preceding chapters beginning with ch. 11.
6. Cf. especially chs. 19-21 and the preceding nos. 10-15.

to some it seems that these communications neither take root nor belong to them until they confer about them and that the communications are then seemingly imparted anew.

17. Second, a soul ordinarily needs instruction pertinent to its experience in order to be guided through the dark night to spiritual denudation and poverty. Without this instruction a person, even without wanting such things, would unknowingly become hardened in the way of the spirit and habituated to that of the senses, in which these communications are partly experienced.

18. Third, for the sake of humility, submission, and mortification, individuals should give a complete account to their director, even if the director disregards or shows no esteem for these communications. Because such communications seem to these individuals to be of little importance, or because of concern about the director's possible reaction, some may dread to tell their director about them. This indicates a lack of humility, and for that very reason one should submit to the ordeal. Others feel abashed about manifesting these favors lest they appear to be saints on account of these experiences, and because of other difficulties they feel in speaking about them. They think that because they themselves pay no attention to these experiences, relating them to their director is unnecessary. But because of this very hardship they ought to mortify themselves and tell their director, and thereby become humble, simple, meek, and prompt in relating these communications. And from then on they will always do so easily.

19. It ought to be noted in this regard that, even though we have greatly stressed rejection of these communications and the duty of confessors to forbid souls from making them a topic of conversation, spiritual fathers should not show severity, displeasure, or scorn in dealing with these souls. With such an attitude they would make them cower and shrink from a manifestation of these experiences, would close the door to these souls, and cause them many difficulties. Since God is leading them by this means, there is no reason to oppose it or become frightened or scandalized over it. The spiritual father should instead proceed with much kindness and calm. He should give these souls encouragement and the opportunity to speak about their experiences, and, if necessary, oblige them to do so, for at times everything is needful on account of the hardship some find in discussing these matters.

Spiritual directors should guide them in the way of faith by giving them good instructions on how to turn their eyes from all these things and on their obligation to denude their appetite and spirit of these communications in order to advance. They should explain how one act done in charity is more precious in God's sight than all the visions and communications possible—since these imply neither merit nor demerit—and how it is that many individuals who have not received these experiences are incomparably more advanced than others who have received many.[7]

CHAPTER 23

Begins the discussion of the intellectual apprehensions that come in a purely spiritual way. Tells what they are.

1. Though our doctrine on the intellectual apprehensions that come from the senses is somewhat brief in comparison with what it ought to be, I have not wanted to enlarge on the matter any more. I believe, rather, that my explanation has been longer than necessary in view of the goal I have in mind, which is to liberate the intellect from these apprehensions and direct it to the night of faith.

Now we will embark on a discussion of those other four kinds of intellectual apprehensions: visions, revelations, locutions, and spiritual feelings. In chapter 10 we called these apprehensions purely spiritual because they are not communicated to the intellect through the corporeal senses as are imaginative corporeal visions. They are clearly, distinctly, and supernaturally imparted to the intellect without any of the exterior or interior bodily senses serving as means; and this is done passively, that is, without the soul's positing any act, at least through its own effort.

2. Let it be known that in a broad sense these four kinds of apprehensions can all be titled visions of the soul because we also call the understanding of the soul its vision. And insofar as all these apprehensions are intelligible, they are called spiritually visible.[1] Accordingly, the understanding formed from them in the intellect can be termed intellectual vision. The objects of the other senses (of sight, hearing, smell, taste, and touch) are objects of the intellect insofar as they bear relation to

---

7. After having forcefully demonstrated that in the Christian plan little attention should be paid to visions and other extraordinary communications, John concludes that nevertheless God communes with each person as he deems best and that the supreme norm is to discover the style in which God is leading one. Strict, then, in his principles, John shows gentleness and flexibility in applying them to the individual case.

1. John adopts the scholastic terminology that considers the apprehensive action of the intellect to be like a vision. In a way analogous to the vision of the bodily eye, the intellect sees what it understands or grasps. Hence he speaks of the intellectual vision.

truth or falsehood. And just as all that is corporeally visible to the material eye causes corporeal vision, so all that is intelligible to the intellect, the spiritual eye of the soul, causes spiritual vision. For, as we said, understanding an object is seeing it. Thus, speaking generally, we can call these four apprehensions visions. This could not be done with the other senses, because none of them is capable of perceiving the object as such of any of the others.

3. But since these apprehensions reach the soul in ways similar to those of the other senses, we can, properly and specifically speaking, apply the term vision to whatever the intellect receives in a manner resembling sight, because the intellect can see objects spiritually just as the eyes can corporeally. And what the intellect receives as though by learning and understanding something new (just as the ears do on hearing what has never before been heard) we call revelation. And what it receives in a way similar to hearing we call a locution. And what it receives after the manner of the other senses, such as the knowledge of a sweet spiritual fragrance, spiritual savor, or spiritual delight that the soul can enjoy supernaturally, we call spiritual feelings. The intellect derives knowledge or spiritual vision from all these communications, without the apprehension of any form, image, or figure of the natural imagination or phantasy. For these experiences are bestowed immediately upon the soul by a supernatural work and by a supernatural means.[2]

4. As was the case with the imaginative corporeal apprehensions, we must disencumber the intellect of these spiritual apprehensions by guiding and directing it past them into the spiritual night of faith, to divine and substantial union with God, lest the solitude and denudation concerning all things, which is a requisite for this union, be impeded by the hindrance and weakness these apprehensions occasion. These apprehensions are nobler, safer, and more advantageous than the imaginative corporeal visions because they are already interior, purely spiritual, and less exposed to the devil's meddling. They are more purely and delicately communicated to the soul and involve none of its own work or imagination—at least not active work. Nonetheless, through lack of caution and by treading such a path, the intellect might be not merely encumbered but highly deceived.

---

2. John speaks of spiritual experiences that are analogous to sense experiences and so of spiritual senses. He completes his classification and applications in ch. 32. Doctrine about the spiritual senses goes back to Origen and Gregory of Nyssa. We find references to these senses in Augustine and the Cistercian mystics. But it is in the theology of Bonaventure that doctrine on the spiritual senses is fully integrated into a system. John's poetic symbols frequently bear the influence of his experiences that came as though through spiritual senses. Cf. e.g. C. 14-15.

5. As a general conclusion, we could give the same counsel for these four kinds of apprehensions that we accorded for the others: they should be the object of neither our aims nor our desires. Yet it can be worthwhile to discuss these apprehensions in particular in order to explain some points about each of them and shed more light on the practice of this counsel. And so we will deal with the first kind, the spiritual or intellectual visions.

CHAPTER 24

Two kinds of supernatural, spiritual visions.

1. Speaking properly, now, of spiritual visions (those that exclude the bodily senses), I find that there are two kinds relating to the intellect: those of corporeal substances, and those of separate or incorporeal substances.

The corporeal visions deal with the material things of heaven and earth. The soul, even while in the body, can see these objects by means of a certain supernatural light derived from God that bestows the power of seeing all heavenly and earthly objects that are absent. We read of such a vision in chapter 21 of the Apocalypse where St. John relates the description and excellence of the heavenly Jerusalem that he beheld as it descended from heaven. We also read that St. Benedict viewed the entire world in a spiritual vision. St. Thomas in the first *Quodlibetum* affirms that this vision was received through a light from above, as we stated.[1]

2. The other visions, those of incorporeal substances, cannot be seen by means of this light derived from God, but by another, higher light, called the light of glory. These visions of incorporeal substances (angels and souls) do not occur in this life, nor can we while in this mortal body view such substances. If God should desire to let the soul see these substances essentially (as they are in themselves), it would immediately depart from the body and be loosed from this mortal life.

God, when asked to show his essence, proclaimed to Moses: *Non videbit me homo, et vivet* (No human person can see me and be able to remain alive) [Ex. 33:20]. When the children of Israel thought they were going to see God, or that they had seen him or some angel, they were afraid of dying. We read of this in Exodus where they fearfully exclaimed: *Non loquatur nobis Dominus, ne forte moriamur* (May God not openly communicate himself to us, lest we die) [Ex. 20:19]. In the Book of Judges we read also that Manoah, Samson's father, thinking he and his wife had seen in

---

1. See St. Gregory the Great, *Dialogus* 2. 35. in Migne, PL 66. 198; Aquinas, *Quodlibetum* 1. 1. ad 1.

its essence the angel that had appeared to them as a most handsome man, declared to his wife: *Morte moriemur, quia vidimus Dominum* (We shall die because we have seen the Lord) [Jgs. 13:22].

3. These visions do not occur in this life, unless in some rare cases and in a transient way. In such an instance, through a dispensation of the natural law, God preserves the nature and life of the individual, abstracts the spirit entirely, and by his own power supplies the natural functions of the soul toward the body.

When, as is the opinion, St. Paul saw them (the separated substances in the third heaven), he accordingly declared: *Sive in corpore, sive extra corpus nescio; Deus scit* (that he was carried up to them, and he does not know if he saw them while in the body or out of the body, God knows) [2 Cor. 12:2,4]. Clearly he was transported above the ways of our natural life through the intervention of God. Also when God, as is believed, revealed his essence to Moses, he declared he would place Moses in the cleft of the rock and cover him with his right hand to protect him from death when the divine glory passed by. This passing indicates both God's transitory manifestation of himself and the concomitant preservation, with his right hand, of Moses' natural life [Ex. 33:22].

Such substantial visions as those of St. Paul, Moses, and our Father Elijah (when he covered his face at the whistling of the gentle breeze of God) [1 Kgs. 19:11-13], even though transitory, occur rarely or hardly ever, and to only a few. For God imparts this kind of vision only to those who are very strong in the spirit of the Church and God's law, as were these three.

4. Though these spiritual substances cannot be unclothed and seen clearly in this life by the intellect, they can nonetheless be felt in the substance of the soul by the most delightful touches and conjunctions. These pertain to the category of spiritual feelings, which with God's help we will discuss later.[2]

For we are directing and guiding our pen toward these, that is, to the divine conjunction and union of the soul with the divine substance. We will speak about this when dealing with the vague or dark mystical knowledge (yet to be expounded) and treating of how, by means of this loving and obscure knowledge, God joins himself to the soul in a high and divine degree. In a way this dark loving knowledge, which is faith,

---

2. The touches were not included in classifying the spiritual feelings in ch. 23. 3; John mentions them now for the first time. Belonging to spiritual feelings, they are experienced in the substance of the soul. He plans a special discussion of them but unfortunately never realizes his plan. Nonetheless he does speak of them, in passing, in many places. But one must be attentive; not all the touches he speaks of are the same as the substantial touches. Cf. ch. 26. 4.

serves as a means for divine union in this life, as does the light of glory for the clear vision of God in the next.[3]

5. Let us discuss now the visions of corporeal substances received spiritually in the soul in a way similar to that of bodily visions. As the eyes behold corporeal objects by means of natural light, so the intellect through supernatural light, as we said,[4] sees interiorly these same objects and others too according to God's wishes. The difference between the two kinds of visions lies in the mode and manner.

Spiritual and intellectual visions are far clearer and more delicate than corporeal ones, for when God desires to bestow this favor upon a soul, he communicates that supernatural light we mentioned so that through it the soul may behold with greater facility and clarity the earthly and heavenly objects he desires it to see. The absence or presence of these objects, then, is of no importance, nor does this hinder the vision. The vision takes place at times as though a door were opened and the soul could see as it would if a flash of lightning were to illumine the dark night and momentarily make objects clearly and distinctly visible, only to leave them all in darkness again, although the forms and images of these objects would remain in the phantasy. This illumination takes place far more perfectly in the soul, for the objects seen in that light are so impressed on it that as often as it adverts to them it beholds them as it did before, just as the forms reflected in a mirror are seen as often as one looks in it. And those objects of the soul's vision are impressed so strongly that they are never entirely removed, although in the course of time they do become somewhat more remote.

6. The effects these visions produce in the soul are: quietude, illumination, happiness resembling that of glory, delight, purity, love, humility, and an elevation and inclination toward God. Sometimes these effects are more intense, sometimes less; sometimes one effect predominates, at other times another. This diversity is due to the spirit that receives them and to God's wishes.

7. Through spiritual suggestion and by means of a certain natural

---

3. John does not fulfill this promise to treat specifically of mystical knowledge. Here in passing he mentions the key themes of his entire work: union with God, the goal to which he is leading the soul; mystical knowledge, the equivalent of both contemplation and the general or dark loving knowledge; faith, which is identified with this dark loving knowledge and serves as the means of union just as the light of glory does for the beatific vision. When faith becomes a "highly illumined faith" through its intensification or purification, it surpasses the general or dark loving knowledge spoken of in chs. 12-15.
4. In no. 1.

light, the devil can also cause these visions in the soul, whether the objects be present or absent. The account in St. Matthew that tells of the devil showing Christ *omnia regna mundi et gloriam eorum* (all the kingdoms of the world and their glory) [Mt. 4:8] is explained by some doctors as an example of spiritual suggestion by the devil because it would have been impossible for him to make Christ see with his bodily eyes all the kingdoms of the world and their glory.

A great difference lies between diabolical and divine visions, for the effects of diabolical visions are unlike those produced by the divine. The devil's visions produce spiritual dryness in one's communion with God and an inclination to self-esteem, to admitting them and considering them important. In no way do they cause the mildness of humility and the love of God. Neither are the forms of these diabolical visions impressed with a delicate clarity upon the soul, as are the others. These impressed forms are not lasting, but are soon obliterated from the soul, except when its esteem causes a natural remembrance of them. But the memory of them is considerably arid, and does not produce the love and humility caused by the remembrance of the good visions.

8. These visions cannot serve the intellect as a proximate means for union with God because they deal with creatures, which bear no proportion or essential conformity to God. Consequently, to advance by the proximate means, which is faith, a person should behave in a purely negative way as with the other visions we mentioned. Souls should not store up or treasure the forms of these visions impressed within, neither should they have the desire to cling to them. In doing so they would impede themselves by what dwells within them (those forms, images, and figures of persons), and they would not journey to God through the negation of all things. Though these forms remain impressed within the soul, they are not a great impediment if one is unwilling to pay heed to them. Even if the remembrance of these visions really does stir the soul to some contemplation and love of God, denudation, pure faith, and darkness regarding them will stir and elevate it much more, and without its knowing how or whence this elevation comes.

It will happen that a person will be enkindled with anxieties of very pure love without knowing their origin or foundation. The reason for this is that just as faith is infused and rooted more deeply in the soul by means of that emptiness, darkness, and nakedness regarding all things, or by spiritual poverty (which are all the same), so too the charity of God is simultaneously infused and deeply rooted in the soul. The more individuals desire darkness and annihilation of themselves regarding all visions, exteriorly or interiorly receivable, the greater will be the infusion of faith and consequently of love and hope, since these three theological virtues increase together.

9. But a person does not always grasp or feel this love, because it does not reside with tenderness in the senses, but resides in the soul with properties of strength and of greater courage and daring than before, though at times it overflows into the senses, imparting a gentle, tender feeling. Accordingly, to attain that love, happiness, and joy caused and produced in the soul by these visions, individuals should possess fortitude, mortification, and love so as to remain in emptiness and darkness regarding all creatures. They should base their love and joy on what they neither see nor feel (nor are capable of seeing or feeling), that is, upon God who is incomprehensible and transcendent. This is why it behooves us to go to God through the negation of all. Even if individuals are so shrewd, humble, and strong that the devil is unable to deceive them by these visions or make them (as he usually does) fall into any presumption, the visions will be an obstacle to their advancement if they fail to practice this denial, since visions are an impediment to spiritual nakedness, poverty of spirit, and emptiness in faith; these are the requisites for union with God.

10. Since the same doctrine we taught about supernatural sensory visions and apprehensions in chapters 19 and 20 is valid also for these visions, we will not spend any more time here in their discussion.[5]

CHAPTER 25

The nature and kinds of revelation.

1. Logically, our next discussion should deal with the second kind of spiritual apprehensions, which are termed revelations and, properly speaking, belong to the spirit of prophecy.
First it should be understood that a revelation is nothing else than the disclosure of some hidden truth, or the manifestation of some secret or mystery, as when God imparts understanding of some truth to the intellect, or discloses to the soul something that he did, is doing, or is thinking of doing.[1]

2. We can affirm, therefore, the existence of two kinds of revelation: first, the disclosure of truths to the intellect (these are properly called intellectual notions or concepts); second, the manifestation of secrets. The term revelation is more properly applied to these latter than to the former. The first kind cannot strictly speaking be called revelations, since

5. The reference should be chs. 17 and 18; ch. 16 also deals with this topic.
1. Cf. C. 14. 15. Linking revelations with the spirit of prophecy corresponds to the thomist outline; cf. Aquinas, *Summa theologiae* 2-2. 171-174.

in them God bestows clear and manifest understanding of naked truths, not only of temporal but of spiritual objects as well. I desire to discuss these under the heading of revelations because of their close alliance and affinity with them, and to avoid a multiplication of divisions.

3. As a result we can divide revelations into two classes of apprehensions: One we shall call intellectual knowledge, and the other, manifestation of God's secrets and hidden mysteries. Beginning with intellectual knowledge, we will deal with these as briefly as possible in the following two chapters.

CHAPTER 26

The two kinds of knowledge of naked truths. The proper conduct of the soul in their regard.

1. For an adequate exposition of this subject (the knowledge of naked truths), God would have to move my hand and pen. For you should know, beloved reader, that what they in themselves are for the soul is beyond words. Since, however, my purpose in speaking of these is only to impart instruction and guide the soul through them to divine union, let me discuss them in a brief and restricted way, which will be sufficient for our purpose.[1]

2. This kind of vision (knowledge of naked truths) is far different from the kind we just dealt with in chapter 24. This intellectual vision is not like the vision of corporeal objects, but rather consists of an intellectual understanding and vision of truths about God, or a vision of present, past, or future events that bears great resemblance to the spirit of prophecy, as we shall perhaps explain later.[2]

3. This type of knowledge is divided into two kinds: The object of one kind is the Creator; and that of the other is the creature, as we said.[3] Both kinds bring intense delight to the soul. Yet those of God produce an incomparable delight. There are no words or terms to describe them, for they are God's own knowledge and God's own delight. And as David says: *there is nothing like unto him* [Ps. 40:5]. God is the direct object of this knowledge in that one of his attributes (his omnipotence, fortitude, goodness, sweetness, and so on) is sublimely experienced. And as often

---

1. In view of the ineffable character of these experiences he speaks in a similar way in C. 26. 3.
2. Here one should keep also in mind the division made in ch. 25. 2.
3. In ch. 25. 1.

as this experience occurs, it remains fixed in the soul. Since this communication is pure contemplation, the soul clearly understands that it is ineffable. Individuals are capable of describing it only through general expressions—expressions caused by the abundance of the delight and good of these experiences. But they realize the impossibility of explaining with these expressions what they tasted and felt in this communication.[4]

4. After David received a similar experience he spoke in these general terms: *Judicia Domini vera, justificata in semetipsa. Desiderabilia super aurum et lapidem pretiosum multum, et dulciora super mel et favum* (God's judgments—the virtues and attributes we experience in God—are true, in themselves justified, more desirable than gold and extremely precious stone, and sweeter than the honey and the honeycomb) [Ps. 19:10].

We read that Moses spoke only in general terms of the lofty knowledge God once gave him while passing by. And it happened that when the Lord passed before him in that knowledge, Moses quickly prostrated himself, crying: *Dominator Domine Deus, misericors et clemens, patiens, et multae miserationis, ac verax. Qui custodis misericordiam in millia,* and so on. (Sovereign Lord God, merciful and clement, patient, and of great compassion, and true. You guard the mercy that you promise to thousands) [Ex. 34:6-7]. Evidently, since Moses could not express with one concept what he knew in God, he did so through an overflow of words.

Although at times individuals use words in reference to this knowledge, they clearly realize that they have said nothing of what they experienced, for no term can give adequate expression to it. And thus when St. Paul experienced that lofty knowledge of God, he did not care to say anything else than that it was not licit for humans to speak of it [2 Cor. 12:4].[5]

5. This divine knowledge of God never deals with particular things, since its object is the Supreme Principle. Consequently one cannot express it in particular terms unless a truth about something less than God is seen together with this knowledge of him. But in no way can anything be said of that divine knowledge.

This sublime knowledge can be received only by a person who has arrived at union with God, for it is itself that very union. It consists in a certain touch of the divinity produced in the soul, and thus it is God

---

4. This is one of the many places in which John describes the loving general knowledge, but here as "pure contemplation," belonging to the state of transformation. For a detailed description of this experience of the divine attributes see F. 3. 2-17, 78-80.

5. On the ineffable character of this experience, cf. C. Prol. 1. In other parallel passages John also cites these same biblical texts. Cf. C. 36. 11; F. 3. 4.

himself who is experienced and tasted there. Although the touch of knowledge and delight that penetrates the substance of the soul is not manifest and clear, as in glory, it is so sublime and lofty that the devil is unable to meddle or produce anything similar (for there is no experience similar or comparable to it), or infuse a savor and delight like it. This knowledge tastes of the divine essence and of eternal life, and the devil cannot counterfeit anything so lofty.

6. He could, nevertheless, ape that experience by presenting to the soul some very sensible feelings of grandeur and fulfillment, trying to persuade it that these are from God. But this attempt of the devil does not enter the substance of the soul and suddenly renew and fill it with love as does a divine touch. Some of these divine touches produced in the substance of the soul are so enriching that one of them would be sufficient not only to remove definitively all the imperfections that the soul would have been unable to eradicate throughout its entire life but also to fill it with virtues and blessings from God.

7. These touches engender such sweetness and intimate delight in the soul that one of them would more than compensate for all the trials suffered in life, even though innumerable. Through these touches individuals become so courageous and so resolved to suffer many things for Christ that they find it a special suffering to observe that they do not suffer.

8. People are incapable of reaching this sublime knowledge through any comparison or imagining of their own, because it transcends what is naturally attainable. Thus God effects in the soul what it is incapable of acquiring. God usually grants these divine touches, which cause certain remembrances of him, at times when the soul is least expecting or thinking of them. Sometimes they are produced suddenly through some remembrance that may concern only some slight detail. They are so sensible that they sometimes cause not only the soul but also the body to tremble. Yet at other times with a sudden feeling of spiritual delight and refreshment, and without any trembling, they occur very tranquilly in the spirit.[6]

9. Or again they may occur on the uttering or hearing of a word from Sacred Scripture or from some other source.[7] These touches do not

---

6. In this section he deals in abbreviated form with the topic he promised in ch. 24. 4. Alongside the touches that are purely spiritual are those that have repercussions in the body. Those that are purely spiritual are proper to the state of perfection or union; cf. F. 4. 12-13.

7. Cf. C. 7. 9.

always have the same efficacy, nor are they always felt so forcefully, because they are often very weak. Yet no matter how weak they may be, one of these divine awakenings and touches is worth more to the soul than numberless other thoughts and ideas about God's creatures and works.

Since this knowledge is imparted to the soul suddenly, without the exercise of free will, individuals do not have to be concerned about desiring it or not. They should simply remain humble and resigned about it, for God will do his work at the time and in the manner he wishes.

10. I do not say that people should behave negatively regarding this knowledge, as they should with the other apprehensions, because this knowledge is an aspect of the union toward which we are directing the soul and which is the reason for our doctrine about denudation and detachment from all other apprehensions. God's means for granting such a grace are humility, suffering for love of him, and resignation as to all recompense. God does not bestow these favors on a possessive soul since he gives them out of a very special love for the recipient. The individual receiving them is one who loves with great detachment. The Son of God meant this when he stated through St. John: *Qui autem diligit me, diligetur a Patre meo, et ego diligam eum et manifestabo ei meipsum* (Whoever loves me will be loved by my Father, and I will love them and manifest myself to them) [Jn. 14:21]. This manifestation includes the knowledge and touches that God imparts to a person who has reached him and truly loves him.

11. The second kind of knowledge, or vision, of interior truths is far different from the type we have just explained because it deals with things inferior to God. This class embodies knowledge of the truth of things in themselves and of human deeds and events. When bestowed, this kind of knowledge is so embedded in the soul—without anyone telling it anything—that if someone were to assert the opposite it would be unable to give interior assent even by force, for it has a spiritual knowledge of this truth that resembles clear vision. This knowledge pertains to the spirit of prophecy and to the grace St. Paul terms the discernment of spirits [1 Cor. 12:10].

Although individuals may consider their knowledge certain and true, as we mentioned, and be unable to cast off that passive interior assent, they must not, because of this conviction, fail to believe and give the assent of reason to the instructions and commands of their spiritual director, even though these may be extremely contrary to what they feel. In this way they will be led by faith to divine union, for a soul must journey to it more by believing than by understanding.

12. We have clear testimonies in Sacred Scripture of both these kinds of knowledge. As for spiritual knowledge of things the Wise Man declares: *Ipse dedit mihi horum quae sunt scientiam veram, ut sciam dispositionem orbis terrarum, et virtutes elementorum, initium et consummationes temporum, vicissitudinum permutationes, et consummationes temporum et morum mutationes, divisiones temporum, et anni cursus, et stellarum dispositiones, naturas animalium et iras bestiarum vim ventorum, et cogitationes hominum, differentias virgultorum, et virtutes radicum, et quaecumque sunt abscondita, et improvisa didici: Omnium enim artifex docuit me sapientia* (God gave me true knowledge of existing things: to know the disposition of the earthly globe and the virtues of the elements, the beginning, ending, and midst of the times, the various vicissitudes and changes of the seasons, the change of customs, the divisions of time, the courses of the year, and the position of the stars, the natures of animals, and the rages of beasts, the power and strength of the winds, the thoughts of people, the diversities of plants and trees, and the healing power of roots; and I learned all hidden and unforeseen things, for Wisdom, the maker of all, taught me) [Wis. 7:17-21].

Although this knowledge of all things, which the Wise Man avows was given to him by God, was infused and general, this passage offers sufficient proof about all the particular knowledge God infuses supernaturally in souls when he desires. It does so not because God gives souls the general habit of knowledge as he did to Solomon, but because he sometimes reveals to them certain truths about the things enumerated here by the Wise Man.

Indeed, our Lord infuses habits about different truths in many souls, although never as general a habit as was Solomon's. These habits are like those different kinds of gifts distributed by God that St. Paul enumerates. Among them he includes wisdom, knowledge, faith, prophecy, discernment or recognition of spirits, knowledge of tongues, interpretation of words, and so on [1 Cor. 12:8-10]. All these kinds of knowledge are infused habits that God grants naturally or supernaturally to whomsoever he wills: naturally, as in the case of Balaam, other idolatrous prophets, and many sibyls, to whom he imparted the spirit of prophecy; and supernaturally, as to the holy prophets, apostles, and other saints.

13. Yet prescinding from these habits or graces *gratis datae*, we affirm that those who have reached perfection or are already close to it usually do possess light and knowledge about events happening in their presence or absence. This knowledge derives from their illumined and purified spirits. That passage from Proverbs can be interpreted as referring to this ability: *Quomodo in aquis resplendent vultus prospicientium, sic corda hominum manifesta sunt prudentibus* (As the faces of those who look in the water are reflected there, so are human hearts manifest to the

prudent) [Prv. 27:19]. These prudent ones are those who possess the wisdom of the saints that Sacred Scripture calls prudence [Prv. 9:10]. Through this ability these persons also come now and then to the knowledge of other truths, although not whenever they desire, for such facility would be proper only to those who have the habit. And even those who possess the habit do not always have this facility in regard to everything, for that would depend on the assistance God wishes to give them.

14. It is worthy of note, though, that individuals whose spirit is purified can naturally perceive—some more than others—the inclinations and talents of other persons and what lies in the heart or interior spirit. They derive this knowledge through exterior indications (even though extremely slight) such as words, gestures, and other signs. Just as the devil, because he is a spirit, is endowed with this skill, so is the spiritual person, according to the Apostle: *Spiritualis autem judicat omnia* (The spiritual person judges all things) [1 Cor. 2:15]. And again he declares: *Spiritus enim omnia scrutatur, etiam profunda Dei* (The spirit searches all things, even the deep things of God) [1 Cor. 2:10].

Although spiritual persons cannot know naturally the thoughts of others or their interior state, they can know this clearly through supernatural enlightenment or through exterior indications. And though they can often be deceived in the knowledge deduced from these indications, they are more often correct in their surmise. But they must not put trust in knowledge acquired through either of these two ways, because, as we will point out,[8] the devil is a notorious and subtle meddler in this area. Consequently they should always renounce such knowledge.

15. We have an example and testimony in the Fourth Book of Kings of how spiritual persons, even when absent, can also possess knowledge of human deeds and events. When Gehazi, the servant of our Father Elisha,[9] desired to hide the money received from Naaman, Elisha said: *Nonne cor meum in praesenti erat, quando reversus est homo de curru suo in occursum tui?* (Was not my heart perchance present when Naaman turned from his chariot and went to meet you?) [2 Kgs. 5:25-26]. This took place spiritually in such a way that the spirit beheld the event as if it had happened right before it. We find another proof of this in the same book where we read that Elisha told the king of Israel everything that the king of Syria discussed with his counselors in his private chamber, and thus these meetings bore no fruit. When the king of Syria realized that their decisions were no longer secret, he complained to his counselors: Why

---

8. In no. 17.
9. In accord with Carmelite tradition, John also sees the prophet Elisha, disciple of the prophet Elijah, as a spiritual Father. See ch. 8. 4. note 4.

do you not tell me who among you is betraying me to the King of Israel? And then one of his counselors exclaimed: *Nequaquam, domine mi rex, sed Elisha propheta, qui est in Israel indicat regi Israel omnia verba quaecumque locutus fueris in conclavi tuo* (Not so, my lord king, but Elisha the prophet who is in Israel reveals to the king everything you say in your private chamber) [2 Kgs. 6:11-12].

16. These kinds of knowledge of things[10] as well as the other kinds come to the soul passively, without it doing anything on its own. For it will happen that, while a person is distracted and inattentive, a keen understanding of what is being heard or read will be implanted in the spirit, an understanding far clearer than that conveyed through the sound of the words. And although sometimes individuals fail to grasp the sense of the words—as when expressed in Latin, a language unknown to them—this meaning is revealed without their understanding the words themselves.[11]

17. We could expound a great deal on the deceptions the devil can and does cause with regard to this kind of knowledge and understanding, for his deceits are gross and singularly concealed. He can through suggestion ingrain many intellectual ideas so deeply in the soul that they will seem to be true; and if the soul is not humble and distrustful he will doubtless bring it to believe a thousand lies.

At times the suggestion produces so strong an impression on individuals—especially when the soul shares somewhat in the weakness of the senses—and embeds the knowledge in them with such power, persuasion, and conviction that they then need a great deal of prayer and strength in order to discard it. Sometimes the devil represents clearly, but falsely, the sins of others, evil consciences, and evil souls in order to calumniate. And he wants these things to be published abroad so that many sins may be committed, and he imparts zeal to these individuals by convincing them that the reason for all of this is so prayer may be offered to God for these people. Now it is true that God sometimes shows holy souls their neighbors' needs so that they might pray for them or provide a remedy. We read, for example, that he revealed to Jeremiah the weakness of the prophet Baruch so that he could instruct Baruch about it [Jer. 45:3]. Nevertheless, the devil does this very frequently and falsely, so as to occasion calumnies, sins, and distress; and of this we have much experience. And again at other times the devil will implant deeply in souls other knowledge, and make them believe it.

18. Regardless of whether this knowledge is from God, it will be of little profit to persons in their advance toward union if they are attached to it.

---

10. Cf. no. 3 and ch. 25. 1-3.
11. For an example, see St. Teresa, *Life*, ch. 15. 8.

If they are careless about denying themselves this knowledge, it will be not only an obstacle but the occasion of serious harm and error. All the dangers and difficulties that we said arise from supernatural apprehensions, which we have discussed up to this point, and even more, can result from this knowledge.

I will not enlarge on this subject any more since we have given sufficient instruction in previous chapters. I only point out that people should be extremely careful always to reject this knowledge, and they should desire to journey to God by unknowing, and always give an account of these revelations to their confessor or spiritual master and abide by his counsel. The director should allow the soul to relate this experience briefly, but should not make it the main factor in the soul's journey toward union with God. The effect God desires to produce through these passive communications will be fixed in the soul without need for efforts of its own.

It seems to me there is no reason, then, to discuss the different effects caused by true and false knowledge, for this would be wearisome and unending. These effects could not be condensed to a few words because the quantity and variety of this knowledge causes a quantity and variety of effects—the good knowledge causing good effects and evil knowledge causing evil effects, and so on. It is sufficient to insist on rejection of all this knowledge as a control against any error.

CHAPTER 27

The second kind of revelation: the disclosure of secrets and hidden mysteries. The ways in which this knowledge can be either a contribution or a hindrance toward union with God. How the devil can greatly deceive souls in this matter.

1. We stated that the second kind of revelation is the disclosure of secrets and hidden mysteries.[1] It can be divided into two further categories:

The first concerns God himself, which includes the revelation of the mystery of the most holy Trinity and unity of God.

The second concerns God in his works. This comprises the remaining articles of our Catholic faith and the propositions of truths that can be explicitly formed about his works. These propositions embody a large number of revelatory prophecies, of promises and threats from God, and of other past and future events in regard to this matter of faith.

We can include in this second category many other particular facts revealed ordinarily by God about the universe in general and, in particu-

---

1. In ch. 25. 3.

lar, about kingdoms, provinces, states, families, and individuals.

We have numerous examples of these manifestations, both general and particular, in the divine Scriptures, especially in the writings of the prophets in which all these kinds of revelations are found. Since this assertion is clear and evident, I do not want to spend time here quoting scriptural passages. I merely want to affirm that these revelations are not given by word only, for God bestows them in a variety of ways and manners: sometimes by word alone; at other times only by signs, figures, images, and likenesses; and sometimes by both together, as is seen in the writings of the prophets. This is particularly evident throughout the Apocalypse where we find examples of all these various kinds of revelations and also of the different ways they are imparted.

2. Even in our time God grants revelations of this second category to whom he wills. He will reveal to some the number of days they have to live, or the trials they will have to endure, or something that will befall a particular person or kingdom, and so on. Even with regard to the mysteries of our faith, he will uncover and declare to the spirit truths concerning them, although properly speaking this would not be a revelation since they are already revealed. It would be instead a manifestation or declaration of the already revealed mysteries.

3. The devil can be a great meddler with this kind of revelation. Since the truths are imparted through words, figures, likenesses, and so on, he can make counterfeits more easily than when the revelations are given solely to the spirit. If, in these two categories we mentioned, some new truth about our faith is revealed, or something at variance with it, we must by no means give assent, even though we may have evidence that it was spoken by an angel from heaven. Thus St. Paul states: *Licet nos, aut angelus de coelo evangelizet vobis praeterquam quod evangelizavimus vobis, anathema sit* (If we, or an angel from heaven, declare or preach something other than what we have preached, let him be anathema) [Gal 1:8].

4. Since there are no more articles to be revealed to the Church about the substance of our faith, people must not merely reject new revelations about the faith, but out of caution repudiate other kinds of knowledge mingled with them. In order to preserve the appropriate purity of faith, a person should not believe already revealed truths because they are again revealed but because they were already sufficiently revealed to the Church. Closing one's mind to them, one should rest simply on the doctrine of the Church and its faith that, as St. Paul says, enters through hearing [Rom. 10:17]. And if individuals want to escape delusion they should not adapt their credence and understanding to those truths of faith revealed again, no matter how true and conformed to the faith they

may seem. To deceive and introduce lies the devil first lures a person with truths and verisimilitudes that give assurance; then he proceeds with his beguilement. These truths of his are like the bristle used in sewing leather: It is put through the holes first in order to pull the soft thread along after it; without the bristle the thread would never pass through.

5. Let this be kept in mind: Even if there is actually no danger of deception to the soul, it greatly behooves souls not to want to understand the truths of faith clearly, so that they may thereby conserve pure and entire the merit of faith and also pass through this night of intellect to the divine light of union.

Closing the eyes to any new revelation and focusing them on former prophecies is so important that even though St. Peter in some way saw the glory of the Son of God on Mount Tabor, he declared in his Second Epistle: *Et habemus firmiorem propheticum sermonem, cui benefacitis attenden-tes,* etc. (Although our vision of Christ on the mount was true, the word of the prophecy revealed to us is more certain and unshaken, and you do well by resting your soul on it) [2 Pt. 1:19].

6. If it is true for the reasons already mentioned that one should close one's eyes to these revelations about the propositions of faith, how much greater need is there to repel and disbelieve other revelations about different things and in which the devil usually meddles! Because of the apparent truth and convincing quality with which the devil clothes them, I consider it impossible for a person who is not striving to reject them to go undeceived. For to make people believe, the devil joins together so many apparent and appropriate facts, and implants them so firmly in the imagination and senses, that it seems the events will undoubtedly occur. And he causes the soul to be so convinced and tenacious about them that if it has no humility it will hardly be torn from its opinion and made to believe the contrary.

The pure, cautious, simple, and humble soul should resist and reject revelations and other visions with as much effort and care as it would extremely dangerous temptations, for in order to reach the union of love there is need not to desire them but to reject them. Solomon meant this when he exclaimed: *What need has one to desire and seek what is above one's natural capacity?* [Eccl. 6:11].[2] This means that to be perfect there is no need to desire to receive goods in a way that is supernatural and beyond one's capacity.

7. Any objection that could be made against these instructions has

---

2. From this point on biblical quotations, with some exceptions, are given only in the vernacular. This becomes an important factor in historical-critical studies.

already been answered in chapters 19 and 20 of this book.[3] Referring to the doctrine given there, I say only that individuals should be on their guard against these revelations so that through the night of faith they may journey to union purely and without error.

CHAPTER 28

The nature and kinds of supernatural locutions received by the spirit.

1. The discreet reader must always keep in mind my intention and goal in this book: to guide the soul in purity of faith through all its natural and supernatural apprehensions, in freedom from deception and every obstacle, to divine union with God. One should understand that though I am not giving abundant instruction about these apprehensions of the soul, nor examining the divisions and subject matter as minutely as may be necessary, I am not being brief on this topic either. For I think I have imparted sufficient advice, light, and instruction on the prudent behavior required for advancement in the midst of these exterior and interior apprehensions.

This is why I discussed prophetic apprehensions so briefly, as I also did the others. There is so much to expound about each of these kinds of prophecy (about their difference and their ways and modes of being received) that I think one would never know it all fully. I am content that, in my opinion, the substantial part of the doctrine has been pointed out, as well as the caution that is necessary in dealing with these apprehensions or anything resembling them.

2. I will now follow the same method with the third kind of apprehension, which we said[1] were the supernatural locutions. These are usually produced in a person's spirit without the use of the bodily senses as means. Although there are many classes, I find they can be reduced to three: successive, formal, and substantial locutions.

Successive locutions are the words and reasonings that the spirit of itself usually forms and deduces while recollected.

Formal locutions are certain distinct and formal words that the spirit receives, whether or not recollected, not from itself but from another.

Substantial locutions are other words that are also produced formally in the spirit, regardless of whether one is recollected, and that cause in the substance of the soul the power and very substance they signify.

---

3. Actually these chapters are 21 and 22. The difference stems from the fact that various manuscripts divide the chapters differently.
1. See ch. 10. 4 and 23. 1-3.

We will discuss all these in due order.

CHAPTER 29

The first kind of locution the recollected spirit sometimes forms. A discussion of its origin and of the profit or harm it may occasion.

1. Successive words always occur when the spirit is recollected and attentively absorbed in some consideration. Individuals will reason about their subject, proceeding thought by thought, forming precise words and judgments, deducing and discovering such unknown truths with so much ease and clarity that it will seem to them they are doing nothing and another person is interiorly reasoning, answering, and teaching them.

Indeed, there is every reason for thinking this, since they reason with themselves and reply as if carrying on a dialogue. In a way they really are speaking with another for, though they reason by using their intellect as the instrument, the Holy Spirit frequently helps them to form true concepts, words, and judgments, and thus they utter them to themselves as though to another person. Since their intellect is recollected and united with the truth, which is the subject of their thought, and the Holy Spirit is also united with them in that truth—for he is in every truth—it results that, while their intellect is thus communing with the divine Spirit by means of that truth, it simultaneously forms interiorly and successively other truths about its subject while the Holy Spirit, the Teacher, leads the way and gives light. This is one of the Holy Spirit's methods of teaching.[1]

2. Thus the intellect, understanding those truths communicated to it from elsewhere, and enlightened and taught by this Master, forms statements by itself about them. Accordingly we could say that the voice is of Jacob, but the hands of Esau [Gn. 27:22]. Anyone having this experience cannot help but think that these statements or words come from another. They do not know about the ease with which the intellect, in dealing with concepts and truths communicated by another, can form words for itself that also seem to come from another.

3. Though in that communication or illumination itself there is actually no deception of the intellect, yet there can be and frequently is deception in the formal words and statements the intellect deduces from it. The light is often so delicate and spiritual that the intellect does not succeed in being completely informed by it; and it is the intellect that

---

1. This chapter deals more directly with the Holy Spirit and his action within the soul.

forms the statements of its own power, as we stated. Consequently the statements are often false, or only apparent, or defective. Since the intellect afterward joins its own lowly capacity and awkwardness to the thread of truth it had already begun to grasp, it can easily change the truth in accordance with this lowly capacity, and all as though another person were speaking to it.

4. I knew a person who in experiencing these successive locutions formed, among some very true and solid ones about the Blessed Sacrament, others that were outright heresies.

I greatly fear what is happening in these times of ours: If any soul whatever after a few pennies worth of reflection experiences one of these locutions in some recollection, it will immediately baptize all as coming from God and, supposing this, say, "God told me," "God answered me." Yet this will not be true but, as we pointed out, these persons will themselves more often be the ones who speak the words.[2]

5. Furthermore, the desire for such locutions and attachment to them will cause these persons to answer themselves and think that God is responding and speaking to them. They will commit serious blunders if they do not practice great restraint and if their directors do not oblige them to renounce such discursive methods. For through these methods they usually derive more vanity of speech and impurity of soul than humility and mortification of spirit. They think something extraordinary has occurred and that God has spoken, whereas in reality little more than nothing will have happened, or nothing at all, or even less than nothing. For whatever does not engender humility, charity, mortification, holy simplicity, silence, and so on, of what value is it?

I say, therefore, that these locutions can be a serious obstacle to souls in their journey toward divine union because by paying attention to them souls are drawn far from the abyss of faith. The intellect should remain in obscurity and journey by love in darkness of faith and not by much reasoning.

6. If you ask me why the intellect must be deprived of those truths since the Spirit of God illumines it through them and thus they are not bad, I answer: The Holy Spirit illumines the recollected intellect, and illumines it according to the mode of its recollection; the intellect can find no better recollection than in faith, and thus the Holy Spirit will not illumine it in any other recollection more than in faith. The purer and more refined a soul is in faith, the more infused charity it has. And the more

---

2. Here John cautions the alumbrados of his time and all those who very easily attribute to God and the Holy Spirit their own ideas, feelings, and insights.

charity it has the more the Holy Spirit illumines it and communicates his gifts because charity is the means by which they are communicated.[3]

Although in that illumination of truths the Holy Spirit does communicate some light to the soul, the light given in faith—in which there is no clear understanding—is qualitatively as different from the other as is the purest gold from the basest metal, and quantitatively as is the sea from a drop of water. In the first kind of illumination, wisdom concerning one, two, or three truths, and so on, is communicated; in the second kind, all of God's Wisdom is communicated in general, that is, the Son of God, who communicates himself to the soul in faith.

7. Should you tell me that everything will be all right since the first kind of illumination is no obstacle to the second, I would reply that it is a serious obstacle if the soul pays attention to it. For this would involve attention to clear things, things of little importance and enough to hinder the communication of the abyss of faith. In this faith God supernaturally and secretly teaches the soul and raises it up in virtues and gifts in a way unknown to it.

The benefit to be gained from a successive locution will not come from focusing one's attention on it. Rather, doing so would drive away the communication, for Wisdom says to the soul in the Song of Songs: *Withdraw your eyes from me, for they make me fly away* [Sg. 6:4], that is, they make me fly far from you and ascend higher. The benefit will be received by refusing to focus the intellect on what is communicated supernaturally and simply centering the will on God with love. For it is in love that these goods are communicated, and indeed more abundantly than before.

If the natural intellect and the other faculties intervene actively in these supernatural and passive communications, they will not attain these heights because of their own mode and obtuseness. Thus they will be forced to modify the communications according to their mode, and consequently change them. The intellect, then, will necessarily err and form judgments of its own that will be neither supernatural nor similar to the supernatural, but singularly natural, erroneous, and base.

8. Yet some intellects are so lively and subtle that, while recollected in meditation, they reason naturally and easily about some concepts, and form locutions and statements very vividly, and think that these are

---

3. John speaks for the first time explicitly of the gifts of the Holy Spirit, relating them directly to charity. As one progresses through the degrees of love the gifts grow in perfection; cf. C. 26. 3. He does not make use of the theological theory about the gifts in which they are considered as principles that dispose one to be moved passively by the Holy Spirit. John also in nos. 5-6 establishes a relationship between faith and charity; in their dynamism they function supernaturally in the way that knowledge and love do naturally.

indeed from God. But that notion is false, for an intellect somewhat freed from the operation of the senses has the capacity to do this and even more with its own natural light and without any other supernatural help. Such an occurrence is frequent. And many are deluded by it into thinking that theirs is the enjoyment of a high degree of prayer and communication from God; consequently they either write the words down themselves or have others do so. But it comes about that the experience amounts to nothing, nothing substantial in the line of virtue comes from it, and it serves for no more than to induce vainglory.

9. These people should learn to give importance to nothing other than sincere effort, the establishment of their wills in humble love, and suffering in imitation of the life and mortifications of the Son of God. This is the road to the attainment of every spiritual good, and not that other one of profuse interior discourse.[4]

10. The devil too meddles a great deal in this kind of interior locution, especially with persons who have a particular attachment to them. When such people begin recollecting themselves, the devil usually offers ample matter for digression by supplying, through suggestion, ideas or words for the intellect. Subtly deceiving them with verisimilitudes, he gradually brings about their ruin. This is one of his ways of communicating with those who have made a tacit or express pact with him, or of informing heretics—or especially heresiarchs—about extremely subtle, false, and erroneous ideas and arguments.

11. Manifestly, then, these successive locutions can originate in the intellect from any of three causes: the divine Spirit, who moves and illumines the intellect; the natural light of the intellect; and the devil, who can speak to it through suggestion.

It would be a difficult task now to discuss completely all the signs for the discernment of the cause from which these locutions proceed, although we can easily give some general ones. They are:

When together with the words and concepts the soul is loving God and simultaneously experiencing this love with humility and reverence, we have an indication that the Holy Spirit is at work within it. Whenever he bestows favors he clothes them with this love. When the locutions originate from the vivacity and light of the intellect, the cause of everything is the intellect and there is no accompanying activity of the virtues. The will can love naturally in the knowledge and light of those truths, yet after the meditation it will remain dry. But the soul will have no inclination toward vanity unless the devil again tempts it about its experience. In the locutions arising from the good spirit this aridity is not

4. Cf. A. 1. 13. 3; A. 2. 7.

felt, because after the locution the will is ordinarily attached to God and inclined toward good. Yet sometimes the will is arid afterward even if the communication is from the good spirit, for God so ordains for reasons that are beneficial to the soul. At other times the soul will not have much experience of the operations or movements of those virtues; nevertheless the locution will be good. This is the reason it is sometimes difficult to discern the cause of these locutions through their varied effects. The effects already referred to are the common ones, though at times they are more abundant and at other times less.

Even locutions caused by the devil are sometimes difficult to discern and recognize. Ordinarily, indeed, they leave the will in dryness as to the love of God, and the intellect inclined toward vanity and self-esteem or complacency; still, they can bring about a false humility and a fervent tendency of the will rooted in self-love. A person in consequence will have to be very spiritual to recognize this. The devil effects these false virtues in order to be more hidden. That he might fix in souls the attachments he desires them to have, he is expert at inducing the flow of tears from the feelings he introduces. He always endeavors to move the will toward an esteem for these interior communications and to get people to place much importance on them so that they will devote and occupy themselves with things that are not virtuous but an occasion for the loss of what virtue there is.

12. Let us conclude then with this precaution necessary for the avoidance of any delusion or hindrance from these variously caused locutions: We should pay no heed to them, but be only interested in directing the will, with fortitude, toward God; we should carry out his law and holy counsels with perfection—for such is the wisdom of the saints—content with knowing the mysteries and truths in the simplicity and verity with which the Church proposes them. An attitude of this kind is sufficient for a vigorous enkindling of the will. Hence we do not have to pry into profundities and curiosities in which there is seldom a lack of danger. St. Paul in regard to this conduct states: *One should not have more knowledge than is fitting* [Rom. 12:3]. What was said should be enough on the subject of successive words.

CHAPTER 30

Interior words formally and supernaturally produced in the spirit. A warning about their danger and a necessary precaution against delusion.

1. The second kind of interior locution is called formal and is produced supernaturally in the spirit without the use of the senses. It comes independently of whether the spirit is recollected or not. I give it

the name "formal locution" because another person formally utters it to the spirit without intervention of the soul. It is consequently far different from the successive locution. It differs not only by the fact that the spirit itself is not involved in the cause but also, as I say, in that it occurs sometimes when there is no recollection and the soul is far from any thought of what is spoken. In successive locutions such is not the case, for they always have to do with the subject of one's reflection.

2. Sometimes these words are very explicit and at other times not. They are often like ideas spoken to the spirit, either as a reply to something or in another manner. At times only one word is spoken, and then again more than one; sometimes the locutions are successive, like the others, for they may endure while the soul is being taught or while something is being discussed. All these words come without any intervention of the spirit because they are received as though one person were speaking to another. Daniel experienced this when, as he says, the angel spoke to him. The angel reasoned formally and successively in his spirit and also declared that he had come to teach him [Dn. 9:22].

3. When these words are no more than formal they bear little effect. Ordinarily they are given merely for the purpose of teaching or shedding light upon some truth. Accordingly the efficacy of their effect need be no more than required to attain their purpose. When God is the cause of the locution this effect is always produced in the soul, for it gives the soul both readiness to accomplish the command and clarity in understanding it. Yet these locutions do not always remove repugnance and difficulty, rather they sometimes augment it. God does this for the further instruction, humility, and good of the soul. God more frequently allows this repugnance when he orders something pertinent to a prelacy or to some other factor that will bring honor to the soul. And in matters of humility and lowliness he imparts more facility and readiness. We read in Exodus that when God ordered Moses to go to Pharaoh and obtain liberation for the people, Moses felt such repugnance that God had to command him three times and show him signs. Yet none of this was of any avail until God gave him Aaron to share in the honor [Ex. 3:10-22; 4:1-18].

4. On the other hand, when the locutions and communications are from the devil, it will happen that both ease and readiness will be given in matters involving prestige, whereas only repugnance will be felt for lowly tasks. God surely abhors the sight of souls inclined toward prelacies. Even when he gives a command in this regard and puts souls in office, he does not want them to be eager to govern. Formal locutions differ from the successive ones with respect to this readiness that God usually bestows. Successive locutions do not move the spirit as much as formal ones do, because the latter are more formal and the intellect does less on

its own. Yet this does not prevent the successive locutions from sometimes producing a greater effect because of a greater communication between the divine Spirit and the human spirit. However, there is considerable difference in the manner in which the effect is produced. The soul has no reason for doubting that these locutions come from another, since it is clearly aware that it does not form them itself, especially because it is not thinking on what is said to it. Even if it does happen to be pondering over this, it still experiences very clearly and distinctly that the locution is from another source.

5. A person should pay no more attention to all these formal locutions than to the other kind, for besides occupying the spirit with matters irrelevant to faith, the legitimate and proximate means to union with God, they will make one an easy victim for the devil's deceits. At times one can hardly discern the locutions spoken by a good spirit or those coming from a bad one. Since these locutions do not produce much effect, they can hardly be discerned by the effect. Sometimes those of the devil will be more effective in imperfect souls than the others will be in spiritual ones. Individuals should not do what these words tell them, nor should they pay attention to them—whether they be from a good or bad spirit. Nevertheless, these locutions should be manifested to a mature confessor or to a discreet and wise person who will give instructions and counsel and consider the appropriate thing to do. But a person's attitude toward them ought to be one of resignation and negation. If such an expert person cannot be found, it is better not to speak of these locutions to anyone, but simply pay no attention to them, for a soul can easily fall into the hands of some persons who will tear it down rather than build it up. Souls should not discuss these locutions with just anyone, since in so serious a matter being right or wrong is of such importance.

6. It should be kept in mind that individuals must never follow their own opinion about these locutions or do or admit anything told through them without ample advice and counsel from another. For in this matter of locutions strange and subtle deceits will occur—so much so that I believe a person who is not opposed to experiencing such things cannot help but be deceived in many of them.

7. Since I intentionally discussed these delusions and dangers, and the necessary precautions concerning them, in chapters 17 to 20 of this book—to which I refer the reader—I will not enlarge any more upon them here.[1] I only repeat that my main teaching is to pay no heed whatever to them.

---

1. The material is actually found in ch. 15-18.

CHAPTER 31

Substantial locutions produced in the spirit. How these differ from formal locutions, the benefit that comes from them, and the resignation and respect that should be had in their regard.

1. The <u>third</u> kind of interior locution, we said,[1] is the substantial locution. Although these locutions are also formal, since they are impressed very formally in the soul, they nevertheless are different in that their effect is vital and substantial, which is not the case with formal locutions. Although every substantial word is formal, it does not follow that every formal word is substantial—only the word that impresses its significance substantially on the soul. For example, if our Lord should say formally to the soul, "Be good," it would immediately be substantially good; or if he should say, "Love me," it would at once have and experience within itself the substance of the love of God; or if he should say to a soul in much fear, "Do not fear," it would without delay feel great fortitude and tranquility. For as the Wise Man declares, God's word and utterance is full of power [Eccl. 8:4], and thus it produces substantially in the soul what is said. David meant this when he stated: *Behold, he will give his voice the voice of power* [Ps. 68:33]. God did this to Abraham. When he said: *Walk in my presence and be perfect* [Gn. 17:1], Abraham immediately became perfect and always proceeded with reverence for God. We note this power of God's word in the Gospel when with a mere expression he healed the sick, raised the dead, and so on.

In this fashion he bestows substantial locutions on certain souls. These locutions are as important and valuable as are the life, virtue, and incomparable blessings they impart to the soul. A locution of this sort does more good for a person than a whole lifetime of deeds.

2. As for these locutions, the soul has nothing to do, desire, refrain from desiring, reject, or fear.

There is nothing to be done, because God never grants them for that purpose, but he bestows them in order to bring about what they express. For this reason they differ from the formal and successive locutions. And there is nothing for the soul to desire or refrain from desiring. A desire for these locutions is not necessary for God to grant them, nor would not wanting them hinder their effect. The soul should rather be resigned and humble about them.

A person has nothing to reject because the effect of these locutions remains substantiated in the soul and replete with God's blessings. Since the soul receives this passively, its activity would be entirely superfluous.

---

1. In ch. 28. 2.

It need not fear any deception because neither the intellect nor the devil can intervene in this communication. The devil is incapable of passively producing the substantial effect of his locution on the soul unless, as it may happen, the soul has surrendered itself to him by a voluntary pact. Thus the devil, dwelling in it as its lord, would produce such effects—not good, but evil ones. Since this soul would already be united with him in voluntary wickedness, he could easily impress in it the evil effects of his locutions and words. From experience we observe that in many matters he has great power through suggestion even with good souls, making these locutions extremely efficacious for them. If these souls were evil, then, he could produce the effect in them completely. But he is unable to produce effects similar to those arising from God's locutions, for there is no comparison between God's words and the devil's. In comparison with God's locutions and their effect, those of the devil and their effect are nothing. God affirms this through Jeremiah: *What has the chaff to do with the wheat? Are not my words perhaps like fire and the hammer that breaks rocks?* [Jer. 23:28-29].[2]

Consequently these substantial locutions are a great aid to union with God. And the more interior and substantial they are, the more advantageous for the soul. Happy the soul to whom God speaks these substantial words. *Speak, Lord, for your servant is listening* [1 Sm. 3:10].

CHAPTER 32

The intellectual apprehensions of the spiritual feelings supernaturally imparted to the soul. The cause of these interior feelings and the attitude necessary to avoid hindering the journey toward union with God.

1. It is time now for a discussion of the fourth and last kind of intellectual apprehension. This kind, we said, the intellect receives from the spiritual feelings that are often granted supernaturally to spiritual persons. We count these spiritual feelings among the distinct apprehensions of the intellect.[1]

2. These distinct spiritual feelings are of two kinds: The first comprises feelings in the affection of the will; the second, feelings in the substance of the soul. The two can take place in many ways.

Those in the will are very sublime when from God, but the feelings in the substance of the soul are the loftiest and are exceptionally advanta-

---

2. In John's opinion the devil struggles more to obstruct blessings given to one who is advanced than to tempt and disturb the imperfect and weak. Cf. C. 16. 2-3; 20. 15; F. 3. 63-65.
1. Cf. ch. 23. 1-3; 24. 4.

geous and good. Neither the soul nor its director can know their origin or the works for which God bestows them.

These favors are not dependent on the works or reflections of the soul, though these exercises do dispose it well to receive such gifts, for God grants them to whom he wills and for the reason he wills. It can happen that someone will have done many works, and yet God will not bestow these touches; and another will have accomplished far fewer works and nevertheless receive an abundance of the most sublime touches. Accordingly, though it may be a better preparation, it is not necessary for a soul to be actually employed and occupied in spiritual matters for God to grant the touches from which it experiences these feelings. Most of the time this favor is given when it is farthest from the mind.

Some of these touches are distinct and of short duration, others are not so distinct and last longer.

3. These feelings, as such, are not allied to the intellect but to the will. Thus it is not my purpose to discuss them here. This I will do in the following book while dealing with the night and purgation of the attachments of the will.[2]

Yet because most of the time the apprehension, knowledge, and understanding of them overflows into the intellect, we ought to mention them here.

It is noteworthy that from these feelings the apprehension of knowledge or understanding frequently overflows, as I say, into the intellect. This is true with both the touches in the will and those in the substance of the soul, whether they be sudden touches or lasting and successive. This apprehension is usually an exceptionally sublime and delightful experience of God in the intellect. It cannot be given a name, nor can the feeling from which it overflows. This knowledge is now of one kind and then again of another. According to the touches produced by God (that cause the feelings from which the knowledge is derived), and according to the property of these touches, this knowledge is sometimes more sublime and clear than at other times.

4. There is no need to waste many words here in cautioning the intellect and directing it through this knowledge to union with God in faith. The feelings we mentioned are produced passively in individuals without their doing anything effectively to receive them. So too the knowledge of these feelings is received passively in the intellect (which philosophers call "possible") without anything being actively done by these individuals. To avoid error as a result of these feelings, and any

---

2. He begins speaking of the purification of the will in ch. 16 of Book Three, but never developed the theme promised here.

impediment to the profit coming from them, the intellect should do nothing about them other than behave passively and refrain from meddling through the use of its natural capacity. For as in the case of successive locutions, the intellect by its own activity easily disturbs and undoes that delicate knowledge, a delightful, supernatural knowing unattainable through one's natural capacity.[3] Nor does the intellect by its own activity find this knowledge comprehensible, but comprehends it only by receiving it.

Thus a person should not strive after this knowledge or want it, lest the intellect begin to form other knowledge on its own, or the devil find an entrance for his varied and false knowledge. The devil can easily effect false knowledge, either by means of these feelings or by others he himself can bestow on the soul that is attached to this knowledge. A person should be resigned, humble, and passive with respect to it. For since it is received passively from God, it will be received when he is pleased to grant it and when he sees that the soul is humble and unpossessive. In this way one will not hinder the tremendous benefit lying in this knowledge with respect to divine union, for all these feelings are touches of union; and the union is produced passively in the soul.

5. The doctrine expounded is sufficient, for in the divisions we gave the soul will find precautions and instructions for any of its intellectual apprehensions. Even though seemingly different or unincluded, there is no intellectual apprehension that cannot be reduced to one of these kinds. A person can therefore obtain the proper instructions by referring to my discussion of it.

---

3. Cf. ch. 28. 2 and ch. 29.

BOOK THREE

This book treats of purgation in the active night of the memory and the will. It presents doctrine about the attitude required in the apprehensions of these two faculties so that a soul may reach union with God in perfect hope and charity.

CHAPTER 1

1. We have already given instructions for the intellect, the first faculty of the soul, so that in all its apprehensions it may be united with God through pure faith, the first theological virtue. The same has to be done for the other two faculties, memory and will. They must undergo a purification of their respective apprehensions in order to reach union with God in perfect hope and charity.

Our exposition in this third book will be brief. It is not necessary to enlarge so much in our treatise on these faculties, since in the instructions given for the intellect (the receptacle in its own way of all the other objects) we have covered a great portion of the matter. If spiritual persons direct their intellects in faith according to the doctrine given them, it is impossible for them not to instruct their other two faculties simultaneously in the other two virtues, for these faculties depend on one another in their operations.[1]

2. To continue the method we have been using and for the sake of clarity, we will discuss each point particularly and list the proper apprehensions of each faculty. We begin with those of the memory and here give a division of them that should suffice for our purpose. We form this division from the three different objects of the memory: natural, imaginative, and spiritual. In accord with these objects the knowledge of the memory is also of three kinds: natural, supernatural imaginative, and spiritual.

---

1. From John's practical viewpoint and that of the contemporary idiom, the three faculties of the soul have proper functions and objects. John does not raise the philosophical question of whether the faculties are specifically different or distinct. What is important for him is their interdependence and interaction. Everything that applies to one on the spiritual plane applies as well, with the proper adjustments, to the others. This threefold division of the faculties with their corresponding virtues appears throughout all of his writings.

3. With God's help we will discuss these three here, beginning with natural knowledge that arises from a more exterior object. Afterward we will deal with the affections of the will, and thereby this third book of the active spiritual night will be brought to a close.

CHAPTER 2

The natural apprehensions of the memory. How to become empty of them in order to reach union with God through this faculty.

1. In each of these books readers must keep in mind the intention we have in writing. Failure to do so will give rise to many doubts about what they read. They may already have them concerning the instructions given for the intellect, or they may experience them on reading what we say about the memory and the will.

Observing how we annihilate the faculties in their operations, it will perhaps seem that we are tearing down rather than building up the way of spiritual exercise. This would be true if our doctrine here were destined merely for beginners who need to prepare themselves by means of these discursive apprehensions.

2. But we are imparting instructions here for advancing in contemplation to union with God. All these sensory means and exercises of the faculties must consequently be left behind and in silence so that God himself may effect divine union in the soul. As a result one has to follow this method of disencumbering, emptying, and depriving the faculties of their natural authority and operations to make room for the inflow and illumination of the supernatural. Those who do not turn their eyes from their natural capacity will not attain to so lofty a communication; rather they will hinder it.

3. Thus, if it is true—as indeed it is—that the soul must journey by knowing God through what he is not rather than through what he is, it must journey, insofar as possible, by way of the denial and rejection of natural and supernatural apprehensions. This is our task now with the memory. We must draw it away from its natural props and boundaries and raise it above itself (above all distinct knowledge and apprehensible possession) to supreme hope in the incomprehensible God.

4. To begin with natural knowledge in the memory, I include under this heading all that can be formed from the objects of the five corporeal senses (hearing, sight, smell, taste, and touch), and everything like this sensory knowledge that the memory can evoke and fashion. It must strip

and empty itself of all this knowledge and these forms and strive to lose the imaginative apprehension of them. It should do this in such a way that no knowledge or trace of them remains in it; rather it should be bare and clear, as though nothing passed through it, forgetful of all and suspended.

There is no way to union with God without annihilating the memory as to all forms. This union cannot be wrought without a complete separation of the memory from all forms that are not God. As we mentioned in the night of the intellect, God cannot be encompassed by any form or distinct knowledge.[1] Since, as Christ affirms, no one can serve two masters [Mt. 6:24], and since the memory cannot at the same time be united with God and with forms and distinct knowledge, and since God has no form or image comprehensible to the memory, the memory is without form and without figure when united with God. Its imagination being lost in great forgetfulness without the remembrance of anything, it is absorbed in a supreme good. This is noted every day through experience. That divine union empties and sweeps the phantasy of all forms and knowledge, and elevates it to the supernatural.

5. It is worthwhile noting what sometimes takes place in this state. When God on occasion produces these touches of union in the memory, a sudden jolt is experienced in the brain (where the memory has its seat), so sensible that it seems the whole head swoons and consciousness and sensibility are lost.[2] This is sometimes more perceptible, sometimes less, according to the force of the touch. Then, owing to the union, the memory is emptied and purged of all knowledge, as I say, and remains in oblivion, at times in such great oblivion that it must occasionally force itself and struggle in order to remember something.

6. Sometimes this forgetfulness of the memory and suspension of the imagination reaches such a degree—because the memory is united with God—that a long time passes without awareness or knowledge of what has happened. Even though others may inflict pain on a person in this state, it is not felt, since the imaginative power is in suspension, and without the imagination there is no feeling. So God may produce these touches of union, the soul must disunite the memory from all apprehensible knowledge. These suspensions, it should be noted, occur at the

---

1. See A. 2. 16. 7.
2. Although John introduces the memory as a spiritual faculty along with the intellect and will, he often identifies it in its functions with the sensible memory and here, in accord with the aristotelian-scholastic system, locates its seat in the brain. Here, too, he is referring to phenomena of a passive and spiritual nature having bodily repercussions. Cf. C. 13.

beginning of union and thus are not found in souls who have reached perfection, because the union is then perfect.

7. Someone may object that this doctrine seems good, but it results in destruction of the natural activity and use of the faculties, so a human person would then be living in oblivion like an animal and, even worse, without remembering natural needs and functions; and in addition, that God does not destroy but perfects nature,[3] and the destruction of nature necessarily follows from this doctrine. For according to these instructions, carrying out natural operations and moral and rational acts would be forgotten. None of this could be remembered, because of the privation of concepts and forms, the means of reminiscence.

8. I answer that this is actually so. The more the memory is united with God, the more the distinct knowledge is perfected, until the memory loses it entirely; that is, when the soul is perfect and has reached the state of union. Thus in the beginning, when this union is in the process of being perfected, a person cannot but experience great forgetfulness of all things since forms and knowledge are gradually being erased from the memory. Owing to the absorption of the memory in God, a person will show many deficiencies in exterior behavior and customs, forgetting to eat and drink or failing to remember if some task was done, or a particular object seen, or something said.

Yet once the habit of union—which is a supreme good—is attained one no longer experiences these lapses of memory in matters concerning the moral and natural life. Rather, such persons will possess greater perfection in actions that are necessary and fitting. These operations, however, are no longer produced through forms and knowledge in the memory, for by possessing habitual union, which is now a supernatural state, the memory and other faculties fail entirely in their natural operations and pass from these natural boundaries to those of God, which are supernatural. Thus, when the memory is transformed in God, the knowledge and forms of things cannot be impressed on it.

As a result all the operations of the memory and other faculties in this state are divine. God now possesses the faculties as their complete lord, because of their transformation in him. And consequently it is he who divinely moves and commands them according to his divine spirit and will. As a result the operations are not different from those of God; but those the soul performs are of God and are divine operations. Since the one who is united with God is one spirit with him, as St. Paul says [1 Cor. 6:17], the operations of the soul united with God are of the divine Spirit and are divine.

---

3. For this principle, see Aquinas, *Summa theologiae* 1. 1. 8 ad 2.

9. These souls, consequently, perform only fitting and reasonable works, and none that are not so. For God's Spirit makes them know what must be known and ignore what must be ignored, remember what ought to be remembered—with or without forms—and forget what ought to be forgotten, and makes them love what they ought to love, and keeps them from loving what is not in God. Accordingly, all the first movements and operations of these faculties are divine. There is no reason to wonder about these movements and operations being divine, since they are transformed into divine being.[4]

10. Here are some examples of these divine operations. A person will ask a soul in this state for prayers. The soul will not remember to carry out this request through any form or idea of that person remaining in the memory. If it is expedient to pray for this one (that is, if God wants to receive prayer for that person), God will move the soul's will and impart a desire to do so; at times God will give it a desire to pray for others whom it has never known or heard of.

The reason is that God alone moves these souls toward those works that are in harmony with his will and ordinance, and they cannot be moved toward others. Thus the works and prayer of these souls always produce their effect.

Such was the prayer and work of our Lady, the most glorious Virgin. Raised from the beginning to this high state, she never had the form of any creature impressed in her soul, nor was she moved by any, for she was always moved by the Holy Spirit.

11. Another example: At a particular time one will have to attend to a necessary business matter. There will be no remembrance through any form, but, without one's knowing how, the time and suitable way of attending to it will be impressed on the soul without fail.

12. The Holy Spirit illumines such souls not merely in these matters but in many other present or future matters and about many events, even distant ones. Although he sometimes accomplishes this through intellectual forms, he often does so without them so that these souls are unaware of how they come by this knowledge. But its origin is divine Wisdom. Since these souls are practiced in not knowing or understanding anything with the faculties, they generally attain, as we mentioned in the drawing of the Mount,[5] to the knowledge of everything; as the Wise Man

---

4. Here John is speaking not about the purification of the memory but of its condition in the state of union in which God works without obstacle in it and the other faculties. Cf. C. 26. 14-18; 27. 6-8; 28. 2-8; 34. 5-7; 38. 4.
5. Cf. A. 1. 13. 10.

states: The artificer of all, who is Wisdom, taught me all things [Wis. 7:21].

13. You may object, perhaps, that the soul cannot so void and deprive the memory of all forms and phantasies as to be able to reach so high a state. In your view there will be two difficulties insurmountable by human strength and capacity: banishment of the natural through one's natural strength, which is impossible, and contact and union with the supernatural, which is far more difficult and, to be truthful, impossible by one's natural ability alone.

I reply that, indeed, God must place the soul in this supernatural state. Nevertheless, individuals must insofar as possible prepare themselves. This they can do naturally, especially with God's help. In the measure that they enter into this negation and emptiness of forms through their own efforts, they will receive from God the possession of union. God effects this union in them passively, as we will explain, *Deo dante*, in the passive night of the soul. Thus God will give the habit of perfect divine union when he is pleased to do so and in accordance with the individual's preparation.[6]

14. We will not discuss in this active night and purgation the divine effects that union, when perfect, produces in the intellect, memory, and will, because divine union is not perfected by this night alone. But we will speak of them in the passive night, for it is by means of this passive night that union with God is wrought.

I will treat here only of the manner in which, through the spiritual person's own efforts, the memory must be brought into this night and purgation. In short, the spiritual person should ordinarily take this precaution: Do not store objects of hearing, sight, smell, taste, or touch in the memory, but leave them immediately and forget them, and endeavor, if necessary, to be as successful in forgetting them as others are in remembering them. This should be practiced in such a way that no form or figure of any of these objects remains in the memory, as though one were not in the world at all. The memory, as though it were nonexistent, should be left free and disencumbered and unattached to any earthly or heavenly consideration. It should be freely left in oblivion, as though it were a hindrance, since everything natural is an obstacle rather than a help to anyone who would desire to use it in the supernatural.

15. If the doubts and objections should arise that we discussed in

---

6. In the measure that the soul tries to dispose itself, God is at work in it, gradually bringing it to the point at which his own action prevails. The soul then, finding itself in the "supernatural state," ceases to work in its connatural mode. John deals with the promised material in the second book of the *Dark Night*.

dealing with the intellect, that is, that nothing is accomplished, time is lost, and the soul is deprived of the spiritual goods receivable through the memory, the answers to them are all in that part.[7] We will also refer to these objections further on, in the passive night. Accordingly there is no reason for delay with them here.

It is only proper to advise here that although at times spiritual persons do not experience the benefit of this suspension of knowledge and forms, they should not grow weary, for God will not fail to come to their aid at a suitable time. And it greatly behooves one to endure and suffer patiently and hopefully for so remarkable a blessing.

16. Although it is true that a soul will hardly be found whose union with God is so continuous that the faculties, without any form, are always divinely moved, nevertheless there are those who are habitually moved by God and not by themselves in their operations, as St. Paul says: The children of God (those who are transformed in God and united to him) are moved by the Spirit of God (that is, moved to divine works in their faculties) [Rom. 8:14]. It is no marvel that the operations are divine, since the union of the soul with God is divine.

CHAPTER 3

Three kinds of harm received by the soul from not darkening the memory in regard to knowledge and discursive reflection. A discussion of the first kind.

1. Spiritual persons who still wish to make use of natural knowledge and discursive reflection in their journey to God, or for anything else, are subject to three kinds of harm and difficulty. Two are positive and one privative. The first kind arises from things of the world, the second from the devil. The third kind, the privative, is the impediment and hindrance to divine union that this knowledge causes.[1]

2. The first, coming from the world, involves subjection to many evils arising from this knowledge and reflection, such as: falsehoods, imperfections, appetites, judgments, loss of time, and numerous other evils engendering many impurities in the soul.

Clearly, spiritual persons allowing themselves this knowledge and reflection will necessarily fall victim to many falsehoods. Often the true will appear false, and the certain doubtful, and vice versa, since we can

---

7. Cf. A. 2. 12-15, where he speaks of doubts arising in the transition from meditation to contemplation.

1. The explanation that follows shows how the division into sense and spirit, with its corresponding books, is not clear-cut.

hardly have complete knowledge of a truth. These persons free them-selves of this if they darken their memory to all knowledge and reflection.

3. Imperfections meet them at every step, if they turn their memory to the objects of hearing, sight, touch, smell, and taste. By so doing some emotion will cling to them, whether it be sorrow, or fear, or hatred, vain hope, vain joy, or vainglory, and so on. All these are at least imperfections, and sometimes real venial sins. They subtly contaminate the soul with impurity even when the knowledge and reflection concern God.

And it is also clear that appetites will be engendered since they naturally arise from this knowledge and reflection. And the mere desire for this knowledge and reflection is already an appetite.

Obviously people also encounter many occasions to judge others, since by using their memory they cannot help but stumble on good or evil deeds of others. And at times evil seems good and good, evil. I am of the opinion that no one can really get free from all these evils without blinding and darkening the memory as to all things.

4. You may say that humans are easily capable of conquering all these dangers when they come upon them. I reply that it is simply impossible to achieve this completely if one pays attention to this knowledge, for intermingled with it are a thousand imperfections and fancies, some so subtle and slight that without one's being aware they stick to the soul just as pitch does to anyone who touches it. These imperfections are better overcome all at once through complete denial of the memory.

You may also object that the soul will suffer the loss of numerous holy thoughts and considerations about God that are helpful toward the reception of favors from him. I answer that purity of soul is more helpful toward this, for purity of soul consists in not having any attachment to creatures—or any temporal things that cling to one—and in not paying attention to them. I think this attachment cannot but adhere to the soul a great deal because of the imperfections the faculties have of themselves in their operations. It is better to learn to silence and quiet the faculties so that God may speak. For in this state, as we pointed out,[2] the natural operations must fade from sight. This is realized when the soul arrives at solitude in these faculties, and God speaks to its heart, as the prophet asserts [Hos. 2:14].

5. If you still insist, claiming that a person will obtain no benefits if the memory does not consider and reflect about God, and that many distractions and weaknesses will gradually find entrance, I answer that this is impossible. If the memory is recollected as to both heavenly and

2. In ch. 3. 3-8.

earthly things, there is no entry for evils, distractions, fancies, or vices—all of which enter through the wandering of the memory. Distractions would result if, on closing the door to reflections and discursive meditation, we opened it to thoughts about earthly matters. But in our case we close the memory to all things—from which distractions and evils arise—by rendering it silent and mute, and listening to God in silence with the hearing of the spirit, saying with the prophet: *Speak Lord, for your servant is listening* [1 Kgs. 3:10]. The Bridegroom in the Song of Songs proclaimed that this was to be the attitude of the bride: *My sister is a garden enclosed and a fountain sealed up* [Sg. 4:12], that is to all the things that can enter it.

6. The soul should remain closed, then, without cares or afflictions, for he who entered the room of his disciples bodily while the doors were closed and gave them peace, without their knowing how this was possible [Jn. 20:19-20], will enter the soul spiritually without its knowing how or using any effort of its own, once it has closed the doors of its intellect, memory, and will to all apprehensions. And he will fill them with peace, *descending on them,* as the prophet says, *like a river of peace* [Is. 66:12]. In this peace he will remove all the misgivings, suspicions, disturbances, and darknesses that made the soul fear it had gone astray. The soul should persevere in prayer and should hope in the midst of nakedness and emptiness, for its blessings will not be long in coming.

CHAPTER 4

The second kind of harm, which comes from the devil through the natural apprehensions of the memory.

1. The second kind of positive harm possible from knowledge in the memory is due to the devil. He has tremendous influence in the soul by this means, for he can add to its knowledge other forms, ideas, and reasonings, and by means of them move it to pride, avarice, anger, envy, and so on, and insert unjust hatred, vain love, and many kinds of delusions. Moreover, he usually so impresses images on the phantasy that the false ones seem true and the true ones false. And finally, all the greatest delusions and evils he produces in the soul enter through the ideas and discursive acts of the memory. If the memory is darkened as to all this knowledge and annihilated through oblivion, the door is closed entirely to this kind of diabolical harm and the soul is liberated from these things, and that is a wonderful blessing.

The devil is unable to do anything in the soul save through the operations of its faculties and principally by means of its knowledge, because almost all the activity of the soul's other faculties depends on its knowledge. If the memory is annihilated concerning this knowledge, the devil is powerless, for he finds no means of getting his grip on the soul and consequently can do nothing.

2. I should like spiritual persons to have full realization of how many evils the devils cause in souls that make much use of their memories; of how much sadness, affliction, vain and evil joy from both spiritual and worldly thoughts these devils occasion; and of the number of impurities they leave rooted in the spirit. They also seriously distract these souls from the highest recollection, a recollection that consists in concentrating all the faculties on the incomprehensible Good and withdrawing them from all apprehensible things, for these apprehensible things are not a good that is beyond comprehension.

Although the good derived from this void is not as excellent as that arising from the application of the soul to God, by the mere fact that such emptiness liberates us from much sorrow, affliction, and sadness—over and above imperfections and sins—it is an exceptional blessing.

CHAPTER 5

The third kind of harm that follows from the natural, distinct knowledge of the memory.

1. The <u>third</u> kind of evil engendered by the natural apprehensions of the memory is privative. These apprehensions can be an impediment to moral good and deprive one of spiritual good.

To explain how these apprehensions are a hindrance to moral good, one must know that moral good consists in bridling the passions and curbing the inordinate appetites. The result for the soul is tranquility, peace, repose, and moral virtue, which is the moral good.

The soul is incapable of truly acquiring control of the passions and restriction of the inordinate appetites without forgetting and withdrawing from the sources of these emotions. Disturbances never arise in a soul unless through the apprehensions of the memory. When all things are forgotten, nothing disturbs the peace or stirs the appetites. As the saying goes: What the eye doesn't see, the heart doesn't want.

2. We experience this all the time. We observe that as often as people begin to think about some matter, they are moved and aroused over it, little or much, according to the kind of apprehension. If the apprehension is bothersome and annoying, they feel sadness or hatred, and so on; if agreeable, they experience desire and joy, and so on.

Accordingly, when the apprehension is changed agitation necessarily results. Thus they will sometimes be joyful, at other times sad, now they will feel hatred, now love. And they are unable to persevere in equanimity, the effect of moral tranquility, unless they endeavor to forget all things. Evidently, then, this knowledge is a serious impediment to possession of the moral virtues.

3. That an encumbered memory is also a hindrance to the possession of spiritual good is clearly proved from our remarks. An unsettled soul that has no foundation of moral good is incapable, as such, of receiving spiritual good, for this spiritual good is impressed only on a restrained and peaceful soul.

Besides, if souls bestow importance and attention on the apprehensions of the memory, they will find it impossible to remain free for the Incomprehensible who is God, for they will be unable to advert to more than one thing. As we have always insisted, souls must go to God by not comprehending rather than by comprehending, and they must exchange the mutable and comprehensible for the Immutable and Incomprehensible.

CHAPTER 6

The benefits derived from forgetting the natural thoughts and knowledge of the memory.

1. From the kinds of harm occasioned by the apprehensions of the memory we can also determine the opposite benefits that come from forgetting them; as the philosophers say: The doctrine for one thing serves also for its contrary.[1]

In contrast to the first kind of harm, spiritual persons enjoy tranquility and peace of soul due to the absence of the disturbance and change arising from thoughts and ideas in the memory, and consequently they possess purity of conscience and soul, which is a greater benefit. As a result they are disposed excellently for human and divine wisdom and virtues.

2. In contrast to the second, they are freed from many suggestions, temptations, and movements that the devil inserts in souls through their thoughts and ideas, thereby occasioning many impurities and sins. As David says: *They thought and spoke wickedness* [Ps. 73:8]. When the thoughts are removed, the devil has nothing naturally with which to wage his war on the spirit.

---

1. For this adage taken from what was called natural philosophy, cf. Aquinas, *Summa theologiae* 1-2. 54. 2 ad 1.

3. Contrary to the third kind of harm, the soul is disposed, by means of this recollection and forgetfulness of all things, to be moved by the Holy Spirit and taught by him. As the Wise Man declares: *He withdraws from thoughts that are without reason* [Wis. 1:5].

Even though no other benefit would come through this oblivion and void of the memory than freedom from afflictions and disturbances, it would be an immense advantage and blessing for a person. For the afflictions and disturbances engendered in a soul through adversities are no help in remedying these adversities; rather, distress and worry ordinarily make things worse and even do harm to the soul itself. Thus David proclaimed: *Indeed every human being is disturbed in vain* [Ps. 39:6]. Clearly, it is always vain to be disturbed, since being disturbed is never any help.

Thus if the whole world were to crumble and come to an end and all things were to go wrong, it would be useless to get disturbed, for this would do more harm than good. Enduring all with tranquil and peaceful equanimity not only reaps many blessings but also helps the soul so that in these very adversities it may manage better in judging them and employing the proper remedy.

4. Solomon, having clear knowledge of this harm and this advantage, exclaimed: *I knew there was nothing better for humans than to rejoice and do good in life* [Eccl. 3:12]. By this he indicates that in all events, however unfavorable, we ought rather to rejoice than be disturbed, and bear them all with equanimity so as not to lose a blessing greater than all prosperity, which is tranquility of soul and peace in all things, adverse or prosperous. People would never lose this tranquility if they were to forget ideas and lay aside their thoughts and also, insofar as possible, withdraw from dealing with others and from hearing and seeing. Our nature is so unstable and fragile that, even when well disciplined, the memory will hardly fail to stumble on things that disturb the soul that was living in peace and tranquility through the forgetfulness of all. As a result Jeremiah proclaimed: *With the memory I will remember, and my soul will faint in me with sorrow* [Lam. 3:20].

CHAPTER 7

The second kind of apprehension, which is of supernatural imaginative knowledge.

1. Though in our discussion of the first kind of apprehension, the natural, we also gave doctrine for the natural imaginative apprehensions, we find this division suitable because of the other forms and ideas the memory preserves. These are from supernatural apprehensions, such as visions, revelations, locutions, and spiritual feelings. When these appre-

hensions occur they usually leave an image, form, figure, or idea impressed either in the soul or in the memory or phantasy. At times this impression is most vivid and efficacious. It is also necessary to give advice about these apprehensions lest they become an encumbrance to the memory and hinder it from union with God in pure and integral hope.

2. I declare that to obtain this blessing individuals should never reflect on clear and distinct supernatural apprehensions for the purpose of preserving within themselves these forms, figures, and ideas. We must always bear in mind this presupposition: The more importance given to any clear and distinct apprehension, natural or supernatural, the less capacity and preparedness the soul has for entering the abyss of faith, where all else is absorbed. As we pointed out,[1] none of the supernatural forms and ideas that can be received by the memory is God, and the soul must empty itself of all that is not God in order to go to God. Consequently the memory must likewise dismiss all these forms and ideas in order to reach union with God in hope. Every possession is against hope. As St. Paul says, *hope is for that which is not possessed* [Heb. 11:1].

In the measure that the memory becomes dispossessed of things, in that measure it will have hope, and the more hope it has the greater will be its union with God; for in relation to God, the more a soul hopes the more it attains. And it hopes more when, precisely, it is more dispossessed of things; when it has reached perfect dispossession it will remain with perfect possession of God in divine union. But there are many who do not want to go without the sweetness and delight of this knowledge in the memory, and therefore they do not reach supreme possession and complete sweetness. For whoever does not renounce all possessions cannot be Christ's disciple [Lk. 14:33].

CHAPTER 8

The harm caused from reflection on this supernatural knowledge. Tells how many kinds of harm there are.

1. Spiritual persons expose themselves to five types of harm if they prize and reflect on the ideas and forms impressed within them through supernatural apprehensions.

2. The first is that they will often be deluded in mistaking the natural for the supernatural.

Second, they put themselves in the occasion of falling into presumption and vanity.

---

1. In ch. 2.3-4.

Third, the devil finds ample power to deceive them through these apprehensions.

Fourth, doing so would impede union with God in hope.

Fifth, for the most part they will be judging God in a lowly way.

3. As for the first, if spiritual persons reflect on these forms and ideas and assign them importance, they will frequently be deceived in their judgment. Since no one is capable of knowing perfectly the things that pass naturally through the imagination, or of forming an integral and certain judgment about them, how much less is one able to make judgments about supernatural things, which transcend our capacity and occur but rarely.

Spiritual persons will often think that the apprehensions are from God, whereas they will be only the product of the imagination. And often they think that what is from God is from the devil and what is from the devil is from God. They will frequently receive, among other images, strong impressions about their own or others' goods and evils. And they hold these to be very certain and true, yet they will not be true but utterly false. Other impressions will be true, yet they will judge them false; although this, I believe, is safer because it is usually the outcome of humility.

4. If they escape delusion about the truth, they can still suffer a quantitative or qualitative delusion. They will think the small, great, and the great, small. Or as to quality, what is in their imagination and judged by them to be this particular kind will in reality be another kind. They will be taking, as Isaiah says, *the darkness for light and the light for darkness, the bitter for the sweet and the sweet for the bitter* [Is. 5:20]. Finally, if they are correct in one matter it will be a wonder if they escape error in another. Even if they do not want to make judgments, it is enough for them to place some importance on these apprehensions for a certain harm to cling to them, at least passively. And if it is not this type of harm it will be one of the four other kinds we shall be discussing.

5. To avoid this evil of being deceived in their judgments, spiritual persons should be unwilling to make judgments about the nature of their experiences or the kind of visions, knowledge, or feeling they have. They should not desire to know this or attribute importance to it except for the sake of informing their spiritual father so he may teach them how to void the memory of these apprehensions. Whatever these apprehensions may in themselves be, they are not as great a help toward the love of God as is the least act of living faith and hope made in the emptiness and renunciation of all things.

CHAPTER 9

The second kind of harm, the danger of falling into self-esteem and vain presumption.

1. These supernatural apprehensions of the memory, if esteemed, are also for spiritual persons a decided occasion for slipping into some presumption or vanity. Since those who do not receive these apprehensions are liberated from falling into this vice because nothing within them warrants this presumption, so, on the other hand, those who receive them will be exposed to the idea that they themselves are now important because of these supernatural communications. Although it is true that one can attribute them to God and be thankful for them and consider oneself unworthy, yet there usually remains in the spirit a certain hidden satisfaction and an esteem both for the communication and for oneself. Consequently, without one's realizing it, an abundant spiritual pride will be bred.

2. This is quite evident from the displeasure and aversion these individuals feel toward anyone who does not laud their spirit or value their communications, and from the affliction they experience on thinking or being told that others receive the same favors or even better ones. All this is born of hidden self-esteem and pride. And these persons are not fully aware that they are steeped in pride. They think that a certain degree of knowledge of one's own misery is sufficient. Yet at the same time they are full of hidden self-esteem and satisfaction, more pleased with their own spirit and spiritual goods than with those of their neighbor. They resemble the pharisee who thanked God that he was not like others and that he had various virtues, and who derived self-satisfaction and presumption from the thought of these virtues [Lk. 18:11-12]. Though they may not express this as the pharisee did, they habitually feel this way in their spirit. Indeed, some become so proud that they are worse than the devil. Since they observe interiorly some apprehensions and devout and sweet feelings that they think are from God, they become self-satisfied to the extent of thinking that they are very close to God and others who do not have these experiences are far beneath them and, like the pharisee, they look down upon these others.

3. To avoid this pestiferous evil, abhorrent in the eyes of God, they should consider two truths:

First, virtue does not consist in apprehensions and feelings of God, however sublime they may be, or in any similar experience. On the contrary, it comprises what they do not experience: that is, deep humility, contempt for themselves and all things (very explicit and conscious to the soul), delight that others feel contempt for them also, and not wanting to be worth anything in the heart of another.

4. Second, all heavenly visions, revelations, and feelings—or whatever else one may desire to think on—are not worth as much as the least act of humility. Humility has the effects of charity: It neither esteems nor seeks its own, it thinks no evil save of self, it thinks no good of self but of others. Consequently souls should not look for their happiness in these supernatural apprehensions, but should strive to forget them for the sake of being free.

CHAPTER 10

The third kind of harm stemming from the imaginative apprehensions of the memory, that which comes from the devil.

1. It can be deduced and easily understood from all we have said above how much evil can come from the devil by way of these supernatural apprehensions. He can present many false ideas and forms to the memory under the guise of their being true and good. This he does by impressing them on the spirit and the senses through suggestion with much certification and efficacy. They then seem so certain that the soul thinks they cannot be false, but that what it feels is in accord with truth. Since the devil transforms himself into an angel of light [2 Cor. 11:14], he seems to be light to the soul. But this is not all. In true visions from God he can also tempt it in many ways by causing inordinate movements of the spiritual and sensory appetites and affections toward these visions. If the soul is pleased with these apprehensions it is very easy for the devil to bring about an increase of the appetites and affections and a lapse into spiritual gluttony and other harmful things.

2. To better accomplish this he usually suggests and places pleasure, savor, and delight in the senses relevant to these things of God so that, sweetened and dazzled by that delight, the soul may become blind and fix its eyes more on the delightful feeling than on the love—or at least not so intensely on the love—and pay more attention to the apprehension than to the nakedness and emptiness that lie in faith, hope, and love. And in so doing the devil deceives the soul little by little and readily makes it believe his falsehoods.

To a blind soul falsehood no longer seems falsehood, and evil no longer evil, and so on, for the darkness appears to be light, and the light darkness [Is. 5:20]. On this account the soul will fall into a thousand blunders in matters natural, moral, and spiritual; and what was wine will have turned into vinegar. All this comes about because of failure from the beginning to deny the pleasure taken in those supernatural apprehensions. Since this satisfaction is slight, or not so evil, at first, the soul is not careful and allows it to remain so that, like the mustard seed, the evil grows into a large tree [Mt. 13:31-32]. As the saying goes, small mistake in the beginning, great one in the end.

3. To flee this gross error of the devil, therefore, it greatly behooves individuals not to want to find satisfaction in these apprehensions, for most certainly this satisfaction will gradually blind them and cause them to fall. Pleasure, delight, and savor blind the soul by their very own nature, without the devil's help. David indicated this when he said: *Darkness will perhaps blind me in my delights and I shall have the night for my light* [Ps. 139:11].

CHAPTER 11

An impediment to union with God, the fourth kind of harm resulting from the distinct supernatural apprehensions of the memory.

1. Little remains to be said about this fourth kind of harm since we are explaining it all along in this third book. We have given proof that a soul must renounce all possession of the memory in order to reach union with God in hope, for if hope is to be centered entirely on God, nothing that is not God should reside in the memory.

And we have also given proof that no form, figure, image, or idea (whether heavenly or earthly, natural or supernatural) that can be grasped by the memory is God or like to him. Accordingly, David teaches: *Lord, among the gods no one is like you* [Ps. 86:8].

Consequently, if the memory desires to pay attention to this knowledge it is hindered from union with God: first, because of the encumbrance; second, because the more possessions it has the less hope it has.

2. The soul, therefore, must live in nakedness and forgetfulness of distinct forms and knowledge about supernatural apprehensions so as not to impede union of the memory with God through perfect hope.

CHAPTER 12

Base and improper judgments about God, the fifth kind of harm arising from supernatural imaginative forms and apprehensions.

1. The fifth kind of harm derived from the desire of preserving in the memory and imagination these forms and images of supernatural

communications is no less evil than the others, especially if the soul
desires to use these images as means toward divine union. It is extremely
easy to judge the being and height of God less worthily and sublimely
than befits his incomprehensibility. Though one may not form an
explicit idea that God is similar to these apprehensions, nevertheless the
very esteem for them—if, in fact, one esteems them—produces in the
soul an estimation and opinion of God less elevated than is given in the
teaching of faith: that he is incomparable, incomprehensible, and so on.

In addition to taking all this attention given to creatures away from
God, the soul will naturally form in its interior, through esteem for these
apprehensions, a certain comparison between them and God. This
comparison prevents it from having as lofty a judgment and esteem of
God as it ought.

Creatures, earthly or heavenly, and all distinct ideas and images,
natural and supernatural, that can be the objects of a person's faculties,
are incomparable and unproportioned to God's being. God does not fall
under the classifications of genus and species, whereas, according to
theologians, creatures do.[1] And the soul is not capable of receiving
clearly and distinctly in this life what does not fall under the classifications
of genus and species. Thus St. John affirms that no one has ever seen God
[Jn. 1:18]. Isaiah declares that it has not entered the human heart what
God is like [Is. 64:4]. And God told Moses: *You cannot see me in this life* [Ex.
33:20]. Therefore anyone encumbering the memory and the other
faculties of the soul with what is comprehensible cannot have a proper
esteem or opinion of God.

2. Here is a poor example. The more people set their eyes on the king's
servants and the more attention they pay to them, the less heed they pay
to the king and the less they esteem him. Though this estimation is not
in the intellect formally and explicitly, it is there practically; because the
more attention they give to the servants, the more they take away from
their lord. And then their judgment of the king is not very high since the
servants seem to them somewhat important in comparison with the king,
their lord. This is what happens in relation to God when a person pays
attention to these creatures, although the comparison is very inadequate
because, as we have mentioned, the being of God is different from the
being of his creatures. God, by his being, is infinitely distant from all of
these creatures. The soul should consequently turn its eyes from these
creatures so as to focus them on God in faith and hope.

3. Those who not only pay heed to these imaginative apprehensions
but think God resembles some of them, and that one can journey to

---

1. Cf. Aquinas, *Summa theologiae* 1. 3. 5; *Contra gentes* 1. 25.

union with God through them, are already in great error and will gradually lose the light of faith in their intellect. And it is by means of faith that the intellect is united with God. Furthermore, they will not increase in the loftiness of hope, the means for union with God in the memory. This union is effected by disuniting oneself from everything imaginative.

CHAPTER 13

The benefits obtained through the rejection of the apprehensions of the imagination. Answers certain objections and explains the difference between the natural and the supernatural imaginative apprehensions.

1. Like the observation we made concerning natural forms, the benefits from voiding the imagination of supernatural apprehensions can be ascertained through the five kinds of harm caused in the soul if it desires to possess these forms interiorly.

But besides these, there are other benefits of deep spiritual repose and quietude. In addition to the tranquility a person naturally enjoys when freed from images and forms, there is a freedom from care about the discernment of good ones from evil, and about how one ought to behave with different kinds. Finally one would be absolved from the drudgery and waste of time that would result from desiring spiritual masters both to discern the good apprehensions from the evil ones and to ascertain the kind of apprehension received. People do not have to know this, since they should not pay attention to any of these apprehensions. The time and energy that would be wasted in trying to discern them can be employed in another, more profitable exercise (the movement of the will toward God), and in solicitude about the search after spiritual and sensory nakedness and poverty (the desire to lack all the consoling support of the apprehensions, both interior and exterior). Individuals practice this latter by desiring and striving after detachment from these forms, since they thereby receive the great gain of approaching God, who has neither image, nor form, nor figure. They will approach God more closely the more they withdraw from all imaginative forms, images, and figures.

2. Perhaps your question will be: Why do many spiritual persons counsel souls to strive for profit in the communications and feelings given by God and to desire favors from him in order to have something to give him, since if God gives nothing to us, we shall have nothing to give to him? And you will establish this with a text from St. Paul: *Do not extinguish the spirit* [1 Thes. 5:19]; also with one from the Song of Songs in which the bridegroom says to the bride: *Put me as a seal upon your heart,*

as a seal upon your arm [Sg. 8:6], for this seal is a certain apprehension. And all of this, you will say, according to our doctrine, must not only be unsought but rejected and put aside even though God bestows it; and evidently, since God grants this gift, he does so for a good purpose and it will be effective. You will add that we must not throw away pearls and it is a kind of pride to refuse God's gifts as though we were self-sufficient without them.

3. In answer to this objection, our explanation in chapters 15 and 16 of Book Two must necessarily be kept in mind.[1] To a great extent the objection is answered there. We stated that the good resulting in the soul from supernatural apprehensions that come from a good source is produced passively, without any operation of the faculties, at the very moment these apprehensions are represented to the senses.

It is consequently unnecessary for the will to act in order to admit them. As we said, if souls were to desire to act with their faculties, through their base natural operation they would impede the supernatural (which God is producing in them by means of these apprehensions) rather than derive profit from their own labor. But since the spirit of these imaginative apprehensions is given passively to the soul, they must maintain a passive attitude without application of their interior or exterior actions to anything.

And this attitude would preserve the spiritual feelings of God, because individuals would not then lose them through their own lowly kind of operation. Nor would they extinguish the spirit. People extinguish the spirit by wanting to conduct themselves in a way different from the way God is leading them. They act this way if they desire, when God gives them the spirit passively—as he does through these apprehensions—to be active by working with the intellect or by desiring something in these apprehensions.

This is clear, for if the soul would then want to work, its activity would necessarily be no more than natural. On its own it can do no more, since a soul does not move itself to a supernatural work, nor can it, but God moves it and places it in this supernatural activity. If spiritual persons, then, were to desire to make use of their own efforts, they would necessarily impede by their activity the passive communication of God, which is the spirit. They would be engaging in their own work, which is of another and lower kind than that which God is communicating to them. The work of God is passive and supernatural, that of the soul is active and natural. This natural activity is what would extinguish the spirit.

4. That this is a more lowly work is also clear, for the faculties of the soul cannot of themselves reflect and work except on some form, figure, and

1. The reference is actually in A. 2. 16 and 17.

image, which would be the rind and accident of the substance and spirit.

This substance and spirit is not united with the faculties of the soul in true understanding and love until the operation of the faculties ceases, for the aim of this operation is the reception of substantial understanding and love through those forms. The difference between the active and passive operation and the advantage of one over the other is the same as that between what is being done and what is already done, or what one intends to attain and what has already been attained.

Thus we also deduce that if individuals were to desire to employ their faculties actively in these supernatural apprehensions by which, as we said, they receive the spirit passively from God, they would be doing nothing less than abandoning what has been accomplished in order to redo it; neither would they be enjoying what was done, nor by their activity doing anything other than impeding God's work. For, as we said, these actions cannot independently attain the spirit God was giving to the soul without them. If the soul pays heed to these imaginative apprehensions, it directly extinguishes the spirit that God infuses by means of them.

Consequently, a person should abandon these apprehensions and behave passively and negatively because then God moves the soul to what transcends its power and knowledge. The prophet accordingly declared: *I will stand on my watch and fix my foot on my tower, and I will contemplate what is said to me* [Hb. 2:1]. This is like saying: I will be raised above the watch of my faculties and take no step forward in my operations; thus I will be able to contemplate what is told me, that is, I will understand and taste what is communicated to me supernaturally.

5. The words of the bridegroom that were quoted in the objection should be interpreted as referring to the love he asks of the bride. It is a characteristic of love to assimilate lovers to one another in their spiritual faculties. As a result he tells her to set him as a mark on her heart [Sg. 8:6], there where all the arrows of love (the actions and motives of love) coming from the quiver strike. He does this so that all the arrows might strike him, who is there as their target, and thus all are directed to him. And the soul would become like him through its actions and movements of love until transformed in him. He tells her to set him also as a mark on her arm because the act of love is on the arm, since by the arm the beloved is held and caressed.

6. In these apprehensions coming from above (imaginative or any other kind—it matters not if they be visions, locutions, spiritual feelings, or revelations), individuals should only advert to the love of God that is interiorly caused. They should pay no attention to the letter and rind (what is signified, represented, or made known). Thus they should pay heed not to the feelings of delight or sweetness, not to the images, but to

the feelings of love that are caused.

Only for the sake of moving the spirit to love should the soul at times recall the images and apprehensions that produced love. The effect produced by the remembrance of this communication is not as strong as the effect at the time the communication was received, yet when the communication is recalled there is a renewal of love and an elevation of the mind to God. This is especially true when the soul remembers some figures, images, or supernatural feelings. These are usually so imprinted on it that they last a long time; some are never erased from the soul. These apprehensions produce, almost as often as remembered, divine effects of love, sweetness, light, and so on—sometimes in a greater degree, sometimes in a lesser—because God impressed them for this reason. This is consequently a great grace, for those on whom God bestows it possess within themselves a mine of blessings.

7. The figures producing such effects are vividly impressed on the soul, for they are not like other images and forms preserved in the phantasy. The soul has no need of recourse to this faculty when it desires to remember them, for it is aware that it has them within itself as an image in a mirror. When a soul possesses these figures formally within itself it can safely recall them to obtain the effect of love I mentioned. They will not be a hindrance to the union of love in faith, providing the soul does not desire to be absorbed with the figure. It must profit from the love by immediately leaving aside the figure. In this way the remembrance will instead be a help to the soul.

8. It is difficult to discern when these images are impressed on the soul and when on the phantasy, for those of the phantasy are also quite frequent. Some persons who usually have imaginative visions find that these same visions are very frequently represented in their phantasy, either because they themselves possess a very lively faculty, so that with little thought the ordinary figure is immediately represented and sketched on it, or because the devil causes these representations, or also because God causes them without impressing them formally in the soul.

They can be discerned through their effects nonetheless, for those that are of natural or diabolical origin produce no good effect or spiritual renewal in the soul, no matter how often they are remembered. The individual beholds them in dryness. When remembered, however, the imaginative apprehensions from God produce some good effect by means of that which they imparted to the soul the first time. Yet the formal apprehensions—those impressed on the soul—yield some effect almost every time they are recalled.

9. Anyone with experience of these will easily be able to tell the difference between the two, for the diversity between them is very clear.

I merely assert that those impressed formally on the soul in a lasting way are of rarer occurrence. But whatever may be their kind, it is good for the soul to have no desire to comprehend anything save God alone in hope through faith.

As for the other point in the objection (that it is apparently pride to reject these apprehensions if they are good), I answer: Rather, it is prudent humility to benefit by them in the best way, as has been mentioned, and be guided along the safest path.

CHAPTER 14

Spiritual knowledge in the memory.

1. We placed apprehensions of spiritual knowledge in the third class not because they pertain to the corporeal phantasy—for they do not have a corporeal image and form—as the others do, but because they are likewise the object of spiritual reminiscence and memory.[1] After the soul receives knowledge of this sort it can freely bring that knowledge back to memory. It does not remember this through the effigy or image left in the corporeal sense faculty, for since it is a corporeal sense faculty the phantasy has no capacity for spiritual forms. But it remembers intellectually and spiritually through the form impressed on the soul (which is also a formal or spiritual form, idea, or image), or through the effect produced. As a result, I classify these apprehensions among those of the memory, even though they do not belong to those of the phantasy.

2. We have given a sufficient explanation in chapter 24 of Book Two,[2] where we discussed intellectual apprehensions, of this kind of knowledge and the attitude toward it required for advancement to union with God. See that chapter, because there we have explained how these apprehensions are of two kinds: one referring to the Creator, and the other to creatures.

Concerning what has to do with our intention here (which is to explain the way the memory should conduct itself in order to advance to union), I merely state, as I have just explained in the preceding chapter about formal images, to which class this knowledge of creatures belongs, that this knowledge may be remembered when it produces a good effect, not in order to retain it but to awaken the knowledge and love of God. But if the remembrance of this knowledge of creatures produces no good

---

1. As John turns now to the spiritual or intellectual memory, apart from the phantasy, it is worth noting that Books Two and Three of this work often extend beyond the topic of purification of the spiritual faculties.
2. Actually in A. 2. 26.

effect, the soul should never desire the memory of it.

But as for knowledge of the Creator, I declare that a person should strive to remember it as often as possible because it will produce in the soul a notable effect. For, as we affirmed there, the communications of this knowledge are touches and spiritual feelings of union with God, the goal to which we are guiding the soul. The memory does not recall these through any form, image, or figure that may have been impressed on the soul, for those touches and feelings of union with the Creator do not have any. It remembers them through the effect of light, love, delight, spiritual renewal, and so on, produced in it. Something of this effect is renewed as often as the soul recalls them.

CHAPTER 15

A general rule of conduct for spiritual persons in their use of the memory.

1. To conclude the discussion of the memory, then, it will be worthwhile to delineate briefly a general method for the use of spiritual persons that they may be united with God according to this sense.[1] Even if clearly understood from what we said, the reader will grasp it more easily in a summary.

The following must be kept in mind: Our aim is union with God in the memory through hope; the object of hope is something unpossessed; the less other objects are possessed, the more capacity and ability there is to hope for this one object, and consequently the more hope; the greater the possessions, the less capacity and ability for hoping, and consequently so much less of hope; accordingly, in the measure that individuals dispossess their memory of forms and objects, which are not God, they will fix it on God and preserve it empty, so as to hope for the fullness of their memory from him. What souls must do in order to live in perfect and pure hope in God is this: As often as distinct ideas, forms, and images occur to them, they should immediately, without resting in them, turn to God with loving affection, in emptiness of everything rememberable. They should not think or look on these things for longer than is sufficient for the understanding and fulfillment of their obligations, if these refer to this. And then they should consider these ideas without becoming attached or seeking gratification in them, lest the effects of them be left in the soul. Thus people are not required to stop recalling and thinking about what they must do and know, for, if they are not attached to the possession of these thoughts, they will not be harmed. The verses of the

---

1. He refers to the memory here as a sense faculty. See ch. 14, note 1.

Mount in chapter 13 of the first book are helpful in this practice.[2]

2. Yet it must be noted here that by our doctrine we are not in agreement, nor do we desire to be, with that of those pestiferous people who, persuaded by the pride and envy of Satan, have sought to remove from the eyes of the faithful the holy and necessary use and renowned cult of images of God and his saints.[3] Our doctrine is far different from theirs. We are not asserting, as they do, that there be no images or veneration of them; we are explaining the difference between these images and God, and how souls should use the painted image in such a way as not to suffer hindrance in their movement toward the living image, and how they should pay no more attention to images than is required for advancing to what is spiritual.

The means are good and necessary for the attainment of the end, as are images for reminding us of God and the saints. But when people use and dwell on the means as though these were more than mere means, their excessive use of them becomes as much an impediment as anything else. The impediment is even greater in the case of supernatural visions and images, with which I am especially dealing here and which are the cause of many delusions and dangers.

There is no delusion or danger in the remembrance, veneration, and esteem of images that the Catholic Church proposes to us in a natural manner, since in these images nothing else is esteemed than the person represented. The memory of these images will not fail to benefit a person, because this remembrance is accompanied with love for whoever is represented. Images will always help individuals toward union with God, provided that no more attention is paid to them than necessary for this love, and that souls allow themselves to soar—when God bestows the favor—from the painted image to the living God, in forgetfulness of all creatures and things pertaining to creatures.

CHAPTER 16

The beginning of the treatise on the dark night of the will. A division of the emotions of the will.

1. We would have achieved nothing by purging the intellect and memory in order to ground them in the virtues of faith and hope had we

---

2. In nos. 10-13. The verses in the sketch of the Mount are applicable at every level and in all dimensions of the purgative process.

3. He is referring to the Iconoclasts of the eighth and ninth centuries who opposed the use of icons, and possibly to the Alumbrados and Protestants of his time.

neglected the purification of the will through charity, the third virtue. Through charity works done in faith are living works and have high value; without it they are worth nothing, as St. James affirms: *Without works of charity, faith is dead* [Jas. 2:20].

For a treatise on the active night and denudation of this faculty, with the aim of forming and perfecting it in this virtue of the charity of God, I have found no more appropriate passage than the one in chapter 6 of Deuteronomy, where Moses commands: *You shall love the Lord, your God, with all your heart, and with all your soul, and with all your strength* [Dt. 6:5]. This passage contains all that spiritual persons must do and all I must teach them here if they are to reach God by union of the will through charity. In it human beings receive the command to employ all the faculties, appetites, operations, and emotions of their soul in God so that they will use all this ability and strength for nothing else, in accord with David's words: *Fortitudinem meam ad te custodiam* (I will keep my strength for you) [Ps. 59:10].

2. The strength of the soul comprises the faculties, passions, and appetites. All this strength is ruled by the will. When the will directs these faculties, passions, and appetites toward God, turning away from all that is not God, the soul preserves its strength for God, and comes to love him with all its might.[1]

So a person may do this, we will discuss here purifying the will of all inordinate emotions. These inordinate emotions are the source of unruly appetites, affections, and operations, and the basis for failure to preserve one's strength for God.

There are four of these emotions or passions: joy, hope, sorrow, and fear. These passions manifestly keep the strength and ability of the soul for God, and direct it toward him, when they are so ruled that a person rejoices only in what is purely for God's honor and glory, hopes for nothing else, feels sorrow only about matters pertaining to this, and fears only God. The more people rejoice over something outside God, the less intense will be their joy in God; and the more their hope goes out toward something else, the less there is of it for God; and so on with the others.[2]

---

1. The will plays a decisive role in the purification process in that it moves the other faculties. Because of the appetitive nature of the will, John speaks of emotions, appetites, and so on, instead of apprehensions. Since the theological virtues, each in its own area, purify the whole person, charity purifies this whole appetitive or affective dimension. In dealing in the following chapters with the purification of the entire affective part, not just of the spiritual faculty, John discusses the active purification of the senses more than he does in the first book.
2. Throughout his works, John accepts the scholastic reduction of the 11 passions defined by Aristotle into four principal ones. See Aquinas, *Summa theologiae* 1-2. 25. 4; 23. 4. Cf. A. 1. 13. 5; A. 2. 21. 8; N. 1. 13. 15; C. 20. 4; 28. 4; 40. 4.

3. To give a complete doctrine on this subject, we will, as is our custom, discuss individually these four passions as well as the appetites of the will. The entire matter of reaching union with God consists in purging the will of its appetites and emotions so that from a human and lowly will it may be changed into the divine will, made identical with the will of God.

4. The less strongly the will is fixed on God and the more dependent it is on creatures, the more these four passions combat the soul and reign in it. A person then very easily rejoices in what deserves no rejoicing, hopes for what brings no profit, sorrows over what should perhaps cause rejoicing, and fears where there is no reason for fear.

5. When these emotions go unbridled they are the source of all vices and imperfections, but when they are put in order and calmed they give rise to all the virtues.

It should be known that, in the measure that one of the passions is regulated according to reason, the others are also. These four passions are so interlinked and brotherly that where one goes actually the others go virtually. If one is recollected actually, the other three in the same measure are recollected virtually. If the will rejoices over something, it must consequently in the same degree hope for it, with the virtual inclusion of sorrow and fear. And in the measure that it loses satisfaction in this object, fear, sorrow, and hope will also be lost.

We find a reference to the will and the four passions in the figure Ezekiel saw: four animals with four faces and only one body, in which the wings of one were bound to those of the other; each one went forward and while going ahead they did not turn back [Ez. 1:6-12]. The feathers of each of these emotions are so connected to those of the others that wherever one actually directs its face (its operations), the others need to go virtually; and when one is lowered, as is affirmed there, all the others must be lowered; and when it is raised, the others are raised too [Ez. 1:19-25]. Where your hope goes, there too will go your joy, fear, and sorrow; and if it turns back, they too will turn back; and so on with each of the other passions.

6. Accordingly, you should keep in mind that wherever one of these passions goes the entire soul (the will and the other faculties) will also go, and they will live as prisoners of this passion; and the other three passions will be alive in the one so as to afflict the soul with their chains and prevent it from soaring to the liberty and repose of sweet contemplation and union. As a result Boethius claimed that if you desire a clear understanding of the truth, you must cast from yourself joys, hope, fear, and sorrow.[3]

---

3. See *The Consolation of Philosophy* 1. 7.

As long as these passions reign in the soul they will not allow it to live in the tranquility and peace necessary for the wisdom it can receive naturally and supernaturally.

CHAPTER 17

The first emotion of the will. The nature of joy and a division of the objects of joy.

1. The first passion of the soul and emotion of the will is joy. Joy—to give a definition suited to our purpose—is nothing else than a delight of the will in an object esteemed and considered fitting. For the will never rejoices unless in something that is valuable and pleasing to it. We are speaking of active joy, which occurs when a person understands distinctly and clearly the object of its joy and has power either to rejoice or not.

There is another joy, which is passive. In this kind of joy the will finds itself rejoicing without any clear and distinct understanding of the object of its joy, except at times. It has no power either to possess this joy or not possess it. We will discuss this passive joy afterward.[1] Our topic now is the joy derived from distinct and clear objects, insofar as it is active and voluntary.

2. Joy can arise from six kinds of objects or goods: temporal, natural, sensory, moral, supernatural, and spiritual. We must treat of these in their proper order, regulating the will according to reason, lest it fail to concentrate the vigor of its joy on God because it is being hindered by these goods. We must in all of this presuppose a fundamental principle that will be like a staff, a continual support for our journey. It must be kept in mind, because it is the light by which we will find guidance and understanding in this doctrine and direct joy to God amid all these goods. The principle is: The will should rejoice only in what is for the honor and glory of God, and the greatest honor we can give him is to serve him according to evangelical perfection; anything unincluded in such service is without value to human beings.[2]

---

1. John does not discuss this passive joy as promised. It would be experienced as the fruit of divine action in the soul.

2. The best way to analyze joy is to observe its activity in relation to the various kinds of goods from which it arises and receives nourishment. The six kinds give a sufficiently complete picture of the affective human situation. The first three refer to more exterior goods, the last three to more interior. The basic principle, that the true motive for rejoicing should be the honor and glory of God and the greatest honor we can pay him is to serve him according to evangelical perfection, is applied throughout the following chapters.

CHAPTER 18

Joy in temporal goods. How a person should direct it to God.

1. We listed the first kind of goods as temporal.[1] By temporal goods we mean: riches, status, positions, and other things claiming prestige; and children, relatives, marriages, and so on. All these are possible objects of joy for the will.

But the vanity of rejoicing over riches, titles, status, positions, and other similar goods after which people usually strive is clear. If people were better servants of God by being richer, they would be obliged to rejoice in riches. But riches are rather the occasion of their offending God, as the Wise Man teaches: *Son, if you be rich you shall not be free from sin* [Ecclus. 11:10]. Though it is true that temporal goods of themselves are not necessarily the cause of sin, yet, because of the weakness of its tendencies, the human heart usually becomes attached to them and fails God, which is sin. Thus the Wise Man says you will not be free from sin.

This is why the Lord in the Gospel calls them thorns; the one who willfully handles them will be wounded with some sin [Mt. 13:22; Lk. 8:14]. In St. Luke's Gospel the exclamation—which ought to be greatly feared—asserts: *How difficult will it be for those who have riches to enter the kingdom of heaven* (those who have joy in them), and demonstrates clearly a person's obligation not to rejoice in riches, since one is thereby exposed to so much danger [Lk. 18:24]. In order to turn us from this danger, David also taught: *If riches abound, do not set your heart on them* [Ps. 62:10].

2. I do not want to add any more references here on so clear a matter, for I would never finish quoting Scripture. When would I ever get through telling of the evils Solomon attributes to them in Ecclesiastes? A man who had abundant riches, and knowledge of what they are, exclaimed that everything under the sun was vanity of vanities, affliction of spirit, and vain solicitude of soul [Eccl. 1:14]; that the lover of riches will not reap fruit from them [Eccl. 5:9]; and that riches are kept to the harm of their owner [Eccl. 5:12]. This last assertion is evident also in the Gospel, where the man who rejoiced because for many years he had stored away a good portion of the harvest heard these words from heaven: *Fool, this night they will seek your soul that you may render an accounting, and whose will be all that you stored away?* [Lk. 12:20]. Finally, David imparts the same teaching, that we should not be envious when our neighbor becomes rich, since being rich is without profit for the next life [Ps. 49:16-17]. He indicates thereby that we ought rather to pity our rich neighbor.

---

1. In ch. 17. 2.

3. People should not rejoice over riches, neither when they possess them nor when their neighbor possesses them, unless God is served through them. If it is in some way tolerable to rejoice in riches, it is when they are spent and employed in the service of God. This is the only way profit will be drawn from them.

The same holds true for other temporal goods, titles and positions, and so on. It is vain for people to rejoice in these goods if they do not serve God by them and walk more securely on the road of eternal life. And because they cannot know with certitude that they are serving God more, it would be vain of them to rejoice over these goods, for such joy cannot be reasonable. As our Lord says, even though one gains the whole world, one can lose one's soul [Mt. 16:26]. The only reason for rejoicing then is the greater service of God.

4. As for children, there is no reason to rejoice in them because they are many, or rich, or endowed with natural talents and gifts, or because they are wealthy. One should rejoice in them if they are serving God. Beauty, riches, and lineage were of no help to Absalom, David's son, since he did not serve God [2 Sm. 14:25]. The joy he found, therefore, in these goods was vain.

It is also vain to desire children, as some do in upsetting and troubling the whole world with their longing for them. For they do not know whether the children will be good and serve God, or whether the expected happiness will instead be sorrow, or the rest and comfort, trial and grief, or the honor, dishonor. And because of the children they might, as many do, offend God more. Christ says of these people that they circle the earth and the sea in order to enrich their children, and they make them children of perdition twice as much as they themselves [Mt. 23:15].

5. Even though all things are smiling and succeeding prosperously, people should have misgivings rather than joy, since the occasion and danger of forgetting God thereby increases. This is the motive Solomon gave in Ecclesiastes for taking precaution: *I judged laughter an error, and to joy I said: Why are you deceived in vain?* [Eccl. 2:2]. This was like saying: When things smiled on me, I considered it error and deceit to be glad over them, for doubtless the error and foolishness of people who are joyous over what apparently brings them prosperity and success is gross, because they do not know whether some eternal good will result or not. The heart of the fool, states the Wise Man, is where there is gladness; but the heart of the wise is where there is sadness [Eccl. 7:4]. Gladness is blinding to the heart and does not allow it to consider and ponder things, while sadness makes people open their eyes and see the advantage or harm in things. Accordingly, the Wise Man also affirms that anger is

better than laughter [Eccl. 7:3]. Hence it is better to go to a house of mourning than a house of feasting, for in the former we see the end of all human life, as the Wise Man also says [Eccl. 7:2].

6. Indeed, it would also be vanity for a husband and wife to rejoice in their marriage when they are uncertain whether God is being better served by it. They should rather be perplexed, for as St. Paul declares, matrimony is the cause of not centering the heart entirely on God, since the hearts of the couple are set on one another [1 Cor. 7:32-34]. He advises consequently: *If you are free from a wife do not seek one, but if you already have one, be as free of heart as if you had none* [1 Cor. 7:27, 29]. He teaches us this together with what, as we affirmed, he teaches about temporal goods: *This, therefore, that I say to you, brothers, is certain, the time is short; what remains is that those who have wives be as those who have them not; and those who weep as those who do not weep; and those who rejoice as those who do not rejoice; and those who buy as those who do not possess; and those who use this world as those who use it not* [1 Cor. 7:29-31].

The reason he says all this is to explain that nothing but what belongs to the service of God should be the object of our joy. Any other joy would be vain and worthless, for joy that is out of harmony with God is of no value to the soul.

CHAPTER 19

The harm caused from joy in temporal goods.

1. We would run out of ink, paper, and time were we to describe the harm that beleaguers the soul because it turns its affection to temporal goods. Something very small can lead into great evils and destroy remarkable blessings, just as an unextinguished spark can kindle immense fires capable of burning up the world.

All this harm has its origin and root in one main private harm embodied in this joy: withdrawal from God. Just as approaching God through the affection of the will gives rise to every good, so withdrawal from him through creature affection breeds every harm and evil in the soul. The measure of the harm reflects the intensity of the joy and affection with which the will is joined to the creature, for in that proportion does it withdraw from God. Hence the harm incurred will be greater or less and, for the most part, in both an extensive and intensive way, according to the degree of one's withdrawal from God.[1]

---

1. Just as there is gradual growth in the spiritual life there may also be gradual deterioration, as the descriptions in this chapter show. Cf. A. 1. 11.

2. This privative harm, from which the other negative and positive kinds arise, has four degrees, one worse than the other. When individuals reach the fourth they have encountered all the harm and evil that can be described in this matter. Moses notes these four degrees very clearly in Deuteronomy with these words: *The beloved was surfeited and hobbled backward; he was surfeited, grew fat, and spread out. He forsook God his Maker, and departed from God his Savior* [Dt. 32:15].

3. The soul, which was previously beloved, becomes surfeited by engulfing itself in the joy of creatures. The first degree of harm to spring from this joy is backsliding: a blunting of the mind in relation to God, by which God's goods become dark to it, just as a cloud darkens the air and prevents the sun from illumining it.

By the very fact that spiritual persons rejoice in something and give reign to the appetite in frivolous things, their relationship with God is darkened and their intellect clouded. This is what the divine Spirit teaches in the Book of Wisdom: *Contact with vanity and deception, and their use, obscures good things, and the inconstancy of the appetite overturns and perverts the sense and judgment that is without malice* [Wis. 4:12]. The Holy Spirit teaches by this that even though the intellect is without the thought of any malice, joy in these vanities and concupiscence for them is alone sufficient to produce the first degree of this harm: dullness of mind and darkness of judgment in understanding truth and judging well of each thing as it is in itself.

4. If human beings give way to concupiscence for temporal goods or take joy in them, their sanctity and keen judgment will be insufficient to prevent this injury. God therefore warned us through Moses: *Do not receive gifts that blind even the prudent* [Ex. 23:8]. This admonition was directed toward those who were to be judges since their judgment must be clear and alert, which would not be the case if they were to covet and rejoice in gifts.

Similarly, God commanded Moses to appoint as judges those who abhorred avarice so their judgment would not be blunted by the gratification of their passions [Ex. 18:21]. He speaks not merely of a lack of desire but of the abhorrence of avarice. To enjoy perfect protection from the emotion of love, individuals must maintain this abhorrence and defend themselves from one contrary by means of another. As the prophet Samuel asserted in the Book of Kings, the reason he was always so upright and enlightened a judge was that he never accepted a gift from anyone [1 Sm. 12:3].

5. The second degree of this privative harm issues from the first. It is disclosed in the passage already quoted: *He was surfeited, grew fat, and*

spread out [Dt. 32:15]. Accordingly, this second degree is a spreading out of the will in temporal things—and in a manner that involves even greater freedom. This consists in making little of joy and pleasure in creatures, in not being afflicted about it nor considering it to be so serious a matter. The root of this injury is the reign that was given to joy in the beginning, for in giving way to it the soul grew fat, as is indicated in Exodus, and that fatness of joy and appetite made the will spread out and extend further to creatures.

The consequences are many kinds of serious harm, for this second degree causes one to withdraw from spiritual exercises and the things of God, to lack satisfaction in these exercises because of the pleasure found in other things, and to give oneself over to many imperfections, frivolities, joys, and vain pleasures.

6. When consummated, this second degree takes away entirely the spiritual practices to which individuals were accustomed, so all their mind and covetousness fix on the secular.

Those in the second degree not only possess darkened intellects and judgment in understanding truths and justice, as do those in the first, but they are now extremely weak, lukewarm, and careless in knowing and practicing true judgment. Isaiah affirms this in these words: *They all love gifts and allow themselves to be carried away by retributions, and they do not judge the orphan, and the widow's cause does not come to them and their attention* [Is. 1:23]. This attitude could not exist without their fault, especially when duty was incumbent on them by their office. Those who have reached this degree are not without malice, as are those in the first degree. Thus they gradually turn from justice and virtue because their will reaches out more and more into affection for creatures.

The trait of those in this second degree is extreme lukewarmness—as well as carelessness—in spiritual matters, observing them through mere formality, force, or habit, rather than through love.

7. The third degree of this privative harm is the complete abandoning of God. These individuals don't care about observing God's law, but attend to worldly goods and allow themselves to fall into mortal sins through covetousness. This third degree is indicated in the next assertion of this passage from Exodus: *He forsook God his Maker* [Dt. 32:15]. This degree includes all who are so engrossed in the things, riches, and affairs of this world that they care nothing about fulfilling the obligations of God's law. Forgetful and sluggish about matters pertaining to their salvation, they become much more alive and astute in the things of the world—so much so that Christ in the Gospel calls them children of this world. He says they are more prudent and keen in their affairs than the children of light are in theirs [Lk. 16:8]. Thus in the affairs of God they

are nothing, and in those of the world they are everything. These, precisely, are the greedy. Their appetite and joy are already so extended and dispersed among creatures—and with such anxiety—that they cannot be satisfied. Rather, their appetite and thirst increase more as they regress further from God, the fount that alone can satisfy them. To these individuals God refers through Jeremiah: *They have abandoned me, the fount of living water, and dug for themselves leaking cisterns that cannot hold water* [Jer. 2:13]. The reason for this dissatisfaction is that creatures do not slake the thirst of the avaricious, but rather intensify it.

These greedy persons fall into thousands of kinds of sins out of love for temporal goods, and the harm they suffer is indeterminable. David says of them: *Transierunt in affectum cordis* [Ps. 73:7].[2]

8. The fourth degree of this privative harm is noted in the final statement of the text: *and departed from God his Savior* [Dt. 32:15]. This is the degree into which the avaricious ones we just mentioned fall. Because of temporal goods, the avaricious do not concern themselves with setting their heart on God's law, and consequently their will, memory, and intellect wander far from God and they forget him, as though he were not their God at all. The reason is that they have made gods for themselves out of money and temporal goods. St. Paul indicates this in declaring that avarice is a form of idolatry [Col. 3:5]. Those who are in this fourth degree forget God and deliberately turn their heart—which ought to be centered on him—to money, as though they had no other God.

9. We find in this fourth degree those who do not hesitate to order divine and supernatural things to temporal things as to gods. They should do just the contrary. They should direct the temporal to God, as is right if God is really their God. Wicked Balaam belongs in this category, for he sold the grace God had given him [Nm. 22:32]. Also Simon Magus, who thought of putting a monetary value on God's grace by contriving to buy it [Acts 18:18-19]. He placed a higher value on money, and he thought he could find someone who by selling grace would esteem money more.

Today many belong in various ways to the category of this fourth degree. Out there in the world, their reason darkened as to spiritual matters through covetousness, they serve money and not God, they are moved by money rather than by God, and they give first consideration to the temporal price and not to the divine value and reward. In countless ways they make money their principal god and goal and give it precedence over God, their ultimate end.

---

2. "They have passed into the affection of the heart."

10. Also included in the category of this last degree are all those miserable souls who value earthly goods as their god and are so enamored of them that they do not hesitate to sacrifice their lives when they observe that this god of theirs undergoes some temporal loss. They despair and commit suicide for wretched reasons, and demonstrate with their own hands the miserable reward that comes from such a god. Since there is nothing to hope for from him, he gives despair and death. And those whom he does not pursue right up to death, the ultimate injury, die from living in the affliction of anxieties and many other miseries. He does not permit gladness to enter their hearts or for any earthly good to bring them joy. Insofar as they are afflicted about money, they are always paying the tribute of their hearts to it. They cling to it unto their final calamity of just perdition, as the Wise Man warns: *Riches are hoarded to the harm of their owner* [Eccl. 5:12].

11. Belonging to this fourth degree are those of whom St. Paul says: *Tradidit illos in reprobum sensum* [Rom. 1:28].[3] For joy in possessions ultimately drags humans down even to these evils.

But even those to whom less harm comes should be pitied greatly, since, as we affirmed, this joy causes the soul to fall far back in the way of God. As David declares: *Do not fear when a man becomes rich* (do not be envious, thinking that he has an advantage over you), *for when he dies he will take nothing with him, nor will his glory and joy descend with him* [Ps. 49:16-17].

CHAPTER 20

Benefits derived through the withdrawal of joy from temporal goods.

1. Spiritual persons must exercise care that in their heart and joy they do not become attached to temporal goods. They must fear lest, through a gradual increase, their small attachments become great. Great things can come from little things, and what is small in the beginning can be immense in the end, just as a spark is enough to set a mountain on fire, and even the whole world [Jas. 3:5]. And they should never assure themselves that, since their attachment is small, they will break away from it in the future even if they do not do so immediately. If they do not have the courage to uproot it when it is small and in its first stages, how do they think and presume they will have the ability to do so when it becomes greater and more deeply rooted? Especially since our Lord affirms in the Gospel that the one who is unfaithful in little things will also be unfaithful

---

3. "He has given them up to a reprobate sense."

in great things [Lk. 16:10]. Those who avoid small attachments will not fall into greater ones. But there is serious harm in little matters since through them the harm has already passed beyond the enclosure wall of the heart. And as the saying goes: Once begun, half done. Accordingly, David warns us that even though riches abound we must not set our heart on them [Ps. 62:10].

2. Even if human beings do not free their heart of joy in temporal goods for the sake of God and the demands of Christian perfection, they ought to do so because of the resulting temporal advantages, prescinding from the spiritual ones. By liberating themselves from joy in temporal goods, they not only free themselves from the pestiferous kinds of harm we mentioned in the preceding chapters, but in addition acquire the virtue of liberality. Liberality is one of God's principal attributes and can in no way coexist with covetousness.

Moreover, they acquire liberty of spirit, clarity of reason, rest, tranquility, peaceful confidence in God, and, in their will, the true cult and homage of God.

They obtain more joy and recreation in creatures through the dispossession of them. They cannot rejoice in them if they behold them with possessiveness, for this is a care that, like a trap, holds the spirit to earth and does not allow wideness of heart [2 Cor. 6:11].

In detachment from things they acquire a clearer knowledge of them and a better understanding of both natural and supernatural truths concerning them. Their joy, consequently, in these temporal goods is far different from the joy of one who is attached to them, and they receive great benefits and advantages from their joy. They delight in these goods according to the truth of them, but those who are attached delight according to what is false in them; they delight in the best, the attached delight in the worst; they delight in the substance of them, those sensibly attached delight in the accidents. The senses cannot grasp or attain to more than the accidents, whereas the spirit, purged of the clouds and appearances of the accidents, penetrates the truth and value of things, which is the object of the spirit. Joy, then, clouds the judgment like a mist. For there can be no voluntary joy over creatures without voluntary possessiveness, just as there can be no joy, insofar as it is a passion, unaccompanied by habitual possessiveness of heart. The denial and purgation of such joy leaves the judgment as clear as the air when vapors vanish.

3. Those, then, whose joy is unpossessive of things rejoice in them all as though they possessed them all; those others, beholding them with a possessive mind, lose all the delight of them all in general. The former,

as St. Paul states, though they have nothing in their heart, possess everything with greater liberty [2 Cor. 6:10]; the others, insofar as they possess things with attachment, neither have nor possess anything. Rather, their heart is held by things and they suffer as a captive. As many as are the joys they long to uncover in creatures, so many will necessarily be the straits and afflictions of their attached and possessed heart.

Cares do not molest the detached, neither in prayer nor outside it, and thus, losing no time, such people easily store up an abundance of spiritual good. Yet those who are attached spend all their time going to and fro about the snare to which their heart is tied, and even with effort they can hardly free themselves for a short while from this snare of thinking about and finding joy in the object to which their heart is attached.

At the first movement of joy toward things, the spiritual person ought to curb it, remembering the principle we are here following: There is nothing worthy of a person's joy save the service of God and the procurement of his honor and glory in all things. One should seek this alone in the use of things, turning away from vanity and concern for one's own delight and consolation.

4. There is another exceptional and principal benefit of detachment from joy in creatures: freedom of the heart for God. With this the soul is disposed for all the favors God will grant it. Without it, he does not bestow them. The favors are such that for each joy the soul renounces out of love of God and evangelical perfection, it will receive a hundredfold in this life, as promised in the Gospel [Mt. 19:29; Mk. 10:30].

Even if such gains were not to be had, the spiritual person would have to quell these joys because of the displeasure given to God through them. In the Gospel we see that merely because the rich man rejoiced in having stored up goods for many years God was so angered he told him he must give an account of his soul that very night [Lk. 12:20].

We should believe, therefore, that as often as we rejoice vainly, God is watching and planning some chastisement and bitter drink according to our merits; for at times the sadness redounding from the joy is a hundred times greater than the joy. What St. John says of Babylon in the Apocalypse is true, that she would receive torment in the measure in which she rejoiced and lived in delights [Rv. 18:7]. Yet the text does not mean that the sadness will not be greater than the joy. It shall be greater, since eternal torments are inflicted for brief pleasures. But it indicates that no fault will escape a particular punishment. For he who will punish the idle word will not pardon vain joy [Mt. 12:36].

CHAPTER 21

The vanity of willful joy in natural goods, and the method of directing oneself through them to God.

1. By natural goods we mean: beauty, grace, elegance, bodily constitution, and all other corporeal endowments; also, in the soul, good intelligence, discretion, and other talents belonging to the rational part of humans.

People are vain and deceitful if they rejoice in these gifts only because they or their relatives have them, without giving thanks to God who grants them in order to be better known and loved. As Solomon says: *Grace is deceitful and beauty vain; she who fears the Lord will be praised* [Prv. 31:30]. We are taught in this text that human beings should rather have misgivings about these natural gifts since through them they can be easily distracted from the love of God and, being allured, fall into vanity and delusion. This is why he says that bodily grace is deceptive, deludes people along the way, and attracts them to inappropriate things through vain joy and complacency with self or with the possession of this grace. And he declares that beauty is vain because it causes people who esteem and rejoice in it to fall in countless ways. People should rejoice only if they serve God or others through it. They ought rather to be diffident and fearful lest their natural gifts and graces occasion their offending God by turning their eyes to these gifts in vain presumption or excessive attachment.

Those possessing these endowments should be careful and live cautiously lest through vain ostentation they be the occasion that someone's heart withdraw even one iota from God. These natural graces and gifts are such a provocation and occasion of sin both to the possessor and the beholder that there is scarcely a heart that escapes from this snare or birdlime. We have observed that many spiritual persons with these endowments have, out of fear, prayed God to disfigure them lest these gifts be an occasion to themselves or others for some vain joy or attachment.

2. Spiritual persons, then, must purge and darken their will of this vain joy, and bear in mind the following: Beauty and all other natural endowments are but earth, arising from the earth and returning to it; grace and elegance are but the smoke and air of this earth, and should be considered and valued as such for the sake of avoiding a lapse into vanity. Regarding these goods, spiritual people must direct their heart to God in joy and gladness that God is himself all this beauty and grace—eminently and infinitely so, above all creatures. As David affirms, all these things will grow old and pass away like a garment, while God alone will remain immutable forever [Ps. 102:26-27]. Accordingly, if one does not turn one's joy to God in all things, it will always be false and illusory. This

is the kind Solomon referred to when he spoke to joy in creatures: *To joy I said: Why do you let yourself be deceived in vain?* [Eccl. 2:2], that is, when you allow the heart to be allured by creatures.

CHAPTER 22

The harm resulting from joy of will in natural goods.

1. A good deal of both the harm and benefit I am describing in each of these kinds of joy is common to them all. Because this harm or benefit is the direct result of either joy or detachment from it, no matter what class the joy belongs to, I am mentioning both in each of these categories since, as I say, this harm or benefit is annexed to all these kinds of joy.

My main intention, however, is to speak of the particular kinds of harm and benefit arising in the soul by rejoicing or not rejoicing in each of these goods. I refer to them as particular because they are the primary and immediate result of a particular kind of joy. They are only caused by other kinds secondarily and indirectly.

For example: Tepidity of spirit is the direct outcome of each and every kind of joy, and so this harm is common to all six; yet fornication is a particular evil that follows directly only from joy in natural goods of which we are now speaking.[1]

2. The spiritual and bodily harm directly and effectively ensuing from joy in natural goods can be reduced to six principal kinds.

The first is vainglory, presumption, pride, and disesteem of neighbor, for a person cannot fasten the eyes of esteem on one object without withdrawing them from others. The result is, at least, a material disesteem of other things, since naturally, when the heart values one thing it turns from others because of its concentration on this esteemed object. And through this material contempt it is exceptionally easy in a general or particular way to slip into intentional and voluntary contempt for some of these other things. Such contempt may not only be internal but manifest itself externally through speech: This is not like that, or so and so is not like so and so.

The second harm is inciting the senses to complacency, sensual delight, and lust.

The third kind of harm is that this joy induces flattery and vain praises involving deception and vanity, as Isaiah warns: *My people, whoever praises you deceives you* [Is. 3:12]. The reason is that even though sometimes the truth is told in lauding natural grace and beauty, this praise rarely fails to contain some harm, either by causing the person praised to fall into vain

---

1. Cf. A. 1. 12. 4-5.

complacency and joy, or by directing one's own imperfect affections and intentions toward the person endowed with this beauty.

The fourth kind of harm is general, for the reason and judgment of the spirit become very dull, as in the case of joy over temporal goods, and in some ways even duller. Since natural goods are more intimate to a person than temporal goods, joy in them produces its imprint more quickly and effectively and ravishes more forcibly. Thus the reason and judgment do not remain free but are clouded by the emotion of a very intimate joy.

This gives rise to the fifth harm: distraction of the mind with creatures.

The next outgrowth is spiritual lukewarmness and weakness. This sixth harm is also general and usually reaches such a point that it causes the soul to find extreme tedium and sadness in the things of God, even to the extent of abhorring them.

Pure spirit is infallibly lost in this kind of joy, at least in the beginning. If some spirituality is felt it will be very sensible, gross, unspiritual, exterior, and unrecollected. It will comprise sensory pleasure more than strength of spirit. The spirit is so lowly and weak that it does not suppress the habit of this joy, for the possession of this imperfect habit is sufficient to impede pure spirit even though the acts of joy are not consented to. Consequently the soul lives more in the weakness of the senses than in the strength it has when occasions of sin arise. Although I do not deny that many virtues can coexist with many imperfections, yet because of the reign of the flesh, which militates against the spirit [Gal. 5:17], there can be neither a pure nor a savory interior spirit dwelling together with these unquelled joys. And even if the spirit is unaware of any harm, distraction is at least secretly caused.

3. Let us go back to that second kind of harm that contains in itself innumerable other indescribable kinds. The extent and enormity of the disaster arising from joy in natural graces and beauty is patent, since on account of this joy we hear every day of many murders, lost reputations, insults, squandered fortunes, rivalries, quarrels, and of so many adulteries, rapes, and fornications, and of fallen saints so numerous that they are compared to the third part of the stars of heaven cast down to earth by the tail of the serpent [Rv. 12:4], to fine gold that has lost its beauty and luster in the mire, and to the illustrious and noble men of Zion clothed with the best gold, yet esteemed as broken clay jars [Lam. 4:1-2].

4. Where does this poisonous harm fail to reach? And who fails to drink little or much from the golden chalice of the Babylonian woman of the Apocalypse [Rv. 17:4]?[2] The fact that she is seated on that large beast with

---

2. The text that continues until the end of no. 4 in ch. 26 is missing from the codex of Alcaudete (11 folios). At this point editors follow the ancient codex of Duruelo.

seven heads and ten crowns signifies that there is hardly anyone of high rank or low, saint or sinner, who does not drink of her wine, subjecting the heart somewhat. For as is pointed out there, all the kings of the earth were inebriated with the wine of her prostitution [Rv. 17:2]. She reaches out to all states, even to the supreme and illustrious state of the sanctuary and divine priesthood, by setting her abominable cup in the holy places, as Daniel asserts [Dn. 9:27], and she hardly leaves a strong person who has not drunk a small or large quantity of wine from her chalice, which is this kind of vain joy. As a result it is said that all the monarchs of the earth were inebriated by this wine, since so few will be found, no matter how holy, who have not been somewhat ravished and perplexed by this drink of joy and pleasure in natural beauty and graces.

5. It is worth remarking that the text says they were inebriated. No matter how small the amount of this wine of joy, it immediately takes hold on the heart and subdues it, producing obscurity in the reason, as happens with those who get drunk from wine. The life of the soul will be in danger if some antidote is not taken immediately, for spiritual weakness will augment and bring such evil on the soul that it will find itself a captive of its enemies, grinding at the mill like Samson with his eyes plucked out and the hair of his first strength cut. And afterward it will perhaps die the second death as he did together with his enemies [Jgs. 16:19-31]. This is the harm the drink of this joy will cause spiritually, as it did physically to Samson and as it does to many today. The enemies of the soul will come and say to it afterward what the Philistines said to Samson, to his great confusion: Were you not the one who snapped the knotted cords, broke the jaws of the lions, killed the thousand Philistines, pulled out the gates, and freed yourself from all your enemies?

6. Let us conclude, then, with necessary instructions for the prevention of this poison. As soon as the heart feels drawn by vain joy in natural goods, it should recall how dangerous and pernicious it is to rejoice in anything other than the service of God. One should consider how harmful it was for the angels to have rejoiced and grown complacent in their natural beauty and goods, since they thereby fell into the ugly abyss; and how many evils come on humans every day because of this very vanity. Therefore take courage and use in time the remedy suggested by the poet for those beginning to grow attached to this joy: "Hurry now in the beginning to apply the remedy, for when evils have had time to increase in the heart, medicine and remedies arrive late."[3] *Look not at wine*, warns the Wise Man, *when its color is scarlet and it shines in the glass; it enters smoothly but bites like a snake and spreads poison like the basilisk* [Prv. 23:31].

---

3. Ovid, *Remedia amoris* 1. 91-92; *"Principiis obsta; sero paratur, cum mala per longas invaluere moras."* Cf. *The Imitation of Christ* 1. 13.

CHAPTER 23

The benefits the soul acquires from not rejoicing in natural goods.

1. Many are the benefits derived through withdrawal of the heart from this joy. Besides preparing the soul for the love of God and for other virtues, it directly paves the way for humility toward self and general charity toward one's neighbor. By not becoming attached to anyone, despite these apparent and deceptive natural goods, a person remains unencumbered and free to love all rationally and spiritually, which is the way God wants them to be loved. As a result one realizes that no one merits love except for virtue. And when one loves with this motive, the love is according to God and exceedingly free. If the love contains some attachment there is greater attachment to God, for as the love of neighbor increases so does the love of God, and as the love of God increases so does the love of neighbor, for what proceeds from God has one and the same reason and cause.

2. Another excellent benefit coming from the denial of this kind of joy is the fulfillment of the counsel our Lord gives in the Gospel of St. Matthew, that those who would follow him should deny themselves [Mt. 16:24]. In no way could a soul do this if it were to rejoice in its natural goods, because those who pay some attention to themselves do not deny themselves or follow Christ.

3. Another notable benefit of the denial of this kind of joy is that such denial begets deep tranquility of soul, empties one of distractions, and brings recollection to the senses, especially to the eyes. By not wanting this joy, souls do not want to look at or occupy the other senses with these things so they may avoid being attracted or ensnared by them and wasting time or thought. They bear resemblance to the prudent serpent that stops its ears so as not to hear the charmers and receive some impression from them [Ps. 58:4-5]. By guarding the senses, the gates of the soul, one safeguards and increases one's peace and purity of soul.

4. There is another benefit of no less importance for those who are already advanced in the mortification of this kind of joy: Obscene objects and ideas do not cause in them the impression and impurity they do in those who still find this joy to their liking. Consequently, from the denial and mortification of this joy, spiritual purity of soul and body (of spirit and sense) arises; a person gradually acquires angelic harmony with God, and the soul and body become a worthy temple of the Holy Spirit. This could not be so were the heart to rejoice in natural goods and graces. It is not necessary that there be consent to some obscene thing or a

remembrance of it in order for the soul's purity to become stained, since this kind of joy along with knowledge of the natural good is sufficient to cause impurity of spirit and sense. The Wise Man declares that the Holy Spirit will withdraw from thoughts that are without understanding, that is, without the superior reason ordered to God [Wis. 1:5].

5. Another general benefit coming to the soul besides freedom from the above-mentioned evils,[1] is freedom from countless vanities and other kinds of spiritual and temporal harm, and especially from being held in disesteem, which is the lot of those who boast about natural endowments and rejoice in them whether they belong to themselves or others. Accordingly, those who pay no attention to such things, but are interested in what is pleasing to God, are considered and esteemed to be discreet and wise—and indeed they are.

6. The last follows on these, that is, freedom of spirit by which the soul easily conquers temptations, passes through trials, and grows prosperously in virtue. This is an excellent good and very necessary in serving God.

CHAPTER 24

Sensory goods, the third kind of good in which the will can place the emotion of joy. A discussion of their nature and number and of how the will should be directed to God through the purgation of this joy.

1. Our next subject is joy in sensory goods, the third kind of good in which the will can rejoice. It should be known that by sensory goods we mean here all the goods apprehensible to the senses of sight, hearing, smell, taste, and touch, and to the interior faculty of discursive imagination. They are goods pertinent to the exterior and interior senses.

2. To darken and purge the will of joy in these sensory goods and lead it through them to God, we must presuppose a truth. It is, as we have often said, that the senses of the lower part of human nature, with which we are dealing, neither are nor can be capable of the knowledge or comprehension of God as he is in himself. The eye cannot see him or anything like him, nor can the hearing perceive his voice or any sound resembling it, nor can the sense of smell apprehend a fragrance so sweet, nor can the sense of taste relish so sublime and delightful a savor, nor can the sense of touch experience a feeling so delicate and ravishing, or anything similar. Neither is God's form or any figure representing it apprehen-

---

1. In chs. 21-22.

sible to thought or imagination. Isaiah thus affirms: *Eye has not seen him, nor ear heard him, nor has it entered into the human heart* [Is. 64:4].[1]

3. It is noteworthy that the senses can receive satisfaction or delight either from the spirit, through some communication received interiorly from God, or from exterior things apprehended by them. And, as was said, the sensory part can have knowledge of God through neither the senses nor the spirit. Being incapable of such an attainment, it receives the spiritual in only a sensible and sensorial way. As a result it would be at least vanity for the will to pause to rejoice in the delight caused by any of these apprehensions. And it would be hindered from centering its strength on God, from placing all its joy in him alone. One cannot concentrate one's joy entirely on God save by purging and darkening oneself with regard to joy in this kind of good, as well as the other kinds.

4. I purposely said that it would be vanity for the will to pause to rejoice in any of these apprehensions. For when the will, in becoming aware of the delight afforded by an object of sight, hearing, or touch, does not stop with this joy but immediately elevates itself to God, being moved and strengthened for this by that delight, it is doing something very good. The will, then, does not have to avoid such experiences when they produce this devotion and prayer, but it can profit by them, and even ought to for the sake of so holy an exercise. For there are souls who are greatly moved toward God by sensible objects.[2]

Yet one should be careful in this matter and take into consideration the effects of such experiences. Frequently, spiritual persons use this refreshment of the senses under the pretext of prayer and devotion to God; and they so perform these exercises that we could call it recreation rather than prayer, and pleasing oneself rather than God. Though the intention of these persons is directed to God, the effect they receive is recreation of the senses, from which they obtain weakness and imperfection more than the quickening of their will and its surrender to God.

5. I should like to offer a norm for discerning when this gratification of the senses is beneficial and when not. Whenever spiritual persons, on hearing music or other things, seeing agreeable objects, smelling sweet fragrance, or feeling the delight of certain tastes and delicate touches, immediately at the first movement direct their thought and the affection of their will to God, receiving more satisfaction in the thought of God than in the sensible object that caused it, and find no delight in the senses save for this motive, it is a sign that they are profiting by the senses and

---

1. This is a key text in John for designating God's transcendence. He sometimes joins it with 1 Cor. 2:9. Cf. A. 2. 4. 4; 8. 4; A. 3. 12. 1; N. 2. 9. 4; C. 38. 6.
2. With his artistic temperament, John probably experienced this himself.

the sensory part is a help to the spirit. The senses can then be used because the sensorial objects serve the purpose for which God created them: that he be more known and loved through them.

It should be understood here that those in whom these sensible objects cause this pure spiritual effect do not on that account have an appetite for them. They care for them hardly at all, even though these objects, by reason of the delight in God they cause, do provide great satisfaction when presented to them. Thus they are not solicitous about these sensible goods; and when, as I say, these goods are offered to them, the will immediately leaves them aside, passing on to God.

6. The reason the soul pays no attention to these sensible motives even though they help it go to God is that the spirit, which has this readiness to go to God in and through all things, is so provided for, nourished, and satisfied by God's spirit that it doesn't miss or want anything else. And if it wants something in order to turn to God, it immediately passes beyond this object, forgetting and paying no attention to it.

Yet anyone who does not feel this freedom of spirit in these objects and sensible delights, but finds that the will pauses in and feeds on them, suffers harm from them and ought to turn from their use. Though according to reason one may want help from them in order to go to God, nonetheless they assuredly prove more a hindrance than a help. They are a harm rather than a benefit in the measure that the appetite delights in them according to the senses; and the effect is always in conformity to the delight. When individuals see that the appetite for these recreations reigns within themselves, they should mortify it, because the stronger their appetite the weaker and more imperfect they are.

7. Spiritual persons, then, in whatever sensory gratification comes their way, whether by chance or through their own intention, ought to benefit from it only for the sake of going to God. They do this by raising their joy of soul to him so that this joy may be useful, profitable, and perfect. They should be aware that every joy unaccompanied by this negation and annihilation of all other joys—even when these concern something apparently very elevated—is vain, without profit, and a hindrance to union of the will with God.

CHAPTER 25

The harm incurred by the desire for willful joy in sensory goods.

1. In the first place, all the general kinds of harm that are born of other types of joy spring as well from this joy in sensory goods if it is not darkened and quelled through direction to God. These kinds of harm are, for

example, obscurity of reason, lukewarmness, spiritual tedium, and so on. But in particular there are many kinds of harm, either spiritual or corporeal and sensory, which can be directly incurred through this joy.

2. First, through failure to deny joy in visible objects for the sake of going to God, the following evils result directly: vanity of spirit, mental distraction, inordinate covetousness, indecency, interior and exterior discomposure, impurity in thought, and envy.

3. Joy in hearing useless things gives direct rise to distraction of the imagination, gossiping, envy, uncertain judgments, and wandering thoughts, from which flow many other pernicious kinds of harm.

4. Joy in sweet fragrance foments disgust for the poor (which is contrary to Christ's doctrine), aversion for servants, unsubmissiveness of heart in humble things, and spiritual insensitivity, at least in the measure of the appetite.

5. Joy in the delights of food directly engenders gluttony and drunkenness, anger, discord, and lack of charity toward one's neighbor and the poor, as toward Lazarus on the part of the rich man who ate sumptuously each day [Lk. 16:19-21]. Accordingly, there arise bodily disorders, infirmities, and impure movements from increasing lustful incentives. A decided spiritual torpor is directly engendered and the desire for spiritual things is so spoiled that one finds no satisfaction in them and is unable to discuss or take part in them. Distraction of the other senses and of the heart and discontent over many things also arise from this joy.

6. Enjoyment in the touch of soft objects foments more numerous and pernicious kinds of harm, and by it the senses more quickly pervert the spirit and extinguish its strength and vigor. The consequence is the abominable vice of effeminacy or incentives toward it in proportion to this kind of joy. This joy foments lust; it makes the spirit cowardly and timid and the senses flattering, honey-mouthed, disposed toward sin and causing harm. It pours vain gladness and mirth into the heart, engenders license of the tongue and freedom of the eyes, and ravishes and stupefies the other senses according to the intensity of the appetite. It confounds the judgment, nurturing it on spiritual incipience and stupidity, and morally engenders cowardice and inconstancy. And by this darkness of soul and weakness of heart it makes one fear where there is no reason for fear.

This joy sometimes begets a spirit of confusion and unresponsiveness of conscience and spirit, since it seriously debilitates reason and reduces it to such a state that one does not know how to take counsel or to give it, and it leaves the soul incapable of moral and spiritual blessings, as useless as a broken jar.

7. All these evils are caused by this kind of joy according to the intensity of the joy and also according to the disposition, weakness, or inconstancy of the individual. Some temperaments receive more detriment from one small occasion than others do from many.

8. Finally from this kind of rejoicing in the sense of touch one can fall into much evil and harm from natural goods, as we pointed out. Since I discussed this harm in speaking of those goods,[1] I will not refer to it here. Neither will I speak of many other kinds of harm caused, such as a decrease in spiritual exercises and corporeal penances, and lukewarmness and lack of devotion in the use of the sacraments of penance and the Eucharist.

CHAPTER 26

The spiritual and temporal benefits resulting from the denial of joy in sensory goods.

1. The benefits acquired from the negation of this joy are admirable; some are spiritual, others temporal.

2. First, by withdrawing their joy from sensible things, individuals are restored from the distraction into which they had fallen through excessive use of their senses. They become recollected in God and conserve the spirit and virtues they had acquired. These virtues increase and the soul advances.

3. The second spiritual benefit people procure from not desiring joy in sensible things is excellent; we can truthfully say that from being sensual they become spiritual, and from animal, rational, and even that from what is human in them they advance to the angelic, and from earthly and human they become heavenly and divine. Since human beings who look for gratification and enjoyment in sensible objects deserve no other title than these we mentioned (sensual, animal, earthly, and so on), they deserve all those other titles (spiritual, heavenly, and so on), when they elevate their joy above these sensible goods.

4. This is obviously true. Since the exercise of the senses and the strength of sensuality are, as the Apostle says, contrary to spiritual exer-

---

1. In chs. 21-22.

cise and vigor [Gal. 5:17], it follows that at the enervation of one of these forces the other, contrary one, unaugmentable because of this impediment, must grow and increase. Thus in perfecting the spirit (the superior portion of the soul, which refers to God and communicates with him), individuals merit all these attributes because they are being perfected in the spiritual and heavenly goods and gifts of God.

St. Paul proves both instances. He calls the sensual person (that is, one who occupies the will with sensory things) the animal person, one who does not perceive the things of God; and the other, who raises the will to God, he calls the spiritual person, and this is the one who penetrates and judges all things, even the deep things of God [1 Cor. 2:10-15]. Consequently the soul possesses here the admirable[1] benefit of a great preparedness for God's spiritual goods and gifts.

5. But the third benefit is that the satisfaction and joy of the will is temporally and exceedingly increased, since, as the Savior says, in this life for one joy they will receive a hundredfold [Mt. 19:29; Mk. 10:29-30]. If you deny one joy, the Lord will give you a hundredfold, spiritually and temporally in this life, as also from one joy taken in these sensible goods, grief and distress will be yours a hundredfold.

Spiritual joy directed to God at the sight of all divine or profane things follows from the eye already purged of enjoyment in seeing things. Resulting from the purgation of enjoyment in hearing things is a most spiritual joy, a hundred times greater, directed to God in all that is heard, divine or profane; and so on with the other senses already purged. In the state of innocence all that our first parents saw, spoke of, and ate in the garden of paradise served them for more abundant delight in contemplation, since the sensory part of their souls was truly subjected and ordered to reason. The person whose sense is purged of sensible objects and ordered to reason procures from the first movements the delight of savory contemplation and awareness of God.

6. In the pure, therefore, all things, high and low, engender greater good and purity. In like manner the impure soul usually derives impurity from things, whether high or low. But anyone who fails to conquer the joy of appetite will fail to experience the serenity of habitual joy in God by means of his creatures and works.

The one who does not live according to the senses directs all the operations of the senses and faculties to divine contemplation. Indeed, in good philosophy, the operation of each thing corresponds to its being

---

1. At this point the text from the codex of Alcaudete resumes.
2. He refers to and adapts the philosophical axiom *operari sequitur esse*. Cf. e.gr., Aquinas, *Summa theologiae* 1. 89. 1.

or life.[2] If the soul through mortification of the animal life lives a spiritual life, it must obviously, without contradiction, go to God in all things, since all its spiritual actions and movements will flow from the spiritual life. Consequently this person, now of pure heart, finds in all things a joyful, pleasant, chaste, pure, spiritual, glad, and loving knowledge of God.

7. I deduce the following doctrine from all that was said: Until individuals are so habituated to the purgation of sensible joy that at the first movement of this joy they gain the benefit spoken of (that these goods turn them immediately to God), they must necessarily deny their joy and satisfaction in sensible goods in order to draw the soul away from the sensory life. Since they are not spiritual, they should be fearful lest through the use of these goods they may perhaps get more satisfaction and strength for the senses than for the spirit. The sensory forces would then have predominance in their activity, increase sensuality, and sustain and nourish it. Our Savior declares: *That which is born of the flesh is flesh; and that which is born of the spirit is spirit* [Jn. 3:6].

And this we should consider carefully, for it is really true. Those who have not yet mortified the delight they find in sensory things should not dare try to gain much through the activity and energy of their senses with the belief that the spirit will be helped by these things. For the soul will find that if it quells its appetite for these sensible things and its joy in them, its energies will increase more.

8. It is unnecessary to discuss the goods of glory that come in the next life through the negation of this joy. Besides the fact that the bodily endowments of glory, such as agility and clarity, will be far more excellent in those who denied themselves than in others who did not, there will be an increase in essential glory in the soul that responds to the love of God and denies sensible goods for him.[3] For every momentary and perishable joy souls deny, as St. Paul states, there will be worked in them eternally an immense weight of glory [2 Cor. 4:17].

Now I do not want to refer here to the additional benefits (moral, temporal, and spiritual) derived from this night regarding joy, for they are the same as those mentioned in dealing with the other kinds of joy. But here they are of a more eminent degree since the sensible joys denied are more closely conjoined with one's nature, and therefore a more intimate purity is acquired through their negation.

---

3. In traditional theological doctrine the distinction was made between essential glory (union of the soul with God in which he is seen and loved perfectly) and accidental glory (endowments over and above the beatific vision); cf. e. g., Aquinas, *Summa theologiae* Suppl. 96. 1.

CHAPTER 27

The nature of moral goods, the fourth kind of goods, and the permissible manner
of rejoicing in them.

1. Moral goods are the fourth kind in which the will can rejoice. By
moral goods we mean: the virtues and their habits insofar as they are
moral; the exercise of any of the virtues; the practice of the works of
mercy; the observance of God's law; political prudence,[1] and all the
practices of good manners.

2. When possessed and practiced, these moral goods perhaps merit
more joy of will than any of the other three kinds spoken of. For either
of two reasons, or for both together, a person can rejoice in these goods;
that is, because of what they are in themselves, or because of the good
effected through their instrumentality.

We discovered that possessing the three kinds of good already mentioned deserves no joy of will. Of themselves, as was said, they neither have
any good nor do they produce any in people, because they are so
perishable and frail. Rather, as was also pointed out, they engender pain,
sorrow, and affliction of spirit. Though they merit some joy for the
second reason, that is, when people make use of them to go to God, this
benefit is so uncertain that, as we commonly observe, a person contracts
harm from them more than help.

But even for the first reason (for what they are in themselves), moral
goods merit some rejoicing by their possessor. For they bring along with
them peace, tranquility, a right and ordered use of reason, and actions
resulting from mature deliberation. Humanly speaking, a person cannot
have any nobler possession in this life.

3. Because virtues in themselves merit love and esteem from a human
viewpoint, and because of their nature and the good they humanly and
temporally effect, a person can well rejoice in the practice and possession
of them. Under this aspect and for this reason philosophers, wise men,
and ancient rulers esteemed, praised, and endeavored to acquire and
practice them.[2] Although they were pagans who only cared for these
goods in a temporal way, because of the temporal, corporeal, and natural
benefits they knew would result, they did not merely acquire these goods
and the renown sought through them. But in addition God, who loves

---

1. The subjective part of prudence by which one directs oneself in relation to the
common good. Cf. Aquinas, *Summa theologiae* 2-2. 48. 1; 50. 2.
2. Here he alludes to the Stoics, such as Seneca, Epictetus, and Marcus Aurelius.
St. Teresa used to refer to John as "my little Seneca." Stoic teaching seems to lie
in the background of some of his observations. Cf. for example A. 3. 6.

every good, even in the barbarian and gentile, and does not hinder any good work from being accomplished, as the Wise Man says [Wis. 7:22], bestowed on them an increase of life, honor, dominion, and peace. He did this with the Romans because of their just laws. He subjected almost the entire world to them, paying them temporally for their commendable customs since, because of their paganism,[3] they were incapable of eternal reward.

God so loves these moral goods that he was exceedingly pleased merely because Solomon asked for wisdom in order to instruct his people, govern them justly, and teach them worthwhile customs. And he told Solomon that he had given it to him and moreover had granted him what had not been asked for, that is, riches and honor, in such a way that no king in the past or future was like him [1 Kgs. 3:11-13].

4. Though Christians ought to rejoice in the moral goods and works they perform temporally, insofar as these are the cause of the temporal goods we spoke of, they ought not stop there as did the gentiles, who with the eyes of their soul did not go beyond the things of this mortal life. Since Christians have the light of faith in which they hope for eternal life and without which nothing from above or below will have any value, they ought to rejoice in the possession and exercise of these moral goods only and chiefly in the second manner: that insofar as they perform these works for the love of God, these works procure eternal life for them.

Thus, through their good customs and virtues they should fix their eyes only on the service and honor of God. Without this aspect the virtues are worth nothing in God's sight. This is evident in the Gospel in the case of the ten virgins. They had all preserved their virginity and done good works, yet because five of them had not rejoiced in this second way (by directing their joy in these works to God), but rather in the first, rejoicing vainly in the possession of these works, they were rejected from heaven and left without any gratitude or reward from their spouse [Mt. 25:1-13]. Also many of the ancients possessed numerous virtues and engaged in good works, and many Christians have them today and accomplish wonderful deeds; but such works are of no profit for eternal life because of failure to seek only the honor and glory of God.

Christians, then, should rejoice not if they accomplish good works and abide by good customs, but if they do these things out of love for God alone, without any other motive. As those who work only for the service of God will receive a more elevated reward of glory, so those who work for other motives will suffer greater shame when they stand before God.

5. For the sake of directing their joy in moral goods to God, Christians

---

3. The source of these ideas may be St. Augustine who developed them in *The City of God* 5. 12-17. 3

should keep in mind that the value of their good works, fasts, alms, penances, and so on, is not based on quantity and quality so much as on the love of God practiced in them; and consequently that these works are of greater excellence in the measure both that the love of God by which they are performed is more pure and entire and that self-interest diminishes with respect to pleasure, comfort, praise, and earthly or heavenly joy. They should not set their heart on the pleasure, comfort, savor, and other elements of self-interest these good works and practices usually entail, but recollect their joy in God and desire to serve him through these means. And through purgation and darkness as to this joy in moral goods they should desire in secret that only God be pleased and joyful over their works. They should have no other interest or satisfaction than the honor and glory of God. Thus all the strength of their will in regard to these moral goods will be recollected in God.

CHAPTER 28

Seven kinds of harm that can result from joy of the will in moral goods.

1. I find there are seven kinds of harm that can be incurred through vain joy in one's good works and customs; and because this harm is spiritual it is particularly ruinous.

2. The first is vanity, pride, vainglory, and presumption, for one is unable to rejoice over one's works without esteeming them. This gives rise to boasting and so on, as is said of the pharisee in the Gospel: He prayed and sought friendship with God by boasting of his fasting and performance of other good works [Lk. 18:11-12].

3. The second is usually linked with the first. It is that people make comparisons judging others to be evil and imperfect, supposing that the deeds and works of others are not as good as their own. Interiorly they have less regard for others, and they sometimes manifest this exteriorly in word. The pharisee also had this defect since he said in his prayer: *I give you thanks that I am not like other men: robbers, unjust, and adulterers* [Lk. 18:11]. Through one act he incurred the two kinds of harm: self-esteem and contempt for others.

Many today also do so when they boast: "I am not like so and so, nor do I do anything similar to what this or that one does." Many are even worse than the pharisee. Though the pharisee not only bore contempt for others in general, but even indicated a particular individual in declaring, *I am not like this publican* [Lk. 18:11], many persons, content with neither of these two attitudes, even become angry and envious in noticing that others receive praise or accomplish more or have greater value than they themselves.

4. The third is that, since they look for satisfaction in their works, they usually do not perform them unless they see that some gratification or praise will result from them. As Christ pointed out, they do everything *ut videantur ab hominibus* (in order to be seen by others) [Mt. 23:5]; and they do not undertake their works only out of love for God.

5. The fourth follows from this third; and it is that they will not find their reward in God since they wished to find, in this life, joy, comfort, honor, or some other thing from their works. Referring to such an attitude, the Savior says that they have received their pay in these goods [Mt. 6:2]. Consequently they are both left alone with the labor of their work and confused without any reward.

There is so much misery among human beings as regards this kind of harm that I believe most of the works publicly achieved are either faulty, worthless, or imperfect in God's sight. The reason is that people are not detached from these human respects and interests. How else can one judge the works performed by some and the memorials constructed at their request, when they do not desire them unless for some honor or human and vain considerations; or when, in the memorials, they perpetuate their own name, lineage, or nobility; or when they even go to the extent of having their coat of arms or heraldry put in the church, as if they want to put themselves there as an image where all may bend the knee?

It can be said that in these works some adore themselves more than God. And this is true if they undertake such works for these reasons and would not do so without them.[1]

Aside from these individuals, who are the worst, how many are there who in various ways suffer this harm in their works? Some want praise for their works; others, thanks; others talk about them and are pleased if this person or that or even the whole world knows about them; at times they want their alms, or whatever they are doing, to pass through the hands of another that it may be better known; others desire all these things together. The Savior in the Gospel compares this to sounding the trumpet, which is the practice of vain persons, and he declares that as a result they will not receive a reward from God for their works [Mt. 6:2].

6. To avoid this kind of harm, then, these persons must hide their work

---

1. Throughout the Middle Ages, as well as in John's time, lay patrons endowed ecclesiastical institutions. Making a donation to a monastery or church, they would ask for burial at a certain altar or chapel. Most important for aristocratic families were the visual embellishments of blazons and heraldic shields, which showed a keen awareness of lineage and family status.

so that only God might see it, and they should not want anyone to pay attention to it. Not only should they hide it from others, but even from themselves: They should desire neither the complacency of esteeming their work as if it had value, nor the procurement of satisfaction. This is the meaning of our Savior's words: *Let not the left hand know what the right hand is doing* [Mt. 6:3], which is like saying: Do not esteem with the temporal and carnal eye the spiritual work you do. The strength of the will is thereby recollected in God, and the work bears fruit in his sight. Consequently a person will not lose the work but reap abundant merit from it.

A passage from Job has this meaning: *I have kissed my hand with my mouth, and my heart rejoiced in secret, which is a great iniquity and sin* [Jb. 31:27-28]. The hand in this affirmation refers to the work, and the mouth to the complacency of the will in it. And because it is self-complacency, as we said, he adds: My heart rejoiced in secret, which is a great iniquity and denial against God. And this was equivalent to saying that he was neither complacent nor secretly glad in his heart.

7. The fifth kind of harm is failure to advance in the way of perfection. As a result of attachment to satisfaction and consolation in their works, some usually become discouraged and lose the spirit of perseverance. This ordinarily happens when God leads them on by giving them hard bread, the bread of the perfect, and takes away the infant's milk so as to prove their strength and purge their weak appetite so they may taste the substantial fare of adults.[2] This is the spiritual interpretation of the Wise Man's words: *Dying flies spoil the sweetness of the ointment* [Eccl. 10:1]. For when the occasion of practicing some mortification is presented to these persons, they die to their good works by ceasing to accomplish them, and they lose the spirit of perseverance, which would give them spiritual sweetness and interior consolation.

8. The sixth is that they are usually deluded by the thought that the exercises and works that give satisfaction are better than those that do not. And they have praise and esteem for the one kind, but disesteem for the other. Yet those works that usually require more mortification from a person (who is not advanced in the way of perfection) are more acceptable and precious in God's sight because of the self-denial exercised in them, than are those from which one can derive consolation, which very easily leads to self-seeking. Apropos of this, Micah asserts:

---

2. What John says here resembles what he says in discussing purgative contemplation; cf. N. 1. 12. 1-2. Purgation deals also with one's works since spiritual sweetness and interior consolation come not only from prayer but from good works as well.

Malum manuum suarum dicunt bonum (What is evil in their works they say is good) [Mi. 7:3]. This evil arises when they seek to please themselves in their works and not God alone.

An account of how this harmful defect reigns in spiritual persons as well as in ordinary people would only end up in my being prolix, for hardly any will be found who are motivated in their work by God alone, without their grasping for the support of some consolation or satisfaction or other consideration of self.

9. The seventh kind of harm is that human beings, insofar as they do not quell vain joy in their moral deeds, become more incapable of taking counsel and receiving reasonable instructions about the works they ought to do. The habitual weakness they have from working with this vain joy so enchains them that they either do not believe that the counsel of another is better, or do not wish to follow it even if in their opinion it is, because they are without the courage to do so.

Such people become very slack in charity toward God and neighbor, for the self-love contained in their works makes them grow cold in charity.

CHAPTER 29

Benefits derived through the removal of joy from moral goods.

1. Great are the benefits derived from restraining the desire for vain rejoicing in this kind of good.

As for the first, the soul is freed from falling into many temptations and deceits of the devil concealed in the joy of these good works. This is understandable from what was said in Job: *He sleeps under the shadow, in the covert of the reed, and in moist places* [Jb. 40:16]. The passage refers to the devil, because in the moisture of joy and the vanity of the reed (of the vain work) he deludes the soul. The devil's hidden deceptiveness in this joy is nothing to marvel at because, prescinding from his suggestion, the vain joy is itself a deception, especially when there is some boastfulness of heart over one's works. As Jeremiah affirms: *Arrogantia tua decepit te* (Your arrogance has deceived you) [Jer. 49:16]. For what greater deception is there than boasting? The soul is freed from this by purging itself of such joy.

2. The second benefit is a more diligent and precise accomplishment of these works. Such is not the case when one takes pleasure in them with the passion of joy. Through this passion of joy the irascible and concupiscible appetites become so strong that they do not allow leeway for the

judgment of reason.[1] As a result people usually become inconstant in their practice of good works and resolutions; they leave these aside and take up others, starting and stopping without ever finishing anything. Since they are motivated by satisfaction, which is changeable—and in some temperaments more so than in others—their work ends when the satisfaction does, and their resolution too, even though it may concern an important endeavor. We can say of those for whom the energy and soul of their work is the joy they find in it that when the joy dies out the good work ceases, and they do not persevere.

Christ spoke of them when he said: *They receive the word with joy, and the devil immediately takes it away from them that they may not persevere* [Lk. 8:12]. And the reason for this lack of perseverance is that they have no other roots or strength than this joy. Withdrawal of the will from such joy, then, is the cause of perseverance and success. This benefit is great, as is also the contrary harm. A wise person is concerned about the substance and benefit of a work, not about the delight and satisfaction it yields. Thus such a one does not beat the air [1 Cor. 9:26], but procures from the work a stable joy without paying the tribute of displeasure.

3. The third is a divine benefit. It is that by extinguishing vain joy in these works a person becomes poor in spirit, which is one of the beatitudes the Son of God mentions: *Blessed are the poor in spirit, for theirs is the kingdom of heaven* [Mt. 5:3].

4. The fourth benefit is that those who deny this joy will be meek, humble, and prudent in their work. For they will act neither impetuously and hastily, compelled by the concupiscible or irascible aspect of joy; nor presumptuously, affected by their esteem for the work due to the joy it gives; nor uncautiously, blinded by joy.

5. The fifth benefit is to become pleasing to both God and other human beings and free of spiritual avarice, gluttony, sloth, envy, and a thousand other vices.[2]

---

1. John alludes fleetingly to the concupiscible and irascible appetites. Aquinas divides the appetite into sensitive and intellectual insofar as things are apprehended by the senses or the intellect. The sensitive appetite in turn is divided into the concupiscible (inclination to seek the good and flee the evil) and irascible (inclination to resist what either hinders the good or inflicts evil). Cf. Aquinas *Summa theologiae* 1. 80. 2; 81. 2; 1-2. 23. 1.
2. John discusses in detail what he calls spiritual vices in N. 1. 2-7.

CHAPTER 30

Supernatural goods, the fifth class of goods in which the will can rejoice. Their nature, the factors distinguishing them from spiritual goods, and how joy in them must be directed to God.

1. Now we ought to discuss the fifth class of goods in which the will can rejoice; these are the supernatural goods. By these we mean all the gifts and graces of God that exceed our natural faculties and powers; they are called *gratiae gratis datae*. Examples of these are the gifts of wisdom and knowledge given by God to Solomon [1 Kgs. 3: 7-12] and the graces St. Paul enumerates: faith, the grace of healing, working of miracles, prophecy, knowledge and discernment of spirits, interpretation of words, and also the gift of tongues [1 Cor. 12: 9-10].

2. Though it is true these goods are also spiritual like the ones we must speak of later, yet I must draw a distinction because there is a considerable difference between them. The exercise of these gifts immediately concerns the benefit of others, and God bestows them for that purpose, as St. Paul points out: *The spirit is given to no one save for the benefit of others* [1 Cor. 12:7]. This assertion is understood in reference to these graces. But the exercise and exchange taking place through spiritual goods flows only between the soul and God and God and the soul, in a communication of intellect and will, and so on, as we shall say afterward.[1]

There is a difference in their objects, since the object of the spiritual goods is only the Creator and the soul, whereas the object of the supernatural goods is the creature. There is a difference, too, in substance, consequently in operation, and also necessarily as regards doctrine.

3. Speaking now of supernatural gifts and graces, as we here understand them, I assert that for the purgation of vain joy regarding them it is appropriate to note two benefits, temporal and spiritual, that are included in this kind of goods.

The temporal includes healing the sick, restoring sight to the blind, raising the dead, expelling devils, prophesying the future so people may be careful, and other similar things.

The spiritual and eternal benefit is the knowledge and love of God caused by these works either in those who perform them or in those in whom, or before whom, they are accomplished.

4. As for the first, the temporal benefit, supernatural works and

---

1. In ch. 33. 2.

miracles merit little or no joy of soul. When the second benefit is excluded they are of little or no importance to human beings, since they are not in themselves a means for uniting the soul with God, as is charity. And the exercise of these supernatural works and graces does not require grace and charity; either God truly bestows them as he did to the wicked prophet Balaam [Nm. 22:20] and to Solomon, or they are effected falsely by means of the devil, as in the case of Simon Magus [Acts 8:9-11], or by means of other secret, natural powers. If any of these marvels were to be beneficial to their agent, they were those that were true, given by God.

St. Paul teaches what their worth is without the second benefit: *If I speak in human and angelic tongues and do not have charity, I am like a sounding metal or bell. And if I have prophecy and know all mysteries and all knowledge, and if I have all faith so as to move mountains, and do not have charity, I am nothing,* and so on [1 Cor. 13:1-2]. When those who esteem their works in this way seek glory from Christ saying: *Lord, did we not prophesy in your name and work many miracles?* He will answer: *Depart from me, workers of iniquity* [Mt. 7:22-23].

5. People should rejoice, then, not in whether they possess and exercise these graces, but in whether they derive the second benefit from them, the spiritual: Serving God through them with true charity, for in charity lies the fruit of eternal life. Accordingly, our Savior reproved the disciples who were glorying in their success at casting out devils: *Do not desire to rejoice that the devils are subject to you, but that your names are written in the book of life* [Lk. 10:20]. In sound theology this is like saying: Rejoice if your names are written in the book of life. Hence it should be understood that people ought not rejoice except in walking along the path that leads to life and in doing works with charity. What profit is there in anything that is not the love of God, and what value has it in God's sight? Love is not perfect if it is not strong and discreet in purifying joy with respect to all things, centering it only on doing God's will. Thus the will is united with God through these supernatural goods.

CHAPTER 31

Harm incurred from rejoicing in this class of goods.

1. It seems to me that three chief kinds of harm follow from rejoicing in supernatural goods: deceiving and being deceived; detriment in the soul with respect to faith; and vainglory or some vanity.

2. As for the first it is very easy to deceive oneself and others by rejoicing in these accomplishments. The reason is that discernment of the true

gifts from the false and knowledge of how and at what time they may be exercised demands much counsel and much light from God, both of which are exceedingly hindered by esteeming and rejoicing in these works.

There are two reasons for this: first, because joy blunts and darkens the judgment; second, because people, on account of their joy in the gift, not only long to believe in it more readily, but even feel impelled to make use of it outside the proper time.

Granted that the wonders and works be genuine, these two defects suffice for one to be deceived often, either by not understanding the gifts as they ought to be understood or by not benefiting from them through an appropriate use as to time and manner. It is true that when God bestows these gifts and graces he gives light for them and an impulse as to the time and manner of their exercise. Yet souls can err seriously because of possible attachment to them and imperfection in their regard, not using them with the perfection desired by God, at the time and in the manner he desires. We read that Balaam was thus at fault when, against God's will, he decided to go and curse the Israelites. Consequently God, being angered, desired to kill him [Nm. 22:22-23]. St. James and St. John wanted to make fire descend from heaven on the Samaritans who refused lodging to our Savior, but the Lord reproved them for this [Lk. 9:54-55].

3. It is clear that in these cases those who were gifted were moved to perform their works at an inopportune time by some imperfect passion that was clothed in joy and esteem for these works. When this imperfection is not present, such persons decide to perform these works when and in the manner that God moves them to do so; until then they should not work them. For this reason God complained of certain prophets through Jeremiah: *I did not send the prophets and they ran; I did not speak and they prophesied* [Jer. 23:21]. Further on he says: *They deceived my people with their lying and prodigies, for I had not commanded it or sent them* [23:32]. He also says of them there that they behold the visions of their own heart and publish them about [23:26]. This would never have happened had they overcome their abominable attachment to these works.

4. Through these passages we learn that the harm engendered by this joy comes not only from the wicked and perverse use of God's graces—as in the case of Balaam and those who deceived the people with their miracles—but even from performing them without God's grace, as in those who prophesied their fancies and spoke of visions manufactured by either themselves or the devil. When the devil observes their attachment to these wonders, he opens a wide field, provides ample material for their endeavors, and meddles extensively. And these individuals with such

means spread wide their sails, become shamelessly audacious, and abound in prodigious works.

5. And this is not all! The joy and covetousness they have in these works reaches such a point that if previously their pact with the devil was secret—for often the works are performed through a secret pact—now through their boldness they make an express and open one with him and by an agreement subject themselves to him as his disciples and friends. Hence we have wizards, enchanters, magicians, soothsayers, and witches.

Joy in these works goes so far that some, as Simon Magus, not merely want to buy gifts and graces with money [Acts 8:18] for the service of the devil, but they even try to get hold of sacred and divine objects—which cannot be mentioned without trembling—as has already been witnessed in the theft of the most sacred body of our Lord Jesus Christ for evil practices and abominations. May God extend and show forth his infinite mercy in this matter![1]

6. Everyone can readily understand how pernicious these individuals are and how detrimental to Christianity. It should be noted that all those magicians and soothsayers who lived among the children of Israel and were expelled from the land by Saul [1 Sm. 28:3] had fallen into many abominations and delusions because of their desire to imitate the genuine prophets.

7. Those, then, who have this supernatural gift should not desire or rejoice in its use, nor should they care about exercising it. God, who grants the grace supernaturally for the usefulness of the Church or its members, will also move the gifted supernaturally as to the manner and time in which they should use their gift. Since the Lord commanded his disciples not to be anxious about what or how to speak, because the matter was a supernatural one of faith, and since these works are also a supernatural matter, he will want these individuals to wait until he

---

1. In 1556, Pedro Ciruelo published in Salamanca *Reprobación de las supersticiones y hechicerías* (a condemnation of superstitions and witchcraft). The book shows the harm that witchcraft caused in Spain especially among the unlettered, but attributes nearly as much influence in human affairs to the devil as to God. When called on to judge particular cases of supposed possession by the devil, John was exceptionally cautious. His judgments varied: in one case (Medina del Campo), he attributed the trouble merely to poor judgment on the part of a nun; in another case (Lisbon), he discovered an egregious fraud; other cases he saw were the results of melancholia. But he did at times find cases of real possession, as, for example, in Avila where a nun whom he exorcised had signed a pact with the devil in her own blood. In one form of devil worship, consecrated hosts were desecrated and profaned. The fear of witchcraft led to unjust accusations and cruel torture.

becomes the worker, by moving their heart [Mt. 10:19; Mk. 13:11]. For it is by the power of God that every other power should be exercised. In the Acts of the Apostles the disciples beseeched him in prayer to extend his hand to work signs and cures through them, so faith in our Lord Jesus Christ would be introduced into hearts [Acts 4:29-30].

8. The second harm proceeds from the first. It is a twofold detriment to the faith.

First, in regard to others: When individuals try to perform the prodigy or exercise the power outside the proper time and without necessity, it can happen that besides tempting God—which is a serious sin—they will be unsuccessful and thereby engender in hearts a distrust and contempt of the faith. Sometimes they are successful because God wishes it for other reasons and motives, as with Saul's sorceress—if it was Samuel who really appeared there [1 Sm. 28:7-15]. But still, they are in error and culpable for using these graces inopportunely.

Second, there is detriment to these individuals themselves as to the merit of faith. By giving importance to these miracles one loses the support of the substantial habit of faith, which is an obscure habit. Where signs and testimonies abound, there is less merit in believing. St. Gregory declares that faith is without merit when it has proof from human reason.[2]

God never works these marvels except when they are a necessity for believing. Lest his disciples go without merit by having sensible proof of his resurrection, he did many things to further their belief before they saw him. Mary Magdalene was first shown the empty sepulcher, and afterward the angels told her about the resurrection so she would, by hearing, believe before seeing. As St. Paul says: *Faith comes through hearing* [Rom. 10:17]. And though she beheld him, he seemed only an ordinary man, so by the warmth of his presence he could finish instructing her in the belief she was lacking [Mt. 28:1-6; Lk. 24:4-10; Jn. 20:11-18]. And the women were sent to tell the disciples first; then these disciples set out to see the sepulcher [Mt. 28:7-8]. And journeying incognito to Emmaus with two of his followers, he inflamed their hearts in faith before allowing them to see [Lk. 24:15-32]. Finally he reproved all his disciples for refusing to believe those who had told them of his resurrection [Mk. 16:14]. And announcing to St. Thomas that they are blessed who believe without seeing, he reprimanded him for desiring to experience the sight and touch of his wounds [Jn. 20:25, 29].

9. Thus God is not inclined to work miracles. When he works them he does so, as they say, out of necessity. He consequently reprimanded the

2. In *Homilia 26 in Evangelium* 1, in Migne, PL 76. 1197.

pharisees because they would not give assent without signs: *If you do not see signs and wonders, you do not believe* [Jn. 4:48]. Those, then, who love to rejoice in these supernatural works suffer a great loss in faith.

10. Third, through joy in these works one ordinarily falls into vainglory or some kind of vanity. Even the very joy in these marvels that is not wholly in and for God is vanity. Our Lord's reproval of the disciples for having rejoiced that the devils were subject to them is a demonstration of this truth; if this joy were not vain he would not have made the reprimand [Lk. 10:20].

CHAPTER 32

Two benefits derived from the negation of joy in supernatural goods.

1. Besides the advantage of being freed from these three kinds of harm, the soul acquires two excellent benefits.

The first refers to the praise and extolling of God; the second to the exaltation of the soul itself.

God is exalted in the soul in two ways. First, the heart and willful joy are withdrawn from all that is not God and concentrated on him alone. David intended this in the verse we quoted at the beginning of the night of this faculty: *The human heart will reach high, and God will be exalted* [Ps. 63:6-7].[1] By lifting the heart above all things, the soul exalts God above them all.

2. And because the soul in this way concentrates only on God, God receives praise and exaltation in manifesting to it his excellence and grandeur. In this elevation of joy in him, God gives the soul testimony of who he is. This is only done when the will is empty of joy and consolation in all things, as he also declares through David: *Leave all and see that I am God* [Ps. 46:10]. And again David says: *In a desert way, dry and pathless, I appeared before you to see your power and glory* [Ps. 63:1-2]. God is truly extolled when joy is withdrawn from all things and centered on him, but he receives much more glory when it is removed from these more marvelous goods and applied to him alone, since by being supernatural they are of higher entity. To leave them behind for the sake of joy in God alone is to attribute greater glory and excellence to God than to them. The greater the quality and quantity of things one despises for the sake of another, the greater the esteem and praise one gives to that other.

3. Moreover, through withdrawing the will from these works, one exalts God in the second manner. The more the soul believes in and

---

1. In fact, these psalm verses are not quoted elsewhere in this work.

serves God without testimonies and signs, the more it extols God, since it believes more of him than signs and miracles can teach.

4. The second benefit, the exaltation of the soul, owes its origin to a withdrawal of the will from all apparent testimonies and signs. Because of this, the soul is exalted in purest faith that God then infuses and augments much more abundantly. And, together with this, he increases the other two theological virtues (charity and hope). As a result the soul enjoys divine and lofty knowledge by means of the dark and naked habit of faith; and the admirable delight of love through charity, by which it rejoices in nothing else than the living God; and satisfaction in the memory by means of hope. All of this is a splendid benefit, essentially and directly required for the perfect union of the soul with God.

CHAPTER 33

The nature and division of the sixth kind of good that is a possible object of joy for the will.

1. Our intention in this work is to guide the soul through spiritual goods to divine union with God. Now that we are about to discuss this sixth kind (those very goods that are the most helpful in this matter), both the reader and I myself will have to pay particular attention. Because of their lack of knowledge, it is a common and certain occurrence with some to let spiritual things serve only for the senses, leaving the spirit empty. Hardly will anyone be found in whom sensory satisfaction does not in some way spoil a good part of what was destined for the spirit, drinking up the waters before they reach the spirit, leaving the spirit dry and empty.

2. To come to our subject then, by spiritual goods I refer to all those that are an aid and motivating force in turning the soul to divine things and communion with God, as well as a help in God's communications to the soul.

3. According to their main headings, I divide spiritual goods into two classes: one delightful, the other painful.[1] Each of these can again be divided into two kinds: the delightful comprise both goods that are clearly and distinctly understood and others that do not afford clear or

---

1. Here John sets aside the procedure followed with the five preceding kinds of goods in which he dedicated three chapters to each. He now so multiplies subdivisions that he allows himself to enter a forest without exit.

distinct understanding; the painful likewise include both those that are clear and distinct and others that are vague and obscure.

4. We can also divide these goods according to the faculties of the soul. Some, those dealing with knowledge, belong to the intellect; others, those dealing with emotions, belong to the will; and others, those dealing with things of the imagination, belong to the memory.

5. We will discuss the painful goods afterward, because they belong to the passive night.[2] The discussion of the vague and indistinct delightful goods will be left for the end since they are pertinent to the general, vague, loving knowledge in which union with God is effected. In the second book we also deferred this to the end when we listed the divisions of intellectual apprehensions.[3] Here we will treat of delightful goods that are clear and distinct.

CHAPTER 34

The proper conduct of the will as to joy in the distinct spiritual goods communicable to the intellect and memory.

1. We would have had to cover a great deal of matter here to instruct the will about proper conduct concerning joy in the multitudinous apprehensions of the intellect and memory if we had not amply discussed these apprehensions in the second and third book. Since we indicated there the conduct suitable for these two faculties in this kind of apprehension, there is no necessity for repetition here. The conduct of the will should be the same in their regard. It is sufficient to remark that wherever it says there that these faculties should be emptied of certain apprehensions, it also means that the will should be emptied of joy in them.

The conduct required of the memory and intellect concerning these apprehensions is also necessary for the will. Since the intellect and other faculties cannot admit or deny anything without the intervention of the will, the same doctrine that serves for one faculty will evidently apply to the others also.

2. In those sections the reader will find what is required in this matter,

---

2. He is thinking of the subject he treats in *The Dark Night,* especially in the second book.
3. Cf. chs. 10. 4; 14. 6, 14. He continues to put off his treatment of this most important topic. Since the *Ascent* was never finished, one must gather what he might have said through his words on the subject in other works.

for the soul will fall into those kinds of harm if it is ignorant of how to direct to God its joy in these apprehensions.

CHAPTER 35

Delightful spiritual goods. A division.

1. All goods giving distinct joy to the will can be reduced to four kinds: motivating, provocative, directive, and perfective. We will discuss them in due order, beginning with motivating goods: statues, paintings of saints, oratories, and ceremonies.

2. There can be considerable vain joy in relation to statues and paintings. Although they are vital to the divine worship and necessary to move the will to devotion, as the approbation and use of our Holy Mother the Church demonstrates (we should always take advantage of them in order to be awakened from our lukewarmness), many rejoice more in the painting and ornamentation than in the object represented.

3. The Church established the use of images for two principal reasons: the reverence given to the saints through them; and both the motivation of the will and the awakening of devotion to the saints by their means. Insofar as they serve this purpose their use is profitable and necessary. We should consequently choose those images that are more lifelike and move the will more to devotion. Our concentration should be centered on this devotion more than on the elaborateness of the workmanship and its ornamentation.

There are, as I say, some people who pay more attention to the workmanship and value of the statue than to the object represented. And the interior devotion, which they should direct spiritually toward the invisible saint in immediate forgetfulness of the statue—since the purpose of the statue is to give motivation—is so taken up with the exterior artistry and ornamentation that the senses receive satisfaction and delight; then both the love and joy of the will dwell on that satisfaction. This is a total obstacle to authentic spirituality, which demands annihilation of the affections in all particular things.

4. Such an attitude is obvious in the abominable custom some have in these times of ours. Without any abhorrence of vain worldly fashions, they adorn statues with the jewelry conceited people in the course of time invent to satisfy themselves in their pastimes and vanities, and they clothe the statues in garments that would be reprehensible if worn by themselves—a practice that was and still is abhorrent to the saints represented

by the statues. In company with the devil they strive to canonize their vanities, not without serious offense to the saints. By this practice the authentic and sincere devotion of the soul, which in itself uproots and rejects every vanity and trace of it, is reduced to little more than doll-dressing. Some use the statues for nothing more than idols upon which they center their joy.

You will see some who never tire of adding statue on statue to their collection, or insist that the statue be of this particular kind and crafts-manship and placed in a certain niche and in a special way—all so these statues will give delight to the senses. As for devotion of heart, there is very little. They are as attached as Micah and Laban were to their idols, for Micah left his house shouting because they were stolen; and Laban, after a long journey and being enraged, turned over all of Jacob's household furnishings in search for them [Jgs. 18:23-24; Gn. 31:23-35].

5. People who are truly devout direct their devotion mainly to the invisible object represented, have little need for many images, and use those that are conformed more to divine traits than to human ones. They bring these images—and themselves through them—into conformity with the fashion and condition of the other world, not with this one. They do this so worldly images will not stir their appetite and so they will not even be reminded of the world, as they would in having before their eyes any object apparently a part of this world. Their heart is not attached to these goods, and if these are taken away, their grief is slight. They seek the living image of Christ crucified within themselves, and thereby they are pleased rather to have everything taken from them and to be left with nothing.

Even when the motives and means that bring the soul closer to God are taken from them, they remain calm. People are more perfect when they remain tranquil and joyous in the privation of these motives than when they possess them with desire and attachment. It is good to be pleased with images that help the soul toward deeper devotion; individuals should always choose the image that they find most devotional. Yet there is no perfection in being so attached to those one possesses as to become sad if they are taken away.

6. Individuals should be certain that the more they are attached with a possessive spirit to the image or motive, the less will their prayer and devotion ascend to God. Indeed, since some statues are truer likenesses than others and excite more devotion, it is appropriate to be attached more to some than to others, but not with that attachment and possessive-ness I mentioned, for to engulf the senses in the joy of the means would expend the good that the spirit should gain by soaring from the image to God in immediate forgetfulness of this thing or that. These means,

which should be an aid in one's flight to God, now become through this imperfection a hindrance, and no less so than in the case of attachment or possessiveness relative to any other object.

7. Although on this subject of statues you may have some objection caused by lack of a clear understanding of the nakedness and spiritual poverty demanded for perfection, at least you will not be able to defend through your objections the imperfection commonly found in the use of rosaries. You will hardly meet anyone who does not have some weakness in this matter. They want the rosary to be made in one style rather than another, or that it be of this color or that metal rather than another, or of this or that particular design. One rosary is no more influential with God than is another. His answer to the rosary prayer is not dependent on the kind of rosary used. The prayer he hears is that of a simple and pure heart that is concerned only about pleasing God and does not bother about the kind of rosary used unless in regard to indulgences.

8. Our vain covetousness is such that it clings to everything. It is like the wood borer that gnaws at what is sound and performs its task in both good and bad objects. What else is your motive in carrying around an overdecorated rosary with the desire that it be this kind rather than another and in wanting to choose this statue instead of that other, if not the joy you find in the instrument? And in your concern about their preciousness and artistry, you neglect to consider their faculty for awakening divine love in you. Were you to employ your appetite and joy only in the love of God, you would be indifferent as to this one or that. It is pitiful to see how attached some persons are to the style and craftsmanship of these instruments and motives as well as to their elaborateness and to the vain satisfaction that is to be gotten from them. You will never see such persons satisfied. They are always setting aside one thing for another and forgetting spiritual devotion because of these visible means. Their attachment and possessive spirit is no different with these religious articles than it is with temporal furnishings. The harm done through such an attitude is by no means slight.

CHAPTER 36

Continues with the discussion of images; the ignorance of some in their use of them.

1. Much could be said about the ignorance of many in their use of images. Their foolishness reaches such a point that they trust more in one statue than in another and think that God will answer them more readily

through it, even when both statues represent the same person, such as those of our Lord or our Blessed Lady. At the bottom of this idea is their greater attachment to the craftsmanship of one over that of the other. Such an attitude entails gross ignorance about communion with God and the worship and honor due him. He looks only on the faith and purity of the prayerful heart.

If God sometimes bestows more favors through one statue than through another, he does not do so because of its greater ability to produce this effect—even though there may be a notable difference in craftsmanship—but because the devotion of individuals is awakened more by means of one statue than the other. Were people to have equal devotion in the presence of both—or even this same devotion without the aid of either statue—God would grant them the same favors.

2. God does not work miracles and grant favors by means of some statues so that these statues may be held in higher esteem than others, but so he may awaken the dormant devotion and affection of the faithful through his wonderful works. Since, consequently, through the instrumentality of a certain statue, devotion is enkindled and prayer prolonged—both means by which God hears and grants one's petitions— God continues to bestow favors and work miracles through that statue. God certainly does not work miracles because of the image, which in itself is no more than a painting, but he does so because of the faith and devotion toward the saint represented. Thus, if you had equal devotion to and faith in our Lady before two different images of her—and even without them, as we said—you would receive the same favors.

Experience even teaches that if God grants some favors and works miracles, he does so through some statues that are not very well carved or carefully painted, or that poorly represent the intended saint, so the faithful will not attribute any of these wonders to the statue or painting.[1]

3. Our Lord frequently bestows these favors by means of images situated in remote and solitary places. The reason for this is that the effort required in journeying to these places makes the affection increase and the act of prayer more intense. Another motive is that a person may withdraw from people and noise in order to pray, as our Lord did [Mt. 14:23; Lk. 6:12].

Whoever makes a pilgrimage, therefore, does well to make it alone,

---

1. The majority of people in 16th-century Spain were illiterate. Paintings, statues, and holy pictures served to remind them of both the content of their faith and the lives of the saints and to awaken their devotion. The people easily grew attached to these means, often becoming superstitious about them, thinking that an image would assure them of a good harvest, or bring about the cure of some illness.

even if this must be done at an unusual time. I would never advise going along with a large crowd, because one ordinarily returns more distracted than before. Many who go on pilgrimage do so more for the sake of recreation than devotion.

Where there is devotion and faith any image will be sufficient, but if they are lacking none will suffice. Our Lord was indeed a living image during his sojourn in this world; nevertheless, those who were faithless received no spiritual gain, even though they frequently went about with him and beheld his wondrous works. This is why he did not perform many mighty works in his own country, as the Evangelists declare [Mt. 13:58; Mk. 6:5-6].

4. I would also like to mention here some supernatural effects that certain images occasionally cause in particular individuals. God gives some images a special spiritual influence on souls so the representations, and the devotion these cause, remain fixed in the mind as though they were present. When a person suddenly recalls the image, it will exercise the same spiritual influence it did when seen, sometimes less and occasionally even more. But that person will not receive the same spiritual influence from another image, even if it is one of more perfect craftsmanship.

5. Many also experience more devotion through statues of one kind of workmanship than another. In some people this devotion will be caused by no more than a natural liking and attachment, just as some will like the face of one person more than that of another and become more attached to it naturally. They will preserve it more readily in their imagination because they are naturally inclined to that type of form and figure, even though the face itself may not be as beautiful as those of others. Thus some people think that the attachment they have to a certain image is devotion, when, in reality, it is perhaps no more than a natural attachment and preference.

Occasionally, when looking at an image, they see it move and make signs and gestures or they hear words and instructions.[2] Although these signs and the supernatural effects produced by the images are authentic and good, destined by God either to increase devotion or to give the soul, because of its weakness, some support against distractions, the devil fre-

---

2. John himself once took from the monastery a painting of Christ carrying his cross and placed it in the church so more people could venerate it. Praying before it afterward, he heard the Lord speak to him: "Fray John, ask of me what you will, for I will grant it in return for this service you have rendered me." John's answer was: "Lord, I desire trials to suffer for you and to be despised and considered unimportant." This painting may still be seen in Segovia.

quently produces them in order to cause deception and harm. We will expound the doctrine regarding all this in the following chapter.

CHAPTER 37

Directing willful joy to God in order to avoid errors and obstacles arising from images.

1. Images are notably beneficial both for remembering God and his saints and for moving the will to devotion if properly used. So too, they will be the cause of serious error if the soul is ignorant of the conduct proper for its journey to God when supernatural phenomena occur relative to these images. One of the means with which the devil readily catches incautious souls, and impedes them in the way of spiritual truthfulness, is the supernatural and extraordinary phenomena he manifests through images, either through the material and corporeal ones the Church uses, or through those he fixes in the phantasy in the guise of a particular saint. He transforms himself into an angel of light so as to deceive [2 Cor. 11:14]. Crafty one that he is, in order to catch us off guard he will disguise himself in the very means we use to procure help for ourselves. In their use of good things, consequently, good souls should be more cautious, for evil in itself gives testimony to itself.

2. The harm that can affect the soul in these circumstances is as follows: hindrance in its flight to God; an ignorant or poor attitude in its use of images; being deceived either naturally or supernaturally by them. These are subjects we dwelt on earlier. So the soul may avoid all this harm, purify its will of the joy it finds in images, and direct itself through them to God, which is the intention of the Church in their use, I wish to set down only one maxim here, which will be sufficient for all cases: Since images serve as a motivating means toward invisible things, we should strive that the motivation, emotion, and joy of will derived from them be directed toward the living object they represent.

The faithful should therefore take this precaution: On seeing the image they should not allow their senses to become absorbed in it (whether it be corporeal or imaginary, of beautiful workmanship or richly adorned, the cause of sensible devotion or spiritual, nor if it make gestures through supernatural power). They should pay no attention to these accidents; they should not dwell on the image but immediately raise the mind to what is represented. They should prayerfully and devoutly center the satisfaction and joy of their will in God, or the saint being invoked, so the painting and senses will not absorb what belongs to both the spirit and the living person represented. They will accordingly be safe from delusion, since they will be paying no attention to what the image supernaturally says to them, nor will they be so employing their senses as to hinder the free elevation of these senses to God, nor be putting more trust in one image than in another. And the image that does excite their devotion will do this more copiously, since their affection will be immediately raised to God. Whenever God bestows these and other favors, he does so by inclining the movement of joy of the will toward the invisible, and he wishes us to do likewise by annihilating the strength and satisfaction of the faculties in regard to all sensory and visible objects.

CHAPTER 38

Continues the discussion of motivating goods. Oratories and dedicated places of prayer.

1. I think I have explained clearly how in these accidental traits, with regard to images, spiritual persons can have as much imperfection—and perhaps more if they look for their satisfaction and joy in them—as in the use of other corporeal and temporal objects. And I add that perhaps these images are more dangerous, for in saying "they are holy objects" these persons become more assured and do not fear natural possessiveness and attachment. Spiritual persons are thus at times seriously deluded by thinking they are filled with devotion because of their satisfaction in the use of these holy objects. Yet perhaps this devotion will be no more than a natural inclination and appetite that is centered on these holy things as it would be on any other object.

2. Hence, to begin our discussion on the subject of oratories, some individuals never grow tired of adding images of one kind or another to their oratories, or of taking delight in the arrangement and adornment of these images so the place of prayer will appear well decorated and attractive. But they do not love God more when it is arranged in this way instead of that, rather they love him less, since the delight they find in these ornate paintings withdraws their attention from the living person represented, as we pointed out.[1] It is true, indeed, that every decoration, adornment, and reverence that can be given to images is very small. Therefore those who show little respect or reverence for their statues deserve sharp reproof, as well as those who carve so inexpertly that the finished statue subtracts from devotion rather than adding to it. Some artisans so unskilled and unpolished in the art of carving should be forbidden to continue their craft. Still, what has this to do with the possessiveness, attachment, and appetite you have in these exterior decorations and adornments that so engross the senses that your heart

---

1. In ch. 37. 2.

is impeded from turning to God, loving him, and forgetting all things out of love for him? If you fail in this love because of these other objects, he will not merely fail to reward you, but will punish you for not having sought his pleasure in all things instead of your own.

We get a clear understanding of this in the festivity that was celebrated in honor of His Majesty when he entered Jerusalem. While they were expressing thanks to him with songs and palm branches, he was weeping because he knew that despite those exterior signs and decorations their hearts were far from him [Lk. 19:35-44]. Evidently they were celebrating themselves more than God, which often happens today when there is a solemn festival in some locality. Many are usually happier because of the recreation derived from the celebration—by seeing or being seen, or by eating, or by some other means—than because of God's pleasure. In these inclinations and intentions they do not please God. This is especially so with those who in organizing the religious festivals invent ridiculous and undevout things to incite laughter among the people, which only adds to the distraction. Others design displays meant to please the people more than to arouse their devotion.

3. What shall I say about the desires for personal profit of some of those who organize these festivals? If they have more concern and covetousness for this than for the service of God they are well aware of the fact, but so is God who sees them. Yet if the right intention is lacking, whatever kind of celebration they may put on, they are having a festival for themselves rather than for God.

God does not record for their merit what they do for their own pleasure or for that of others. On the contrary, many taking part in festivals in honor of God will be only diverting themselves, and God will be angry with them. He was angry in this way with the children of Israel when he killed many thousands of them while they were celebrating a festival singing and dancing to their idol, thinking their festivity was in honor of God [Ex. 32:7-28]. God also killed the priests Nadab and Abihu, children of Aaron, while they still held the censers in their hands, because they offered strange fire [Lv. 10:1-2]. And the one who came to the wedding feast badly dressed and without the wedding garment was commanded by the king to be bound hand and foot and cast into exterior darkness [Mt. 22:12-13]. We learn from these instances how intolerable to God these irreverences are in gatherings organized for his service.

How many festivals, my God, do the children of this earth celebrate in your honor in which the devil has a greater role than you! And the devil, like a merchant, is pleased with these gatherings because he does more business on those days. How many times will you say of them: *This people honors me with their lips alone, but their heart is far from me, because they serve me without cause* [Mt. 15:8-9]. God must be served because of who he is, and other motives must not be intermingled with this one. Not serving God only because of who he is, is the same as serving God without having God as the final cause.

4. Returning, then, to the subject of oratories, I say that some persons decorate them more for their own pleasure than for God's pleasure. Some pay so little attention to the devotional aspect of their oratories that they have no more regard for them than they do for their profane dressing rooms. Some do not even have this much interest in them, since they find more gratification in profane things than in divine.

5. Let us turn our discussion rather to more spiritual persons, those who are considered devout. Many of them in their desire and gratification grow so attached to their oratory and its decoration that all their energy, which should be employed in prayer and interior recollection, is expended on these things. They do not realize that, by not arranging their oratory in a way that would further interior recollection and peace of soul, they receive as much distraction as they would from other things. And at every step they become disquieted over this satisfaction, and even more so if anyone wants to take it away from them.

CHAPTER 39

How a person should use oratories and churches, directing the spirit to God through them.

1. To direct the spirit to God in this kind of good, we should keep in mind that for beginners it is permissible and even fitting to find some sensible gratification and satisfaction in the use of images, oratories, and other visible objects of devotion. With this delight they are assisted in renouncing worldly things from whose taste they are not yet weaned or detached. This is what we do with a child when we desire to take something away from it; we give it another thing to play with so it will not begin to cry when left empty-handed.

But in order to advance, spiritual persons should divest themselves also of all these satisfactions and appetites, for the pure spirit is bound to none of these objects but turns only to interior recollection and mental communion with God. Although they derive profit from images and oratories, this is very transitory, for their spirit is immediately elevated to God in forgetfulness of all sensory objects.

2. Even though it is better to pray in a place that is more respectable, one should, in spite of this, choose the place that hinders least the

elevation of sense and spirit to God. This is the interpretation we should give to Christ's reply to the query of the Samaritan woman about the place best suited for prayer—the temple or the mountains. His answer was that true prayer is annexed neither to the temple nor to the mountain, but that the adorers who please the Father are those who adore him in spirit and truth [Jn. 4:20-24].

Churches and quiet places are dedicated and suitable for prayer, for the church should be used for no other purpose. Nevertheless, in a matter of communion with God as interior as this, that place should be chosen that least occupies and attracts the senses. Spiritual persons should not look for a spot pleasant and delightful to the senses, as some usually do, lest they become absorbed in the recreation, gratification, and delight of the senses rather than in God in spiritual recollection. A solitary and austere location is beneficial for the sure and direct ascent of the spirit to God without the impediment or detainment caused by visible things. Sometimes visible objects do aid in the elevation of the spirit, but this elevation is the result of immediately forgetting them in order to remain recollected in God. To give us an example, our Savior chose for his prayer solitary places, those that raised the soul to God and were undistracting to the senses (such as mountains that are elevated above the earth and usually barren of objects that would provide recreation for the senses) [Mt. 14:23].

3. Persons who are truly spiritual never consider or become attached to the particular comfort of a place of prayer, for this would result from attachment to the senses. Their interest is interior recollection in the forgetfulness of other things. They choose the site that is freest of sensible objects and satisfactions and turn their attention from all these considerations so that, unimpeded by any creature, they may rejoice more in solitude with God. Some spiritual persons noticeably spend all their time in adorning oratories and making places agreeable to their own temperament or inclination and pay little heed to interior recollection, which is the important factor. They are not very recollected, for if they were they would be unable to find any satisfaction in these ways, but would grow tired of them.

CHAPTER 40

Continues directing the spirit in this matter toward interior recollection.

1. The reason some spiritual persons never entirely enter into the true joys of the spirit is that they never manage to renounce their desire for joy in these exterior and visible things. These persons should keep in

mind that although the place dedicated and suited to prayer is the visible oratory or church and the motivating good is the image, these means should not be so used that the satisfaction and delight of the soul stems entirely from them, thereby causing one to forget to pray in the living temple, which is interior recollection of soul.

To remind us of this, the Apostle said: *Behold, your bodies are living temples of the Holy Spirit, who dwells within you* [1 Cor. 3:16]. This thought brings to mind the affirmation of Christ that we quoted:[1] *The true adorers should adore in spirit and truth* [Jn. 4:24]. God pays little attention to your oratories and places arranged for prayer if through your desire and the delight you take in them you become attached and, in consequence, have less interior nakedness, that is, spiritual poverty, in the renunciation of things that can be possessed.

2. To purge the will of its desire and vain joy in these objects and direct it to God, you should strive in your prayer for a pure conscience, a will that is wholly with God, and a mind truly set on him.

And, as I mentioned,[2] you ought to choose the most withdrawn and solitary place possible, convert all your joy of will into glorifying and invoking God. And you should pay no attention to these other little exterior satisfactions; you should rather seek to deny them. Should a soul become bound to the delight of sensory devotion, it will never succeed in passing on to the strength of spiritual delight, which is discovered through interior recollection in spiritual nakedness.

CHAPTER 41

Some harm resulting from surrender to sensible gratification in the use of devotional objects and places.

1. Spiritual persons incur many kinds of interior and exterior harm by their desire to get sensible delight from the use of devotional objects. As for interior harm, one will never reach inward recollection of spirit, which consists in passing beyond all these sensory delights, making the soul forget them, entering into the living temple of spiritual recollection, and acquiring solid virtue. With regard to exterior harm, individuals will be rendered incapable of praying everywhere. They will be able to pray only in those places suited to their taste, and thus be frequently wanting in prayer. As the saying goes, the only book he knows is his own village.

2. Moreover, the appetites of these individuals will be the occasion of

---

1. In ch. 39. 2.
2. In ch. 39. 2.

considerable instability. Some never persevere in one place—nor even at times in one state—but now you see them in one spot, now in another; now choosing one hermitage, now another; now decorating one oratory, and now another.

Some also pass their time here below changing states and modes of life. The fervor and joy they find in their spiritual practices is merely sensible, and they have never made any effort to reach spiritual recollection through denial of their wills and submission to suffering discomforts. Consequently, as often as they see a seemingly devotional place, or way, or state of life that fits their disposition and inclination, they immediately leave what they have and follow after it. And since they are motivated by sensible gratification they soon begin to look for something else, for sensible satisfaction is inconstant and quickly fails.

CHAPTER 42

The proper conduct of the will in the use of three different kinds of devotional places.

1. There are three different kinds of places, I find, by which God usually moves the will.

The first includes sites that have pleasant variations in the arrangement of the land and trees and provide solitary quietude, all of which naturally awakens devotion. It is advantageous to use these places if one immediately directs the will to God in forgetfulness of the place itself, since one should not be detained by the means and motive more than necessary to attain the end. If individuals strive for recreation of their appetites and sensory satisfaction, they will rather find spiritual dryness and distraction; for spiritual satisfaction and contentment are found only in interior recollection.[1]

2. Therefore when people pray in a beautiful site, they should endeavor to be interiorly with God and forget the place, as though they were not there at all, for when they wander about looking for delight and gratification from a particular site they are searching for sensory recreation and spiritual instability more than for spiritual tranquility.

The anchorites and other holy hermits, while in the loveliest and vastest wildernesses, chose for themselves as small an area as possible, built narrow cells and caves, and enclosed themselves within. St. Benedict

---

1. John himself had a deep aesthetic sense and used to take his religious out to solitary places of natural beauty for their prayer. The recollection he urges is not of a mere exterior sort that renounces the perception and use of things but a theological recollection in which nature mediates the transcendent.

lived in one of these for three years, and St. Simon tied himself with a cord so as not to use up more space or go farther than the cord allowed him. There are many other examples of this kind of mortification of which we would never finish speaking. For those saints clearly understood that without extinguishing their appetite and covetousness for spiritual gratification and delight they would never become truly spiritual.[2]

3. The second kind of place in which God moves the will to devotion is more particular. It includes those localities, whether wildernesses or not, in which God usually grants some very delightful spiritual favors to particular individuals. He grants his favor so the heart of the recipient will have a natural inclination toward that place, and will sometimes experience intense desires and longings to return there. But on returning, that person discovers that the place is not what it was before because these favors do not lie within one's own power. God bestows these graces when and how and where he wills without being bound to place or time or to the free will of the recipient.

Yet it is good sometimes to return there for prayer, provided one's soul is divested of the desire for spiritual possessions. There are three reasons for this: First, it seems that God desires, in granting the favor, to receive praise there from that soul, although he is not bound to any place. Second, when there, the soul will be more mindful of thanking God for his favors. Third, while one remembers there the graces that were received, a more fervent devotion will be awakened.

4. These are the reasons for returning to that place. Consequently one should not think that God is bound to grant favors there as if he were unable to do so wherever he wishes, for the soul is a more becoming and suitable place for God than any material site. We read in Sacred Scripture that Abraham built an altar in the very place God appeared and there called on God's holy name. Afterward, on his return from Egypt, he went to the same place where God had appeared and invoked him again at that very altar he had built there [Gn. 12:7-8; 13:3-4]. By setting up a stone anointed with oil, Jacob also marked the place where God, leaning upon a ladder, had appeared to him [Gn. 28:13-18]. Hagar, with highest esteem for that place where the angel appeared to her, gave it a name, saying: *Certainly, here have I seen the shoulder of him who sees me* [Gn. 16:7-14].

5. The third kind of place comprises those in which God chooses to be invoked and worshipped. Examples are Mount Sinai, where he presented the law to Moses [Ex. 24:12]; the place he marked for the sacrifice of Abraham's son [Gn. 22:2]; also Mount Horeb, to which he sent our

---

2. These examples could have been found in the Breviary, the *Lives of the Desert Fathers,* or in the *Dialogues* of St. Gregory the Great.

Father Elijah that he might appear to him there [1 Kgs. 19:8]; and Mount Garganus, the place St. Michael dedicated to God's worship by appearing to the Bishop of Siponto and telling him how he guarded that place so a chapel might be dedicated to God there in memory of the angels; and the site in Rome that the Blessed Virgin, through the miracle of snow, pointed out for a church she wanted Patritius to build in her name.[3]

6. God alone knows why he chooses one place in which to receive praise more than another. What we should know is that he does all for our own benefit and so he may hear our prayers in these places—or anywhere we beseech him with integral faith. Yet those places consecrated to his worship are more appropriate as places for our prayers to be heard since the Church has so marked and dedicated them.

CHAPTER 43

The large variety of ceremonies that many people use as another motivating means for prayer.

1. The useless joy and imperfect possessiveness of many apropos of the goods we have mentioned is perhaps somewhat tolerable because of their innocence in the matter. Yet the strong attachment of some to many kinds of ceremonies that were introduced by people uninstructed and wanting in the simplicity of faith is insufferable.

We will prescind from those ceremonies that make use of extravagant names or terms without meaning and other unsacred things that ignorant, rude, and questionable persons usually intermingle with their prayers, since these ceremonies are obviously evil and sinful. And in many of them there is a secret pact with the devil by which God is provoked to anger and not to mercy.

2. I want to speak only of those ceremonies that are used by many today with indiscreet devotions, since these are not included in those other suspect kinds. These people attribute so much efficacy to methods of carrying out their devotions and prayers and so trust in them that they believe that if one point is missing or certain limits have been exceeded their prayer will be profitless and go unanswered. As a result they put more trust in these methods than they do in the living prayer, not without great disrespect and offense toward God. For example, they demand that the Mass be said with a certain number of candles, no more nor less; or that it be celebrated at a particular hour, no sooner nor later; or that it

---

3. These events concerning St. Michael on Mt. Gargano and Our Lady of the Snows were commemorated in the liturgy.

be said after a certain day, not before; or that the prayers and stations be a particular number and kind and that they be recited at certain times and with certain ceremonies, and neither before nor after, nor in any other way; and that the person performing the ceremonies have certain endowments and characteristics. And they are of the opinion that nothing will be accomplished if one of these points is lacking.

3. What is worse—and intolerable—is that some desire to experience an effect in themselves: either the granting of their petition or the knowledge that it will be granted at the end of those superstitious ceremonies. Such a desire would amount to nothing more than tempting God and would thereby seriously provoke his wrath. Sometimes God gives the devil permission to deceive them through an experience and knowledge of things far from profitable to their souls. They deserve this because of the possessiveness they bring into their prayer, by not willing what God wills but what they themselves will. Hence, because they do not put all their trust in God, nothing turns out well for them.[1]

CHAPTER 44

The manner of directing the joy and strength of the will to God in these devotions.

1. These individuals should know, then, that the more trust they put in these ceremonies the less confidence they have in God, and that they will not obtain from him the object of their desire.

Some pray more for their own aims than for the honor of God. Although they pray with the supposition that if God is to be served their petition will be granted, and if otherwise it will not, they nevertheless overmultiply their prayers. They are praying in this way because of their attachment to the desired object and their vain joy in it. It would be better to convert these prayers into practices of greater importance, such as purification of their consciences and serious concentration on matters pertinent to their salvation. Thus they ought to have far less regard for all these other petitions irrelevant to this concentration and purification. Through the attainment of more important goals, they will also obtain all that in this other aim is good for them even though they do not ask for it. And they receive this answer to their prayer sooner and in a better way than if they had put all their strength praying for their desire.

2. The Lord has promised in the Gospel: *Seek first, and chiefly, the*

---

1. Here the codex of Alcaudete as copied by Fray Juan Evangelista ends. What follows was taken from the ancient manuscript of Duruelo and added to Alcaudete in 1762.

kingdom of God and his justice, and all these other things will be added unto you [Mt. 6:33]. This is the aim and petition that is most pleasing to God. To obtain an answer to the requests we bear in our hearts, there is no better means than to concentrate the strength of our prayers on what is more pleasing to God. Then he will give us not only the salvation we beg for but whatever else he sees is fit and good for us, even though we do not ask for it. David shows this clearly in a psalm: *The Lord is near to those who call on him in truth* [Ps. 145:18], to those who ask for things that are most true, such as things pertinent to salvation. Of these individuals he says afterward: *He will fulfill the will of those who fear him, and he will hear their prayers and save them. For God is the guardian of those who love him* [Ps. 145:19-20]. God's being near, of which David speaks, is nothing more than his satisfying them and granting what it did not even enter their minds to ask for. We read that because Solomon had asked for something pleasing to God (that is, wisdom) so as to be certain of ruling the people justly, God answered him: *Because wisdom pleased you more than any other thing, and you did not seek victory through the death of your enemies, or riches, or a long life, not only will I give you the wisdom you seek to rule my people justly, but I will even give you what you have not asked for, that is, riches and substance and glory so that no king, either before you or after you, will be like you* [2 Chron. 1:11-12]. And God in fact did this and pacified Solomon's enemies, too, so that all who were around him paid him tribute and did not perturb him [1 Kgs. 4:21-24]. Similarly, we read in Genesis that God, promising to multiply the offspring of Abraham's legitimate son like the stars of heaven, told Abraham in response to his request: *I will also multiply the offspring of the son of the bondwoman because he is your son* [Gn. 15:2, 5; 21:13].

3. In one's petitions, then, the energies of the will and its joy should be directed to God in the manner described. One should be distrustful of ceremonies unapproved by the Catholic Church; and the manner of saying Mass should be left to the priest who represents the Church at the altar, for he has received directions from her as to how Mass should be said. And persons should not desire new methods as if they knew more than the Holy Spirit and his Church. If in such simplicity God does not hear them, let them be convinced that he will not answer them no matter how many ceremonies they invent. For God is such that if people live in harmony with him and do his will he will give them whatever they want, but if they seek their own interests it will be useless for them to speak to God.

4. And regarding other ceremonies in vocal prayers and other devotions, one should not become attached to any ceremonies or modes of prayer other than those Christ taught us. When his disciples asked him to teach them to pray, Christ obviously, as one who knew so well his Father's will, would have told them all that was necessary in order to

obtain an answer from the Eternal Father. And, in fact, he taught them only those seven petitions of the *Pater Noster,* which include all our spiritual and temporal needs, and he did not teach numerous other kinds of prayers and ceremonies [Lk. 11:1-4]. Instead, at another time he told them that in praying they should not desire much speaking because our heavenly Father clearly knows our needs [Mt. 6:7-8]. He only charged us with great insistence to persevere in prayer—that is, in the *Pater Noster*—teaching in another place that one should pray and never cease [Lk. 18:1]. He did not teach us a quantity of petitions but that these seven be repeated often, and with fervor and care. In these, as I say, are embodied everything that is God's will and all that is fitting for us. Accordingly, when His Majesty had recourse three times to the Eternal Father, all three times he prayed with the same petition of the *Pater Noster,* as the Evangelists recount: *Father, if it cannot be but that I drink this chalice, may your will be done* [Mt. 26:39; Mk. 14:36; Lk. 22:42].

And the ceremonies he taught us for use in our prayers are either of two. Our prayer should be made either in the concealment of our inner room (where without noise and without telling anyone we can pray with a more perfect and pure heart, as he said: *When you pray enter your inner room, and having closed the door, pray* [Mt. 6:6]); or, if not in one's room, it should be made in the solitary wilderness, and at the best and most quiet time of night, as he did [Lk. 6:12]. No reason exists, hence, for designating fixed times or set days, or for choosing some days more than others for our devotions; neither is there reason for using other kinds of prayer, or phrases having a play on words, but only those prayers that the Church uses, and as she uses them, for all are reducible to the *Pater Noster.*

5. By this I do not condemn—but rather approve—the custom of setting aside certain days for devotions, such as novenas, fasting, and other similar practices. I condemn the fixed methods and ceremonies with which the devotions are carried out, just as Judith reproved the Bethulians for having established a certain time to await God's mercy: *You have fixed a time for God's mercies. This does not serve to move God to clemency, but to stir up his wrath* [Jdt. 8:11-13].

CHAPTER 45

The second kind of distinct goods in which the will can vainly rejoice.

1. The second kind of distinct delightful goods in which the will can vainly rejoice comprises those that arouse or persuade one to serve God. We call these provocative goods. Preachers belong to this class, and we can speak of them in two ways: with reference to the preacher himself, and with reference to his hearers. It is needful to counsel both preacher

and hearer as to how joy of will should be directed to God in this practice.

2. As for the preacher, in order to benefit the people and avoid the impediment of vain joy and presumption, he should keep in mind that preaching is more a spiritual practice than a vocal one. For although it is practiced through exterior words, it has no force or efficacy save from the interior spirit. No matter how lofty the doctrine preached, or polished the rhetoric, or sublime the style in which the preaching is clothed, the profit does not ordinarily increase because of these means in themselves; it comes from the spirit. God's word is indeed efficacious of itself according to David, who says that *God will give to his voice the voice of power* [Ps. 68:33]; yet fire also has power to burn but will not burn if the material is unprepared.

3. A twofold preparation is required if the doctrine is to communicate its force: that of the preacher and that of his hearers. For the one who teaches, the profit is usually commensurate with his preparation. For this reason it is commonly said that as the master, so usually is the disciple.

In the Acts of the Apostles, when those seven sons of the Jewish high priest were casting out devils with the same formula St. Paul used, the devil was enraged against them, crying: *Jesus I know, and Paul I know; but you, who are you? And he attacked and stripped and wounded them* [Acts 19:14-16]. This unfortunate outcome was due to their lack of proper attitudes, and not because Christ was unwilling that they perform these works in his name. Once the Apostles forbade a man who was not a disciple to continue casting out devils in the name of Christ, and the Lord in turn reproved them: *Do not forbid him, for no one who does mighty works in my name will at the same time be able to speak badly of me* [Mk. 9:38-39]. But he is opposed to those who preach the law of God yet do not keep it, and who preach to others the good spirit yet do not possess it themselves. He admonishes consequently through St. Paul: *You teach others, but you do not teach yourselves. You who preach that others must not steal, steal* [Rom. 2:21]. And the Holy Spirit says through David: God said to the sinner: *Why do you preach my statutes and take my law in your mouth though you have abhorred discipline and cast my words behind you?* [Ps. 50:16-17]. From this we deduce that he will not give them the spirit from which they may bear fruit.

4. We frequently see, insofar as it is possible to judge here below, that the better the life of the preacher the more abundant the fruit, no matter how lowly his style, poor his rhetoric, and plain the doctrine. For the living spirit enkindles fire. But when this spirit is wanting the gain is small, however sublime the style and doctrine. Although it is true that good style, gestures, sublime doctrine, and well-chosen words are more moving and productive of effect when accompanied by this good spirit, yet

without it the sermon imparts little or no devotion to the will even though it may be delightful and pleasing to the senses and the intellect. For the will in this case will ordinarily be left as weak and remiss as before, even though wonderful things were wonderfully spoken; and the sermon merely delights the sense of hearing, like a musical concert or sounding bells. But the spirit, as I said, will not leave its natural ties any more than previously, since the voice does not possess the power to raise a dead man from his sepulcher.

5. It is of little significance that one kind of music is more pleasing to me than another if it fails to move me to the practice of works more than the other. Although the preacher may speak remarkable truths, these will soon be forgotten since they do not enkindle the will. Besides the fact of their unproductivity, the sensory adherence to the gratification provided by the doctrine hinders any effect the doctrine may have on the spirit, and people are left only with esteem for the mode and accidents of the sermon. They praise the preacher and listen to him for these reasons more than for the motivation they receive to amend their lives.

St. Paul gives an exceptionally clear explanation of this doctrine to the Corinthians: *I, brothers, when I came to you, did not come preaching with sublimity of doctrine and wisdom, and my words and my preaching were not in the rhetoric of human wisdom, but in the manifestation of the spirit and of truth* [1 Cor. 2:1-4]. Indeed, it is neither the Apostle's intention nor mine to condemn good style and rhetoric and effective delivery; these, rather, are most important to the preacher, as they are in all matters. Elegant style and delivery lift up and restore even those things that have fallen into ruin, just as poor presentation spoils what is good and destroys.[1]

---

1. Here *The Ascent of Mount Carmel* ends abruptly. In regard to the four passions (ch. 16. 3), John did not get beyond that of joy; nor, in treating of joy, did he complete his discussion of the directive and perfective spiritual goods (ch. 35. 1).

The Dark Night

INTRODUCTION
TO
THE DARK NIGHT

A work called *The Dark Night* has come down to us from John of the Cross in manuscripts separate from *The Ascent of Mount Carmel*. Explaining the passive purifications of both the senses and the spirit, this work fulfills John's several promises in the *Ascent* to treat of the passive nights. That the passive purifications are necessary to attain union with God seems obvious from the first chapter of the *Ascent*, where the author proposes to explain the active and passive nights. And a number of times as he moves through his material, he asserts that active purification alone is insufficient for attainment of union. This work, *The Dark Night*, then, describes how God purifies the soul passively and brings the theological life to the perfection delineated in the *Ascent*. The far-reaching demands of the *Ascent*, which John never finished expounding, are fully met through the passive purifications of the *Night*. Though different in literary style, this latter work furnishes a necessary complement to *The Ascent of Mount Carmel*.

A Commentary

The divisions that John set up in the *Ascent* took him far away from his original promise of commenting on the stanzas of the poem. In the *Night*, turning to the poem once again, he states his intention to explain its stanzas. And this time the exposition of the subject matter follows the poem more closely and is more influenced by it.

In a broad division of the poem, John gives us a clue to what we might expect in his commentary. He tells us in a brief prologue that the first two stanzas refer to the effects of the two kinds of purification, sensory and spiritual; and the last six speak of the effects, wonderful though ineffable, of illumination and union. Thus the poem describes two fundamental conditions in the spiritual process: the painful passage through the night, and the unspeakable joy of encountering God. In commenting on the stanzas, he pays particular attention to these conditions to which the poem intuitively and creatively alludes. But the verses of the poem do not set out a program to be rigorously embraced. John composed them after he had passed along the constricted path that leads to eternal life, the path he called a dark night. From the height of a blessed union with God, in this poem he sings of his happiness in having escaped from himself and other enemies, disguised and by a secret ladder, at night, in darkness. He then uses his own experience as a paradigm for others, souls who must find their freedom in this same way.

Reading the work, we have to be aware from the start that the text as written by John contained no divisions into chapters or books, no chapter headings. The conventional divisions, introduced by Diego de Salablanca in the first edition of 1618 and still used today, help to present and refer to the work in a more manageable form. Though editors could possibly devise other, better arrangements, the preservation of the traditional divisions is undoubtedly useful for references and quotations. In his actual composition of the work, John proceeded as he did in his commentaries on *The Spiritual Canticle* and *The Living Flame of Love;* that is, he used the stanzas and verses as the only dividing marks. But this commentary on the *Night* turns out to be much more uneven than the others. In fact, John comments on the first stanza twice, and gives as the reason that the symbol, though it speaks mainly of the purification of the spirit, can refer as well to the first night or purification of the senses. Differently explained in the *Ascent* and the *Night,* the poem, as we read along, begins to find its genuine meaning when the commentary turns its focus on the passive purification of the spirit. Other explanations are more distant from this dynamic moment.

The *Ascent,* then, beginning as a commentary, moved outside the span of the poetic verses and shifted into a treatise in its own right. The *Night* maintains its link with the poem and its style as commentary, but at times digresses into its own little treatises noticeably removed from the poem itself.

In contrast to our expectations, hardly does John begin to comment on the third stanza of the poem when he sets aside the work. Of the eight stanzas, he explains only two. These two alone enable him to give a thorough presentation, though somewhat repetitious, of the subject that in this work most interests him: the dark night of purgative contemplation. In a way, the commentary for the second stanza resembles a musical variation on a theme. And we can suppose that an explanation of the remaining stanzas would have drawn him into a lengthy elaboration of the life of union, a subject whose features he treats extensively in other works.

The Doctrine

While dealing with his material, John works on two levels: his personal experience and his doctrinal reflections. His personal experience expressed in the poem, seen from the perspective of one who has escaped in the night and is looking back, becomes the framework on which he builds his doctrine applicable to others. Woven into the description, then, of the spiritual experience symbolized by the dark night image, we find the doctrinal explanation, on a theological level, of the phenomena described. These levels become particularly evident in chapters 4-18 of the second book, the central texts of the work.

Two basic allegories serve to illustrate the purifications. In the one, regarding the initial purgation, God is likened to a loving mother who first nurses her child, carries and caresses it in her arms, but who then must wean it, teach it both to walk on its own and to put aside the ways of childhood. In the other, the purification of the spirit, God's action is likened to fire working on and transforming a log of wood.

In his exposition, John does not present a program of detailed asceticism for attaining the poverty of spirit implied by the radical purification. His emphasis is on allowing God to lead, on accepting the Lord's work with all its consequences. At the same time the teaching must be seen in relation to the main focus of the *Ascent,* as a prolongation and complement to it.

The main topics of the book are: the experience of the night; the theological principles underlying both its causes and its purpose; analyses of a person before, during, and after the purification; and the fruits of love and illumination. *Night* is divided into Book One and Book Two. The first book, consisting of 14 chapters, explains what refers to the passive night of the senses; the second, containing 25 chapters, explains what refers to the passive night of the spirit. What is really at stake in the spiritual journey to union with God is an ongoing work of purification, a cleansing of all that is repugnant to God's holiness. The purity implied is impossible without personal effort, but this effort, however intense, does not achieve the radical stripping demanded by the union. God's own intervention is necessary through a purifying communication that works passively, beyond the realm of what human effort can achieve. Human effort does little more than dispose one for the divine action.

The negation (poverty, purity, nakedness, void, death, and so on) of the dark night is in reality theological communion. The emptying of self is transformed into the fullness of God. We find in John's vocabulary and style the paradoxical language of St. Paul: light/darkness, life/death, spirit/flesh, new self/old self.

The human work and the divine action are not perfectly successive; rather, they are parallel and simultaneous. It is the predominance of one over the other that permits the establishing of a certain relative succession, which of course means that in the final stage of the purification the divine is clearly prevalent. Since the divine intervention may also come with greater or lesser intensity and efficacy, we can speak of parts or periods of passive night. The high point of the dark night, being the passive night of the spirit, from the viewpoint of time belongs within that period of the spiritual life that John calls the spiritual betrothal, borrowing from the tradition of commentary on the *Song of Songs*. Though the verses of the poem refer directly to this high point, their author, as a teacher, extends their meaning, adjusting them that they may speak to other periods or situations as well.

What the person undergoing the dark night experiences is a painful lack or privation: darkness in the intellect; aridity in the will regarding the exercise of love; emptiness of all possessions in the memory; and a general affliction and torment as a consequence. Such persons receive a vivid understanding of their own misery and think they will never escape from it. Their faculties seem powerless and bound; all outside help appears useless; they feel no hope for any breakthrough or remedy in the future. The effect of all this is the dread-filled experience of being abandoned by God. This feeling of being abandoned by God becomes the worst part of the suffering since we are dealing with one who longs for God with utmost love.

All these painful experiences as well as the beneficial fruits of the transformation are attributable to contemplation. This contemplation is an inpouring of God into the soul, a divine, loving knowledge that is general, without images or concepts, obscure and hidden from the one who receives it, a knowledge that both purifies and illumines. If John speaks of this knowledge as general, he does so not because contemplation refers to something imprecise but because it embraces the totality of the relationship: an attitude of personal and complete receptivity before God who is communicating himself in his personal infinitude. Seen thus, "general" points to the totality or whole, not to the generic or imprecise. The novelty of the knowledge then does not lie in the information, but in a new sense of the presence of God through faith and love. The one who receives it is in a kind of passive activity. There are no adequate human controls; before God, only poverty, confidence, and abandonment remain. But contemplation is not identifiable with dark night; it may be given in forms that produce effects different from these purifying ones. In addition, it is worth saying that if this night darkens, it does so only to give light; if it humiliates, it does so only to exalt; if it impoverishes, it does so only to enrich.

The point of arrival to which the night leads is the "new self," divinized in being and operation, living now a life of faith, hope, and love, fortified and pure.

John's exposition of the night may seem to disengage that experience from the rest of life. But the night cannot occur apart from the external happenings of every day, nor can we forget, while reading, the event of John's imprisonment in Toledo with all its social and material deprivations. Our horizons open to many possible forms in which we may experience a dark night, according to the grace, state in life, and historical or personal circumstances of the individual. John leaves to each reader and each age the task of making the suitable applications. What is essential is that the sufferings and privations bring about a growing response of faith, hope, and love; without this transforming theological life the night would fail to purify and produce fruit.

The work may be divided this way:

Book One:
Introductory description of the dark night.
Necessity of the passive night demonstrated by way of the imperfec
    tions (seven capital vices) of beginners (ch. 1-7).
The passive night of the senses (ch. 8).
The signs for recognizing this night (ch. 9).
The appropriate response (ch. 10).
Experiences of love (ch. 11).
Benefits of the night: knowledge of God and of self; virtues (ch. 12-
    13).
Duration and accompanying trials (ch. 14).

Book Two:
Introductory description of the proficient's experience (ch. 1).
Necessity of the passive night of the spirit, demonstrated by way of the
    imperfections of proficients (ch. 1-3).
The passive night of the spirit (ch. 4).
Nature (ch. 5).
Afflictions (ch. 5-8).
Positive content (ch. 9).
Illustration as fire acting on wood (ch. 10).
The enkindling of love and its fruits (ch. 11-14).
Description of the passive night of the spirit based on the second
    stanza: darkness, secure, secret, ladder, disguised (ch. 15-24).
Summary explanation of the third stanza (ch. 25).

The manuscript copies of *The Dark Night* generally receiving the most credit from scholars are *Hispalensis* and *Roma*. The first is conserved in the National Library of Madrid; the second, in the general archives of the discalced Carmelite Friars in Rome.

THE DARK NIGHT

An explanation of the stanzas describing a soul's conduct along the spiritual road that leads to the perfect union with God through love, insofar as it is attainable in this life. A description also of the characteristics of one who has reached this perfection.

PROLOGUE FOR THE READER

In this book we will first cite the entire poem, then each stanza will be repeated separately and explained, and finally we will do the same thing with the individual verses.

The first two stanzas describe the effects of the two kinds of spiritual purgation that take place in a person: one, a purification of the sensory part; the other, a purification of the spiritual part. The remaining six stanzas speak of some of the marvelous results obtained from spiritual illumination and union with God through love.

STANZAS OF THE SOUL

1. One dark night,
fired with love's urgent longings
—ah, the sheer grace!—
I went out unseen,
my house being now all stilled.

2. In darkness, and secure,
by the secret ladder, disguised,
—ah, the sheer grace!—
in darkness and concealment,
my house being now all stilled.

3. On that glad night,
in secret, for no one saw me,
nor did I look at anything,
with no other light or guide
than the one that burned in my heart.

4. This guided me
more surely than the light of noon
to where he was awaiting me
—him I knew so well—
there in a place where no one appeared.

5. O guiding night!
O night more lovely than the dawn!
O night that has united
the Lover with his beloved,
transforming the beloved in her Lover.

6. Upon my flowering breast
which I kept wholly for him alone,
there he lay sleeping,
and I caressing him
there in a breeze from the fanning cedars.

7. When the breeze blew from the turret,
as I parted his hair,
it wounded my neck
with its gentle hand,
suspending all my senses.

8. I abandoned and forgot myself,
laying my face on my Beloved;
all things ceased; I went out from myself,
leaving my cares
forgotten among the lilies.

Beginning of the explanation of the stanzas that deal with the way a soul must conduct itself along the road leading to union with God through love, by Padre Fray John of the Cross.

Before embarking on an explanation of these stanzas, we should remember that the soul recites them when it has already reached the state of perfection—that is, union with God through love—and has now passed through severe trials and conflicts by means of the spiritual exercise that leads one along the constricted way to eternal life, of which our Savior speaks in the Gospel [Mt. 7:14]. The soul must ordinarily walk this path to reach that sublime and joyous union with God. Recognizing the narrowness of the path and the fact that so very few tread it—as the Lord himself says [Mt. 7:14]—the soul's song in this first stanza is one of happiness in having advanced along it to this perfection of love. Appropriately, this constricted road is called a dark night, as we shall explain in later verses of this stanza. The soul, therefore, happy at having trod this narrow road from which it derived so much good, speaks in this manner:

BOOK ONE

[A treatise on the night of the senses]

> One dark night,
> fired with love's urgent longings
> —ah, the sheer grace!—
> I went out unseen,
> my house being now all stilled.

[Explanation]

1. In this first stanza, the soul speaks of the way it followed in its departure from love of both self and all things. Through a method of true mortification, it died to all these things and to itself. It did this so as to reach the sweet and delightful life of love with God. And it declares that this departure was a dark night. As we will explain later,[1] this dark night signifies here purgative contemplation, which passively causes in the soul this negation of self and of all things.

2. The soul states that it was able to make this escape because of the strength and warmth gained from loving its Bridegroom in this obscure

---

1. In N. 2. 4. 1.

contemplation. It emphasizes its good fortune in having journeyed to God through this dark night. So great was the soul's success that none of the three enemies (the world, the devil, and the flesh, which are always in opposition to the journey along this road) could impede it, for that night of purifying contemplation lulled to sleep and deadened all the inordinate movements of the passions and appetites in the house of sense. The verse then states:

One dark night,

CHAPTER 1

[Quotes the first verse and begins to discuss the imperfections of beginners.]

1. Souls begin to enter this dark night when God, gradually drawing them out of the state of beginners (those who practice meditation on the spiritual road), begins to place them in the state of proficients (those who are already contemplatives), so that by passing through this state they might reach that of the perfect, which is the divine union of the soul with God.

We should first mention here some characteristics of beginners, for the sake of a better explanation and understanding of the nature of this night and of God's motive for placing the soul in it. Although our treatment of these things will be as brief as possible, it will help beginners understand the feebleness of their state and take courage and desire that God place them in this night where the soul is strengthened in virtue and fortified for the inestimable delights of the love of God. And, although we will be delayed for a moment, it will be for no longer than our discussion of this dark night requires.

2. It should be known, then, that God nurtures and caresses the soul, after it has been resolutely converted to his service, like a loving mother who warms her child with the heat of her bosom, nurses it with good milk and tender food, and carries and caresses it in her arms. But as the child grows older, the mother withholds her caresses and hides her tender love; she rubs bitter aloes on her sweet breast and sets the child down from her arms, letting it walk on its own feet so that it may put aside the habits of childhood and grow accustomed to greater and more important things. The grace of God acts just as a loving mother by re-engendering in the soul new enthusiasm and fervor in the service of God. With no effort on the soul's part, this grace causes it to taste sweet and delectable milk and to experience intense satisfaction in the performance of spiritual exercises, because God is handing the breast of his tender love to the

soul, just as if it were a delicate child [1 Pt. 2:2-3].[1]

3. The soul finds its joy, therefore, in spending lengthy periods at prayer, perhaps even entire nights; its penances are pleasures; its fasts, happiness; and the sacraments and spiritual conversations are its consolations. Although spiritual persons do practice these exercises with great profit and persistence, and are very careful about them, spiritually speaking, they conduct themselves in a very weak and imperfect manner. Since their motivation in their spiritual works and exercises is the consolation and satisfaction they experience in them, and since they have not been conditioned by the arduous struggle of practicing virtue, they possess many faults and imperfections in the discharge of their spiritual activities. Assuredly, since everyone's actions are in direct conformity with the habit of perfection that has been acquired, and since these persons have not had time to acquire those firm habits, their work must of necessity be feeble, like that of weak children.

For a clearer understanding of this and of how truly imperfect beginners are, insofar as they practice virtue readily because of the satisfaction attached to it, we will describe, using the seven capital vices as our basis, some of the numerous imperfections beginners commit. Thus we will clearly see how very similar their deeds are to those of children. The benefits of the dark night will become evident, since it cleanses and purifies the soul of all these imperfections.

CHAPTER 2

[Some of the imperfections of pride possessed by beginners.]

1. These beginners feel so fervent and diligent in their spiritual exercises and undertakings that a certain kind of secret pride is generated in them that begets a complacency with themselves and their accomplishments, even though holy works do of their very nature cause humility. Then they develop a somewhat vain—at times very vain—desire to speak of spiritual things in others' presence, and sometimes even to instruct rather than be instructed; in their hearts they condemn others who do not seem to have the kind of devotion they would like them to have, and sometimes they give expression to this criticism like the pharisee who despised the publican while he boasted and praised God

---

1. As he has previously, John describes the state of beginners by using the image of a mother lovingly nursing and caring for her child; cf. A. 2. 14. 3; 17. 6-7; A. 3. 28. 7.

for the good deeds he himself accomplished [Lk. 18:11-12].[1]

2. The devil, desiring the growth of pride and presumption in these beginners, often increases their fervor and readiness to perform such works, and other ones, too. For he is quite aware that all these works and virtues are not only worthless for them, but even become vices. Some of these persons become so evil-minded that they do not want anyone except themselves to appear holy; and so by both word and deed they condemn and detract others whenever the occasion arises, seeing the little splinter in their brother's eye and failing to consider the wooden beam in their own eye [Mt. 7:3]; they strain at the other's gnat and swallow their own camel [Mt. 23:24].

3. And when at times their spiritual directors, their confessors, or their superiors disapprove their spirit and method of procedure, they feel that these directors do not understand, or perhaps that this failure to approve derives from a lack of holiness, since they want these directors to regard their conduct with esteem and praise. So they quickly search for some other spiritual advisor more to their liking, someone who will congratulate them and be impressed by their deeds; and they flee, as they would death, those who attempt to place them on the safe road by forbidding these things—and sometimes they even become hostile toward such spiritual directors. Frequently, in their presumption, they make many resolutions but accomplish very little. Sometimes they want others to recognize their spirit and devotion, and as a result occasionally contrive to make some manifestations of it, such as movements, sighs, and other ceremonies; sometimes, with the assistance of the devil, they experience raptures, more often in public than in private, and they are quite pleased, and often eager, for others to take notice of these.

4. Many want to be the favorites of their confessors, and thus they are consumed by a thousand envies and disquietudes. Embarrassment forbids them from relating their sins clearly, lest their reputation diminish in their confessor's eyes. They confess their sins in the most favorable light so as to appear better than they actually are, and thus they approach the confessional to excuse themselves rather than accuse themselves. Sometimes they confess the evil things they do to a different confessor so that their own confessor might think they commit no sins at all. Therefore, in their desire to appear holy, they enjoy relating their good behavior to their confessor, and in such careful terms that these good deeds appear greater than they actually are. It would be more humble of them, as we will point out later,[2] to make light of the good they do and

---

1. For a related passage, cf. A. 3. 28. 2-3.
2. In nos. 6-8 and ch. 12. 7-9.

to wish that no one, neither their confessor nor anybody else, should consider it of any importance at all.

5. Sometimes they minimize their faults, and at other times they become discouraged by them, since they felt they were already saints, and they become impatient and angry with themselves, which is yet another fault.

They are often extremely anxious that God remove their faults and imperfections, but their motive is personal peace rather than God. They fail to realize that were God to remove their faults they might very well become more proud and presumptuous.

They dislike praising anyone else, but they love to receive praise, and sometimes they even seek it. In this they resemble the foolish virgins who had to seek oil from others when their own lamps were extinguished [Mt. 25:8].

6. The number of these imperfections is serious in some people and causes them a good deal of harm. Some have fewer, some have more, and yet others have little more than the first movements toward them. But there are scarcely any beginners who at the time of their initial fervor do not fall victim to some of these imperfections.

But souls who are advancing in perfection at this time act in an entirely different manner and with a different quality of spirit.[3] They receive great benefit from their humility, by which they not only place little importance on their deeds, but also take very little self-satisfaction from them. They think everyone else is far better than they are, and usually possess a holy envy of them and would like to emulate their service of God. Since they are truly humble, their growing fervor and the increased number of their good deeds and the gratification they receive from them only cause them to become more aware of their debt to God and the inadequacy of their service to him, and thus the more they do, the less satisfaction they derive from it. Their charity and love makes them want to do so much for God that what they actually do accomplish seems as nothing. This loving solicitude goads them, preoccupies them, and absorbs them to such an extent that they never notice what others do or do not accomplish, but if they should, they then think, as I say, that everyone is better than they. They think they themselves are insignificant, and want others to think this also and to belittle and slight their deeds. Moreover, even though others do praise and value their works, these souls are unable to believe them; such praises seem strange to them.

7. These souls humbly and tranquilly long to be taught by anyone who

---

3. Here for comparison John begins to describe traits of proficients and the perfect.

might be a help to them. This desire is the exact opposite of that other desire we mentioned above, of those who want to be themselves the teachers in everything. When these others notice that someone is trying to give them some instruction, they themselves take the words from their very mouths as though they already know everything.

Yet these humble souls, far from desiring to be anyone's teacher, are ready to take a road different from the one they are following, if told to do so. For they do not believe they could ever be right themselves. They rejoice when others receive praise, and their only sorrow is that they do not serve God as these others do. Because they consider their deeds insignificant, they do not want to make them known. They are even ashamed to speak of them to their spiritual directors because they think these deeds are not worth mentioning. They are more eager to speak of their faults and sins, and reveal these to others, than of their virtues. They have an inclination to seek direction from one who will have less esteem for their spirit and deeds. Such is the characteristic of a pure and simple and true spirit, one very pleasing to God. Since the wise Spirit of God dwells within these humble souls, he moves them to keep these treasures hidden, and to manifest only their faults. God gives this grace to the humble, together with the other virtues, just as he denies it to the proud.

8. These souls would give their life's blood to anyone who serves God, and they will do whatever they can to help others serve him. When they see themselves fall into imperfections, they suffer this with humility, with docility of spirit, and with loving fear of God and hope in him.

Yet I believe very few souls are so perfect in the beginning. We would be happy enough if they managed not to fall into these imperfections of pride. As we will point out later, then, God places these souls in the dark night so as to purify them of these imperfections and make them advance.

CHAPTER 3

[Some imperfections of spiritual avarice commonly found in beginners.]

1. Many beginners also at times possess great spiritual avarice. They hardly ever seem content with the spirit God gives them. They become unhappy and peevish because they don't find the consolation they want in spiritual things. Many never have enough of hearing counsels, or learning spiritual maxims, or keeping them and reading books about them. They spend more time in these than in striving after mortification and the perfection of the interior poverty to which they are obliged.

Furthermore, they weigh themselves down with overdecorated images and rosaries. They now put these down, now take up others; at one moment they are exchanging, and at the next re-exchanging. Now they want this kind, now they want another. And they prefer one cross to another because of its elaborateness. Others you see who are decked out in *agnusdeis* and relics and lists of saints' names, like children in trinkets.[1]

What I condemn in this is possessiveness of heart and attachment to the number, workmanship, and overdecoration of these objects. For this attachment is contrary to poverty of spirit, which is intent only on the substance of the devotion, benefits by no more than what procures this sufficiently, and tires of all other multiplicity and elaborate ornamentation. Since true devotion comes from the heart and looks only to the truth and substance represented by spiritual objects, and since everything else is imperfect attachment and possessiveness, any appetite for these things must be uprooted if some degree of perfection is to be reached.

2. I knew a person who for more than ten years profited by a cross roughly made out of a blessed palm and held together by a pin twisted around it. That person carried it about and never would part with it until I took it—and the person was not someone of poor judgment or little intelligence. I saw someone else who prayed with beads made out of bones from the spine of a fish. Certainly, the devotion was not for this reason less precious in the sight of God.[2] In neither of these two instances, obviously, did these persons base their devotion on the workmanship and value of a spiritual object.

They, therefore, who are well guided from the outset do not become attached to visible instruments or burden themselves with them. They do not care to know any more than is necessary to accomplish good works, because their eyes are fixed only on God, on being his friend and pleasing him; this is what they long for. They very generously give all they have. Their pleasure is to know how to live for love of God or neighbor without these spiritual or temporal things. As I say, they set their eyes on the substance of interior perfection, on pleasing God and not themselves.

3. Yet until a soul is placed by God in the passive purgation of that dark night, which we will soon explain, it cannot purify itself completely of these imperfections or others. But people should insofar as possible strive to do their part in purifying and perfecting themselves and thereby merit God's divine cure. In this cure God will heal them of what through their own efforts they were unable to remedy. No matter how much

---

1. Cf. A. 3. 35-37 for further descriptions. An *agnusdei* was a small wax disk with the image of a lamb. Blessed by the pope in special ceremonies that took place every seven years, it was worn as protection against natural disasters.
2. The identity of these persons is unknown; some think the first one might have been St. Teresa.

individuals do through their own efforts, they cannot actively purify themselves enough to be disposed in the least degree for the divine union of the perfection of love. God must take over and purge them in that fire that is dark for them, as we will explain.

CHAPTER 4

[The imperfections of lust, the third capital vice, usually found in beginners.]

1. A number of these beginners have many more imperfections in each vice than those I am mentioning. But to avoid prolixity, I am omitting them and touching on some principal ones that are as it were the origin of the others.

As for the vice of lust—aside from what it means for spiritual persons to fall into this vice, since my intent is to treat of the imperfections that have to be purged by means of the dark night—spiritual persons have numerous imperfections, many of which can be called spiritual lust, not because the lust is spiritual but because it proceeds from spiritual things. It happens frequently that in a person's spiritual exercises themselves, without the person being able to avoid it, impure movements will be experienced in the sensory part of the soul, and even sometimes when the spirit is deep in prayer or when receiving the sacraments of Penance or the Eucharist. These impure feelings arise from any of three causes outside one's control.[1]

2. First, they often proceed from the pleasure human nature finds in spiritual exercises. Since both the spiritual and the sensory part of the soul receive gratification from that refreshment, each part experiences delight according to its own nature and properties. The spirit, the superior part of the soul, experiences renewal and satisfaction in God; and the sense, the lower part, feels sensory gratification and delight because it is ignorant of how to get anything else, and hence takes whatever is nearest, which is the impure sensory satisfaction. It may happen that while a soul is with God in deep spiritual prayer, it will conversely passively experience sensual rebellions, movements, and acts in the senses, not without its own great displeasure.

This frequently happens at the time of Communion. Since the soul receives joy and gladness in this act of love—for the Lord grants the grace and gives himself for this reason—the sensory part also takes its share, as we said, according to its mode. Since, after all, these two parts form one suppositum, each one usually shares according to its mode in what the

---

1. For a fuller treatment of related material cf. A. 3. 21-23.

other receives. As the Philosopher says: *Whatever is received, is received according to the mode of the receiver.*[2] Because in the initial stages of the spiritual life, and even more advanced ones, the sensory part of the soul is imperfect, God's spirit is frequently received in this sensory part with this same imperfection. Once the sensory part is reformed through the purgation of the dark night, it no longer has these infirmities. Then the spiritual part of the soul, rather than the sensory part, receives God's spirit, and the soul thus receives everything according to the mode of the spirit.

3. The second origin of these rebellions is the devil. To bring disquietude and disturbance on a soul when it is praying, or trying to pray, he endeavors to excite impure feelings in the sensory part. And if people pay any attention to these, the devil does them great harm. Through fear, some souls grow slack in their prayer—which is what the devil wants—in order to struggle against these movements, and others give it up entirely, for they think these feelings come while they are engaged in prayer rather than at other times. And this is true because the devil excites these feelings while souls are at prayer, instead of when they are engaged in other works, so that they might abandon prayer. And that is not all; to make them cowardly and afraid, he brings vividly to their minds foul and impure thoughts. And sometimes the thoughts will concern spiritually helpful things and persons. Those who attribute any importance to such thoughts, therefore, do not even dare look at anything or think about anything lest they thereupon stumble into them.

These impure thoughts so affect people who are afflicted with melancholia that one should have great pity for them; indeed, these people suffer a sad life. In some who are troubled with this bad humor the trial reaches such a point that they clearly feel that the devil has access to them without their having the freedom to prevent it. Yet some of these melancholiacs are able through intense effort and struggle to forestall this power of the devil. If these impure thoughts and feelings arise from melancholia, individuals are not ordinarily freed from them until they are cured of that humor—unless they enter the dark night, which in time deprives them of everything.[3]

4. The third origin from which these impure feelings usually proceed and wage war on the soul is the latter's fear of them. The fear that springs

---

2. This axiom as such has not been found in Aristotle. Aquinas makes use of it several times, for example, in *Summa theologiae* 1. 79. 6. The principle is important in John's teaching; cf. N. 2. 16. 4; F. 3. 34.

3. The term melancholia, or melancholy, was used for the whole gamut of emotional disturbances believed to be caused by an excess of black bile. Cf. A. prol. 4; A. 2. 13. 6; N. 1. 9. 2-3; also Teresa of Avila's *Foundations*, ch. 7.

up at the sudden remembrance of these thoughts, caused by what one sees, is dealing with, or thinking of, produces impure feelings without the person being at fault.

5. Some people are so delicate that when gratification is received spiritually, or in prayer, they immediately experience a lust that so inebriates them and caresses their senses that they become as it were engulfed in the delight and satisfaction of that vice; and this experience continues passively with the other. Sometimes these individuals become aware that certain impure and rebellious acts have taken place. The reason for such occurrences is that since these natures are, as I say, delicate and tender, their humors and blood are stirred up by any change. These persons also experience such feelings when they are inflamed with anger or are agitated by some other disturbance or affliction.

6. Sometimes, too, in their spiritual conversations or works, they manifest a certain sprightliness and gallantry on considering who is present, and they carry on with a kind of vain satisfaction. Such behavior is also a by-product of spiritual lust (in the way we here understand it), which generally accompanies complacency of the will.

7. Some spiritually acquire a liking for other individuals that often arises from lust rather than from the spirit. This lustful origin will be recognized if, on recalling that affection, there is remorse of conscience, not an increase in the remembrance and love of God. The affection is purely spiritual if the love of God grows when it grows, or if the love of God is remembered as often as the affection is remembered, or if the affection gives the soul a desire for God—if by growing in one the soul grows also in the other. For this is a trait of God's spirit: The good increases with the good since there is likeness and conformity between them. But when the love is born of this sensual vice it has the contrary effects. As the one love grows greater, the other lessens, and the remembrance of it lessens too. If the inordinate love increases, then, as will be seen, the soul grows cold in the love of God and, because of the recollection of that other love, forgets him—not without feeling some remorse of conscience. On the other hand, as the love of God increases, the soul grows cold in the inordinate affection and comes to forget it. For not only do these loves fail to benefit each other, but, since they are contrary loves, the predominating one, while becoming stronger itself, stifles and extinguishes the other, as the philosophers say.[4] Hence our Savior proclaimed in the Gospel: *That which is born of the flesh is flesh, and that which is born of the spirit*

---

4. Cf. A. 1. 4. 2.

is spirit [Jn. 3:6], that is: Love derived from sensuality terminates in sensuality, and the love that is of the spirit terminates in the spirit of God, and brings it increase. And this, then, is the difference between these two loves, which enables us to discern one from the other.

8. When the soul enters the dark night, all these loves are placed in reasonable order. This night strengthens and purifies the love that is of God, and takes away and destroys the other. But in the beginning it causes the soul to lose sight of both of them, as will be explained.

CHAPTER 5

[The imperfections of the capital vice of anger into which beginners fall.]

1. Because of the strong desire of many beginners for spiritual gratification, they usually have many imperfections of anger. When the delight and satisfaction procured in their spiritual exercises passes, these beginners are naturally left without any spiritual savor. And because of this distastefulness, they become peevish in the works they do and easily angered by the least thing, and occasionally they are so unbearable that nobody can put up with them. This frequently occurs after they have experienced in prayer some recollection pleasant to the senses.

After the delight and satisfaction are gone, the sensory part of the soul is naturally left vapid and zestless, just as a child is when withdrawn from the sweet breast. These souls are not at fault if they do not allow this dejection to influence them, for it is an imperfection that must be purged through the dryness and distress of the dark night.

2. Among these spiritual persons there are also those who fall into another kind of spiritual anger. Through a certain indiscreet zeal they become angry over the sins of others, reprove these others, and sometimes even feel the impulse to do so angrily, which in fact they occasionally do, setting themselves up as lords of virtue. All such conduct is contrary to spiritual meekness.

3. Others, in becoming aware of their own imperfections, grow angry with themselves in an unhumble impatience. So impatient are they about these imperfections that they want to become saints in a day. Many of these beginners make numerous plans and great resolutions, but since they are not humble and have no distrust of themselves, the more resolves they make the more they break, and the greater becomes their anger. They do not have the patience to wait until God gives them what they need, when he so desires. Their attitude is contrary to spiritual

meekness and can only be remedied by the purgation of the dark night. Some, however, are so patient about their desire for advancement that God would prefer to see them a little less so.

CHAPTER 6

[The imperfections of spiritual gluttony.]

1. A great deal can be said on spiritual gluttony, the fourth vice. There are hardly any persons among these beginners, no matter how excellent their conduct, who do not fall into some of the many imperfections of this vice. These imperfections arise because of the delight beginners find in their spiritual exercises.

Many, lured by the delight and satisfaction procured in their religious practices, strive more for spiritual savor than for spiritual purity and discretion; yet it is this purity and discretion that God looks for and finds acceptable throughout a soul's entire spiritual journey. Besides the imperfection of seeking after these delights, the sweetness these persons experience makes them go to extremes and pass beyond the mean in which virtue resides and is acquired. Some, attracted by the delight they feel in their spiritual exercises, kill themselves with penances, and others weaken themselves by fasts and, without the counsel or command of another, overtax their weakness; indeed, they try to hide these penances from the one to whom they owe obedience in such matters. Some even dare perform these penances contrary to obedience.

2. Such individuals are unreasonable and most imperfect. They subordinate submissiveness and obedience (which is a penance of reason and discretion, and consequently a sacrifice more pleasing and acceptable to God) to corporeal penance. But corporeal penance without obedience is no more than a penance of beasts. And like beasts, they are motivated in these penances by an appetite for the pleasure they find in them. Since all extremes are vicious and since by such behavior these persons are doing their own will, they grow in vice rather than in virtue. For through this conduct they at least become spiritually gluttonous and proud, since they do not tread the path of obedience.

The devil, increasing the delights and appetites of these beginners and thereby stirring up this gluttony in them, so impels many of them that when they are unable to avoid obedience they either add to, change, or modify what was commanded. Any obedience in this matter is distasteful to them. Some reach such a point that the mere obligation of obedience to perform their spiritual exercises makes them lose all desire and devotion. Their only yearning and satisfaction is to do what they feel inclined to do, whereas it would be better in all likelihood for them not to do this at all.

3. Some are very insistent that their spiritual director allow them to do what they themselves want to do, and finally almost force the permission from him. And if they do not get what they want, they become sad and go about like testy children. They are under the impression that they do not serve God when they are not allowed to do what they want. Since they take gratification and their own will as their support and their god, they become sad, weak, and discouraged when their director takes these from them and desires that they do God's will. They think that gratifying and satisfying themselves is serving and satisfying God.

4. Others, too, because of this sweetness, have so little knowledge of their own lowliness and misery and such lack of the loving fear and respect they owe to God's grandeur that they do not hesitate to insist boldly that their confessors allow them the frequent reception of Communion. And worse than this, they often dare to receive Communion without the permission and advice of the minister and dispenser of Christ. They are guided here solely by their own opinion, and they endeavor to hide the truth from him. As a result, with their hearts set on frequent Communion, they make their confessions carelessly, more eager just to receive Communion than to receive it with a pure and perfect heart. It would be sounder and holier of them to have the contrary inclination and to ask their confessor not to let them receive Communion so frequently. Humble resignation, though, is better than either of these two attitudes. But the boldnesses referred to first will bring great evil and chastisement on one.

5. In receiving Communion they spend all their time trying to get some feeling and satisfaction rather than humbly praising and reverencing God dwelling within them. And they go about this in such a way that, if they do not procure any sensible feeling and satisfaction, they think they have accomplished nothing. As a result they judge very poorly of God and fail to understand that the sensory benefits are the least among those that this most blessed Sacrament bestows, for the invisible grace it gives is a greater blessing. God often withdraws sensory delight and pleasure so that souls might set the eyes of faith on this invisible grace. Not only in receiving Communion, but in other spiritual exercises as well, beginners desire to feel God and taste him as if he were comprehensible and accessible. This desire is a serious imperfection and, because it involves impurity of faith, is opposed to God's way.

6. They have the same defect in their prayer, for they think the whole

matter of prayer consists in looking for sensory satisfaction and devotion. They strive to procure this by their own efforts, and tire and weary their heads and their faculties. When they do not get this sensible comfort, they become very disconsolate and think they have done nothing. Because of their aim they lose true devotion and spirit, which lie in distrust of self and in humble and patient perseverance so as to please God. Once they do not find delight in prayer, or in any other spiritual exercise, they feel extreme reluctance and repugnance in returning to it and sometimes even give it up. For after all, as was mentioned,[1] they are like children who are prompted to act not by reason but by pleasure.

All their time is spent looking for satisfaction and spiritual consolation; they can never read enough spiritual books, and one minute they are meditating on one subject and the next on another, always hunting for some gratification in the things of God. God very rightly and discreetly and lovingly denies this satisfaction to these beginners. If he did not, they would fall into innumerable evils because of their spiritual gluttony and craving for sweetness. This is why it is important for these beginners to enter the dark night and be purged of this childishness.[2]

7. Those who are inclined toward these delights have also another serious imperfection, which is that they are weak and remiss in treading the rough way of the cross. A soul given up to pleasure naturally feels aversion toward the bitterness of self-denial.

8. These people incur many other imperfections because of this spiritual gluttony, of which the Lord in time will cure them through temptations, aridities, and other trials, which are all a part of the dark night. So as not to be too lengthy, I do not want to discuss these imperfections any more, but only point out that spiritual sobriety and temperance beget another very different quality, one of mortification, fear, and submissiveness in all things. Individuals thereby become aware that the perfection and value of their works do not depend on quantity or the satisfaction found in them but on knowing how to practice self-denial in them. These beginners ought to do their part in striving after this self-denial until God in fact brings them into the dark night and purifies them. In order to get to our discussion of this dark night, I am passing over these imperfections hurriedly.

---

1. In ch. 5. 1.
2. Throughout these chapters, describing the situation of beginners in regard to each capital vice, John repeatedly points out their need for the purification of the dark night, which he begins to treat in ch. 8.

CHAPTER 7

[The imperfections of spiritual envy and sloth.]

1. As for the other two vices, spiritual envy and sloth, these beginners also have many imperfections. In regard to envy, many of them feel sad about the spiritual good of others and experience sensible grief in noting that their neighbor is ahead of them on the road to perfection, and they do not want to hear others praised. Learning of the virtues of others makes them sad. They cannot bear to hear others being praised without contradicting and undoing these compliments as much as possible. Their annoyance grows because they themselves do not receive these plaudits and because they long for preference in everything. All of this is contrary to charity, which, as St. Paul says, *rejoices in the truth* [1 Cor. 13:6]. If any envy accompanies charity, it is a holy envy by which they become sad at not having the virtues of others, rejoice that others have them, and are happy that all others are ahead of them in the service of God, since they themselves are so wanting in his service.

2. Also, regarding spiritual sloth, these beginners usually become weary in exercises that are more spiritual and flee from them since these exercises are contrary to sensory satisfaction. Since they are so used to finding delight in spiritual practices, they become bored when they do not find it. If they do not receive in prayer the satisfaction they crave— for after all it is fit that God withdraw this so as to try them—they do not want to return to it, or at times they either give up prayer or go to it begrudgingly. Because of their sloth, they subordinate the way of perfection (which requires denying one's own will and satisfaction for God) to the pleasure and delight of their own will. As a result they strive to satisfy their own will rather than God's.

3. Many of these beginners want God to desire what they want, and they become sad if they have to desire God's will. They feel an aversion toward adapting their will to God's. Hence they frequently believe that what is not their will, or brings them no satisfaction, is not God's will, and, on the other hand, that if they are satisfied, God is too. They measure God by themselves and not themselves by God, which is in opposition to his teaching in the Gospel that those who lose their life for his sake will gain it and those who desire to gain it will lose it [Mt. 16:25].

4. Beginners also become bored when told to do something unpleasant. Because they look for spiritual gratifications and delights, they are extremely lax in the fortitude and labor perfection demands. Like those who are reared in luxury, they run sadly from everything rough, and they

are scandalized by the cross, in which spiritual delights are found. And in the more spiritual exercises their boredom is greater. Since they expect to go about in spiritual matters according to the whims and satisfactions of their own will, entering by the narrow way of life, about which Christ speaks, is saddening and repugnant to them [Mt. 7:14].[1]

5. It is enough to have referred to the many imperfections of those who live in this beginner's state to see their need for God to put them into the state of proficients. He does this by introducing them into the dark night, of which we will now speak. There, through pure dryness and interior darkness, he weans them from the breasts of these gratifications and delights, takes away all these trivialities and childish ways, and makes them acquire the virtues by very different means. No matter how earnestly beginners in all their actions and passions practice the mortification of self, they will never be able to do so entirely—far from it—until God accomplishes it in them passively by means of the purgation of this night. May God be pleased to give me his divine light that I may say something worthwhile about this subject, for in a night so dark and a matter so difficult to treat and expound, his enlightenment is very necessary. The verse, then, is:

One dark night.

CHAPTER 8

[The beginning of the exposition of this dark night. An explanation of verse 1 of the first stanza.]

1. This night, which as we say is contemplation, causes two kinds of darkness or purgation in spiritual persons according to the two parts of the soul, the sensory and the spiritual. Hence one night of purgation is sensory, by which the senses are purged and accommodated to the spirit; and the other night or purgation is spiritual, by which the spirit is purged and denuded as well as accommodated and prepared for union with God through love. The sensory night is common and happens to many. These are the beginners of whom we will treat first. The spiritual night is the lot of very few, those who have been tried and are proficient, and of whom we will speak afterward.[1]

---

1. Cf. A. 2. 7.
1. As John goes on he makes it clearer that his arrangement of the nights coincides with that mentioned in A. 1. 1. 2-3. This passive night of the senses marks a transition from the stage of beginners to that of proficients; the passive night of the spirit, the transition from the stage of proficients to that of the perfect.

2. The first purgation or night is bitter and terrible to the senses. But nothing can be compared to the second, for it is horrible and frightful to the spirit. Because the sensory night is first in order, we will speak of it now briefly. It is a more common occurrence, so one finds more written on it. Then we will pass on to discuss more at length the spiritual night, for hardly anything has been said of it in sermons or in writing; and even the experience of it is rare.

3. Since the conduct of these beginners in the way of God is lowly and not too distant from love of pleasure and of self, as we explained,[2] God desires to withdraw them from this base manner of loving and lead them on to a higher degree of divine love. And he desires to liberate them from the lowly exercise of the senses and of discursive meditation, by which they go in search of him so inadequately and with so many difficulties, and lead them into the exercise of spirit, in which they become capable of a communion with God that is more abundant and more free of imperfections. God does this after beginners have exercised themselves for a time in the way of virtue and have persevered in meditation and prayer. For it is through the delight and satisfaction they experience in prayer that they have become detached from worldly things and have gained some spiritual strength in God. This strength has helped them somewhat to restrain their appetites for creatures, and through it they will be able to suffer a little oppression and dryness without turning back. Consequently, it is at the time they are going about their spiritual exercises with delight and satisfaction, when in their opinion the sun of divine favor is shining most brightly on them, that God darkens all this light and closes the door and the spring of sweet spiritual water they were tasting as often and as long as they desired. For since they were weak and tender, no door was closed to them, as St. John says in the Book of Revelation [Rv. 3:8]. God now leaves them in such darkness that they do not know which way to turn in their discursive imaginings. They cannot advance a step in meditation, as they used to, now that the interior sense faculties are engulfed in this night. He leaves them in such dryness that they not only fail to receive satisfaction and pleasure from their spiritual exercises and works, as they formerly did, but also find these exercises distasteful and bitter. As I said,[3] when God sees that they have grown a little, he weans them from the sweet breast so that they might be strengthened, lays aside their swaddling bands, and puts them down from his arms that they may grow accustomed to walking by themselves. This change is a surprise to them because everything seems to be functioning in reverse.

---

2. In chaps. 1-7.
3. In ch. 1. 2.

4. This usually happens to recollected beginners sooner than to others since they are freer from occasions of backsliding and more quickly reform their appetites for worldly things. A reform of the appetites is the requirement for entering the happy night of the senses. Not much time ordinarily passes after the initial stages of their spiritual life before beginners start to enter this night of sense. And the majority of them do enter it because it is common to see them suffer these aridities.

5. We could adduce numerous passages from Sacred Scripture, for since this sensory purgation is so customary we find a great many references to it throughout, especially in the Psalms and the Prophets. But I do not want to spend time citing them, because the prevalence of the experience of this night should be enough for those who are unable to find the scriptural references to it.

CHAPTER 9

[Signs for discerning whether a spiritual person is treading the path of this sensory night and purgation.]

1. Because these aridities may not proceed from the sensory night and purgation, but from sin and imperfection, or weakness and lukewarmness, or some bad humor or bodily indisposition, I will give some signs here for discerning whether the dryness is the result of this purgation or of one of these other defects. I find there are three principal signs for knowing this.

2. The first is that since these souls do not get satisfaction or consolation from the things of God, they do not get any from creatures either. Since God puts a soul in this dark night in order to dry up and purge its sensory appetite, he does not allow it to find sweetness or delight in anything. Through this sign it can in all likelihood be inferred that this dryness and distaste is not the outcome of newly committed sins and imperfections. If this were so, some inclination or propensity to look for satisfaction in something other than the things of God would be felt in the sensory part, for when the appetite is allowed indulgence in some imperfection, the soul immediately feels an inclination toward it, little or great in proportion to the degree of its satisfaction and attachment.

Yet, because the want of satisfaction in earthly or heavenly things could be the product of some indisposition or melancholic humor, which frequently prevents one from being satisfied with anything, the second sign or condition is necessary.

3. The second sign for the discernment of this purgation is that the memory ordinarily turns to God solicitously and with painful care, and the soul thinks it is not serving God but turning back, because it is aware of this distaste for the things of God. Hence it is obvious that this aversion and dryness is not the fruit of laxity and tepidity, for lukewarm people do not care much for the things of God nor are they inwardly solicitous about them.

There is, consequently, a notable difference between dryness and lukewarmness. The lukewarm are very lax and remiss in their will and spirit, and have no solicitude about serving God. Those suffering from the purgative dryness are ordinarily solicitous, concerned, and pained about not serving God. Even though the dryness may be furthered by melancholia or some other humor—as it often is—it does not thereby fail to produce its purgative effect in the appetite, for the soul will be deprived of every satisfaction and concerned only about God. If this humor is the entire cause, everything ends in displeasure and does harm to one's nature, and there are none of these desires to serve God that accompany the purgative dryness. Even though in this purgative dryness the sensory part of the soul is very cast down, slack, and feeble in its actions because of the little satisfaction it finds, the spirit is ready and strong.

4. The reason for this dryness is that God transfers his goods and strength from sense to spirit. Since the sensory part of the soul is incapable of the goods of spirit, it remains deprived, dry, and empty. Thus, while the spirit is tasting, the flesh tastes nothing at all and becomes weak in its work.[1] But through this nourishment the spirit grows stronger and more alert, and becomes more solicitous than before about not failing God.

If in the beginning the soul does not experience this spiritual savor and delight, but dryness and distaste, the reason is the novelty involved in this exchange. Since its palate is accustomed to these other sensory tastes, the soul still sets its eyes on them. And since, also, its spiritual palate is neither purged nor accommodated for so subtle a taste, it is unable to experience the spiritual savor and good until gradually prepared by means of this dark and obscure night. The soul instead experiences dryness and distaste because of a lack of the gratification it formerly enjoyed so readily.

5. Those whom God begins to lead into these desert solitudes are like the children of Israel. When God began giving them the heavenly food, which contained in itself all savors and changed to whatever taste each

---

1. This same maxim is followed in A. 2. 17. 5; C. 16. 5; F. 3. 39.

one hungered after [Wis. 16:20-21], as is there mentioned, they nonetheless felt a craving for the tastes of the fleshmeats and onions they had eaten in Egypt, for their palate was accustomed and attracted to them more than to the delicate sweetness of the angelic manna. And in the midst of that heavenly food, they wept and sighed for fleshmeat [Nm. 11:4-6]. The baseness of our appetite is such that it makes us long for our own miserable goods and feel aversion for the incommunicable heavenly good.

6. Yet, as I say, when these aridities are the outcome of the purgative way of the sensory appetite, the spirit feels the strength and energy to work, which is obtained from the substance of that interior food, even though in the beginning it may not experience the savor, for the reason just mentioned. This food is the beginning of a contemplation that is dark and dry to the senses. Ordinarily this contemplation, which is secret and hidden from the very one who receives it, imparts to the soul, together with the dryness and emptiness it produces in the senses, an inclination to remain alone and in quietude. And the soul will be unable to dwell on any particular thought, nor will it have the desire to do so.

If those in whom this occurs know how to remain quiet, without care or solicitude about any interior or exterior work, they will soon in that unconcern and idleness delicately experience the interior nourishment. This refection is so delicate that usually if the soul desires or tries to experience it, it cannot do so. For, as I say, this contemplation is active while the soul is in idleness and unconcern. It is like air that escapes when one tries to grasp it in one's hand.

7. In this sense we can interpret what the Spouse said to the bride in the Song of Songs: *Turn your eyes from me, because they make me fly away* [Sg. 6:4]. God conducts the soul along so different a path, and so puts it in this state, that a desire to work with the faculties would hinder rather than help his work; whereas in the beginning of the spiritual life everything was quite the contrary. The reason is that now in this state of contemplation, when the soul leaves discursive meditation and enters the state of proficients, it is God who works in it.

He therefore binds the interior faculties and leaves no support in the intellect, nor satisfaction in the will, nor remembrance in the memory. At this time a person's own efforts are of no avail, but are an obstacle to the interior peace and work God is producing in the spirit through that dryness of sense. Since this peace is something spiritual and delicate, its fruit is quiet, delicate, solitary, satisfying, and peaceful, and far removed from all the other gratifications of beginners, which are very palpable and sensory. This is the peace that David says God speaks in the soul in order to make it spiritual [Ps. 85:8]. The third sign follows from this one.

8. The third sign for the discernment of this purgation of the senses is the powerlessness, in spite of one's efforts, to meditate and make use of the imagination, the interior sense, as was one's previous custom. At this time God does not communicate himself through the senses as he did before, by means of the discursive analysis and synthesis of ideas, but begins to communicate himself through pure spirit by an act of simple contemplation in which there is no discursive succession of thought. The exterior and interior senses of the lower part of the soul cannot attain to this contemplation. As a result the imaginative power and phantasy can no longer rest in any consideration or find support in it.[2]

9. From the third sign it can be deduced that this dissatisfaction of the faculties is not the fruit of any bad humor. If it were, people would be able with a little care to return to their former exercises and find support for their faculties when that humor passed away, for it is by its nature changeable. In the purgation of the appetite this return is not possible, because on entering it the powerlessness to meditate always continues. It is true, though, that at times in the beginning the purgation of some souls is not continuous in such a way that they are always deprived of sensory satisfaction and the ability to meditate. Perhaps, because of their weakness, they cannot be weaned all at once. Nevertheless, if they are to advance, they will ever enter further into the purgation and leave further behind their work of the senses.

Those who do not walk the road of contemplation act very differently. This night of the aridity of the senses is not so continuous in them, for sometimes they experience the aridities and at other times not, and sometimes they can meditate and at other times they cannot. God places them in this night solely to exercise and humble them, and reform their appetite lest in their spiritual life they foster a harmful attraction toward sweetness. But he does not do so in order to lead them to the life of the spirit, which is contemplation. For God does not bring to contemplation all those who purposely exercise themselves in the way of the spirit, nor even half. Why? He best knows. As a result he never completely weans their senses from the breasts of considerations and discursive meditations, except for some short periods and at certain seasons, as we said.

---

2. Of these three signs two are negative (lack of satisfaction, inability to practice discursive meditation) and one positive (solicitude about not failing God). The positive sign is the best indicator of God's communication (faith, hope, and love). These signs coincide with those explained in A. 2. 13, except that here the positive sign represents an earlier phase of the transition to contemplation.

CHAPTER 10

The conduct required of souls in this dark night.

1. At the time of the aridities of this sensory night, God makes the exchange we mentioned[1] by withdrawing the soul from the life of the senses and placing it in that of spirit—that is, he brings it from meditation to contemplation—where the soul no longer has the power to work or meditate with its faculties on the things of God. Spiritual persons suffer considerable affliction in this night, owing not so much to the aridities they undergo as to their fear of having gone astray. Since they do not find any support or satisfaction in good things, they believe there will be no more spiritual blessings for them and that God has abandoned them.

They then grow weary and strive, as was their custom, to concentrate their faculties with some satisfaction on a subject of meditation, and they think that if they do not do this and do not feel that they are at work, they are doing nothing. This effort of theirs is accompanied by an interior reluctance and repugnance on the part of the soul, for it would be pleased to dwell in that quietude and idleness without working with the faculties.

They consequently impair God's work and do not profit by their own. In searching for spirit, they lose the spirit that was the source of their tranquility and peace. They are like someone who turns from what has already been done in order to do it again, or like one who leaves a city only to re-enter it, or they are like a hunter who abandons the prey in order to go hunting again. It is useless, then, for the soul to try to meditate because it will no longer profit by this exercise.

2. If there is no one to understand these persons, they either turn back and abandon the road or lose courage, or at least they hinder their own progress because of their excessive diligence in treading the path of discursive meditation. They fatigue and overwork themselves, thinking that they are failing because of their negligence or sins. Meditation is now useless for them because God is conducting them along another road, which is contemplation and is very different from the first, for the one road belongs to discursive meditation and the other is beyond the range of the imagination and discursive reflection.

3. Those who are in this situation should feel comforted; they ought to persevere patiently and not be afflicted. Let them trust in God who does not fail those who seek him with a simple and righteous heart; nor will he fail to impart what is needful for the way until getting them to the clear and pure light of love. God will give them this light by means of that other night, the night of spirit, if they merit that he place them in it.

1. In ch. 8. 3-4.

4. The attitude necessary in the night of sense is to pay no attention to discursive meditation since this is not the time for it. They should allow the soul to remain in rest and quietude even though it may seem obvious to them that they are doing nothing and wasting time, and even though they think this disinclination to think about anything is due to their laxity. Through patience and perseverance in prayer, they will be doing a great deal without activity on their part.

All that is required of them here is freedom of soul, that they liberate themselves from the impediment and fatigue of ideas and thoughts, and care not about thinking and meditating. They must be content simply with a loving and peaceful attentiveness to God, and live without the concern, without the effort, and without the desire to taste or feel him. All these desires disquiet the soul and distract it from the peaceful, quiet, and sweet idleness of the contemplation that is being communicated to it.

5. And even though more scruples come to the fore concerning the loss of time and the advantages of doing something else, since it cannot do anything or think of anything in prayer, the soul should endure them peacefully, as though going to prayer means remaining in ease and freedom of spirit. If individuals were to desire to do something themselves with their interior faculties, they would hinder and lose the goods that God engraves on their souls through that peace and idleness.

If a model for the painting or retouching of a portrait should move because of a desire to do something, the artist would be unable to finish and the work would be spoiled. Similarly, any operation, affection, or thought a soul might cling to when it wants to abide in interior peace and idleness would cause distraction and disquietude, and make it feel sensory dryness and emptiness. The more a person seeks some support in knowledge and affection the more the soul will feel the lack of these, for this support cannot be supplied through these sensory means.

6. Accordingly, such persons should not mind if the operations of their faculties are being lost to them; they should desire rather that this be done quickly so they may be no obstacle to the operation of the infused contemplation God is bestowing, so they may receive it with more peaceful plenitude and make room in the spirit for the enkindling and burning of the love that this dark and secret contemplation bears and communicates to the soul. For contemplation is nothing else than a secret and peaceful and loving inflow of God, which, if not hampered, fires the soul in the spirit of love, as is brought out in the following verse:[2]

Fired with love's urgent longings

---

2. In this number, John uses the term infused contemplation for the first time. The terms "infused," "supernatural," and "passive" are used similarly. Here he

CHAPTER 11

[Explains three verses of the stanza.]

1. The fire of love is not commonly felt at the outset, either because it does not have a chance to take hold, owing to the impurity of the sensory part, or because the soul for want of understanding has not made within itself a peaceful place for it; although at times with or without these conditions a person will begin to feel a certain longing for God. In the measure that the fire increases, the soul becomes aware of being attracted by the love of God and enkindled in it, without knowing how or where this attraction and love originates. At times this flame and enkindling increase to such an extent that the soul desires God with urgent longings of love, as David, while in this night, said of himself: *Because my heart was inflamed* (in contemplative love), *my reins were likewise changed* [Ps. 73:21]. That is, my appetites of sensible affection were changed from the sensory life to the spiritual life, which implies dryness and cessation of all those appetites we are speaking of. And, he says: *I was brought to nothing and annihilated, and I knew not* [Ps. 73:22]. For, as we pointed out,[1] the soul, with no knowledge of its destination, sees itself annihilated in all heavenly and earthly things in which it formerly found satisfaction; and it only sees that it is enamored, but knows not how.

Because the enkindling of love in the spirit sometimes increases exceedingly, the longings for God become so intense that it will seem to such persons that their bones are drying up in this thirst, their nature withering away, and their ardor and strength diminishing through the liveliness of the thirst of love. They will feel that this is a living thirst. David also had such experience when he proclaimed: *My soul thirsts for the living God* [Ps. 43:3], as though to say, this thirst my soul experiences is a living thirst. Since this thirst is alive, we can assert that it is a thirst that kills. Yet it should be noted that its vehemence is not continual, but only experienced from time to time, although usually some thirst is felt.

2. Yet it must be kept in mind that, as I began to say here, individuals generally do not perceive this love in the beginning, but they experience rather the dryness and void we are speaking of. Then, instead of this love which is enkindled afterward, they harbor, in the midst of the dryness and emptiness of their faculties, a habitual care and solicitude for God accompanied by grief or fear about not serving him. It is a sacrifice most pleasing to God—that of a spirit in distress and solicitude for his love [Ps. 51:17].

---

gives a definition of what he means by infused contemplation. In considering the effects it produces in the soul, he will employ other terms, such as purgative, illuminative, and unitive.

1. In ch. 10.

Secret contemplation produces this solicitude and concern in the soul until, after having somewhat purged the sensory part of its natural propensities by means of this aridity, it begins to enkindle in the spirit this divine love. Meanwhile, however, as in one who is undergoing a cure, all is suffering in this dark and dry purgation of the appetite, and the soul being relieved of numerous imperfections acquires many virtues, thereby becoming capable of this love, as will be shown in the explanation of the following verse: —ah, the sheer grace!—

3. God introduces people into this night to purge their senses, and to accommodate, subject, and unite the lower part of the soul to the spiritual part by darkening it and causing a cessation of discursive meditation (just as afterward, in order to purify the spirit and unite it to himself, he brings it into the spiritual night). As a result they gain so many benefits— though at the time this may not be apparent—that they consider their departure from the fetters and straits of the senses a sheer grace.

The verse therefore proclaims: "—ah, the sheer grace!—"

We ought to point out the benefits procured in this night, for it is because of them that the soul says it was a sheer grace to have passed through it.[2] All these benefits are included in the next verse:

I went out unseen,

4. This going out bears reference to the subjection the soul had to its senses, in seeking God through operations so feeble, limited, and exposed to error as are those of this lower part, for at every step it stumbled into numerous imperfections and much ignorance, as was noted above in relation to the seven capital vices.[3] This night frees the soul from all these vices by quenching all its earthly and heavenly satisfactions, darkening its discursive meditations, and producing in it other innumerable goods through its acquiring of the virtues, as we will now explain. For it will please and comfort one who treads this path to know that a way seemingly so rough and adverse and contrary to spiritual gratification engenders so many blessings.

These blessings are attained when by means of this night the soul departs from all created things, in its affections and operations, and walks on toward eternal things. This is a great happiness and grace: first, because of the signal benefit of quenching one's appetite and affection for all things; second, because there are very few who will endure the night and persevere in entering through this narrow gate and treading

---

2. John begins now to discuss a third topic: the fruits of this night. The basic benefit is knowledge of self and of God (ch. 12). The other benefits are the virtues (ch. 13) opposite the imperfections of which he spoke.
3. In chs. 2-7.

this constricted road that leads to life, as our Savior says [Mt. 7:14].

This narrow gate is the dark night of sense, in which the soul is despoiled and denuded—in order to enter it—and grounded in faith, which is foreign to all sense, that it may be capable of walking along the constricted road, which is the night of spirit. The soul enters this second night so that it may journey to God in pure faith, for pure faith is the means whereby it is united with God. Few there are who walk along this road, because it is so narrow, dark, and terrible that, in obscurities and trials, the night of sense cannot be compared to it, as will be explained. Yet the benefits of this night are incomparably greater than those of the night of sense.

We will say something now about the benefits of the night of sense as briefly as possible in order to pass on to our exposition of the other night.

CHAPTER 12

[The benefits this night causes in the soul.]

1. This glad night and purgation causes many benefits even though to the soul it seemingly deprives it of them. So numerous are these benefits that, just as Abraham made a great feast on the day of his son Isaac's weaning [Gn. 21:8], there is rejoicing in heaven that God has now taken from this soul its swaddling clothes; that he has put it down from his arms and is making it walk alone; that he is weaning it from the delicate and sweet food of infants and making it eat bread with crust; and that the soul is beginning to taste the food of the strong (the infused contemplation of which we have spoken[1]), which in these sensory aridities and darknesses is given to the spirit that is dry and empty of the satisfactions of sense.

2. The first and chief benefit this dry and dark night of contemplation causes is the knowledge of self and of one's own misery. Besides the fact that all the favors God imparts to the soul are ordinarily wrapped in this knowledge, the aridities and voids of the faculties in relation to the abundance previously experienced and the difficulty encountered in the practice of virtue make the soul recognize its own lowliness and misery, which was not apparent in the time of its prosperity.

There is a good figure of this in Exodus where God, desiring to humble the children of Israel and make them know themselves, ordered them to remove their festive garments and the adornments they had been wearing in the desert: *From now on leave aside your festive ornaments and put on common working garments that you may be aware of the treatment you deserve*

---

1. In ch. 10. 6.

[Ex. 33:5]. This was like saying: Since the clothing you wear, being of festivity and mirth, is an occasion for your not feeling as lowly as you in fact are, put it aside, so that seeing the vileness of your dress you may know yourself and your just deserts.

As a result the soul recognizes the truth about its misery, of which it was formerly ignorant. When it was walking in festivity, gratification, consolation, and support in God, it was more content, believing that it was serving God in some way. Though this idea of serving God may not be explicitly formed in a person's mind, at least some notion of it is deeply embedded within, owing to the satisfaction derived from one's spiritual exercises. Now that the soul is clothed in these other garments of labor, dryness, and desolation, and its former lights have been darkened, it possesses more authentic lights in this most excellent and necessary virtue of self-knowledge. It considers itself to be nothing and finds no satisfaction in self because it is aware that of itself it neither does nor can do anything.

God esteems this lack of self-satisfaction and the dejection persons have about not serving him more than all their former deeds and gratifications, however notable they may have been, since they were the occasion of many imperfections and a great deal of ignorance. Not only the benefits we mentioned result from this garment of dryness but also those of which we will now speak, and many more, for they flow from self-knowledge as from their fount.

3. First, individuals commune with God more respectfully and courteously, the way one should always converse with the Most High. In the prosperity of their satisfaction and consolation as beginners, they did not act thus, for that satisfying delight made them somewhat more daring with God than was proper, and more discourteous and inconsiderate. This is what happened to Moses: When he heard God speaking to him, he was blinded by that gratification and desire and without any further thought would have dared to approach God, if he had not been ordered to stop and take off his shoes [Ex. 3:4-5]. This instance denotes the respect and discretion, the nakedness of appetite, with which one ought to commune with God. Consequently when Moses was obedient to this command, he was so discreet and cautious that Scripture says he not only dared not approach but did not even dare look [Ex. 3:6; Acts 7:32]. Having left aside the shoes of his appetites and gratifications, he was fully aware of his misery in the sight of God, for this was the manner in which it was fitting for him to hear God's word.

Similarly, Job was not prepared for converse with God by means of those delights and glories that he says he was accustomed to experience in his God. But the preparation for this converse embodied nakedness on a dunghill, abandonment and even persecution by his friends, the fullness of anguish and bitterness, and the sight of the earth round about him covered with worms [Jb. 2:8; 30:17-18]. Yet the most high God, he who raises the poor from the dunghill [Ps. 112:7], was then pleased to descend and speak face to face with him and reveal the deep mysteries of his wisdom, which he never did before in the time of Job's prosperity [Jb. 38-41].

4. Since this is the proper moment, we ought to point out another benefit resulting from this night and dryness of the sensory appetite. So that the prophecy—*your light will illumine the darkness* [Is. 58:10]—may be verified, God will give illumination by bestowing on the soul not only knowledge of its own misery and lowliness but also knowledge of his grandeur and majesty. When the sensory appetites, gratifications, and supports are quenched, the intellect is left clean and free to understand the truth, for even though these appetites and pleasures concern spiritual things, they blind and impede the spirit. Similarly, the anguish and dryness of the senses illumine and quicken the intellect, as Isaiah affirms: *Vexation makes one understand* [Is. 28:19]. But God also, by means of this dark and dry night of contemplation, supernaturally instructs in his divine wisdom the soul that is empty and unhindered (which is the requirement for his divine inpouring), which he did not do through the former satisfactions and pleasures.

5. Isaiah explains this clearly: *To whom will God teach his knowledge? And to whom will he explain his message? To them that are weaned*, he says, *from the milk, and to them who are drawn away from the breasts* [Is. 28:9]. This passage indicates that the preparation for this divine inpouring is not the former milk of spiritual sweetness or aid from the breast of the discursive meditations of the sensory faculties that the soul enjoyed, but the privation of one and a withdrawal from the other.

In order to hear God, people should stand firm and be detached in their sense life and affections, as the prophet himself declares: *I will stand on my watch* (with detached appetite) and *will fix my foot* (I will not meditate with the sensory faculties) *in order to contemplate* (understand) *what God says to me* [Hb. 2:1].

We conclude that self-knowledge flows first from this dry night, and that from this knowledge as from its source proceeds the other knowledge of God. Hence St. Augustine said to God: *Let me know myself, Lord, and I will know you.*[2] For as the philosophers say, one extreme is clearly known by the other.[3]

6. For a more complete proof of the efficacy of this sensory night in

---

2. See *Soliloquia*, 2. 1. 1, in Migne, PL 32. 885.

3. From the philosophical axiom: *Contrariorum eadem est ratio.*

producing through its dryness and destitution the light here received from God, we will quote that passage from David in which the great power of this night in relation to the lofty knowledge of God is clearly shown. He proclaims: *In a desert land, without water, dry, and without a way, I appeared before you to be able to see your power and your glory.* [Ps. 63:1-2]. David's teaching here is admirable: that the means to the knowledge of the glory of God were not the many spiritual delights and gratifications he had received, but the sensory aridities and detachments referred to by the dry and desert land. And it is also wonderful that, as he says, the way to the experience and vision of the power of God did not consist in ideas and meditations about God, of which he had made extensive use. But it consisted in not being able either to grasp God with ideas or walk by means of discursive, imaginative meditation, which is here indicated by the land without a way.

Hence the dark night with its aridities and voids is the means to the knowledge of both God and self. However, the knowledge given in this night is not as plenteous and abundant as that of the other night of spirit, for the knowledge of this night is as it were the foundation of the other.[4]

7. In the dryness and emptiness of this night of the appetite, a person also procures spiritual humility, that virtue opposed to the first capital vice, spiritual pride. Through this humility acquired by means of self-knowledge, individuals are purged of all those imperfections of the vice of pride into which they fell in the time of their prosperity. Aware of their own dryness and wretchedness, the thought of their being more advanced than others does not even occur in its first movements, as it did before; on the contrary, they realize that others are better.

8. From this humility stems love of neighbor, for they esteem them and do not judge them as they did before when they were aware that they enjoyed an intense fervor while others did not.

These persons know only their own misery and keep it so much in sight that they have no opportunity to watch anyone else's conduct. David while in this night gives an admirable manifestation of such a state of soul: *I became dumb, and was humbled, and I kept silent in good things, and my sorrow was renewed* [Ps. 39:2]. He says this because it seemed to him that his blessings had so come to an end that not only was he unable to find words for them, but he also became silent concerning his neighbor, in the sorrow he experienced from the knowledge of his own misery.

These individuals also become submissive and obedient in their spiritual journey. Since they are so aware of their own wretchedness, they

---

4. Here John concludes his treatment of the basic benefit. The following numbers deal with the benefits opposite the imperfections and more properly belong in ch. 12.

not only listen to the teaching of others but even desire to be directed and told what to do by anyone at all. The affective presumption they sometimes had in their prosperity leaves them. And, finally, as they proceed on their journey, all the other imperfections of this first vice, spiritual pride, are swept away.

CHAPTER 13

[Other benefits of this night of the senses.]

1. In this arid and obscure night the soul undergoes a thorough reform in its imperfections of avarice, in which it craved various spiritual objects and was never content with many of its spiritual exercises because of the covetousness of its appetite and the gratification it found in spiritual things. Since it does not obtain the delight it formerly did in its spiritual practices, but rather finds them distasteful and laborious, it uses them so moderately that now perhaps it might fail through defect rather than excess. Nevertheless, God usually imparts to those whom he brings into this night the humility and the readiness, even though they feel displeasure, to do what is commanded of them for his sake alone, and they become detached from many things because of this lack of gratification.

2. It is also evident regarding spiritual lust that through the sensory dryness and distaste experienced in its spiritual exercises, the soul is freed of those impurities we noted.[1] For we said that they ordinarily proceed from the delight of the spirit redounding in the senses.

3. The imperfections of the fourth vice, spiritual gluttony, from which a person is freed in this dark night, are listed above,[2] although not all of them since they are innumerable. Thus I will not refer to them here, since I am eager to conclude this dark night in order to pass on to the important doctrine we have concerning the other night.

To understand the countless benefits gained in this night in regard to the vice of spiritual gluttony, let it suffice to say that the soul is liberated from all the imperfections we mentioned and from many other greater evils and foul abominations not listed, into which many have fallen, as we know from experience, because they did not reform their desire for this spiritual sweetness.

God so curbs concupiscence and bridles the appetite through this arid

---

1. In ch. 4.
2. In ch. 6.

and dark night that the soul cannot feast on any sensory delight from earthly or heavenly things, and he continues this purgation in such a way that the concupiscence and the appetites are brought into subjection, reformed, and mortified. The passions, as a result, lose their strength and become sterile from not receiving any satisfaction, just as the courses of the udder dry up when milk is not drawn through them daily.

Once the soul's appetites have withered, and it lives in spiritual sobriety, admirable benefits besides those mentioned result. For when the appetites and concupiscences are quenched, the soul dwells in spiritual peace and tranquility. Where neither the appetites nor concupiscence reign, there is no disturbance but only God's peace and consolation.

4. A second benefit following on this one is that the soul bears a habitual remembrance of God, accompanied by a fear and dread of turning back on the spiritual road. This is a notable benefit and by no means one of the least in this dryness and purgation of the appetite, because the soul is purified of the imperfections that of themselves make it dull and dark, and cling to it by means of appetites and affections.

5. Another very great benefit for the soul in this night is that it exercises all the virtues together. In the patience and forbearance practiced in these voids and aridities, and through perseverance in its spiritual exercises without consolation or satisfaction, the soul practices the love of God, since it is no longer motivated by the attractive and savory gratification it finds in its work, but only by God. It also practices the virtue of fortitude, because it draws strength from weakness in the difficulties and aversions experienced in its work, and thus becomes strong. Finally, in these aridities the soul practices corporeally and spiritually all the virtues, theological as well as cardinal and moral.

6. David affirms that a person obtains in this night these four benefits: the delight of peace; a habitual remembrance of God and solicitude concerning him; cleanness and purity of soul; and the practice of virtue. For David himself had such experience by being in this night: *My soul refused consolations, I remembered God and found consolation, and exercised myself, and my soul swooned away;* and then he adds: *I meditated at night in my heart, and I exercised myself, and swept and purified my spirit* (of all its imperfections) [Ps. 77:2-6].

7. In relation to the imperfections of the other three vices (anger, envy, and sloth), the soul is also purged in this dryness of appetite, and it acquires the virtues to which these vices are opposed. Softened and humbled by aridities and hardships and by other temptations and trials

in which God exercises the soul in the course of this night, individuals become meek toward God and themselves and also toward their neighbor. As a result they no longer become impatiently angry with themselves and their faults or with their neighbor's; neither are they displeased or disrespectfully querulous with God for not making them perfect quickly.

8. As for envy, these individuals also become charitable toward others. For if they do have envy, it will not be vicious as before, when they were distressed that others were preferred to them and more advanced. Now, aware of how miserable they are, they are willing to concede this about others. The envy they have—if they do have any—is a holy envy that desires to imitate others, which indicates solid virtue.

9. The sloth and tedium they feel in spiritual things is not vicious as before. Previously this sloth was the outcome of the spiritual gratification they either enjoyed or tried to obtain when not experienced. Yet this wearisomeness does not flow from any weakness relative to sensory gratification, for in this purgation of the appetite God takes from the soul all its satisfaction.

10. Besides these benefits, innumerable others flow from this dry contemplation. In the midst of these aridities and straits, God frequently communicates to the soul, when it least expects, spiritual sweetness, a very pure love, and a spiritual knowledge that is sometimes most delicate. Each of these communications is more valuable than all the soul previously sought. Yet in the beginning one will not think so because the spiritual inflow is very delicate and the senses do not perceive it.

11. Finally, insofar as these persons are purged of their sensory affections and appetites, they obtain freedom of spirit in which they acquire the twelve fruits of the Holy Spirit.

They are also wondrously liberated from the hands of their enemies, the devil, the world, and the flesh. For when the sensory delight and gratification regarding things is quenched, neither the devil, nor the world, nor sensuality has arms or power against the spirit.

12. These aridities, then, make people walk with purity in the love of God. No longer are they moved to act by the delight and satisfaction they find in a work, as perhaps they were when they derived this from their deeds, but by the desire of pleasing God. They are neither presumptuous nor self-satisfied, as was their custom in the time of their prosperity, but fearful and disquieted about themselves and lacking in any self-satisfaction. This is the holy fear that preserves and gives increase to the virtues.

This dryness also quenches the natural concupiscences and vigor, as we also said. Were it not for the satisfaction God himself sometimes infuses, it would be a wonder if the soul through its own diligence could get any sensible gratification or consolation out of its spiritual works and exercises.

13. In this arid night solicitude for God and longings about serving him increase. Since the sensory breasts (through which the appetites pursued by these souls were sustained and nurtured) gradually dry up, only the anxiety about serving God remains, in dryness and nakedness. These yearnings are very pleasing to God, since as David proclaims: *The afflicted spirit is a sacrifice to God* [Ps. 51:17].

14. Since the soul knows that, from this dry purgation through which it passed, it procured so many and such precious benefits, as are referred to here, the verse of this stanza is no exaggeration: "—Ah, the sheer grace!—I went out unseen." That is, I went forth from subjection to my sensory appetites and affections unseen, so that the three enemies were unable to stop me. These three enemies entrap the soul—as with snares—in its appetites and gratifications and keep it from going forth to the freedom of the love of God. But without these satisfactions and appetites the enemies cannot fight against the soul.

15. Having calmed the four passions (joy, sorrow, hope, and fear) through constant mortification, and lulled to sleep the natural sensory appetites, and having achieved harmony in the interior senses by discontinuing discursive operations (all of which pertains to the household or dwelling of the lower part of the soul, here referred to as its house), the soul says:

My house being now all stilled.

CHAPTER 14

[An explanation of the last verse of the first stanza.]

1. When this house of the senses was stilled (that is, mortified), its passions quenched, and its appetites calmed and put to sleep through this happy night of the purgation of the senses, the soul went out in order to begin its journey along the road of the spirit, which is that of proficients and which by another terminology is referred to as the illuminative way or the way of infused contemplation. On this road God himself pastures and refreshes the soul without any of its own discursive meditation or active help.

Such is the sensory night and purgation of the soul. For those who must afterward enter into the other more oppressive night of the spirit in order to reach the divine union of love—because not everyone but only a few usually reach this union—this night is ordinarily accompanied by burdensome trials and sensory temptations that last a long time, and with some longer than with others.[1]

An angel of Satan [2 Cor. 12:7], which is the spirit of fornication, is given to some to buffet their senses with strong and abominable temptations, and afflict their spirit with foul thoughts and very vivid images, which sometimes is a pain worse than death for them.

2. At other times a blasphemous spirit is added; it commingles intolerable blasphemies with all one's thoughts and ideas. Sometimes these blasphemies are so strongly suggested to the imagination that the soul is almost made to pronounce them, which is a grave torment to it.

3. Sometimes another loathsome spirit, which Isaiah calls *spiritus vertiginis* [Is. 19:14], is sent to these souls, not for their downfall but to try them.[2] This spirit so darkens the senses that such souls are filled with a thousand scruples and perplexities, so intricate that such persons can never be content with anything, nor can their judgment receive the support of any counsel or idea. This is one of the most burdensome goads and horrors of this night—very similar to what occurs in the spiritual night.

4. God generally sends these storms and trials in this sensory night and purgation to those whom he will afterward put in the other night—although not all pass on to it—so that thus chastised and buffeted, the senses and faculties may gradually be exercised, prepared, and inured for the union with wisdom that will be granted there. For if a soul is not tempted, tried, and proved through temptations and trials, its senses will not be strengthened in preparation for wisdom. It is said therefore in Ecclesiasticus: *He who is not tempted, what does he know? And he who is not tried, what are the things he knows?* [Ecclus. 34:9-10]. Jeremiah gives good testimony of this truth: *You have chastised me, Lord, and I was instructed* [Jer. 31:18].

And the most fitting kind of chastisement for entering into wisdom consists of the interior trials we mentioned, since they most efficaciously purge the senses of all the satisfaction and consolation the soul was attached to through natural weakness. By these trials it is truly humbled in preparation for its coming exaltation.

---

1. The general principles previously explained allow for a wide variety in the ways they are actually realized. Here John mentions three kinds of temptations, but there can be many others, and the degree of intensity will also differ.
2. This is a spirit of confusion; cf. A. 2. 21. 11.

5. Yet we cannot say certainly how long the soul will be kept in this fast and penance of the senses. Not everyone undergoes this in the same way, neither are the temptations identical. All is meted out according to God's will and the greater or lesser amount of imperfection that must be purged from each one. In the measure of the degree of love to which God wishes to raise a soul, he humbles it with greater or less intensity, or for a longer or shorter period of time.

Those who have more considerable capacity and strength for suffering, God purges more intensely and quickly. But those who are very weak he keeps in this night for a long time. Their purgation is less intense and their temptations abated, and he frequently refreshes their senses to keep them from backsliding. They arrive at the purity of perfection late in life. And some of them never reach it entirely, for they are never wholly in the night or wholly out of it. Although they do not advance, God exercises them for short periods and on certain days in those temptations and aridities to preserve them in humility and self-knowledge; and at other times and seasons he comes to their aid with consolation, lest through loss of courage they return to their search for worldly consolation. God acts with other weaker souls as though he were showing himself and then hiding; he does this to exercise them in his love, for without these withdrawals they would not learn to reach him.

6. Yet, as is evident through experience, souls who will pass on to so happy and lofty a state as is the union of love must usually remain in these aridities and temptations for a long while no matter how quickly God leads them. It is time to begin our treatise on the second night.

BOOK TWO

CHAPTER 1

[The beginning of the treatise on the dark night of the spirit. Explains when this night commences.]

1. If His Majesty intends to lead the soul on, he does not put it in this dark night of spirit immediately after its going out from the aridities and trials of the first purgation and night of sense. Instead, after having emerged from the state of beginners, the soul usually spends many years exercising itself in the state of proficients. In this new state, as one liberated from a cramped prison cell, it goes about the things of God with much more freedom and satisfaction of spirit and with more abundant interior delight than it did in the beginning before entering the night of sense. Its imagination and faculties are no longer bound to discursive meditation and spiritual solicitude, as was their custom. The soul readily finds in its spirit, without the work of meditation, a very serene, loving contemplation and spiritual delight. Nonetheless, the purgation of the soul is not complete. The purgation of the principal part, that of the spirit, is lacking, and without it the sensory purgation, however strong it may have been, is incomplete because of a communication existing between the two parts of the soul that form only one suppositum. As a result, certain needs, aridities, darknesses, and conflicts are felt. These are sometimes far more intense than those of the past and are like omens or messengers of the coming night of the spirit.[1]

But they are not lasting, as they will be in the night that is to come. For after enduring the short period or periods of time, or even days, in this night and tempest, the soul immediately returns to its customary serenity. Thus God purges some individuals who are not destined to ascend to so lofty a degree of love as are others. He brings them into this night of contemplation and spiritual purgation at intervals, frequently causing the night to come and then the dawn so that David's affirmation might be fulfilled: *He sends his crystal* (contemplation) *like morsels* [Ps. 147:17].

---

1. The interchange between sense and spirit highlights the intrinsic unity of the human person. This contemplation, sometimes dry and dark, sometimes serene and loving, invites comparison with the absence and presence of the Beloved in the drama of *The Spiritual Canticle*. The active night of the spirit explained at length in the *Ascent* also deals with the state of proficients.

These morsels of dark contemplation, though, are never as intense as is that frightful night of contemplation we are about to describe, in which God places the soul purposely in order to bring it to divine union.

2. The delight and interior gratification that these proficients enjoy abundantly and readily is communicated more copiously to them than previously and consequently overflows into the senses more than was usual before the sensory purgation. Since the sensory part of the soul is now purer, it can, after its own mode, experience the delights of the spirit more easily.

But since, after all, the sensory part of the soul is weak and incapable of vigorous spiritual communications, these proficients, because of such communications experienced in the sensitive part, suffer many infirmities, injuries, and weaknesses of stomach, and as a result fatigue of spirit. The Wise Man says: *The corruptible body is a load upon the soul* [Wis. 9:15]. Consequently the communications imparted to proficients cannot be very strong or very intense or very spiritual, as is required for divine union, because of the weakness and corruption of the senses that have their share in them.

Thus we have raptures and transports and the dislocation of bones, which always occur when the communications are not purely spiritual (communicated to the spirit alone) as are those of the perfect, who are already purified by the night of spirit. The perfect enjoy freedom of spirit without their senses being clouded or transported, for in them these raptures and bodily torments cease.[2]

3. To point out why these proficients must enter this night of spirit, we will note some of their imperfections and some of the dangers they confront.[3]

CHAPTER 2

[Other imperfections of these proficients.]

1. The imperfections in these proficients are of two kinds: habitual and actual. The habitual are the imperfect affections and habits still remaining like roots in the spirit, for the sensory purgation could not reach the spirit. The difference between the two purgations is like the difference between pulling up roots or cutting off a branch, rubbing out a fresh stain

---

2. Cf. C. 13 for a further explanation. There he refers us to St. Teresa's treatment of these matters. See her *Life,* ch. 20; *Interior Castle,* VI, chs. 4-6.

3. As in Book 1, to explain the need for the purification John pauses first to speak of imperfections, in this case of the proficients.

or an old, deeply embedded one. As we said,[1] the purgation of the senses is only the gate to and beginning of the contemplation that leads to the purgation of spirit. This sensitive purgation, as we also explained, serves more for the accommodation of the senses to the spirit than for the union of the spirit with God. The stains of the old self still linger in the spirit, although they may not be apparent or perceptible. If these are not wiped away by the use of the soap and strong lye of this purgative night, the spirit will be unable to reach the purity of divine union.

2. These proficients also have the *hebetudo mentis,* the natural dullness everyone contracts through sin, and a distracted and inattentive spirit.[2] The spirit must be illumined, clarified, and recollected by means of the hardships and conflicts of this night. All those who have not passed beyond the state of proficients possess these habitual imperfections that cannot, as we said, coexist with the perfect state of the union of love.

3. Not all these proficients fall into actual imperfections in the same way. Some encounter greater difficulties and dangers than those we mentioned, for their experience of these goods in the senses is so exterior and easily come by. They receive an abundance of spiritual communications and apprehensions in the sensory and spiritual parts of their souls and frequently behold imaginative and spiritual visions. All of this as well as other delightful feelings are the lot of those who are in this state, and a soul is often tricked through them by its own phantasy as well as by the devil. The devil finds it pleasing to suggest to souls and impress on them apprehensions and feelings. As a result of all this, these proficients are easily charmed and beguiled if they are not careful to renounce such apprehensions and feelings and energetically defend themselves through faith.

This is the stage in which the devil induces many into believing vain visions and false prophecies. He strives to make them presume that God and the saints speak with them, and frequently they believe their phantasy. It is here that the devil customarily fills them with presumption and pride. Drawn by vanity and arrogance, they allow themselves to be seen in exterior acts of apparent holiness, such as raptures and other exhibitions. They become audacious with God and lose holy fear, which is the key to and guardian of all the virtues. Illusions and deceptions so multiply in some, and they become so inveterate in them, that it is very doubtful whether they will return to the pure road of virtue and authentic spirituality. They fall into these miseries by being too secure in their

---

1. In N. 1. 11. 4.
2. An important factor in John's anthropology is that sin lies at the root of all the defects mentioned both here and in the first book.

surrender to these apprehensions and spiritual feelings, and do this just when they were beginning to make progress along the way.[3]

4. So much could be said about the imperfections of these proficients and of how irremediable they are—since proficients think their blessings are more spiritual than formerly—that I desire to pass over the matter. I only assert, in order to establish the necessity of the spiritual night (the purgation) for anyone who is to advance, that no proficients, however strenuous their efforts, will avoid many of these natural affections and imperfect habits. These must be purified before one may pass on to divine union.

5. Furthermore, to repeat what was said above,[4] these spiritual communications cannot be so intense, so pure, and so vigorous as is requisite for this union, because the lower part of the soul still shares in them. Thus, to reach union, the soul must enter the second night of the spirit. In this night both the sensory and spiritual parts are despoiled of all these apprehensions and delights, and the soul is made to walk in dark and pure faith, which is the proper and adequate means to divine union, as God says through Hosea: *I will espouse you* (unite you) *to me through faith* [Hos. 2:20].

CHAPTER 3

[An explanation for what is to follow.]

1. These souls, then, are now proficients. Their senses have been fed with sweet communications so that, allured by the gratification flowing from the spirit, they could be accommodated and united to the spirit. Each part of the soul can now in its own way receive nourishment from the same spiritual food and from the same dish of only one suppositum and subject. These two parts thus united and conformed are jointly prepared to suffer the rough and arduous purgation of the spirit that awaits them. In this purgation, these two portions of the soul will undergo complete purification, for one part is never adequately purged without the other. The real purgation of the senses begins with the spirit. Hence the night of the senses we explained should be called a certain reformation and bridling of the appetite rather than a purgation. The reason is that all the imperfections and disorders of the sensory part are rooted in the spirit and from it receive their strength. All good and evil habits reside

---

3. John deals with these matters more at length, and from the active perspective of the journey in faith, in A. 2. 16-32.
4. In ch. 1. 2.

in the spirit and until these habits are purged, the senses cannot be completely purified of their rebellions and vices.

2. In this night that follows both parts are jointly purified. This was the purpose of the reformation of the first night and the calm that resulted from it: that the sensory part, united in a certain way with the spirit, might undergo purgation and suffering with greater fortitude. Such is the fortitude necessary for so strong and arduous a purgation that if the lower part in its weakness is not reformed first, and afterward strengthened in God through the experience of sweet and delightful communion with him, it has neither the fortitude nor the preparedness to endure it.

3. These proficients are still very lowly and natural in their communion with God and in their activity directed toward him because the gold of the spirit is not purified and illumined. They still think of God and speak of him as little children, and their knowledge and experience of him is like that of little children, as St. Paul asserts [1 Cor. 13:11]. The reason is that they have not reached perfection, which is union of the soul with God. Through this union, as fully grown, they do mighty works in their spirit since their faculties and works are more divine than human, as we will point out. Wishing to strip them in fact of this old self and clothe them with the new, which is created according to God in the newness of sense, as the Apostle says [Col. 3:9-10; Eph. 4:22-24; Rom. 12:2], God divests the faculties, affections, and senses, both spiritual and sensory, interior and exterior. He leaves the intellect in darkness, the will in aridity, the memory in emptiness, and the affections in supreme affliction, bitterness, and anguish by depriving the soul of the feeling and satisfaction it previously obtained from spiritual blessings. For this privation is one of the conditions required that the spiritual form, which is the union of love, may be introduced into the spirit and united with it.

The Lord works all of this in the soul by means of a pure and dark contemplation, as is indicated in the first stanza. Although we explained this stanza in reference to the first night of the senses, the soul understands it mainly in relation to this second night of the spirit, since this night is the principal purification of the soul. With this in mind, we will quote it and explain it again.[1]

---

1. John explains this first stanza three times, each time from a different perspective (A. 1; N. 1; N. 2). The stanza refers mainly to the night of the spirit.

CHAPTER 4

[The first stanza and its explanation.]

First Stanza

> One dark night,
> fired with love's urgent longings
> —ah, the sheer grace!—
> I went out unseen,
> my house being now all stilled.

[Explanation]

1. Understanding this stanza now to refer to contemplative purgation or nakedness and poverty of spirit (which are all about the same),[1] we can thus explain it, as though the soul says:

Poor, abandoned, and unsupported by any of the apprehensions of my soul (in the darkness of my intellect, the distress of my will, and the affliction and anguish of my memory), left to darkness in pure faith, which is a dark night for these natural faculties, and with my will touched only by sorrows, afflictions, and longings of love of God, I went out from myself. That is, I departed from my low manner of understanding, and my feeble way of loving, and my poor and limited method of finding satisfaction in God. I did this unhindered by either the flesh or the devil.

2. This was great happiness and a sheer grace for me, because through the annihilation and calming of my faculties, passions, appetites, and affections, by which my experience and satisfaction in God were base, I went out from my human operation and way of acting to God's operation and way of acting. That is:

My intellect departed from itself, changing from human and natural to divine. For united with God through this purgation, it no longer understands by means of its natural vigor and light, but by means of the divine wisdom to which it was united. And my will departed from itself and became divine. United with the divine love, it no longer loves in a lowly manner, with its natural strength, but with the strength and purity of the Holy Spirit; and thus the will does not operate humanly in relation to God.

The memory, too, was changed into presentiments of eternal glory.

And finally, all the strength and affections of the soul, by means of this night and purgation of the old self, are renewed with divine qualities and

---

1. Equivalents of this contemplative purgation of the night are poverty of spirit and dark, pure faith.

delights.²

An explanation of the first verse follows:
One dark night,

CHAPTER 5

[Begins to explain how this dark contemplation is not only night for the soul but also affliction and torment.]

1. This dark night is an inflow of God into the soul, which purges it of its habitual ignorances and imperfections, natural and spiritual, and which the contemplatives call infused contemplation or mystical theology.¹ Through this contemplation, God teaches the soul secretly and instructs it in the perfection of love without its doing anything or understanding how this happens.

Insofar as infused contemplation is loving wisdom of God, it produces two principal effects in the soul: by both purging and illumining, this contemplation prepares the soul for union with God through love. Hence the same loving wisdom that purges and illumines the blessed spirits purges and illumines the soul here on earth.

2. Yet a doubt arises: Why, if it is a divine light (for it illumines souls and purges them of their ignorance), does the soul call it a dark night? In answer to this, there are two reasons this divine wisdom is not only night and darkness for the soul but also affliction and torment. First, because of the height of the divine wisdom that exceeds the abilities of the soul; and on this account the wisdom is dark for the soul. Second, because of the soul's baseness and impurity; and on this account the wisdom is painful, afflictive, and also dark for the soul.²

3. To prove the first reason, we must presuppose a certain principle of the Philosopher: that the clearer and more obvious divine things are in themselves, the darker and more hidden they are to the soul naturally.³

---

2. Underlying this teaching on purification are the Pauline assertions about taking off the old self and putting on the new. Cf. A. 1. 5. 7; N. 2. 3. 3

1. John identifies infused contemplation with mystical theology; and both of them with the dark night from the viewpoint of the cause of the night, not its effects. Cf. A. 2. 8. 6; N. 2. 12. 5; 17. 2, 6; C. 39. 12.

2. Darkness and affliction are the two negative effects of the night. These stem from a conflict between the divine and the human (chs. 5-6); the remembrance of past prosperity with a hopeless feeling about the present situation (ch. 7); and the powerlessness of the soul's faculties, unprepared to perceive the divine object (ch. 8).

3. See Aristotle *Metaphysics* 2. 1.

The brighter the light, the more the owl is blinded; and the more one looks at the brilliant sun, the more the sun darkens the faculty of sight, deprives and overwhelms it in its weakness.

Hence when the divine light of contemplation strikes a soul not yet entirely illumined, it causes spiritual darkness, for it not only surpasses the act of natural understanding but it also deprives the soul of this act and darkens it. This is why St. Dionysius and other mystical theologians call this infused contemplation a "ray of darkness"—that is, for the soul not yet illumined and purged.[4] For this great supernatural light overwhelms the intellect and deprives it of its natural vigor.

David also said that clouds and darkness are near God and surround him [Ps. 18:11], not because this is true in itself, but because it appears thus to our weak intellects, which in being unable to attain so bright a light are blinded and darkened. Hence he next declared that clouds passed before the great splendor of his presence [Ps. 18:12], that is, between God and our intellect. As a result, when God communicates this bright ray of his secret wisdom to the soul not yet transformed, he causes thick darkness in its intellect.

4. It is also evident that this dark contemplation is painful to the soul in these beginnings. Since this divine infused contemplation has many extremely good properties, and the still unpurged soul that receives it has many extreme miseries, and because two contraries cannot coexist in one subject, the soul must necessarily undergo affliction and suffering. Because of the purgation of its imperfections caused by this contemplation, the soul becomes a battlefield in which these two contraries combat one another. We will prove this by induction in the following way.

5. In regard to the first cause of one's affliction: Because the light and wisdom of this contemplation is very bright and pure, and the soul in which it shines is dark and impure, a person will be deeply afflicted on receiving it. When eyes are sickly, impure, and weak, they suffer pain if a bright light shines on them.

The soul, because of its impurity, suffers immensely at the time this divine light truly assails it. When this pure light strikes in order to expel all impurity, persons feel so unclean and wretched that it seems God is against them and they are against God.

Because it seems that God has rejected it, the soul suffers such pain and grief that when God tried Job in this way it proved one of the worst of Job's trials, as he says: *Why have You set me against You, and I am heavy and burdensome to myself?* [Jb. 7:20]. Clearly beholding its impurity by means of this pure light, although in darkness, the soul understands distinctly

---

4. See Pseudo-Dionysius, *The Mystical Theology* 1. 1.

that it is worthy neither of God nor of any creature. And what most grieves it is that it thinks it will never be worthy, and there are no more blessings for it. This divine and dark light causes deep immersion of the mind in the knowledge and feeling of one's own miseries and evils; it brings all these miseries into relief so the soul sees clearly that of itself it will never possess anything else. We can interpret that passage from David in this sense: *You have corrected humans because of their iniquity and have undone and consumed their souls, as a spider is eviscerated in its work* [Ps. 39:11].

6. Persons suffer affliction in the second manner because of their natural, moral, and spiritual weakness. Since this divine contemplation assails them somewhat forcibly in order to subdue and strengthen their soul, they suffer so much in their weakness that they almost die, particularly at times when the light is more powerful. Both the sense and the spirit, as though under an immense and dark load, undergo such agony and pain that the soul would consider death a relief. The prophet Job, having experienced this, declared: *I do not desire that he commune with me with much strength lest he overwhelm me with the weight of his greatness* [Jb. 23:6].

7. Under the stress of this oppression and weight, individuals feel so far from all favor that they think, and so it is, that even that which previously upheld them has ended, along with everything else, and there is no one who will take pity on them. It is in this sense that Job also cried out: *Have pity on me, at least you, my friends, for the hand of the Lord has touched me* [Jb. 19:21].

How amazing and pitiful it is that the soul be so utterly weak and impure that the hand of God, though light and gentle, should feel so heavy and contrary. For the hand of God does not press down or weigh on the soul, but only touches it; and this mercifully, for God's aim is to grant it favors and not to chastise it.

CHAPTER 6

[Other kinds of affliction suffered in this night.]

1. The two extremes, divine and human, which are joined here, produce the third kind of pain and affliction the soul suffers at this time. The divine extreme is the purgative contemplation, and the human extreme is the soul, the receiver of this contemplation. Since the divine extreme strikes in order to renew the soul and divinize it (by stripping it of the habitual affections and properties of the old self to which the soul is strongly united, attached, and conformed), it so disentangles and

dissolves the spiritual substance—absorbing it in a profound darkness—that the soul at the sight of its miseries feels that it is melting away and being undone by a cruel spiritual death. It feels as if it were swallowed by a beast and being digested in the dark belly, and it suffers an anguish comparable to Jonah's in the belly of the whale [Jon. 2:1-3]. It is fitting that the soul be in this sepulcher of dark death in order that it attain the spiritual resurrection for which it hopes.

2. David describes this suffering and affliction—although it is truly beyond all description—when he says: *The sighs of death encircled me, the sorrows of hell surrounded me, in my tribulation I cried out* [Ps. 18:5-6].

But what the sorrowing soul feels most is the conviction that God has rejected it, and with abhorrence cast it into darkness. The thought that God has abandoned it is a piteous and heavy affliction for the soul. When David also felt this affliction he cried: *In the manner of the wounded, dead in the sepulchers, abandoned now by your hand so that you remember them no longer, so have you placed me in the deepest and lowest lake, in the darkness and shadow of death, and your wrath weighs on me, and all your waves you have let loose on me* [Ps. 88:4-7].

When this purgative contemplation oppresses a soul, it feels very vividly indeed the shadow of death, the sighs of death, and the sorrows of hell, all of which reflect the feeling of God's absence, of being chastised and rejected by him, and of being unworthy of him, as well as the object of his anger. The soul experiences all this and even more, for now it seems that this affliction will last forever.

3. Such persons also feel forsaken and despised by creatures, particularly by their friends. David immediately adds: *You have withdrawn my friends and acquaintances far from me; they have considered me an abomination* [Ps. 88:8]. Jonah, as one who also underwent this experience, both physically and spiritually in the belly of the whale, testifies: *You have cast me out into the deep, into the heart of the sea, and the current surrounded me; all its whirlpools and waves passed over me and I said: I am cast from the sight of your eyes; yet I shall see your holy temple again* (he says this because God purifies the soul that it might see his temple); *the waters encircled me even to the soul, the abyss went round about me, the open sea covered my head, I descended to the lowest parts of the mountains, the locks of the earth closed me up forever* [Jon. 2:4-7]. The "locks" refer to the soul's imperfections that hinder it from enjoying the delights of this contemplation.

4. Another excellence of dark contemplation, its majesty and grandeur, causes a fourth kind of affliction to the soul. This property makes the soul feel within itself the other extreme—its own intimate poverty and misery. Such awareness is one of the chief afflictions it suffers in the purgation.

The soul experiences an emptiness and poverty in regard to three classes of goods (temporal, natural, and spiritual) which are directed toward pleasing it, and is conscious of being placed in the midst of the contrary evils (the miseries of imperfections, aridities and voids in the apprehensions of the faculties, and an abandonment of the spirit in darkness).

Since God here purges both the sensory and spiritual substance of the soul, and its interior and exterior faculties, it is appropriately brought into emptiness, poverty, and abandonment in these parts, and left in dryness and darkness. For the sensory part is purified by aridity, the faculties by the void of their apprehensions, and the spirit by thick darkness.

5. God does all this by means of dark contemplation. And the soul not only suffers the void and suspension of these natural supports and apprehensions, which is a terrible anguish (like hanging in midair, unable to breathe), but it is also purged by this contemplation. As fire consumes the tarnish and rust of metal, this contemplation annihilates, empties, and consumes all the affections and imperfect habits the soul contracted throughout its life. Since these imperfections are deeply rooted in the substance of the soul, in addition to this poverty, this natural and spiritual emptiness, it usually suffers an oppressive undoing and an inner torment. Thus the passage of Ezekiel may be verified: *Heap together the bones, and I shall burn them in the fire, the flesh shall be consumed, and the whole composition burned, and the bones destroyed* [Ez. 24:10). He refers here to the affliction suffered in the emptiness and poverty of both the sensory and the spiritual substance of the soul. And he then adds: *Place it also thus empty on the embers that its metal may become hot and melt and its uncleanness be taken away from it and its rust consumed* [Ez. 24:11]. This passage points out the heavy affliction the soul suffers from the purgation caused by the fire of this contemplation. For the prophet asserts that in order to burn away the rust of the affections the soul must, as it were, be annihilated and undone in the measure that these passions and imperfections are connatural to it.

6. Because the soul is purified in this forge *like gold in the crucible,* as the Wise Man says [Wis. 3:6], it feels both this terrible undoing in its very substance and extreme poverty as though it were approaching its end. This experience is expressed in David's cry: *Save me, Lord, for the waters have come in even unto my soul; I am stuck in the mire of the deep, and there is nowhere to stand; I have come unto the depth of the sea, and the tempest has overwhelmed me. I have labored in crying out, my throat has become hoarse, my eyes have failed while I hope in my God* [Ps. 69:1-3].

God humbles the soul greatly in order to exalt it greatly afterward. And if he did not ordain that these feelings, when quickened in the soul, be soon put to sleep again, a person would die in a few days. Only at intervals is one aware of these feelings in all their intensity. Sometimes this experience is so vivid that it seems to the soul that it sees hell and perdition open before it. These are the ones who go down into hell alive [Ps. 55:15], since their purgation on earth is similar to what takes place there. For this purgation is what would have to be undergone there. The soul that endures it here on earth either does not enter that place, or is detained there for only a short while. It gains more in one hour here on earth by this purgation than it would in many there.

CHAPTER 7

[A continuation of the same subject; other afflictions and straits of the will.][1]

1. The afflictions and straits of the will are also immense. Sometimes these afflictions pierce the soul when it suddenly remembers the evils in which it sees itself immersed, and it becomes uncertain of any remedy. To this pain is added the remembrance of past prosperity, because usually persons who enter this night have previously had many consolations in God and rendered him many services. They are now sorrowful in knowing that they are far from such good and can no longer enjoy it. Job tells also of his affliction: *I who was wont to be wealthy and rich am suddenly undone and broken; he has taken me by the neck, he has broken me and set me up as his mark so as to wound me. He has surrounded me with his lances, he wounded all my loins, he has not pardoned, he has scattered my bowels on the ground, he has torn me with wound upon wound, he has attacked me like a strong giant. I sewed sackcloth upon my skin and covered my flesh with ashes. My face is swollen with weeping, and my eyes blinded* [Jb. 16:12-16].

2. So numerous and burdensome are the pains of this night, and so many are the scriptural passages we could cite that we would have neither the time nor the energy to put it all in writing; and, doubtless, all that we can possibly say would fall short of expressing what this night really is. Through the texts already quoted we have some idea of it.

To conclude my commentary on this verse[2] and further explain what this night causes in the soul, I will refer to what Jeremiah felt in it. Because his tribulations were so terrible, he speaks of them and weeps over them profusely: *I am the man who sees my poverty in the rod of his indignation. He has led me and brought me into darkness and not into light. He has turned and turned again his hand against me all the day. He has made my skin and my flesh old; he*

---

1. The afflictions arise from the memory and overflow into the will.
2. John began commenting on verse 1 in ch. 4 and continues until ch. 11.

has broken my bones. He has built a fence round about me; and he has surrounded me with gall and labor. He has set me in darkness, as those who are dead forever. He has made a fence around me and against me that I might not go out; he has made my fetters heavy. And also when I might have cried out and entreated, he has shut out my prayer. He has closed up my exits and ways with square stones; he has destroyed my paths. He is become to me like a bear lying in wait, as a lion in hiding. He has turned aside my paths, and broken me in pieces; he has made me desolate. He has bent his bow and set me as a mark for his arrow. He has shot into my reins the daughters of his quiver. I have become a derision to all the people, and laughter and scorn for them all the day. He has filled me with bitterness, he has inebriated me with absinthe. One by one he has broken my teeth; he has fed me with ashes. My soul is far removed from peace. I have forgotten good things. And I said: My end, my aim and my hope from the Lord is frustrated and finished. Remember my poverty and my distress, the absinthe and the gall. I shall be mindful and remember, and my soul will languish within me in afflictions [Lam. 3:1-20].

3. Jeremiah gives vent to all these lamentations about his afflictions and trials and depicts very vividly the sufferings of a soul in this purgation and spiritual night.

One ought to have deep compassion for the soul God puts in this tempestuous and frightful night. It may be true that the soul is fortunate because of what is being accomplished within it, for great blessings will proceed from this night; and Job affirms that out of darkness God will raise up in the soul profound blessings and change the shadow of death into light [Jb. 12:22]; and God will do this in such a way that, as David says, *the light will become what the darkness was* [Ps. 139:12]. Nevertheless, the soul is deserving of great pity because of the immense tribulation and the suffering of extreme uncertainty about a remedy. It believes, as Jeremiah says [Lam. 3:18], that its evil will never end. And it feels as David that God has placed it in darkness like the dead of old, and that its spirit as a result is in anguish within it and its heart troubled [Ps. 143:3-4].

Added to this, because of the solitude and desolation this night causes, is the fact that individuals in this state find neither consolation nor support in any doctrine or spiritual master. Although their spiritual director may point out many reasons for comfort on account of the blessings contained in these afflictions, they cannot believe this. Because they are engulfed and immersed in that feeling of evil by which they so clearly see their own miseries, they believe their directors say these things because they do not understand them and do not see what they themselves see and feel. Instead of consolation they experience greater sorrow, thinking that the director's doctrine is no remedy for their evil. Indeed, it is not a remedy, for until the Lord finishes purging them in the way he desires, no remedy is a help to them in their sorrow. Their helplessness is even greater because of the little they can do in this situation. They resemble one who is imprisoned in a dark dungeon, bound hands and feet, and able neither to move nor see nor feel any favor from heaven or earth. They remain in this condition until their spirit is humbled, softened, and purified, until it becomes so delicate, simple, and refined that it can be one with the Spirit of God, according to the degree of union of love that God, in his mercy, desires to grant. In conformity with this degree, the purgation is of greater or lesser force and endures for a longer or shorter time.

4. But if it is to be truly efficacious, it will last for some years, no matter how intense it may be; although there are intervals in which, through God's dispensation, this dark contemplation ceases to assail the soul in a purgative mode and shines upon it illuminatively and lovingly. Then the soul, like one who has been unshackled and released from a dungeon and who can enjoy the benefit of spaciousness and freedom, experiences great sweetness of peace and loving friendship with God in a ready abundance of spiritual communication.

This illumination is for the soul a sign of the health the purgation is producing within it and a foretaste of the abundance for which it hopes. Sometimes the experience is so intense that it seems to the soul that its trials are over. For when the graces imparted are more purely spiritual they have this trait: When they are trials, it seems to a soul that it will never be liberated from them and that no more blessings await it, as was mentioned in the passages previously cited; when they are spiritual goods, the soul believes its evils have passed and it will no longer lack blessings, as David confessed on being aware of these goods: *I said in my abundance: I shall never move* [Ps. 30:6].

5. The soul experiences this because in the spirit the possession of one contrary removes of itself the actual possession and feeling of the other contrary. This does not occur in the sensory part because of the weakness of its apprehensive power. But since the spirit is not yet completely purged and cleansed of affections contracted from the lower part, it can, insofar as it is affected by them, be changed and suffer affliction, although insofar as it is a spirit it does not change. We note that David changed and experienced many afflictions and evils, although in the time of his abundance he had thought and said he would never be moved. Since the soul beholds itself actuated with that abundance of spiritual goods, and is unable to see the imperfection and impurity still rooted within, it thinks its trials have ended.

6. But this thought is rare, for until the spiritual purification is completed, the tranquil communication is seldom so abundant as to conceal the roots that still remain. The soul does not cease to feel that something is lacking or remains to be done, and this feeling keeps it from fully enjoying the alleviation. It feels as though an enemy is within it who,

although pacified and put to sleep, will awaken and cause trouble.

And this is true, for when a person feels safest and least expects it, the purgation returns to engulf the soul in another degree more severe, dark, and piteous than the former, lasting for another period of time, perhaps longer than the first. Such persons believe thereby that their blessings are gone forever. The enjoyment of blessing that was theirs after the first trial, in which they thought they no longer had anything more to suffer, was not sufficient to prevent them from thinking in this second degree of anguish that now all is over and the blessings formerly experienced will never return. As I say, this strong conviction is caused by the actual apprehension of the spirit, which annihilates within itself everything contrary to this conviction.

7. This is the reason that souls in purgatory suffer great doubts about whether they will ever leave and whether their afflictions will end. Although they habitually possess the three theological virtues (faith, hope, and charity), the actual feeling of both the privation of God and the afflictions does not permit them to enjoy the actual blessing and comfort of these virtues. Although they are aware that they love God, this gives them no consolation, because they think that God does not love them and they are unworthy of his love. Because they see themselves deprived of him and established in their own miseries, they feel that they truly bear within themselves every reason for being rejected and abhorred by God.

Thus, although persons suffering this purgation know that they love God and that they would give a thousand lives for him (they would indeed, for souls undergoing these trials love God very earnestly), they find no relief. This knowledge instead causes them deeper affliction. For in loving God so intensely that nothing else gives them concern, and aware of their own misery, they are unable to believe that God loves them. They believe that they neither have nor ever will have within themselves anything deserving of God's love, but rather every reason for being abhorred not only by God but by every creature forever. They grieve to see within themselves reasons for meriting rejection by him whom they so love and long for.

CHAPTER 8

[Other afflictions that trouble the soul in this state.]

1. Yet something else grieves and troubles individuals in this state, and it is that, since this dark night impedes their faculties and affections, they cannot beseech God or raise their mind and affection to him. It seems as

it did to Jeremiah that God has placed a cloud in front of the soul so that its prayer might not pass through [Lam. 3:44]. The passage we already cited refers to this difficulty also: *He closed and locked my ways with square stones* [Lam. 3:9]. And if sometimes the soul does beseech God, it does this with so little strength and fervor that it thinks God does not hear or pay any attention to it, as the prophet Jeremiah also lamented: *When I cried out and entreated, he excluded my prayer* [Lam. 3:8].

Indeed, this is not the time to speak with God, but the time to put one's mouth in the dust, as Jeremiah says, that perhaps there might come some actual hope [Lam. 3:29], and the time to suffer this purgation patiently. God it is who is working now in the soul, and for this reason the soul can do nothing. Consequently, these persons can neither pray vocally nor be attentive to spiritual matters, nor still less attend to temporal affairs and business. Furthermore, they frequently experience such absorption and profound forgetfulness in the memory that long periods pass without their knowing what they did or thought about, and they know not what they are doing or about to do, nor can they concentrate on the task at hand, even though they desire to.

2. Since this night purges not only the intellect of its light and the will of its affections but also the memory of its discursive knowledge, it is fitting that the memory be annihilated in all things to fulfill what David said of this purgation: *I was annihilated and knew not* [Ps. 73:22]. David's unknowing refers to forgetfulness and a lack of knowledge in the memory. This abstraction and oblivion is caused by the interior recollection in which this contemplation absorbs the soul.

That the soul with its faculties be divinely tempered and prepared for the divine union of love, it must first be engulfed in this divine and dark spiritual light of contemplation, and thereby be withdrawn from all creature affections and apprehensions. The duration of this absorption is proportionate to the intensity of the contemplation. The more simply and purely the divine light strikes the soul, the more it darkens and empties and annihilates it in its particular apprehensions and affections concerning both earthly and heavenly things; and, also, the less simply and purely it shines, the less it deprives and darkens the soul.

It seems incredible that the brighter and purer the supernatural, divine light is, the darker it is for the soul; and that the less bright it is, the less dark it is to the soul. We can understand this truth clearly if we consider what we proved above from the teaching of the Philosopher: that the clearer and more evident supernatural things are in themselves, the darker they are to our intellects.[1]

3. A comparison with natural light will illustrate this. We observe that

---

1. See N. 2. 5. 3.

the more a ray of sunlight shining through a window is void of dust particles, the less clearly it is seen, and that it is perceived more clearly when there are more dust particles in the air. The reason is that the light in itself is invisible and is rather the means by which the objects it strikes are seen. But, then, it is also seen through its reflection off them. Were the light not to strike these objects, it would not be seen and neither would they. As a result, if a ray of sunlight should enter through one window, traverse the room, and go out through another window without coming in contact with any object or dust particles off which it could reflect, the room would have no more light than previously; neither would the ray be visible. Instead, upon close observation one notes that there is more darkness where the ray is present, because the ray takes away and darkens some of the other light; and this ray is invisible, as we said, because there are no objects off which it can reflect.

4. This is precisely what the divine ray of contemplation does. In striking the soul with its divine light, it surpasses the natural light and thereby darkens and deprives a soul of all the natural affections and apprehensions it perceived by means of its natural light. It leaves a person's spiritual and natural faculties not only in darkness, but in emptiness too. Leaving the soul thus empty and dark, the ray purges and illumines it with divine spiritual light, while the soul thinks that it has no light and is in darkness, as illustrated in the case of the ray of sunlight that is invisible even in the middle of a room if the room is pure and void of any object off which the light may reflect. Yet when this spiritual light finds an object on which to shine, that is, when something is to be understood spiritually concerning perfection or imperfection, no matter how slight, or about a judgment on the truth or falsity of some matter, persons will understand more clearly than they did before they were in this darkness. And easily recognizing the imperfection that presents itself, they grow conscious of the spiritual light they possess; for the ray of light is dark and invisible until a hand or some other thing passes through it, and then both the object and the ray are recognized.

5. Since this light is so simple, so pure, and so general, and is unaffected and unrestricted by any particular intelligible object, natural or divine, and since the faculties are empty and annihilated of all these apprehensions, the soul with universality and great facility perceives and penetrates anything, earthly or heavenly, that is presented to it. Hence the Apostle says that the spiritual person penetrates all things, even the deep things of God [1 Cor. 2:10]. What the Holy Spirit says through the Wise Man applies to this general and simple wisdom, that is, that it touches everywhere because of its purity [Wis. 7:24], because it is not particularized by any distinct object of affection.

And this is characteristic of the spirit purged and annihilated of all particular knowledge and affection: Not finding satisfaction in anything or understanding anything in particular, and remaining in its emptiness and darkness, it embraces all things with great preparedness. And St. Paul's words are verified: *Nihil habentes, et omnia possidentes* (Having nothing, yet possessing all things) [2 Cor. 6:10]. Such poverty of spirit deserves this blessedness.

CHAPTER 9

[Although this night darkens the spirit, it does so to give light.]

1. It remains to be said, then, that even though this happy night darkens the spirit, it does so only to impart light concerning all things; and even though it humbles individuals and reveals their miseries, it does so only to exalt them; and even though it impoverishes and empties them of all possessions and natural affection, it does so only that they may reach out divinely to the enjoyment of all earthly and heavenly things, with a general freedom of spirit in them all.

That elements be commingled with all natural compounds, they must be unaffected by any particular color, odor, or taste, and thus they can concur with all tastes, odors, and colors. Similarly, the spirit must be simple, pure, and naked as to all natural affections, actual and habitual, in order to be able to communicate freely in fullness of spirit with the divine wisdom in which, on account of the soul's purity, the delights of all things are tasted to a certain eminent degree. Without this purgation the soul would be wholly unable to experience the satisfaction of all this abundance of spiritual delight. Only one attachment or one particular object to which the spirit is actually or habitually bound is enough to hinder the experience or reception of the delicate and intimate delight of the spirit of love that contains eminently in itself all delights.

2. Because of their one attachment to the food and fleshmeat they had tasted in Egypt [Ex. 16:3], the children of Israel were unable to get any taste from the delicate bread of angels—the manna of the desert, which, as Scripture says, contained all savors and was changed to the taste each one desired [Wis. 16:20-21]. Similarly the spirit, still affected by some actual or habitual attachment or some particular knowledge or any other apprehension, is unable to taste the delights of the spirit of freedom.

The reason is that the affections, feelings, and apprehensions of the perfect spirit, because they are divine, are of another sort and are so eminent and so different from the natural that their actual and habitual possession demands the annihilation and expulsion of the natural affections and apprehensions; for two contraries cannot coexist in one subject.

Hence, so the soul may pass on to these grandeurs, this dark night of contemplation must necessarily annihilate it first and undo it in its lowly ways by putting it into darkness, dryness, conflict, and emptiness. For the light imparted to the soul is a most lofty divine light that transcends all natural light and does not belong naturally to the intellect.

3. That the intellect reach union with the divine light and become divine in the state of perfection, this dark contemplation must first purge and annihilate it of its natural light and bring it actually into obscurity. It is fitting that this darkness last as long as is necessary for the expulsion and annihilation of the intellect's habitual way of understanding, which was a long time in use, and that divine light and illumination take its place. Since that strength of understanding was natural to the intellect, the darkness it here suffers is profound, frightful, and extremely painful. This darkness seems to be substantial darkness, since it is felt in the deep substance of the spirit.

The affection of love that is bestowed in the divine union of love is also divine, and consequently very spiritual, subtle, delicate, and interior, exceeding every affection and feeling of the will and every appetite. The will, as a result, must first be purged and annihilated of all its affections and feelings in order to experience and taste, through union of love, this divine affection and delight, which is so sublime and does not naturally belong to the will. The soul is left in a dryness and distress proportional to its habitual natural affections (whether for divine or human things), so that every kind of demon may be debilitated, dried up, and tried in the fire of this divine contemplation, as when Tobias placed the fish heart in the fire [Tb. 6:16-17], and the soul may become pure and simple, with a palate purged and healthy and ready to experience the sublime and marvelous touches of divine love. After the expulsion of all actual and habitual obstacles, it will behold itself transformed in these divine touches.

4. Furthermore, in this union for which the dark night is a preparation, the soul in its communion with God must be endowed and filled with a certain glorious splendor embodying innumerable delights. These delights surpass all the abundance the soul can possess naturally, for nature, so weak and impure, cannot receive these delights, as Isaiah says: *Eye has not seen, nor ear heard, nor has it entered any human heart what he has prepared,* etc. [Is. 64:4]. As a result the soul must first be set in emptiness and poverty of spirit and purged of every natural support, consolation, and apprehension, earthly and heavenly. Thus empty, it is truly poor in spirit and stripped of the old self, and thereby able to live that new and blessed

life which is the state of union with God, attained by means of this night.[1]

5. Extraneous to its common experience and natural knowledge, the soul will have a very abundant and delightful divine sense and knowledge of all divine and human things. It must then be refined and inured, as far as its common and natural experience goes (for the eyes by which it now views these things will be as different from those of the past as is spirit from sense and divine from human), and placed in terrible anguish and distress by means of this purgative contemplation. And the memory must be abstracted from all agreeable and peaceful knowledge and feel interiorly alien to all things, in which it will seem that all things are different than before.

This night withdraws the spirit from its customary manner of experience to bring it to the divine experience that is foreign to every human way. It seems to the soul in this night that it is being carried out of itself by afflictions. At other times the soul wonders if it is not being charmed, and it goes about with wonderment over what it sees and hears. Everything seems very strange even though a person is the same as always. The reason is that the soul is being made a stranger to its usual knowledge and experience of things so that, annihilated in this respect, it may be informed with the divine, which belongs more to the next life than to this.

6. Individuals suffer all these afflictive purgations of spirit that they may be reborn into the life of the spirit by means of this divine inflow, and through these sufferings the spirit of salvation is brought forth in fulfillment of the words of Isaiah: *In your presence, O Lord, we have conceived and been in the pains of labor and have brought forth the spirit of salvation* [Is. 26:17-18].

Moreover, the soul should leave aside all its former peace, because it is prepared by means of this contemplative night to attain inner peace, which is of such a quality and so delightful that, as the Church says, it surpasses all understanding [Phil. 4:7].[2] That peace was not truly peace, because it was clothed with many imperfections, although to the soul walking in delight it seemed to be peace. It seemed to be a twofold peace, sensory and spiritual, since the soul beheld within itself a spiritual abundance. This sensory and spiritual peace, since it is still imperfect, must first be purged; the soul's peace must be disturbed and taken away. In the passage we quoted to demonstrate the distress of this night,

---

1. The key ideas here are poverty of spirit, transformation of the old self into the new, and the natural incompatibility of the human and limited with the divine and spiritual. Dealing with these ideas elsewhere, John also quotes this Isaian text. Cf. A. 2. 4. 4; 8. 4; A. 3. 24. 2.

2. This Pauline passage was recited in the Divine Office at None on the Third Sunday of Advent. Perhaps that is why John attributes the words to the Church.

Jeremiah felt disturbed and wept over his loss of peace: *My soul is withdrawn and removed from peace* [Lam. 3:17].

7. This night is a painful disturbance involving many fears, imaginings, and struggles within these persons. On account of the apprehension and feeling of their miseries, they suspect that they are lost and their blessings are gone forever. The sorrow and moaning of their spirit is so deep that it turns into vehement spiritual roars and clamoring, and sometimes they pronounce them vocally and dissolve in tears (if they have the strength and power to do so), although such relief is less frequent.

David, one who also had experience of this trial, refers to it very clearly in one of the psalms: *I was very afflicted and humbled; I roared with the groaning of my heart* [Ps. 38:8]. This roaring embodies great suffering. Sometimes on account of the sudden and piercing remembrance of their wretchedness, the roaring becomes so loud and the affections so surrounded by suffering and pain that I know not how to describe it save by the simile holy Job used while undergoing this very trial: *As the overflowing waters, so is my roaring* [Jb. 3:24]. As the waters sometimes overflow in such a way that they inundate everything, this roaring and feeling so increase that in seeping through and flooding everything, they fill all one's deep affections and energies with indescribable spiritual anguish and suffering.

8. These are the effects produced in the soul by this night, which enshrouds the hopes one has for the light of day. The prophet Job also proclaims: *In the night my mouth is pierced with sufferings, and they that feed upon me do not sleep* [Jb. 30:17]. The mouth refers to the will pierced through by these sufferings that neither sleep nor cease to tear the soul to shreds. For these doubts and fears that penetrate the soul are never at rest.

9. This war or combat is profound because the peace awaiting the soul must be exceedingly profound; and the spiritual suffering is intimate and penetrating because the love to be possessed by the soul will also be intimate and refined. The more intimate and highly finished the work must be, so the more intimate, careful, and pure must the labor be; and commensurate with the solidity of the edifice is the energy involved in the work. As Job says, *the soul is withering within itself and its inmost parts boiling without any hope* [Jb. 30:16, 27].

Because in the state of perfection toward which it journeys by means of this purgative night the soul must reach the possession and enjoyment of innumerable blessings of gifts and virtues in both its substance and its faculties, it must first in a general way feel a withdrawal, deprivation, emptiness, and poverty regarding these blessings. And such persons must be brought to think that they are far removed from them, and become so convinced that no one can persuade them otherwise or make them believe anything but that their blessings have come to an end. Jeremiah points this out when he says in the passage already cited: *I have forgotten good things* [Lam. 3:17].

10. Let us examine now why this light of contemplation, which is so gentle and agreeable that there is nothing more to desire and which is the same light the soul must be united to and in which it will find all its blessings in the desired state of perfection, produces such painful and disagreeable effects when in these initial stages it shines upon the soul.

11. We can answer this question easily by repeating what we already explained in part:[3] There is nothing in contemplation or the divine inflow that of itself can give pain; contemplation rather bestows sweetness and delight, as we shall say afterward.[4] The cause for not experiencing these agreeable effects is the soul's weakness and imperfection at the time, its inadequate preparation, and the qualities it possesses that are contrary to this light. Because of these the soul has to suffer when the divine light shines upon it.

CHAPTER 10

[Explains this purgation thoroughly by means of a comparison.]

1. For the sake of further clarity in this matter, we ought to note that this purgative and loving knowledge, or divine light we are speaking of, has the same effect on a soul that fire has on a log of wood. The soul is purged and prepared for union with the divine light just as the wood is prepared for transformation into the fire. Fire, when applied to wood, first dehumidifies it, dispelling all moisture and making it give off any water it contains. Then it gradually turns the wood black, makes it dark and ugly, and even causes it to emit a bad odor. By drying out the wood, the fire brings to light and expels all those ugly and dark accidents that are contrary to fire. Finally, by heating and enkindling it from without, the fire transforms the wood into itself and makes it as beautiful as it is itself. Once transformed, the wood no longer has any activity or passivity of its own, except for its weight and its quantity that is denser than the fire. It possesses the properties and performs the actions of fire: It is dry and it dries; it is hot and it gives off heat; it is brilliant and it illumines; it is also

3. In ch. 5.
4. This promise indicates John's plan to comment on the entire poem, the final stanzas of which refer to union. But the work is unfinished.

much lighter in weight than before. It is the fire that produces all these properties in the wood.[1]

2. Similarly, we should philosophize about this divine, loving fire of contemplation. Before transforming the soul, it purges it of all contrary qualities. It produces blackness and darkness and brings to the fore the soul's ugliness; thus one seems worse than before and unsightly and abominable. This divine purge stirs up all the foul and vicious humors of which the soul was never before aware; never did it realize there was so much evil in itself, since these humors were so deeply rooted. And now that they may be expelled and annihilated they are brought to light and seen clearly through the illumination of this dark light of divine contemplation. Although the soul is no worse than before, either in itself or in its relationship with God, it feels clearly that it is so bad as to be not only unworthy that God see it but deserving of his abhorrence. In fact, it feels that God now does abhor it. This comparison illustrates many of the things we have been saying and will say.

3. First, we can understand that the very loving light and wisdom into which the soul will be transformed is what in the beginning purges and prepares it, just as the fire that transforms the wood by incorporating it into itself is what first prepares it for this transformation.

4. Second, we discern that the experience of these sufferings does not derive from this wisdom—for as the Wise Man says: *All good things come to the soul together with her* [Wis. 7:11]—but from the soul's own weakness and imperfection. Without this purgation it cannot receive the divine light, sweetness, and delight of wisdom, just as the log of wood until prepared cannot be transformed by the fire that is applied to it. And this is why the soul suffers so intensely. Ecclesiasticus confirms our assertion by telling what he suffered in order to be united with wisdom and enjoy it: *My soul wrestled for her, and my entrails were disturbed in acquiring her; therefore shall I possess a good possession* [Ecclus. 51:25, 29].

5. Third, we can infer the manner in which souls suffer in purgatory. The fire, when applied, would be powerless over them if they did not have imperfections from which to suffer. These imperfections are the fuel that catches on fire, and once they are gone there is nothing left to burn. So it is here on earth; when the imperfections are gone, the soul's suffering terminates, and joy remains.

---

1. This simile effectively describes the whole spiritual life in reference to God's action in the soul, especially as presented in the *Night* and the *Living Flame*. Cf. Fl. Pro. 3; 1. 3-4, 19, 22-23, 25, 33; also A. 1. 11. 6; A. 2. 8. 2.

6. Fourth, we deduce that as the soul is purged and purified by this fire of love, it is further enkindled in love, just as the wood becomes hotter as the fire prepares it. Individuals, however, do not always feel this enkindling of love. But sometimes the contemplation shines less forcibly so they may have the opportunity to observe and even rejoice over the work being achieved, for then these good effects are revealed. It is as though one were to stop work and take the iron out of the forge to observe what is being accomplished. Thus the soul is able to perceive the good it was unaware of while the work was proceeding. So too, when the flame stops acting upon the wood, there is a chance to see how much the wood has been enkindled by it.

7. Fifth, we can also gather from this comparison why, as we mentioned earlier,[2] after this alleviation the soul suffers again, more intensely and inwardly than before. After that manifestation and after a more exterior purification of imperfections, the fire of love returns to act more interiorly on the consumable matter of which the soul must be purified. The suffering of the soul becomes more intimate, subtle, and spiritual in proportion to the inwardness, subtlety, spirituality, and deep-rootedness of the imperfections that are removed. This more interior purgation resembles the action of fire on wood: As the fire penetrates more deeply into the wood its action becomes stronger and more vehement, preparing the innermost part in order to gain possession of it.

8. Sixth, we discover the reason it seems to the soul that all blessings are past and it is full of evil. At this time it is conscious of nothing but its own bitterness, just as in the example of the wood, for neither the air nor anything else gives it more than a consuming fire. Yet, when other manifestations like the previous ones are made, the soul's joy will be more interior because of the more intimate purification.

9. Seventh, we deduce that when the purification is soon to return, even though the soul's joy is ample during these intervals (so much so that it sometimes seems, as we pointed out, that the bitterness will never recur), there is a feeling, if one adverts (and sometimes one cannot help adverting), that some root remains. And this advertence does not allow complete joy, for it seems that the purification is threatening to assail the soul again. And when the soul does have this feeling, the purification soon returns. Finally, that more inward part still to be purged and illumined cannot be completely concealed by the portion already purified, just as there is a very perceptible difference between the inmost part of the wood still to be illumined and that which is already purged. When

2. In ch. 7. 4-6.

this purification returns to attack more interiorly, it is no wonder that once again the soul thinks all its good has come to an end and its blessings are over. Placed in these more interior sufferings, it is blinded as to all exterior good.

10. With this example in mind as well as the explanation of verse 1 of the first stanza concerning this dark night and its terrible properties, it will be a good thing to leave these sad experiences and begin now to discuss the fruit of the soul's tears and the happy traits about which it begins to sing in this second verse:

fired with love's urgent longings

CHAPTER 11

[The beginning of an explanation of verse 2 of the first stanza. Tells how the fruit of these dark straits is a vehement passion of divine love.]

1. This second verse refers to the fire of love that, like material fire acting on wood, penetrates the soul in this night of painful contemplation. Although this enkindling of love we are now discussing is in some way similar to what occurs in the sensory part of the soul, it is as different from it, in another way, as is the soul from the body or the spiritual part from the sensory part.[1] For this enkindling of love occurs in the spirit. Through it the soul in the midst of these dark conflicts feels vividly and keenly that it is being wounded by a strong divine love, and it has a certain feeling and foretaste of God. Yet it understands nothing in particular, for as we said the intellect is in darkness.

2. The spirit herein experiences an impassioned and intense love because this spiritual inflaming engenders the passion of love. Since this love is infused, it is more passive than active and thus generates in the soul a strong passion of love. This love is now beginning to possess something of union with God and thereby shares to a certain extent in the properties of this union. These properties are actions of God more than of the soul and they reside in it passively, although the soul does give its consent. But only the love of God that is being united to the soul imparts the heat, strength, temper, and passion of love, or fire, as it is termed here. This love finds that the soul is equipped to receive the wound and union in the

---

1. In these chapters John refers to the various degrees of love. These main degrees are evident in this work: feelings of fervor on the sensory level (N. 1. 1. 2); a dry solicitude about serving God (N. 1. 11. 2); an enkindling of love on the sense level (N. 1. 11. 1); an esteeming love (N. 2. 13. 5); an impassioned enkindling of love in the spirit (N. 2. 11. 1-5; 13. 3-9).

measure that all its appetites are brought into subjection, alienated, incapacitated, and unable to be satisfied by any heavenly or earthly thing.

3. This happens very particularly in this dark purgation, as was said, since God so weans and recollects the appetites that they cannot find satisfaction in any of their objects. God proceeds thus so that by both withdrawing the appetites from other objects and recollecting them in himself, he strengthens the soul and gives it the capacity for this strong union of love, which he begins to accord by means of this purgation. In this union the soul loves God intensely with all its strength and all its sensory and spiritual appetites. Such love is impossible if these appetites are scattered by their satisfaction in other things. In order to receive the strength of this union of love, David exclaimed to God: *I will keep my strength for you* [Ps. 59:9], that is, all the ability, appetites, and strength of my faculties, by not desiring to make use of them or find satisfaction in anything outside of you.[2]

4. One might, then, in a certain way ponder how remarkable and how strong this enkindling of love in the spirit can be. God gathers together all the strength, faculties, and appetites of the soul, spiritual and sensory alike, so the energy and power of this whole harmonious composite may be employed in this love. The soul consequently arrives at the true fulfillment of the first commandment which, neither disdaining anything human nor excluding it from this love, states: *You shall love your God with your whole heart, and with your whole mind, and with your whole soul, and with all your strength* [Dt. 6:5].

5. When the soul is wounded, touched, and impassioned, all its strength and its appetites are recollected in this burning of love. How will we be able to understand the movements and impulses of all this strength and these appetites? They are aroused when the soul becomes aware of the fire and wound of this forceful love and still neither possesses it nor gets satisfaction from it, but remains in darkness and doubt. Certainly, suffering hunger like dogs, as David says, these souls wander about the city and howl and sigh because they are not filled with this love [Ps. 59:6, 14-15].

The touch of this divine love and fire so dries up the spirit and so enkindles the soul's longings to slake its thirst for this love that such persons go over these longings in their mind a thousand times and pine for God in a thousand ways. David expresses this state very well in a psalm: *My soul thirsts for you; in how many ways does my flesh long for you* [Ps. 63:1],

---

2. Cf. A. 1. 10. 1; A. 2. 16. 1; C. 8. 8.

that is, in its desires. And another translation puts it this way: *My soul thirsts for you, my soul loses itself or dies for you.*[3]

6. As a result the soul proclaims in this verse: "with love's urgent longings," and not, "with an urgent longing of love." In all its thoughts and in all its business and in all events, it loves in many ways, and desires, and also suffers in its desire in many ways, and at all times and in many places. It finds rest in nothing, for it feels this anxiety in the burning wound, as the prophet Job explains: *As the servant desires the shade and as the hireling desires the end of his work, so have I had empty months and numbered to myself long and wearisome nights. If I lie down to sleep I shall say: When will I arise? And then I will await the evening and will be filled with sorrows until the darkness of the night* [Jb. 7:2-4].

Everything becomes narrow for this soul: There is no room for it within itself, neither is there any room for it in heaven or on earth; and it is filled with sorrows unto darkness, as Job says speaking spiritually and from our point of view. This affliction the soul undergoes here is a suffering unaccompanied by the comfort of certain hope for some spiritual light and good.

One's anxiety and affliction in this burning of love are more intense because they are doubly increased: first, through the spiritual darknesses in which the soul is engulfed and which afflict it with doubts and fears; second, through the love of God that inflames and stimulates and wondrously stirs it with a loving wound.

7. Isaiah clearly explains these two ways of suffering in this state when he says: *My soul desired you in the night* [Is. 26:9], that is, in the midst of misery. This is one way of suffering in this dark night. *Yet within my spirit,* he says, *until the morning I will watch for you* [Is. 26:9]. And this is a second way of suffering: with desire and anxiety of love in the innermost parts of the spirit, which are the spiritual feelings.

Nonetheless, in the midst of these dark and loving afflictions, the soul feels a certain companionship and an interior strength; these so fortify and accompany it that when this weight of anxious darkness passes, the soul often feels alone, empty, and weak. The reason is that since the strength and efficacy of the dark fire of love that assails it is communicated and impressed on it passively, the darkness, strength, and warmth of love cease when the assault terminates.

---

3. The only time John refers to another translation. This could have been a Latin version of the Septuagint.

CHAPTER 12

[The resemblance of this frightful night to purgatory. How the divine wisdom illumines those who suffer this night on earth by the same illumination with which it illumines and purges the angels in heaven.]

1. We can therefore understand that just as this dark night of loving fire purges in darkness, it also in darkness does its work of enkindling. We can also note that as the spirits in the other life are purged with a dark material fire, so in this life souls are purged and cleansed with a dark, loving spiritual fire. For such is the difference: Souls are cleansed in the other life by fire, but here on earth they are cleansed and illumined only by love. David asked for this love when he said: *Cor mundum crea in me Deus,* etc. (A clean heart create for me, O God) [Ps. 51:12]. Cleanness of heart is nothing less than the love and grace of God. The pure of heart are called blessed by our Savior [Mt. 5:8], and to call them blessed is equivalent to saying they are taken with love, for blessedness is derived from nothing else but love.

2. Jeremiah shows clearly that the soul is purged by the illumination of this fire of loving wisdom (for God never bestows mystical wisdom without love, since love itself infuses it) where he says: *He sent fire into my bones and instructed me* [Lam. 1:13]. And David says that God's wisdom is silver tried in the fire [Ps. 11:6], that is, in the purgative fire of love. This contemplation infuses both love and wisdom in each soul according to its capacity and necessity. It illumines the soul and purges it of its ignorance, as the Wise Man declares it did to him [Ecclus. 51:25-27].

3. Another deduction is that this very wisdom of God, which purges and illumines these souls, purges the angels of their ignorances and gives them understanding by illumining them on matters they are ignorant of. This wisdom descends from God through the first hierarchies unto the last, and from these last to humans. It is rightly and truly said in Scripture that all the works of the angels and the inspirations they impart are also accomplished or granted by God. For ordinarily these works and inspirations are derived from God by means of the angels, and the angels also in turn give them one to another without delay. This communication is like that of a ray of sunlight shining through many windows placed one after the other. Although it is true that of itself the ray of light passes through them all, nevertheless each window communicates this light to the other with a certain modification according to its own quality. The communication is more or less intense insofar as the window is closer to or farther from the sun.

4. Consequently, the nearer the higher spirits (and those that follow) are to God, the more purged and clarified they are by a more general purification; the last spirits receive a fainter and more remote illumination. Humans, the last to whom this loving contemplation of God is communicated, when God so desires, must receive it according to their own mode, in a very limited and painful way.

God's light, which illumines the angels by clarifying and giving them the sweetness of love—for they are pure spirits prepared for this inflow—illumines humans, as we said, by darkening them and giving them pain and anguish, since naturally they are impure and feeble. The communication affects them as sunlight affects a sick and bleared eye. This very fire of love enamors these individuals both impassionedly and afflictively until it spiritualizes and refines them through purification, and thus they become capable of the tranquil reception of this loving inflow, as are the angels and those already purified. With the Lord's help we will explain this state later.[1] In the meantime, however, the soul receives this contemplation and loving knowledge in distress and longing of love.

5. The soul does not always feel this inflaming and anxious longing of love. In the beginning of the spiritual purgation, the divine fire spends itself in drying out and preparing the wood—that is, the soul—rather than in heating it. Yet as time passes and the fire begins to give off heat, the soul usually experiences the burning and warmth of love.

As the intellect becomes more purged by means of this darkness, it happens sometimes that this mystical and loving theology, besides inflaming the will, also wounds the intellect by illumining it with some knowledge and light so delightfully and delicately that the will is thereby marvelously enkindled in fervor. This divine fire burns in the will—while the will remains passive—like a living flame and in such a way that this love now seems to be a live fire because of the living knowledge communicated. David says in the psalm: *My heart grew hot within me and a certain fire was enkindled while I was knowing* [Ps. 39:3].

6. This enkindling of love and the union of these two faculties, the intellect and the will, is something immensely rich and delightful for the soul, because it is a certain touch of the divinity and already the beginning of the perfection of the union of love for which the soul hopes.[2] Thus one does not receive this touch of so sublime an experience and love of God without having suffered many trials and a great part of the purgation. But

---

1. Again, John did not complete this part of his planned work. The doctrine about the hierarchical illumination has its basis in Pseudo-Dionysius' work *The Celestial Hierarchy*.
2. With respect to the divine touches, cf. A. 2. 24.4; 26. 3-10; 32. 2-4.

so extensive a purgation is not required for other inferior and more common touches.

7. You may deduce from our explanation that when God infuses these spiritual goods the will can very easily love without the intellect understanding, just as the intellect can know without the will loving. Since this dark night of contemplation consists of divine light and love—just as fire gives off both light and heat—it is not incongruous that this loving light, when communicated, sometimes acts more upon the will through the fire of love. Then the intellect is left in darkness, not being wounded by the light. At other times, this loving light illumines the intellect with understanding and leaves the will in dryness. All of this is similar to feeling the warmth of fire without seeing its light or seeing the light without feeling the fire's heat. The Lord works in this way because he infuses contemplation as he wills.

CHAPTER 13

[Other delightful effects of this dark night of contemplation in the soul.]

1. Through this inflaming of love we can understand some of the delightful effects this dark night of contemplation now gradually produces in the soul. Sometimes, as we said, it illumines in the midst of these darknesses, and the light shines in the darkness [Jn. 1:5], serenely communicating this mystical knowledge to the intellect and leaving the will in dryness, that is, without the actual union of love. The serenity is so delicate and delightful to the feeling of the soul that it is ineffable. This experience of God is felt now in one way and now in another.

2. Sometimes, as we said, this contemplation acts on both the intellect and will together, and sublimely, tenderly, and forcibly enkindles love. We already pointed out that once the intellect is purged more these two faculties are sometimes united; and in the measure that they are both purged, this union becomes so much more perfect and deeper in quality. Yet before reaching this degree, it is more common to experience the touch of burning in the will than the touch of understanding in the intellect.

3. A question arises here: Why does one in the beginning more commonly experience in purgative contemplation an inflaming of love in the will rather than understanding in the intellect, since these two faculties are being purged equally?

We may answer that this passive love does not act upon the will directly because the will is free, and this burning love is more the passion of love than a free act of the will. The warmth of love wounds the substance of the soul and thus moves the affections passively. As a result the enkindling of love is called the passion of love rather than a free act of the will. An act of the will is such only insofar as it is free. Yet, since these passions and affections bear a relation to the will, it is said that if the soul is impassioned with some affection, the will is. This is true, because the will thus becomes captive and loses its freedom, carried away by the impetus and force of the passion. As a result we say that this enkindling of love takes place in the will, that is, the appetites of the will are enkindled. This enkindling is called the passion of love rather than the free exercise of the will. Since the receptive capacity of the intellect can only take in the naked and passive knowledge, and since the intellect, unless purged, cannot receive this knowledge, the soul, prior to the purgation of the intellect, experiences the touch of knowledge less frequently than the passion of love. For to feel the passion of love it is unnecessary that the will be so purged in relation to the passions; the passions even help it experience impassioned love.

4. Since this fire and thirst of love is spiritual, it is far different from the other enkindling of love we discussed in the night of the senses. Although the sensory part shares in this love, because it does not fail to participate in the work of the spirit, the root and keenness of the thirst is felt in the higher part of the soul. The spirit so feels and understands what it experiences and the lack that this desire causes in it that all the suffering of sense—even though incomparably greater than that of the night of the senses—is nothing in comparison to this spiritual suffering. For the soul is conscious deeply within itself of the lack of an immense and incomparable good.

5. We ought to point out that the burning of love is not felt at the beginning of this spiritual night because the fire of love has not begun to catch. Nevertheless, God gives from the outset an esteeming love by which he is held in such high favor that, as we said, the soul's greatest suffering in the trials of this night is the anguish of thinking it has lost God and been abandoned by him. We can always assert, then, that from the commencement of this night the soul is touched with urgent longings of love: of esteeming love, sometimes; at other times, also of burning love.

The soul is aware that the greatest suffering it experiences in these trials is this fear. If such persons could be assured that all is not over and lost but that what they suffer is for the better—as indeed it is—and that God is not angry with them, they would be unconcerned about all these sufferings; rather, they would rejoice in the knowledge that God is pleased with them. Their love of esteem for God is so intense, even though obscure and imperceptible, that they would be happy not only to suffer these things but even to die many times in order to please him.

When the fire now inflames the soul together with the esteem of God already possessed, individuals usually acquire such strength, courage, and longings relative to God, through the warmth of the love that is being communicated, that with singular boldness they do strange things, in whatever way necessary, in order to encounter him whom they love. Because of the strength and inebriation of their love and desire, they perform these actions without any consideration or concern.

6. Mary Magdalene, in spite of her past, paid no heed to the crowds of people, prominent as well as unknown, at the banquet. She did not consider the propriety of weeping and shedding tears in the presence of our Lord's guests. Her only concern was to reach him for whom her soul was already wounded and on fire, without any delay and without waiting for another more appropriate time [Lk. 7:37-38].[1] And such is the inebriation and courage of love: Knowing that her Beloved was shut up in the tomb by a huge sealed rock and surrounded by guards so the disciples could not steal his body, she did not permit this to keep her from going out with ointments before daybreak to anoint him [Mt. 27:64-66; Mk. 16:1-2; Jn. 20:1].

7. Finally, this inebriation and urgent longing of love prompted her to ask the man she thought was the gardener if he had stolen him and, if he had, to tell her where he had put him so she could take him away [Jn. 20:15]. She did not stop to realize that her question in the light of sound judgment was foolish, for obviously if he had stolen the Lord he would not have told her, and still less would he have allowed her to take him away.

The strength and vehemence of love has this trait: Everything seems possible to it, and it believes everyone is occupied as it is; it does not believe anyone could be employed in any other way or seek anyone other than him whom it seeks and loves; it believes there is nothing else to desire or to occupy it and that everyone is engaged in seeking and loving him. When the bride went searching for her Beloved in the plazas and suburbs, she thought that others were doing the same and told them that if they found him they should tell him she was suffering for love of him [Sg. 3:2; 5:8]. Mary's love was so ardent that she thought she would go and take Jesus away, however great the impediments, if the gardener would tell where he was hidden.

8. Such are the traits of these longings of love that the soul experiences when it is advanced in this spiritual purgation. The wounded soul rises up at night, in this purgative darkness, according to the affections of the will;

---

1. Following St. Gregory the Great, the Latin Church in the past has generally identified Mary Magdalene with the repentant woman in Luke.

as the lioness or she-bear that goes in search of her cubs when they are taken away and cannot be found [2 Sm. 17:8; Hos. 13:8], it anxiously and forcibly goes out in search of its God. Since it is immersed in darkness, it feels his absence and feels that it is dying with love of him. Such is impatient love, which one cannot long endure without either receiving its object or dying. Rachel bore this love for children when she said: *Give me children, otherwise I shall die* [Gn. 30:1].[2]

9. It should be explained here why, even though the soul feels as miserable and unworthy of God as it does in these purgative darknesses, it possesses an energy bold enough to go out to be joined with God.

The reason is that since love now imparts a force by which the soul loves authentically, and since it is the nature of love to seek to be united, joined, equaled, and assimilated to the loved object in order to be perfected in the good of love, the soul hungers and thirsts for this union or perfection of love still unattained. And the strength now bestowed by love, and by which the will has become impassioned, makes this inflamed will daring. Yet since the intellect is not illumined but in darkness, the soul feels unworthy and knows that it is miserable.

10. I do not want to fail to explain why this divine light, even though it is always light for the soul, does not illumine immediately on striking as it will afterward, but instead causes trials and darkness. We already said something on this matter.[3] Yet we may reply particularly that the darknesses and evils the soul experiences when this light strikes are not darknesses and evils of the light but of the soul itself. And it is this light that illumines the soul so that it may see these evils. From the beginning the divine light illumines the soul; yet at the outset it can only see through this light what is nearest—or rather within—itself, namely, its own darknesses and miseries. It sees these by the mercy of God, and it did not see them before because this supernatural light did not shine in it. Accordingly, it only feels darknesses and evils at the outset. After being purged through the knowledge and feeling of these darknesses and evils, it will have eyes capable of seeing the goods of the divine light. Once all these darknesses and imperfections are expelled, it seems that the immense benefits and goods the soul is acquiring in this happy night of contemplation begin to appear.

11. It is clear, consequently, how God grants the soul a favor by cleansing and curing it. He cleanses it with a strong lye and a bitter purge in its sensory and spiritual parts of all imperfect affections and habits relative to temporal, natural, sensory, and spiritual things. He does this

---

2. This impatient love is the theme of the first 12 stanzas of *The Spiritual Canticle*.
3. See especially ch. 5. 2-3 and ch. 9.

by darkening the interior faculties and emptying them of all these objects, and by restraining and drying up the sensory and spiritual affections, and by weakening and refining the natural forces of the soul with respect to these things. A person would never have been able to accomplish this work alone, as we shall soon explain.[4] Accordingly, God makes the soul die to all that he is not, so that when it is stripped and flayed of its old skin, he may clothe it anew. Its youth is renewed like the eagle's [Ps. 103:5], clothed in the new self, which is created, as the Apostle says, according to God [Eph. 4:24]. This renovation illumines the human intellect with supernatural light so it becomes divine, united with the divine; informs the will with love of God so it is no longer less than divine and loves in no other way than divinely, united and made one with the divine will and love; and is also a divine conversion and changing of the memory, the affections, and the appetites according to God. And thus this soul will be a soul of heaven, heavenly and more divine than human.

As we have gradually seen, God accomplishes all this work in the soul by illumining it and firing it divinely with urgent longings for God alone. Rightly and reasonably does the soul add the third verse of the stanza:

—Ah, the sheer grace!—

CHAPTER 14

[An explanation of the three last verses of the first stanza.]

1. This sheer grace resulted from what is expressed in the following verses: I went out unseen,

my house being now all stilled.

We have the metaphor of one who, in order to execute a plan better and without hindrance, goes out at night, in darkness, when everybody in the house is sleeping.[1]

The soul had to go out to accomplish so heroic and rare a feat—to be united with its divine Beloved outside—because the Beloved is not found except alone, outside, and in solitude. The bride accordingly desired to find him alone, saying: *Who will give you to me, my brother, that I may find you alone outside and communicate to you my love?* [Sg. 8:1]. The enamored soul must leave its house, then, in order to reach its desired goal. It must go out at night when all the members of its house are asleep, that is, when the lower operations, passions, and appetites of its soul are put to sleep or quelled by means of this night. These are the people of its household who when awake are a continual hindrance to the reception of any good,

---

4. In ch. 16.
1. John's escape at night from prison seems to have influenced the poem. Cf. A. 1. 15. note 1.

and hostile to the soul's departure in freedom from them. Our Savior declares that one's enemies are those of one's own household [Mt. 10:36]. The operations and movements of these members had to be put to sleep in order not to keep the soul from receiving the supernatural goods of the union of love of God, for this union cannot be wrought while they are awake and active. All the soul's natural activity hinders rather than helps it to receive the spiritual goods of the union of love. All natural ability is insufficient to produce the supernatural goods that God alone infuses in the soul passively, secretly, and in silence. All the faculties must receive this infusion, and in order to do so they must be passive and not interfere through their own lowly activity and vile inclinations.

2. It was a sheer grace for this soul that God in this night puts to sleep all the members of its household, that is, all the faculties, passions, affections, and appetites that live in its sensory and spiritual parts. God puts them to sleep to enable the soul to go out to the spiritual union of the perfect love of God without being seen, that is, without the hindrance of these affections, and so on. For these members of the household are put to sleep and mortified in this night, which leaves them in darkness, so they may not be able to observe or experience anything in their lowly, natural way that would impede the soul's departure from itself and the house of the senses.

3. Oh, what a sheer grace it is for the soul to be freed from the house of its senses! This good fortune, in my opinion, can only be understood by the ones who have tasted it. For then such persons will become clearly aware of the wretched servitude and the many miseries they suffered when they were subject to the activity of their faculties and appetites. They will understand how the life of the spirit is true freedom and wealth and embodies inestimable goods. In the following stanzas we will specify some of these goods and see more clearly how right the soul is in singing about the journey through this horrendous night as being a great grace.

CHAPTER 15

Second Stanza

In darkness, and secure,
by the secret ladder, disguised,
—ah, the sheer grace!—
in darkness and concealment,
my house being now all stilled.

Explanation

1. The soul in its song continues to recount some of the properties of the darkness of this night and mentions again the happiness resulting from them.[1] It speaks of these traits in response to a certain tacit objection. It says that we should not think a person runs a more serious risk of being lost because of the torments of anguish, the doubts, the fears, and the horrors of this night and darkness; rather a person is saved in the darkness of this night. In this night the soul subtly escapes from its enemies, who were always opposed to its departure. In its journey in the darkness of this night, its garb is changed and thus it is disguised by three different colored garments, which we will discuss later;[2] and it departs by a very secret ladder of which no one in the house knows. This ladder, as we will also explain,[3] is the living faith by which it departs in so concealed a way in order to carry out its plan successfully, and by which it cannot but escape very securely. The soul is particularly secure in this purgative night because its appetites, affections, passions, and so on, were put to sleep, mortified, and deadened. These are the members of the household that when awake and alive would not consent to this departure. The following verse then states:

In darkness, and secure,

CHAPTER 16

[An explanation of how the soul is secure when it walks in darkness.]

1. We already said that the darkness the soul mentions here relates to the sensory, the interior, and the spiritual appetites and faculties, because this night darkens their natural light so that through the purgation of this light they may be illumined supernaturally. It puts the sensory and spiritual appetites to sleep, deadens them, and deprives them of the ability to find pleasure in anything. It binds the imagination and impedes it from doing any good discursive work. It makes the memory cease, the intellect become dark and unable to understand anything, and hence it causes the will also to become arid and constrained, and all the faculties empty and useless. And over all this hangs a dense and burdensome cloud that afflicts the soul and keeps it withdrawn from God. As a result the soul asserts that in darkness it walks securely.

---

1. This stanza, then, does not represent any new stage in the experience of the night. It is only a variation on the same theme.
2. In ch. 21.
3. In ch. 18.

2. The reason for this security has been clearly explained. Usually a soul never strays except through its appetites, its gratifications, or its discursive meditation, or through its knowledge or affections. By these, people usually fail through excess or defect, or they change because of them or go astray, or experience inordinate inclinations. Once all these operations and movements are impeded, individuals are obviously freed from error in them, because they are not only liberated from themselves but also from their other enemies, the world and the devil. The world and the devil have no other means of warring against the soul when its affections and operations are deadened.

3. In the measure that the soul walks in darkness and emptiness in its natural operations, it walks securely. As the prophet says, the soul's perdition comes only from itself (from its senses and interior and sensory appetites); and its good, says God, comes only from me [Hos. 13:9]. Since the soul's evils are thus impeded, only the goods of union with God are imparted to the appetites and faculties; these appetites and faculties become divine and heavenly in this union. If they observe closely at the time of these darknesses, individuals will see clearly how little the appetites and faculties are distracted with useless and harmful things and how secure they are from vainglory, from pride and presumption, from an empty and false joy, and from many other evils. By walking in darkness the soul not only avoids going astray but advances rapidly, because it thus gains the virtues.

4. A question immediately arises here: Since the things of God in themselves produce good in the soul, are beneficial, and give assurance, why does God in this night darken the appetites and faculties so that these derive no satisfaction in such good things and find it difficult to be occupied with them—in some ways even more difficult than to be occupied with other things? The answer is that at this time there should be no activity or satisfaction relative to spiritual objects, because the soul's faculties and appetites are impure, lowly, and very natural. And even were God to give these faculties the activity and delight of supernatural, divine things, they would be unable to receive them except in their own way, very basely and naturally. As the Philosopher says, *Whatever is received is received according to the mode of the receiver.*[1]

Since these natural faculties do not have the purity, strength, or capacity to receive and taste supernatural things in a supernatural or divine mode, but only according to their own mode, which is human and lowly, as we said, these faculties must also be darkened regarding the divine, so that weaned, purged, and annihilated in their natural way they

---

1. See N. 1. 4. 2.

might lose that lowly and human mode of receiving and working. Thus all these faculties and appetites of the soul are tempered and prepared for the sublime reception, experience, and savor of the divine and supernatural, which cannot be received until the old self dies.

5. Consequently, if all spiritual communication does not come from on high, from the Father of lights, from above the free will and human appetite [Jas. 1:17], humans will not taste it divinely and spiritually but rather humanly and naturally, no matter how much their faculties are employed in God and no matter how much satisfaction they derive from this. For goods do not go from humans to God, but they come from God to humans.

Here we could explain, if this were the place, how many persons have numerous inclinations toward God and spiritual things, employ their faculties in them, derive great satisfaction by so doing, and think their actions and appetites are supernatural and spiritual when perhaps they are no more than natural and human. Because of a certain natural facility they have for moving the appetites and faculties toward any object at all, their activity with spiritual things and the satisfaction they derive are the same as with other things.

6. If by chance the opportunity arises we will give some signs for recognizing when the movements and interior actions of the soul in its communion with God are only natural and when only spiritual, and when they are both natural and spiritual.[2] Here it is sufficient to know that if the soul in its interior acts is to be moved by God divinely, it must be obscured, put to sleep, and pacified in regard to its natural ability and operations until these lose their strength.

7. Oh, then, spiritual soul, when you see your appetites darkened, your inclinations dry and constrained, your faculties incapacitated for any interior exercise, do not be afflicted; think of this as a grace, since God is freeing you from yourself and taking from you your own activity. However well your actions may have succeeded, you did not work so completely, perfectly, and securely—because of their impurity and awkwardness—as you do now that God takes you by the hand and guides you in darkness, as though you were blind, along a way and to a place you know not. You would never have succeeded in reaching this place no matter how good your eyes and your feet.

8. Another reason the soul not only advances securely when it walks in darkness but even gains and profits is that when in a new way it receives

---

2. He never did deal explicitly with these signs.

some betterment, it usually does so in a manner it least understands, and thus ordinarily thinks it is getting lost. Since it has never possessed this new experience, which makes it go out, blinds it, and leads it astray with respect to its first method of procedure, it thinks it is getting lost rather than advancing successfully and profitably. Indeed, it is getting lost to what it knew and tasted, and going by a way in which it neither tastes nor knows.

To reach a new and unknown land and journey along unknown roads, travelers cannot be guided by their own knowledge; instead, they have doubts about their own knowledge and seek the guidance of others. Obviously they cannot reach new territory or attain this added knowledge if they do not take these new and unknown roads and abandon those familiar ones. Similarly, people learning new details about their art or trade must work in darkness and not with what they already know. If they refuse to lay aside their former knowledge, they will never make any further progress. The soul, too, when it advances, walks in darkness and unknowing.

Since God, as we said, is the master and guide of the soul,[3] this blind one can truly rejoice now that it has come to understand as it has here, and say: in darkness, and secure.

9. There is another reason the soul walks securely in these darknesses: It advances by suffering. Suffering is a surer and even more advantageous road than that of joy and action. First, in suffering, strength is given to the soul by God. In its doing and enjoying, the soul exercises its own weakness and imperfections. Second, in suffering, virtues are practiced and acquired, and the soul is purified and made wiser and more cautious.

10. Another more basic reason the soul walks securely in darkness is that this light, or obscure wisdom, so absorbs and engulfs the soul in the dark night of contemplation and brings it so near God that it is protected and freed from all that is not God. Since the soul, as it were, is undergoing a cure to regain its health, which is God himself, His Majesty restricts it to a diet, to abstinence from all things, and causes it to lose its appetite for them all. This effect resembles the cure of sick people when esteemed by members of their household: They are kept inside so that neither air nor light may harm them; others try not to disturb them by the noise of their footsteps or even whisperings, and give them a very delicate and limited amount of food, substantial rather than tasty.

11. Because dark contemplation brings the soul closer to God, it has all these characteristics; it safeguards and cares for the soul. Because of

3. In no. 7. This is an important element in John's teaching about spiritual direction; cf. F. 3. 29.

their weakness, individuals feel thick darkness and more profound obscurity the closer they come to God, just as they would feel greater darkness and pain, because of the weakness and impurity of their eyes, the closer they approached the immense brilliance of the sun. The spiritual light is so bright and so transcendent that it blinds and darkens the natural intellect as this latter approaches it.

Accordingly, David says in Psalm 17 [Ps. 18:11] that God made darkness his hiding place and covert, and dark waters in the clouds of the air his tabernacle round about him. The dark water in the clouds of the air signifies dark contemplation and divine wisdom in these souls. When God is joining them closer to himself they feel that this darkness is near him as though it were a tabernacle in which he dwells. That which is light in God and of the loftiest clarity is dense darkness for the soul, as St. Paul affirms [1 Cor. 2:14], and as David points out immediately in the same psalm: *Because of the splendor encircling his presence, the clouds and cataracts came out* [Ps. 18:12], that is, they came out over the natural intellect, whose light, as Isaiah says in chapter 5, *obtenebrata est in caligine ejus* [Is. 5:30].[4]

12. Oh, what a miserable lot this life is! We live in the midst of so much danger and find it so hard to arrive at truth. The clearest and truest things are the darkest and most dubious to us, and consequently we flee from what most suits us. We embrace what fills our eyes with the most light and satisfaction and run after what is the very worst thing for us, and we fall at every step. In how much danger and fear do humans live, since the very light of their natural eyes, which ought to be their guide, is the first to deceive them in their journey to God, and since they must keep their eyes shut and tread the path in darkness if they want to be sure of where they are going and be safeguarded against the enemies of their house, their senses and faculties.

13. The soul, then, is well hidden and protected in this dark water, for it is close to God. Since the dark water serves God himself as a tabernacle and dwelling place, it will serve the soul in this way and also as a perfect safeguard and security, even though it causes darkness. In this darkness the soul is hidden and protected from itself and the harm of creatures.

David's assertion in another psalm is also applicable to these souls: *You will hide them in the secret of your face from the disturbance of people. You will protect them in your tabernacle from the contradiction of tongues* [Ps. 31:20]. This passage applies to every kind of protection. To be hidden in the face of God from the disturbance of people refers to the fortification this dark contemplation provides against all the occasions that may arise because

---

4. "is darkened by its clouds."

of others. To receive protection in his tabernacle from the contradiction of tongues indicates the absorption of the soul in this dark water. This dark water is the tabernacle we said David mentions, in which the soul, with weaned appetites and affections and darkened faculties, is freed of all imperfections contradictory to the spirit, whether they originate with its own flesh or with other creatures. The soul can therefore truly say that its journey is in darkness, and secure.

14. There is another no less efficacious reason to help us understand clearly that this soul's journey is in darkness, and secure, that is, the fortitude this obscure, painful, and dark water of God bestows on the soul from the beginning. After all, even though it is dark, it is water, and thereby refreshes and fortifies the soul in what most suits it—although in darkness, and painfully.

From the outset individuals are conscious of a true determination and power to do nothing they recognize as an offense against God and to omit nothing that seems to be for his service. That dark love enkindles in the soul a remarkably vigilant care and interior solicitude about what to do or omit in order to please God. They will ponder whether they may have angered God and go over this in their minds a thousand times. They do this with much greater care and solicitude than before, as we mentioned in discussing the longings of love.[5] In this dark contemplation the soul's appetites, strength, and faculties are withdrawn from all other things, and its efforts and strength are expended only in paying homage to God. This is the way it goes out from itself and from all created things to the sweet and delightful union with God through love:

> In darkness, and secure,
> By the secret ladder, disguised,

CHAPTER 17

[An explanation of the secrecy of this dark contemplation.]

1. We ought to explain three properties of this night indicated in the three terms of this verse. Two of them, "secret" and "ladder," pertain to the dark night of contemplation now under discussion; the third, "disguised," refers to the soul and the way it conducts itself in this night.

Relative to the first two, it should be known that in this verse the soul calls dark contemplation a "secret ladder." By dark contemplation it goes out to the union of love because of two properties found in this contemplation: It is secret, and it is a ladder. We will discuss them separately.

---

5. In ch. 13. 5.

2. First, it calls this dark contemplation "secret" since, as we mentioned,[1] contemplation is mystical theology, which theologians call secret wisdom and which St. Thomas says is communicated and infused into the soul through love.[2] This communication is secret and dark to the work of the intellect and the other faculties. Insofar as these faculties do not acquire it but the Holy Spirit infuses it and puts it in order in the soul, as the bride says in the Song of Songs [Sg. 2:4], the soul neither knows nor understands how this comes to pass and thus calls it secret. Indeed, not only does the soul fail to understand, but no one understands, not even the devil, since the Master who teaches the soul dwells within it substantially where neither the devil nor the natural senses nor the intellect can reach.

3. Contemplation is called "secret" not only because of one's inability to understand but also because of the effects it produces in the soul. The wisdom of love is not secret merely in the darknesses and straits of the soul's purgation (for the soul does not know how to describe it) but also afterward in the illumination, when it is communicated more clearly. Even then it is so secret that it is ineffable. Not only does a person feel unwilling to give expression to this wisdom, but one finds no adequate means or simile to signify so sublime an understanding and delicate a spiritual feeling. Even if the soul should desire to convey this experience in words and think up many similes the wisdom would always remain secret and still to be expressed.

Since this interior wisdom is so simple, general, and spiritual that in entering the intellect it is not clothed in any sensory species or image, the imaginative faculty cannot form an idea or picture of it in order to speak of it. This wisdom did not enter through these faculties, nor did they behold any of its apparel or color. Yet the soul is clearly aware that it understands and tastes that delightful and wondrous wisdom. On beholding an object never before seen in itself or in its likeness, one would be unable to describe it or give it a name no matter how much one tried, even though understanding and satisfaction were found in it. And if people find it so difficult to describe what they perceive through the senses, how much more difficult is it to express what does not enter through the senses. The language of God has this trait: Since it is very spiritual and intimate to the soul, transcending everything sensory, it immediately silences the entire ability and harmonious composite of the exterior and interior senses.

4. We have examples of this ineffability of divine language in Sacred

---

1. In ch. 5. 1.
2. The most probable source is in his *Summa theologiae* 2-2. 45. 2.

Scripture. Jeremiah manifested his incapacity to describe it when, after God had spoken to him, he knew of nothing more to say than *ah, ah, ah!* [Jer. 1:6]. Moses also declared before God, present in the burning bush, his interior inability (the inability of both his imagination and his exterior senses) [Ex. 4:10]. He asserted that not only was he unable to speak of this conversation but that he did not even dare consider it in his imagination, as is said in the Acts of the Apostles [Acts 7:32]. He believed that his imagination was not only unable to speak, as it were, in the matter of forming some image of what he understood in God, but also incapable of receiving this knowledge.

Since the wisdom of this contemplation is the language of God to the soul, of Pure Spirit to pure spirit, all that is less than spirit, such as the sensory, fails to perceive it. Consequently this wisdom is secret to the senses; they have neither the knowledge nor the ability to speak of it, nor do they even desire to do so because it is beyond words.

5. We understand, then, why some persons who tread this road and desire to give an account of this experience to their director—for they are good and God-fearing—are unable to describe it. They feel great repugnance in speaking about it, especially when the contemplation is so simple that they are hardly aware of it. All they can manage to say is they are satisfied, quiet and content, and aware of God, and in their opinion all goes well. But the experience is ineffable, and one will hear from the soul no more than these general terms. It is a different matter when the communications the soul receives are particular, such as visions, feelings, and so on. These communications are ordinarily received through some species in which the sense participates and are describable through that species or a similar one. Yet pure contemplation is indescribable, as we said, and on this account called "secret."

6. Not for this reason alone do we call mystical wisdom "secret"—and it is actually so—but also because it has the characteristic of hiding the soul within itself. Besides its usual effect, this mystical wisdom occasionally so engulfs souls in its secret abyss that they have the keen awareness of being brought into a place far removed from every creature. They accordingly feel that they have been led into a remarkably deep and vast wilderness unattainable by any human creature, into an immense, unbounded desert, the more delightful, savorous, and loving, the deeper, vaster, and more solitary it is. They are conscious of being so much more hidden, the more they are elevated above every temporal creature.

Souls are so elevated and exalted by this abyss of wisdom, which leads them into the heart of the science of love, that they realize that all the conditions of creatures in relation to this supreme knowing and divine experience are very base, and they perceive the lowliness, deficiency, and inadequacy of all the terms and words used in this life to deal with divine things. They also note the impossibility, without the illumination of this mystical theology, of a knowledge or experience of these divine things as they are in themselves, through any natural means, no matter how wisely or loftily one speaks of them. Beholding this truth—that it can neither grasp nor explain this wisdom—the soul rightly calls it secret.

7. This divine contemplation has the property of being secret and above one's natural capacity, not merely because it is supernatural but also because it is the way that guides the soul to the perfections of union with God, toward which one must advance humanly by not knowing and divinely by ignorance, since these perfections are not humanly knowable.

8. Speaking mystically, as we are here, the divine things and perfections are not known as they are in themselves while they are being sought and acquired, but when they are already found and acquired. Accordingly, the prophet Baruch speaks of this divine wisdom: *There is no one able to know her ways or think of her paths* [Bar. 3:31]. The Royal Prophet of this road also speaks of this kind of wisdom in his converse with God: *And your illuminations enlightened and illumined the entire world; the earth shook and trembled. Your way is in the sea and your paths are in many waters, and your footsteps shall not be known* [Ps. 77:18-19]. Spiritually speaking, this passage refers to our subject. The lightning of God illumining the whole earth signifies the illumination this divine contemplation produces in the faculties of the soul; the shaking and trembling of the earth applies to the painful purgation it causes in the soul; and to assert that the way and road of God, by which the soul travels toward him, is in the sea, and his footsteps in many waters, and thereby unknowable, is similar to stating that the way to God is as hidden and secret to the senses of the soul as are the footsteps of one walking on water imperceptible to the senses of the body. The traces and footsteps God leaves in those whom he desires to bring to himself, by making them great in the union with his wisdom, are unrecognizable. In the Book of Job this fact is stressed in these words: *Do you perchance know the paths of the great clouds or the perfect sciences?* [Jb. 37:16]. This passage refers to the ways and roads by which God exalts souls (here referred to by the clouds) and perfects them in his wisdom. Consequently, this contemplation that is guiding the soul to God is secret wisdom.

CHAPTER 18

[An explanation of how this secret wisdom is also a ladder.]

1. The second characteristic has yet to be discussed, that is, how this secret wisdom is also a ladder. It should be known that there are many

reasons for calling this secret contemplation a ladder.

First, as one ascends a ladder to pillage the fortresses containing goods and treasures, so too, by this secret contemplation, the soul ascends in order to plunder, know, and possess the goods and treasures of heaven. The Royal Prophet points this out clearly in saying: *Blessed are those who receive your favor and help. In their heart they have prepared their ascent, in the vale of tears, in the place which they set. For in this way the Lord of the Law will give a blessing, and they will go from virtue to virtue (as from step to step) and the God of gods will be seen on Zion* [Ps. 84:6-8]. He is the treasure of the fortress of Zion, and this treasure is beatitude.

2. We can also call this secret wisdom a "ladder" because as the same steps of a ladder are used for both ascent and descent, so also the same communications produced by this secret contemplation extol the soul in God and humiliate it within itself. Communications that are truly from God have this trait: They simultaneously exalt and humble the soul. For on this road, to descend is to ascend and to ascend is to descend, since those who humble themselves are exalted and those who exalt themselves are humbled [Lk. 14:11]. Besides this (that the virtue of humility exalts), God, in order to exercise the soul in humility, usually makes it ascend by this ladder so that it might descend, and he makes it descend that it might ascend. Accordingly, the Wise Man's words are fulfilled: *Before the soul is exalted, it is humbled, and before it is humbled, it is exalted* [Prv. 18:12].

3. Naturally speaking, and disregarding the spiritual, which it does not feel, the soul, if it desires to pay close attention, will clearly recognize how on this road it suffers many ups and downs, and how immediately after prosperity some tempest and trial follows, so much so that seemingly the calm was given to forewarn and strengthen it against the future penury. It sees, too, how abundance and tranquility succeed misery and torment, and in such a way that it thinks it was made to fast before celebrating that feast. This is the ordinary procedure in the state of contemplation until one arrives at the quiet state: The soul never remains in one state, but everything is ascent and descent.

4. The reason is that since the state of perfection, which consists in perfect love of God and contempt of self, cannot exist without knowledge of God and of self, the soul necessarily must first be exercised in both. It is now given the one, in which it finds satisfaction and exaltation, and now made to experience the other, humbled until the ascent and descent cease through the acquiring of the perfect habits. For the soul will then have reached God and united itself with him. He is at the end of the ladder and it is in him that the ladder rests.

This ladder of contemplation, derived as we have said from God, is prefigured in that ladder Jacob saw in his sleep and by which the angels were ascending and descending from God to human beings and from human beings to God, while God leaned on the top [Gn. 28:12-13]. The divine Scriptures say that all this happened at night, while Jacob was sleeping, to disclose how secret is the way and ascent to God and how it differs from human knowledge. The secrecy of this ascent is evident, since ordinarily the losing and annihilation of self, which bring the most profit to individuals, are considered the worst for them, whereas consolation and satisfaction (which are of less value and in which one ordinarily loses rather than gains if attachment is present) are considered the best.

5. Speaking now somewhat more particularly of this ladder of secret contemplation, we declare that the principal property involved in calling contemplation a "ladder" is its being a science of love, which as we said is an infused loving knowledge that both illumines and enamors the soul, elevating it step by step to God, its Creator. For it is only love that unites and joins the soul to God.

For greater clarity we will note the steps of this divine ladder and briefly point out the signs and effects of each so that one may surmise which of these steps one is on. We will distinguish them by their effects, as do St. Bernard and St. Thomas.[1] Knowing these steps in themselves is impossible naturally, because this ladder of love is, as we said, so secret that God alone measures and weighs it.

CHAPTER 19

[An explanation of the first five of the ten steps on the mystical ladder of divine love.]

1. We mentioned that there are ten successive steps on this ladder of love by which the soul ascends to God.

The first step of love makes the soul sick in an advantageous way. The bride speaks of this step of love when she says: *I conjure you, daughters of*

---

1. The text closely followed by John in the next two chapters was an apocryphal work attributed by some to St. Bernard and by others to St. Thomas Aquinas. The author is now known to be a Dominican of the 13th or 14th century named Helvicus Teutonicus. The work, entitled *De dilectione Dei et proximi* (On the Love of God and Neighbor) contains the section *De decem gradibus amoris secundum Bernardum* (On the ten degrees of love according to Bernard). It may be found in the Vives edition of Aquinas' works, vol. 28, Paris, 1889.

Jerusalem, if you encounter my Beloved, to tell him that I am lovesick [Sg. 5:8].
Yet this sickness is not unto death but for the glory of God [Jn. 11:4],
because in this sickness the soul's languor pertains to sin and to all the
things that are not God. It languishes for the sake of God himself, as David
testifies: *My soul has languished* (in regard to all things) *for Your salvation*
[Ps. 119:81]. As a sick person changes color and loses appetite for all
foods, so on this step of love the soul changes the color of its past life and
loses its appetite for all things. The soul does not get this sickness unless
an excess of heat is sent to it from above, as is brought out in this verse
of David: *Pluviam voluntariam segregabis, Deus, haereditati tuae, et infirmata
est,* and so on [Ps. 68:9].[1]

We clearly explained this sickness and languor in respect to all things
when we mentioned the annihilation of which the soul becomes aware
when it begins to climb this ladder of contemplation.[2] It becomes unable
then to find satisfaction, support, consolation, or a resting place in
anything. The soul therefore begins immediately to ascend from this step
to the next.

2. The second step causes a person to search for God unceasingly.
When the bride said that seeking him by night in her bed (when in accord
with the first step of love she was languishing), she did not find him, she
added: *I will rise up and seek him whom my soul loves* [Sg. 3:1-2], which as we
said the soul does unceasingly, as David counsels: *Seek the face of God always*
[Ps. 105:4]. Searching for him in all things, it pays heed to nothing until
it finds him. It resembles the bride who, after asking the guards for him,
immediately passed by and left them behind [Sg. 3:3-4]. Mary Magdalene
did not even pay attention to the angels at the sepulcher [Jn. 20:14].

The soul goes about so solicitously on this step that it looks for its
Beloved in all things. In all its thoughts it turns immediately to the
Beloved; in all converse and business it at once speaks about the Beloved;
when eating, sleeping, keeping vigil, or doing anything else, it centers all
its care on the Beloved, as we pointed out in speaking of the anxious
longings of love.[3]

Since the soul is here convalescing and gaining strength in the love
found in this second step, it immediately begins to ascend to the third
through a certain degree of new purgation in the night, as we will point
out, which produces the following effects.

3. The third step of this loving ladder prompts the soul to the
performance of works and gives it fervor that it might not fail. The Royal

---

1. "You shall set aside for your inheritance a free rain, O God, and it was
weakened."
2. In ch. 10. 2.
3. Cf., for example, ch. 11. 6.

Prophet exclaims: *Blessed are they who fear the Lord, because in his command-ments they long to work* [Ps. 112:1]. If fear, a child of love, produces this eagerness in the soul, what will love itself do? On this step the soul thinks the great works it does for the Beloved are small; its many works, few; the long time spent in his service, short. It believes all of this because of the fire of love in which it is now burning. Thus because of the intensity of his love, Jacob, obliged to serve seven more years in addition to the seven years he had already served, did not think these were many [Gn. 29:20, 30]. If Jacob's love for a creature could do so much, what will love of the Creator do when it takes hold of the soul on this third step?

Because of such intense love for God, individuals at this stage feel deep sorrow and pain about the little they do for him, and if it were licit they would destroy themselves a thousand times for God and be greatly consoled. They consequently consider themselves useless in all their works and think their lives worthless.

Another admirable effect produced here is that such persons think inwardly that they are really worse than all others. One reason for this effect is that love is teaching them what God deserves; another is that because the works they perform for God are many and they know them to be wanting and imperfect, they are confused and pained by them all, conscious that their work is so lowly for so high a Lord. On this third step the soul is far removed from vainglory, presumption, and the practice of condemning others. This third step causes these effects of solicitude and many other similar ones in the soul. And thus one acquires the courage and strength to ascend to the fourth step.

4. On the fourth step of this ladder of love a habitual yet unwearisome suffering is engendered on account of the Beloved. As St. Augustine says: *Love makes all burdensome and heavy things nearly nothing.*[4] The bride spoke of this step when, desiring to reach the last step, she said to her Spouse: *Put me as a seal upon your heart, as a seal upon your arm, for love* (the act and work of love) *is as strong as death, and emulation and importunity endure as long as hell* [Sg. 8:6].

The spirit possesses so much energy on this step that it brings the flesh under control and takes as little account of it as would a tree of one of its leaves. The soul in no way seeks consolation or satisfaction either in God or in anything else; neither does it desire or ask favors of God, for it is clearly aware that it has already received many from him. All its care is directed toward how it might give some pleasure to God and render him some service because of what he deserves and the favors he has bestowed, even though the cost might be high. These persons proclaim in their heart and spirit: "Ah, my Lord and my God! How many go to you looking for their own consolation and gratification and desiring that you grant

---

4. See *Sermo 70, De verbis Domini in Evangelium S. Matthei*, in Migne, PL 38. 444.

them favors and gifts, but those wanting to give you pleasure and something at a cost to themselves, setting aside their own interests, are few. What is lacking is not that you, O my God, desire to grant us favors again, but that we make use of them for your service alone and thus oblige you to grant them to us continually."

This degree of love is a very elevated step. For as the soul at this stage through so genuine a love pursues God in the spirit of suffering for his sake, His Majesty frequently gives it joy by paying it visits of spiritual delight. For this immense love that Christ, the Word, has cannot long endure the sufferings of his beloved without responding. God affirms this through Jeremiah: *I have remembered you, pitying your youth and tenderness when you followed me in the desert* [Jer. 2:2]. Spiritually speaking, the desert is an interior detachment from every creature in which the soul neither pauses nor rests in anything. This fourth step so inflames and enkindles individuals with desire for God that it enables them to ascend to the fifth step.

5. The fifth step of this ladder of love imparts an impatient desire and longing for God. On this step the desire of the lover to apprehend and be united with the Beloved is so ardent that any delay, no matter how slight, is long, annoying, and tiresome. The soul is ever believing that it is finding its Beloved; and when it sees its desire frustrated, which is at almost every step, it faints in its longing, as the Psalmist declares: *My soul longs and faints for the dwelling places of the Lord* [Ps. 84:2]. On this step the lover must either see its love or die. With such love Rachel in her immense longing for children declared to Jacob, her spouse: *Give me children or I will die* [Gn. 30:1]. On this step, *they suffer hunger like dogs and encircle the city of God* [Ps. 58:6]. On this step of hunger, the soul so feeds on love—for in accord with its hunger is its satisfaction—that it can ascend to the sixth step, which produces the following effects.

CHAPTER 20

[The remaining five steps of love.]

1. The sixth step makes the soul run swiftly toward God and experience many touches in him. And it runs without fainting by reason of its hope. The love that has invigorated it makes it fly swiftly. The prophet Isaiah also speaks of this step: *The saints who hope in God shall renew their strength. They shall take wings like the eagle and shall fly and not faint* [Is. 40:31], as is characteristic of the fifth step. The following verse of the psalm also pertains to this step: *As the hart desires the waters, so does my soul desire you, my God* [Ps. 42:1], for the hart when thirsty races toward the waters.

The reason for the swiftness of love on this step is that the soul's charity is now highly increased and almost completely purified, as is also stated in the psalm: *Sine iniquitate cucurri* (Without iniquity have I run) [Ps. 59:4]; and in another psalm: *I have run the way of your commandments, when you enlarged my heart* [Ps. 119:32]. The soul is soon brought from the sixth to the seventh step.

2. The seventh step of the ladder gives it an ardent boldness. At this stage love neither profits by the judgment to wait nor makes use of the counsel to retreat, neither can it be curbed through shame. For the favor God now gives it imparts an ardent daring. Hence the Apostle says: *Charity believes all things, hopes all things, and endures all things* [1 Cor. 13:7]. Moses spoke from this step when he besought God to forgive the people or else strike his name out of the book of life [Ex. 32:32]. These souls obtain from God what, with pleasure, they ask of him. David accordingly declares: *Delight in God, and he will grant you the petitions of your heart* [Ps. 37:4]. On this step the bride became bold and exclaimed: *Osculetur me osculo oris sui* [Sg. 1:1].[1] It is illicit for the soul to become daring on this step if it does not perceive the divine favor of the king's scepter held out toward it (Est. 5:2; 8:4), for it might then fall down the step it has already climbed. On these steps it must always conserve humility.

From the free hand and boldness God gives on this seventh step, that one may be daring in his presence with an ardent love, follows the eighth step. Here the soul captures the Beloved and is united with him as follows.

3. The eighth step of love impels the soul to lay hold of the Beloved without letting him go, as the bride proclaims: *I found him whom my heart and soul loves, I held him and did not let him go* [Sg. 3:4]. Although the soul satisfies its desire on this step of union, it does not do so continually. Some manage to get to it, but soon turn back and leave it. If one were to remain on this step, a certain glory would be possessed in this life, and so the soul rests on it for only short periods of time. Because the prophet Daniel was a man of desires, God ordered him to stay on this step: *Daniel, remain on your step, because you are a man of desires* [Dn. 10:11]. After this step comes the ninth, which is that of the perfect.

4. The ninth step of love causes the soul to burn gently. It is the step of the perfect who burn gently in God. The Holy Spirit produces this gentle and delightful ardor by reason of the perfect soul's union with God. St. Gregory accordingly says of the Apostles that when the Holy Spirit came upon them visibly, they burned interiorly and gently with love.[2]

---

1. "Let him kiss me with the kiss of his mouth."
2. See *Homilia 30 in Evangelium*, in Migne, PL 76. 1220.

We cannot speak of the goods and riches of God a person enjoys on this step because even were we to write many books about them the greater part would remain unsaid. For this reason and also because we will say something about them later, I will mention no more here than that this step of the ladder of love is succeeded by the tenth and final step, which is no longer of this life.

5. The tenth and last step of this secret ladder of love assimilates the soul to God completely because of the clear vision of God that a person possesses at once on reaching it. After arriving at the ninth step in this life, the soul departs from the body. Since these souls—few that there be—are already extremely purged through love, they do not enter purgatory. St. Matthew says: *Beati mundo corde, quoniam ipsi Deum videbunt,* etc. [Mt. 5:8].[3] As we mentioned, this vision is the cause of the soul's complete likeness to God. St. John says: *We know that we shall be like him* [1 Jn. 3:2], not because the soul will have as much capacity as God—this is impossible—but because all it is will become like God. Thus it will be called, and shall be, God through participation.

6. Such is the secret ladder of which the soul here speaks, although on these higher steps it is not very secret to the soul, for love reveals a great deal through the remarkable effects it produces. But on this last step of clear vision at the top of the ladder, where God rests, as we said,[4] nothing is any longer hid from the soul, and this because of its total assimilation. Accordingly our Savior exclaimed: *On that day you will not ask me anything,* etc. [Jn. 16:23]. Nevertheless, until that day, however high the soul may ascend, something will still be hidden in proportion to one's lack of total assimilation to the divine essence.

Thus, by means of this mystical theology and secret love, the soul departs from itself and all things and ascends to God. For love is like a fire that always rises upward as though longing to be engulfed in its center.

CHAPTER 21

[An explanation of the term "disguised" and a description of the colors of the disguise the soul wears in this night.]

1. Now then, after having explained why the soul calls this contemplation a secret ladder, we have still to comment on the third word of this

---

3. "Blessed are the clean of heart, for they will see God."
4. In ch. 18. 4.

verse, "disguised," and tell why it also says that it departed by this "secret ladder, disguised."

2. It should be known for the sake of understanding this verse that people disguise themselves by simply dissembling their identity under a garb and appearance different from their own. And they do this either to show exteriorly by means of that garment their will and aspiration toward gaining the favor and good pleasure of their beloved, or also to hide from rivals and better execute their plan. They then choose the garments and livery that most represent and signify their heart's affections and with which they can better dissemble themselves from their enemies.

3. The soul, then, touched with love for Christ, her Spouse, and aspiring to win his favor and friendship, departs in the disguise that more vividly represents the affections of her spirit.[1] Her advance in this disguise makes her more secure against her adversaries: the devil, the world, and the flesh. The livery she thus wears is of three principal colors: white, green, and red. These three colors stand for the three theological virtues: faith, hope, and charity, by which she not only gains the favor and good will of her Beloved but also advances very safely, fortified against her three enemies.

4. Faith is an inner tunic of such pure whiteness that it blinds the sight of every intellect. When the soul is clothed in faith the devil is ignorant of how to hinder her, neither is he successful in his efforts, for faith gives her strong protection—more than do all the other virtues—against the devil, who is the mightiest and most astute enemy.

As a result, St. Peter found no greater safeguard than faith in freeing himself from the devil, when he advised: *Cui resistite fortes in fide* [1 Pt. 5:9].[2] To obtain the favor of the Beloved and union with him, the soul can have no better inner tunic than this white garment of faith, the foundation and beginning of the other garments or virtues. *Without faith,* as the Apostle says, *it is impossible to please God* [Heb. 11:6]; and with faith it is impossible not to please him, since he himself declares through the prophet Hosea, *Desponsabo te mihi in fide* [Hos. 2:20], which is similar to saying: If you desire, soul, union and espousal with me, you must come interiorly clothed in faith.

---

1. As he moves out of his discussion of purgative contemplation, John begins to speak more in the style of *The Spiritual Canticle,* referring to Christ in terms of "Beloved" or "Bridegroom" and to the soul as "bride," although this symbolism in itself is basic to the poem.
2. "Resist him, steadfast in faith."

5. The soul wore her white tunic of faith when she departed on this dark night and walked, as we said, in the midst of interior darknesses and straits, without the comfort of any intellectual light—neither from above, because heaven seemed closed and God hidden, nor from below, because she derived no satisfaction from her spiritual teachers, and suffered with constancy and perseverance, passing through these trials without growing discouraged or failing the Beloved. The Beloved so proves the faith of his bride in tribulations that she can afterward truthfully declare what David says: *Because of the words of your lips I have kept hard ways* [Ps. 17:4].

6. Over this white tunic of faith the soul puts on a second colored garment, a green coat of mail. Green, as we said, signifies the virtue of hope, by which one in the first place is defended and freed from the second enemy, the world. This greenness of living hope in God imparts such courage and valor and so elevates the soul to the things of eternal life that in comparison with these heavenly hopes all earthly things seem, as they truly are, dry, withered, dead, and worthless. The soul is thus divested of all worldly garments and does not set her heart on anything there is, or will be, in the world; she lives clothed only in the hope of eternal life. Having her heart so lifted up above the things of the world, she is not only unable to touch or take hold of worldly things, but she cannot even see them.

7. By this green livery and disguise, the soul is therefore protected against its second enemy, the world. St. Paul calls hope the *helmet of salvation* [1 Thes. 5:8]. A helmet is a piece of armor that protects the entire head and covers it so there is no opening except for a visor through which to see.

Hope has this characteristic: It covers all the senses of a person's head so they do not become absorbed in any worldly thing, nor is there any way some arrow from the world might wound them. Hope allows the soul only a visor that it may look toward heavenly things, and no more. This is the ordinary task of hope in the soul; it raises the eyes to look only at God, as David asserts it did with him: *Oculi mei semper ad Dominum*[3] [Ps. 25:15]. David hoped for nothing from anyone else, as he says in another psalm: *Just as the eyes of the handmaid are fixed on the hands of her mistress, so are our eyes on the Lord our God until he has mercy on us who hope in him* [Ps. 123:2].

8. As a result, this green livery, by which one always gazes on God, looks at nothing else, and is not content save with him alone, so pleases the Beloved that it is true to say the soul obtains from God all that she hopes

---

3. "My eyes are ever toward the Lord."

for from him. The Bridegroom of the Canticle consequently says of his bride that she wounded his heart by merely the look of her eyes [Sg. 4:9]. Without this green livery of hope in God alone, it would not behoove anyone to go out toward this goal of love; a person would obtain nothing, since what moves and conquers is unrelenting hope.

9. The soul advances through this dark and secret night in the disguise of the green livery of hope, for she walks along so empty of all possessions and support that neither her eyes nor her care are taken up with anything but God. She places her mouth in the dust that there might be hope [Lam. 3:29], as we previously quoted from Jeremiah.[4]

10. Over the white and green, as the finishing touch and perfection of this disguise, the soul puts on a third color, a precious red toga. This color denotes charity, the third virtue, which not only adds elegance to the other two colors but so elevates the soul as to place her near God. Charity makes her so beautiful and pleasing to God that she dares to say: *Although I am black, O daughters of Jerusalem, I am beautiful, and for this reason the king has loved me and brought me into his chamber* [Sg. 1:5].[5]

With this livery of charity, a livery that by manifesting love increases love in the Beloved, the soul receives protection and concealment from the flesh, her third enemy. For where there is true love of God, love of self and of one's own things finds no entry. Not only does charity protect her, but it even makes the other virtues genuine, strengthens and invigorates them in order to fortify the soul, and bestows on them loveliness and charm so as to please the Beloved thereby. For without charity no virtue is pleasing to God. This is the seat draped in purple on which God rests, as is said in the Song of Songs [Sg. 3:10].

The soul is clothed in this red livery when, as explained in the first stanza, she departs in the dark night from herself and from all creatures, fired with love's urgent longings, and advances by the secret ladder of contemplation to perfect union with God, who is her Beloved salvation.

11. This, then, is the disguise the soul says she wore on this secret ladder in the night of faith, and these are its colors. These colors are a most suitable preparation for union of the three faculties (intellect, memory, and will) with God.

Faith darkens and empties the intellect of all its natural understanding and thereby prepares it for union with the divine wisdom.

Hope empties and withdraws the memory from all creature possessions, for as St. Paul says, hope is for that which is not possessed [Rom.

4. In ch. 8. 1.
5. As it stands the text comes from an antiphon in the Divine Office of the Blessed Virgin Mary.

8:24]. It withdraws the memory from what can be possessed and fixes it on what it hopes for. Hence only hope in God prepares the memory perfectly for union with him.

Charity also empties and annihilates the affections and appetites of the will of whatever is not God and centers them on him alone. Thus charity prepares the will and unites it with God through love.

Because these virtues have the function of withdrawing the soul from all that is less than God, they consequently have the mission of joining it with God.

12. Without walking sincerely in the garb of these three virtues, it is impossible to reach perfect union with God through love. This garb and disguise worn by the soul was very necessary for her to reach her goal, which was this loving and delightful union with her Beloved. It was a great grace for the soul to have put on this vesture, and to have persevered in it until attaining her end or goal, the union of love, which she so desired. Consequently she proclaims in the next verse:

—ah, the sheer grace!—

CHAPTER 22

[An explanation of verse 3 of the second stanza.]

1. It was manifestly a great grace for the soul to have successfully undertaken this departure, in which she liberated herself from the devil, the world, and her own sensuality. In having reached the happy freedom of spirit desired by all, the soul went from the lowly to the sublime; being earthly, she became heavenly; and being human, she became divine, and arrived at having her conversation in heaven [Phil. 3:20], as is proper to this state of perfection, which we will now discuss, although somewhat more briefly.

2. What was more important and the reason I undertook this task was to explain this night to many souls who in passing through it do not understand it, as is pointed out in the prologue.[1] The nature of this night has now been explained to some extent. We have also discussed the many blessings this night brings to the soul—though in a way that makes them

---

1. John must be referring to the long prologue of the *Ascent* because it is there that he pointed out the matter. From this reference, one may note how the *Ascent* and *Dark Night*, although different works, deal with the material of a comprehensive initial plan in which the purification was to be treated from both active and passive perspectives. Neither of these works can be interpreted apart from the other.

seem less than what they in fact are—and how great a grace it is for one who passes through it. We have written of these blessings so that when souls become frightened by the horror of so many trials they might take courage in the sure hope of the many advantageous blessings obtained from God through these trials.

This night was, besides, a sheer grace for the soul on account of what she says in the next verse:

in darkness and concealment,

CHAPTER 23

[An explanation of the fourth verse. Tells of the soul's wondrous hiding place during this night and how, though the devil enters other very high places, he is unable to gain entry to this one.]

1. "In concealment" amounts to saying in hiding or under cover. As a result, departing in darkness and concealment more truly indicates the security the soul speaks of in the first verse of this stanza. She received this security along the way toward union with God through love by means of this dark contemplation. "In darkness and concealment" is like saying that since the soul walked in darkness in the way we mentioned, she was concealed and hidden from the devil, and from his deceits and wiles.[1]

2. The reason the darkness of this contemplation frees and hides the soul from the wiles of the devil is that the contemplation experienced here is infused passively and secretly without the use of the exterior and interior faculties of the sensory part of the soul. The soul's journey, consequently, is not only hidden and freed from the obstacle these faculties in their natural weakness can occasion, but also from the devil, who without these faculties of the sensory part cannot reach the soul or know what is happening within it. Accordingly, the more spiritual and interior the communication and the more removed it is from the senses, the less the devil understands it.

3. It is very important to the soul's security that in its inner communion with God its senses remain in darkness, without this communication, and that they do not attain to it. First, so that there may be room for a more abundant spiritual communication, without any hindrance to freedom of spirit from the weakness of the sensory part. Second, so that, as we say, the soul might journey more securely, since the devil cannot

---

1. This chapter presents John's most detailed analysis of the interference of the devil in the spiritual life.

enter so far within it. Hence we can understand spiritually those words of our Savior: *Let not your left hand know what your right hand is doing* [Mt. 6:3]. This is like saying: Do not allow the left side, the lower portion of your soul, to know or attain to what happens on the right side, the superior and spiritual part of the soul; let this be a secret between the spirit and God alone.

4. It is quite true that even though the devil is ignorant of the nature of these very interior and secret spiritual communications, he frequently perceives that one is receiving them because of the great quietude and silence some of them cause in the sensory part. And since he is aware that he cannot impede them in the depths of the soul, he does everything possible to excite and disturb the sensory part, which he can affect with sufferings, horrors, and fears. He intends by this agitation to disquiet the superior and spiritual part of the soul in its reception and enjoyment of that good.

Yet when the communication of such contemplation shines in the spirit alone and produces strength in it, the devil's diligence in disturbing the soul is often of no avail. It receives instead new benefits and a deeper, more secure peace. For what a wonderful thing it is! In experiencing the troublesome presence of the enemy, the soul enters more deeply into its inner depths without knowing how and without any efforts of its own, and it is sharply aware of being placed in a certain refuge where it is more hidden and withdrawn from the enemy. There the peace and joy that the devil planned to undo increase. All that fear remains outside; and the soul exults in a very clear consciousness of secure joy, in the quiet peace and delight of the hidden Spouse that neither the world nor the devil can either give or take away. The soul experiences the truth of the bride's exclamation in the Song of Songs: *Behold, sixty men surround the bed of Solomon,* etc., *because of the fears of the night* [Sg. 3:7-8]. She is aware of this strength and peace even though she frequently feels that her flesh and bones outside are being tormented.

5. At other times, when the spiritual communication is not bestowed exclusively on the spirit but on the senses too, the devil more easily disturbs and agitates the spirit with these horrors by means of the senses. The torment and pain he then causes is immense, and sometimes it is ineffable. For since it proceeds nakedly from spirit to spirit, the horror the evil spirit causes within the good spirit (in that of the soul), if he reaches the spiritual part, is unbearable. The bride of the Song of Songs also speaks of this disturbance in telling of her desire to descend to interior recollection and enjoy these goods: *I went down into the garden of nuts to see the apples of the valleys and if the vineyard was in flower; I knew not;*

my soul was troubled by the chariots (by the carts and roaring) *of Aminadab* (the devil) [Sg. 6:11-12].[2]

6. At other times, when the communications are accorded by means of the good angels, the devil detects some of the favors God desires to grant the soul. God ordinarily permits the adversary to recognize favors granted through the good angels so this adversary may do what he can, in accord with the measure of justice, to hinder them. Thus the devil cannot protest his rights, claiming that he is not given the opportunity to conquer the soul, as was his complaint in the story of Job [Jb. 1:9-11; 2:4-5]. He could do this if God did not allow a certain parity between the two warriors (the good angel and the bad) in their struggle for the soul. Hence the victory of either one will be more estimable, and the soul, victorious and faithful in temptation, will receive a more abundant reward.

7. We must note that this is why God permits the devil to deal with the soul in the same measure and mode in which he himself conducts and deals with it. True visions ordinarily come from the good angel, even if Christ is represented, for he hardly ever appears in his own Person. If a person receives true visions from the good angel, God permits the bad angel to represent false ones of the same kind. Thus an incautious person can be deceived, as many have been. There is a figure of this in Exodus where it says that all the true signs Moses worked were seemingly worked by Pharaoh's magicians: If he produced frogs, they also did; if he turned water into blood, they also did so [Ex. 7:11-12, 19-22; 8:6-7].

8. Not only does the devil imitate this kind of corporeal vision, but he also simulates and interferes with spiritual communications coming from a good angel, since he can discern them, as we said; and as Job said, *omne sublime videt*[3] [Jb. 41:25], imitates and interferes with them. Yet he cannot imitate and form these spiritual communications as he can those granted under some appearance or figure, for these are without form and figure, and it is of the nature of the spirit to be formless and figureless.

He represents his frightful spirit to the soul in order to attack it in the same way in which it receives the spiritual communication, and to assail and destroy the spiritual with the spiritual.

In this case, when the good angel communicates spiritual contemplation, the soul cannot enter the hiding place of this contemplation quickly enough to go unnoticed by the devil. He then presents himself to it with

---

2. Cf. C. 40. 3.
3. "Every high thing he sees."

some spiritual horror and disturbance, at times very painful. Sometimes the soul can withdraw speedily without giving this horror of the evil spirit an opportunity to make an impression on it, and it recollects itself by the efficacious favor the good angel then gives it.

9. At other times the devil prevails, and disturbance and horror seize upon it. This terror is a greater suffering than any other torment in life. Since this horrendous communication proceeds from spirit to spirit manifestly and somewhat incorporeally, it surpasses all sensory pain. This spiritual suffering does not last long, for if it did the soul would depart from the body on account of this violent communication. Afterward the soul can recall this diabolic communication; doing so is enough to cause great suffering.

10. All we have mentioned here takes place passively without one's doing or undoing anything. Yet it should be understood that when the good angel allows the devil the advantage of reaching the soul with this spiritual horror, he does so that it may be purified and prepared, through this spiritual vigil, for some great feast and spiritual favor that God, who never mortifies but to give life or humbles but to exalt [1 Sam. 2:6-7], desires to give. This favor will be granted a short time afterward, and the soul, in accord with the dark and horrible purgation it suffered, will enjoy a wondrous and delightful spiritual communication, at times ineffably sublime. The preceding horror of the evil spirit greatly refines the soul so it can receive this good. These spiritual visions belong more to the next life than to this, and each is a preparation for the one following.

11. We have been speaking of God's visits by means of the good angel, in which the soul does not walk in such complete darkness and conceal-ment that the enemy cannot somehow reach it. Yet when God visits the soul directly, this verse is fully verified. In receiving spiritual favors from God, the soul is in total darkness and concealment as far as the enemy is concerned.

The reason for this concealment is that since His Majesty dwells substantially in that part of the soul to which neither the angel nor the devil can gain access and thereby see what is happening, the enemy cannot learn of the intimate and secret communications there between the soul and God. Since the Lord grants these communications directly, they are wholly divine and sovereign. They are all substantial touches of divine union between God and the soul. In one of these touches, since this is the highest degree of prayer, the soul receives greater good than in all else.

12. These are the touches the soul began to ask for in the Song of Songs

on saying: *Osculetur me osculo oris sui,* etc.[4] [Sg. 1:1]. Since a substantial touch is wrought in such close intimacy with God, for which the soul longs with so many yearnings, a person will esteem and covet a touch of the divinity more than all God's other favors. After the bride in the Song had received many favors, which she related there, she was unsatisfied and asked for these divine touches: *Who will give you to me, my brother, that I might find you alone, outside nursing at the breasts of my mother so that with the mouth of my soul I might kiss you and no one might despise me or attack me?* [Sg. 8:1]. This passage refers to the communication God gives to the soul by himself alone, outside and exclusive of all creatures, for this is the meaning of the terms "alone" and "outside nursing at the breasts." The breasts of the appetites and affections of the sensory part are dried up when in freedom of spirit the soul enjoys these blessings with intimate delight and peace, unhindered by the sensory part or the devil (who opposes them through the senses). The devil, then, would not assail the soul, because he would be unable to reach these blessings or come to understand these divine touches of the loving substance of God in the substance of the soul.

13. No one attains to this blessing except through an intimate nakedness, purgation, and spiritual hiding from all that is of creatures. Accordingly, one reaches this good in "darkness" (as we have explained at length and now repeat in reference to this verse), "and concealment" (in which the hidden soul, as we said, is confirmed in its union with God through love). The soul in its song consequently exclaims: "In darkness and concealment."

14. When these favors are bestowed in concealment (only in the spirit, as we said), a person is usually aware, without knowing how, that the superior and spiritual part of the soul is withdrawn and alienated from the lower and sensory part. This withdrawal makes one conscious of two parts so distinct that one seemingly has no relation to the other and is far removed from it. And, indeed, this is in a way true, for in the activity that is then entirely spiritual there is no communication with the sensory part. A person in this way becomes wholly spiritual, and in these hiding places of unitive contemplation, and by their means, the passions and spiritual appetites are to a great degree eliminated. Referring thus to the superior part, the soul says in this last verse:

> my house being now all stilled;

---

4. "Let him kiss me with the kiss of his mouth."

CHAPTER 24

[The concluding explanation of this second stanza.]

1. This is like saying: Since the superior portion of my soul is now, like the lower, at rest in its appetites and faculties, I went out to divine union with God through love.

2. Insofar as the soul is buffeted and purged through the war of the dark night in a twofold way (in the sensory and spiritual parts with their senses, faculties, and passions), she also attains a twofold peace and rest in the faculties and appetites of both the sensory and spiritual parts. Consequently the soul repeats this verse of the first stanza. The sensory and spiritual parts of the soul, in order to go out to the divine union of love, must first be reformed, put in order, and pacified, as was their condition in Adam's state of innocence. This verse, which in the first stanza refers to the quiet of the lower and sensory part, refers particularly in this second stanza to the superior and spiritual part, and consequently the soul has repeated it.

3. By means of the acts of substantial touches of divine union, the soul obtains habitually and perfectly (insofar as the condition of this life allows) the rest and quietude of her spiritual house. In concealment and hiding from the disturbance of both the devil and the senses and passions, she receives these touches from the divinity. By their means the soul is purified, quieted, strengthened, and made stable so she may receive permanently this divine union, which is the divine espousal between the soul and the Son of God.[1]

As soon as these two parts of the soul are wholly at rest and strengthened, together with all the members of the household, the faculties and appetites (also put to sleep and in silence regarding earthly and heavenly things), Divine Wisdom is united with the soul in a new bond of the possession of love. This union is wrought, as is asserted in the Book of Wisdom, *Dum quietum silentium contineret omnia, et nox in suo cursu medium iter haberet, omnipotens sermo tuus, Domine, a regalibus sedibus prosilivit*[2] [Wis. 18:14-15]. The bride in the Song of Songs explains the same thing when she states that after she passed by those who took away her veil and wounded her, she found him whom her soul loved [Sg. 5:7; 3:4].

---

1. This divine espousal now refers to spiritual marriage rather than spiritual betrothal. The state of spiritual marriage, which John explains in more detail in *The Spiritual Canticle,* is identical with that of the perfect.
2. "When peaceful stillness compassed everything and the night in its course was half spent, your all-powerful word, O Lord, leapt down from your royal throne."

4. One cannot reach this union without remarkable purity, and this purity is unattainable without vigorous mortification and nakedness regarding all creatures. "Taking off the bride's veil" and "wounding her at night," in her search and desire for her Spouse, signify this denudation and mortification, for she could not put on the new bridal veil without first removing her other one. Persons who refuse to go out at night in search for the Beloved and to divest and mortify their will, but rather seek the Beloved in their own bed and comfort, as did the bride [Sg. 3:1], will not succeed in finding him. As this soul declares, she found him when she departed in darkness and with longings of love.

CHAPTER 25

[A brief explanation of the third stanza.]

Third Stanza

> On that glad night,
> in secret, for no one saw me,
> nor did I look at anything,
> with no other light or guide
> than the one that burned in my heart.

Explanation

1. Still using the metaphor and simile of temporal night to describe this spiritual night, the soul enumerates and extols the good properties of the night. She found and made use of these properties by means of this night and thereby obtained her desired goal securely and quickly. We will list three of these properties here.

2. The first is that in this glad contemplative night, God conducts her by so solitary and secret a contemplation, one so remote and alien to all the senses, that nothing pertinent to the senses, nor any touch of creature, can reach or detain her on the route leading to the union of love.

3. The second property of this night, mentioned in this stanza, has as its cause the spiritual darkness of this night, in which all the faculties of the higher part of the soul are in obscurity. In neither looking nor being able to look at anything, the soul is not detained in her journey to God by anything outside of him, for in her advance she is free of hindrance from the forms and figures of the natural apprehensions, which are those

that usually prevent her from being always united with the being of God.

4. The third property is that, although the soul in her progress does not have the support of any particular interior light of the intellect, or of any exterior guide that may give her satisfaction on this lofty path—since these dense darknesses have deprived her of all satisfaction—love alone, which at this period burns by soliciting the heart for the Beloved, is what guides and moves her, and makes her soar to God in an unknown way along the road of solitude.

The next verse is:

On that glad night,[1]

---

1. The work ends here. John has achieved his goal, to explain the purification of the dark night.

The
Spiritual
Canticle

INTRODUCTION TO
THE SPIRITUAL CANTICLE

The Theme and Origin of the Poem

Though the lyric verses of *The Spiritual Canticle* do not mention Christ explicitly, St. John of the Cross, according to his commentary, sings in them about the loving exchange between a soul and Christ, the Bridegroom. The soul undoubtedly represents John himself and the stanzas disclose the colloquy of love that must have occurred between himself and Christ.

Asking ourselves why John expressed this loving communication in poetry, we find the clue to an answer in his Prologue. There he explains that the stanzas are utterances of love flowing from mystical understanding. In stanza 25, he tells how the Beloved can set the soul ablaze by a loving touch, like a hot spark leaping from a fire. The will is then enkindled in loving, desiring, praising, and thanking God. The bride calls these acts "flowings from the balsam of God." Born out of the mystical understanding that was communicated to John's soul in the touch of the spark, these stanzas or canticles are, then, like flowings or outpourings from the balsam of God.

St. Teresa in chapter 16 of her *Life* tells explicitly how the mystic sometimes feels the impulse to express in poetry a deep spiritual experience, even though talent as a poet may be lacking: "Oh, help me God! What is the soul like when it is in this state! It would want to be all tongues so as to praise the Lord. It speaks folly in a thousand holy ways, ever trying to find means of pleasing the one who thus possesses it. I know a person who though not a poet suddenly composed some deeply felt verses well expressing her pain."

Expression of the Ineffable

Although these canticles resulted from a love flowing out of abundant mystical understanding, they cannot declare fully the understanding or experience. John asks in the Prologue: "Who can describe in writing the understanding he [the Beloved] gives to loving souls in whom he dwells? And who can express with words the experience he imparts to them?

Who, finally, can explain the desires he gives them? Certainly, no one can! Not even they who receive these communications." Always, as John explains in stanza 7, there is an "I-don't-know-what" that strives to be articulated, something further to say, something unknown, not yet spoken, a sublime trace of God still uninvestigated but revealed to the mystic. The effort to convey the contents of the experience becomes sheer stammering.

Faced with an inability to make their experience clearly known and at the same time feeling a loving impulse to convey it outwardly, these persons who speak of mysteries and secrets seem to be uttering absurdities. But the apparent absurdities of the poetic images and similes are a more powerful means than rational explanations for expressing the mystical experience; they can suggest so much more about its contents. John, in fact, points out that his is the method of the Holy Spirit who, "unable to express the plenitude of his meaning in ordinary words, utters mysteries in strange figures and likenesses," as for example in the Song of Songs.

In fact the Song of Songs is the principal source of *The Spiritual Canticle*. In this biblical work John found an expression of his own profound experience, and also found the scenes, images, and words, even though sometimes foreign to his environment, with which to create his own work.

That the figures and similitudes of poetry speak about the inexpressible exchange of love between Christ and John of the Cross more adequately than do ordinary words does not mean that every mystic must be a poet. The work of art, as such, is the creation of the poet, not of the mystic. Still, the mystical understanding and experience will doubtless have an impact on the activity of the poet. The lines of poetry may flow from the impulse of the mystical understanding or they may be composed in the love that endures for some days after the spark of the divine touch has passed. This love, says John, lasts together with its effect a long while, and sometimes a day or two, or many days, though not always in the same degree of intensity.

A Story About Love

In the form of an eclogue, the poem tells a story of love between two lovers, bridegroom and bride. The story unfolds through dialogue between them. In this way John recounts, somewhat mysteriously, the history of his love for Christ, a love in response to Christ's love for him. Essentially dynamic, the love moves forward, marking degrees or stages of John's spiritual life, which develops along lines parallel with love and dependent on it. This movement of love sustains the poem and supplies the direction and framework for the stanzas. Although the verses uncover a personal story by describing the advance in love, they do not set forth explicitly every moment of communion with Christ. Nor do they present a precise temporal perspective; they do not reveal in their sequence a progressive chronological order, verse by verse, stanza by stanza. The development appears rather in blocks of stanzas that focus on some of the vibrant moments in the life of divine love.

The bride speaks in 32 of the stanzas, the bridegroom in 7, and creatures in 1. The stanzas contain both narration and supplication. The bride tells of her anxious search for her beloved, describes her encounters with him, the qualities of the beloved, and the gifts she receives from him. She beseeches the beloved to surrender and reveal himself, to free her from her enemies, from obstacles, and from all ties that impede union with him; she begs above all for a greater communion with him.

The bridegroom speaks at three places in the poem where a shift in the action occurs. His words bring about the union that the bride seeks; they have transforming power. He also gives himself with his words, in peace, solitude, and unreserved love,

The first 13 stanzas show a state of anxious, hurried searching. The two stanzas that follow express the joy of union, and they delay over it through the use of many adjectives and the absence of verbal activity. Then the poet returns to images of restlessness conveying the incompleteness of the union. Beginning with stanza 22, where full union takes place, the rhythm slows and the images turn inward: the bed, the inner wine cellar, the garden. The poem in this way moves between two extremes, one moment turning to the whole realm of nature, and the next concentrating on one tiny part. The first stanza bursts forth abruptly in interrogation and action, the last provides a scene of complete peace; it is in fact anticlimactic and gives a sense of relaxation, termination, and rest.

More precisely, the four phases of the action dealt with in the blocks of stanzas are: The bride goes out searching for her beloved to the mountains and the watersides, learning many things about him but never satisfied; this knowledge only increases her longings for him, wounds her with deeper love (stanzas 1-12). After all this searching and longing, she catches sight of him on the hill. Her condition changes; he is for her like mountains, lonely wooded valleys, strange islands, silent music, the tranquil night. Yet the bride and her beloved are not wholly free from disturbances, the foxes, the deadening north wind, the girls of Judea, the swift-winged birds, lions, stags, fears of night; all seek to unsettle the communion of love (stanzas 13-21). Ultimately the bride enters the sweet garden of her desire, laying her neck on the gentle arms of her beloved, and in the inner wine cellar drinks of her beloved. There he gives her his breast, and there teaches her a sweet, living knowledge. She is no longer seen or found on the common (stanzas 22-35). In the end she desires to go with her beloved to the mountain and the hill, further, deep into the thicket, and then on to the high caverns in the rock—there where he will show her and give the vision of his beauty in glory (stanzas 36-40).

This overall plan of the poem embodies four main aspects of the life of love. From the viewpoint of the communion of love between Christ and the soul we have: 1) the anxious loving search for the Beloved; 2) the first encounter with him, called the spiritual betrothal, and the life of union with him that is nonetheless disturbed by many outward and inward impediments; 3) perfect union with the Bridegroom, or the spiritual marriage, the mutual and total gift of self, various facets of the communion of love; 4) desire for perfect union with the Beloved in glory.

The poetic symbols delineate this development of love and represent the gracious gifts the soul receives from her Beloved. These gifts are the communications of knowledge and love: the favors, visits, wounds, and touches of love. The increasingly intimate communion with the divine Bridegroom is wrought by means of an increasingly elevated knowledge and love of him. First, such loving knowledge arises from the consideration of creatures; second, it flows from consideration of God's works manifested in the mysteries of faith, particularly the Incarnation; third, it originates with a touch of supreme knowledge of the divinity. As the loving knowledge of God grows in depth and power, the soul withdraws from every affection contrary to her good, which is the will of the divine Bridegroom.

The Time of Composition

In the confinement of his cramped prison cell in Toledo, John had to look inward for a feeling of expansion. What helped him were the images of the *Song of Songs*, a work he knew by heart: mountains, valleys, rivers, fountains, flowers—all that we associate with being outside, free in the open country. Rearranging these images, he began composing his own song based on them. The result was the first 31 stanzas of the *Spiritual Canticle*. Later, with writing materials supplied by a sympathetic guard, he jotted down these stanzas along with other poems he had composed there. Not long after the night that John escaped from his prison, the discalced Carmelite nuns in Beas read his little notebook of poems; they at once made copies of them. In the following years, at various times, John added more stanzas.

With regard to the last five stanzas, the story is told that while John was prior of Granada and was passing through Beas, he asked Madre Francisca de la Madre de Dios her manner of prayer. She answered simply that it consisted in beholding God's beauty and rejoicing that he possessed it. John so exulted in her answer that for several days he spoke sublime and wonderful things concerning the beauty of God. Carried away by love, he wrote five stanzas on this beauty, beginning with: "Let us rejoice, be-loved,/and let us go forth to behold ourselves in your beauty."

The Commentary

The first ones to read the *Canticle*, the Carmelite nuns in Beas, were in awe over its lines, recognizing in them something of astounding depth. What lay hidden behind these words that to some might seem absurdi-ties? They begged the poet for some enlightenment. How could they, left to themselves, probe deeply enough to catch all the meaning hidden in the rich symbols? Thus Fray John of the Cross began his commentary. At first in spiritual conferences, later in writing, he drew out the treasures contained in his verses. In the end, at the request of Madre Ana de Jesús, he compiled a complete commentary.

In the commentary, the Carmelite friar wishes to do no more than shed some general light on the meaning of his poem by interpreting the symbols. Translating the imagery verse by verse, he discloses the basic order of the poem, which, he assures us, corresponds to the personal experience of the poet and, in its general plan, to the common path that leads to spiritual perfection. In addition to his proposal in the prologue to give a commentary on the poem, he promises to dwell at length on some matters concerning prayer and its effects, making use of scholastic theology.

Shaping the commentary and the poem into a unified whole did not come easily to the master of spiritual theology. A lyric creation by a poet does not necessarily show concern for the logical demands of a theolo-gian. Finally, in an effort to present an orderly analysis of the evolution of the spiritual life, John rearranged the stanzas to establish more precise order. He did this while revising the first commentary he composed. The result is that two redactions of *The Spiritual Canticle* have been preserved for posterity.

Some think that the change of sequence in the stanzas has harmed the poetic spontaneity and inspiration of the poem. Whether or not this is true, the doctrinal underpinnings have been enhanced in the second version. Despite the improvement, though, some imprecision in the order of the stanzas still remains. In an attempt to explain the arrange-ment of the verses, John asserts that the soul begins with the practice of mortification and meditation, referred to in the first four stanzas, then walks along the paths and straits of love until stanza 13. But the first two stanzas do not speak of mortification and meditation. They speak clearly of the pains, longings, and straits of love. The condition alluded to in the first two stanzas is that of "impatient love." If any of these stanzas speak of mortification and meditation, they are stanzas 3 and 4. In stanza 7,

John speaks of a touch of supreme knowledge of the divinity, a favor belonging more properly to those stanzas in the general plan that describe a higher period of the spiritual life. Stanza 22 speaks of spiritual marriage, a state, in his teaching, far surpassing spiritual betrothal. Still in stanzas 27, 28, and 30, we find John speaking again, not precisely, of spiritual betrothal.

The stanzas in themselves do not have to be held hostage within the strict confines of the period designated for them in the commentary. The lines pulsating with impatient love need not apply only to the first period of searching; nothing prevents them from being uttered again in those absences of the Beloved that the soul suffers in the period of spiritual betrothal when the torment is greater because of a more intense love. The luxuriant images used in describing the abundant communication received in the state of spiritual betrothal could just as well apply to a communication received in the state of spiritual marriage.

This difficulty involved in attempting to fit the poetic work of art into the logical framework of the commentary calls for caution in any endeavor to determine the period of the spiritual life to which the stanzas refer, even though these periods are specified both at the beginning of the work in the *Theme* and in stanza 22.

The Elements of the Commentary

The chief elements constituting the commentary are:

1) After the particular quotation of each stanza a *general summary* of its meaning brings into relief its content and relation to the previous or following stanza.

2) A *detailed explanation* of each verse presents a literal interpretation of the words in relation to the narrative as a whole. Focusing on the various moments of the spiritual life to which the poem alludes, it may be separate from or united to the doctrinal clarifications.

3) The *doctrinal clarifications* seek to justify theologically the teaching contained in the explanation of the verse; in addition, they seek to accommodate the teaching as much as possible to the actual development of the spiritual life. With the use of texts from Sacred Scripture and through theoretical reasoning they enlarge considerably the doctrinal scope of the simple commentary. It is important to note these teachings, for they do not always correspond to the spiritual moment laid before us in the lines of the stanza. Sometimes these explanations are patent digressions forming something apart from the commentary on the verses. They become the lengthier explanations promised in the prologue about "some matters concerning prayer and its effects." More frequently they appear in immediate relation to the literary and doctrinal

content of the stanza. In these cases the additional elucidation suits well the spiritual moment described in the poem; but at the same time establishes general principles that do not belong to this moment alone, as for example in stanza 1, numbers 4-11.

4) Finally, the *introductions* placed before most of the stanzas mold them into a systematic whole. These introductions, with the exception of the one to stanzas 13 and 14, are proper to the revised version of the *Canticle* known as the second redaction, or *Canticle B*. In his second redaction, after quoting the entire poem, John also adds a few paragraphs under the title *Theme* that tell generally how the stanzas refer to the classic stages of the spiritual life. But keeping in mind all the elements that go to make up the commentary, one can expect and will find doctrine about a particular spiritual period in stanzas other than those ascribed to that period.

The Two Redactions of the Commentary

The two redactions of *The Spiritual Canticle,* commonly distinguished as *Canticle A* and *Canticle B,* differ from one another in both the sequence and the number of stanzas. Moreover, the commentary of the second redaction, *Canticle B,* incorporates more detail. *Canticle A* comprises 39 stanzas; *Canticle B,* 40, the additional one being stanza 11. The first 14 stanzas follow the same sequence in both redactions; the final seven stanzas also follow the same sequence. The reorganization of the stanzas occurs, then, in the middle section of the poem, from stanza 16 (or 15 in *Canticle A*) to stanza 33 (or 32 in *Canticle A*).

No one has ever seriously questioned the authenticity of the first redaction, but that of the second did come under debate, although with arguments that scholarship has shown to be unacceptable. No reason now exists for doubting that the revision is the work of John himself. The historical documentation in manuscripts and testimonies supporting the authorship of John of the Cross is plentiful and trustworthy. The style of the work, the language, the thought, are inimitably John's. The attempts made to attribute the work to some other author have either lacked a concrete historical foundation or failed to establish even the slightest similarity in style.

That John might review his writings and make additions and revisions should bring no surprise. We find an excellent example of his doing so in the *Codex of Sanlúcar de Barrameda* (a copy of *Canticle A*). Here in his handwriting are a number of marginal and interlinear corrections, changes, and additions. These paved the way for *Canticle B* and the developments made therein.

All the codices of both redactions state that the commentary was written at the request of Madre Ana de Jesús, prioress of the discalced Carmelite nuns in Granada, and they add the date 1584. As for the second redaction, it must have been written sometime in 1585-86, after the first redaction of the *Living Flame of Love*, since in the revised commentary on stanza 31 John refers to this latter work.

Clearer, better arranged, and more valuable from a doctrinal viewpoint, *Canticle B* best suits our purposes for this collection of John's works. The translation follows the *Codex of Jaén*, the most trustworthy copy of the second redaction.

The *Spiritual Canticle* may be divided this way:

I. The Search for the Beloved (stanzas 1-12).
> The initial burst into song; the bride laments the absence of her bridegroom.
> First steps of the spiritual journey.
> Longings and the weariness of impatient love.

II. Preparations for Perfect Union (stanzas 13-21).
> Encounters of loving union.
> Urgent desires for complete freedom from inner and outer obstacles.

III. Full Union (stanzas 22-40).
> The mutual, total surrender and gift of self in spiritual marriage.
> Comparison of the present with the past.
> Delights of union and desires for the vision of glory.

THE SPIRITUAL CANTICLE

This commentary on the stanzas that deal with the exchange of love between the soul and Christ, its Bridegroom, explains certain matters about prayer and its effects. It was written at the request of Mother Ana de Jesús, prioress of the discalced Carmelite nuns of St. Joseph's in Granada, in the year 1584.

PROLOGUE

1. These stanzas, Reverend Mother,[1] were obviously composed with a certain burning love of God. The wisdom and charity of God is so vast, as the Book of Wisdom states, that it reaches from end to end [Wis. 8:1], and the soul informed and moved by it bears in some way this very abundance and impulsiveness in her words. As a result, I do not plan to expound these stanzas in all the breadth and fullness that the fruitful spirit of love conveys to them. It would be foolish to think that expressions of love arising from mystical understanding, like these stanzas, are fully explainable. The Spirit of the Lord, who abides in us and aids our weakness, as St. Paul says [Rom. 8:26], pleads for us with unspeakable groanings in order to manifest what we can neither fully understand nor comprehend.

Who can describe in writing the understanding he gives to loving souls in whom he dwells? And who can express with words the experience he imparts to them? Who, finally, can explain the desires he gives them? Certainly, no one can! Not even they who receive these communications. As a result these persons let something of their experience overflow in figures, comparisons and similitudes, and from the abundance of their spirit pour out secrets and mysteries rather than rational explanations.

If these similitudes are not read with the simplicity of the spirit of knowledge and love they contain, they will seem to be absurdities rather than reasonable utterances, as will those comparisons of the divine Song

---

1. He is alluding to Mother Ana de Jesús (Lobera). She was born in Medina del Campo on November 25, 1545, and entered the Teresian Carmel on August 1, 1570. In 1575 she went to Beas as prioress, where she became an intimate friend of St. John of the Cross. She later served as prioress also in Granada and Madrid. In 1604 she went to France and Belgium where she made numerous foundations. She died in Brussels on March 4, 1621. The cause for her beatification is in process.

of Solomon and other books of Sacred Scripture where the Holy Spirit, unable to express the fullness of his meaning in ordinary words, utters mysteries in strange figures and likenesses. The saintly doctors, no matter how much they have said or will say, can never furnish an exhaustive explanation of these figures and comparisons, since the abundant meanings of the Holy Spirit cannot be caught in words. Thus the explanation of these expressions usually contains less than what they embody in themselves.

2. Since these stanzas, then, were composed in a love flowing from abundant mystical understanding, I cannot explain them adequately, nor is it my intention to do so. I only wish to shed some general light on them, since Your Reverence has desired this of me. I believe such an explanation will be more suitable. It is better to explain the utterances of love in their broadest sense so that each one may derive profit from them according to the mode and capacity of one's own spirit, rather than narrow them down to a meaning unadaptable to every palate. As a result, though we give some explanation of these stanzas, there is no reason to be bound to this explanation. For mystical wisdom, which comes through love and is the subject of these stanzas, need not be understood distinctly in order to cause love and affection in the soul, for it is given according to the mode of faith through which we love God without understanding him.

3. I will then be very brief, although I do intend to give a lengthier explanation when necessary and the occasion arises for a discussion of some matters concerning prayer and its effects. Since these stanzas refer to many of the effects of prayer, I ought to treat of at least some of these effects.

Yet, passing over the more common effects, I will briefly deal with the more extraordinary ones that take place in those who with God's help have passed beyond the state of beginners. I do this for two reasons: first, because there are many writings for beginners; second, because I am addressing Your Reverence, at your request. And our Lord has favored you and led you beyond the state of beginners into the depths of his divine love.

I hope that, although some scholastic theology is used here in reference to the soul's interior converse with God, it will not prove vain to speak in such a manner to the pure of spirit. Even though Your Reverence lacks training in scholastic theology, through which the divine truths are understood, you are not wanting in mystical theology, which is known through love and by which these truths are not only known but at the same time enjoyed.

4. And that my explanations—which I desire to submit to anyone with better judgment than mine and entirely to Holy Mother the Church—may be worthy of belief, I do not intend to affirm anything of myself or trust in any of my own experiences or in those of other spiritual persons whom I have known or heard of. Although I plan to make use of these experiences, I want to explain and confirm at least the more difficult matters through passages from Sacred Scripture. In using these passages, I will quote the words in Latin,[2] and then interpret them in regard to the matter being discussed.

I will now record the stanzas in full and then in due order quote each one separately before its explanation; similarly, I will quote each verse before commenting on it.

THE END OF THE PROLOGUE

Stanzas between the Soul and the Bridegroom

Bride

1. Where have you hidden,
Beloved, and left me moaning?
You fled like the stag
after wounding me;
I went out calling you, but you were gone.

2. Shepherds, you who go
up through the sheepfolds to the hill,
if by chance you see
him I love most,
tell him I am sick, I suffer, and I die.

3. Seeking my Love
I will head for the mountains and for watersides,
I will not gather flowers,
nor fear wild beasts;
I will go beyond strong men and frontiers.

---

2. In this second redaction of his work, John quotes in Latin those passages that so appear in Canticle A, but the new or modified scriptural passages, proper to this work, are quoted only in the vernacular. The change in procedure accords with that of the *Ascent* 2. 28.

4. O woods and thickets,
planted by the hand of my Beloved!
O green meadow,
coated, bright, with flowers,
tell me, has he passed by you?

5. Pouring out a thousand graces,
he passed these groves in haste;
and having looked at them,
with his image alone,
clothed them in beauty.

6. Ah, who has the power to heal me?
now wholly surrender yourself!
Do not send me
any more messengers,
they cannot tell me what I must hear.

7. All who are free
tell me a thousand graceful things of you;
all wound me more
and leave me dying
of, ah, I-don't-know-what behind their stammering.

8. How do you endure
O life, not living where you live,
and being brought near death
by the arrows you receive
from that which you conceive of your Beloved?

9. Why, since you wounded
this heart, don't you heal it?
And why, since you stole it from me,
do you leave it so,
and fail to carry off what you have stolen?

10. Extinguish these miseries,
since no one else can stamp them out;
and may my eyes behold you,
because you are their light,
and I would open them to you alone.

11. Reveal your presence,
and may the vision of your beauty be my death;
for the sickness of love
is not cured
except by your very presence and image.

12. O spring like crystal!
If only, on your silvered-over faces,
you would suddenly form
the eyes I have desired,
which I bear sketched deep within my heart.

13. Withdraw them, Beloved,
I am taking flight!

Bridegroom
    Return, dove,
    the wounded stag
    is in sight on the hill,
    cooled by the breeze of your flight.

Bride
    14. My Beloved, the mountains,
    and lonely wooded valleys,
    strange islands,
    and resounding rivers,
    the whistling of love-stirring breezes,

    15. the tranquil night
    at the time of the rising dawn,
    silent music,
    sounding solitude,
    the supper that refreshes, and deepens love.

    16. Catch us the foxes,
    for our vineyard is now in flower,
    while we fashion a cone of roses
    intricate as the pine's;
    and let no one appear on the hill.

    17. Be still, deadening north wind;
    south wind, come, you that waken love,
    breathe through my garden,
    let its fragrance flow,
    and the Beloved will feed amid the flowers.

18. You girls of Judea,
while among flowers and roses
the amber spreads its perfume,
stay away, there on the outskirts:
do not so much as seek to touch our thresholds.

19. Hide yourself, my love;
turn your face toward the mountains,
and do not speak;
but look at those companions
going with her through strange islands.

Bridegroom

20. Swift-winged birds,
lions, stags, and leaping roes,
mountains, lowlands, and river banks,
waters, winds, and ardors,
watching fears of night:

21. By the pleasant lyres
and the siren's song, I conjure you
to cease your anger
and not touch the wall,
that the bride may sleep in deeper peace.

22. The bride has entered
the sweet garden of her desire,
and she rests in delight,
laying her neck
on the gentle arms of her Beloved.

23. Beneath the apple tree:
there I took you for my own,
there I offered you my hand,
and restored you,
where your mother was corrupted.

Bride

24. Our bed is in flower,
bound round with linking dens of lions,
hung with purple,
built up in peace,
and crowned with a thousand shields of gold.

25. Following your footprints
maidens run along the way;
the touch of a spark,
the spiced wine,
cause flowings in them from the balsam of God.

26. In the inner wine cellar
I drank of my Beloved, and, when I went abroad
through all this valley
I no longer knew anything,
and lost the herd that I was following.

27. There he gave me his breast;
there he taught me a sweet and living knowledge;
and I gave myself to him,
keeping nothing back;
there I promised to be his bride.

28. Now I occupy my soul
and all my energy in his service;
I no longer tend the herd,
nor have I any other work
now that my every act is love.

29. If, then, I am no longer
seen or found on the common,
you will say that I am lost;
that, stricken by love,
I lost myself, and was found.

30. With flowers and emeralds
chosen on cool mornings
we shall weave garlands
flowering in your love,
and bound with one hair of mine.

31. You considered
that one hair fluttering at my neck;
you gazed at it upon my neck
and it captivated you;
and one of my eyes wounded you.

32. When you looked at me
your eyes imprinted your grace in me;
for this you loved me ardently;
and thus my eyes deserved
to adore what they beheld in you.

33. Do not despise me;
for if, before, you found me dark,
now truly you can look at me
since you have looked
and left in me grace and beauty.

Bridegroom

34. The small white dove
has returned to the ark with an olive branch;
and now the turtledove
has found its longed-for mate
by the green river banks.

35. She lived in solitude,
and now in solitude has built her nest;
and in solitude he guides her,
he alone, who also bears
in solitude the wound of love.

Bride

36. Let us rejoice, Beloved,
and let us go forth to behold ourselves in your beauty,
to the mountain and to the hill,
to where the pure water flows,
and further, deep into the thicket.

37. And then we will go on
to the high caverns in the rock
which are so well concealed;
there we shall enter
and taste the fresh juice of the pomegranates.

38. There you will show me
what my soul has been seeking,
and then you will give me,
you, my life, will give me there
what you gave me on that other day:

39. the breathing of the air,
the song of the sweet nightingale,
the grove and its living beauty
in the serene night,
with a flame that is consuming and painless.

40. No one looked at her,
nor did Aminadab appear;
the siege was still;
and the cavalry,
at the sight of the waters, descended.

THEME

1. These stanzas begin with a person's initial steps in the service of God and continue until the ultimate state of perfection is reached, which is spiritual marriage. They refer, consequently, to the three states or ways of spiritual exercise (purgative, illuminative, and unitive) through which a person passes in advancing to this state, and they describe some of the characteristics and effects of these ways.

2. The initial stanzas treat of the state of beginners, that of the purgative way.
The subsequent ones deal with the state of proficients, in which the spiritual betrothal is effected, that is, the illuminative way.
The stanzas following these refer to the unitive way, that of the perfect, where spiritual marriage takes place. This unitive way of the perfect follows the illuminative way of the proficients.
The final stanzas speak of the beatific state, that sole aspiration of a person who has reached perfection.

The beginning of the commentary
on the love songs between the bride and Christ, the Bridegroom.

STANZA 1

Introduction

1. The soul at the beginning of this song has grown aware of her obligations and observed that life is short [Jb. 14:5], the path leading to eternal life constricted [Mt. 7:14], the just one scarcely saved [1 Pt. 4:18],

the things of the world vain and deceitful [Eccl. 1:2], that all comes to an end and fails like falling water [2 Sam. 14:14], and that the time is uncertain, the accounting strict, perdition very easy, and salvation very difficult. She knows on the other hand of her immense indebtedness to God for having created her solely for himself, and that for this she owes him the service of her whole life; and because he redeemed her solely for himself she owes him every response of love. She knows, too, of the thousand other benefits by which she has been obligated to God from before the time of her birth, and that a good part of her life has vanished, that she must render an account of everything—of the beginning of her life as well as the later part—unto the last penny [Mt. 5:26], when God will search Jerusalem with lighted candles [Zeph. 1:12], and that it is already late—and the day far spent [Lk. 24:29]—to remedy so much evil and harm. She feels on the other hand that God is angry and hidden because she desired to forget him so in the midst of creatures. Touched with dread and interior sorrow of heart over so much loss and danger, renouncing all things, leaving aside all business, and not delaying a day or an hour, with desires and sighs pouring from her heart, wounded now with love for God, she begins to call her Beloved and say:

> Where have you hidden,
> Beloved, and left me moaning?
> you fled like the stag
> after wounding me;
> I went out calling you, but you were gone.

Commentary

2. In this first stanza the soul, enamored of the Word, her Bridegroom, the Son of God, longs for union with him through clear and essential vision. She records her longings of love and complains to him of his absence, especially since his love wounds her. Through this love she went out from all creatures and from herself, and yet she must suffer her Beloved's absence, for she is not freed from mortal flesh as the enjoyment of him in the glory of eternity requires.[1] Accordingly she says:

> Where have you hidden?

3. This is like saying: O Word, my Spouse, show me where you are hidden. In her petition she seeks the manifestation of his divine essence, because the hiding place of the Word of God is, as St. John asserts [Jn. 1:18], the bosom of the Father, that is, the divine essence, which is alien to every mortal eye and hidden from every human intellect. Isaiah

---

1. From this perspective, she considers, in looking back, the journey that was undertaken in order to reach her goal. The commentary on the last five stanzas treats more directly of this desire to be dissolved and to be with Christ.

proclaimed in speaking to God: *Indeed, you are a hidden God* [Is. 45:15].

It is noteworthy that, however elevated God's communications and the experiences of his presence are, and however sublime a person's knowledge of him may be, these are not God essentially, nor are they comparable to him because, indeed, he is still hidden to the soul. Hence, regardless of all these lofty experiences, a person should think of him as hidden and seek him as one who is hidden, saying: "Where have You hidden?"

Neither the sublime communication nor the sensible awareness of his nearness is a sure testimony of his gracious presence, nor are dryness and the lack of these a reflection of his absence. As a result, the prophet Job exclaims: *If he comes to me I shall not see him, and if he goes away I shall not understand* [Jb. 9:11].

4. It must be understood that if a person experiences some elevated spiritual communication or feeling or knowledge, it should not be thought that the experiences are similar to the clear and essential vision or possession of God, or that the communication, no matter how remarkable it is, signifies a more notable possession of God or union with him. It should be known too that if all these sensible and spiritual communications are wanting and individuals live in dryness, darkness, and dereliction, they must not thereby think that God is any more absent than in the former case. People, actually, cannot have certain knowledge from the one state that they are in God's grace or from the other that they are not. As the Wise Man says, *We do not know if we are worthy of love or abhorrence before God* [Eccl. 9:1].

The soul's chief aim in this verse is not to ask for sensible devotion, in which there is neither certain nor clear possession of the Bridegroom in this life, but for the manifest presence and vision of his divine essence, in which she desires to be secure and satisfied in the next life.

5. The bride of the divine Song of Songs had this very idea when, longing for union with the divinity of the Word, her Bridegroom, she asked the Father: *Show me where you pasture and where you rest at midday* [Sg. 1:7]. In requesting him to disclose his place of pasture, she wanted him to reveal the essence of the divine Word, his Son. For the Father does not pasture anywhere else than in his only Son, for the Son is the glory of the Father. And in begging that he show her his place of rest, she was asking to see that same Son. The Son is the only delight of the Father, who rests nowhere else nor is present in any other than in his beloved Son. He rests wholly in his Son, communicating to him his essence at midday, which is eternity, where he ever begets him and has begotten him.

When the soul, the bride, cries: "Where have you hidden?" she seeks this pasture, the Word, her Bridegroom, where the Father feeds in infinite glory, and she seeks the flowering bosom where he rests with infinite delight of love, deeply hidden from every mortal eye and every creature.

6. So this thirsting soul might find her Bridegroom and be united with him in this life through union of love insofar as possible, so she might slake her thirst with the drop of him that can be received in this life, it would be well for us to answer for her Bridegroom since she asks him, and point out the place where he is most surely hidden. She may then surely find him there with the perfection and delight possible in this life, and thus not wander in vain after the footprints of her companions [Sg. 1:7].

It should be known that the Word, the Son of God, together with the Father and the Holy Spirit, is hidden by his essence and his presence in the innermost being of the soul. Individuals who want to find him should leave all things through affection and will, enter within themselves in deepest recollection, and let all things be as though not. St. Augustine, addressing God in the *Soliloquies*, said: *I did not find you without, Lord, because I wrongly sought you without, who were within.*[2] God, then, is hidden in the soul, and there the good contemplative must seek him with love, exclaiming: "Where have you hidden?"

7. Oh, then, soul, most beautiful among all creatures, so anxious to know the dwelling place of your Beloved so you may go in search of him and be united with him, now we are telling you that you yourself are his dwelling and his secret inner room and hiding place. There is reason for you to be elated and joyful in seeing that all your good and hope is so close as to be within you, or better, that you cannot be without him. *Behold,* exclaims the Bridegroom, *the kingdom of God is within you* [Lk. 17:21]. And his servant, the apostle St. Paul, declares: *You are the temple of God* [2 Cor. 6:16].

8. It brings special happiness to a person to understand that God is never absent, not even from a soul in mortal sin (and how much less from one in the state of grace).

What more do you want, O soul! And what else do you search for outside, when within yourself you possess your riches, delights, satisfaction, fullness, and kingdom—your Beloved whom you desire and seek? Be joyful and gladdened in your interior recollection with him, for you have him so close to you. Desire him there, adore him there. Do not go in pursuit of him outside yourself. You will only become distracted and wearied thereby, and you shall not find him, or enjoy him more securely, or sooner, or more intimately than by seeking him within you. There is

2. This passage is from Pseudo-Augustine, *Soliloquiorum animae ad Deum* 1. 30, in Migne, PL 40. 888.

but one difficulty: Even though he does abide within you, he is hidden. Nevertheless, it is vital for you to know his hiding place so you may search for him there with assuredness. And this, soul, is also what you ask, when with the affection of love you question: "Where have you hidden?"

9. Yet you inquire: Since he whom my soul loves is within me, why don't I find him or experience him? The reason is that he remains concealed and you do not also conceal yourself in order to find and experience him. If you want to find a hidden treasure you must enter the hiding place secretly, and once you have discovered it, you will also be hidden just as the treasure is hidden. Since, then, your beloved Bridegroom is the treasure hidden in a field for which the wise merchant sold all his possessions [Mt. 13:44], and that field is your soul, in order to find him you should forget all your possessions and all creatures and hide in the secret inner room of your spirit and there, closing the door behind you (your will to all things), you should pray to your Father in secret [Mt. 6:6]. Remaining hidden with him, you will experience him in hiding, that is, in a way transcending all language and feeling.

10. Come, then, O beautiful soul! Since you know now that your desired Beloved lives hidden within your heart, strive to be really hidden with him, and you will embrace him within you and experience him with loving affection. Note that through Isaiah he calls you to this hiding place: *Come, enter into your inner rooms, shut the door behind you* (your faculties to all creatures), *hide yourself a little, even for a moment* [Is. 26:20], for this moment of life on earth. If, O soul, in this short space of time you keep diligent watch over your heart, as the Wise Man advises [Prv. 4:23], God will undoubtedly give you what he also promises further on through Isaiah: *I will give you hidden treasures and reveal to you the substance and mysteries of the secrets* [Is. 45:3]. The substance of the secrets is God himself, for God is the substance and concept of faith, and faith is the secret and the mystery. And when that which faith covers and hides from us is revealed—that which is perfect concerning God, spoken of by St. Paul [1 Cor. 13:10]—then the substance and mysteries of the secrets will be uncovered to the soul.

However much the soul hides herself, she will never in this mortal life attain to so perfect a knowledge of these mysteries as she will possess in the next. Nevertheless, if like Moses she hides herself in the cavern of the rock (in real imitation of the perfect life of the Son of God, her Bridegroom), she will merit that, while he protects her with his right hand, God will show her his shoulders [Ex. 33:22-23], that is, he will bring her to the high perfection of union with the Son of God, her Bridegroom, and transformation in him through love. In this union she experiences such closeness to him and is so instructed and wise in his mysteries that, as for knowing him in this life, she has no need to say, "Where have you hidden?"

11. You have been told, O soul, of the conduct you should observe if you want to find the Bridegroom in your hiding place. Still, if you want to hear this again, listen to a word abounding in substance and inaccessible truth: Seek him in faith and love, without desiring to find satisfaction in anything, or delight, or desiring to understand anything other than what you ought to know. Faith and love are like the blind person's guides. They will lead you along a path unknown to you, to the place where God is hidden. Faith, the secret we mentioned,[3] is comparable to the feet by which one journeys to God, and love is like one's guide. In dealing with these mysteries and secrets of faith, the soul will merit through love the discovery of the content of faith, that is, the Bridegroom whom she desires to possess in this life through the special grace of divine union with God, as we said,[4] and in the next life through the essential glory, by which she will rejoice in him not in a hidden way, but face to face [1 Cor. 13:12].

In the meantime, even though the soul reaches union in this life (the highest state attainable here below), she always exclaims; "Where have You hidden?" For even in the state of union he is still hidden from her, in the bosom of the Father, as we said,[5] which is how she wants to enjoy him in the next life.

12. You do very well, O soul, to seek him ever as one hidden, for you exalt God and approach very near him when you consider him higher and deeper than anything you can reach. Hence pay no attention, neither partially nor entirely, to anything your faculties can grasp. I mean that you should never seek satisfaction in what you understand about God, but in what you do not understand about him. Never pause to love and delight in your understanding and experience of God, but love and delight in what you cannot understand or experience of him. Such is the way, as we said,[6] of seeking him in faith. However surely it may seem that you find, experience, and understand God, because he is inaccessible and concealed you must always regard him as hidden, and serve him who is hidden in a secret way. Do not be like the many foolish ones who, in their lowly understanding of God, think that when they do not understand, taste, or experience him, he is far away and utterly concealed. The contrary belief would be truer. The less distinct is their understanding of him, the closer they approach him, since in the words of the prophet

---

3. In no. 10.
4. In no. 10.
5. In no. 3.
6. In no. 11.

David, *he made darkness his hiding place* [Ps. 18:11]. Thus in drawing near him you will experience darkness because of the weakness of your eye.

You do well, then, at all times, in both adversity and prosperity, whether spiritual or temporal, to consider God as hidden, and call after him thus:

> Where have you hidden,
> Beloved, and left me moaning?

13. She calls him "Beloved" to move him more to answer her prayer. When God is loved he very readily answers the requests of his lover. This he teaches through St. John: *If you abide in me, ask whatever you want and it shall be done unto you* [Jn. 15:7]. You can truthfully call God Beloved when you are wholly with him, do not allow your heart attachment to anything outside of him, and thereby ordinarily center your mind on him. This is why Delilah asked Samson how he could say he loved her, since his spirit was not with her [Jgs. 16:15], and this spirit includes the mind and the affection.

Some call the Bridegroom beloved when he is not really their beloved because their heart is not wholly set on him. As a result their petition is not of much value in his sight. They do not obtain their request until they keep their spirit more continually with God through perseverance in prayer, and their heart with its affectionate love more entirely set on him. Nothing is obtained from God except by love.

14. It is noteworthy of her next remark, "and left me moaning," that the absence of the Beloved causes continual moaning in the lover. Since she loves nothing outside of him, she finds no rest or relief in anything. This is how we recognize persons who truly love God: if they are content with nothing less than God. But what am I saying, if they are content? Even if they possess everything they will not be content; in fact the more they have, the less satisfied they will be. Satisfaction of heart is not found in the possession of things, but in being stripped of them all and in poverty of spirit. Since perfection consists in this poverty of spirit, in which God is possessed by a very intimate and special grace, the soul, having attained it, lives in this life with some satisfaction, although not complete. For David, in spite of all his perfection, hoped to have this fullness in heaven, saying: *When your glory appears, I shall be filled* [Ps. 17:15].

As a result, the peace, tranquility, and satisfaction of heart attainable in this life is insufficient to prevent the soul from moaning within itself—although this moan may be tranquil and painless—hoping for what it lacks.[7] Moaning is connected with hope, and the Apostle affirmed that he

---

7. This moaning of hope remains even in the highest stage of the spiritual life; cf. F. 1. 27.

and others moaned even though they were perfect: *We ourselves who have the first fruits of the spirit moan within ourselves, hoping for the adoption of the children of God* [Rom. 8:23].

The soul, then, bears this moan within herself, in her enamored heart. For there where love wounds is the moan rising from the wound, and it ever cries out in the feeling of his absence; especially when the soul, after the taste of some sweet and delightful communication of the Bridegroom, suffers his absence and is left alone and dry. She thus says:

You fled like the stag

15. It is noteworthy that in the Song of Songs the bride compares the Bridegroom to the stag and the mountain goat: *My beloved is like a gazelle or a young stag* [Sg. 2:9]. She makes this comparison not only because he is withdrawn and solitary and flees from companions like the stag, but also because of the swiftness with which he shows and then hides himself. He usually visits devout souls in order to gladden and liven them, and then leaves in order to try, humble, and teach them. Because of his visits his withdrawals are felt with keener sorrow, as is evident in the following verse: After wounding me;

16. This is like saying: The pain and sorrow I ordinarily suffer in your absence was not enough for me, but having inflicted on me a deeper wound of love with your arrow, and increasing my desire to see you, you flee as swiftly as the stag and do not let yourself be captured even for a moment.

17. In further explanation of this verse, it should be known that besides the many other different kinds of visits God grants to the soul, in which he wounds and raises it up in love, he usually bestows some secret touches of love that pierce and wound it like fiery arrows, leaving it wholly cauterized by the fire of love. And these wounds, mentioned here, are properly called wounds of love.[8] They so inflame the will in its affection that it burns up in this flame and fire of love. So intense is this burning that the soul is seemingly consumed in that flame, and the fire makes it go out of itself, wholly renews it, and changes its manner of being, as in the case of the phoenix that burns itself in the fire and rises anew from the ashes. David said in this regard: *My heart was inflamed and my reins have been changed, and I was brought to nothing, and I knew not* [Ps. 73:21-22].

18. The appetites and affections, which the prophet refers to as reins, are all changed to divine ones in that inflammation of the heart, and the

---

8. The wounds of love so frequently mentioned in this work are equivalent for the most part to the touches of love mentioned in the *Ascent* and *Dark Night*. The "moanings," "sore wounds," and "sickness" refer to these graces.

soul, through love, is brought to nothing, knowing nothing save love. The change of these reins at this time is accompanied by a kind of immense torment and yearning to see God. So extreme is this torment that love seems to be unbearably rigorous with the soul, not because it has wounded her—she rather considers these wounds to be favorable to her health—but because it left her thus suffering with love, and did not slay her for the sake of her seeing and being united with him in the life of perfect love. In stressing or declaring her sorrow, she says, "After wounding me," that is, leaving me thus wounded, thus dying with wounds of love for you, you have hidden as swiftly as the stag.

19. This feeling is so strong because in the love-wound that God produces in the soul, the affection of the will rises with sudden rapidity toward the possession of the Beloved, whose touch was felt. Just as quickly, she feels his absence and the impossibility of possessing him here as she wants. And together with this feeling, she then experiences "moaning" over his absence. These visits are not like others in which God refreshes and satisfies the soul. He bestows these to wound more than heal and afflict more than satisfy, since they serve to quicken the knowledge and increase the appetite (consequently the sorrow and longing) to see God.

These are termed spiritual wounds of love and are very delightful and desirable. The soul would desire to be ever dying a thousand deaths from these thrusts of the lance, for they make her go out of herself and enter into God. She explains this in the following verse:

I went out calling you, but you were gone.

20. No medicine can be gotten for these wounds of love except from the One who causes them. Thus the wounded soul, strengthened from the fire caused by the wound, went out after her Beloved who wounded her, calling for him that he might heal her.

This spiritual departure, it should be pointed out, refers to the two ways of going after God: one consists of a departure from all things, effected through an abhorrence and contempt for them; the other of going out from oneself through self-forgetfulness, which is achieved by the love of God. When the love of God really touches the soul, as we are saying, it so raises her up that it not only impels her to go out from self in this forgetfulness, but even draws her away from her natural supports, manners, and inclinations, thus inducing her to call after God.

Accordingly, this verse is like saying: My Spouse, in that touch and wound of your love you have not only drawn my soul away from all things, but have also made it go out from self—indeed, it even seems that you draw it out of the body—and you have raised it up to yourself while it was calling after you, now totally detached so as to be attached to you.

"But you were gone."

21. This is like saying: At the time I desired to hold fast to your presence I could not find you, and the detachment from one without attachment to the other left me suspended in air and suffering, without any support from you or from myself.

What the soul refers to as going out in search of the Beloved, the bride of the Song of Songs calls "rising": *I will rise and seek him whom my soul loves, by going about the city, through the squares and the suburbs. But,* she adds, *I did not find him, and they wounded me* [Sg. 3:2; 5:6-7]. The rising of the soul, the bride, is spiritually understood as rising from the lowly to the sublime. The same is understood of the soul's words here, "I went out," that is, from her lowly manner and love to the sublime love of God.

Yet the bride states that she was wounded because she did not find him. And the soul also declares that she was wounded with love and he left her thus. The loving soul lives in constant suffering at the absence of her Beloved, for she is already surrendered to him and hopes for the reward of that surrender: the surrender of the Beloved to her. Yet he does not do so. Now lost to herself and to all things for the sake of her loved one, she has gained nothing from her loss, since she does not possess him.

22. The suffering and pain arising from God's absence is usually so intense in those who are nearing the state of perfection at the time of these divine wounds that they would die if the Lord did not provide. Since the palate of their will is healthy and their spirit is cleansed and well prepared for God, and they have been given some of the sweetness of divine love, which they desire beyond all measure, they suffer beyond all measure. An immense good is shown them, as through a crevice, but not granted them. Thus their pain and torment is unspeakable.

STANZA 2

Shepherds, you who go
up through the sheepfolds to the hill,
if by chance you see
him I love most,
tell him I am sick, I suffer, and I die.

Commentary

1. The soul in this stanza desires the advantage of intercessors and intermediaries with her Beloved by begging them to bring him word of her grief and pain. This is the trait of a lover: When she herself cannot converse with her loved one, she does so through the best means

possible. The soul wants to take advantage of her desire, affections, and moanings as messengers that know so well how to manifest to the Beloved the secret of the lover's heart. She entreats them to go, crying:

Shepherds, you who go

2. She calls her desires, affections, and moanings "shepherds," because they pasture the soul with spiritual goods—a shepherd or pastor is one who feeds or pastures—and by means of these yearnings God communicates himself to her and gives her the divine pasture. Without them he communicates little to her.

"You who go," is like saying, you that go out through pure love. Not all the affections and desires reach him, but only those that go out through true love.

up through the sheepfolds to the hill,

3. She calls the hierarchies and choirs of angels "sheepfolds." Through them, from choir to choir, our moanings and prayers go to God. She refers to God as "the hill," because he is the supreme height and in him, as on a hill, one has a view of all things and of both the higher and the lower sheepfolds. Our prayers rise up to him through the angels who offer them to him, as we said. The angel told Tobias: *When you were praying with tears and burying the dead, I was offering your prayer to God* [Tb. 12:12].

These shepherds can also be the angels who carry not only our messages to God but also God's messages to us. They feed our souls, like good shepherds, with sweet communications and inspirations from God—they are the means by which God grants them—and they protect us from the wolves, which are the devils.

Whether, then, these shepherds refer to the affections or to the angels, the soul longs that they all be helps and intermediaries with her Beloved. She pleads with them all:

if by chance you see

4. This means: If by my good luck you so reach his presence that he sees and hears you. It is noteworthy that even though God has knowledge and understanding of all, and even sees the very thoughts of the soul, as Moses asserts [Dt. 31:21], it is said when he provides a remedy for us in our needs that he sees them, and when he answers our prayers that he hears them. Not all needs and petitions reach the point at which God, in hearing, grants them. They must wait until in his eyes they arrive at the suitable time, season, and number, and then it is said that he sees and hears them.[1] This is evident in Exodus. After the 400 years in which the children of

---

1. Here the lover is reminded that the search for the Beloved involves a long journey in which love only gradually matures.

Israel had been afflicted by their slavery in Egypt, God declared to Moses: *I have seen the affliction of my people and have come down to free them* [Ex. 3:7-8], even though he had always seen it.

And St. Gabriel, too, told Zechariah not to fear, because God had heard his prayer and given him the son for whom he had prayed those many years, even though God had always heard that prayer [Lk. 1:13]. Every soul should know that even though God does not answer its prayer immediately, he will not on that account fail to answer it at the opportune time if it does not become discouraged and give up its prayer. He is, as David remarks, *a helper in opportune times and tribulations* [Ps. 9:10].[2]

The soul means in saying "If by chance you see" that if by chance the time is at hand for my petition to be heard by
> him I love most,

5. That is, by him I love more than all things. She loves him more than all things when nothing intimidates her in doing and suffering for love of him whatever is for his service. And when she can also say truthfully what she proclaims in the following verse, it is a sign that she loves him above all things. The verse is:
> tell him I am sick, I suffer, and I die.

6. In this line the soul discloses three needs: sickness, suffering, and death. The soul that truly loves God with some perfection usually suffers from his absence in three ways, with respect to the three faculties of the soul: intellect, will, and memory.

With respect to the intellect, she says she is sick because she does not see God, the health of the intellect. God says through David: *I am your health* [Ps. 35:3].

With respect to the will, she declares she suffers because she does not possess God, the will's refreshment and delight. David also says: *You shall fill us with the torrent of your delight* [Ps. 36:9].

With respect to the memory, she says she dies because she suffers a distress that resembles death on remembering that she lacks all the goods of the intellect (the vision of God) and the delights of the will (the possession of God), and it is highly possible, among the dangers and sinful occasions of this life, to be without him forever. For she sees her lack of the sure and perfect possession of God, who, as Moses affirms, is the soul's life: *He is certainly your life* [Dt. 30:20].

7. Jeremiah also indicated these three kinds of needs in Lamentations, saying: *Remember my poverty, the wormwood, and the gall* [Lam. 3:19].

---

2. This teaching applies, of course, to the most significant petition, the prayer for full union with the Beloved.

The poverty relates to the intellect because to the intellect belong the riches of the wisdom of the Son of God, *in whom,* as St. Paul says, *are hidden all the treasures of God* [Col. 2:3].

The wormwood, a most bitter herb, refers to the will because to this faculty belongs the sweetness of the possession of God. When this possession is lacking, the will is left in bitterness. And the fact that bitterness pertains to the will is understood spiritually in the Apocalypse when the angel told St. John that eating the book would bring bitterness to the belly [Rv. 10:9], meaning to the will.

The gall refers not only to the memory but to all a person's faculties and strength. Gall signifies the death of the soul, as Moses indicates, speaking of the condemned in Deuteronomy: *Their wine will be the gall of dragons and the incurable poison of asps* [Dt. 32:33]. Gall refers to their lack of God, which is death to the soul.

These three needs and sufferings are based on the three theological virtues (faith, charity, and hope) that reside in the three faculties of the soul in the order given here, intellect, will, and memory.

8. It should be pointed out that in this verse the soul does no more than disclose to the Beloved her need and suffering. The discreet lover does not care to ask for what she lacks and desires, but only indicates this need so the Beloved may do what he pleases. When the Blessed Virgin spoke to her beloved Son at the wedding feast at Cana in Galilee, she did not ask directly for the wine, but merely remarked: *They have no wine* [Jn. 2:3]. And the sisters of Lazarus did not send to ask our Lord to cure their brother, but to tell him that Lazarus whom he loved was sick [Jn. 11:3]. There are three reasons for this: First, the Lord knows what is suitable for us better than we do; second, the Beloved has more compassion when he beholds the need and resignation of a soul that loves him; third, the soul is better safeguarded against self-love and possessiveness by indicating its lack, rather than asking for what in its opinion is wanting. The soul, now, does likewise by just indicating her three needs. Her words are similar to saying: Tell my Beloved, since I am sick and he alone is my health, to give me health; and, since I suffer and he alone is my joy, to give me joy; and, since I die and he alone is my life, to give me life.

STANZA 3

Seeking my Love
I will head for the mountains and for watersides,
I will not gather flowers,
nor fear wild beasts;
I will go beyond strong men and frontiers.

Commentary

1. The soul is aware that neither her sighs and prayers nor the help of good intermediaries, about which she spoke in the first and second stanzas, are sufficient for her to find her Beloved. Since the desire in which she seeks him is authentic and her love intense, she does not want to leave any possible means untried. The soul that truly loves God is not slothful in doing all she can to find the Son of God, her Beloved. Even after she has done everything, she is dissatisfied and thinks she has done nothing.

And accordingly in this third stanza she says that she herself through works desires to look for him, and she describes the method to be employed in order to find him: She must practice the virtues and engage in the spiritual exercises of both the active and the contemplative life. As a result she must tolerate no delights or comforts, and the powers and snares of her three enemies (the world, the devil, and the flesh) must neither detain nor impede her. She says,

> Seeking my love

That is, seeking my Beloved, and so on.

2. She points out here that for the attainment of God it is not enough to pray with the heart and the tongue or receive favors from others, but that together with this a soul must through its own efforts do everything possible. God usually esteems the work persons do by themselves more than many other works done for them. And mindful of the words of the Beloved, *Seek and you shall find* [Lk. 11:9], the soul decides to go out searching for him in the way we mentioned, to seek him through works that she may not be left without finding him. Many desire that God cost them no more than words, and even these they say badly. They desire to do for him scarcely anything that might cost them something. Some would not even rise from a place of their liking if they were not to receive thereby some delight from God in their mouth and heart. They will not even take one step to mortify themselves and lose some of their satisfactions, comforts, and useless desires.

Yet, unless they go in search for God, they will not find him, no matter how much they cry out for him. The bride of the Song of Songs cried after him, but did not find him until she went out looking for him. She affirms: *In my bed by night I sought him whom my soul loves; I sought him and did not find him. I will rise up and go about the city; in the suburbs and the squares I will look for him whom my soul loves* [Sg. 3:1-2]. And she says that after undergoing some trials she found him [Sg. 3:4].

3. Those who seek God and yet want their own satisfaction and rest seek him at night and thus will not find him. Those who look for him

through the practice and works of the virtues and get up from the bed of their own satisfaction and delight seek him by day and thus will find him. What is not found at night appears during the day. The Bridegroom himself points this out in the Book of Wisdom: *Wisdom is bright and never fades and is easily seen by them that love her, and found by them that seek her. She goes out before them that covet her that she might first show herself to them. Those who awake early in the morning to seek her shall not labor, because they will find her seated at the door of their house* [Wis. 6:12-14]. This passage indicates that when the soul has departed from the house of her own will and the bed of her own satisfaction, outside she will find divine Wisdom, the Son of God, her Spouse. As a result, she says here: "Seeking my Love"

I will head for the mountains and for watersides,

4. The mountains, which are high, refer to the virtues: first, because of their height; second, because of the difficulty and labor one undergoes in climbing them. She says she will exercise the contemplative life by means of these virtues.

The watersides, which are low, refer to the mortifications, penances, and spiritual exercises by which she says she will practice the active life, joined with the contemplative life that she mentioned. To seek God in the right way and acquire the virtues both are necessary.

These words, then, are like saying: Seeking my Beloved, I will both practice the high virtues and humble myself by lowly mortifications and humble exercises.

She recites this line because the way to look for God is to do good works for him and mortify evil within oneself in this manner:

I will not gather flowers,

5. Since seeking God demands a heart naked, strong, and free from all evils and goods that are not purely God, the soul speaks in this and the following verses of the freedom and fortitude one should possess in looking for him.

She declares she will not gather the flowers she sees along the way. The flowers are all the gratifications, satisfactions, and delights that may be offered to her in this life and will hinder her should she desire to gather and accept them. They are of three kinds: temporal, sensory, and spiritual. All three occupy the heart and hinder the spiritual nakedness required for the direct way of Christ, if the soul pays attention to them or becomes attached. Consequently she says that in order to seek him she will not gather these things. This line is equivalent to saying: I will not set my heart on the riches and goods the world offers, neither will I tolerate the pleasures and delights of my flesh, nor will I pay heed to the satisfactions and consolations of my spirit in a way that may detain me from seeking my Love in the mountains and riversides of virtues and trials.

She makes this declaration in order to take the advice the prophet David gives those who journey along this path: *Divitiae si affluent, nolite cor apponere* (If riches abound, do not set your heart on them) [Ps. 62:10]. These riches refer to both sensory and temporal goods and to spiritual consolation.

It should be known that not only are temporal goods and bodily delights contradictory to the path leading to God, but so also are spiritual consolations, if possessed or sought with attachment, an obstacle to the way of the cross of Christ, the Bridegroom. Those who are to advance must not gather these flowers. More than this, they must also have the courage and fortitude to say:

> nor fear wild beasts;
> I will go beyond strong men and frontiers.

6. In these verses she records the soul's three enemies: the world, the devil, and the flesh. They are causes of war and hardship along the road. The wild beasts refer to the world, the strong men to the devil, and the frontiers to the flesh.

7. She calls the world "wild beasts" because in the imagination of the soul that begins to tread the path leading to God the world is pictured as wild animals threatening and scaring her. The world frightens her principally in three ways:

First, it makes her think she must live without its favor, and lose her friends, reputation, importance, and even wealth.

Second, through another beast, no less ferocious, it makes her wonder how she will ever endure the permanent lack of the consolations and delights of the world and all its comforts.

Third, which is still worse, it makes her think that tongues will rise up against her and mock her, there will be many remarks and jeers, and she will be considered almost worthless.

These fears are brought before some souls in such a way that not only does persevering against these wild beasts become most difficult, but so does being able to get started on the journey.

8. Yet some generous souls will be faced with other wild beasts, more interior and spiritual: hardships and temptations and many kinds of trials through which they must pass. God sends these to those he wants to raise to high perfection by trying them like gold in the fire. According to David, *Multae tribulationes justorum* (Many are the tribulations of the just), *but out of these the Lord will deliver them* [Ps. 34:19]. Yet the truly loving soul, esteeming her Beloved above all things, trusting in his love and friendship, does not find it hard to say: "Nor fear wild beasts," and "I will go beyond strong men and frontiers."

9. She calls devils, the second enemy, "strong men" because they strive mightily to entrap her on this road and also because their temptations are stronger and their wiles more baffling than those of the world and the flesh and, finally, because the devils reinforce themselves with these other two enemies, the world and the flesh, in order to wage a rugged war.

David, in alluding to them, calls them strong men: *Fortes quaesierunt animam meam* (The strong men sought after my soul) [Ps. 54:3]. The prophet Job also remarked concerning this strength that there is no power on earth comparable to that of the devil, who was made to fear no one [Jb. 41:25]; that is, no human strength is comparable to his. Only divine power is sufficient to conquer him and only divine light can understand his wiles.

A soul that must overcome the devil's strength will be unable to do so without prayer, nor will it be able to understand his deceits without mortification and humility. St. Paul counsels the faithful: *Induite vos armaturam Dei, ut possitis stare adversus insidias diaboli, quoniam non est nobis colluctatio adversus carnem et sanguinem* (Put on the armor of God that you may be able to resist the wiles of the devil, for this struggle is not against flesh and blood) [Eph. 6:11-12]. By blood he means the world, and by the armor of God, prayer and the cross of Christ, in which are found the humility and mortification we mentioned.[1]

10. The soul affirms also that she will pass by frontiers, which refer to the natural rebellions of the flesh against the spirit. As St. Paul says: *Caro enim concupiscit adversus spiritum* [Gal. 5:17], which is like saying: The flesh covets against the spirit and sets itself up as though on the frontier to oppose the spiritual journey. A person must pass these frontiers by breaking through these difficulties and throwing down with willful strength and determination all sensory appetites and natural affections. In the measure that these are present in the soul, the spirit is impeded by them and cannot go on to true life and spiritual delight. St. Paul indicated this clearly: *Si spiritu facta carnis mortificaveritis, vivetis* (If by the spirit you mortify the inclinations and appetites of the flesh, you shall live) [Rom. 8:13].

Such is the method the soul, in this stanza, claims she must follow in order to seek her Beloved on this road. The method, in sum, consists of steadfastness and courage in not stooping to gather flowers; of bravery in not fearing the wild beasts; of strength in passing by strong men and frontiers; and of the sole intention to head for the mountains and watersides of virtues, as we explained.

---

1. In no. 4; John enlarges the perspective of the stanzas so as to comment on the whole spiritual journey, from the beginner afraid to set out to the truly loving soul.

STANZA 4

O woods and thickets,
Planted by the hand of my Beloved!
O green meadow,
Coated, bright, with flowers,
Tell me, has he passed by you?

Commentary

1. The soul has made known the manner of preparing oneself to begin this journey: to pursue delights and satisfactions no longer, and to overcome temptations and difficulties through fortitude. This is the practice of self-knowledge, the first requirement of advancing to the knowledge of God. Now, in this stanza, she begins to walk along the way of the knowledge and consideration of creatures that leads to the knowledge of her Beloved, the Creator.[1]

On this spiritual road the consideration of creatures is first in order after the exercise of self-knowledge. The soul thereby advances in the knowledge of God by considering his greatness and excellence manifested in creatures, as is brought out in that passage of St. Paul: *Invisibilia enim ipsius a creatura mundi, per ea quae facta sunt intellecta conspiciuntur* (The invisible things of God are known by the soul through creatures, both visible and invisible) [Rom. 1:20].

She addresses creatures, then, in this stanza, asking them about her Beloved. And it is noteworthy, as St. Augustine says, that the soul's interrogation of creatures is the reflection about the Creator that it makes through them.[2] This stanza contains a meditation on the elements and other inferior creatures, on the heavens together with the other material things in them that God created, and also on the heavenly spirits.

O woods and thickets

2. She calls the elements (earth, water, air, and fire) "woods," because like pleasant woods they are thickly populated with creatures. She labels these creatures "thickets" because of their vast number and the notable difference among them in each of the elements. On the earth there are

---

1. After the practice of self-knowledge, the soul seeks knowledge of God. The stanzas that follow define, in retrospect, some steps in the search for knowledge of the Beloved: asking irrational creatures, without satisfaction (4-6); asking rational creatures, still without satisfaction (7-8); asking for the Beloved in person, who alone can fill the heart with presence and communion, not just information (9-11).

2. Cf. Pseudo-Augustine, *Soliloquiorum animae ad Deum* 1. 31, in Migne, 40. 888.

countless varieties of animals and plants; in the water, numberless kinds of fish; and in the air, a remarkable diversity of birds; and the element fire concurs with the others for the animation and preservation of these creatures. Each kind of animal lives in its element and is placed and planted in it as in the woods and region where it is born and nurtured. Indeed, God commanded this when he created the elements. He ordered the earth to produce the plants and the animals; and the sea and water, the fish; and he made the air a habitation for birds [Gn. 1:11-12, 20-21, 24]. Seeing that as he commanded it was done, the soul says in the following verse:

> planted by the hand of my Beloved!

3. This verse contains the following reflection: Only the hand of God, her Beloved, was able to create this diversity and grandeur. It is noteworthy that she deliberately says "by the hand of my Beloved." Although God often acts through the hand of another—as through those of angels and humans—he never created, nor does he carry on this work of creation by any other hand than his own. This reflection on creatures, this observing that they are things made by the very hand of God, her Beloved, strongly awakens the soul to love him. She then continues:

> O green meadow,

4. This verse refers to her reflection on the heavens. She calls them a "green meadow" because the created things in them are as green growing plants that neither die nor fade with time, and in them, as in cool green meadows, the just find their recreation and delight. The diversity of the beautiful stars and other heavenly planets is also included in this meditation.

5. The Church likewise uses the word "green" to express heavenly things. In praying to God for the souls of the faithful departed, she says, speaking to them: *Constituat vos Dominus inter amoena virentia*, which means: May God set you in delightful green places.[3] And she says that this green meadow is also

> coated, bright, with flowers,

6. By these "flowers" she understands the angels and saintly souls that adorn and beautify that place like a costly enamel on a vase of fine gold.

> tell me, has he passed by you?

7. This question is the reflection mentioned above; it is similar to saying: Tell me of the excellent qualities he has created in you.

---

3. A modified version of the *Ordo commendationis animae* in the *Rituale Romanum* 6. 7.

STANZA 5

Pouring out a thousand graces,
he passed these groves in haste;
and having looked at them,
with his image alone,
clothed them in beauty.

Commentary

1. In this stanza the creatures answer the soul. Their answer, as St. Augustine also declares in that same place, is the testimony they in themselves give the soul of God's grandeur and excellence.[1] It is for this testimony that she asked in her reflections. The substance of this stanza is: God created all things with remarkable ease and brevity, and in them he left some trace of who he is, not only in giving all things being from nothing, but even by endowing them with innumerable graces and qualities, making them beautiful in a wonderful order and unfailing dependence on one another. All of this he did through his own Wisdom, the Word, his only begotten Son by whom he created them. She then says:
Pouring out a thousand graces,

2. These "thousand graces" she says he was pouring out refer to the numberless multitude of creatures. She records the high number, a thousand, to indicate their multitude. She calls them graces because of the many graces he has endowed creatures with. Pouring these out, that is, stocking the whole world with them,
he passed these groves in haste;

3. To "pass the groves" is to create the elements, which are here termed "groves." She declares that he passed by them pouring out a thousand graces because he adorned them with all the creatures, for these groves are favored with graces. And, in addition, he poured out on them a thousand graces by giving them the power to concur in generation and conservation.
And she says "he passed" because creatures are like a trace of God's passing. Through them one can track down his grandeur, might, wisdom, and other divine attributes.
She declares that this passing was "in haste." Creatures are the lesser works of God because he made them as though in passing. The greater works, in which he manifested himself more and to which he gave greater attention, were those of the Incarnation of the Word and the mysteries

---

1. See Pseudo-Augustine, *Soliloquiorum animae ad Deum* 1. 31, in Migne, PL 40. 888.

of the Christian faith. Compared to these, all the others were done as though in passing and with haste.

> and having looked at them,
> with his image alone,
> clothed them in beauty.

4. St. Paul says: *the Son of God is the splendor of his glory and the image of his substance* [Heb. 1:3]. It should be known that only with this figure, his Son, did God look at all things, that is, he communicated to them their natural being and many natural graces and gifts, and made them complete and perfect, as is said in Genesis: *God looked at all things that he made, and they were very good* [Gn. 1:31]. To look and behold that they were very good was to make them very good in the Word, his Son.

Not only by looking at them did he communicate natural being and graces, as we said, but also, with this image of his Son alone, he clothed them in beauty by imparting to them supernatural being. This he did when he took on our human nature and elevated it in the beauty of God, and consequently all creatures, since in human nature he was united with them all. Accordingly, the Son of God proclaimed: *Si ego exaltatus a terra fuero omnia traham ad me ipsum* (If I be lifted up from the earth, I will elevate all things to myself) [Jn. 12:32]. And in this elevation of all things through the Incarnation of his Son and through the glory of his resurrection according to the flesh not only did the Father beautify creatures partially, but, we can say, he clothed them entirely in beauty and dignity.

STANZA 6
Introduction to the Following Stanza[1]

1. In addition to all this, from the viewpoint of contemplative experience it should be known that in the living contemplation and knowledge of creatures the soul sees such fullness of graces, powers, and beauty with which God has endowed them that seemingly all are arrayed in wonderful beauty and natural virtue. The beauty and virtue derive from above and are imparted by that infinite supernatural beauty of the Image of God; his look clothes the world and all the heavens with beauty and gladness, just as he also, on opening his hand, fills every animal with blessing, as David says [Ps. 145:16]. The soul, wounded with love through a trace of the beauty of her Beloved, which she has known through creatures, and anxious to see the invisible beauty that caused this visible beauty, declares in the following verse:

---

1. This is the first stanza in *Canticle B* that begins with an introduction, a practice that becomes standard.

Ah, who has the power to heal me?
now wholly surrender yourself!
Do not send me
any more messengers,
they cannot tell me what I must hear.

Commentary

2. Since creatures gave the soul signs of her Beloved and showed within themselves traces of his beauty and excellence, love grew in her and, consequently, sorrow at his absence. The more the soul knows of God the more the desire and anxiety to see him increase. Since she is conscious that nothing can cure her grief other than her Beloved's presence and the sight of him, she asks him in this stanza, distrusting any other remedy, to surrender his presence so she may possess him. She asks him that from henceforth he no longer detain her with any other knowledge, communications, and traces of his excellence since, rather than bringing her satisfaction, these increase her longings and suffering. The will is content with nothing less than his presence and the sight of him. She asks, therefore, if it be his will, that he truly surrender himself to her in complete and perfect love. She says:

Ah, who has the power to heal me?

3. This is like saying: Among all worldly delights and sensible satisfactions and spiritual gratification and sweetness, there is certainly nothing with the power to heal me, nothing to satisfy me. And then she adds:

Now wholly surrender yourself!

4. It is noteworthy that any soul with authentic love cannot be satisfied until it really possesses God. Everything else not only fails to satisfy it but, as we said,[2] increases the hunger and appetite to see him as he is. Every glimpse of the Beloved received through knowledge or feeling or any other communication (which is like a messenger bringing the soul news of who he is) further increases and awakens her appetite, like the crumbs given to someone who is famished. Finding it difficult to be delayed by so little, she pleads: "Now wholly surrender yourself!"

5. All the knowledge of God possible in this life, however extensive it may be, is inadequate, for it is only partial knowledge and very remote. Essential knowledge of him is the real knowledge for which the soul asks here, unsatisfied by these other communications. She says next:

Do not send me
any more messengers,

---

2. In no. 2.

6. This is like saying: Do not let my knowledge of you, communicated through these messengers of news and feelings about you, be any longer so measured, so remote, and alien to what my soul desires. How well you know, my Spouse, that messengers augment the sorrow of one who grieves over your absence: first, through knowledge they enlarge the wound; second, they seem to postpone your coming. From now on do not send me this remote knowledge. If up to this time I could be content with it, because I did not have much knowledge or love of you, now the intensity of my love cannot be satisfied with these messages; therefore: "Now wholly surrender yourself!"

More clearly, this is like saying: My Lord, my Spouse, you have given yourself to me partially; now may you give yourself completely. You have revealed yourself to me as through fissures in a rock; now may you give me that revelation more clearly. You have communicated by means of others, as if joking with me; now may you do so truly, communicating yourself by yourself. In your visits, at times, it seems you are about to give me the jewel of possessing you; but when I become aware of this I find myself without possessing it, for you hide this jewel as if you had been joking. Now wholly surrender yourself by giving yourself entirely to all of me, so my entire soul may have complete possession of you. "Do not send me any more messengers,"
    they cannot tell me what I must hear.

7. This verse is equivalent to saying: I desire complete knowledge of you, and they have neither knowledge nor ability to tell of you entirely. Nothing in heaven or earth can give the soul the knowledge she desires of you. Thus "they cannot tell me what I must hear." Instead of these other messengers, may you, then, be both the messenger and the message.

STANZA 7

All who are free,
tell me a thousand graceful things of you;
all wound me more
and leave me dying
of, ah, I-don't-know-what behind their stammering.

Commentary

1. In the previous stanza the soul showed her sickness, or wound of love for her Bridegroom, caused by the knowledge irrational creatures

gave of him. In this stanza she asserts that she is wounded with love because of another higher knowledge she receives of the Beloved through rational creatures (angels and humans), creatures more noble than the others. She also asserts that she is not merely wounded, but is dying of love. This dying of love is due to an admirable immensity these creatures disclose to her, yet do not completely disclose. Because this immensity is indescribable she calls it an "I-don't-know-what." And because of it the soul is dying of love.

2. We can deduce that in this matter of love there exist three ways of suffering for the Beloved corresponding to three kinds of knowledge of him.

The first is called a wound. It is the mildest and heals the most quickly, as does a wound. This wound arises from the knowledge the soul receives from creatures, the lowest of God's works. The bride of the Song of Songs refers to this wound, which we also call sickness, saying: *Adjuro vos, filiae Jerusalem, si inveneritis dilectum meum ut nuntietis ei quia amore langueo* (I adjure you, daughters of Jerusalem, if you find my Beloved that you tell him I am sick with love) [Sg. 5:8]. By "the daughters of Jerusalem" she refers to creatures.

3. The second is called a sore wound and cuts more deeply into the soul than the simple wound. As a result it is longer-lasting because it is like a wound that has now become sore, from which she feels she is indeed sorely wounded by love. This sore wound is produced in the soul by knowledge of the Incarnation of the Word and the mysteries of faith. Since these are more remarkable works of God, embodying in themselves a greater love than that shown forth in creatures, they produce in the soul a more intense love. Thus, if the first is like a wound, this second is like a sore wound, which lasts longer. Speaking of this to the soul in the Song of Songs, the Bridegroom says: *You have wounded my heart, my sister, with one of your eyes and with one hair of your neck* [Sg. 4:9]. The "eye" refers to faith in the Incarnation of the Bridegroom, and the "hair" signifies love for this very Incarnation.

4. The third kind of suffering of love is like dying. It is equivalent to having a festered wound, since the soul is now like a wound wholly festered. She lives by dying until love, in killing her, makes her live the life of love, transforming her in love. This death of love is caused in the soul by means of a touch of supreme knowledge of the divinity, the "I-don't-know-what" that she says lies behind their stammering. This touch is not continual or prolonged, for if it were the soul would be loosed from the body. It passes quickly, and she is left dying of love. And she dies the more

in realizing that she does not wholly die of love.[1]

This love is called impatient love. Genesis points to it in telling that Rachel's longing to conceive was so intense that she pleaded with her spouse Jacob: *Da mihi liberos, alioquin moriar* (Give me children, otherwise I will die) [Gn. 30:1]. And the prophet Job exclaimed: *Quis mihi det ut qui coepit, ipse me conterat* (Who will grant that he who gave me a beginning might destroy me?) [Jb. 6:8-9].

5. The soul says in this stanza that these rational creatures cause two kinds of suffering of love in her, the sore wound and death; the sore wound because, as she asserts, they relate a thousand graces of the Beloved in their teaching about both the mysteries of faith and the wisdom of God; death, from what, as she says, lies "behind their stammering": the feeling and knowledge of the divinity sometimes unveiled in what she hears about God. She says then:

> All who are free

6. She refers here to rational creatures (angels and humans) as those "who are free." For they alone among all creatures are free to engage in knowing God. This is the significance of the term "are free," which rendered in Latin is *vacant*. This verse, as a result, is like saying: All of them are free for God. Some, the angels, are free for God in contemplating and enjoying him in heaven; others, human beings, by loving and desiring him on earth.

Through these rational creatures the soul acquires a more vivid knowledge of God, sometimes through the consideration of their excellence, which transcends all created things; at other times through what the rational creatures teach about God. The angels teach us interiorly through secret inspirations; others teach exteriorly, through the truths of Scripture. As a result she says:

> tell me a thousand graceful things of you;

7. This line means: They teach me choice things about your grace and mercy manifested in both the works of your Incarnation and the truths of faith. And they forever tell more, because the more they desire to tell, the more of your graces they are able to reveal.

> all wound me more

8. Insofar as angels inspire me and humans teach me about you, they

---

1. The "touches," graces or communications received from God, are bestowed in contemplation, be it purgative, illuminative, or unitive. Here the effects are characteristic of the state of spiritual betrothal: impatient love, wounds of love.

inspire me to love you more. Thus all wound me more with love.
       and leave me dying
       of, ah, I-don't-know-what behind their stammering.

9. These lines amount to saying: Besides the fact that these creatures wound me with the thousand graceful things they explain about you, there is a certain "I-don't-know-what" that one feels is yet to be said, something unknown still to be spoken, and a sublime trace of God as yet uninvestigated but revealed to the soul, a lofty understanding of God that cannot be put into words. Hence she calls this something "I-don't-know-what." If what I understand wounds me with love, what I do not understand completely, yet have sublime experience of, is death to me.

Sometimes God favors advanced souls through what they hear, see, or understand—and sometimes independently of this—with a sublime knowledge by which they receive an understanding or experience of the height and grandeur of God. Their experience of God in this favor is so lofty that they understand clearly that everything remains to be understood. This understanding and experience that the divinity is so immense as to surpass complete understanding is indeed a sublime knowledge.

One of the outstanding favors God grants briefly in this life is an understanding and experience of himself so lucid and lofty that one comes to know clearly that God cannot be completely understood or experienced. This understanding is somewhat like that of the Blessed in heaven: Those who understand God more understand more distinctly the infinitude that remains to be understood; those who see less of him do not realize so clearly what remains to be seen.

10. I do not think anyone who has not had such experience will understand this well. But, since the soul experiencing this is aware that what she has so sublimely experienced remains beyond her understanding, she calls it "I-don't-know-what." Since it is not understandable, it is indescribable, although, as I say, one may know what the experience of it is. As a result, she says the creatures are stammering, for they do not make it completely known. "Stammering," a trait we notice in children's speech, means that one is unsuccessful in saying and explaining what one has to say.

STANZA 8

Introduction

1. When God favors the soul by disclosing to it a spiritual knowledge and experience of other creatures, he gives it some illuminations con-

cerning these creatures in the way we mentioned,[1] although these illuminations are not always so sublime as the others. It seems these creatures impart to the soul an understanding of the grandeurs of God, which are not entirely understandable; and it is as if they were making these grandeurs understood while yet they remain to be understood. Hence there is an "I-don't-know-what behind their stammering." The soul continues with her complaint, and in the following stanza speaks to her life, saying:

> How do you endure
> O life, not living where you live,
> and being brought near death
> by the arrows you receive
> from that which you conceive of your Beloved?

Commentary

2. Since the soul is aware that she is dying of love, as she has just declared, but she does not die entirely and thus enjoy love freely, she complains about the duration of life in the body, on account of which the spiritual life is delayed.

In this stanza she addresses her own life, stressing the grief it causes her. The meaning of the stanza is: Life of my soul, how can you endure in this bodily life, for it is death to you and a privation of that true spiritual life of God, in which through essence, love, and desire you live more truly than in the body? And now that this understanding of God's grandeur has not caused you to go out and be freed from the body of this death [Rom. 7:24] so as to live and enjoy the life of your God, how can you still live in a body so fragile? Moreover, the wounds of love that you receive from the grandeurs of the Beloved communicated to you are in themselves alone enough to end your life. For all of them leave you wounded with vehement love. And the things you experience and understand of him are as numerous as the touches and wounds you receive of a love that slays. The verse follows:

> How do you endure
> O life, not living where you live?

3. To understand these lines it should be known that the soul lives where she loves more than in the body she animates; for she does not live in the body, but rather gives life to the body and lives through love in the object of her love.

Yet besides this life of love through which the soul that loves God lives in him, her life is radically and naturally centered in God, like that of all

---

1. In 7. 2-4, 6-8.

created things, as St. Paul says: *In him we live and move and are* [Acts 17:28]. This was like saying: In God we have our life and our movement and our being. And St. John says that all that was made was life in God [Jn. 1:3-4]. Since the soul knows she has her natural life in God by the being she has in him, and her spiritual life through the love by which she loves him, she complains and laments that so fragile a life in the mortal body can achieve so much as to hinder her from the enjoyment of a life so strong, true, and delightful as the one she lives in God through nature and love.

The soul puts great stress on this complaint, for she announces here that she suffers from two contraries: natural life in the body and spiritual life in God. They are contraries insofar as one wars against the other [Rom. 7:23]. And living both in the body and in God, she necessarily feels great torment, since the one painful life thwarts the other delightful one, so much so that the natural life is like death to her, because through it she is deprived of the spiritual life in which she has all her being and life through nature, and all her operations and affections through love. To indicate further the hardship of this fragile life, she says next:

> and being brought near death
> by the arrows you receive

4. This is like saying: Moreover, how can you endure in the body, since the touches of love (indicated by the arrows) that the Beloved causes in your heart are enough to take away your life? These touches so impregnate the soul and heart with the knowledge and love of God that she can truthfully say she conceives of God, as she does in the following verse:

> from that which you conceive of your Beloved?

5. That is, from the grandeur, beauty, wisdom, grace, and virtues you understand of him.

STANZA 9

Introduction

1. A stag wounded by a poison arrow neither rests nor remains calm, but searches everywhere for remedies, plunging now into these waters, now into those, and the effect of the poison arrow ever increases in all circumstances and with all remedies taken until finally it seizes upon the heart and the stag dies. Similarly, the soul touched by the poison arrow of love, as is this soul we are discussing, never stops seeking remedies for her sorrow. Yet she not only fails to find them, but everything she thinks, says, and does brings her greater sorrow. Conscious of this, and knowing she has no other remedy than to put herself in the hands of the one who

wounded her, so that in relieving her he may slay her now entirely with the force of love, she turns to her Beloved, the cause of all this, and speaks to him in the following stanza:

> Why, since you wounded
> this heart, don't you heal it?
> And why, since you stole it from me,
> do you leave it so,
> and fail to carry off what you have stolen?

Commentary

2. The soul, then, in this stanza, still complaining of her grief, turns once more to speak with the Beloved. For the impatient love here manifested will endure no idleness and allow no rest to the soul in its affliction, but shows its longings in every way until it discovers a remedy. Aware that she is sorely wounded and alone, without any other remedy or medicine than her Beloved, the one who wounded her, she questions him: Why didn't he heal her with the vision of his presence, since he wounded her heart with love coming from knowledge of himself? She also asks, since he stole her through the love by which he captivated her and carried her away from her own power, why he leaves her thus drawn out of her own power (for the lover does not possess her heart but has given it to the beloved) and does not truly place her heart in his own, taking it for himself in complete transformation of love in glory. She asks then:

> Why, since you wounded
> this heart, don't you heal it?

3. Her complaint is not that he wounded her—for the more a loving soul is wounded the more its love is repaid—but that in sorely wounding her heart, he did not heal her by slaying her completely. The wounds of love are so sweet and delightful that if they do not cause death they cannot satisfy. Yet they are so delightful that she would want them to wound her sorely until they slay her completely. Consequently she says: "Why, since you wounded this heart, don't you heal it?" This is equivalent to saying: Why, since you wounded this heart until it has become sorely wounded, do you not heal it by wholly slaying it with love? Since you cause the sore wound in the sickness of love, may you cause health in the death of love. As a result the heart, wounded with the sorrow of your absence, will be healed with the delight and glory of your sweet presence. And she adds:

> And why, since you stole it from me,
> do you leave it so,

4. To steal is to dispossess an owner of something and take possession of it oneself. This is the complaint the soul here sets before the Beloved in asking, since he has stolen her heart through love and taken it out of her power and possession, why he left it so without really taking possession of it, as the thief does, in fact, by carrying off the stolen goods.

5. Lovers are said to have their heart stolen or seized by the object of their love, for the heart will go out from self and become fixed on the loved object. Thus their heart or love is not for themselves but for what they love. Accordingly, the soul can know clearly whether or not she loves God purely. If she loves him her heart or love will not be set on herself or her own satisfaction and gain, but on pleasing God and giving him honor and glory. In the measure she loves herself, that much less she loves God.

6. Whether the heart has been truly stolen by God will be evident in either of these two signs: if it has longings for God or if it finds no satisfaction in anything but him, as the soul demonstrates here. The reason is that the heart cannot have peace and rest while not possessing, and when it is truly attracted it no longer has possession of self or of any other thing. And if it does not possess completely what it loves, it cannot help being weary, in proportion to its loss, until it possesses the loved object and is satisfied. Until this possession the soul is like an empty vessel waiting to be filled, or a hungry person craving for food, or someone sick moaning for health, or like one suspended in the air with nothing to lean on.[1] Such is the truly loving heart. The soul experiencing this love exclaims: "Why do you leave it so," that is, empty, hungry, alone, sorely wounded and sick with love, suspended in the air,

> and fail to carry off what you have stolen?

7. That is, Why do you fail to carry off the heart you have stolen through love; and why do you fail to fill, satisfy, accompany, and heal it, giving it complete stability and repose in you?

The loving soul, however great her conformity to the Beloved, cannot cease longing for the wages of her love, for which she serves the Beloved. Otherwise there would not be true love, for the wages of love are nothing else—neither can the soul desire anything else—than more love, until perfect love is reached. Love is paid only with love itself, as the prophet Job brought out when he exclaimed with the same yearning and desire the soul has: *Just as the servant desires the shade, and the day laborer waits for*

---

1. These expressions refer characteristically to the painful void caused by the passive night of the spirit; cf. N. 2. 6. 5. The emphasis here is not on the darkness but on the impassioned love that seems to go unheeded.

the end of his work, so I had empty months and I counted the nights wearisome for myself. If I lie down to sleep, I shall say: When will the day come that I might arise? Then again I turn to awaiting the evening and I shall be full of sorrows till the darkness of night [Jb. 7:2-4]. The soul, then, enkindled with love of God, yearns for the fulfillment and perfection of love in order to have complete refreshment therein. As the servant, wearied by the summer heat, longs for the refreshing shade, and as the hireling awaits the end of his work, the soul awaits the end of hers.

It is noteworthy that the prophet Job did not say the hireling was awaiting the end of his labor, but the end of his work, in order to indicate what we are explaining, that is, that the soul that loves does not await the end of her labor but the end of her work. Her work is to love, and of this work, which is love, she awaits the end, which is the perfection and completeness of it. Until this work is accomplished the soul is always in the condition of the picture Job paints in this passage; she considers her days and months empty and counts her nights as long and wearisome.

We have explained how the soul that loves God must not desire or hope for any other reward for her services than the perfect love of God.

STANZA 10

Introduction

1. The soul in this condition of love, then, is like a sick person who is extremely tired and, having lost the taste and appetite for all food, finds it nauseating and everything a disturbance and annoyance. In all that sick people think or see they have only one desire, the desire for health, and everything that does not lead to this is a bother and burden to them.

Since the soul has reached this sickness of love of God, she has three traits: In all things that are offered to her or with which she deals, she has ever before her that longing for her health, which is her Beloved, and even though she cannot help being occupied with things, she always has her heart fixed on him. The second trait, arising from this first, is the loss of taste for all things. The third, then, which follows from these, is that all these things bother her and all dealings with others are burdensome and annoying.

2. The reason for these traits, deduced from what has been said, is that, since the palate of the soul's will has tasted this food of love of God, her will is inclined immediately to seek and enjoy her Beloved in everything that happens and in all her occupations, without looking for any satisfaction or concern of her own. Mary Magdalene acted similarly when with ardent love she was searching for him in the garden. Thinking that he was

the gardener, without any further reasoning or consideration she pleaded with him: *If you have taken him from me, tell me, and I will take him away* [Jn. 20:15]. Having a similar yearning to find him in all things, and not immediately finding him as she desires—but rather quite the contrary—not only does the soul fail to find satisfaction in these things, but they also become a torment to her, and sometimes a very great one. Such souls suffer much in dealing with people and with business matters, for these contacts hinder rather than help them to their goal.

3. The bride clearly indicates in the Song of Songs these three traits she had when searching for her Bridegroom: *I looked for him and did not find him. But they who go about the city found me and wounded me, and the guards of the walls took my mantle from me* [Sg. 5:6-7]. "Those who go about the city" refers to the affairs of the world. When they find the soul who is searching for God, they inflict on her many wounds of sorrow, pain, and displeasure, for not only does she fail to find her desire in them, but she is also impeded by them. Those who guard the wall of contemplation, to prevent the soul from entering, are the devils and the negotiations of the world, and they take away the mantle of the peace and quietude of loving contemplation. The soul that loves God derives a thousand displeasures and annoyances from all of these. Conscious that as long as she is in this life without the vision of God she cannot free herself from them to either a small or great degree, she continues her prayers to the Beloved and recites the following stanza:

> Extinguish these miseries,
> since no one else can stamp them out;
> and may my eyes behold you,
> because you are their light,
> and I would open them to you alone.

Commentary

4. She continues in this stanza to ask the Beloved to put an end to her longings and pains, since he alone can do this, no one else; and to accomplish this so that the eyes of her soul may be able to see him, since he alone is the light they behold and she wants to employ them in him alone:

> Extinguish these miseries,

5. A characteristic of the desires of love is that all deeds and words unconformed with what the will loves will weary, tire, annoy, and displease the soul as she beholds that her desire goes unfulfilled. She refers to this weariness and annoyance she suffers in order to see God as "these miseries." And nothing but possession of the Beloved can extin-

guish them. She says he extinguishes them by his presence and refreshes her as cool water soothes a person exhausted from the heat. She uses the word "extinguish" to indicate that she is suffering from the fire of love.

since no one else can stamp them out;

6. To further urge and persuade her Beloved to grant her petition, she declares that he must be the one to extinguish these miseries, since he alone suffices to satisfy her need. It is noteworthy that God is very ready to comfort and satisfy the soul in her needs and afflictions when she neither has nor desires consolation and satisfaction outside of him. The soul possessing nothing that might withhold her from God cannot remain long without a visit from her Beloved.

and may my eyes behold you,

7. That is: May I see you face to face with the eyes of my soul,

because you are their light,

8. In addition to the fact that God is the supernatural light of the soul's eyes, and without this light she is enveloped in darkness, she affectionately calls him here the light of her eyes, just as a lover would call her loved one the light of her eyes in order to show her affection.

These two verses are like saying: Since my eyes have no other light (neither through nature nor through love) than you, "may my eyes behold you because you are their light" in every way. David noted the absence of this light when he lamented: *The light of my eyes itself is not with me* [Ps. 37:10]. Tobit did the same: *What joy can be mine, since I am seated in darkness and do not see the light of heaven?* [Tb. 5:12]. Through these words he gave expression to his desire for the clear vision of God, because the light of heaven is the Son of God, as St. John says: *The heavenly city has no need of the sun or the moon to shine in it, because the brightness of God illumines it, and the Lamb is the lamp thereof* [Rv. 21:23].

and I would open them to you alone.

9. With this line the soul desires to oblige the Bridegroom to reveal this light of her eyes, not only because she lives in darkness in that her eyes have no other light, but also because she wants to keep her eyes for him alone. As the soul longing to focus the eyes of her will on the light of something outside of God is justly deprived of the divine light—insofar as the spiritual power she has for receiving God's light is occupied with this other light—so also does the soul that closes its eyes to all things in order to open them to God alone merit congruously the illumination of the divine light.

STANZA 11

Introduction

1. It should be known that the loving Bridegroom of souls cannot long watch them suffering alone—as this soul is suffering—because, as he says through Zechariah, their afflictions touch him in the apple of his eye [Zech. 2:8], especially when these afflictions are the outcome of love for him, as are those of this soul.[1] He also declares through Isaiah: *Before they call, I will hear; while they are yet with the word in their mouth, I will hear them* [Is. 65:24]. The Wise Man says of him that if the soul seeks him as money, she will find him [Prv. 2:4-5].

Apparently God granted a certain spiritual feeling of his presence to this loving soul whose prayers are so enkindled and who seeks him more covetously than people seek money, since she has left herself and all things for him. In this spiritual sense of his presence, he revealed some deep glimpses of his divinity and beauty by which he greatly increased her fervor and desire to see him. As a man throws water into the forge to stir up and intensify the fire, so the Lord usually grants certain signs of his excellence to some souls that walk in these fiery longings of love to make them more fervent and further prepare them for the favors he wishes to grant them later. Since the soul saw and experienced through that obscure presence the supreme good and beauty hidden there, she recites the following stanza, dying with the desire to see him:

> Reveal your presence,
> and may the vision of your beauty be my death;
> for the sickness of love
> is not cured
> except by your very presence and image.

Commentary

2. The soul desiring to be possessed by this immense God, for love of whom she feels that her heart is stolen and wounded, unable to suffer her sickness any longer, deliberately asks him in this stanza to show her his beauty, his divine essence, and to kill her with this revelation and thereby free her from the flesh, since she cannot see and enjoy him as she wants. She makes this request by displaying before him the sickness and yearning of her heart, in which she perseveres in suffering for love of him,

---

1. This is the new stanza added to *Canticle B,* giving this version of the poem 40 stanzas. The stanza fits well at this point of the poem. And the doctrinal content of the commentary is of special merit, forming a bridge between all that preceded and the change that takes place in the following stanza.

unable to find a cure in anything less than this glorious vision of his divine essence. The verse follows:

Reveal your presence,

3. In explanation of this verse it should be known that God's presence can be of three kinds:

The first is his presence by essence. In this way he is present not only in the holiest souls but also in sinners and all other creatures. With this presence he gives them life and being. Should this essential presence be lacking to them, they would all be annihilated. Thus this presence is never wanting to the soul.

The second is his presence by grace, in which he abides in the soul, pleased and satisfied with it. Not all have this presence of God; those who fall into mortal sin lose it. The soul cannot know naturally if it has this presence.

The third is his presence by spiritual affection, for God usually grants his spiritual presence to devout souls in many ways by which he refreshes, delights, and gladdens them.

Yet these many kinds of spiritual presence, just as the others, are all hidden, for in them God does not reveal himself as he is, since the conditions of this life will not allow such a manifestation. Thus the above verse "reveal your presence" could be understood of any of these three ways in which God is present.

4. Since it is certain that at least in the first way God is ever present in the soul, she does not ask him to be present in her but that he so reveal his hidden presence, whether natural, spiritual, or affective, that she may be able to see him in his divine being and beauty. Since he both gives the soul natural being through his essential presence and perfects her through his presence by grace, she begs him to glorify her also with his manifest glory.

Yet insofar as this soul is full of fervor and tender love of God, we should understand that this presence she asks the Beloved to reveal refers chiefly to a certain affective presence the Beloved accords her. This presence is so sublime that the soul feels an immense hidden being from which God communicates to her some semi-clear glimpses of his divine beauty. And these bear such an effect on the soul that she ardently longs and faints with desire for what she feels hidden there in that presence. This is similar to what David felt when he exclaimed: *My soul longs and faints for the courts of the Lord* [Ps. 84:2].

At this time the soul faints with longing to be engulfed in that supreme good she feels present and hidden, for although it is hidden she has a notable experience of the good and delight present there. Accordingly she is drawn and carried toward this good more forcibly than any material object is pulled toward its center by gravity. With this longing and heartfelt desire, unable to contain herself any longer, the soul begs:

Reveal your presence

5. Moses had this very experience on Mount Sinai. While standing in God's presence, he was able to get such sublime and profound glimpses of the height and beauty of the hidden divinity that, unable to endure it, he asked God twice to reveal his glory: *You say that you know me by name and that I have found favor before you. If therefore I have found favor in your presence, show me your face that I may know you and find before your eyes the grace which I desire fulfilled* [Ex. 33:12-13], that is, to reach the perfect love of the glory of God. Yet the Lord answered: *You shall not be able to see my face, for no human shall see me and live* [Ex. 33:20]. This is like saying: You ask a difficult thing of me, Moses, for such is the beauty of my face and the delight derived from the sight of my being that your soul will be unable to withstand it in a life as weak as this.

The soul knows that she cannot see him in his beauty in this kind of life. She knows this either through God's answer to Moses or through her experience of what is hidden here in the presence of God. For even though he appears only vaguely, she faints. Hence she anticipates the reply that can be made to her as it was to Moses and says:

and may the vision of your beauty be my death;

6. This is like saying: Since the delight arising from the sight of your being and beauty is unendurable, and since I must die in seeing you, may the vision of your beauty be my death.

7. It is known that there are two sights that will kill humans because of the inability of human nature to suffer their force and vigor: one is the sight of the basilisk, from which it is said a person dies immediately; the other is the vision of God. Yet the causes are very different, for the sight of one kills through a terrible poison, and the vision of the other kills by an untold health and glorious good.

The soul does nothing very outstanding by wanting to die at the vision of the beauty of God in order to enjoy him forever. Were she to have but a glimpse of the height and beauty of God, she would not only desire death in order to see him now forever, as she here desires, but she would very gladly undergo a thousand singularly bitter deaths to see him only for a moment; and having seen him, she would ask to suffer just as many more that she might see him for another moment.

8. To shed further light on this verse, it should be known that when the soul asks that the vision of his beauty be her death she speaks conditionally, under the supposition that she cannot see him without dying. Were

she able to see him without dying, she would not ask him to slay her, for to desire death is a natural imperfection. Yet with the supposition that this corruptible human life is incompatible with the other incorruptible life of God, she says: May the vision of your beauty be my death.

9. St Paul teaches this doctrine to the Corinthians, saying: *We do not wish to be unclothed, but we desire to be clothed over, so that which is mortal may be absorbed in life* [2 Cor. 5:4]. This is like saying: We do not desire to be despoiled of the flesh, but to be clothed over with glory. Yet, observing that one cannot live simultaneously in glory and in the mortal flesh, he says to the Philippians that he desires to be set free and to be with Christ [Phil. 1:23].

Yet one may question: Why did the children of Israel formerly flee God and fear to see him lest they die, as Manoah and his wife did [Jgs. 13:22], whereas this soul desires to die at the sight of God? We reply that there are two reasons for this: First, even though the children of Israel at that time died in the grace of God, they were not to see him until the coming of Christ. It was much better for them to live in the flesh, increasing their merits and enjoying their natural life, than to be in limbo, without ability to merit and suffering the darkness and spiritual absence of God. As a result they considered it a wonderful gift and favor from God to live for many years.

10. The second reason is based on love. Since the Israelites were not so fortified in love or so close to God through love, they feared to die upon seeing him. But because now in the law of grace the soul can see God when separated from the body, the desire to live but a short while and die in order to see him is more perfect.[2] And even if this were false, the soul loving God as intensely as this one does would not fear to die from seeing him. True love receives all things that come from the Beloved—prosperity, adversity, even chastisement—with the same evenness of soul, since they are his will. And they afford her joy and delight because, as St. John says: *Perfect charity casts out all fear* [1 Jn. 4:18].

Death cannot be bitter to the soul that loves, for in it she finds all the sweetness and delight of love. The thought of death cannot sadden her, for what she finds is that gladness accompanies this thought. Neither can the thought of death be burdensome and painful to her, for death will put an end to all her sorrows and afflictions and be the beginning of all her bliss. She thinks of death as her friend and bridegroom, and at the thought of it she rejoices as she would over the thought of her betrothal and marriage, and she longs for the day and the hour of her death more than earthly kings long for kingdoms and principalities.

---

2. For the source of this classic theory on limbo, see Aquinas, *Summa theologiae* Suppl. 69.

The Wise Man proclaims of this kind of death: *O death, your sentence is welcome to the person who feels need* [Ecclus. 41:2]. If it is welcome to those who feel need for earthly things, even though it does not provide for these needs but rather despoils such persons of the possessions they have, how much better will its sentence be for the soul in need of love, as is this one who is crying out for more love. For death will not despoil her of the love she possesses, but rather will be the cause of love's completeness, which she desires, and the satisfaction of all her needs.

The soul is right in daring to say, "may the vision of your beauty be my death," since she knows that at the instant she sees this beauty she will be carried away by it, and absorbed in this very beauty, and transformed in this beauty, and made beautiful like this beauty itself, and enriched and provided for like this very beauty. David declares, consequently, that the death of the saints is precious in the sight of the Lord [Ps. 116:15]. This would not be true if they did not participate in God's own grandeurs, for in the sight of God nothing is precious but what he in himself is.

Accordingly, the soul does not fear death when she loves; rather she desires it. Yet sinners are always fearful of death. They foresee that death will take everything away and bring them all evils. As David says, *the death of sinners is very evil* [Ps. 34:21]. And hence, as the Wise Man says, *the remembrance of it is bitter* [Ecclus. 41:1]. Since sinners love the life of this world intensely and have little love for that of the other, they have an intense fear of death. But the soul that loves God lives more in the next life than in this, for a soul lives where it loves more than where it gives life, and thus takes little account of this temporal life. She says then: May the vision of your beauty be my death.

> for the sickness of love
> is not cured
> except by your very presence and image.

11. The reason lovesickness has no other remedy than the presence and the image of the beloved is that, since this sickness differs from others, its medicine also differs. In other sicknesses, following sound philosophy, contraries are cured by contraries, but love is incurable except by things in accord with love.[3]

The reason for this is that love of God is the soul's health, and the soul does not have full health until love is complete. Sickness is nothing but the lack of health, and when the soul has not even a single degree of love she is dead. But when she possesses some degrees of love of God, no matter how few, she is then alive, yet very weak and infirm because of her little love. In the measure that love increases she will be healthier, and when love is perfect she will have full health.

---

3. Cf. A. 3. 6. 1; N. 1. 12. 5; F. 3. 18.

12. It should be known that love never reaches perfection until the lovers are so alike that one is transfigured in the other. And then the love is in full health. The soul experiences within herself a certain sketch of love, which is the sickness she mentions, and she desires the completion of the sketch of this image, the image of her Bridegroom, the Word, the Son of God, who, as St. Paul says, *is the splendor of his glory and the image of his substance* [Heb. 1:3]; for this is the image referred to in this verse and into which the soul desires to be transformed through love. As a result she says: For the sickness of love is not cured except by your very presence and image.

13. She does well to call imperfect love "sickness," for just as a sick person is too weak for work, so is the soul that is feeble in love too weak to practice heroic virtue.

14. It is also noteworthy that those who feel in themselves the sickness of love, a lack of love, show they have some love, because they are aware of what they lack through what they have. Those who do not feel this sickness show they either have no love or are perfect in love.

STANZA 12

Introduction

1. At this period the soul feels that she is rushing toward God as rapidly as a falling stone when nearing its center. She also feels that she is like wax in which an impression, though being made, is not yet complete. She knows, too, that she is like a sketch or the first draft of a drawing and calls out to the one who did this sketch to finish the painting and image. And her faith is so enlightened that it gives her a glimpse of some clear divine reflections of the height of her God. As a result she does not know what to do other than turn to this very faith that contains and hides the image and the beauty of her Beloved and from which she also receives these sketches and tokens of love, and speak to it in the following stanza:[1]

> O spring like crystal!
> If only, on your silvered-over faces,
> you would suddenly form
> the eyes I have desired,
> which I bear sketched deep within my heart.

---

1. Here the first phase of anxious searching draws to a close, and the bride turns again to faith, although the faith is now further enlightened.

Commentary

2. Since the soul longs so ardently for union with the Bridegroom and is aware that she finds no means or remedy in any creature, she turns to speak to faith, as to that which most vividly sheds light concerning her Beloved, and takes it as a means toward this union. Indeed, there is no other means by which one reaches true union and spiritual espousal with God, as Hosea indicates: *I will espouse you to me in faith* [Hos. 2:20]. With this burning desire she exclaims, which is the meaning of the stanza: O faith of Christ, my Bridegroom, would that you might show me clearly now the truths of my Beloved that you have infused in my soul and are covered with obscurity and darkness (for faith, as the theologians say, is an obscure habit),[2] in such a way that what you communicate to me in inexplicit and obscure knowledge, you would show suddenly, clearly, and perfectly, changing it into a manifestation of glory! Would that you might do this by drawing back from these truths (for faith is the covering and veil over the truths of God)! The verse then runs:

O spring like crystal!

3. She says faith is like crystal for two reasons: first, because it concerns Christ, her Bridegroom; second, because it has the characteristics of crystal, being pure in its truths, strong, clear, and cleansed of errors and natural forms.

And she calls it a spring because from it the waters of all spiritual goods flow into the soul. Christ our Lord, speaking with the Samaritan woman, called faith a spring, declaring that in those who believe in him he would make a fountain whose waters would leap up unto life everlasting [Jn. 4:14]. This water was the Spirit that believers were to receive through faith [Jn. 7:39].[3]

If only, on your silvered-over faces,

4. She calls the propositions and articles of faith "silvered-over faces." To understand this verse as well as the others, it should be known that faith is compared to silver in the propositions it teaches us, and the truths and substance it contains are compared to gold. For in the next life we shall see and enjoy openly this very substance that, clothed and covered with the silver of faith, we now believe.

David says of faith: *If you sleep between the two choirs, the feathers of the dove will be silvery and the hinder parts will be of the color of gold* [Ps. 68:13]. This means that if we close the eyes of the intellect to earthly and heavenly things, which he terms "sleeping between," we shall remain in faith. He

2. Cf. A. 2. 3. 1 and note 1.
3. Cf. F. 3. 8.

calls faith the dove; and its feathers (the truths it tells us) are silvery because in this life faith proposes these truths to us covered and in darkness. As a result she calls these truths silvered-over faces. Yet when faith comes to an end, when it terminates through the clear vision of God, the substance of faith, having been stripped of the veil of silver, will have the color of gold.

Faith, consequently, gives and communicates God himself to us but covered with the silver of faith. Yet it does not for this reason fail to give him to us truly. Were someone to give us a gold vase plated with silver, we would not fail to receive a gold vase merely because of its being silver-plated. When the bride of the Song of Songs wanted this divine possession, God promised to make her, insofar as possible in this life, gold earrings plated with silver [Sg. 1:11]. He thereby promised to give himself to her, but hidden in faith.

The soul, then, exclaims to faith: Oh, if only on your silvered-over faces (the articles we mentioned) by which you cover the gold of the divine rays (the eyes I have desired), and adds:

> you would suddenly form
> the eyes I have desired,

5. The eyes refer to the divine truths and rays. Faith, as we mentioned, proposes these truths to us in its covered and inexplicit articles. The soul, in other words, says: Oh, if only the truths hidden in your articles, which you teach me in an inexplicit and dark manner, you would give me now completely, clearly, and explicitly, freed of their covering, as my desire begs!

She calls these truths "eyes" because of the remarkable presence of the Beloved she experiences. It seems that he is now always looking at her. Thus she says:

> which I bear sketched deep within my heart.

6. She says these truths are sketched deep within her, that is, in her soul, in her intellect and will. For these truths are infused by faith into her intellect. And since the knowledge of them is imperfect, she says they are sketched. Just as a sketch is not a perfect painting, so the knowledge of faith is not perfect knowledge. Hence the truths infused in the soul through faith are as though sketched, and when clearly visible they will be like a perfect and finished painting in the soul. As the Apostle says: *Cum autem venerit quod perfectum est evacuabitur quod ex parte est* [1 Cor. 13:10]; this means that when what is perfect, the clear vision, comes, what is in part, the knowledge of faith, will end.

7. Over this sketch of faith the sketch of love is drawn in the will of the lover. When there is union of love, the image of the Beloved is so sketched

in the will, and drawn so intimately and vividly, that it is true to say that the Beloved lives in the lover and the lover in the Beloved. Love produces such likeness in this transformation of lovers that one can say each is the other and both are one. The reason is that in the union and transformation of love each gives possession of self to the other and each leaves and exchanges self for the other. Thus each one lives in the other and is the other, and both are one in the transformation of love.

8. This is the meaning of St. Paul's affirmation: *Vivo autem, iam non ego; vivit vero in me Christus* (I live, now not I, but Christ lives in me) [Gal. 2:20]. In saying, "I live, now not I," he meant that even though he had life it was not his because he was transformed in Christ, and it was divine more than human. He consequently asserts that he does not live but Christ lives in him. In accord with this likeness and transformation, we can say that his life and Christ's were one life through union of love. This transformation into divine life will be effected perfectly in heaven in all those who merit the vision of God. Transformed in God, these blessed souls will live the life of God and not their own life—although, indeed, it will be their own life because God's life will be theirs. Then they will truly proclaim: We live, now not we, but God lives in us.

Although transformation in this life can be what it was in St. Paul, it still cannot be perfect and complete even though the soul reaches such transformation of love as is found in the spiritual marriage, the highest state attainable in this life.[4] Everything can be called a sketch of love in comparison with that perfect image, the transformation in glory. Yet the attainment of such a sketch of transformation in this life is a great blessing, for with this transformation the Beloved is very pleased. Desiring the bride to put him as a sketch in her soul, he said in the Song of Songs: *Put Me as a seal upon your heart, as a seal upon your arm* [Sg. 8:6]. The "heart" signifies the soul in which God dwells in this life as a seal, which is the sketch of faith mentioned above; the "arm" signifies the strong will in which he is present as the seal, which is the sketch of love we just discussed.

9. The soul's state at this time is such that I do not want to neglect saying something about it, even though briefly, regardless of the fact that it is indescribable. It seems to the soul that its bodily and spiritual substance is drying up with thirst for this living spring of God. Its thirst is like David's when he said: *As the hart longs for the fount of waters, so does my soul long for you, my God. My soul has thirsted for God the living fount; when shall I see and*

---

4. The expression "spiritual marriage" appears here for the first time, being identified with the state of union or transformation. This is not the state in which the bride finds herself at this point in the poem.

appear before the face of God? [Ps. 42:1-2]. This thirst so exhausts the soul that she would think nothing of breaking through the midst of the camp of the Philistines, as did David's strong men to fill their containers with water from the cistern of Bethlehem, which was Christ [1 Chr. 11:18]. She would consider all the difficulties of the world, the fury of demons, and infernal afflictions nothing if by passing through them she could plunge into the unfathomable spring of love. In this respect it is said in the Song of Songs: *Love is as strong as death and its jealousy as hard as hell* [Sg. 8:6].

It is incredible how ardent the longing and pain is that the soul experiences when she sees she is near the enjoyment of that good, yet it is not given to her. The more the object of her desire comes into sight and the closer it draws, while still being denied her, so much more pain and torment does it cause. In this spiritual sense Job says: *Before I eat, I sigh; and the roaring and bellowing of my soul is like overflowing waters* [Jb. 3:24], that is, on account of its craving for food. By the food is meant God because the yearning for food, or the knowledge of God, is commensurate with suffering for him.

STANZA 13

Introduction

1. The reason the soul suffers so intensely for God at this time is that she is drawing nearer to him; so she has greater experience within herself of the void of God, of very heavy darkness, and of spiritual fire that dries up and purges her so that thus purified she may be united with him. Inasmuch as God does not communicate some supernatural ray of light from himself, he is intolerable darkness to her when he is spiritually near her, for the excess of supernatural light darkens the natural light. David indicated all this when he said: *Clouds and darkness are round about him; fire goes before him* [Ps. 97:2-3]. And in another psalm he asserts: *He made darkness his covert and hiding place, and his tent round about him is dark water in the clouds of the air; because of his great splendor there are in his presence clouds, hail, and coals of fire* [Ps. 18:12-13], that is, for the soul drawing near him. As the soul comes closer to him, and until God introduces her into his divine splendors through transformation of love, she experiences within herself all that David described. In the meanwhile, like Job, she exclaims over and over: *Who will grant me to know him and find him and come unto his throne?* [Jb. 23:3].[1]

---

1. This paragraph recalls the teaching and descriptions contained in *The Dark Night*. The visits of the Bridegroom in the following stanzas characterize the stage of spiritual betrothal. The sufferings related to these divine communications stem from the soul's not being totally purified.

Just as God through his immense mercy grants the soul favors and consolations in the measure of her darknesses and voids, for *sicut tenebrae ejus, ita et lumen ejus* (as is the darkness, so is the light) [Ps. 139:12], and because in exalting and glorifying her he humbles and wearies her, so in like manner he sent the soul that was suffering these fatigues some of his divine rays with such strong love and glory that he stirred her completely and caused her to go out of her senses. Thus in great fear and trembling, she spoke to her Beloved the first part of the following stanza, and her Beloved then spoke the remaining verses.

> Withdraw them, Beloved,
> I am taking flight!

Bridegroom

> Return, dove,
> the wounded stag
> is in sight on the hill,
> cooled by the breeze of your flight.

Commentary

2. The Beloved usually visits his bride chastely, delicately, and with strong love amid the intense loving desires and ardors she showed in the previous stanzas. God's favors and visits are generally in accord with the intensity of the yearnings and ardors of love that precede them.

Since, as she just finished saying in the previous stanza, the soul desired these divine eyes with such yearnings, the Beloved revealed to her some rays of his grandeur and divinity. He communicated these so sublimely and forcibly that he carried her out of herself in rapture and ecstasy. At the beginning this is accompanied by great pain and fear in one's natural makeup. Unable in her weakness to endure such excess, she proclaims in this stanza: "Withdraw them, Beloved," that is, your divine eyes, "for they cause me to take flight and go out of myself to lofty contemplation, which is beyond what human nature can endure." She makes this plea because seemingly the soul is flying away from the body. This flight from the body is what she desired; this is why she begged him to withdraw his eyes, to cease communicating them to her in the body in which she is unable to suffer and enjoy them as she would, and to communicate them to her in her flight outside the body.

The Bridegroom, then, impedes this desire and flight, saying: "Return, dove, for the communication you receive from me is not yet of the state of glory to which you now aspire. Return to me, for I am he whom you, wounded with love, seek. For I, too, like the stag, wounded by your love, begin to reveal myself to you in your high contemplation, and I am refreshed and renewed in the love that arises from your contemplation."

The soul, then, says to the Bridegroom:
Withdraw them, Beloved,

3. As we mentioned, the soul in accordance with her intense desire for these divine eyes, for the divinity, received interiorly from the Beloved such divine communication and knowledge that she had to say, "Withdraw them, Beloved."

The misery of human nature is such in this life that when the communication and knowledge of the Beloved, which means more life for the soul and for which she longs so ardently, is about to be imparted, she cannot receive it save almost at the cost of her life. When she receives the eyes she has been searching for so anxiously and in so many ways, she cries: Withdraw them, Beloved!

4. The torment experienced in these rapturous visits is such that no other so disjoins the bones and endangers human nature. Were God not to provide, she would die. And indeed, it seems so to the soul in which this happens, that she is being loosed from the flesh and is abandoning the body.

The reason for this is that such favors cannot be received wholly in the body, for the spirit is elevated to commune with the divine Spirit who comes to the soul. Thus the soul must in some fashion abandon the body. As a result the body must suffer and, consequently, the soul in the body because of their unity in one suppositum.[2] The torment she experiences at the time of this visit and the terror arising from her awareness of being treated in this supernatural way make her cry: Withdraw them, Beloved!

5. Yet, it should not be thought that because she says "withdraw them" she desires him to do so. Those words spring from natural fear, as we said.[3] No matter what the cost, she would not want to lose these visits and favors of the Beloved. Although human nature suffers, the spirit takes flight to supernatural recollection and enjoyment of the Beloved's spirit, which is what she desired and sought.

Yet she would not want to receive the spirit in the body, for there she cannot receive it fully, but only in a small degree and with considerable suffering. But she would want to receive it in the flight of the spirit, outside the body, where she can rejoice freely. Accordingly she says "withdraw them, Beloved," that is, cease communicating them to me in the body,
I am taking flight!

---

2. The basic unity of the human person and the lack of adaptation of the sensory to the spiritual are the two reasons for this suffering. The latter reason is highlighted in *The Dark Night*.
3. In no. 2.

6. This is like saying: I am taking flight from the body so you may communicate them to me outside it, since they cause me to fly out of the body.

For a better understanding of the nature of this flight, it should be noted that, as we said,[4] in this visit of the divine Spirit, the spirit of the soul is carried away violently to communicate with him, and it abandons the body and ceases to have its feelings and actions in it, for they are in God. Thus St. Paul said that in his rapture he did not know if his soul was receiving the communication in the body or out of the body [2 Cor. 12:2].

However, it should not be thought because of this that the soul forsakes the body of its natural life, but rather that the soul's actions are not in the body. This is why in these raptures and flights the body has no feeling and even though severely painful things are done to it, it does not feel them. This rapture is not like other natural transports and swoons in which one returns to self when pain is inflicted.

These feelings are experienced in such visits by those who have not yet reached the state of perfection but are moving along in the state of proficients.[5] Those who have reached perfection receive all communications in peace and gentle love. There these raptures cease, for they are communications that prepare one to receive the total communication.

7. This would be an apt place to treat of the different kinds of raptures, ecstasies, and other elevations and flights of the soul that are customarily experienced by spiritual persons. But since, as I promised in the prologue,[6] my intention is only to give a brief explanation of these stanzas, such a discussion will have to be left for someone who knows how to treat the matter better than I. Then too, the blessed Teresa of Jesus, our Mother, left writings about these spiritual matters that are admirably done and which I hope will soon be printed and brought to light.[7]

What the soul thus says about flight here should be understood in reference to rapture and ecstasy of the spirit in God. And next, the Beloved says:

Return, dove.

---

4. In nos. 2 and 5.

5. The divine communications mentioned in this stanza correspond to the state of proficients or the illuminative way and alternate with the trials of the purifying night. Cf. A. 2. 23. 1; N. 1. 14. 1; N. 2. 1. 1-2.

6. In prol. 4.

7. On September 1, 1586, the Discalced Carmelite Definitory, of which St. John of the Cross was a member, decreed that St. Teresa's writings be published. She speaks of the matters referred to here especially in her *Life*, ch. 20, and in the *Interior Castle*, VI. chs. 4-5. He refers to her as "our Mother" because she was the foundress and spiritual teacher of the Discalced Carmelites.

8. The soul went out of the body very willingly in that spiritual flight, and thought that now her life was at an end and she would be able to see her Bridegroom openly and enjoy him forever. But the Bridegroom intercepted her flight, saying "Return, dove." This is like saying: In your sublime and swift contemplation and in your burning love and in the simplicity of your advance—for the dove has these three properties—return from this lofty flight in which you aim after true possession of me; the time has not yet come for such high knowledge. Adapt yourself to this lower knowledge that I am communicating to you in this rapture of yours. And it is this:

the wounded stag

9. The Bridegroom in this verse compares himself to a stag. It is characteristic of the stag that he climbs to high places and when wounded races in search of refreshment and cool waters. If he hears the cry of his mate and senses that she is wounded, he immediately runs to her to comfort and caress her.

The Bridegroom now acts similarly. Beholding that the bride is wounded with love for him, because of her moan he also is wounded with love for her. Among lovers, the wound of one is a wound for both, and the two have but one feeling. Thus, in other words, he says: Return to me, my bride, because if you go about wounded with love for me, I too, like the stag, will come to you wounded by your wound. Also by appearing in a high place I am like the stag. Hence he says:

is in sight on the hill,

10. That is, on the height of your contemplation that you experience in this flight. For contemplation is a high place where God begins to communicate and show himself to the soul in this life, but not completely. Hence he does not say that he has appeared fully but that he is in sight. However sublime may be the knowledge God gives the soul in this life, it is but like a glimpse of him from a great distance.

The third characteristic of the stag is contained in the next verse:

cooled by the breeze of your flight.

11. By the "flight," he means the contemplation received in that ecstasy; and by the "breeze," the spirit of love that this flight of contemplation causes in the soul. He very appropriately terms this love caused by the flight a "breeze," because the Holy Spirit, who is love, is also compared to a breeze in Scripture, for the Holy Spirit is the breath of the Father and the Son. And just as the Holy Spirit is like a breeze from the flight (that is, he proceeds through spiration from the contemplation and wisdom of the Father and the Son), so the Bridegroom calls this love of the soul a breeze because it proceeds from the contemplation and

knowledge she has of God at this time.

It is noteworthy that the Bridegroom does not say he comes at the flight, but at the breeze of the flight, because, properly speaking, God does not communicate himself to the soul through its flight (the knowledge it has of him), but through the love it has from this knowledge. For just as love is the union of the Father and the Son, so is it the union of the soul with God. Hence even though a soul may have the highest knowledge and contemplation of God and know all mysteries but does not love, this knowledge will be of no avail to her union with God, as St. Paul teaches [1 Cor. 13:2]. St. Paul also says: *Caritatem habete quod est vinculum perfectionis* (Have this charity that is the bond of perfection) [Col. 3:14].

This charity, then, causes the Bridegroom to run to the spring of his bride's love just as the cool waters cause the wounded and thirsty stag to run seeking refreshment. Consequently he uses the word "cooled."

12. As a breeze cools and refreshes a person worn out by the heat, so this breeze of love refreshes and renews the one burning with the fire of love. The fire of love bears this property: The breeze by which it is cooled and refreshed makes it increase, for in the lover, love is a flame that burns with a desire to burn more, like the flame of natural fire. He refers to the fulfillment of this desire to burn more in his ardent love for his bride as being "cooled." In other words he says: In the ardor of your flight it burns more, because one love enkindles another.

It is worthy of note that God does not place his grace and love in the soul except according to its desire and love. Those who truly love God must strive not to fail in this love, for they will thereby induce God, if we may so express it, to further love them and find delight in them. And to acquire this charity, one ought to practice what St. Paul taught: *Charity is patient, is kind, is not envious, does no evil, does not become proud, is not ambitious, seeks not its own, does not become disturbed, thinks no evil, rejoices not in iniquity, but rejoices in the truth, suffers all things* (that are to be suffered), *believes all things* (that must be believed), *hopes all things, and endures all things* (that are in accord with charity) [1 Cor. 13:4-7].

STANZAS 14 and 15

Introduction

1. Since this little dove was flying in the breeze of love above the flood waters of her loving fatigues and yearnings, which she has shown until now, and could find nowhere to alight, the compassionate father Noah, stretching out his merciful hand, caught her on her last flight and placed

her in the ark of his charity [Gn. 8:9]. This occurred when in the stanza we just explained the Bridegroom said, "Return, dove."

Finding in this recollection all she desired and more than is expressible, the soul begins to sing the praises of her Beloved in the following stanzas. They apply to his grandeurs, which she experiences and enjoys in this union.

Bride

> My Beloved, the mountains,
> and lonely wooded valleys,
> strange islands,
> and resounding rivers,
> the whistling of love-stirring breezes,
>
> the tranquil night
> at the time of the rising dawn,
> silent music,
> sounding solitude,
> the supper that refreshes, and deepens love.

2. Before commenting on these stanzas, we should call to mind for the sake of a clearer understanding of them and those following that this spiritual flight denotes a high state and union of love in which, after much spiritual exercise, the soul is placed by God. This state is called spiritual betrothal with the Word, the Son of God.

And at the beginning, when this flight is experienced the first time, God communicates to the soul great things about himself, beautifies her with grandeur and majesty, adorns her with gifts and virtues, and clothes her with the knowledge and honor of God, as the betrothed is clothed on the day of her betrothal. Not only do her vehement yearnings and complaints of love cease but, in being graced with the blessings mentioned, a state of peace and delight and gentleness of love begins in her. This state is indicated in these stanzas, in which she does no more than tell in song her Beloved's grandeurs, which she knows and enjoys in him through this union of betrothal. In the remaining stanzas she no longer speaks of sufferings and longings as she did before, but of the communion and exchange of sweet and peaceful love with her Beloved, because now in this state all those sufferings have ceased.[1]

It should be noted that these two stanzas describe the most God communicates to the soul at this time. Yet it must not be thought that he communicates to all those who reach this state everything declared in these two stanzas, or that he does so in the same manner and measure of

---

1. In fact, as will become clear, the sufferings and longings continue because the soul is still not completely purified. For further clarification, cf. F. 3. 24-26.

knowledge and feeling. To some souls he gives more and to others less, to some in one way and to others in another, although all alike may be in this same state of spiritual betrothal. But the greatest possible communication is recorded here because it includes everything else. The commentary follows.[2]

Commentary on the Two Stanzas

3. In Noah's ark, as the divine Scripture says, there were many rooms for different kinds of animals, and all the food that could be eaten [Gn. 6:14,19-21]. It should be noted that, similarly, the soul in her flight to the divine ark, the bosom of God, not only sees there the many mansions that His Majesty through St. John declared were in his Father's house [Jn. 14:2], but sees and knows there all the foods (all the grandeurs the soul can enjoy), that is, all the things included in these two stanzas and signified by these common terms. In substance, these are:

4. The soul sees and tastes abundance and inestimable riches in this divine union. She finds all the rest and recreation she desires, and understands secrets and strange knowledge of God, which is another of the foods that taste best to her. She experiences in God an awesome power and a strength that sweep away every other power and strength. She tastes there a splendid spiritual sweetness and gratification, discovers true quiet and divine light, and tastes sublimely the wisdom of God reflected in the harmony of his creatures and works. She has the feeling of being filled with blessings and being empty of evils and far removed from them. And, above all, she understands and enjoys inestimable refreshment of love, which confirms her in love. These in substance are the affirmations of the two stanzas.

5. The bride says in these stanzas that the Beloved is all these things in himself, and he is so also for her, because in such superabundant communications from God the soul experiences and knows the truth of St. Francis' prayer: My God and all things.[3] Since God is all things to the soul and the good that is in all things, the communication of this superabundance is explained through the likeness that the goodness of the things mentioned in these stanzas has to it, which we shall explain in our commentary on each of the verses. It should be known that what is explained here is present in God eminently and infinitely, or better, each

---

2. These are important observations that can serve as principles for interpreting John's descriptions of these mystical experiences.
3. Bartholomew of Pisa tells how St. Francis of Assisi spent an entire night in prayer repeating the words *Deus meus et omnia.*

of these sublime attributes is God, and all of them together are God.[4]

Inasmuch as the soul in this case is united with God, she feels that all things are God, as St. John experienced when he said: *Quod factum est, in ipso vita erat* (That which was made, in him was life) [Jn. 1:4]. It should not be thought that what the soul is said to feel here is comparable to seeing things by means of the light, or creatures by means of God; rather in this possession the soul feels that God is all things for her. Neither must it be thought that, because the soul has so sublime an experience of God, we are asserting that she has essential and clear vision of him. This experience is nothing but a strong and overflowing communication and glimpse of what God is in himself, in which the soul feels the goodness of the things mentioned in these verses, which we will now comment upon.[5]

My Beloved, the mountains,

6. Mountains have heights and they are affluent, vast, beautiful, graceful, bright, and fragrant. These mountains are what my Beloved is to me.

and lonely wooded valleys,

7. Lonely valleys are quiet, pleasant, cool, shady, and flowing with fresh waters; in the variety of their groves and in the sweet song of the birds, they afford abundant recreation and delight to the senses, and in their solitude and silence they refresh and give rest. These valleys are what my Beloved is to me.

strange islands,

8. Strange islands are surrounded by water and situated across the sea, far withdrawn and cut off from communication with others. Many things very different from what we have here are born and nurtured in these islands; these things are of many strange kinds and powers never before seen by humans, and they cause surprise and wonder in anyone who sees them. Thus, because of the wonderful new things and the strange knowledge (far removed from common knowledge) that the soul sees in God, she calls him "strange islands."[6]

People are called strange for either of two reasons: They are with-

---

4. John accepts the scholastic theory that everything that consists of a perfection pure and simple may be attributed to God in an eminent degree (or analogously). The divine attributes do not designate perfections really distinct from one another; in God all reality is his very being.

5. In John's opinion the direct vision of God in this life is impossible, and so he speaks of these experiences as "glimpses." Cf. A. 2. 24. 2-4; C. 7. 9; 12. 7-8; 13. 10.

6. John could have had in mind the Americas or the Philippines.

drawn from others; or, compared with others, they are singular and superior in their deeds and works. The soul calls God "strange" for these two reasons. Not only is he all the strangeness of islands never seen before, but also his ways, counsels, and works are very strange and new and wonderful to humans.

It is no wonder that God is strange to humans who have not seen him, since he is also strange to the holy angels and to the blessed. For the angels and the blessed are incapable of seeing him fully, nor will they ever be capable of doing so. Until the day of the Last Judgment they will see so many new things in him concerning his deep judgments and his works of mercy and justice that they will forever be receiving new surprises and marveling the more. Hence not only humans but also the angels can call him "strange islands." Only to himself is he neither strange nor new.

> and resounding rivers,

9. Rivers have three properties: first, they besiege and inundate everything they encounter; second, they fill up all the low and empty spots found along their path; third, they are so loud that they muffle and suppress every other sound. Since in this communication in God the soul has a delightful experience of these three properties, she says that her Beloved is the resounding rivers.

As for the first property, it should be known that the soul is conscious at this time that the torrent of God's spirit is besieging and taking possession of her so forcibly that all the rivers of the world seem to have flooded in upon her and to be assailing her. She feels that all the actions and passions in which she was formerly occupied are drowned therein. Although it is a thing of tremendous force, this is not a torment to her because these rivers are rivers of peace, as God declared of this onslaught through Isaiah: *Ecce ego declinabo super eam quasi fluvium pacis, et quasi torrentem inundantem gloriam* (See that I will descend and besiege her— the soul—like a river of peace and like a torrent overflowing with glory) [Is. 66:12]. Hence this divine onslaught caused by God in the soul, like resounding rivers, fills everything with peace and glory.

The second property the soul experiences at this time is the divine water filling the low places of her humility and the voids of her appetites, as St. Luke says: *Exaltavit humiles; esurientes implevit bonis* (he exalted the humble and filled the hungry with good things) [Lk. 1:52-53].

The third property she experiences in these resounding rivers of her Beloved is a spiritual clamor and outcry louder than any other sound or call. This cry prevails against all other cries and its sound exceeds all the sounds of the world. To explain how this comes about we will have to delay a short while.

10. This clamor, or resounding of these rivers, that the soul refers to

here is such an abundant plenitude that she is filled with goods, and it is so powerful a force that she is possessed by it, for it seems to be not merely the sound of rivers but the sound of roaring thunder. Nevertheless this cry is a spiritual cry that does not contain these other material sounds, or their pain and disturbance, but rather grandeur, strength, power, delight, and glory. It is like an immense interior clamor and sound that clothes the soul in power and strength.

This spiritual cry and noise was made in the souls of the Apostles when the Holy Spirit descended like a mighty wind, as is related in the Acts of the Apostles [Acts 2:2]. To manifest the spiritual voice bestowed on them interiorly, that sound was heard exteriorly as a fierce wind by all who were in Jerusalem [Acts 2:5-6]. This sound denoted what the Apostles received interiorly, a fullness of power and fortitude.

St. John says that while the Lord Jesus was praying to his Father in the conflict and anguish occasioned by his enemies, an inner voice came to him from heaven and comforted him in his humanity. The sound of this voice, which the Jews heard as though coming from outside, was so deep and loud that some said it had thundered and others that an angel from heaven had spoken [Jn. 12:27-29]. The reason is that the voice, which was heard as though coming from without, denoted and manifested the fortitude and strength that was interiorly bestowed on Christ in his humanity.

It must not be thought on this account that the soul fails to receive in its spirit the sound of the spiritual voice. It should be noted that the spiritual voice is the effect produced in the spirit, just as the sound in the ear and knowledge in the spirit are effects of the material voice. David meant this when he said: *Ecce dabit voci suae vocem virtutis* (Behold that God will give to his voice the voice of power) [Ps. 68:33]. This power is the interior voice, because when David said he will give to his voice the voice of power, he meant that to the exterior voice, heard from without, he will give the voice of power that is heard from within.

Hence it should be known that God is an infinite voice, and by communicating himself to the soul in this way he produces the effect of an immense voice.

11. St. John heard this voice and says in the Apocalypse that the voice he heard from heaven *erat tanquam vocem aquarum et tanquam vocem tonitrui magni* (was like the voice of many waters and like the voice of a great thunder) [Rv. 14:2]. So it might not be thought that because this voice was so great it was harsh and painful, he immediately adds that it was so gentle it sounded *sicut citharoedorum citharizantium in citharis suis* (like many harpists playing on their harps) [Rv. 14:2]. And Ezekiel says that this sound as of many waters was *quasi sonum sublimis Dei* (like the sound of the most high God); that is, the infinite voice was communicated in a

most lofty and gentle way. For, as we said,[7] it is God himself who communicates himself by producing this voice in the soul. But he limits himself in each soul, measuring out the voice of power according to the soul's capacity, and this voice produces great delight and grandeur. As a result he said to the bride in the Song of Songs: *Sonet vox tua in auribus meis, vox enim tua dulcis* (Let your voice sound in my ears, for your voice is sweet) [Sg. 2:14].

The whistling of love-stirring breezes,

12. The soul refers to two things in this verse: the breezes and the whistling. By "love-stirring breezes" are understood the attributes and graces of the Beloved that by means of this union assail the soul and lovingly touch her in her substance.

This most sublime and delightful knowledge of God and his attributes, which overflows into the intellect from the touch produced in the substance of the soul by these attributes of God, is called by the soul the whistling of these breezes. Of all the delight the soul here enjoys, this delight is the most exalted.

13. To understand this better it should be noted that just as two things are felt in the breeze (the touch and the whistling or sound), so in this communication of the Bridegroom two things are experienced: knowledge and a feeling of delight. As the feeling of the breeze delights the sense of touch, and its whistling the sense of hearing, so the feeling of the Beloved's attributes are felt and enjoyed by the soul's power of touch, which is in its substance, and the knowledge of these attributes is experienced in its hearing, which is the intellect.

It should also be known that the love-stirring breeze is said to come when it wounds in a pleasant way by satisfying the appetite of the one desiring such refreshment, for the sense of touch is then filled with enjoyment and refreshment; and the hearing, at the moment of this delectable touch, experiences great pleasure and gratification in the sound and whistling of the breeze. The delight of hearing is much greater than that of feeling because the sound in the sense of hearing is more spiritual; or, better, it more closely approaches the spiritual than does feeling. Consequently, the delight of hearing is more spiritual than that of feeling.

14. Since this touch of God gives intense satisfaction and enjoyment to the substance of the soul and gently fulfills her desire for this union, she calls this union or these touches "love-stirring breezes." As we have said, the Beloved's attributes are lovingly and sweetly communicated in this

---

7. In no. 10.

breeze, and from it the intellect receives the knowledge or whistling.

She calls the knowledge a "whistling" because just as the whistling of the breeze pierces deeply into the hearing organ, so this most subtle and delicate knowledge penetrates with wonderful savoriness into the innermost part of the substance of the soul, and the delight is greater than all others.[8]

The reason for the delight is that the substance, understood and stripped of accidents and phantasms, is bestowed. For this knowledge is given to the intellect that philosophers call the passive or possible intellect, and the intellect receives it passively without any effort of its own. This knowing is the soul's main delight because it is pertinent to the intellect, and, as theologians say, fruition, the vision of God, is proper to the intellect.[9] Since this whistling refers to the substantial knowledge mentioned, some theologians think our Father Elijah saw God in the whistling of the gentle breeze heard on the mount at the mouth of his cave [1 Kgs. 19:11-13].[10] Scripture calls it "the whistling of the gentle breeze" because knowledge was begotten in his intellect from the delicate spiritual communication. The soul calls this knowledge "the whistling of love-stirring breezes" because it flows over into the intellect from the loving communication of the Beloved's attributes. As a result she calls the knowledge "the whistling of the love-stirring breezes."

15. This divine whistling, which enters through the soul's hearing, is not only the substance understood, as I have said, but also an unveiling of truths about the divinity and a revelation of God's secrets.[11] When Scripture refers to a communication of God that enters by hearing, this communication ordinarily amounts to a manifestation of these naked truths to the intellect, or a revelation of the secrets of God. These are pure spiritual revelations or visions, which are given only to the spirit without the service and help of the senses. Thus what is called the communication of God through hearing is very certain and lofty.

---

8. Here John distinguishes between knowledge that is present in the intellect and knowledge in the substance of the soul. He is referring to both a conceptual and an experiential knowledge of the divine realities; cf. A. 2. 32. 3

9. Cf. Aquinas *Summa theologiae* 1-2. 3. In this explanation, moreover, John uses the scholastic theory of knowing through the process of abstraction. The active (or agent intellect) through illumination extracts from the phantasm the nature of the object. This process results in an intelligible species that the active intellect impresses on the passive (or possible) intellect, thus giving rise in this passive intellect to the universal, immaterial concept of the object.

10. Cf. A. 2. 8. 4; 24. 3.

11. These graces are amply classified and explained in A. 2. 24-27. They form a part of the totality of graces that accompany the stage of spiritual betrothal.

Accordingly, St. Paul in order to declare the height of his revelation did not say, *vidit arcana verba,* and still less, *gustavit arcana verba,* but: *audivit arcana verba quae non licet homini loqui* (he heard secret words that people are not permitted to utter) [2 Cor. 12:4]. It is thought that he saw God there as our Father Elijah also did in the whistling.

Since faith, as St. Paul also says [Rom. 10:17], comes though hearing, so too what faith tells us, the substance understood, comes through spiritual hearing. The prophet Job indicates this clearly in speaking with God who revealed himself: *Auditu auris audivi te, nunc autem oculus meus videt te* (With the hearing of the ear I heard you and now my eye sees you) [Jb. 42:5]. This passage points out clearly that to hear him with the hearing of the soul is to see him with the eye of the passive intellect. Consequently, he does not say I heard you with the hearing of my ears, but of my ear; or, I saw you with my eyes, but with my eye, which is the intellect. This hearing of the soul, therefore, is the vision of the intellect.

16. It must not be thought that, because what the soul understands is the naked substance, there is perfect and clear fruition as in heaven. Although the knowledge is stripped of accidents, it is not clear because of this, but dark, for it is contemplation, which in this life is a ray of darkness, as St. Dionysius says.[12] We can say that it is a ray and image of fruition, since it is in the intellect that fruition takes place.

This substance understood, which the soul calls "whistling," is equivalent to "the eyes I have desired," of which the soul said when they were being revealed to her, "Withdraw them, Beloved," because her senses could not endure them.

17. Because it seems to me that a passage from Job, which confirms a great deal of what I said about this rapture and betrothal, is very appropriate, I will refer to it here, even though we may be detained some more, and explain its pertinent parts. First, I will cite the entire passage in Latin, and then render it in the vernacular; afterward I will offer a brief explanation of what interests us. After this I will continue with the commentary on the verses of the other stanza.

In the Book of Job, then, Eliphaz the Temanite speaks in the following way: *Porro ad me dictum est verbum absconditum et quasi furtive suscepit auris mea venas susurri ejus. In horrore visionis nocturnae, quando solet sopor occupare homines, pavor tenuit me et tremor, et omnia ossa mea perterrita sunt; et cum spiritus, me praesente, transiret, inhorruerunt pili carnis meae. Stetit quidam, cujus non agnoscebam vultum, imago coram oculis meis, et vocem quasi aurae lenis audivi* (Truly a hidden word was spoken to me, and my ear as though by stealth received the veins of his whisper. In the horror of the nocturnal

---

12. See Pseudo-Dionysius, *The Mystical Theology* 1. 1.

vision, when sleep usually occupies people, fear and trembling took hold of me and all my bones were disturbed; and as the spirit passed before me the hair of my flesh shriveled. There stood one before me whose countenance I knew not, an image before my eyes, and I heard the voice of a gentle wind) [Jb 4:12-16]. The passage contains almost everything we have said about this rapture from stanza 13 (which says, "Withdraw them, Beloved") up to this point.

18. What Eliphaz the Temanite refers to (in saying that a hidden word was spoken to him) was given to the soul when, unable to endure it, she said, "Withdraw them, Beloved."

By saying that his ear, as though by stealth, received the veins of his whisper, he refers to the naked substance received by the intellect. The veins here denote the interior substance, and the whisper signifies that communication and touch of attributes by which the substance understood is imparted to the intellect. He calls the communication a "whisper" because it is very gentle, just as the soul calls it "love-stirring breezes" because it is lovingly bestowed. He says he received it as though by stealth because just as a stolen article is not one's own, so that secret, from a natural viewpoint, is foreign to humans, for Eliphaz received what did not belong to him naturally. Thus it was unlawful for him to receive it just as it was unlawful for St. Paul to disclose the secret words he heard [2 Cor. 12:4]. Hence the other prophet twice declared: *My secret for myself* [Is. 24:16].

In saying that fear and trembling took hold of him in the horror of the nocturnal vision when sleep usually occupies people, he refers to the fear and trembling naturally caused in the soul by that rapturous communication, unendurable to nature, in the imparting of God's spirit. The prophet here indicates that just as people are oppressed and frightened by the vision called a nightmare that occurs when they are about to sleep (at the moment between sleeping and waking, the point at which sleep begins), so at the time of this spiritual transport, between the sleep of natural ignorance and the wakefulness of supernatural knowledge, which is the beginning of the rapture or ecstasy, the communication of a spiritual vision gives rise to this fear and trembling.

19. And he adds that all his bones were terrified or disturbed, which amounts to saying that they were shaken and dislocated. He refers here to the great disjuncture of the bones that we said they suffer at this time.[13] Daniel clearly indicates this when he says on seeing the angel: *Domine in visione tua dissolutae sunt compages meae* (Lord, on seeing you the joints of my bones are loosed) [Dn. 10:16].

---

13. In 13. 4-7; cf N. 2. 1. 2.

And in what Eliphaz says next, that is, "and as the spirit passed before me" (by making my spirit pass beyond its natural limits and ways through the rapture we have mentioned), "the hair of my flesh shriveled," he attests to our teaching concerning the body: that in this transport, as in death, it remains frozen, and the flesh stiff.

20. And he continues, "there stood before me one whose countenance I knew not, an image before my eyes." He who stood before him was God, who communicated himself in the manner mentioned. And he says he did not know his countenance in order to signify that in such a communication and vision, even though most sublime, the countenance and essence of God is neither known nor seen. Yet he says it was an image before his eyes, because the knowledge of the hidden word was most high, like an image and trace of God, but he is not referring to the essential vision of God.

21. Then he concludes, saying, "and I heard the voice of a gentle wind." This voice of the gentle wind refers to the whistling of love-stirring breezes, which the soul says is her Beloved.

It must not be thought that these visits are always accompanied by natural tremblings and torments; for, as we said,[14] these are found only in those who are beginning to enter the state of illumination and perfection and this kind of communication; in others, they are very gentle. The commentary continues:

the tranquil night

22. In this spiritual sleep in the bosom of the Beloved, the soul possesses and relishes all the tranquility, rest, and quietude of the peaceful night; and she receives in God, together with this peace, a fathomless and obscure divine knowledge. As a result she says that her Beloved is a tranquil night to her.

at the time of the rising dawn,

23. Yet she does not say that the tranquil night is equivalent to a dark night, but rather that it is like the night that has reached the time of the rising dawn. This quietude and tranquility in God is not entirely obscure to the soul as is a dark night; but it is a tranquility and quietude in divine light, in the new knowledge of God, in which the spirit elevated to the divine light is in quiet.

She very appropriately calls this divine light "the rising dawn," which means the morning. Just as the rise of morning dispels the darkness of night and unveils the light of day, so this spirit, quieted and put to rest in

---

14. In 13. 6.

God, is elevated from the darkness of natural knowledge to the morning light of the supernatural knowledge of God.[15] This morning light is not clear, as was said, but dark as night at the time of the rising dawn. Just as the night at the rise of dawn is not entirely night or entirely day, but is, as they say, at the break of day, so this divine solitude and tranquility, informed by the divine light, has some share in that light, but not its complete clarity.

24. In this tranquility the intellect is aware of being elevated to the divine light in a strangely new way above all natural understanding, just as after a long sleep one opens one's eyes to the unexpected light.

I think David was referring to this knowledge when he said: *Vigilavi et factus sum sicut passer solitarius in tecto* (I have kept watch and am become like a solitary sparrow on the housetop) [Ps. 102:7]. This was like saying: I opened the eyes of my intellect and found myself above all natural knowledge, without this knowledge, and alone on the housetop, which is above all low things.[16]

He says he became like the solitary sparrow because in this contemplation the spirit has the traits of a solitary sparrow. There are five of these traits:

First, the sparrow ordinarily perches on the highest things. And so the spirit at this stage is placed in the highest contemplation.

Second, it always turns its beak toward the wind. Thus the spirit ever turns the beak of its affection toward the Spirit of Love, who is God.

Third, it is usually alone and allows no other bird close to it; when another perches nearby, it flies away. Thus the spirit in this contemplation is alone in regard to all things, stripped of them all, nor does it allow within itself anything other than solitude in God.

The fourth trait is that it sings very sweetly. And so does the spirit sing sweetly to God at this time, for the praises it renders him are of the most delightful love, pleasant to the soul and precious in God's eyes.

The fifth is that it possesses no definite color. So neither does the perfect spirit, in this excess, have any color of sensible affection or self-love; it does not even have any particular consideration in either its lower or higher part, nor will it be able to describe the mode or manner of this excess, for what it possesses is an abyss of the knowledge of God.

silent music,

25. In that nocturnal tranquility and silence and in knowledge of the divine light the soul becomes aware of Wisdom's wonderful harmony and sequence in the variety of her creatures and works. Each of them is en-

---

15. Cf. A. 1. 2. 5; A. 2. 2. 1-2.
16. Cf. A. 2. 14. 11; and also St. Teresa, *Life* 20. 10.

dowed with a certain likeness of God and in its own way gives voice to what God is in it. So creatures will be for the soul a harmonious symphony of sublime music surpassing all concerts and melodies of the world. She calls this music "silent" because it is tranquil and quiet knowledge, without the sound of voices. And thus there is in it the sweetness of music and the quietude of silence. Accordingly, she says that her Beloved is silent music because in him she knows and enjoys this symphony of spiritual music. Not only is he silent music, but he is also

Sounding solitude,

26. This is almost identical with silent music, for even though that music is silent to the natural senses and faculties, it is sounding solitude for the spiritual faculties. When these spiritual faculties are alone and empty of all natural forms and apprehensions, they can receive in a most sonorous way the spiritual sound of the excellence of God, in himself and in his creatures. We said above[17] that St. John speaks of this spiritual vision in the Apocalypse, that is: *the voice of many harpists playing on their harps* [Rv. 14:2]. This vision was spiritual and had nothing to do with material harps. It involved a knowledge of the praises that the blessed, each in an individual degree of glory, give continually to God. This praise is like music, for as each one possesses God's gifts differently, each one sings God's praises differently, and all of them together form a symphony of love, as of music.

27. In this same way the soul perceives in that tranquil wisdom that all creatures, higher and lower ones alike, according to what each in itself has received from God, raise their voice in testimony to what God is. She beholds that each in its own way, bearing God within itself according to its capacity, magnifies God. And thus all these voices form one voice of music praising the grandeur, wisdom, and wonderful knowledge of God.

This is the meaning of the Holy Spirit in the Book of Wisdom when he said: *Spiritus Domini replevit orbem terrarum, et hoc quod continet omnia, scientiam habet vocis* (The Spirit of the Lord filled the whole earth, and this world, which contains all things, has knowledge of the voice) [Wis. 1:7]. This voice is the sounding solitude the soul knows here; that is, the testimony to God that, in themselves, all things give.

Since the soul does not receive this sonorous music without solitude and estrangement from all exterior things, she calls it "silent music" and "sounding solitude," which she says is her Beloved. And what is more:

The supper that refreshes, and deepens love.

28. Supper affords lovers refreshment, satisfaction, and love. Since in

---

17. In no. 11.

this gentle communication the Beloved produces these three benefits in the soul, she calls it "the supper that refreshes, and deepens love."

It should be known that in divine Scripture this term "supper" refers to the divine vision [Rv. 3:20-21]. Just as supper comes at the end of a day's work and the beginning of evening rest, this tranquil knowledge causes the soul to experience a certain end of her evils and the possession of good things in which her love of God is deepened more than before. As a result, he is the supper that refreshes by being the end of evils for her, and deepens love by being to her the possession of all goods.

29. Yet for a better understanding of what this supper is to the soul—it is, as we said, her Beloved—we should note in this appropriate place what the beloved Bridegroom says in the Apocalypse: *I stand at the door and knock; if anyone opens, I shall enter and we shall sup together* [Rv. 3:20]. In this text he indicates that he carries his supper with him, and it is nothing but his very own delights and savors that he himself enjoys. In uniting himself with the soul he imparts them, and she likewise enjoys them. For such is the meaning of the words, "we shall sup together." Hence these words declare the effect of the divine union of the soul with God, in which God's very own goods are graciously and bounteously shared in common with his bride, the soul. He himself is for her the supper that refreshes and deepens love, for in being bounteous he refreshes her, and in being gracious he deepens love in her.

30. Before continuing with the commentary on the remaining stanzas, we ought to point out here that even though we have said that in this state of betrothal the soul enjoys complete tranquility and receives the most abundant communication possible in this life, it should be understood that this tranquility refers only to the superior part. Until the state of spiritual marriage the sensory part never completely loses the dross left from bad habits or brings all its energies into subjection, as will be said later. The communication being referred to is the most abundant possible in the state of betrothal. In spiritual marriage there are striking advantages over this state of betrothal, for although the bride, the soul, enjoys so much good in these visits of the state of betrothal, she still suffers from her Beloved's withdrawal and from disturbances and afflictions in her sensory part and from the devil; all of these cease in the state of marriage.[18]

---

18. This number appears in the style of the introductions preceding the stanzas. Its purpose is to further clarify the characteristics of spiritual betrothal as distinct from spiritual marriage. The rest of the poem and commentary deals with either spiritual betrothal or spiritual marriage. The differences between the two are more obvious in the following arrangement of the stanzas than they were in John's first draft of this work.

STANZA 16

Introduction

1. Since the virtues of the bride are perfect and she enjoys habitual peace in the visits of her Beloved, she sometimes has a sublime enjoyment of their sweetness and fragrance when her Beloved touches these virtues, just as a person will enjoy the sweetness and beauty of flowers and lilies when they have blossomed and are handled. In many of these visits the soul sees within her spirit all her virtues by means of the light the Bridegroom causes. And then in a wonderful delight of love she gathers them together and offers them to him as a bouquet of beautiful flowers. And he, in accepting them—for indeed he accepts them—receives great service.

All of this goes on interiorly. The soul feels that the Beloved is within her as in his own bed. She offers herself together with her virtues, which is the greatest service she can render him. Thus one of the most remarkable delights she receives in her interior communion with God comes from this gift of herself to her Beloved.

2. The devil, who in his great malice is envious of all the good he sees in the soul, knowing of her prosperity, now employs all his ability and engages all his crafts to disturb this good, even if only a slight part of it. It is worth more to him to hinder a small fraction of this soul's rich and glorious delight than to make many others fall into numerous serious sins, for these others have little or nothing to lose; but this soul has very much to lose because of all her precious gain. The loss of a little pure gold is much worse than the loss of many other base metals.

The devil at this point takes advantage of the sensory appetites, although most of the time he can do very little or nothing, since these appetites are already deadened in persons who have reached this state. When he is unable to stir these appetites, he produces a great variety of images in the imagination. He is sometimes the cause of many movements of the sensory part of the soul and of many other disturbances, spiritual as well as sensory. It is not in a person's power to be free of these until the Lord sends his angel, as is said in the psalm, round about them that fear him and delivers them [Ps. 34:7], and until he brings peace and tranquility in both the sensory and spiritual parts of the soul.

Referring to the devil's disturbances and distrustful of the wiles he uses to cause her harm at this time, the soul, seeking this favor from God, speaks to the angels whose duty it is to assist her now by putting the devil to flight. She recites the following stanza:

Catch us the foxes,
for our vineyard is now in flower,
while we fashion a cone of roses
intricate as the pine's;
and let no one appear on the hill.

Commentary

3. Desirous that neither envious and malicious devils nor wild sensory appetites nor the various wanderings of the imagination nor any other knowledge or awareness hamper the continuance of this interior delight of love, which is the flower of her vineyard, the bride invokes the angels, telling them to catch all these disturbances and keep them from interfering with the interior exercise of love, in the delight of which the virtues and graces are communicated and enjoyed by both the soul and the Son of God. And thus she says:

Catch us the foxes,
for our vineyard is now in flower,

4. The vineyard spoken of is the nursery of all the virtues in this holy soul; these virtues supply her with a sweet-tasting wine. This vineyard is in flower when the soul is united with her Bridegroom according to the will and gladdened in him according to all these virtues together.

At times, as we said, many various kinds of images are brought to the memory and phantasy and many appetites and inclinations are stirred up in the sensory part. These are of so many kinds that when David was drinking this delicious spiritual wine with intense thirst for God, he proclaimed on experiencing the hindrance caused by them: *My soul has thirsted for you; oh, how many ways my flesh for you!* [Ps. 63:1].

5. The soul calls all this harmonious composite of appetites and sensory movements "foxes" because of the great resemblance. As foxes pretend to be asleep when they are out to catch their prey, so all these appetites and sensory powers are tranquil and asleep until these flowers of virtues rise and blossom in the soul in an exercise of love. At that moment, then, it seems that the sensual flowers of the appetites and sense powers awaken and arise in the sensory part of the soul in an effort to contradict the spirit and to reign. Covetousness will reach such a point, as St. Paul says, that the flesh covets against the spirit [Gal. 5:17]. Since the flesh has a strong inclination to sensory things, once the spirit finds delight the flesh becomes distasteful and unpleasant.[1] As a result these

---

1. Cf. N. 1. 9. 4. note 1. The maxim *gustato spiritu disipit omnis caro* seems to come from St. Bernard, *Epistola* 111, in Migne, PL 182. 2558.

appetites are a notable disturbance to the sweet spirit. Thus she says: "Catch us the foxes."

6. The malicious devils on their part disturb the soul in two ways: They vehemently incite and stimulate these appetites and, by means of them and other imaginations, and so on, wage war on this peaceful and flowering kingdom of the soul.

In the second way, which is worse, when it is impossible for these devils to disturb her in the first way, they assail her with bodily torments and noises in order to distract her. And what is still worse, they struggle against her with spiritual terrors and horrors that sometimes become a frightful torment. If permission is given them they can do this very easily, for since the soul at this time enters into great nakedness of spirit for the sake of this spiritual exercise, the devil can easily show himself to her, because he is also spirit.[2]

At other times he attacks her with different horrors before she begins to enjoy these sweet flowers, when God is beginning to withdraw her from the house of the senses that she may enter, through this interior exercise, the garden of her Bridegroom. The devil knows that once the soul has entered into that recollection, she is so fortified that however much he may try he cannot do her harm. Frequently when he goes out to block the soul she recollects herself very quickly in her deep interior hiding place, where she finds intense delight and protection. Then the terrors she suffers seem so exterior and far away that the devils not only fail to frighten her but cause her happiness and joy.

7. The bride of the Song of Songs spoke of these terrors, saying: *My soul troubles me because of the chariots of Aminadab* [Sg. 6:12]. By Aminadab she refers to the devil, and she call his attacks and assaults chariots because of the terrible violence and clamor he produces with them.

The soul afterward says here: "Catch us the foxes"; this very request was made by the bride of the Song of Songs: *Catch us the little foxes that damage the vines, for our vineyard is in flower* [Sg. 2:15]. She does not say "catch me" but "catch us," because she is speaking of both herself and the Beloved. They are united and enjoying the flower of the vine.

The reason she says the vine is in flower rather than with fruit is that, even though the virtues in this life are enjoyed with all this perfection we have been discussing, she merely enjoys them as though in flower. Only in the next life will they be enjoyed as the fruit. And she adds:

> while we fashion a cone of roses
> intricate as the pine's;

---

2. Cf. St. Teresa's *Life*, chs. 30. 9-22; 31. 1-11.

8. While the soul at this stage is enjoying the flower of this vineyard and delighting on the bosom of her Beloved, it will happen that all her virtues are suddenly and clearly revealed in their perfection and give her immense sweetness and delight. The soul feels that these virtues are both in her and in God so they seem to form a very pleasant and flowering vineyard belonging to the Bridegroom as well as to herself in which they both feed and delight. She then gathers all these virtues and makes very delightful acts of love in each of them and in all together. She offers this bouquet to the Beloved with remarkable tenderness and sweetness of love. The Beloved himself helps her, for without his favor and help she would not be able to gather these virtues and offer them to him. Hence she says: "While we fashion a cone of roses."

9. She fashions this bouquet in the shape of a pine cone, for as a pine cone is something sturdy with many pieces, or pine kernels, firmly fastened together, so this cone or bouquet of virtues that the soul arranges for her Beloved forms one perfect whole embodying in itself many perfect and strong virtues and very rich gifts. All perfections and virtues are incorporated in orderly fashion in the one solid perfection of the soul. This perfection, while being formed through the practice of the virtues—as well as when already formed—is offered by the soul to the Beloved in that spirit of love we are discussing. These foxes should, then, be caught so they do not hinder the interior communion of the two.

The bride asks not only for the ability to make a good bouquet but also for what follows in the next verse:

and let no one appear on the hill.

10. To attain this divine interior exercise there is also need for solitude and withdrawal from all things presentable to the soul, whether from the lower, sensory portion, or from the higher, rational part. These two parts comprise the entire compound of human faculties and senses, and she calls this compound a "hill." All the natural knowledge and the appetites dwelling on the hill in this harmonious composite are like prey to the devil, who hunts and catches them in order to harm the soul.

She says: "And let no one appear on the hill," that is, let no image of any object belonging to any of these faculties or senses we have mentioned appear before the soul and the Bridegroom. This is like saying: Let there be no particular knowledge or affection or other consideration in any of the spiritual faculties (memory, intellect, and will); and let there be no other digressions, forms, images, or figures of objects, or other natural operations in any of the bodily senses and faculties, either interior or exterior (the imaginative power and phantasy, and so on, sight and hearing, and so on).

11. The soul says this because, for the perfect enjoyment of this communion with God, all the senses and faculties, interior and exterior, should be unoccupied, idle, and empty of their own operations and objects. The more active they are in themselves at such a time, the more they hinder communication. When the soul reaches a certain degree of interior union of love, the spiritual faculties are no longer active, and much less the corporeal ones, since the union of love is already wrought and the soul is actuated in love. Thus the faculties cease their work, since on attaining the end the activity of the means ceases. Then the soul attends to God with love, which is to love in the continuance of unitive love.

"And let no one appear on the hill" then. Let only the will appear, attending to the Beloved in a surrender of self and of all the virtues in the way described.

STANZA 17

Introduction

. 1. For a greater understanding of the following stanza it should be pointed out that the experiences of the Beloved's absence, which the soul suffers in this state of spiritual betrothal, are very painful; some are of such a kind that no suffering is comparable to them. The reason for such affliction is that since she has a singular and intense love for God in this state, his absence is a singular and intense torment for her. Added to this torment is the disturbance that she receives at this time from any kind of converse or communication with creatures. Since she lives with that driving force of a fathomless desire for union with God, any delay whatever is very burdensome and disturbing, just as anything in the path of a stone that is racing on toward its center would cause a violent jolt in that void. Since the soul has already received the delight of these sweet visits, they are more desirable than gold and all beauty. Fearing as a result the great lack—even if momentary—of so precious a presence, she speaks in this stanza both to dryness and to the spirit of her Bridegroom:

> Be still, deadening north wind;
> south wind come, you that waken love,
> breathe through my garden,
> let its fragrance flow,
> and the Beloved will feed amid the flowers.

Commentary

2. Besides what was said in the previous stanza, spiritual dryness also

hampers the interior satisfaction and sweetness of which she spoke.[1] Dreading this, she does two things here:

First, she impedes dryness by closing the door to it through continual prayer and devotion.

Second, she invokes the Holy Spirit; it is he who will dispel this dryness and sustain and increase her love for the Bridegroom. He also moves the soul to the interior exercise of the virtues, so that the Son of God, her Bridegroom, may rejoice and delight more in his bride. She invokes the Holy Spirit because her entire aim is to please her Bridegroom.

> Be still, deadening north wind;

3. The north wind is very cold; it dries up and withers the flowers and plants, or at least makes them shrink and close when striking them. Because the spiritual dryness and affective absence of the Beloved produce this same effect in the soul by extinguishing the satisfaction, delight, and fragrance of the virtues she was enjoying, she calls it a "deadening north wind." It deadens the virtues and affective exercise, and as a result the soul pleads, "Be still, deadening north wind."

It should be understood that this plea of the soul flows from prayer and the spiritual exercises and is directed toward a detainment of the dryness. Yet since God's communications to the soul are so interior that she cannot actively move her own faculties to the enjoyment of these communications unless the Spirit of the Bridegroom causes this movement of love, she invokes him, saying:

> south wind, come, you that waken love,

4. The south wind is a delightful breeze: it causes rain, makes herbs and plants germinate, opens flowers, and spreads their fragrance. Its effects are the opposite of those of the north wind. The soul, by this breeze, refers to the Holy Spirit, who awakens love. When this divine breeze strikes her, it wholly enkindles and refreshes her, quickens and awakens the will, and elevates the previously fallen appetites that were asleep to the love of God; it does so in such a way that she can easily add, "you that waken love," both his love and hers. What she asks of the Holy Spirit is expressed in this verse:

> breathe through my garden,

5. This garden is the soul. As the soul above calls herself a "vineyard in flower" because the flower of her inner virtues supplies sweet-tasting wine, here she calls herself a garden because the flowers of perfections and virtues planted within her come to life and begin to grow.

It should be noted that the bride does not say "breathe into my garden"

---

1. Cf. C. 16. 2.

but "breathe through my garden," for there is a considerable difference between God's breathing into the soul and his breathing through the soul. To breathe into the soul is to infuse graces, gifts, and virtues. To breathe through the soul is to touch and put in motion the virtues and perfections already given, renewing and moving them in such a way that of themselves they afford the soul a wonderful fragrance and sweetness, as when you shake aromatic spices and they spread their abundant fragrance that before this was neither so strong nor so highly perceptible. The soul is not always actually experiencing and enjoying the acquired or infused virtues because, as we shall say later, they remain within her in this life like flowers enclosed in the bud or like aromatic spices whose scent is not perceived until shaken and uncovered.

6. God sometimes grants these favors to the soul, his bride. With his Spirit he breathes through her flowering garden, opens all these buds of virtues, and uncovers these aromatic spices of gifts, perfections, and riches; and, disclosing this interior treasure and wealth, he reveals all her beauty. And then it is something wonderful to behold and pleasant to feel: the richness of her gifts unveiled to the soul and the beauty of these flowers of virtues now in full bloom. And the fragrant scent each one with its own characteristics gives to her is inestimable. She calls this the flowing of the garden's fragrance when she says in the following verse:
> let its fragrance flow,

7. Sometimes the fragrance is so abundant that it seems to the soul that she is clothed with delight and bathed in inestimable glory to such an extent that the experience is not only within her but overflows and becomes manifest outside her, and those capable of recognizing it are aware of her experience. It seems to them that she is in a pleasant garden filled with the delights and riches of God. And not only when these flowers are open can you see this in these holy souls, but they ordinarily bear in themselves an "I-don't-know-what" of greatness and dignity. This causes awe and respect in others because of the supernatural effect diffused in such persons from their close and familiar conversation with God. It is said of Moses in Exodus that others were unable to look on his countenance because of the honor and glory that remained with him after he conversed face to face with God [Ex. 34:29-30; 2 Cor. 3:7].

8. In this breathing through the soul, which is the Holy Spirit's visit of love, the Bridegroom, the Son of God, is himself sublimely communicated. He sends his Spirit, as he sent his Apostles [Lk. 22:8], to act as his quartermaster, to prepare his dwelling, the bride-soul, by raising her up in delight and adorning this garden, opening its flowers, uncovering the gifts, and decorating her with the tapestry of graces and riches.

And thus the bride has immense longing that the north wind be stilled and the south wind come and breathe through her garden. For then the soul gains many things together: She gains the agreeable exercise of the perfect virtues; she gains enjoyment of the Beloved in them, since by their means he communicates himself to her with more intimate love and grants her a more particular favor than before; her Beloved delights more in her through this exercise of the virtues, and this is what she most enjoys (pleasing the Beloved); and she also gains the continuation of this delight and sweetness of the virtues. This endures as long as the Bridegroom thus sustains his bride and gives her sweetness in her virtues, as she says in the Song of Songs: *While the king was at his repose* (in the soul), *my flowering spikenard gave forth its fragrance* [Sg. 1:12]. This fragrant spikenard refers to the soul herself, who from the flowers of the virtues within her gives forth the scent of sweetness to her Beloved dwelling in her in this union.

9. Hence this divine breeze of the Holy Spirit should be greatly desired. Let each soul petition that he breathe through her garden so the divine fragrance might flow. Since this is so necessary and brings such glory and good to the soul, the bride in the Song of Songs desired and asked for it in the same terms as here, saying: *Arise north wind, come south wind and blow through my garden, and its fragrance and precious spices will flow* [Sg. 4:16].

The soul desires this, not for her own pleasure and glory but because she knows that her Bridegroom delights in this, and it is a preparation and foretelling of the coming of the Son of God to take his delight in her. She says next:

and the Beloved will feed amid the flowers.

10. The soul applies the word "feed" to the delight the Son of God takes in her at this time. This term provides an appropriate description, since food is something that not only gives pleasure but also sustains. The Son of God finds delight in the soul in these her delights, and is sustained in her; that is, he dwells in her as in a place that pleases him, for the soul is indeed pleasing to him. This, I believe, is what he meant through what Solomon said in Proverbs: *My delights are with the children of this earth* [Prv. 8:31], that is, when their delight is to be with me, who am the Son of God.

It should be noted that the soul does not say the Beloved will feed on the flowers, but amid the flowers. Since the Bridegroom communicates himself to the soul by means of the adornment of these virtues, he feeds on the soul, transforming her into himself, now that she is prepared and seasoned with the flowers of virtues, gifts, and perfections; these are the seasonings with which, and among which, he feeds on her. By means of the Holy Spirit, who prepares the dwelling, these virtues delight the Son of God so that through them he may feed more on the love of the soul. This is characteristic of the Bridegroom: to unite himself with the soul amid the fragrance of these flowers.

The bride of the Song of Songs, as one who knows so well, notes this characteristic in these words: *My Beloved is gone down into the garden, to the small threshing floor and the air scented with the aromatic spices, to pasture in the gardens and gather lilies* [Sg. 6:2]. And again she says: *I for my Beloved and my Beloved for me, who feeds among the lilies* [Sg. 6:3], that is, who feeds and delights in my soul, which is his garden, amid the lilies of my virtues, perfections, and graces.

STANZA 18

Introduction

1. Since in this state of spiritual betrothal the soul is able to see her excellent qualities and ample riches and also that she does not possess and enjoy them as she would like because she still dwells in the body, her suffering is often intense, especially so when her awareness of this lack is heightened. Her presence in the body makes her feel like a noble lord held in prison. Such a prisoner is subject to a thousand miseries, while his dominions are confiscated and he is prevented from making use of his lordship and wealth; all he gets from his riches is a little food, and that very sparingly. The extent of his suffering is obvious, for even the members of his own household are not submissive to him, and his servants and slaves without respect turn against him every chance they have, even to the point of taking from his plate the morsel of food meant for him. For at the moment God favors the soul with the taste of a morsel of the goods and riches he has prepared for her, a bad servant or appetite, sometimes an inordinate movement, sometimes other sensory rebellions, rises up in the lower part to impede this good.

2. As a result the soul feels as though she were in the land of enemies and tyrannized among strangers and like one dead among the dead. She has a definite experience of what the prophet Baruch discloses in stressing the misery of Jacob's captivity: *How is it, Israel, that you are in enemy land? You have grown old in a foreign land, you are defiled with the dead, you are counted with those who go down into hell* [Bar. 3:10-11]. And Jeremiah, feeling this miserable treatment the soul suffers because of its captivity in the body, speaks in a spiritual sense to Israel: *Is Israel perhaps a servant or a slave? Why is he thus imprisoned? The lions have roared upon him,* and so on [Jer. 2:14-15]. By "the lions" he refers here to the appetites and rebellions of this tyrant king, sensuality.

To manifest the trouble she receives and her desire that this kingdom of sensuality with all its armies and disturbances come to an end or be entirely subjected to her, she raises her eyes to the Bridegroom as to one who will accomplish all of this and speaks against those movements and rebellions:

> You girls of Judea,
> while among flowers and roses
> the amber spreads its perfume,
> stay away, there on the outskirts:
> do not so much as seek to touch our thresholds.

Commentary

3. It is the bride who speaks in this stanza; aware in the spiritual part of her being of rich and beneficial gifts and delights from her Beloved, she desires to preserve the security and possession found in them. She referred to these gifts and delights, of which the Bridegroom makes her conscious, in the two preceding stanzas.[1] Realizing that because of the lower, sensory part this good can be disturbed and in fact is, she begs the operations and movements of the lower faculties and senses to be still and not transcend the limits of this sensory region to molest and disquiet the higher and spiritual part. She asks this so that the good and delight enjoyed will not be impeded by even the slightest motion in this lower part. When the spirit is rejoicing, the movements of the senses and its faculties, in the measure that they are active and lively, molest and disquiet it. She says, then:

> You girls of Judea,

4. The lower, sensory part of the soul is Judea because it is weak and carnal and, of itself, blind like the Judean people. She names the imaginations, phantasies, movements, and affections of the lower part "girls." She calls them all girls because as girls attract lovers to themselves by their affection and grace, so these pleasant sensory operations and movements strive persistently to attract the will of the rational part to themselves. They try to draw it out of its interior to a desire for the exterior things that they crave. They also endeavor to move and attract the intellect so it may be wed to them in their base way of feeling, and they strive to bring the rational part into conformity and union with the sensory. You, then, O sensory operations and movements, she says,

> while among flowers and roses

5. The flowers, as we said,[2] are the soul's virtues. The rose bushes are

---

1. This reference is to the two stanzas that preceded this one in the arrangement of the first draft.
2. Throughout stanza 17.

the faculties (memory, intellect, and will) that bear and nurture in themselves the flowers of divine concepts, acts of love, and these same virtues. Then, while among these virtues and faculties of my soul

the amber spreads its perfume,

6. By "the amber" she refers to the Bridegroom's divine Spirit abiding within her. The divine amber spreading its perfume among the flowers and rose bushes is a reference to the overflow and communication of the Spirit in the faculties and virtues of the soul, by which he imparts through them the perfume of divine sweetness. While the divine Spirit is giving my soul this sweetness,

stay away, there on the outskirts:

7. The "outskirts" of Judea (and Judea, we said, refers to the lower or sensory part of the soul) are the interior senses (memory, phantasy, and imagination) in which the forms, images, and phantasms of objects gather and reside. By means of these images the sensory appetites are moved. These forms are what she refers to as girls. When they are quiet and tranquil, the appetites are also asleep. These images enter the outskirts, the interior senses, through the gates of the exterior senses—hearing, sight, smell, and so on. They do so in such a way that we can call both the interior and exterior sense faculties "outskirts," for they are the districts outside the walls of the city. That part of the soul called the city is the innermost part, the rational portion, which is capable of communion with God; its operations are contrary to those of the sensory part.

Yet because there is a natural communication of the people, or girls, dwelling in these outskirts of the sensory part with the superior part or city, this communication is of such a kind that what occurs in this lower part is usually felt in the interior part, and consequently distracts and deprives this part of the peace derived from its spiritual activity and attentiveness to God. As a result she tells those dwelling in the outskirts, in the interior and exterior senses, to remain quiet.

do not so much as seek to touch our thresholds.

8. This means that they should not even touch the superior part through the first movements. The first movements are the entrances and thresholds of the soul. When these girls pass beyond first movements to the rational part of the soul, they cross the thresholds. But in the case of first movements, it is said that they merely set foot on the thresholds or knock at the door. This happens when the sensory part attacks the rational for the sake of some inordinate act. The soul not only tells these girls not to enter, but also tells them not to distract the quietude and good she enjoys.

STANZA 19

Introduction

1. The soul in this state becomes such an enemy of the lower part and its operations that she does not want God to communicate to that part any of the spiritual good he gives to the higher part. Because of its weak condition the sensory part is unable to endure an abundant spiritual communication without fainting. Consequently the spirit suffers and is afflicted and cannot enjoy the communication peacefully. As the Wise Man says: *The body on account of its corruption is a burden to the soul* [Wis. 9:15]. Since the soul desires the highest and most excellent communications from God, and is unable to receive them in the company of the sensory part, she desires God to bestow them apart from it.

St. Paul states of his sublime vision of the third heaven, in which he saw God, that he does not know whether he received it in the body or out of it [2 Cor. 12:2]. Nevertheless, in whatever way it did take place, it occurred outside the body. For if the body had participated, St. Paul would have known of this and the vision would not have been as sublime as he implied by stating that he heard such secret words that it is unlawful for anyone to speak of them [2 Cor. 12:4]. Knowing full well that such favors cannot be received by so fragile a vessel [2 Cor. 4:7], and desiring that the Bridegroom grant them outside her, or at least without her, the soul asks him in this stanza:

> Hide yourself, my love;
> turn your face toward the mountains,
> and do not speak;
> but look at those companions
> going with her through strange islands.

Commentary

2. The bride-soul asks four things of the Bridegroom in this stanza:

First, that he be pleased to communicate himself to her very inwardly, in the hiding place of the soul.

Second, that he inform and shine on her faculties with the glory and excellence of his divinity.

Third, that this communication be so sublime and profound that she may neither desire nor know how to give a description of it, and that the sensory and exterior part be incapable of receiving it.

Fourth, that he be enamored of the many virtues and graces he has placed in her. These accompany her in her ascent to God through a very lofty and elevated knowledge of the divinity and through excesses of love that are very strange and extraordinary in comparison with those she ordinarily has. Thus she says:

> Hide yourself, my love;

3. This is like saying: My dear Spouse, withdraw to the innermost part of my soul and communicate yourself in secret, manifest your hidden wonders, alien to every mortal eye.

> turn your face toward the mountains,

4. The "face" of God is the divinity, and "the mountains" are the soul's faculties (memory, intellect, and will). This verse is like saying: Let your divinity shine on my intellect by giving it divine knowledge, and on my will by imparting to it divine love, and on my memory with the divine possession of glory.

The soul asks in this line for everything she possibly can ask of him. She is no longer satisfied with the knowledge and communication of the "back" of God—which was his communication to Moses [Ex. 33:23]—and is knowledge of him in his effects and works; she can only be satisfied with God's face, which is an essential communication of the divinity to the soul. This communication is not brought about through any means, but through a certain contact of the soul with the divinity. This contact is something foreign to everything sensory and accidental, since it is a touch of naked substances—of the soul and the divinity.[1] Consequently she adds:

> and do not speak;

5. This means: Do not speak as before when the communications you granted me were such that you spoke them to the exterior senses; that is, you spoke things apprehensible to the senses since these things were not so high and deep that the sensory part could not attain to them. But now let these communications be so lofty and substantial and interior that you do not say anything to the senses, that is, let not the senses attain knowledge of them. Spiritual substance cannot be communicated to the senses, and anything imparted to sense, especially in this life, cannot be pure spirit, since sense is incapable of it.

The soul, then, desiring this communication of God that is so substantial and essential it is imperceptible to sense, asks the Bridegroom to refrain from speaking, which is like saying: Let the depth of this hiding place, which is spiritual union, be of such a kind that the senses will be unable to feel or speak of it, as were the secrets heard by St. Paul about which it was unlawful for anyone to speak [2 Cor. 12:4].

> but look at those companions

---

1. Cf. parallel texts in A. 2. 24. 3-4; C. 1. 10; F. 4. 12.

6. When God looks, he loves and grants favors. And the companions whom the soul tells God to look at are the many virtues, gifts, perfections, and other spiritual riches he has placed in her as the pledges, tokens, and jewels of betrothal. Thus this verse is like saying: But Beloved, first turn to the interior of my soul, and be enamored of the company—the riches—you have placed there, so that loving the soul through them you may dwell and hide in her. For, indeed, even though they are yours, since you gave them to her, they also belong to her,

> going with her through strange islands.

7. That is, they belong to my soul that goes to you by means of strange knowledge of you and by modes and ways that are foreign to all the senses and to common natural knowledge. And thus it is as though, desiring to oblige him, she were to say: Since I go to you through a spiritual knowledge strange and foreign to the senses, let your communication be so interior and sublime as to be foreign to all of them.

STANZAS 20 and 21

Introduction

1. The attainment of so high a state of perfection as that for which the soul here aims, which is spiritual marriage, requires the purification of all the imperfections, rebellions, and imperfect habits of the lower part, which, by being stripped of the old self [Eph. 4:22-23], is surrendered and made subject to the higher part; but a singular fortitude and a very sublime love are also needed for so strong and intimate an embrace from God. For in this state the soul obtains not only a very lofty purity and beauty but also an amazing strength because of the powerful and intimate bond effected between God and her by means of this union.

2. In order that she reach him, it is necessary for her to attain an adequate degree of purity, fortitude, and love. The Holy Spirit, he who intervenes to effect this spiritual union, desiring that the soul attain the possession of these qualities in order to merit this union, speaks to the Father and the Son in the Song of Songs: *What shall we do for our sister on the day of her courtship, for she is little and has no breasts? If she is a wall, let us build upon it silver bulwarks and defenses; and if she is a door, let us reinforce it with cedar wood* [Sg. 8:8-9]. The silver bulwarks and defenses refer to the strong and heroic virtues covered with faith, which is signified by the silver. These heroic virtues are those of spiritual marriage, and their foundation is in the strong soul, referred to by the wall. The peaceful Bridegroom rests in the strength of these virtues without any weakness

disturbing him. The cedar wood applies to the affections and properties of lofty love. This lofty love is signified by cedar and it is the love proper to spiritual marriage. The bride must first be a door in order to receive the reinforcement of cedar wood; that is, she must hold the door of her will open to the Bridegroom so he may enter through the complete and true "yes" of love. This is the yes of betrothal that is given before the spiritual marriage. The breasts of the bride also refer to this perfect love that she should possess in order to appear before the Bridegroom, Christ, for the consummation of this state.

3. The text, however, mentions that the bride answered immediately by stating her desire to be courted: *I am a wall and my breasts are as a tower* [Sg. 8:10]. This means: My soul is strong and my love lofty, and so I should not be held back. Desiring this perfect union and transformation, the bride also manifested this strength in the preceding stanzas, especially in the one just explained, in which to oblige her bridegroom further she sets before him the virtues and preparative riches received from him. As a result the Bridegroom, desiring to conclude this matter, speaks the two following stanzas in which he finishes purifying the soul, strengthening and disposing her in both sensory and spiritual parts for this state. He speaks these lines against all the oppositions and rebellions from the sensory part and the devil.

Bridegroom

> Swift-winged birds,
> lions, stags, and leaping roes,
> mountains, lowlands, and river banks,
> waters, winds, and ardors,
> watching fears of night:
>
> By the pleasant lyres
> and the siren's song, I conjure you
> to cease your anger
> and not touch the wall,
> that the bride may sleep in deeper peace.

Commentary

4. In these two stanzas the Bridegroom, the Son of God, gives the bride-soul possession of peace and tranquility by conforming the lower part to the higher, cleansing it of all its imperfections, bringing under rational control the natural faculties and motives, and quieting all the other appetites mentioned in these two stanzas. The meaning of these stanzas is:

First, the Bridegroom conjures and commands the useless wanderings of the phantasy and imaginative power to cease once and for all.

He also puts under the control of reason the two natural powers, the irascible and the concupiscible, which were previously somewhat of an affliction to the soul.[1]

And, insofar as is possible in this life, he perfects the three faculties (memory, intellect, and will) in regard to their objects.

What is more, he conjures and commands the four passions (joy, hope, fear, and sorrow) so from now on they will be mitigated and controlled by reason.

Such is the meaning of the terms used in the first of these stanzas. The Bridegroom makes these disturbing activities and movements cease by means of the immense delight and sweetness and strength received in the spiritual communication and surrender he makes of himself at this time. Because God vitally transforms the soul into himself, all these faculties, appetites, and movements lose their natural imperfection and are changed to divine. And thus he says:

> Swift-winged birds,

5. He calls the wanderings of the imagination "swift-winged birds," for these digressions are quick and restless in flying from one place to another. When the will is enjoying the delightful communication of the Beloved in quietude, these wanderings usually displease her by their restless flights and put an end to her satisfaction. The Bridegroom says that he conjures them by the pleasant lyres, and so on (by sweetness and delight so abundant and frequent that they cannot be the impediment they were before she reached so high a state), to cease their restless flights, impulses, and excesses. This should be understood similarly regarding the other verses we will comment on here, such as:

> lions, stags, and leaping roes,

6. By the "lions" he refers to the acrimony and impetuosity of the irascible power, for in its acts this power is bold and daring like the lion.

By the "stags" and the "leaping roes" he refers to that other power, the concupiscible, which is an appetitive power. This faculty causes two classes of effects: one of cowardice and the other of daring. It produces the effects of cowardice when things are found difficult, for it then retires, withdraws within itself, and becomes cowardly. Because of these effects this faculty is comparable to stags, for since the stag has a more intense concupiscible power than many other animals, it is very cowardly and withdrawn. This faculty produces the effects of daring when things are found easy, for then it does not withdraw and become cowardly but makes bold to accept these things with its appetites and affections. And

---

1. Cf. A. 3. 29. 2, note 1.

because of these effects this faculty is compared to the roes, which have such concupiscence that they do not merely run after their desires but even leap after them. And thus he calls them leaping roes.

7. In conjuring the lions he bridles the impulses and excesses of anger. And in conjuring the stags he strengthens the concupiscible power against the cowardice and pusillanimity that previously made it withdrawn. And in conjuring the leaping roes he satisfies the appetites, previously restless and leaping like roes from one thing to another, trying to satisfy concupiscence. This concupiscence is now satisfied by the pleasant lyres whose sweetness it enjoys, and by the siren's song, the delight of which it feeds on.

It should be observed that the Bridegroom does not conjure anger and concupiscence to cease, for these powers are never wanting to the soul. But he conjures their disturbances and inordinate actions, signified by the lions, stags, and leaping roes, to cease. It is necessary that in this state these inordinate movements be lacking.

> mountains, lowlands, and river banks,

8. These expressions denote the vicious and inordinate acts of the three faculties, memory, intellect, and will. These acts are inordinate and vicious when they reach either a high level or a low level, or even when they are inclined toward one of them without actually reaching it.

Thus the "mountains," which are high, refer to acts that are extreme through an inordinate excess. The "lowlands," being low, refer to acts that are extreme through defect. The "river banks," which are neither high nor low but still not level, participate somewhat in both extremes and refer to the acts that exceed or lack something of the mean or right measure. Although these are not extremely inordinate, as would be the case with mortal sin, they are nonetheless partly so, either through venial sin or through imperfection, however slight, in the intellect, memory, and will.

He also conjures, by means of the pleasant lyres and the siren's song, all these acts in excess of the just measure to cease. These lyres perfect the three faculties of the soul by bringing them to an operation that lies in the just measure, without extremes or even any part in extremes. The remaining verses follow:

> waters, winds, and ardors,
> watching fears of night:

9. These four references indicate the four passions: sorrow, hope, joy, and fear.[2] The "waters" denote the emotions of sorrow that afflict the

---

2. Cf. A. 3. 16. 2, note 2.

soul, for they enter like water. David, referring to them, says to God: *Salvum me fac, Deus, quoniam intraverunt aquae usque ad animam meam* (Save me, my God, for the waters have come in even unto my soul) [Ps. 69:1].

The "winds" allude to the emotions of hope, for like the wind they fly toward the absent object. David also says: *Os meum aperui et attraxi spiritum, quia mandata tua desiderabam* (I opened the mouth of my hope and drew in the breath of my desires because I longed and hoped for your commandments) [Ps. 119: 131].

The "ardors" refer to the emotions of the passion of joy that inflame the heart like fire. David says: *Concaluit cor meum intra me, et in meditatione mea exardescet ignis* (My heart grew hot within me, and in my meditation a fire shall be enkindled) [Ps. 39:3]. This is like saying: In my meditation joy shall be enkindled.

By the "watching fears of night" are understood the emotions of fear, the other passion. These fears are usually very great in spiritual persons who have not reached this state of spiritual marriage of which we are speaking. Sometimes when God wishes to grant them some favors, he causes fear and trembling in the spirit and also shriveling of the flesh and the senses, because the sensory part is not fortified, perfected, and habituated to such favors. Sometimes, too, the devil, being envious and sad over the soul's peace and good when God grants it recollection and sweetness in himself, strives to put horror and fear in the spirit so as to hinder that good. And sometimes he does this as though he were threatening her there in the spirit. When he becomes aware of his inability to reach the inmost part of the soul because of her deep recollection and union with God, he tries to cause distraction, wanderings, conflicts, sorrows, and dread, at least in the sensory part, to see if in this way he can disturb the bride in her bridal chamber.

He calls these emotions "fears of night" because they are produced by the devil, who endeavors by their means to diffuse obscurity in the soul and darken the divine light she enjoys.

He calls them "watching fears" because of themselves they awaken her from her peaceful interior sleep, and also because the devils are always awake and watching for their chance to cause these fears. These fears, as I said, are passively introduced by God or the devil into the souls of those who are already spiritual. I am not speaking here of other temporal or natural fears, for such fears are not characteristic of spiritual people; but these spiritual fears are.

10. The Beloved also conjures these four passions of the soul and makes them cease and be calm insofar as he gives the bride in this state riches, strength, and satisfaction through the pleasant lyres of his sweetness and the siren's song of his delight. He does this so they may not only cease to reign in her but also cease to cause her any displeasure.

If previously the waters of sorrow over something reached the soul—especially concerning her own sins or those of others, since sin is what usually causes the most sorrow in spiritual persons—her grandeur and stability are now so great that even though she knows what these sins are, they do not produce sorrow or grief. And she does not have compassion, that is, the feeling of compassion, even though she possesses its work and perfection. In this state the soul lacks what involved weakness in her practice of the virtues, though the strength, constancy, and perfection of them remains. For the soul in this transformation of love resembles the angels who judge perfectly the things that give sorrow without the feeling of sorrow, and exercise the works of mercy without the feeling of compassion. Sometimes, however, and at certain periods, God allows her to feel things and suffer from them so she might gain more merit and grow in the fervor of love, or for other reasons, as he did with the Virgin Mother, St. Paul, and others. Yet in itself the state does not include this feeling of sorrow.[3]

11. Neither is she afflicted with the desires of hope. Being now satisfied in this union with God insofar as is possible in this life, she has neither anything to hope for from the world nor anything to desire spiritually, for she has the awareness and experience of the fullness of God's riches. In life and in death she is conformed to the will of God, saying in both the sensory and spiritual part without the impulse of any other longing or appetite: *Fiat voluntas tua* [Mt. 6:10]. Thus her desire for the vision of God is painless.

Neither do the emotions of joy, which usually caused her a feeling of possessing more or less, make her aware of any want; nor do they add a sense of new abundance. What she ordinarily enjoys is so great that, like the sea, she neither decreases by the outflow of waters nor increases by the inflow. For this is the soul in which is established the fount whose waters, as Christ says through St. John, leap up unto life everlasting [Jn. 4:14].

12. Because I asserted that this soul does not receive anything new in this state of transformation, in which it seems that accidental joys are taken from her (which are not lacking even in the glorified), it should be pointed out that even though these joys and accidental sweetnesses are not lacking—ordinarily they are numberless—they do not on this account add anything to the substantial spiritual communication. She

---

3. Although this resemblance to the angels may be true theoretically for the reasons mentioned, other factors enter in so that the Virgin Mother and St. Paul, in their feelings of sorrow, are not the exceptions but the norm; cf. C. 36. 10-13. With regard to the angels, see Aquinas, *Summa theologiae* 1. 59. 4.

already possesses everything that could come to her anew. Thus what she possesses within herself is more than what comes to her anew.

Hence, every time joyous and happy things are offered to this soul, whether they are exterior or interior and spiritual, she immediately turns to the enjoyment of the riches she already has within herself, and experiences much greater gladness and delight in them than in those new joys. She in some way resembles God who, even though he has delight in all things, does not delight in them as much as he does in himself, for he possesses within himself a good eminently above all others. Thus all new joys and satisfactions serve more to awaken the soul to a delight in what she already possesses and experiences within herself than to new delights, for, as I say, what she already possesses is greater than these.

13. If something gives the soul joy and contentment but she esteems another even more, it would be natural for her, on enjoying the former, to turn her thoughts at once to the latter and find her satisfaction and joy in that. Thus what is accidental in these new spiritual joys is so little in comparison with the substantial good the bride already has within herself that we can call it a nothing. The soul that has attained this fulfillment, which is transformation, in which she has reached full stature, does not grow through these new spiritual things as do others who have not arrived. Yet it is a wonderful thing to behold how, although the soul receives no new delights, it always seems to her that she receives them anew and also that she has had them before. The reason is that she ever takes pleasure in them anew, since they are her good that is ever new. Thus it seems to her that she is always receiving new things without need.

14. Yet were we to desire to speak of the glorious illumination he sometimes gives to the soul in this habitual embrace, which is a certain spiritual turning toward her in which he bestows the vision and enjoyment of this whole abyss of riches and delight he has placed within her, our words would fail to explain anything about it. As the sun shining brightly on the sea lights up great depths and caverns and reveals pearls and rich veins of gold and other minerals, and so on, the Bridegroom, the divine sun, in turning to the bride so reveals her riches that even the angels marvel and utter those words of the Song of Songs: *Who is she that comes forth like the morning rising, beautiful as the moon, resplendent as the sun, terrible as the armies set in array?* [Sg. 6:10]. In spite of the excellence of this illumination, it gives no increase to the soul; it only brings to light what was previously possessed so she may have enjoyment of it.

15. Finally, the "watching fears of night" do not reach her, for she is now so clearly illumined and strong and rests so firmly in her God that the devils can neither cause her obscurity through their darkness, nor

frighten her with their terrors, nor awaken her by their attacks. Nothing can reach or molest her now that she has withdrawn from all things and entered into her God where she enjoys all peace, tastes all sweetness, and delights in all delights insofar as this earthly state allows. The Wise Man's words refer to this soul: *The peaceful and tranquil soul is like a continual banquet* [Prv. 15:15]. As one at a banquet enjoys the taste of a variety of foods and the sweetness of many melodies, the soul at this banquet, which she now receives at the bosom of her Beloved, enjoys every delight and tastes every sweetness.

So little of this is describable that we would never succeed in fully explaining what takes place in the soul that has reached this happy state. If she attains the peace of God that, as the Church says, surpasses all understanding,[4] all understanding will be inadequate and mute when it comes to explaining this peace.

Verses from the stanza follow:

> By the pleasant lyres
> and the siren's song, I conjure you

16. We have already explained that by "the pleasant lyres" the Bridegroom refers here to the sweetness bestowed on the soul in this state. By it he causes all the disturbances we mentioned to cease. As the music of the lyres fills the soul with sweetness and refreshment and so absorbs and suspends her as to keep her away from bitterness and sorrow, so this sweetness takes such an inward hold on her that nothing painful can reach her. These words are like saying: May all bitter things cease for the soul by means of the sweetness I place in her.

We also said that the "siren's song" signifies the soul's habitual delight. He calls this delight the "siren's song" because, as they say, this song is so charming that it enraptures and enamors its hearers and makes them forget all things as though they were in a transport. Similarly, the delight of this union absorbs the soul within herself and gives her such refreshment that it makes her insensible to the disturbances and troubles mentioned. These disturbances are referred to in this verse:

> to cease your anger

17. He calls these troubles and disturbances of the inordinate passions and operations "anger." Just as anger is a certain impulse that troubles peace by going beyond its limits, so all the passions and so on that we mentioned exceed by their movements the limits of peace and tranquility, and when they touch the soul they cause disquietude. As a result he says:

> and not touch the wall,

---

4. The text from Philippians 4:7 was then used in the liturgy on the third Sunday of Advent.

18. By "the wall" he refers to the enclosure of peace and the fence of virtues and perfections by which the soul is shut in and protected, for she is the garden mentioned above that is enclosed and protected solely for the Beloved, among whose flowers he browses. In the Song of Songs he calls her an enclosed garden: *My sister is an enclosed garden* [Sg. 4:12]. Thus he tells them here not to touch even the wall of his garden

that the bride may sleep in deeper peace.

19. That she may delight more freely in the quietude and sweetness she enjoys in her Beloved. It should be known that now no door is closed to the soul, but it is in her power to enjoy this gentle sleep of love at will, as the Bridegroom indicates in the Song of Songs: *I conjure you, daughters of Jerusalem, by the roes and harts of the fields that you do not stir up or wake the beloved until she wishes* [Sg. 3:5].

STANZA 22

Introduction

1. Great was the desire of the Bridegroom to free and ransom his bride completely from the hands of sensuality and the devil.[1] Like the good shepherd rejoicing and holding on his shoulders the lost sheep for which he had searched along many winding paths [Lk. 15:4-5], and like the woman who, having lit the candle and hunted through her whole house for the lost drachma, holding it up in her hands with gladness and calling her friends and neighbors to come and celebrate, saying, rejoice with me, and so on [Lk. 15:8-9], now, too, that the soul is liberated, this loving Shepherd and Bridegroom rejoices. And it is wonderful to see his pleasure in carrying the rescued, perfected soul on his shoulders, held there by his hands in this desired union.

Not only does he himself rejoice, but he also makes the angels and saintly souls share in his gladness, saying in the words of the Song of Songs: *Go forth, daughters of Zion, and behold king Solomon in the crown with which his mother crowned him on the day of his espousal and on the day of the joy in his heart* [Sg. 3:11]. By these words he calls the soul his crown, his bride, and the joy of his heart, and he takes her now in his arms and goes forth with her as the bridegroom from his bridal chamber [Ps. 19:5]. He refers to all this in the following stanza:

---

1. The long road traveled up to this point appeared as an effort of the bride in anxious search of her hidden Beloved. Here we find that the Bridegroom was seeking the bride even more, and it was she who was hiding (cf. F. 3. 28). The commentary now begins to describe the state of spiritual marriage.

The bride has entered
the sweet garden of her desire,
and she rests in delight,
laying her neck
on the gentle arms of her Beloved.

Commentary

2. Now that the bride has diligently sought to catch the foxes, still the north wind, and calm the girls of Judea, all of which are obstacles to the full delight of the state of spiritual marriage; and now that she has also invoked and obtained the breeze of the Holy Spirit, as in the preceding stanzas, which entails the proper preparation and instrument for the perfection of this state, we must treat of this marriage by explaining this stanza. Here the Bridegroom speaks and, in calling the soul "bride," declares two things:

First, he tells how, now victorious, she has reached this pleasant state of spiritual marriage, which was his as well as her ardent longing.

And second, he enumerates the properties of this state that the soul now enjoys, such as resting in delight and laying her neck on the gentle arms of her Beloved, as we shall explain.

The bride has entered

3. To offer a more lucid explanation of the order of these stanzas and of what the soul usually passes through before reaching this state of spiritual marriage, which is the highest (which we will now speak of with divine help), it should be noted that before the soul reaches this state she first exercises herself in the trials and bitterness of mortification and in meditation on spiritual things. This is referred to from the first stanza until that which says: "Pouring out a thousand graces." Afterward she enters the contemplative way. Here she passes through the paths and straits of love about which she sings in the sequence of the verses until the stanza that begins, "Withdraw them, Beloved," where the spiritual betrothal is wrought. Then she advances along the unitive way, in which she receives many remarkable communications, visits, gifts, and jewels from her Bridegroom, and, as one betrothed, learns of her Beloved and becomes perfect in loving him. All of this she relates from the stanza in which the betrothal was made ("Withdraw them, Beloved") to the present one beginning with, "The bride has entered," where the spiritual marriage between this soul and the Son of God is effected.

This spiritual marriage is incomparably greater than the spiritual betrothal, for it is a total transformation in the Beloved, in which each surrenders the entire possession of self to the other with a certain consummation of the union of love. The soul thereby becomes divine,

God through participation, insofar as is possible in this life. And thus I think that this state never occurs without the soul's being confirmed in grace, for the faith of both is confirmed when God's faith in the soul is here confirmed. It is accordingly the highest state attainable in this life.

Just as in the consummation of carnal marriage there are two in one flesh, as Sacred Scripture points out [Gn. 2:24], so also when the spiritual marriage between God and the soul is consummated, there are two natures in one spirit and love, as St. Paul says in making this same comparison: *Whoever is joined to the Lord becomes one spirit with him* [1 Cor. 6:17]. This union resembles the union of the light of a star or candle with the light of the sun, for what then sheds light is not the star or candle, but the sun, which has absorbed the other lights into its own.

4. The Bridegroom speaks of the state in this verse, saying, "the bride has entered," that is, she has entered, leaving behind everything temporal and natural and all spiritual affections, modes, and manners, and has set aside and forgotten all temptations, disturbances, pains, solicitude, and cares, and is transformed in this high embrace. Wherefore the next line follows:

<blockquote>the sweet garden of her desire,</blockquote>

This is like saying: She has been transformed into her God, here referred to as "the sweet garden," because of the sweet and pleasant dwelling she finds in him.

One does not reach this garden of full transformation, which is the joy, delight, and glory of spiritual marriage, without first passing through the spiritual betrothal and the loyal and mutual love of betrothed persons. For after the soul has been for some time the betrothed of the Son of God in gentle and complete love, God calls her and places her in his flowering garden to consummate this most joyful state of marriage with him. The union wrought between the two natures and the communication of the divine to the human in this state is such that even though neither changes its being, both appear to be God. Yet in this life the union cannot be perfect, although it is beyond words and thought.

5. The Bridegroom points this out clearly in the Song of Songs where he invites the soul, now his betrothed, to this state: *Veni in hortum meum, mea soror, mea sponsa, messui myrrham meam cum aromatibus meis* (Come and enter my garden, my sister, my bride, for now I have gathered my myrrh with my fragrant spices) [Sg. 5:1]. He calls her "sister" and "bride" because she was a sister and bride in the love and surrender she had made of herself to him before he called her to this state of spiritual marriage, where, as he says, he has now gathered his fragrant myrrh and aromatic spices, the fruits of the flowers now ripe and ready for the soul. These are the delights and grandeurs that of himself and in himself he communi-

cates to her in this state. Consequently he is for her an enchanting, desirable garden. Her entire aim, and God's as well, in all her works is the consummation and perfection of this state. She never rests until reaching it. She finds in this state a much greater abundance and fullness of God, a more secure and stable peace, and an incomparably more perfect delight than in the spiritual betrothal; here it is as though she were placed in the arms of her Bridegroom. As a result she usually experiences an intimate spiritual embrace, which is a veritable embrace, by means of which she lives the life of God. The words of St. Paul are verified in this soul: *I live, now not I, but Christ lives in me* [Gal. 2:20].

Therefore, since the soul lives in this state a life as happy and glorious as is God's, let each one consider here, if this be possible, how pleasant her life is. Just as God is incapable of feeling any distaste, neither does she feel any, for the delight of God's glory is experienced and enjoyed in the substance of the soul now transformed in him. As a result the next verse continues:

> and she rests in delight,
> laying her neck

6. The "neck" refers here to the soul's strength by means of which, as we said, is effected this union with her Bridegroom. She would be unable to endure so intimate an embrace if she were not now very strong. And because the soul labored by means of this strength, practiced the virtues, and conquered, it is right that with the strength by which she struggled and conquered she rest, laying her neck

> on the gentle arms of her Beloved.

7. To recline her neck on the arms of God is to have her strength, or better, her weakness, now united to the strength of God, for the "arms" of God signify God's strength. Accordingly this state of spiritual marriage is very aptly designated by the laying of her neck on the gentle arms of the Beloved, for now God is the soul's strength and sweetness in which she is sheltered and protected against all evils, and habituated to the delight of all goods.

Desirous of this state, the bride spoke to the Bridegroom in the Song of Songs: *Who will give you to me for my brother, nursed at the breasts of my mother, that I may find you alone outside and kiss you, and no one despise me?* [Sg. 8:1]. In calling him "brother," she indicates the equality of love between the two in the betrothal before this state is reached. And in saying, "nursed at the breasts of my mother," she means: You dried up and subdued in me the appetites and passions that in our flesh are the breasts and milk of mother Eve, and an impediment to this state. And when this is accomplished "that I may find you alone outside," that is, outside of all things and of myself, in solitude and nakedness of spirit, which is attained when the appetites are dried up. And alone there, "kiss you" alone, that is, that my nature now alone and denuded of all temporal, natural, and spiritual impurity may be united with you alone, with your nature alone, through no intermediary. This union is found only in the spiritual marriage, in which the soul kisses God without contempt or disturbance from anyone. For in this state neither the devil, the flesh, the world, nor the appetites molest her. Here we find also the fulfillment of what is said in the Song of Songs: *Winter is now past, the rain is gone, and the flowers have appeared in our land* [Sg. 2:11-12].

STANZA 23

Introduction

1. In this high state of spiritual marriage the Bridegroom reveals his wonderful secrets to the soul as to his faithful consort, with remarkable ease and frequency, for true and perfect love knows not how to keep anything hidden from the beloved. He mainly communicates to her sweet mysteries of his Incarnation and the ways of the redemption of humankind, one of the loftiest of his works and thus more delightful to the soul. Even though he communicates many other mysteries to her, the Bridegroom in the following stanza mentions only the Incarnation as the most important. In speaking to the soul he says:

> Beneath the apple tree:
> there I took you for my own,
> there I offered you my hand,
> and restored you,
> where your mother was corrupted.

Commentary

2. The Bridegroom explains to the soul in this stanza his admirable plan in redeeming and espousing her to himself through the very means by which human nature was corrupted and ruined, telling her that as human nature was ruined through Adam and corrupted by means of the forbidden tree in the Garden of Paradise, so on the tree of the cross it was redeemed and restored when he gave it there, through his passion and death, the hand of his favor and mercy, and broke down the barriers between God and humans that were built up through original sin. Thus he says:

> Beneath the apple tree:

3. That is: beneath the favor of the tree of the cross (referred to by the

apple tree), where the Son of God redeemed human nature and consequently espoused it to himself, and then espoused each soul by giving it through the cross grace and pledges for this espousal. And thus he says:

> there I took you for my own,
> there I offered you my hand,

4. That is: There I offered you my kind regard and help by raising you from your low state to be my companion and spouse.

> and restored you,
> where your mother was corrupted.

5. For human nature, your mother, was corrupted in your first parents under the tree, and you too under the tree of the cross were restored. If your mother, therefore, brought you death under the tree, I brought you life under the tree of the cross. In such a way God manifests the decrees of his wisdom; he knows how to draw good from evil so wisely and beautifully, and to ordain to a greater good what was a cause of evil.

The Bridegroom himself literally speaks this stanza to the bride in the Song of Songs: *Sub arbore malo suscitavi te; ibi corrupta est mater tua, ibi violata est genitrix tua* (Under the apple tree I raised you up; there your mother was corrupted, there she who bore you was violated) [Sg. 8:5].

6. The espousal made on the cross is not the one we now speak of. For that espousal is accomplished immediately when God gives the first grace that is bestowed on each one at baptism. The espousal of which we speak bears reference to perfection and is not achieved save gradually and by stages. For though it is all one espousal, there is a difference in that one is attained at the soul's pace, and thus little by little, and the other at God's pace, and thus immediately.

This espousal we are dealing with is what God makes known through Ezekiel by saying to the soul: *You were cast out upon the earth in contempt of your soul on the day you were born. And passing by you I saw you trodden under foot in your blood. And I said to you as you were in your blood: Love and be as multiplied as the grass of the field. Increase and grow great and enter and reach the stature of womanhood. And your breasts grew and your hair increased, and you were naked and full of confusion. And I passed by you and looked at you and saw that your time was the time of lovers, and I held my mantle over you and covered your ignominy. And I swore to you and entered into a pact with you and made you mine. And I washed you with water and cleansed the blood from you and anointed you with oil; and I clothed you in color and shod you with violet shoes, girded you with fine linen and clothed you with fine woven garments. And I adorned you with ornaments, put bracelets on your hands and a chain on your neck. And above your mouth I placed a ring, and I put earrings in your ears and a beautiful crown on your head. And you were adorned with gold and silver and clothed with fine linen and embroidered silk and many colors. You ate very choice bread and honey and oil, and you became exceedingly beautiful, and advanced to rule and be a queen. And your name was spread among the people because of your beauty* [Ez. 16:5-14]. These are the words of Ezekiel. And so it happens with the soul of which we are speaking.

STANZA 24

Introduction

1. But what immediately follows this delightful surrender of the bride and the Beloved is their bed, in which the bride tastes in a more stable manner the delights of her Bridegroom. In the following stanza she speaks of their bed, which is divine, pure, and chaste, and in which the soul is divine, pure, and chaste. For the bed is nothing else but her very Bridegroom, the Word, the Son of God, as will soon be said, on whom she reclines through the union of love. She calls her bed a flourishing one because her Bridegroom is not only flourishing but the very *flower of the fields and the lily of the valleys,* as he himself says in the Song of Songs [Sg. 2:1]. Thus the soul reclines not merely on the bed in flower but on the flower itself, the Son of God, who bears within himself divine fragrance, grace, and beauty, as he likewise declares through David: *The beauty of the field is with me* [Ps. 50:11]. The soul thus relates in song the properties and graces of her bed:

> Bride
>
> Our bed is in flower,
> bound round with linking dens of lions,
> hung with purple,
> built up in peace,
> and crowned with a thousand shields of gold.

Commentary

2. In the two preceding stanzas the bride-soul's song told of the graces and grandeurs of her Beloved, the Son of God. In this stanza the theme continues but also includes the happy and high state in which she has been placed, and its security. Third, she tells of the rich gifts and virtues with which she sees herself endowed and adorned in the nuptial chamber of her Bridegroom, for she says she is now in union with God and possesses the virtues with fortitude. Fourth, she relates that she now has perfect love. Fifth, that she has perfect spiritual peace, and all is enriched and made beautiful with gifts and virtues to the measure that can be

possessed and enjoyed in this life, as will be said in commenting on the verses. First, then, she tells about her delight in the union with her Beloved, saying:

> Our bed is in flower,

3. We have already mentioned that this bed of the soul is the Bridegroom, the Son of God, who is in flower for the soul. For now that she is united with and reclines on him and has become his bride, her Beloved's breast and love is communicated to her. This means that he communicates to her his wisdom, secrets, graces, virtues, and gifts, and through them he makes her so beautiful and rich and so imbues her with delights that it seems to her that she rests on a bed made of a variety of sweet divine flowers that delights with its touch and refreshes with its fragrance. Very appropriately does she call this union with God through love a "bed in flower," for this is what the bride speaking to the Bridegroom in the Song of Songs calls it: *Lectulus noster floridus* (our bed in flower) [Sg. 1:16].

She calls it "our," because both have the same virtues and the same love (which are the Beloved's), and both have the same delight, as the Holy Spirit says in Proverbs: *My delights are with the children of the earth* [Prv. 8:31].

She also says that it is in flower because the virtues of the soul in this state are now perfect and heroic. This, though, could not have come about until the bed was in flower in the perfect union with God. Next she declares the second property of this union:

> bound round with linking dens of lions,

4. By the "dens of lions," she understands the virtues possessed in this state of union with God, for dens of lions are very safe and protected against all other animals. Fearful of the strength and boldness of the lion within, not only do these animals dare not enter but they dare not even stay nearby. Thus when the soul possesses the perfect virtues, each of them is like a den of lions in which Christ, the Bridegroom, united with the soul in that virtue and in each of the others, dwells and assists like a strong lion. And the soul herself, united with him in these same virtues, is also like a strong lion because she thereby receives the properties of God.

In this state the soul is so protected and strong in each of the virtues and in all of them together—while at rest on this "bed in flower" of union with God—that the devils not only fear to attack her but do not even venture to appear before her. For they become greatly frightened on seeing her so exalted, courageous, and bold, with the perfect virtues in the bed of her Beloved. When she is united with God in transformation they fear her as much as they do him, and they dare not even look at her. The devil has an extraordinary fear of the perfect soul.

5. She also says that the bed is bound round with linking dens of lions because in this state the virtues are bound together, united, and fortified by each other, and fitted to the full perfection of the soul, sustaining one another in such a way that no part remains open or weak. They are so fastened that not only does the devil fail to find entry, but nothing in the world, high or low, can disquiet, molest, or even move the soul. Liberated from all the disturbance of the natural passions, and estranged from and stripped of the torment and variety of temporal cares, she enjoys in security and quietude the participation of God.

This is what the bride wanted to say in the Song of Songs: *Who will give you to me for my brother, nursed at the breasts of my mother, that I may find you alone outside and kiss you, and no one despise me?* [Sg. 8:1]. This kiss is the union of which we speak, in which the soul is made equal with God through love. Because of this desire she asks who will give her the Beloved as her brother (which would both signify equality and produce it), nursed at the breasts of her mother (which is a destroying of all her natural imperfections and appetites received from her mother Eve), so she may find him alone outside (be united with him alone, outside of all things, stripped of all things according to the appetite and will). Thus no one will despise her, that is, neither the world nor the flesh nor the devil will dare attack her. For none of these can disturb the soul that is liberated and purged of all things and united with God. She enjoys now in this state habitual sweetness and tranquility that is never lost or lacking to her.

6. Besides this habitual satisfaction and peace, the flowers of the virtues of this garden are so wont to open within her and spread their fragrance, it seems—and so it is—that she is filled with the delights of God.

And I said that the flowers of the virtues within her are wont to open, because even though she is filled with perfect virtues she is not always enjoying them actually although, as I said, she ordinarily does enjoy the peace and tranquility they cause. We can say that in this life they are present in the soul as flower buds in a garden. It is sometimes a wonderful thing to see them all open through the Holy Spirit and diffuse a marvelous variety of fragrance.

The soul will behold in herself the mountain flowers mentioned above, which are the abundance, grandeur, and beauty of God; and, intertwined among them, the lilies of the wooded valleys, which stand for rest, refreshment, and protection; and next, interspersed there, the fragrant roses of the strange islands, referring to the strange knowledge of God. Then too she will be struck by the scent of the lilies beside the resounding rivers, which we said represented the greatness of God filling every soul. And she will perceive from the jasmine interwoven there a fragrance diffused by the whistling of love-stirring breezes, which we also said the soul enjoys in this state. Likewise she is aware of all the other virtues and gifts we mentioned: the tranquil knowledge, silent music, sounding solitude, and the delightful and loving supper.[1]

And sometimes her experience and enjoyment of these flowers united together is such that she can very truthfully say: "Our bed is in flower, bound round with linking dens of lions." Happy is the soul who in this life merits at some time the enjoyment of the fragrance of these divine flowers! And she says that this bed is also

> hung with purple,

7. In Scripture purple denotes charity, and kings use and clothe themselves in purple. The soul says that this bed in flower is hung with purple because it is only by the charity and love of the King of heaven that all the virtues, riches, and goods flourish, receive sustenance, and give enjoyment. Without such love the soul could not enjoy this bed and its flowers. Thus all these virtues are present in her as though hung with the love of God, as in a subject in which they are well preserved. And they are as though bathed in love because each one of them is ever enkindling her love of God, and in all things and in all works they move her with love to love God more.

Such is the meaning of "hung with purple." A clear reference to this is found in the divine Song of Songs. For there it is said that the couch or bed Solomon made for himself was of wood from Lebanon, and the columns were of silver; the seat, of gold; and the hangings, purple; and it is said that he put order in all by means of charity [Sg. 3:9-10]. The virtues and endowments, signified by the wood from Lebanon and the silver columns, and which God places in the soul, have their couch and reclining place made of gold. For, as we have said, the firm seat of the virtues is love, and by love they are conserved. And all of them are put in order and exercised by means of the charity of both God and the soul. And she also says of this bed

> built up in peace,

8. Here she lists the fourth excellence of this bed, which is dependent on the third. The third was perfect love; and from perfect love, whose property, as St. John says, is to cast out all fear [1 Jn. 4:18], stems perfect peace of soul, the fourth characteristic of this bed.

For a greater understanding of this, it should be known that each of the virtues is of itself peaceful, meek, and strong; consequently, each produces in the soul these three effects: peace, meekness, and fortitude. And because this bed is in flower, made from the flowers of virtues, and all these virtues are peaceful, meek, and strong, the bed itself is built up

---

1. Cf. C. 14-15. In the first arrangement of the Canticle this stanza immediately followed stanzas 14 and 15, which explains why the images from those verses appear here in these combinations.

in peace; and the soul peaceful, meek, and strong. These are three properties against which no war can be waged, neither by the world nor the devil nor the flesh. And the virtues keep the soul so tranquil and safe that to her it seems she is built up in peace. To what has already been said, she adds the fifth property of this bed in flower:

And crowned with a thousand shields of gold.

9. These shields are the virtues and gifts. Even though these virtues and gifts, as we said, are the flowers, and so on, of this bed, they also serve as the soul's crown and her reward for having struggled to acquire them. Not only this, but they also have a defensive value, like strong shields, against the vices that were conquered through the practice of virtue. As a result the bride's bed in flower is crowned with them as her reward and protected by them as by a shield.

She states that they are gold in order to designate the high value of the virtues. The bride made this same assertion in other terms in the Song of Songs: *Behold that 60 strong men of the strongest in Israel surround the bed of Solomon, each with a sword at his thigh in defense against the fears of night* [Sg. 3:7-8].

And she asserts there are "a thousand" to denote the multitude of virtues, graces, and gifts with which God endows the soul in this state. To signify the vast number of the bride's virtues, the same term was used in the Song of Songs: *Thy neck is like the tower of David that is built with defenses; a thousand shields hang from it and all the armor of the strong men* [Sg. 4:4].

STANZA 25

Introduction

1. The soul that has reached this state of perfection is not content with extolling and praising the excellence of her Beloved, the Son of God, or of telling in song and rendering thanks for the favors she receives from him and the delights she enjoys in him; for she makes references also to those he bestows on other souls. In this blessed union of love she is aware of both. In praising and thanking him for the favors he grants to other souls, she recites this stanza:

> Following your footprints
> maidens run along the way;
> the touch of a spark,
> the spiced wine,
> cause flowings in them from the balsam of God.

Commentary

2. In this stanza the bride praises the Beloved for the three favors devout souls receive from him, which animate them further and raise them to the love of God. Because she herself has experience of them in this state, she mentions them here.

The first, she says, is his sweetness he gives them that is so efficacious it makes them run along the road to perfection. The second is a visit of love by which he suddenly inflames them in love. The third is an abundance of charity that he infuses in them and by which he so inebriates them that he causes the spirit—as in the visit of love—to be elevated and burst forth in praise and delightful affections of love before God. Thus she says:

following your footprints

3. A footprint is a trace by which we can track the one to whom it belongs. God's sweetness and knowledge, given to the soul seeking him, is a trace by which she goes on knowing and searching for him. Yet the soul says to the Word, her Bridegroom: Following your footprints (the traces of your sweetness that you infuse and leave impressed on them) and the fragrance that flows from you,

maidens run along the way;

4. This means that devout souls run along by the youthful strength received from the sweetness of your footprints, that is, run from place to place and in many ways. This is the meaning of "run along": Each runs along according to the way and kind of spirit and state God gives, with many differences of spiritual practices and works. They run along the way of eternal life, the way of evangelical perfection, by which they encounter the Beloved in union of love after their spirit has been stripped of all things.

This sweetness and trace of himself that God leaves in the soul greatly lightens her and makes her run after him. For then the soul does very little or nothing of her own in order to advance on this road; rather, she is moved and attracted by the divine footprints, not only to go out, but even to run along this road in many ways, as we said. The bride in the Song of Songs sought this divine attraction from the Bridegroom, saying: *Trahe me; post te curremus in odorem unguentorum tuorum* (Draw me, and we shall run after you in the fragrance of your ointments) [Sg. 1:3-4]. And after he gave her this divine fragrance she says: *In odorem unguentorum tuorum currimus: adolescentulae dilexerunt te nimis* (We run in the odor of your ointments; the maidens have loved you exceedingly). And David says: *I have run the way of your commandments when you enlarged my heart* [Ps. 119:32].

> The touch of a spark,
> the spiced wine,
> cause flowings in me from the balsam of God.

5. Commenting on the first two verses, we explained that souls, following his footprints, run along the way by external practices and works. And now in these three verses the soul speaks of the interior exercise of will when moved by two other inward favors and visits bestowed by the Beloved. She calls these favors "the touch of a spark" and "the spiced wine." And she calls the interior exercise of the will arising from these two visits "flowings in me from the balsam of God."

As for the first, it should be known that this touch of a spark is a very subtle touch that the Beloved sometimes produces in the soul, even when least expected, and which inflames her in the fire of love, as if a hot spark were to leap from the fire and set her ablaze. Then with remarkable speed, as when one suddenly remembers, the will is enkindled in loving, desiring, praising, and thanking God, and reverencing, esteeming, and praying to him in the savor of love. She calls these acts "flowings from the balsam of God." These flowings result from the touch of the sparks shot forth by the divine love that enkindles the fire. This divine love is the balsam of God that with its fragrance and substance comforts and cures the soul.

6. In the Song of Songs the bride speaks of this divine touch: *Dilectus meus misit manum suam per foramen, et venter meus intremuit ad tactum eius* (My Beloved put his hand through the opening, and my heart trembled at his touch) [Sg. 5:4].

The Beloved's touch is the touch of love that we said he produces in the soul. The hand is the favor he grants her by this touch. The opening through which this hand entered is the manner, mode, and degree of the soul's perfection, for the touch is usually greater or less and of one kind of spiritual quality or another in accordance with the manner of perfection. Her heart, which she says trembled, is the will in which this touch is produced. And the trembling is the elevation of her appetites and affections toward God through the desire, love, and praise of him, and all the other acts we mentioned, which are the flowings from the balsam of God redounding from this touch.

> the spiced wine.

7. This spiced wine is another much greater favor that God sometimes grants to advanced souls, in which he inebriates them in the Holy Spirit with a wine of sweet, delightful, and fortified love. Accordingly, she calls this love "spiced wine." As this wine is seasoned and strengthened with many diverse, fragrant, and fortified spices, so this love, which God

accords to those who are already perfect, is fermented and established in these souls and spiced with the virtues they have gained. Prepared with these precious spices, this wine gives such strength and abundance of sweet inebriation in these visits granted by God to the soul that they cause her to direct toward him, efficaciously and forcefully, flowings or outpourings of praise, love, and reverence, and so on, which we have mentioned. And she does this with admirable desires to work and suffer for him.

8. It should be known that this favor of sweet inebriation, because it has more permanence, does not pass away as quickly as the spark. The spark touches and then passes, although its effect lasts for a while, and sometimes for a long while; but the spiced wine—which, as I say, is sweet love in the soul—usually lasts, together with its effect, a long while, and sometimes a day or two, or many days, though not always in the same degree of intensity, because its lessening and increasing are beyond the soul's power. Sometimes without doing anything on their own, persons feel in their intimate substance that their spirit is being sweetly inebriated and inflamed by this divine wine. As David says: *My heart grew hot within me, and in my meditation a fire shall be enkindled* [Ps. 39:3].

The flowings from this inebriation of love sometimes last as long as the inebriation itself. At other times, even though this love is present, these flowings are absent; but when they are present their intensity is greater or less in accordance with the intensity of the inebriation. But the flowings, or effects of the spark, ordinarily last longer than the spark itself; in fact, the spark leaves these flowings in the soul, and they are more ardent than those derived from the inebriation, for this divine spark sometimes sets souls on fire and leaves them burning up with love.

9. And since we have mentioned fermented wine, it will be worthwhile to note briefly the difference between fermented wine, which is called old wine, and new wine. The difference will be the same as that between old and new lovers. This will help us in giving some instructions to spiritual persons.

With new wine, the lees are not yet completely fermented and settled. Thus the wine is still in the process of fermentation, and one cannot know its good quality and value until the effervescence stops and the lees are entirely fermented. Until then the wine is in danger of going bad, has a rough, sharp savor, and is harmful to one who drinks much of it. A great deal of its strength lies in the sediment.

In old wine the lees are settled and the process of fermentation finished, and thus there is no effervescence as in new wine. The good quality of the wine is now evident and there is no danger of its going bad, since the fermentation that could have spoiled it has now ceased. The wine that is well fermented is hardly ever spoiled or lost; it has a smooth savor; its strength lies in the substance and no longer in the taste. Drinking it fortifies one and gives a good disposition.

10. New lovers are comparable to new wine. They are the beginners in the service of God. The fervors of the wine of love are very exterior, in the sensory part of the soul. The lees of the weak and imperfect sensory part have not yet finished their work of fermentation. These new lovers find their strength in the savor of love, and this sensible savor is what really motivates and strengthens them for the performance of their works. One should not trust this love until these fervors and coarse sensory tastes have passed. Just as this fervor and the warmth of sense can incline one to good and perfect love and serve as a beneficial means for such love by a thorough fermentation of the lees of imperfection, so too it is very easy in these beginnings and in this novelty of tastes for the new wine of love to fail and lose its fervor and delight.

These new lovers always carry about the anxieties and fatigues of sensible love. In this regard they ought to be moderate in their drinking, for if, prompted by the agitation of the wine, they do a great deal of work, their nature will be ruined by these anxieties and fatigues of love, that is, of the new wine. As we said, this new wine is sharp, coarse, and unsmooth until completely fermented, that is, when these anxieties of love have passed, as we shall soon say.

11. The Wise Man in the Book of Ecclesiasticus makes this same comparison, saying: *A new friend is like new wine; it will grow old and become a smooth drink* [Ecclus. 9:10].

Now, then, the old lovers, those who are exercised and tried in the service of the Bridegroom, are like old wine. The lees of this wine are already fermented, and it does not have the sensitive effervescence or fermentation or the ardent external fires. What is more, these lovers taste the sweetness of the wine of love, the substance of which is now well fermented, so their love is based not on sensible delights, as is the love of new lovers, but settled within the soul in spiritual substance and savor and truly good works. And these individuals do not want to be attached to this sensory taste and fervor, nor do they desire to take pleasure in it lest weariness and distaste become their lot. For they who give reign to their appetite for some sensory taste will necessarily suffer affliction and displeasure in both sense and spirit.

Since these old lovers now lack the spiritual sweetness that has its roots in the sensory part, they do not have the anxieties or afflictions of love in the sense and spirit. These old lovers hardly ever fail God, for they now stand above all that would make them fail him, that is, above sensuality. And their wine of love is not only fermented and purged of the lees, but even spiced, as is said in the verse, with the perfect virtues that do not let it go bad as does the new wine. In God's sight, as a result, the old friend is highly esteemed, and thus the Book of Ecclesiasticus says of him: *Do not forsake an old friend, for a new one will not be like him* [Ecclus. 9:14].

With this wine of love, then, now tried in the soul and spiced, the Beloved causes the divine inebriation we mentioned. By its strength, the soul directs toward God sweet and delightful outpourings. Thus the meaning of these three verses is: The touch of the spark by which you awaken the soul, and the spiced wine by which you lovingly inebriate her cause her to direct to you the flowings of the movements and acts of love that you cause in her.

STANZA 26

Introduction

1. What, then, is the state of this happy soul in her bed of flowers where these things and so many others take place, in which she has for her couch the Bridegroom, the Son of God, and for a covering and hanging, love of this very Bridegroom? She can certainly repeat the words of the bride: *His left hand is under my head* [Sg. 2:6]. We can therefore assert truly that this soul is here clothed with God and bathed in divinity, not as though on the surface, but in the interior of her spirit, superabounding in divine delights. In the fullness of the spiritual waters of life, she experiences what David says of those who have reached God: *They shall be inebriated with the plenty of your house; and you will give them to drink of the torrent of your delight, because with you is the fountain of life* [Ps. 36:8-9]. What fulfillment will the soul have in her being, since the drink given her is no less than a torrent of delight! This torrent is the Holy Spirit, because, as St. John says, *He is a resplendent river of living water that flows from the throne of God and of the Lamb* [Rv. 22:1]. These waters, since they are the intimate love of God, flow intimately into the soul and give her to drink of this torrent of love that, as we said, is the Spirit of her Bridegroom infused in this union. As a result she sings this stanza with abundant love:

> In the inner wine cellar
> I drank of my Beloved, and, when I went abroad
> through all this valley
> I no longer knew anything,
> and lost the herd which I was following.

Commentary

2. In this stanza the soul relates the sovereign favor God granted by

recollecting her in the intimacy of his love, which is the union with God, or transformation, through love.[1] And she notes two effects of this union: forgetfulness or withdrawal from all worldly things, and mortification of all her appetites and gratifications.

In the inner wine cellar

3. To explain something about this wine cellar, and what the soul wishes to make known here, it will be necessary for the Holy Spirit to take my hand and guide my pen.

This wine cellar is the last and most intimate degree of love in which the soul can be placed in this life. Accordingly she calls this degree of love "the inner wine cellar," that is, the most interior. As a result, there are other steps of love not so interior by which one ascends to this last.

And we can assert that there are seven of these degrees or wine cellars of love. They are all possessed when the seven gifts of the Holy Spirit are possessed perfectly according to the soul's capacity for receiving them. Thus when the soul attains to the perfect possession of the spirit of fear, she has the spirit of love insofar as that fear, which is the last of the seven gifts, is filial. And perfect filial fear arises from perfect paternal love. So when the divine Scripture wishes to point out that a person is perfect in charity, it says such a one is God-fearing. Isaiah, in prophesying the perfection of Christ, said: *Replebit eum spiritus timoris Domini* (The spirit of the fear of God will fill him) [Is. 11:3]. St. Luke likewise called Simeon a God-fearing man: *Erat vir justus et timoratus* [Lk. 2:25]. And so with many others.

4. It should be known that many people reach and enter the first wine cellars according to the perfection of their love, but few in this life reach this last and most interior; for in it is wrought the perfect union with God, called spiritual marriage, of which the soul is now speaking. What God communicates to the soul in this intimate union is totally beyond words. One can say nothing about it, just as one can say nothing about God himself that resembles him. For in the transformation of the soul in God, it is God who communicates himself with admirable glory; the two become one, as we would say of the window united with the ray of sunlight, or the coal with the fire, or the starlight with the light of the sun. But this union is not as essential and perfect as in the next life.

---

1. After stanza 22, which presented a kind of synthesis of everything contained in this third phase, the most direct description of this state is contained in stanzas 26-30. Stanzas 26 and 27 speak of the gifts of the Beloved that correspond to the surrender of the bride. Stanzas 28 and 29 speak further of the surrender of love: love as the highest personal fulfillment (28), and love as the highest form of service to the Church (29). Stanza 30 speaks of the bride and Bridegroom working together as one.

Thus to explain what she receives from God in the interior cellar of union, the soul says nothing else—nor do I think she can say anything more adequate—than the following:

I drank of my Beloved,

5. As the drink is diffused through all the members and veins of the body, so this communication is diffused substantially in the whole soul, or better, the soul is transformed in God. In this transformation she drinks of God in her substance and in her spiritual faculties. With the intellect she drinks wisdom and knowledge; with the will, sweetest love; and with the memory she drinks refreshment and delight in the remembrance and the feeling of glory.[2]

As for the first, that the soul receives and drinks delight substantially, the bride speaks of it in the Song of Songs: *Anima mea liquefacta est, ut sponsus locutus est* (My soul delighted as soon as the bridegroom spoke) [Sg. 5:6]. This speaking of the bridegroom is equivalent to God's communication of himself to the soul.

6. In the same book the bride says that the intellect drinks wisdom when, in desiring to attain this kiss of union and seeking it from the bridegroom, she said: *There you will teach me* (wisdom and knowledge and love), *and I shall give you a drink of spiced wine* (my love spiced with yours, transformed in yours) [Sg. 8:2].

7. Regarding the third, the will drinks love as the bride says in the Song of Songs: *He put me in the secret wine cellar and set in order charity in me* [Sg. 2:4]. The meaning is that when I was put in his love, he gave me love to drink; or, more clearly and properly speaking: He put his charity in order in me, making his own charity fit and suit me. Hence the soul drinks of the Beloved's very own love that he infuses in her.

8. It should be known that the teaching of some about the will's inability to love what the intellect does not first know ought to be understood naturally. Naturally, it is impossible to love without first understanding what is loved, but, supernaturally, God can easily infuse and increase love without the infusion or increase of particular knowledge.

This is the experience of many spiritual persons; they frequently feel they are burning in love of God, with no more particular knowledge than before. They understand little but love a great deal, or understand a great deal but love little. As a matter of fact those spiritual persons whose

---

2. For more on these experiences of union, cf. some parallel texts: A. 2. 5. 2; 11. 1; 24. 4-5; 26. 5-6; N. 2. 17. 6; 23. 11; F. 3. 68-69; 4. 14-15.

understanding of God is not very advanced usually make progress according to their wills, while infused faith suffices for their knowledge. By means of this faith God infuses charity in them and augments this charity and its act, which means greater love, although, as we said, their knowledge is not increased. Thus the will can drink love without the intellect again drinking knowledge, although in our case, in which the soul says she drank of her Beloved, all three faculties drink together insofar as there is union in the inner wine cellar.

9. As to the fourth, in which the memory drinks of the Beloved, it is clear that the memory is illumined by the intellectual light in remembrance of the goods the soul possesses and enjoys in the union with her Beloved.

10. This divine drink so deifies, elevates, and immerses her in God that she says:

> and, when I went abroad

11. That is, when this favor had passed. For even though the soul is always in this sublime state of spiritual marriage once God has placed her in it, the faculties are not always in actual union although the substance is. Yet in this substantial union of the soul the faculties are frequently united too; and they drink in this inner wine cellar, the intellect understanding, the will loving, and so on. But in saying "when I went abroad" she does not refer to the essential or substantial union, which is this state she already has, but to the union of the faculties, which is not, nor can be, continuous in this life. "And when I went abroad," then

> through all this valley

12. That is, through this vast world.

> I no longer knew anything,

13. The reason is that the drink of highest wisdom makes her forget all worldly things. And it seems that her previous knowledge, and even all the knowledge of the world, is pure ignorance in comparison with this knowledge.

For a better understanding of this, it should be known that the most formal cause of the soul's knowing nothing of the world when in this state is that she is being informed with supernatural knowledge, in the presence of which all natural and political knowledge of the world is ignorance rather than knowledge. When the soul is brought into this lofty knowing, she understands by means of it that all other knowledge, which has not the taste of this knowledge, is not knowledge but ignorance, and there is nothing to know in it. She declares the truth of the

Apostle's words, that what is greater wisdom in the sight of humans is foolishness before God [1 Cor. 3:19]. Hence she asserts that she no longer knew anything after drinking of that divine wisdom. And this truth (that the wisdom of humans and of the whole world is pure ignorance and unworthy of being known) cannot be understood except by this favor of God's presence in the soul, by which he communicates his wisdom and comforts her with the drink of love so that she may behold this truth clearly, as Solomon explains: *This is the vision that the man who is with God saw and spoke. And being comforted by God's dwelling within him, he said: I am the most foolish of all, and human wisdom is not with me* [Prv. 30:1-3].

The reason is that, in the excess of the lofty wisdom of God, the lowly wisdom of humans is ignorance. The natural sciences themselves and the very works of God, when set beside what it is to know God, are like ignorance. For where God is unknown nothing is known. *The high things of God are foolishness and madness to humans,* as St. Paul also says [1 Cor. 2:14]. Hence the wise people of God and the wise people of the world are foolish in the eyes of each other; one group cannot perceive the wisdom and knowledge of God, and the other cannot perceive the wisdom and knowledge of the world. The wisdom of the world is ignorance to the wisdom of God, and the wisdom of God is ignorance to the wisdom of the world.

14. On the other hand, the elevation and immersion of the mind in God in which the soul is as though carried away and absorbed in love, entirely transformed in God, does not allow attention to any worldly thing. The soul is not only annihilated with respect to all things and estranged from them, but undergoes the same even with respect to herself, as if she had vanished and been dissolved in love; all of which consists in passing out of self to the Beloved. Thus the bride, in the Song of Songs, after having treated of the transformation of her love in the Beloved, refers to this unknowing, in which she was left, by the word, *nescivi* (I did not know) [Sg. 6:12].

In a way, the soul in this state resembles Adam in the state of innocence, who did not know evil. For she is so innocent that she does not understand evil, nor does she judge anything in a bad light. And she will hear very evil things and see them with her own eyes and be unable to understand that they are so, since she does not have within herself the habit of evil by which to judge them; for God, by means of the perfect habit of true wisdom, has destroyed her habitual imperfections and ignorances that include the evil of sin.

15. And so too in regard to her words, "I no longer knew anything." She takes little part in the affairs of others, for she is not even mindful of her

own. This is characteristic of God's spirit in the soul: He gives her an immediate inclination toward ignoring and not desiring knowledge of the affairs of others, especially that which brings her no benefit. God's spirit is turned toward the soul to draw her away from external affairs rather than involve her in them. Thus she remains in an unknowing, in the manner she was accustomed to.

16. It should not be thought that because she remains in this unknowing she loses there her acquired knowledge of the sciences; rather, these habits are perfected by the more perfect habit of supernatural knowledge infused in her. Yet they do not reign in such a way that she must use them in order to know, although at times she may still use them. For in this union with divine wisdom these habits are joined to the superior wisdom of God. When a faint light is mingled with a bright one, the bright light prevails and is what illumines. Yet the faint light is not lost; rather, it is perfected even though it is not the light that illumines principally. Such, I believe, will be the case in heaven. The habits of acquired knowledge of the just will not be supplanted, but they will not be of great benefit either, since the just will have more knowledge through divine wisdom than through these habits.

17. Yet particular knowledge, forms of things, imaginative acts, and any other apprehensions involving form and figure are all lost and ignored in that absorption of love. There are two reasons for this:

First, since the soul is absorbed and imbibed in that drink of love she cannot advert actually to any other thing.

Second, and principally, transformation in God makes her so consonant with the simplicity and purity of God, in which there is no form or imaginative figure, that it leaves her clean, pure, and empty of all forms or figures, purged and radiant in simple contemplation. The effect of this contemplation is like that of the sun on a window. In shining on the window, the sun makes it look bright, and all the stains and smudges previously apparent are lost sight of; yet when the sunlight passes, the stains and smudges reappear.

Since the effect of that act of love lasts for a while, the unknowing also continues so the soul cannot advert to anything in particular until the effect of that act of love passes. Since the act of love inflamed and transformed her into love, it annihilated her and did away with all that was not love, as is understood in what we mentioned above concerning David: *Because my heart was inflamed, my reins were also changed, and I was brought to nothing and knew not* [Ps. 73:21-22]. The change of reins because of this inflaming of the heart is a change of the soul according to her operations and appetites into God, into a new kind of life in which she is undone and annihilated before all the old things she formerly made use of. The prophet thus says that he was brought to nothing and did not know, for these are the two effects we mentioned of this drink from the wine cellar of God. Not only is all her old knowing annihilated, seeming to her to be nothing, but her old life and imperfections are annihilated, and she is renewed in the new self [Col. 3:10], which is the second effect contained in this verse.

                 and lost the herd that I was following.

18. It should be known that however spiritual a soul may be there always remains, until she reaches this state of perfection, some little herd of appetites, satisfactions, and other imperfections, natural or spiritual, after which she follows in an effort to pasture and satisfy it.

In the intellect there usually reside some imperfect appetites for knowing things.

The will is usually allowed to be captivated by some small appetites and gratifications of its own. These may involve temporal things, such as some little possession, or the attachment to one object more than to another, or some presumptions, judgments, punctilios, and other small things having a worldly savor or tinge. These latter may concern natural things, such as eating, drinking, finding more gratification in this than in that, choosing and desiring the best. Or they may concern spiritual things, such as the desire for spiritual satisfactions or other trifles we would never finish listing that are characteristic of spiritual persons who are not yet perfect.

In the memory there are usually many wanderings, cares, and useless imaginings after which she follows.

19. Regarding, too, the four passions of the soul, there are many useless hopes, joys, sorrows, and fears that she follows.

Some have more and others less of this herd, and they follow until, having entered the interior wine cellar to drink, all transformed in love, they lose it entirely. In this wine cellar these herds of imperfections are more easily consumed than are the rust and tarnish of metal consumed by fire. Thus the soul now feels free of all the childish likes and trifles she pursued; and she can say: "And lost the herd which I was following."

STANZA 27

Introduction

1. In this interior union God communicates himself to the soul with such genuine love that neither the affection of a mother, with which she so tenderly caresses her child, nor a brother's love, nor any friendship is comparable to it. The tenderness and truth of love by which the immense

Father favors and exalts this humble and loving soul reaches such a degree—O wonderful thing, worthy of all our awe and admiration!—that the Father himself becomes subject to her for her exaltation, as though he were her servant and she his lord. And he is as solicitous in favoring her as he would be if he were her slave and she his god. So profound is the humility and sweetness of God!

In this communication of love, he exercises in some way that very service that he says in the Gospel he will render to his elect in heaven; that is, girding himself and passing from one to another, he will minister to them [Lk. 12:37]. He is occupied here in favoring and caressing the soul like a mother who ministers to her child and nurses it at her own breasts. The soul thereby comes to know the truth of Isaiah's words: *You shall be carried at the breast of God and upon his knees you will be caressed* [Is. 66:12].

2. What then will be the soul's experience among such sovereign graces! How she will be dissolved in love! How thankful she will be to see the breasts of God given to her with such supreme and generous love! Aware that she has been set among so many delights, she makes a complete surrender of herself and gives him the breast of her will and love. She experiences this surrender to her Bridegroom in the way the Bride did in the Song of Songs when speaking to her Bridegroom: *I to my Beloved, and his turning is toward me. Come, my Beloved, let us go into the field, let us abide together on the grange; let us rise very early and go to the vineyards to see if the vine is in flower and if the flowers bear fruit, if the pomegranates flourish; there will I give you my breasts* (that is, I will employ the delights and strength of my will in your love) [Sg. 7:10-12]. Because this mutual surrender of God and the soul is made in this union, she refers to it in the following stanza:

> There he gave me his breast;
> there he taught me a sweet and living knowledge;
> and I gave myself to him,
> keeping nothing back;
> there I promised to be his bride.

Commentary

3. In this stanza the bride tells of the mutual surrender made in this spiritual espousal between the soul and God, saying that in the interior wine cellar of love they were joined by the communication he made of himself to her, by freely offering her the breast of his love in which he taught her wisdom and secrets, and by the complete surrender she made of herself to him, keeping nothing back for herself or for any other, promising to be his forever. The verse follows:

> There he gave me his breast;

4. Giving one's breast to another signifies the giving of love and friendship to another and the revealing of secrets to him as to a friend. When the soul says there he gave her his breast, she means that he communicated his love and secrets to her there. God grants this communication to the soul in this state, and also that of which she speaks in the following verse:

there he taught me a sweet and living knowledge;

5. The sweet and living knowledge that she says he taught her is mystical theology, the secret knowledge of God that spiritual persons call contemplation. This knowledge is very delightful because it is a knowledge through love. Love is the master of this knowledge and what makes it wholly agreeable. Since God communicates this knowledge and understanding in the love with which he communicates himself to the soul, it is very delightful to the intellect since it is a knowledge belonging to the intellect, and it is delightful to the will since it is communicated in love, which pertains to the will. Then she says:

and I gave myself to him,
keeping nothing back;

6. In that sweet drink of God, in which the soul is imbibed in him, she most willingly and with intense delight surrenders herself wholly to him in the desire to be totally his and never to possess in herself anything other than him. God causes in this union the purity and perfection necessary for such a surrender. And since he transforms her in himself, he makes her entirely his own and empties her of all she possesses other than him.

Hence, not only in her will but also in her works she is really and totally given to God without keeping anything back, just as God has freely given himself entirely to her. This union is so effected that the two wills are mutually paid, surrendered, and satisfied (so that neither fails the other in anything) with the fidelity and stability of an espousal. She therefore adds:

there I promised to be his bride.

7. Just as one who is espoused does not love, care, or work for any other than her bridegroom, so the soul in this state has no affections of the will or knowledge in the intellect or care or work or appetite that is not entirely inclined toward God. She is as it were divine and deified, in such a way that in regard to all she can understand she does not even suffer the first movements contrary to God's will.

As an imperfect soul is ordinarily inclined toward evil, at least in the first movements of its will, intellect, memory, and appetites, and as it has imperfections, so conversely the soul in this state ordinarily inclines and moves toward God in the first movements of its intellect, memory, will, and appetites, because of the great help and stability it has in God and its perfect conversion toward him.

David clarified all this when he said, speaking of the soul in this state: *Shall not my soul be subject to God? Yes; for from him do I receive salvation, and because he is my God and my Savior and my rock I shall no longer move* [Ps. 62:1-2]. By using the expression "my rock," he indicates that since his soul is set firmly in God and united to him, it will no longer suffer any movement contrary to God.

8. Obviously, then, the soul that has reached this state of spiritual espousal knows how to do nothing else than love and walk always with its Bridegroom in the delights of love. Since in this state she has reached perfection, the form and nature of which, as St. Paul says, is love [Col. 3:14], and since the more a soul loves the more completely it loves, this soul that is now perfect is all love, if one may express it so, and all her actions love. She employs all her faculties and possessions in loving, in giving up everything like the wise merchant [Mt. 13:44], for this treasure of love has been found by her, hidden in God. She is conscious that love is so valuable in her Beloved's sight that he neither esteems nor makes use of anything else but love, and so she employs all her strength in the pure love of God, desiring to serve him perfectly.

She does this not merely because he desires it, but also because the love by which she is united to him moves her to the love of God in and through all things. Like the bee that sucks honey from all the wildflowers and will not use them for anything else, the soul easily extracts the sweetness of love from all the things that happen to her; that is, she loves God in them. Thus everything leads her to love. And being informed and fortified as she is with love, she neither feels nor tastes nor knows the things that happen to her, whether delightful or bitter, since as we said the soul knows nothing else but love. And her pleasure in all things and in all transactions is always the delight of loving God. To illustrate this she speaks the following stanza.

STANZA 28

Introduction

1. Because we said that God makes use of nothing other than love, it may prove beneficial to explain the reason for this before commenting on the stanza. The reason is that all our works and all our trials, even though they be the greatest possible, are nothing in the sight of God. For through them we cannot give him anything or fulfill his only desire,

which is the exaltation of the soul. Of these other things he desires nothing for himself, since he has no need of them. If anything pleases him, it is the exaltation of the soul. Since there is no way by which he can exalt her more than by making her equal to himself, he is pleased only with her love. For the property of love is to make the lover equal to the object loved.[1] Since the soul in this state possesses perfect love, she is called the bride of the Son of God, which signifies equality with him. In this equality of friendship the possessions of both are held in common, as the Bridegroom himself said to his disciples: *I have now called you my friends, because all that I have heard from my Father I have manifested to you* [Jn. 15:15]. She then recites the stanza:

> Now I occupy my soul
> and all my energy in his service;
> I no longer tend the herd,
> nor have I any other work
> now that my every act is love.

Commentary

2. Since in the last stanza the soul—or better, the bride—said she surrendered herself entirely to the Bridegroom without keeping anything back, she now tells her mode and method of accomplishing this, saying that now she occupies her soul and body, her faculties and all her ability, in nothing other than the service of her Bridegroom. And she says that on this account she no longer goes about in search of her own gain or pleasures, nor occupies herself with things and matters foreign to God; and even in dealing with God himself she has no other style or manner than the exercise of love, since she has now traded and changed all her first manner of dealing with him into love, as is now said:

> Now I occupy my soul

3. By saying that she occupies her soul, she refers to her surrender to the Beloved in that union of love where now the soul and all the faculties (intellect, memory, and will) are dedicated and devoted to his service. She employs the intellect in understanding and carrying out the things that are more for his service, and the will in loving all that is pleasing to him, attaching it to him in all things, and her memory and care in what most pleases and serves him.

> and all my energy in his service;

4. By all her "energy" she refers to all that pertains to the sensory part of the soul. The sensory part includes the body with all its senses and

---

1. This is a general principle on which John bases his demonstration of the spiritual process; cf. A. 1. 4. 3 and note 2.

faculties, interior and exterior, and all natural ability (the four passions, the natural appetites, and other energies).

All of this, she says she occupies, as she does the rational and spiritual part referred to in the preceding verse, in the service of her Beloved. By directing the activity of the interior and exterior senses toward God, her use of the body is now conformed to his will. She also binds the four passions of the soul to him, for she does not rejoice except in God or hope in anything other than God; she fears only God and has no sorrow unless in relation to him. And likewise all her appetites and cares go out only to God.

5. All this energy is occupied in God and so directed to him that even without advertence all its parts, which we have mentioned, are inclined from their first movements to work in and for God. The intellect, will, and memory go out immediately toward God; and the affections, senses, desires, appetites, hope, joy, and all the energy from the first instant incline toward God, although, as I say, the soul may not advert to the fact that she is working for him. As a result she frequently works for God, and is occupied in him and in his affairs, without thinking or being aware that she is doing so. For her custom and habit of acting in this way causes her to lack advertence and care and even the fervent acts she used to make in beginning some work. Because this energy is now all employed in God, the soul necessarily achieves the condition described in the following verse:

I no longer tend the herd,

6. This is like saying: I no longer follow after my pleasures and appetites. For having placed them in God and given them to him, she no longer feeds them or keeps them for herself. She does not merely say she no longer tends this herd, but even more:

nor have I any other work

7. Before reaching this gift and surrender of herself and her energy to the Beloved, the soul usually has many unprofitable occupations by which she endeavors to serve her own appetite and that of others. For we can say she had as much work as she had many habitual imperfections. These habitual imperfections can be, for example, the trait or "work" of speaking about useless things, thinking about them, and also carrying them out, not making use of such actions in accord with the demands of perfection. She usually has desires to serve the appetites of others, which she does through ostentation, compliments, flattery, human respect, the effort to impress and please people by her actions, and many other useless things. In this fashion she strives to please people, employing for them all her care, desires, work, and finally energy.

She says she no longer has all this "work" because all her words, thoughts, and works are of God and are directed toward him without any of the former imperfections. Thus the verse means: I no longer go about satisfying my appetite or that of others, nor am I occupied or detained with other useless pastimes or things of the world.

now that my every act is love.

8. This is like saying that now all this work is directed to the practice of love of God, that is: All the ability of my soul and body (memory, intellect, and will, interior and exterior senses, appetites of the sensory and spiritual parts) move in love and because of love. Everything I do I do with love, and everything I suffer I suffer with the delight of love. David meant this when he said: *I shall keep my strength for you* [Ps. 59:10].

9. It should be known that when the soul reaches this state, all the activity of the spiritual and sensory parts (in what she does or in what she suffers and in whatever manner) always causes more love and delight in God, as we have said. Even the very exercise of prayer and communion with God, in which she was accustomed to considerations and methods, is now wholly the exercise of love.[2] Hence whether her work is temporal or spiritual, this soul can always say, "Now that my every act is love."

10. Happy is the life and state, and happy the person who attains it, where everything is now the substance of love and the pleasure and delight of espousal. The bride in this state can indeed say to the divine Bridegroom those words she spoke to him out of pure love in the Song of Songs: *All the new and old apples I have kept for you* [Sg. 7:13], which is equivalent to saying: My Beloved, all that is rough and toilsome I desire for your sake, and all that is sweet and pleasant I desire for your sake. Yet the accommodated sense of this verse is that the soul in this state of spiritual espousal ordinarily walks in the union of love of God, which is a habitual and loving attentiveness of the will to God.

STANZA 29

Introduction

1. The soul, indeed, lost to all things and won over to love, no longer

---

2. St. Thérèse of Lisieux discovered the portrait of her soul in the verses of this stanza, a favorite of hers. See *Story of a Soul*, ch. 8. This love is not merely a matter of feeling but of one's entire person in the whole of existence.

occupies her spirit in anything else.[1] She even withdraws in matters pertinent to the active life and other exterior exercises for the sake of fulfilling the one thing the Bridegroom said was necessary [Lk. 10:42], and that is: attentiveness to God and the continual exercise of love in him. This the Lord values and esteems so highly that he reproved Martha when she tried to call Mary away from her place at his feet in order to busy her with other active things in his service; and Martha thought that she herself was doing all the work and Mary, because she was enjoying the Lord's presence, was doing nothing [Lk. 10:39-41]. Yet, since there is no greater or more necessary work than love, the contrary is true. The Lord also defends the bride in the Song of Songs, conjuring all creatures of the world, referred to by the daughters of Jerusalem, not to hinder the bride's spiritual sleep of love or cause her to awaken or open her eyes to anything else until she desire [Sg. 3:5].[2]

2. It should be noted that until the soul reaches this state of union of love, she should practice love in both the active and contemplative life. Yet once she arrives she should not become involved in other works and exterior exercises that might be of the slightest hindrance to the attentiveness of love toward God, even though the work be of great service to God. For a little of this pure love is more precious to God and the soul and more beneficial to the Church, even though it seems one is doing nothing, than all these other works put together.

Because of her determined desire to please her Bridegroom and benefit the Church, Mary Magdalene, even though she was accomplishing great good by her preaching and would have continued doing so, hid in the desert for 30 years in order to surrender herself truly to this love. It seemed to her, after all, that by such retirement she would obtain much more because of the notable benefit and gain that a little of this love brings to the Church.[3]

3. Great wrong would be done to a soul who possesses some degree of this solitary love, as well as to the Church, if we were to urge her to become

---

1. This stanza complements the previous one. Love of God is the supreme value in one's personal life and in the service of the Church. This is the longest introduction in the whole Canticle and is written with passion and conviction.
2. For St. Teresa's reflections on Martha and Mary and how the two must work together, cf. *Meditations on the Song of Songs* 7. 3; *Interior Castle* VII. 1. 10-11; 4. 12-15.
3. Here John follows the traditional legend about St. Mary Magdalene that passed from the lives of the saints into the breviary. St. Thérèse of Lisieux longed for this pure love in the desert of Carmel, cf. *Story of a Soul*, chs. 3 & 19; but she also sees this pure love expressed in the labors of her missionary brother P. Roulland in China, cf. *General Correspondence*, vol. II, LT 221.

occupied in exterior or active things, even if the works were very important and required only a short time. Since God has solemnly entreated that no one awaken a soul from this love [Sg. 3:5], who will dare do so and remain without reproof? After all, this love is the end for which we were created.

Let those, then, who are singularly active, who think they can win the world with their preaching and exterior works, observe here that they would profit the Church and please God much more, not to mention the good example they would give, were they to spend at least half of this time with God in prayer, even though they might not have reached a prayer as sublime as this. They would then certainly accomplish more, and with less labor, by one work than they otherwise would by a thousand. For through their prayer they would merit this result, and themselves be spiritually strengthened. Without prayer they would do a great deal of hammering but accomplish little, and sometimes nothing, and even at times cause harm. God forbid that the salt should begin to lose its savor [Mt. 5:13]. However much they may appear to achieve externally, they will in substance be accomplishing nothing; it is beyond doubt that good works can be performed only by the power of God.

4. Oh, how much could be written here on this subject! But this is not the place. I have mentioned it only in explanation of the next stanza. In this stanza the soul replies to all those who impugn her holy idleness and desire every work to be the kind that shines outwardly and satisfies the eye, and do not know the secret source from which both the water flows and all fruit is produced.[4] And thus she recites the stanza.

> If, then, I am no longer
> seen or found on the common,
> you will say that I am lost;
> that, stricken by love,
> I lost myself, and was found.

Commentary

5. In this stanza the soul answers a tacit reproof of those in the world who customarily criticize persons who give themselves entirely to God. They think these persons are excessive in their conduct, estrangement, and withdrawal, and assert that they are useless in important matters and lost to what the world esteems. The soul skillfully answers this reprimand, boldly facing it and all the other possible reproofs of the world; for in

---

4. This pure love demands a serious consideration of one's options and a deep conviction that God is the power behind every good work.

having reached the intimate love of God, she considers everything else of little consequence.

But this is not all. She even proclaims how she has acted, and rejoices and glories in having lost the world and herself for her Beloved. This is what she means in the stanza when she addresses the worldly: that, if they no longer see her engaged in her former worldly conversations and pastimes, they should believe and declare that she has lost these things and withdrawn; and she has counted this loss such a good that she herself, searching for her Beloved and intensely enamored of him, desired it. So they might see the gain of her loss and not think it an absurdity or a delusion, she declares that her loss was her gain, and as a result she became lost purposely.

> If, then, I am no longer
> seen or found on the common,

6. The place where people often gather for diversion and recreation, and where shepherds also feed their flocks, is usually called "the common." Thus, by the common the soul refers to the world, where worldlings engage in their pastimes and conversations and feed the flock of their appetites. In this verse she tells those who are of the world that if they neither see nor find her as they did before her complete surrender to God, they should consider her by this fact lost, and they should therefore say (because she rejoices in their saying this and desires them to do so):

> You will say that I am lost;

7. Those who love are not abashed before the world because of the works they perform for God, nor even if everybody condemns these works do they hide them in shame. Those who are ashamed to confess the Son of God before others, by failing to perform their works, will discover that the Son of God, as is recorded in Luke, will be ashamed to confess them before the Father [Lk. 9:26]. The soul possessing the spirit of love glories rather in beholding that she has achieved this work in praise of her Beloved and lost all things of the world.[5] Hence she says: "You will say that I am lost."

8. Few spiritual persons reach such daring and determination in their works. Though some do act this way, and are considered far advanced, they never lose themselves entirely in some matters, whether worldly or natural, and never execute works for Christ with perfection and nakedness of spirit; they think about what others will say or how their work will

---

5. Now John speaks of the soul's happiness in performing works in praise of God. The topic discussed in the introduction to this stanza differs slightly from the subject matter presented in the commentary.

appear. Since these persons are not lost to themselves in their work, they cannot declare: "You will say that I am lost." They are still ashamed to confess Christ before others by their works. Because of their human respect they do not live entirely in Christ.

that, stricken by love,

9. This means that, through the practice of virtue, stricken with love, I lost myself, and was found.

10. Aware of the Bridegroom's words in the Gospel, that no one can serve two masters but must necessarily fail one [Mt. 6:24], the soul claims here that in order not to fail God she failed all that is not God, that is, herself and all other creatures, losing all these for love of him.

Anyone truly in love will let all other things go in order to come closer to the loved one. On this account the soul affirms here that she lost herself. She achieved this in two ways: she became lost to herself by paying no attention to herself in anything, by concentrating on her Beloved and surrendering herself to him freely and disinterestedly, with no desire to gain anything for herself; second, she became lost to all creatures, paying no heed to all her own affairs but only to those of her Beloved. And this is to love herself purposely, which is to desire to be found.

11. The one who walks in the love of God seeks neither gain nor reward, but seeks only to lose with the will all things and self for God; and this loss the lover judges to be a gain. Thus it is, as St. Paul asserts: *Mori lucrum* [Phil. 1:21], that is, my death for Christ is my gain, spiritually, of all things and of myself. Consequently the soul declares: I was found. The soul that does not know how to lose herself does not find herself but rather loses herself, as Our Lord teaches in the Gospel: *Those who desire to gain their soul shall lose it, and those who lose it for my sake shall gain it* [Mt. 16:25].

Should we desire to interpret this verse more spiritually and in closer accord with what we are discussing here, it ought to be known that when a soul treading the spiritual road has reached such a point that she has lost all roads and natural methods in her communion with God, and no longer seeks him by reflections or forms or feelings or by any other way of creatures and the senses, but has advanced beyond them all and beyond all modes and manners, and enjoys communion with God in faith and love, then it is said that God is her gain, because she has certainly lost all that is not God.

STANZA 30

Introduction

1. Everything is a gain for the soul whose gain is God, because all the strength of her faculties is converted into a spiritual communion of exceedingly agreeable interior love with him. These interior exchanges between God and the soul bear such delicate and sublime delight that no mortal tongue can describe it or human intellect understand it. For the espoused one on the day of her espousal understands nothing else than what belongs to the festivity and delight of love and to the revealing of all her jewels and graces for the sake of pleasing and gladdening the Bridegroom. And similarly, her Bridegroom manifests to her all his wealth and excellent qualities in order to bring her consolation and happiness. In this spiritual espousal then, in which the soul truly experiences what the bride says in the Song of Songs—*I for my Beloved and my Beloved for me* [Sg. 6:3]—the virtues and graces of the bride as well as the grandeurs and graces of the Bridegroom, the Son of God, are brought to light. They both display these riches in order to celebrate the feast of this espousal, and they mutually communicate their goods and delights with a wine of savory love in the Holy Spirit. The soul declares this by addressing the Bridegroom in this stanza:

> With flowers and emeralds
> chosen on cool mornings
> we shall weave garlands
> flowering in your love,
> and bound with one hair of mine.

Commentary

2. In this stanza the bride returns to address the Bridegroom in the communion and refreshment of love. She describes the solace and fruition the bride-soul and the Son of God possess in the wealth of the virtues and gifts of each other, and in the interchange of these treasures that they enjoy mutually in the communion of love. In speaking to him, therefore, she asserts that they will weave rich garlands of gifts and virtues, acquired and gained at a pleasant and suitable time, made beautiful and attractive in the love he bears for her, and sustained and preserved through her love for him. She calls this enjoyment of the virtues a weaving of garlands from them, for both the bride and the Bridegroom enjoy them together in their love for each other, as though these virtues were flowers twisted into garlands.

> With flowers and emeralds

3. The flowers are the soul's virtues, and the emeralds are the gifts received from God. These flowers and emeralds are

chosen on cool mornings

4. This means they are acquired at the time of youth, which is life's cool morning. She points out that they are chosen because she obtained them during her youth when the vices put up more strenuous opposition and nature is more inclined and ready to lose them; also by beginning to gather the virtues at this early season, she acquired more perfect and choice ones.

She terms this time of youth "cool mornings." For just as fresh spring mornings are more pleasant than other times of day, so too the virtue of youth pleases God more. And these cool mornings can even refer to the acts of love by which the virtues are acquired. These acts of love give more pleasure to God than do cool mornings to the children of the earth.

5. The cool mornings also bear reference to works done in difficulty and dryness of spirit. God highly esteems these works denoted by the chill of the winter mornings and done for him in aridity and hardship, for by such means the virtues and gifts are acquired in a high degree. Those acquired through this labor are for the most part more select, refined, and stable than if they were obtained with spiritual relish and enjoyment, for virtue takes root in dryness, difficulty, and labor, as God says to St. Paul: *Virtue is made perfect in weakness* [2 Cor. 12:9]. To stress, then, the excellence of the virtues from which garlands for the Beloved are woven, the words "chosen on cool mornings" are very apt, because the Beloved rejoices only in these flowers and emeralds of select and perfect virtues and gifts, and not in imperfect ones. As a result the bride declares here that with them

we shall weave garlands

6. To understand this verse it should be known that all the virtues and gifts the soul (and God within her) acquires are like a garland of various flowers within her with which she is wonderfully adorned, as though in a robe of rich variety. For a better understanding it should be noted that while gathering material flowers one weaves them into the garland being made at the same time, so too while one acquires the spiritual flowers of virtues and gifts, they are at the same time fixed firmly in the soul. And when these spiritual flowers are wholly obtained, the garland of perfection in the soul is complete. Both the soul and the Bridegroom rejoice in the beauty and adornment of this garland, as is proper to the state of perfection.

These are the garlands she declares they must weave, that is, she must be girded, surrounded with an assortment of flowers and emeralds that are perfect virtues and gifts, so that, wearing this beautiful and costly adornment, she may appear worthily before the King and deserve that he make her his equal and place her at his side like a queen; this she merits through the beauty of such variety. Hence David speaks to Christ on this subject: *Astitit regina a dextris tuis in vestitu deaurato, circumdata varietate* (The queen stood at your right hand, clothed in a garment of gold, surrounded with variety) [Ps. 45:9]. This would be similar to saying: She stood at your right, clothed in perfect love and surrounded with a variety of perfect gifts and virtues.

And she does not say I alone shall weave the garlands, or you alone will, but we shall weave them together. The soul cannot practice or acquire the virtues without the help of God, nor does God effect them alone in the soul without her help. Although it is true that every good gift and every perfect gift is from above, having come down from the Father of lights, as St. James says [Jas. 1:17], yet this gift is not received without the ability and help of the soul receiving it. So the bride in the Song of Songs said to the bridegroom: *Draw me; we shall run after you* [Sg. 1:4]. The movement toward good, therefore, comes only from God, as is declared here. But she does not state that he alone or she alone runs, but that we shall both run, which means that God and the soul work together.

7. This verse most appropriately refers to the Church and Christ, for in it the Church, the Bride of Christ, addresses him, saying: Let us weave garlands (understanding by garlands, all the holy souls engendered by Christ in the Church). Each holy soul is like a garland adorned with the flowers of virtues and gifts, and all of them together form a garland for the head of Christ, the Bridegroom.

The lovely garlands can refer as well to what we call aureoles; these are also woven by Christ and the Church and are of three kinds:

The first kind is made from the beautiful white flowers of all the virgins. Each virgin possesses her own aureole of virginity, and all these aureoles together will be joined into one and placed on the head of Christ, the Bridegroom.

The second aureole contains the resplendent flowers of the holy doctors. All these aureoles will be entwined into one and set upon the head of Christ over that of the virgins.

The third is fashioned from the crimson carnations of the martyrs. Each martyr has the aureole of martyrdom, and all these red aureoles woven together will add the final touch to the aureole of Christ, the Bridegroom.

So beautiful and fair will Christ the Bridegroom be with these three garlands that the bride's words in the Song of Songs will be repeated in heaven: *Go forth, daughters of Zion, and behold king Solomon in the crown with which his mother crowned him on the day of his espousal and on the day of the joy*

of his heart [Sg. 3:11]. We shall weave these garlands, she says:
flowering in your love,

8. The flower of these works and virtues is the grace and power they possess from the love of God. Without love these works will not only fail to flower but will all wither and become valueless in God's sight, even though they may be perfect from a human standpoint. Yet because God bestows his grace and love, they are works that have blossomed in his love.
and bound with one hair of mine.

9. This hair is her will and the love she has for the Beloved. This love assumes the task of the thread in a garland. As the thread binds the flowers together, so love fastens and sustains the virtues in the soul. In St. Paul's words: *Charity is the bond of perfection* [Col. 3:14]. The supernatural virtues and gifts are so necessarily tied together in this soul's love that if the love should break, by an offense against God, the virtues would immediately become loose and fall away, just as the flowers would fall away if the thread of the garland were broken. Consequently it is insufficient that God love us and thereby give us virtues, for we must also love him in order to receive and preserve them.

She says they were held with only one hair, not with many, in order to point out that now her will is alone, detached from all other strands of hair, that is, from all extraneous loves. She clearly stresses here the value of these garlands of virtues, for when love is fixed solely and firmly in God, as she says, the virtues are also perfect, complete, and full-flowering in the love of God. Then God's love for the soul is inestimable, as she also experiences.

10. Even if I wanted to, I could not find words to express the beauty arising from the interweaving of these flowers of virtues and these emeralds, nor could I describe the strength and majesty their order and arrangement give to the soul or the loveliness and charm in which this garment of variety clothes her.

In the Book of Job, God declares that the devil's body is like shields of molten metal protected with scales closely knit and so joined that air cannot pass through [Jb. 41:6-7]. If the devil, since he is clothed with evils (the scales) that are bound and ordained one to the other, is so strong that his body is comparable to a shield of molten metal, and since all evils in themselves are weakness, how tremendous will be the might of this soul that is all clothed with strong virtues and has them so fastened and interwoven that no ugliness or imperfection can get between them! By its strength every virtue adds strength to the soul, by its beauty it adds beauty, by its value it enriches her, and by its majesty it imparts power and grandeur to her. How marvelous, then, to the spiritual eye will this bride-soul appear, at the right hand of the King, her Bridegroom, in the charm of these gifts. *How beautiful are your steps in sandals, O prince's daughter,* exclaims the bridegroom in the Song of Songs [Sg. 7:1]. He calls her "prince's daughter" to denote her royal inheritance. And if he calls her beautiful because of her sandals, what will be the beauty afforded her by her garment!

11. Not only does her beauty in this robe of flowers stir one's admiration, but the strength she possesses from the orderly arrangement of these flowers interspersed with both emeralds and innumerable divine gifts fills one with terror. On this account the groom declares of her in the Song of Songs: *You are terrible, like an army in array* [Sg. 6:4]. As these virtues and gifts of God give refreshment by their spiritual fragrance, so too, when they are joined together in the soul, they impart strength by their substance. As a result the bride in the Song of Songs, when she was weak and love-sick over not having attained the union and interweaving of these flowers and emeralds by means of the hair of love, desired to be strengthened by this union and joining of them, and asked for this, saying: *Strengthen me with flowers, surround me with apples, because I languish with love* [Sg. 2:5]. By "flowers" she means the virtues, and by "apples," the remaining gifts.

STANZA 31

Introduction

1. I believe it is clear that by means of these garlands, interwoven and placed in the soul, the bride wishes to describe the divine union of love between herself and God. The flowers represent the Bridegroom; he is the flower of the fields and the lily of the valleys, as he affirms [Sg. 2:1]. The hair of the soul's love is what unites and fastens her to this flower of flowers, for as the Apostle teaches: *Love is the bond of perfection* (which is union with God) [Col. 3:14]. The soul is like the peg on which the garlands are hung, since she is the subject of this glory and no longer appears to be what she was before. But by the perfection and beauty of all the flowers, she resembles the perfect flower himself. This thread of love joins and binds God and the soul so strongly that it unites and transforms them. So great is this union that even though they differ in substance, in glory and appearance the soul seems to be God and God seems to be the soul.

2. This union is more wonderful than all that can be said of it. Scripture mentions something about it in the First Book of Kings in reference to

Jonathan and David. The love Jonathan bore David was so intimate that it knitted his soul to David's [1 Sm. 18:1]. If the love of one man for another was that strong, what will be the tie caused through the soul's love for God, the Bridegroom; especially since God here is the principal lover,[1] who in the omnipotence of his fathomless love absorbs the soul in himself more efficaciously and forcibly than a torrent of fire would devour a drop of morning dew that usually rises and dissolves in the air! Undoubtedly the hair that so joins them must be thin and very strong, since it penetrates with such forcefulness the parts it binds. Accordingly, the soul describes in the following stanza the properties of this beautiful strand of hair.

> You considered
> that one hair fluttering at my neck;
> you gazed at it upon my neck
> and it captivated you;
> and one of my eyes wounded you.

Commentary

3. The soul wishes to express three things in this stanza:

First, she wishes to explain that the love that binds the virtues is no other love than solitary and strong love, for it must be this if it is to preserve them.

Second, she wishes to state that God was greatly captivated by this single hair of love when he beheld it alone and strong.

Third, she wishes to declare that God was intimately taken with love for her when he marked the purity and integrity of her faith. And thus she proclaims:

> You considered
> that one hair fluttering at my neck;

4. The neck, where the hair of love was fluttering, signifies fortitude. This hair of love weaves the virtues together, that is to say, loves with fortitude. In order to preserve the virtues it is not enough that love be alone; it must also be strong so that no contrary vice on any side of the garland of virtue may be able to break it. This hair of love binds the virtues in such a way that if it breaks where one of these virtues lies, it will immediately, as we said, fail in regard to them all. Just as all the virtues are present where one is, so they all fail where one fails.[2]

---

1. Though it may often seem that the Beloved is passive and inactive while the bride searches for him, John reminds us again that in reality Christ is the principal lover.

2. For more on this doctrine about the connection and interdependence of the virtues, see Aquinas *Summa theologiae* 1-2. 65.

And she says that it was fluttering and flying about at her neck because in the soul's fortitude this love flies to God mightily and speedily without anything detaining it. And as the breeze causes the hair to flutter and fly about the neck, so too the breeze of the Holy Spirit moves and arouses the strong love to make its flight to God. Without this divine breeze to stir the faculties to the exercise of divine love, the virtues do not produce their effects, even though they are present in the soul.

In saying that the Beloved considered this hair fluttering at her neck, she points out how much God cherishes a strong love, for to consider an object is to look with very particular attention and esteem; and the strong love urges God to turn his eyes to look at it. And thus:

> you gazed at it upon my neck

5. The soul makes this affirmation to show that God not only values this love of hers because he sees that it is alone, but also cherishes it because he sees that it is strong. With God, to gaze at is to love, just as to consider an object is to value it. She repeats the word "neck" in this verse, in speaking of the hair—"You gazed at it upon my neck"— because, as we mentioned, this is why he loved her so much; he saw that her love was strong. Thus it is like saying: You loved it on seeing that it was strong, without cowardice or fear; and alone, without other loves; and fluttering about quickly and fervently.

6. Until now this hair had not captivated God because he had not gazed at it, nor had he seen it alone and detached from other strands of other loves, appetites, affections, and pleasures, nor did it flutter about alone at the neck of fortitude. But after love, through mortifications, trials, and penance, becomes so detached and strong that no force or occasion can break it, then God looks at it and takes the flowers of these garlands and binds them with it, since it is strong enough to keep them fastened in the soul.

7. In the explanation of the four stanzas that begin "O Living Flame of Love," we mentioned something about the nature of these temptations and trials, and about how deeply they reach the soul that she might come to this fortitude of love in which God unites himself to her.[3] Having passed through these tribulations, the soul has reached such a degree of love that she merits divine union. Hence she says:

> and it captivated you;

---

3. See F. 1. 18-25; 2. 23-30. At the time in which John worked on this second redaction, the *Living Flame* was his more recent work. There (1. 25), he refers to what he said at greater length on this matter in a previous work, "The Dark Night of the Ascent of Mount Carmel."

8. Oh, how worthy of utter admiration and joy! God is taken captive by a hair! The reason this captivity is so estimable is that God wished to stop and gaze at the fluttering of the hair, as the preceding verse asserts. And as we pointed out: For God, to gaze at is to love. If in his infinite mercy he had not gazed at us and loved us first—as St. John declares [1 Jn. 4:10,19]—and descended, the hair of our lowly love would not have taken him prisoner, for this love was not so lofty in its flight as to be able to capture this divine bird of heights. But because he came down to gaze at us and arouse the flight of our love by strengthening and giving it the courage for this [Dt. 32:11], he himself as a result was captivated by the flight of the hair, that is, he was satisfied and pleased. Such is the meaning of the verses: "You gazed at it upon my neck and it captivated you." It is indeed credible that a bird of lowly flight can capture the royal eagle of the heights if this eagle descends with the desire of being captured. And she continues:

And one of my eyes wounded you.

9. The eye refers to faith. She says she wounded him with only one eye because if the soul's faith and fidelity toward God were not single, but mixed with some other human respect, it would not attain such an effect as to wound God with love. Thus it is only one eye that wounds the Beloved, just as it is only one hair that captivates him. And so intimate is the love with which the Bridegroom is captivated by the bride in this single-hearted fidelity he beholds in her that, if the hair of her love captivates him, the eye of her faith so tightens the bonds of his captivity as to cause a wound of love. This wound of love is the result of the tenderest affection with which he loves her, which means he introduces her further into his love.

10. The Bridegroom in addressing the bride in the Song of Songs makes this same statement about the hair and the eye: *You have wounded my heart, my sister; you have wounded my heart with one of your eyes and with one hair of your neck* [Sg. 4:9]. In this passage he declares twice that his heart was wounded—by the eye and by the hair. The soul accordingly mentions in this stanza the eye and the hair, for through them she denotes her union with God in the intellect and the will. Faith or fidelity, signified by the eye, resides in the intellect, and love, signified by the hair, resides in the will. She is then united with God in the intellect through faith, and in the will through love. She glories here in this union and thanks her Spouse for this favor received from his hands, and she values highly the fact that he should be satisfied and captivated by her love. Consider the joy, happiness, and delight the soul finds in such a prisoner, she who for so long had been his prisoner.

STANZA 32

Introduction

1. The power and the tenacity of love is great, for love captures and binds God himself.[1] Happy is the loving soul, since she possesses God for her prisoner, and he is surrendered to all her desires. God is such that those who act with love and friendship toward him will make him do all they desire, but if they act otherwise there is no speaking to him or power with him, even though they go to extremes. Yet by love they bind him with one hair. Knowing this, and knowing how far beyond her merits it was that he should have favored her with such sublime love and rich tokens of virtues and gifts, she attributes all to him in this stanza:

> When you looked at me
> your eyes imprinted your grace in me;
> for this you loved me ardently;
> and thus my eyes deserved
> to adore what they beheld in you.

Commentary

2. It is the property of perfect love to be unwilling to take anything for self, nor does it attribute anything to self, but all to the beloved. If we find this characteristic in base loves, how much more in love of God, where reason so strongly obliges us to this. Because, therefore, it seems in the two previous stanzas that the bride attributed something to herself (saying that she would make garlands with the Bridegroom, and weave them together with one of her hairs—a work of no small importance— and afterward announcing and glorying in the fact that her hair captivated the Beloved and her eye wounded him, in which she also takes some credit), she desires in this stanza to explain her intention and to remove the false impression that may have been received. For she is anxious and fearful lest she give herself some credit and attribute less to God than is his due and her desire. So she accredits all to him and thanks him, stating that the reason the hair of her love captivated him and the eye of her faith wounded him was that he favored her by looking at her with love. By this look of love he made her gracious and pleasing to himself. And she adds that from this grace and value she received from him, she merited his love and a value within herself enabling her to adore her Beloved in a fashion pleasing to him and to perform works worthy of his grace and love. The verse follows:

> When you looked at me

---

1. Cf. A. 3. 44. 3 for a similar text on the power of the prayer of one who thus loves God.

3. That is, with the affection of love, because we have already pointed out that here for God to look is for him to love.[2]

> your eyes imprinted your grace in me;

4. By the eyes of the Bridegroom she refers to God's mercy: He descends in mercy on the soul, impressing and infusing his love and grace in her, making her beautiful and lifting her so high as to make her a partaker of his very divinity [2 Pt. 1:4]. Seeing the height and dignity in which he has placed her, the soul proclaims:

> for this you loved me ardently;

5. To love ardently is to love very much. It is more than loving simply; it is like loving doubly, for two reasons. In this verse the soul points to the two motives or causes of the Bridegroom's love for her. Not only did he love her in being captivated by her hair, but he loved her ardently in being wounded by her eye.

And she states in this verse that the cause of his loving her so ardently and intimately was his desire in looking at her to give her grace by which he could find his pleasure in her. Thus he gave her love, which is her hair, and he gave her faith, which is her eye, formed with his charity. She says therefore: "For this you loved me ardently." By infusing his grace in the soul, God makes it worthy and capable of his love. This verse, then, is like saying: Because you have infused your grace into me, which was a worthy token of your love, you loved me ardently, that is, you gave me more grace on this account. St. John makes the same affirmation: *He gives grace for the grace he has given* [Jn. 1:16], which is to give more grace. Without his grace one cannot merit his grace.

6. It should be noted for an understanding of this that just as God loves nothing outside himself, he bears no love for anything lower than the love he has for himself. He loves all things for himself; thus love becomes the purpose for which he loves. He therefore does not love things because of what they are in themselves. With God, to love the soul is to put her somehow in himself and make her his equal. Thus he loves the soul within himself, with himself, that is, with the very love by which he loves himself. This is why the soul merits the love of God in all her works insofar as she does them in God. Placed in this height, this grace, she merits God himself in every work. Consequently, she continues:

> and thus my eyes deserved

7. That is, by the favor and grace the eyes of your mercy granted me,

---

2. In 31. 5-8.

when you looked at me and made me pleasing to your eyes and worthy of your sight, my eyes deserved
> to adore what they beheld in you.

8. This is like saying: My faculties, the eyes through which I can see you, my Spouse, merited this elevation that enables them to look at you. These faculties were previously fallen and lowly in the misery of their inferior operation and natural ability, for the power to look at God is, for the soul, the power to do works in the grace of God. The faculties of the adoring soul merited this because they adored in the grace of God, by which every work becomes meritorious. Illumined and elevated by his grace and favor, they adored what they saw in him, which they did not previously see because of their blindness and lowliness.

What was it, then, they beheld? They beheld in God sublime virtues, abundant sweetness, immense goodness, love, and mercy, and the numberless benefits received from him, either before or since these close ties with him were wrought. The soul's eyes now deserved to adore all this meritoriously, for they were now gracious and pleasing to the Bride-groom. Previously they did not merit to adore or behold this; they did not even deserve to reflect on some of these things about God. Great is the rudeness and the blindness of the soul without God's grace!

9. There is much to note here and much to grieve over in observing how far from the fulfillment of its obligations is the soul unillumined by the love of God. Having the obligation to know these and countless other favors, both temporal and spiritual, she has received and continues to receive from God at every step, and to adore and serve God ceaselessly with all her faculties, she fails to do so. Not only this, she does not even merit to look at and know him or even to be aware of the possibility; such is the misery of those who live, or better are dead, in sin.

STANZA 33

Introduction

1. For a better understanding of both what we have said and will say, it should be known that God's gaze produces four goods in the soul: It cleanses, endows with grace, enriches, and illumines, like the sun that dries and provides warmth and beauty and splendor when it pours down its rays.

After God places these three last kinds of good in the soul, he no longer remembers her former ugliness and sin, as he declares through

Ezekiel [Ez. 18:22], for on account of these goods she is very agreeable to him. And once he has blotted out this sin and ugliness, he no longer reproaches her for it, or fails to impart more favors, since he never judges a thing twice [Na. 1:9].

Yet even though God forgets evil and sin once it is pardoned, the soul should not become oblivious of her former sins. As the Wise Man says: *Be not without fear for sin forgiven* [Ecclus. 5:5]. There are three reasons she should not forget her sins: first, so as always to have a motive against presumption; second, to have cause for rendering thanks; third, to incite herself to greater confidence, for if while in sin the soul received so much good from God, how many more remarkable favors will she be able to hope for now that God has placed her in his love, outside of sin?

2. Remembering here all these mercies and aware that she has been placed with so much dignity close to the Bridegroom, she rejoices immeasurably in the delight of thanksgiving and love. The memory of that former state, so unsightly and abject, notably promotes this gratitude and love. She was not only unprepared for and unworthy of God's gaze, but she did not even deserve that he pronounce her name, as he says through David [Ps. 16:4]. Conscious that in herself there is no reason, or possibility of a reason, why God should look at and exalt her, but that this reason is only in God, in his mere will and beautiful grace, she ascribes her misery to herself, and all her good possessions to the Beloved. Aware that through them she now merits what previously she did not, she takes courage and becomes bold to request the continuation of the divine spiritual union in which he will go on multiplying his favors in her. She declares all this in this stanza:

> Do not despise me;
> for if, before, you found me dark,
> now truly you can look at me
> since you have looked
> and left in me grace and beauty.

Commentary

3. Taking courage and appraising herself by the tokens and value she has from her Beloved and observing that since they belong to him she deserves esteem on their account—although in herself she is of small value and merits no esteem—the bride dares to tell her Beloved not to consider her any longer of little account and not to despise her. If she previously merited this treatment because of the ugliness of her faults and the lowliness of her nature, now, after he has looked at her the first time, by which he arrayed her in his grace and clothed her in his beauty, he can easily look at her the second time and many more times, making

this grace and beauty grow. Now there is reason enough for him to look at her, if we consider that he looked at her when she did not have these qualities, or merit that he do so.

> Do not despise me;

4. The soul does not declare this out of a desire to be held in high regard (on the contrary, those with a genuine love of God greatly esteem and rejoice in being hated and reviled because they are aware that of themselves they deserve nothing else), but because of the gifts and graces of God that she possesses, as she points out in saying:

> for if, before, you found me dark,

5. That is, if before you graciously looked on me, you found in me the unsightliness of sins and imperfections and the lowness of the natural condition.

> now truly you can look at me
> since you have looked

6. Since you have looked (rubbed out this dark and wretched color of sin that made me unsightly), in which you bestowed grace on me the first time, "now truly you can look at me." That is, now I can indeed be seen, and I merit being seen by receiving more grace from your eyes. The first time you not only rubbed out the dark color with those eyes, but you made me worthy to be seen since you looked with love.

> and left in me grace and beauty.

7. The soul's affirmation in the two preceding verses explains what St. John states in his Gospel, that God gives grace for grace [Jn. 1:16], because when God beholds the soul made attractive through grace, he is impelled to grant her more grace, for he dwells within her well pleased with her. Knowing this, Moses begged God for more grace, desiring to oblige him by the grace he had already received from him: *You say that you know me by name and I have found grace before you; if, therefore, I have found grace in your sight, show me your face that I might know you and find grace in your sight* [Ex. 33:12-13].

Because this grace exalts, honors, and beautifies her in his sight, God loves her ineffably. If prior to her being in grace, he loved her only on account of himself, now that she is in grace he loves her not only on account of himself but also on account of herself. And thus enamored by means of the effects and works of grace, or without them, he ever continues to communicate more love and more graces. And as he continues to honor and exalt her, he becomes continually more captivated by and enamored of her. God manifests this in speaking to his friend Jacob through Isaiah: *Since you have become honorable and glorious in my sight, I have loved you* [Is. 43:4]. In other words, after I had turned my eyes toward you, thus giving you grace and making you glorious and worthy of honor and my presence, you merited the grace of more of my favors.

The bride in the Song of Songs explains the same thing, saying: *I am dark but beautiful, daughters of Jerusalem; wherefore the King has loved me and brought me to his inner chamber* [Sg. 1:4-5]. This is like saying: Souls, you who do not know of or recognize these favors, do not marvel that the heavenly King has granted such admirable ones as even to bring me to his inner love. For though of myself I am dark, he so frequently fixed his eyes on me, after having looked at me the first time, that he was not satisfied until he had espoused me to himself and brought me to the inner chamber of his love.

8. Who can express how much God exalts the soul that pleases him? It is impossible to do so, nor can this even be imagined, for after all, he does this as God, to show who he is. One can only explain something of it through that characteristic God has of giving more to whoever has more. And his gifts are multiplied in proportion to what the soul possesses, as the Gospel makes clear: *To those who have, more will be given until they abound; and from those who have not, even what they have shall be taken from them* [Mt. 13:12; Lk. 19:26]. Thus the money of the servant who did not stand in the lord's good graces was taken from him and given to the servant who had the most money of all those who pleased the lord [Lk. 19:24].

God gathers together in the one who is his closest friend the best and principal goods of his house, of both the Church Militant and the Church Triumphant. He makes arrangements so that these goods will give more honor and glory to his friend, who becomes like a brilliant light absorbing in itself countless fainter lights. God also declared this, according to the spiritual sense, in the passage of Isaiah, quoted above, when he spoke to Jacob: *I am your Lord God, the Holy One of Israel, your Savior; I have given Egypt for your propitiation, Ethiopia and Saba for you, and I will give men for you and people for your soul* [Is. 43:3-4].

9. Now, my God, you can easily look on and bear high esteem for the soul you behold, for by your look you present her with valuables and jewels and then esteem her and are captivated. After you have looked at her she no longer merits that you look at her only once, but that you look at her often. The Holy Spirit observes in the Book of Esther: *Worthy of such honor is the one whom the king honors* [Est. 6:11].

STANZA 34

Introduction

1. The gifts of friendship the Bridegroom bestows on the soul in this state are inestimable, and the praises and endearing expressions of love that frequently pass between the two are indescribable. She praises and thanks him; and he extols, praises, and thanks her, as is apparent in the Song of Songs where he tells her: *Behold you are beautiful, my love, behold you are beautiful and your eyes are those of doves.* And she replies: *Behold you are beautiful, my Beloved, and fair* [Sg. 1:14-15]. There are many other expressions of gratitude and praise they repeat to each other throughout the Song of Songs. In the preceding stanza she belittled herself, calling herself dark and ugly, and lauded him for his beauty and grace since with his regard he gave her beauty and grace. And since he customarily exalts those who humble themselves [Lk. 14:11; Mt. 23:12], he fixes his eyes on her as she requested, and in the next stanza he extols her and does not call her dark, as she called herself, but a white dove, praising her good characteristics that are like those of the dove and the turtledove. Thus he says:

Bridegroom
> The small white dove
> has returned to the ark with an olive branch;
> and now the turtledove
> has found its longed-for mate
> by the green river banks.

Commentary

2. It is the Bridegroom who takes up the song here and describes the soul's purity in this state and her riches and reward for laboring and preparing herself to come to him. He also tells of her good fortune in having found her Bridegroom in this union, and of the fulfillment of her desires and of the delight and refreshment she possesses in him, now that the trials of this life and time are over. And thus he says:

> The small white dove

3. He calls the soul a "white dove" because of the whiteness and purity imparted by the grace she has found in God. And he calls her "dove," because this is the name he gives her in the Song of Songs [Sg. 2:10] to denote both the simplicity and meekness of her character and her loving contemplation. For not only is the dove simple and meek, without gall, but also it has bright and loving eyes. As a result the Bridegroom in

addition remarked there that she had dove's eyes to denote this property of loving contemplation by which she looks at God [Sg. 4:1]. He declares that this dove

> has returned to the ark with an olive branch;

4. Here the Bridegroom compares the soul to the dove of Noah's ark, taking that flight back and forth from the ark as a figure of what has happened to the soul in this case. For the dove flew back and forth from the ark because it found no place among the waters of the flood where it could alight, until it returned with an olive branch in its beak as a sign of God's mercy in the cessation of the deluge [Gn. 8:8-11]. Similarly this soul that left the ark of God's omnipotence when he created her passed through the waters of sin and imperfection and, finding no place for her appetite to rest, flew back and forth through the air of the anxieties of love from the ark of the Creator's breast. And he did not take her in until he made the waters of all the imperfections on the land of the soul to cease, and she returned with the olive branch (which denotes her victory over all things through the clemency and mercy of God) to this happy and perfect recollection at the breast of her Beloved. She returns not only victorious over her enemies but with the reward of her merits, for both are denoted by the olive branch. Thus the small dove, the soul, not only returns to the ark of her God as clean and white as when he created her before her departure, but also carries in addition the olive branch that signifies the reward and peace obtained in her victory over self.

> and now the turtledove
> has found its longed-for mate
> by the green river banks.

5. The Bridegroom calls the soul a "turtledove" because, in looking for her Beloved, she acted as the turtledove when it does not find the mate it longs for. To make this clear we ought to recall what they say about the turtledove: When it does not find its mate, it will not perch on the green branch or drink the cool, clear water, nor does it rest in the shade or join the company of others; but when it finds its mate, then it will enjoy all these other goods.

The soul possesses all these traits, and it is necessary for her to possess them in order to reach this union with her Bridegroom, the Son of God. For she must advance with such love and solicitude as not to set the foot of her appetite on the green branch of any delight, or drink the clear water of any worldly honor and glory, nor should she desire to taste the cool water of any temporal refreshment or comfort, or to settle in the shade of any creature's favor and protection, nor should she desire in any way to rest in anything or have the company of other affections; but she should always sigh for solitude in all things until she reaches her

Bridegroom in complete satisfaction.

6. Because the soul, before reaching this high state, went about with deep love in search of her Beloved and was satisfied with nothing else than him, the Bridegroom himself describes in song the end of her fatigues and the fulfillment of her desires, saying that now the turtledove has found its longed-for mate by the green river banks. This is similar to saying: Now the bride alights on the green branch, delighting in her Beloved; now she drinks the clear water of sublime contemplation and wisdom of God, and the cool water of her refreshment and comfort in God; and she also rests in the shade of his protection and favor that she so longed for, where she is divinely and delightfully consoled, fed, and refreshed, as she happily declares in the Song of Songs: *I sat down in the shade of him whom I desired, and his fruit was sweet to my palate* [Sg. 2:3].

STANZA 35

Introduction

1. The Bridegroom continues the explanation of his happiness over the blessing the bride has obtained through the solitude in which she formerly desired to live. This blessing is a stable peace and unchanging good. When the soul has become established in the quietude of solitary love of her Bridegroom, as has this one of whom we are speaking, she is settled in God, and God in her, with so much delight that she has no need of other masters or means to direct her to him, for now God is her guide and her light. He accomplishes in her what he promised through Hosea: *I shall lead her into solitude and there speak to her heart* [Hos. 2:14]. In this promise he reveals that he communicates and unites himself to the soul in solitude. To speak to the heart is to satisfy the heart, which is dissatisfied with anything less than God. Thus the Bridegroom continues:

> She lived in solitude,
> and now in solitude has built her nest;
> and in solitude he guides her,
> he alone, who also bears
> in solitude the wound of love.

Commentary

2. The Bridegroom does two things in this stanza:

First, he praises the solitude in which the soul formerly desired to live, telling how it was a means for her to find and rejoice in her Beloved alone, withdrawn from all her former afflictions and fatigues. Since she wished to live in solitude, apart from every satisfaction, comfort, and support of creatures in order to reach companionship and union with her Beloved, she deserved to discover the possession of peaceful solitude in her Beloved, in whom she rests, alone and isolated from all these disturbances.[1]

Second, he states that, insofar as she desired to live apart from all created things, in solitude for her Beloved's sake, he himself was enamored of her because of this solitude and took care of her by accepting her in his arms, feeding her in himself with every blessing, and guiding her to the high things of God. He asserts not only that he guides her, but does so alone without other means (angels, humans, forms, or figures), for she now possesses, through this solitude, true liberty of spirit that is not bound to any of these means. The verse states:

> She lived in solitude,

3. The soul, represented by the turtledove, lived in solitude before encountering the Beloved in this state of union. There is no companionship that affords consolation to the soul that longs for God; indeed, until she finds him, everything causes greater solitude.

> and now in solitude has built her nest;

4. The solitude in which she lived consisted of the desire to go without the things of the world for her Bridegroom's sake—as we said of the turtledove—by striving for perfection, acquiring perfect solitude in which she reaches union with the Word.[2] She consequently attains to complete refreshment and rest, signified here by the nest that refers to repose. It is similar to saying: She formerly practiced this solitude, in which she lived, in trial and anguish because she was imperfect, but now she has built her nest in it and has found refreshment and repose in having acquired it perfectly in God. David, speaking spiritually, says: *Truly the sparrow has found a house and the turtledove a nest where she can nurture her young* [Ps. 84:3], that is: The soul has found a place in God where she can satisfy her appetites and faculties.

> and in solitude he guides her,

5. In this solitude, away from all things, the soul is alone with God and he guides, moves, and raises her to divine things. That is: he elevates her intellect to divine understanding, because it is alone and divested of other contrary and alien knowledge; he moves her will freely to the love

---

1. By repeating the word "solitude" in this stanza and throughout the commentary, John heightens the impression of a peaceful solitude. This authentic solitude is not necessarily physical but a solitude of detachment, or poverty of spirit, for the sake of the Bridegroom. Cf. F. 3. 46.
2. Cf. 34. 5.

of God, because it is alone and freed from other affections; and he fills her memory with divine knowledge, because it is now alone and empty of other images and phantasies. Once the soul disencumbers these faculties and empties them of everything inferior and of possessiveness in regard to superior things, leaving them alone without these things, God engages them in the invisible and divine. It is God who guides her in this solitude, as St. Paul declares of the perfect: *Qui spiritu Dei aguntur,* and so on (they are moved by the Spirit of God) [Rom. 8:14]. This is like saying; In solitude he guided her,

> he alone, who also bears

6. The meaning of this is not only that he guided her in her solitude, but it is he alone who works in her without any means. This is a characteristic of the union of the soul with God in spiritual marriage: God works in and communicates himself to her through himself alone, without using as means the angels or natural ability, for the exterior and interior senses, and all creatures, and even the soul herself do very little toward the reception of the remarkable supernatural favors that God grants in this state. These favors do not fall within the province of the soul's natural ability or work or diligence, but God alone grants them to her. And the reason he does so is that he finds her alone and does not want to give her any other company, nor does he want her to trust in or profit by any other than himself alone.

Since the soul has left all and passed beyond all means, ascending above them all to God, it is fitting that God himself be the guide and means of reaching himself. And having ascended above all things, in solitude from all things, she profits by no other than the Word, the Bridegroom, who helps her to ascend further. He is taken with love for her and wants to be the only one to grant her these favors. And he goes on:

> in solitude the wound of love.

7. That is, he is wounded with love for the bride. The Bridegroom bears a great love for the solitude of the soul; but he is wounded much more by her love since, being wounded with love for him, she desired to live alone in respect to all things. And he does not wish to leave her alone, but wounded by the solitude she embraces for his sake, and observing that she is dissatisfied with any other thing, he alone guides her, drawing her to and absorbing her in himself. Had he not found her in spiritual solitude, he would not have wrought this in her.

STANZA 36

Introduction

1. Strange it is, this property of lovers, that they like to enjoy each other's companionship alone, apart from every creature and all company. If some stranger is present they do not enjoy each other freely, even though they are together and may speak to each other just as much as when the other is absent, and even though the other does not talk to them. The reason they desire to commune with each other alone is that love is a union between two alone.

Once the soul is placed at the peak of perfection and freedom of spirit in God, and all the repugnances and contradictions of sensuality have ceased, she no longer has any other activity to engage her than surrender to the delights and joys of intimate love of her Bridegroom. As it is written of the holy Tobit, that after he had undergone the trials of his poverty and temptations he was enlightened by God and spent all the rest of his days in joy [Tb. 14:4], so does the soul of whom we are now speaking, since the goods she beholds in herself are of such joy and delight.

2. Isaiah declares this of the one who has practiced the works of perfection and arrived at the summit of which we are discussing. Addressing the soul, he says of this perfection: *Then your light will rise up in darkness, and your darkness will be as the noonday. And your Lord God will give you rest always and will fill your soul with brightness, and deliver your bones; and you will be like a watered garden and an unfailing fount of water. And the solitudes of ages will be built in you. You will raise up the beginnings and foundations of generation and generation, and you will be called the builder of the fences, withdrawing your paths and ways to quietude. If you separate your labor from the day of rest and from doing your will on my holy day, and call yourself the delicate, holy, and glorious Lord's day of rest, and if you glorify him by not doing your own ways and not fulfilling your own will, then you will delight in the Lord, and I will extol you above the heights of the earth and feed you with the inheritance of Jacob* [Is. 58:10-14]. These are the words of Isaiah. Jacob's inheritance here is God himself. Accordingly, as we said, this soul is no longer engaged in anything else than joy in the delights of this pasture. One thing only is left for her to desire: perfect enjoyment of God in eternal life. In the remaining stanzas she asks her Beloved for this beatific pasture of the manifest vision of God.[1] Thus she exclaims:

---

1. In these final stanzas the focus shifts from the state of spiritual marriage to prayer for the beatific vision.

Let us rejoice, Beloved,
and let us go forth to behold ourselves in your beauty
to the mountain and to the hill,
to where the pure water flows,
and further, deep into the thicket.

Commentary

3. Now that the perfect union of love between God and the soul is wrought, she desires to employ herself in those things proper to love. She it is who addresses the Bridegroom in this stanza, asking for three things proper to love.

First, she desires to receive the joy and savor of love, which is what she asks for in saying, "Let us rejoice, Beloved."

Second, she desires to become like the Beloved, and she asks for this in stating, "And let us go forth to behold ourselves in your beauty."

Third, she desires to look closely at and know the things and secrets of the Beloved himself, which is what she requests in saying, "And further, deep into the thicket." The verse follows:

Let us rejoice, Beloved,

4. That is: Let us rejoice in the communication of the sweetness of love, not only in that sweetness we already possess in our habitual union but in that which overflows into the effective and actual practice of love, either interiorly with the will in the affective act or exteriorly in works directed to the service of the Beloved. As we mentioned, when love takes root it has this characteristic: It makes one always desire to taste the joys and sweetnesses of love in the inward and outward exercise of love.[2] All this the lover does in order to resemble the Beloved more. And thus she continues:

Let us go forth to behold ourselves in your beauty,

5. This means: Let us so act that by means of this loving activity we may attain to the vision of ourselves in your beauty in eternal life. That is: That I be so transformed in your beauty that we may be alike in beauty, and both behold ourselves in your beauty, possessing then your very beauty; this, in such a way that each looking at the other may see in the other their own beauty, since both are your beauty alone, I being absorbed in your beauty; hence, I shall see you in your beauty, and you will see me in your beauty, and I shall see myself in you in your beauty, and you will see yourself in me in your beauty; that I may resemble you in your beauty, and

---

2. She wants to rejoice in the love expressed not only in contemplation but also in action. On active and contemplative life, cf. 3. 1; 29. 1-2.

you resemble me in your beauty, and my beauty be your beauty and your beauty my beauty; wherefore I shall be you in your beauty, and you will be me in your beauty, because your very beauty will be my beauty; and thus we shall behold each other in your beauty.[3]

This is the adoption of the children of God, who will indeed declare to God what the very Son said to the Eternal Father through St. John: *All my things are yours, and yours mine* [Jn. 17:10]. He says this by essence, since he is the natural Son of God, and we say it by participation, since we are adopted children. He declared this not only for himself, the Head, but for his whole mystical body, the Church, which on the day of her triumph, when she sees God face to face, will participate in the very beauty of the Bridegroom. Hence the soul makes the petition that she and her Bridegroom go forth to behold each other in his beauty.

to the mountain and to the hill,

6. That is: to the morning and essential knowledge of God, which is knowledge in the divine Word, who in his height is signified here by the mountain. That they may know the Son of God, Isaiah urges all: *Come, let us ascend to the mountain of the Lord* [Is. 2:3]; in another passage: *The mountain of the house of the Lord shall be prepared* [Is. 2:2].

"And to the hill," that is, to the evening knowledge of God, which is God's wisdom in his creatures, works, and wondrous decrees. The hill suggests this wisdom because it is not as high as the morning wisdom. Yet the soul asks for both the evening and the morning wisdom when she says: "To the mountain and to the hill."

7. The soul in urging the Bridegroom, "Let us go forth to the mountain to behold ourselves in your beauty," means: Transform me into the beauty of divine Wisdom and make me resemble that which is the Word, the Son of God. And in adding "to the hill," she asks that he inform her with the beauty of this other, lesser wisdom contained in his creatures and other mysterious works. This wisdom is also the beauty of the Son of God by which the soul desires to be illumined.

8. The soul cannot see herself in the beauty of God unless she is transformed into the wisdom of God, in which she sees herself in possession of earthly and heavenly things. The bride wanted to come to this mountain and to this hill when she asserted: *I shall go to the mountain of myrrh and to the hill of incense* [Sg. 4:6]. The mountain of myrrh refers to

---

3. John expresses here his mystical experience of the beauty of God not through a mere description but rather through a kind of intense prayer in which he forgets the reader in concentration on his Beloved. In this outpouring of his heart the word "beauty" appears 23 times.

the clear vision of God and the hill of incense to the knowledge of creatures, for the myrrh on the mountain is more choice than the incense on the hill.

> to where the pure water flows,

9. That is, to where God bestows on the intellect knowledge and wisdom, called water here because it cleanses and removes accidents and phantasies and clears away the clouds of ignorance. The soul always possesses this desire to have clear and pure understanding of the divine truths; and the greater her love, the more she longs to enter further into these truths. Because of this desire she asks for the third property of love, saying:

> and further, deep into the thicket.

10. Into the thicket of your splendid works and profound judgments, whose multitude and variety are such that we can use the term "thicket." In these works and judgments there is abundant wisdom, so full of mysteries, that not only is the term "thicket" apt, but even "curdled thicket," which David uses: *Mons Dei, mons pinguis, mons coagulatus* (The mountain of God is a fat mountain and a curdled mountain) [Ps. 68:16].

This thicket of God's wisdom and knowledge is so deep and immense that no matter how much the soul knows, she can always enter it further; it is vast and its riches incomprehensible, as St. Paul exclaims: *O height of the riches of the wisdom and knowledge of God, how incomprehensible are his judgments and unsearchable his ways* [Rom. 11:33].

11. Yet the soul wants to enter this thicket and incomprehensibility of judgments and ways because she is dying with the desire to penetrate them deeply. Knowledge of them is an inestimable delight surpassing all understanding. David, therefore, in speaking of the savoriness of these judgments, says: *The judgments of the Lord are true and in themselves justified. They are more to be desired and coveted than gold and precious stone of great price; and they are sweeter than honey and the honeycomb, so much so that your servant loved and kept them* [Ps. 19:9-11]. Hence the soul ardently wishes to be engulfed in these judgments and know them from further within. And, in exchange, it will be a singular comfort and happiness for her to enter all the afflictions and trials of the world and everything, however difficult and painful, that might be a means to this knowledge, even the anguish and agony of death, all in order to see herself further within her God.

12. This thicket into which the soul thus wants to enter also signifies very appropriately the thicket and multitude of trials and tribulations, for suffering is very delightful and beneficial to her. Suffering is the means of her penetrating further, deep into the thicket of the delectable

wisdom of God. The purest suffering brings with it the purest and most intimate knowing, and consequently the purest and highest joy, because it is a knowing from further within. Not being content with just any kind of suffering, she insists: "And further, deep into the thicket," that is, even to the agony of death in order to see God. The prophet Job, desirous of this suffering in order to see God, exclaimed: *Who will grant that my request be fulfilled and that God will give me what I hope for and that he who began me may destroy me, and let loose his hand and put an end to me. And that I may have this comfort, that in afflicting me with sorrow he might not spare me?* [Jb. 6:8-10].

13. Oh! If we could but now fully understand how a soul cannot reach the thicket and wisdom of the riches of God, which are of many kinds, without entering the thicket of many kinds of suffering, finding in this her delight and consolation; and how a soul with an authentic desire for divine wisdom wants suffering first in order to enter this wisdom by the thicket of the cross! Accordingly, St. Paul admonished the Ephesians not to grow weak in their tribulations and to be strong and rooted in charity in order to comprehend with all the saints what is the breadth and height and depth, and to know also the supereminent charity of the knowledge of Christ, in order to be filled with all the fullness of God [Eph. 3:13, 17-19]. The gate entering into these riches of his wisdom is the cross, which is narrow, and few desire to enter by it, but many desire the delights obtained from entering there.[4]

STANZA 37

Introduction

1. One of the main reasons for the desire to be dissolved and to be with Christ [Phil. 1:23] is to see him face to face and thoroughly understand the profound and eternal mysteries of his Incarnation, which is by no means the lesser part of beatitude. As Christ himself says to the Father in St. John's Gospel: *This is eternal life, that they know you, the one true God, and your Son Jesus Christ whom you have sent* [Jn. 17:3]. The first thing a person desires to do after having come a long distance is to see and converse with a deeply loved one; similarly, the first thing the soul desires on coming to the vision of God is to know and enjoy the deep secrets and mysteries of the Incarnation and the ancient ways of God dependent on it. Hence, after expressing her desire to see herself in the beauty of God, the soul declares in the following stanza:

---

4. Cf. A. 2. 7. 5.

And then we will go on
to the high caverns in the rock
which are so well concealed;
there we shall enter
and taste the fresh juice of the pomegranates.

Commentary

2. One of the reasons urging the soul most to enter this thicket of God's wisdom and to know its beauty from further within is her wish to unite her intellect with God in the knowledge of the mysteries of the Incarnation, in which is contained the highest and most savory wisdom of all his works. The bride states in this stanza that once she has entered further into the divine wisdom (further into the spiritual marriage she now possesses, which in glory will be the face-to-face vision of God as well as union with this divine wisdom who is the Son of God), she will know the sublime mysteries of God and human beings. These mysteries are exalted in wisdom, and the soul enters the knowledge of them, engulfing and immersing herself in them. And both the bride and the Bridegroom will taste the savoriness and the delight caused by the knowledge of these mysteries together with the powers and attributes of God uncovered in them, such as: justice, mercy, wisdom, power, charity, and so on.

And then we will go on
to the high caverns in the rock

3. The rock mentioned here, as St. Paul says, is Christ [1 Cor. 10:4]. The high caverns of this rock are the sublime, exalted, and deep mysteries of God's wisdom in Christ, in the hypostatic union of the human nature with the divine Word, and in the corresponding union of human beings with God, and the mystery of the harmony between God's justice and mercy with respect to the manifestations of his judgments in the salvation of the human race. These mysteries are so profound that she very appropriately calls them high caverns: high, because of the height of the sublime mysteries; and caverns, because of the depth of God's wisdom in them. As caverns are deep and have many recesses, so each of the mysteries in Christ is singularly deep in wisdom and contains many recesses of his secret judgments of predestination and foreknowledge concerning the children of the earth. She then adds:

which are so well concealed;

4. They are so well concealed that however numerous are the mysteries and marvels that holy doctors have discovered and saintly souls understood in this earthly life, all the more is yet to be said and understood. There is much to fathom in Christ, for he is like an abundant mine with

many recesses of treasures, so that however deep individuals may go they never reach the end or bottom, but rather in every recess find new veins with new riches everywhere. On this account St. Paul said of Christ: *In Christ dwell hidden all treasures and wisdom* [Col. 2:3]. The soul cannot enter these caverns or reach these treasures if, as we said, she does not first pass over to the divine wisdom through the straits of exterior and interior suffering. For one cannot reach in this life what is attainable of these mysteries of Christ without having suffered much and without having received numerous intellectual and sensible favors from God, and without having undergone much spiritual activity; for all these favors are inferior to the wisdom of the mysteries of Christ in that they serve as preparations for coming to this wisdom.

When Moses asked God to reveal his glory, God told Moses that he would be unable to receive such a revelation in this life, but that he would be shown all good, that is, all the good that can be revealed in this life. So God put Moses in the cavern of the rock, which is Christ, as we said, and showed his back to him, which was to impart knowledge of the mysteries of the humanity of Christ.

5. The soul, then, earnestly longs to enter these caverns of Christ in order to be absorbed, transformed, and wholly inebriated in the love of the wisdom of these mysteries, and hide herself in the bosom of the Beloved. In the Song of Songs he invites her to these clefts, saying: *Arise, make haste, my love, my beautiful one, and come into the clefts of the rock and into the cavern of the wall* [Sg. 2:13-14]. These clefts are the caverns we are discussing here of which the soul says next:

there we shall enter

6. That is, "there," into that knowledge and those mysteries, "we shall enter." And she does not declare, I alone shall enter—which would seem more suitable since the Bridegroom does not enter again—but we (the Beloved and I) shall enter. Thereby she shows that she does not do this work alone but that the Bridegroom does it with her. Furthermore, since the soul and God are now united in this state of spiritual marriage that we are discussing, the soul performs no work without God.

To say, "there we shall enter," is to say that there we shall be transformed; that is, I shall be transformed in you through love of these divine and delightful judgments. In her knowledge about the predestination of the just and the foreknowledge of the damned, in which the Father predisposed the just with the blessings of his sweetness [Ps. 21:3], in his Son Jesus Christ, the soul is most sublimely and intimately transformed in the love of God. And with unspeakable delight she thanks and loves the Father again through his Son Jesus. She does this united with Christ, together with Christ. And the savor of this praise is so delicate as to be

totally beyond words. Yet the soul states in the following verse:
and taste the fresh juice of the pomegranates.

7. The pomegranates stand for the mysteries of Christ, the judgments of the wisdom of God, and the virtues and attributes uncovered in the knowledge of these innumerable mysteries and judgments. Just as pomegranates have many little seeds formed and sustained within the circular shell, so each of the attributes, mysteries, judgments, and virtues of God, like a round shell of power and mystery, holds and sustains a multitude of marvelous decrees and wondrous effects.

We observe here the circular or spherical figure of the pomegranate and by each pomegranate understand here some divine attribute and power; each divine attribute and power is God himself, who is represented by the circular or spherical figure because he has no beginning or end.[1]

Since in God's wisdom there are such countless judgments and mysteries, the bride told the Bridegroom in the Song of Songs: *Your belly is of ivory set with sapphires* [Sg. 5:14]. The sapphires represent these mysteries and judgments of the divine wisdom, signified by the belly; for the sapphire is a precious stone, the color of a clear and serene sky.

8. The juice from these pomegranates that the bride and the Bridegroom will taste is the fruition and delight of the love of God overflowing from the knowledge of his attributes. In eating a pomegranate, one juice alone is tasted from its many seeds; similarly, from all the infused wonders and grandeurs of God there redounds to the soul one fruition and delight of love, which is the drink of the Holy Spirit. With glowing tenderness of love she at once offers this drink to her God, the Word, her Spouse. She had promised him this divine drink in the Song of Songs if he would lead her into this lofty knowledge: *There you will teach me; and I shall give you the drink of spiced wine and of juice from my pomegranates* [Sg. 8:2]. She calls the pomegranates (the divine knowledge) her own because even though they are his, God has given them to her. She offers as a drink to God her joy in and fruition of this knowledge in the wine of love. Such is the meaning of the words, "And taste the fresh juice of the pomegranates." Tasting it himself, he gives it to her to taste; and she in tasting it turns and offers it to him. And thus they both taste it together.

---

1. A sphere drawn twice in the Jaén copy of this paragraph suggests that John illustrated what he was describing here.

STANZA 38

Introduction

1. In the two preceding stanzas the bride's song focused on the good the Bridegroom will offer her in that eternal bliss. That is, the Bridegroom will really transform her into the beauty of both his created and uncreated wisdom, and also into the beauty of the union of the Word with his humanity in which she will know him face to face as well as from the back.

In the next stanza she discusses two things: first, the manner in which she will taste that divine juice of the sapphires, or rather the pomegranates; second, the glory she will give her Bridegroom through her predestination. It should be noted that even though she refers to these goods as successive parts, they are all contained in one essential glory. She says:

> There you will show me
> what my soul has been seeking,
> and then you will give me,
> you, my life, will give me there
> what you gave me on that other day:

Commentary

2. The reason the soul desired to enter these caverns was to reach the consummation of the love of God, which she had always been seeking; that is, to love God as purely and perfectly as he loves her in order to repay him by such love. She declares to the Bridegroom in this stanza that there he will show her that which was her aim in all her acts: to love the Bridegroom as perfectly as he loves her. The second gift she will receive there is the essential glory to which he predestined her from the day of his eternity. Thus she declares:

> There you will show me
> what my soul has been seeking,

3. The soul's aim is a love equal to God's. She always desired this equality, naturally and supernaturally, for lovers cannot be satisfied without feeling that they love as much as they are loved. Since the soul sees through her transformation in God in this life that she cannot, even though her love is immense, equal the perfection of God's love for her, she desires the clear transformation of glory in which she will reach this equality. Even though there is a true union of will in this high state she now enjoys, she cannot attain the excellence and power of love that she will possess in the strong union of glory. Just as the soul, according to St. Paul, will know then as she is known by God [1 Cor. 13:12], so she will also

love God as she is loved by him. As her intellect will be the intellect of God, her will then will be God's will, and thus her love will be God's love. The soul's will is not destroyed there, but is so firmly united with the strength of God's will, with which he loves her, that her love for him is as strong and perfect as his love for her; for the two wills are so united that there is only one will and love, which is God's. Thus the soul loves God with the will and strength of God himself, united with the very strength of love with which God loves her. This strength lies in the Holy Spirit in whom the soul is there transformed, for by this transformation of glory he supplies what is lacking in her, since he is given to the soul for the sake of the strength of this love. Even in the perfect transformation of this state of spiritual marriage, which the soul reaches in this life, she superabounds with grace and, as above, loves in some way through the Holy Spirit who is given to her [Rom. 5:5] in this transformation of love.

4. It should be noted that the soul does not say that there he will give her his love—although he really does—because she would thereby manifest only that God loves her. She states rather that there he will show her how to love him as perfectly as she desires. It is precisely by giving her his love there that he shows her how to love as she is loved by him. Besides teaching her to love purely, freely, and disinterestedly, as he loves us, God makes her love him with the very strength with which he loves her. Transforming her into his love, as we said, he gives her his own strength by which she can love him. As if he were to put an instrument in her hands and show her how it works by operating it jointly with her, he shows her how to love and gives her the ability to do so.

Until attaining this equality of love the soul is dissatisfied, nor would she be satisfied in heaven if, as St. Thomas affirms in the opuscule *De Beatitudine*,[1] she did not feel that she loved God as much as she is loved by him. And even though in this state of spiritual marriage we are discussing there is not that perfection of glorious love, there is nonetheless a living and totally ineffable semblance of that perfection.

> and then you will give me,
> you, my Life, will give me there
> what you gave me on that other day:

5. What the soul says he will then give her is essential glory, consisting

---

1. Here is the only place that John cites this apocryphal work of St. Thomas Aquinas. With the exception of Scripture, this is the work that has most visibly influenced John. He makes use of it particularly in these last stanzas and in the *Flame*, 3. 82-85. The probable author is Helvicus Theutonicus, O.P. The work may be found in *D. Thomae Aquinatis Opera Omnia*, vol. 28 (Paris: Vives, 1875). The section John refers to here may be found on pages 405-26.

in the vision of God's being. But before proceeding we ought to resolve a doubt: Why, since essential glory lies in seeing God and not in loving, does the soul declare at the beginning of the stanza that her aim was this love and not the essential glory, and afterward request, as something of less importance, essential glory? There are two reasons:

First, just as the ultimate reason for everything is love (which is seated in the will), whose property is to give and not to receive, whereas the property of the intellect (which is the subject of essential glory) lies in receiving and not giving, the soul in the inebriation of love does not put first the glory she will receive from God, but rather the surrender of herself to him through true love without concern for her own profit.

Second, the desire to see is included in the desire to love and already presupposed in the preceding stanzas, for it is impossible to reach the perfect love of God without the perfect vision of God. Thus the force of this doubt is resolved by the first answer. With love the soul pays God what she owes him; with the intellect, on the contrary, she receives from him.

6. But returning to the commentary, let us see what day "that other day" is, which she here mentions, as well as the meaning of the "what" God gave her on that other day and which she asks to have afterward in glory.

By "that other day," she means the day of God's eternity, which is different from this temporal day. In that day of eternity God predestined the soul to glory, decreed the glory he would bestow on her, and gave it to her freely from all eternity before he created her. And this "what" is so proper to the soul that no event or adversity, whether great or insignificant, will suffice to take it from her; rather, she will attain the endless possession of the "what" to which God predestined her from eternity. And this is the "what" that she says he gave her on that other day and she now desires to possess openly in glory.

As for understanding the nature of the "what" he there gave her: *Neither eye has seen, nor ear heard, nor has it entered into the human heart,* as the Apostle says [1 Cor. 2:9]. And again Isaiah says: *Eye has not seen, outside of you, Lord, what you have prepared,* and so on [Is. 64:4]. Since it has no name, the soul calls it "what." The "what" is in point of fact the vision of God, but that which the vision of God is to the soul has no other name than "what."

7. Yet in order to say something about it, let us repeat what Christ said of it to St. John seven times in the Apocalypse with many expressions and words and comparisons, for this "what" cannot be understood by one word, nor at one time, for even with all these terms it still remains to be expressed. Christ then says: *To him that overcomes I will give to eat of the tree of life, which is in the paradise of my God* [Rv. 2:7].

But since this expression does not explain the "what" suitably, he immediately adds another: *Be faithful unto death and I will give you the crown of life* [Rv. 2:10].

Because this expression is inadequate also, he uses another that is more obscure, yet explains it better: *To the one who overcomes I will give the hidden manna and a white stone, and on the stone a new name will be written, which no one knows save the one who receives it* [Rv. 2:17].

And because this is also an insufficient expression of the "what," the Son of God uses another indicating great happiness and power: *To the one who overcomes and keeps my commandments until the end will I give power over the nations. That one will rule them with a rod of iron, and as a vessel of clay they shall be smashed, as I also received of my Father. And I will give that one the morning star* [Rv. 2:26-28].

And discontented with these expressions for explaining this "what," he then states: *The one who overcomes will thus be clothed in white garments, and I will not cross the name of that one from the book of life. And I will confess this name before my Father* [Rv. 3:5].

8. But since everything he said falls short of the mark, he then employs many terms to explain the "what," and they include in themselves unspeakable majesty and grandeur: *And I will make the one who overcomes a pillar in the temple of my God, and this victor shall go out no more. And I will write upon this one the name of my God and the name of the city of my God, the new Jerusalem, which comes down out of heaven from my God, and also my new name* [Rv. 3:12].

And then he makes use of the seventh expression to explain the "what": *To the one who overcomes I will give to sit with me on my throne, as I also have conquered and sat with my Father on his throne. Let whoever has ears to hear, hear,* and so on [Rv. 3:21-22].

These are the words of the Son of God, explaining the "what." They cast the "what" in very perfect terms, but they still do not explain it. This is a peculiarity of a thing that is immense: All the expressions of excellence, grandeur, and goodness are fitting, but do not explain it, not even when taken together.

9. Let us see if David makes any affirmations about this "what." In a psalm he exclaims: *How great is the multitude of your sweetness that you have hidden for them who fear you* [Ps. 31:19]. And so in another place he calls the "what" a torrent of delight: *You will give them to drink from the torrent of your delight* [Ps. 36:8]. And because David finds this term inadequate as well, he calls it the prevenient blessings of God's sweetness [Ps. 21:3].

Consequently, a suitable expression for the "what" of which the soul here speaks (the happiness to which God predestined her) is undiscoverable.

Let us set aside this term "what" that the soul uses and explain the verse in this way: What you gave me (that weight of glory to which you predestined me, O my Spouse, on the day of your eternity when you considered it good to decree my creation), you will give me then on the day of my espousals and nuptials and on my day of gladness of heart [Sg. 3:11], when loosed from the flesh and within the high caverns of your chamber, gloriously transformed in you, I shall drink with you the juice of the sweet pomegranates.

STANZA 39

Introduction

1. Yet since the soul in this state of spiritual marriage knows something of this "what," she desires to say something about it, for by her transformation in God something of this "what" occurs within her. She now feels within herself the signs and traces of the "what," for as it is said in the book of Job: *Who can keep back the word conceived within and not say it?* [Jb. 4:2]. In the following stanza she says something about the fruition she will enjoy in the beatific vision, by explaining insofar as possible the nature and mode of the "what" that she will there possess.

> the breathing of the air,
> the song of the sweet nightingale,
> the grove and its living beauty
> in the serene night,
> with a flame that is consuming and painless.

Commentary

2. In this stanza the soul declares with five expressions the "what" she says the Bridegroom will bestow on her in that beatific transformation.

First, she says it is the breath or spiration of the Holy Spirit from God to her and from her to God.

Second, jubilation in the fruition of God.

Third, the knowledge of creatures and of their orderly arrangement.

Fourth, pure and clear contemplation of the divine essence.

Fifth, a total transformation in the immense love of God. The verse then is:

> the breathing of the air,

3. This breathing of the air is an ability that the soul states God will give her there in the communication of the Holy Spirit. By his divine breath-like spiration, the Holy Spirit elevates the soul sublimely and informs her

and makes her capable of breathing in God the same spiration of love that the Father breathes in the Son and the Son in the Father. This spiration of love is the Holy Spirit himself, who in the Father and the Son breathes out to her in this transformation in order to unite her to himself. There would not be a true and total transformation if the soul were not transformed in the three Persons of the Most Holy Trinity in an open and manifest degree.

And this kind of spiration of the Holy Spirit in the soul, by which God transforms her into himself, is so sublime, delicate, and deep a delight that a mortal tongue finds it indescribable, nor can the human intellect, as such, in any way grasp it. Even what comes to pass in the communication given in this temporal transformation is unspeakable, for the soul united and transformed in God breathes out in God to God the very divine spiration that God—she being transformed in him—breathes out in himself to her.

4. In the transformation that the soul possesses in this life, the same spiration passes from God to the soul and from the soul to God with notable frequency and blissful love, although not in the open and manifest degree proper to the next life. Such I believe was St. Paul's meaning when he said: *Since you are children of God, God sent the Spirit of his Son into your hearts, calling to the Father* [Gal. 4:6]. This is true of the Blessed in the next life and of the perfect in this life according to the ways described.

One should not think it impossible that the soul be capable of so sublime an activity as this breathing in God through participation as God breathes in her. For, granted that God favors her by union with the Most Blessed Trinity, in which she becomes deiform and God through participation, how could it be incredible that she also understand, know, and love—or better that this be done in her—in the Trinity, together with it, as does the Trinity itself! Yet God accomplishes this in the soul through communication and participation. This is transformation in the three Persons in power and wisdom and love, and thus the soul is like God through this transformation. He created her in his image and likeness that she might attain such resemblance.

5. No knowledge or power can describe how this happens, unless by explaining how the Son of God attained and merited such a high state for us, *the power to be children of God,* as St. John says [Jn. 1:12]. Thus the Son asked of the Father in St. John's Gospel: *Father, I desire that where I am those you have given me may also be with me, that they may see the glory you have given me* [Jn. 17:24], that is, that they may perform in us by participation the same work that I do by nature; that is, breathe the Holy Spirit. And he adds: *I do not ask, Father, only for those present, but for those also who will believe*

in me through their doctrine; that all of them may be one as you, Father, in me and I in you, that thus they be one in us. The glory which you have given me I have given them that they may be one as we are one, I in them and you in me; that they may be perfect in one; that the world may know that you have sent me and loved them as you have loved me [Jn. 17:20-23].[1] The Father loves them by communicating to them the same love he communicates to the Son, though not naturally as to the Son but, as we said, through unity and transformation of love. It should not be thought that the Son desires here to ask the Father that the saints be one with him essentially and naturally as the Son is with the Father, but that they may be so through the union of love, just as the Father and the Son are one in unity of love.

6. Accordingly, souls possess the same goods by participation that the Son possesses by nature. As a result they are truly gods by participation, equals and companions of God. Wherefore St. Peter said: *May grace and peace be accomplished and perfect in you in the knowledge of God and of our Lord Jesus Christ, as all things of his divine power that pertain to life and piety are given us through the knowledge of him who called us with his own glory and power, by whom he has given us very great and precious promises, that by these we may be made partakers of the divine nature* [2 Pt. 1:2-4]. These are words from St. Peter in which he clearly indicates that the soul will participate in God himself by performing in him, in company with him, the work of the Most Blessed Trinity because of the substantial union between the soul and God. Although this participation will be perfectly accomplished in the next life, still in this life when the soul has reached the state of perfection, as has the soul we are here discussing, she obtains a foretaste and noticeable trace of it in the way we are describing, although as we said it is indescribable.[2]

7. O souls, created for these grandeurs and called to them! What are you doing? How are you spending your time? Your aims are base and your possessions miseries! O wretched blindness of your eyes! You are blind to so brilliant a light and deaf to such loud voices because you fail to discern that insofar as you seek eminence and glory you remain miserable, base, ignorant, and unworthy of so many blessings! The next expression the soul uses to explain the "what" is:

    the song of the sweet nightingale,

---

1. This important New Testament passage helps John express his experience of union that he found so difficult to put into words. Jerónimo de la Cruz, John's companion on many journeys, testifies that Fray John of the Cross used to recite quietly along the road and with great devotion the 17th chapter of St. John's Gospel.

2. Cf. 22. 6-7; F. 1. 28.

8. The result of the soul's breathing the air is that she hears the sweet voice of her Beloved calling to her. And she in this voice expresses to him her delightful jubilation and calls both voices the song of the nightingale. Just as the nightingale begins its song in the spring, once the wintery cold, rain, and changes have passed, and provides melody for the ear and refreshment for the spirit, so in this actual communication and transformation of love that the bride has now attained in this life, in which she is freed from and protected against all temporal disturbances and changes, and divested and purged of imperfections, penalties, and clouds in the senses and the spirit, she feels a new spring in spiritual freedom and breadth and gladness. She hears the sweet voice of her Bridegroom who is her sweet nightingale. Renewing and refreshing the substance of the soul with the sweetness and mellowness of his voice, he calls her as he would call one now disposed to make the journey to eternal life, and she hears this pleasant voice urge: *Arise, make haste, my love, my dove, my beautiful one, and come; for now the winter has passed, the rains have gone far off, the flowers have appeared in our land, the time of pruning has come, and the voice of the turtledove is heard in our land* [Sg. 2:10-12].

9. The bride feels that this voice of the Bridegroom speaking within her is the end of evil and the beginning of good. In the refreshment, protection, and delightful sentiment afforded by this voice, she too, like the sweet nightingale, sings a new and jubilant song together with God, who moves her to do this. He gives his voice to her that so united with him she may give it together with him to God.

This is the Bridegroom's aim and desire, that the soul may intone to God with a spiritual voice of jubilation, as he requests in the Song of Songs: *Arise, make haste my love, and come, my dove; in the clefts of the rock; in the hollow of the wall show me your face, let your voice sound in my ears* [Sg. 2:13-14].

The ears of God signify his desires to have the soul sing to him with this voice of perfect jubilation. That this voice be perfect, the Bridegroom asks that she sing and let it resound in the caverns of the rock, that is, in the transformation into the mysteries of Christ. Since the soul rejoices in and praises God with God himself in this union (as we said in speaking of love),[3] it is a praise highly perfect and pleasing to God, for a soul in this state of perfection performs very perfect works. This voice of jubilation, thus, is sweet both to God and to the soul. As a result the Bridegroom declared: *Your voice is sweet* [Sg. 2:14], that is, not only to you but to me as well, since through union with me you sing for me—and with me—like the sweet nightingale.

---

3. In 38. 3-4.

10. Such is the song of the soul in the transformation that is hers in this life, the delight of which is beyond all exaggeration. Yet since this song is not as perfect as the new song of the glorious life, the soul in this bliss becomes mindful of the new song of glory, hearing faintly in the song of this life the excellence of the possession of glory, which is incomparably more precious. And she states that the "what" that he will give her is the song of the sweet nightingale. She continues:

the grove and its living beauty

11. This is the third gift the Bridegroom will bestow on the soul. Since many plants and animals are nurtured in it, the "grove" refers to God, for he nurtures and gives being to all creatures rooted and living in him. Through this gift God shows himself to her and reveals himself as Creator.

By the "living beauty" of this grove, for which she asks the Bridegroom here, she intends to beg for the grace, wisdom, and beauty that every earthly and heavenly creature not only has from God but also manifests in its wise, well ordered, gracious, and harmonious relationship to other creatures. We find this accord among the lower creatures and among the higher, and we find it as well in the relationships between the higher and the lower. The knowledge of this harmony fascinates and delights the soul. The fourth gift follows:

in the serene night,

12. This night is the contemplation in which the soul desires to behold these things. Because of its obscurity, she calls contemplation night. On this account contemplation is also termed mystical theology, meaning the secret or hidden knowledge of God. In contemplation God teaches the soul very quietly and secretly, without its knowing how, without the sound of words, and without the help of any bodily or spiritual faculty, in silence and quietude, in darkness to all sensory and natural things. Some spiritual persons call this contemplation knowing by unknowing.[4] For this knowledge is not produced by the intellect that the philosophers call the agent intellect, which works on the forms, phantasies, and apprehensions of the corporal faculties; rather it is produced in the possible or passive intellect. This possible intellect, without the reception of these forms, and so on, receives passively only substantial knowledge, which is divested of images and given without any work or active function of the intellect.[5]

---

4. In this vein, St. Teresa gives a famous description of contemplation; see *Life* 18. 14.

5. Cf. 14 & 15. 14 and note 9.

13. This contemplation, in which the soul, by means of her transformation, has sublime knowledge in this life of the divine grove and its living beauty, is consequently called "night." Yet however sublime this knowledge may be, it is still a dark night when compared with the beatific knowledge she asks for here. In seeking clear contemplation, she asks that this enjoyment of the grove and its living beauty, as well as the other goods mentioned, take place now in the serene night; that is, in beatific and clear contemplation, the night of the dark contemplation of this earth changing into the contemplation of the clear and serene vision of God in heaven. Therefore, by saying "in the serene night," she means in the clear and serene contemplation of the vision of God. David declares of this night of contemplation: *The night will be my illumination in my delights* [Ps. 139:11], which is like saying: When I shall delight in the essential vision of God, then the night of contemplation will have changed into day and light for my intellect. The fifth good follows:

with a flame that is consuming and painless.

14. By the "flame" she here understands the love of the Holy Spirit. "To consummate" means to bring to completion or perfection. The soul, then, in affirming that the Beloved will give her all the things she mentioned in this stanza and she will possess them with consummate and perfect love and these goods will all be absorbed—and she with them— in perfect love that is painless, affirms all this in order to reveal the complete perfection of this love. That love be perfect, it must have these two properties: It must consummate and transform the soul in God; and the inflammation and transformation engendered by this flame must give no pain to the soul, which cannot be true except in the beatific state where this flame is delightful love. For by the transformation of the soul in this flame, there is a beatific conformity and satisfaction of both lover and Beloved, and thus the flame gives no pain from the variety of greater or lesser intensity, as it did before the soul reached the capacity for this perfect love. Having reached perfection, the soul possesses a love so comforting and conformed to God that, even though God is a consuming fire, as Moses says [Dt. 4:24], he is now a consummator and restorer. This transformation is not like the one the soul possesses in this life, for although the flame in this life is perfect and consummating in love, it is still also somewhat consuming and tends to take away, acting as fire does on coal; although the coal is conformed with and transformed into the fire, and does not fume as it did before the transformation, still the flame that consummated the coal in fire consumed and reduced it to ashes.

This is what happens to the soul that in this life is transformed through the perfection of love. Although it is conformed, it still suffers a kind of pain and detriment: first, because of the lack of the beatific transformation, the absence of which is always felt in the spirit; second, because of the detriment the weak and corruptible sense suffers from the strength and height of so much love, for any excellent thing is a pain and detriment to natural weakness, as it is written: *Corpus quod corrumpitur, aggravat animam* [Wis. 9:15].[6] Yet in that beatific life she will feel no detriment or pain, although her understanding will be very deep and her love immense. For God will equip her for one and strengthen her for the other, consummating her intellect with his wisdom and her will with his love.

15. Since in the preceding stanzas as well as in this one the bride sought from God immense communications and knowledge for which she needs the strongest and highest love, a love commensurate with the greatness and height of this knowledge, she asks that this knowledge be communicated in consummated, perfect, and strong love.

STANZA 40

No one looked at her,
nor did Aminadab appear;
the siege was still;
and the cavalry,
at the sight of the waters, descended.

Introduction and Commentary

1. The bride knows that now her will's desire is detached from all things and attached to her God in most intimate love; that the sensory part of her soul, with all its strengths, faculties, and appetites, is in harmony with the spirit, and its rebelliousness brought into subjection; that the devil is now conquered and far withdrawn as a result of her varied and prolonged spiritual activity and combat; that her soul is united and transformed with an abundance of heavenly riches and gifts; and that consequently she is now well prepared, disposed, and strong, leaning on her Beloved, so as to come up from the desert of death, flowing with delights, to the glorious thrones of her Bridegroom [Sg. 8:5]. Desiring the Bridegroom to conclude this matter now, she sets all these facts before him in this last stanza in order to urge him the more to do so. In this stanza she mentions five blessings:[1]

---

6. For the corruptible body is a load upon the soul.
1. In this final stanza we have a little summary in retrospect of the spiritual journey as presented in this poem.

First, her soul is detached and withdrawn from all things.

Second, the devil is conquered and put to flight.

Third, the passions are subjected and the natural appetites mortified.

Fourth and fifth, the sensory and lower part is reformed, purified, and brought into conformity with the spiritual part. The sensory part not only offers no obstacle to the reception of these spiritual blessings but is even accommodated to them, since it participates according to its capacity in the goods the soul now possesses. She thus says:

> No one looked at her,

2. This is like saying: My soul is now divested, detached, alone, and withdrawn from all created things, both from those above and from those below; and it has entered so deeply into interior recollection with you that none of them can discern the intimate delight I now possess in you; that is, these creatures cannot move my soul to relish their sweetness or become displeased and disturbed by their misery and lowness. Since my soul stays so far from them and abides in such profound delight with you, none of them can get a view of me. Not this alone, but:

> nor did Aminadab appear;

3. In Sacred Scripture [Sg. 6:11], speaking spiritually, Aminadab signifies the devil, the soul's adversary. He continually disturbed and waged war against her with the countless ammunition of his artillery to prevent her entry into this fort and hiding place of interior recollection with the Bridegroom. But in this place where she now dwells, she is so favored, strong, and victorious with the virtues, and with God's embrace, that the devil dares not come, but with immense fear flees and does not dare appear. Also, because of the practice of virtue and the state of perfection, the soul has so conquered and routed him that he no longer appears before her. And thus Aminadab did not appear with any right to hinder this blessing I aim after.

> the siege was still;

4. By "the siege" the soul means the passions and appetites. When these passions and appetites are not conquered and calmed, they surround and fight against her on all sides, and for this reason she calls them a siege. She says "the siege is now still," that is, the passions are put in order according to reason and the appetites mortified. She asks God not to fail to communicate his favors to her since the siege is no longer capable of impeding them. She says this because she is incapable of the vision of God until her four passions are directed to him and her appetites mortified and purged. And the stanza continues:

> and the cavalry,
> at the sight of the waters, descended.

5. "The waters" refers here to the spiritual goods and delights that the soul enjoys inwardly with God in this state. "The cavalry" signifies the bodily senses, interior as well as exterior, because they bear the phantasms and figures of their objects.

The bride declares that in this state the cavalry descended at the sight of the spiritual waters because in this state of spiritual marriage the sensory and lower part of the soul is so purified and spiritualized that it recollects the sensory faculties and natural strength, and they thereby share in and enjoy in their own fashion the spiritual grandeurs that God is communicating in the inwardness of the spirit. David described this when he said: *My heart and my flesh have rejoiced in the living God* [Ps. 84:2].

6. It should be noted that the bride does not state that the cavalry descended to taste the waters, but that it descended at the sight of the waters. For this sensory part with its faculties has no capacity in this life, nor even in the next, for the essential and proper taste of spiritual goods. It can, though, through a certain spiritual overflow, receive sensible refreshment and delight from them. This delight attracts the corporeal senses and faculties to the inner recollection where the soul drinks the waters of spiritual goods, and so they descend at the sight of the waters rather than drink and taste them as they are.

The soul declares that they descended—she does not say "they went," or use some other word—in order to point out that in this share that the sensory part has in the spiritual communication, when the soul takes this drink of spiritual goods, the senses discontinue their natural operations and go down from them to spiritual recollection.

7. The bride sets all this perfection and preparedness before her Beloved, the Son of God, with the desire that he transfer her from the spiritual marriage, to which he desired to bring her in this Church Militant, to the glorious marriage of the Triumphant. May the most sweet Jesus, Bridegroom of faithful souls, be pleased to bring all who invoke his name to this marriage. To him be honor and glory, together with the Father and the Holy Spirit, in saecula saeculorum. Amen.

The
Living Flame
of
Love

INTRODUCTION TO

THE LIVING FLAME OF LOVE

The Poem

The stanzas of *The Living Flame of Love* sing of an elevated union within the intimate depths of the spirit. The subject matter is exalted, so much so that John dares speak of it only with a deeply recollected soul. The image of flame, working on the wood, dispelling the moisture, turning it black, then giving it the qualities of fire, appeared first in the *Dark Night*. In the *Canticle* it turns up again in the serene night toward the end of the poem, a flame that is painless, comforting, and conformed to God. This flame, John told us there, is the love of the Holy Spirit. Now, having grown hotter and sometimes flaring up, it impels the Carmelite friar to write more verses about the sublime communion taking place in his deepest center.

At this depth he lives in both stable serenity and exalted activity; the tone is prolonged admiration and holy ardor. The six-line length of each stanza, the sounds, the rhythm, convey these characteristics.

All the verses of the poem point to the same profundity; there is no progressive movement from stage to stage. The focus is on the present, on what is taking place now. Only a few times is there a glance toward what went before, and then merely for the sake of stating that the past has unfolded into the peace and plenitude of the present.

John wrote this brief lyric creation that so ardently and closely approaches the mystery of divine union for Doña Ana de Peñalosa, a devout laywoman whom he directed. It is the only instance we know of in which he composed a poem for another, although we do not know whether he did so in answer to a request from her. What is certain is that he composed these stanzas burning in love's flame, with the intimate and delicate sweetness of love.

The Commentary

As John composed his commentary on the stanzas of the *Spiritual Canticle*, those close to him made copies and circulated them. It is not surprising that Ana de Peñalosa would ask for another commentary, one on the magnificent stanzas John had written for her. If we consider the mentality of the times, when many frowned on the practice of mental prayer among women (as we know from St. Teresa's experience) and thought of sanctity as a pursuit more suited to monks and friars, it is surprising that John wrote this loftiest of his works for a laywoman. The only thing that made him hesitate to respond to her pleadings was his difficulty in speaking of what pertained to the intimate depths of one's being. He waited for a spirit of recollection and fervor to descend on him, as seems to have been the case with his poems. Then he wrote the work, immersed in the flame, in the shortest space of time, within a span of two weeks (according to Fray Juan Evangelista), and at a time, in 1586, when he had many other duties as vicar provincial of Andalusia. The profound recollection he required of himself referred to the interior quality of his life, not to a freedom from business matters and concerns. He waited for an opportunity in which he could almost relive the moment of the poem, and thus the commentary bears much of the poetry's light and heat, its symbolism and lyric tone.

As with the *Dark Night* and the *Spiritual Canticle*, he follows his customary procedure: first he cites the entire poem; then, repeating each stanza separately, he sums up its content; finally, he explains each verse in particular. The commentary of the *Flame* is more prolonged than that of the *Canticle*, but not as extended as in the *Night*. At times, rather than adhere to a simple interpretation of these expressions of his own experience, he heeds the call to be a spiritual teacher and enters into digressions that enlarge the commentary. The paramount one occurs in the third stanza, njmbers 27-67. There he explains how souls must watch what they are doing and into whose hands they commit themselves so as not to impede God's work and thereby stumble and slip back on their journey.

John also teaches about some other topics that lie outside the immediate scope of the poem: the soul's purgation wrought previously by the flame (1. 19-25); the cause and mode of death of those who have reached the state of transformation (1. 30); transpiercing of the soul and impression of the stigmata (2. 9-14); the necessity of suffering in order to reach transformation in God (2. 25-30); the thirst, hunger, and longing of the spiritual faculties experienced toward the end of purification and illumination (3. 18-26).

On the whole, as with the poem itself, John's concentration is on the present, the high goal from which he may glance fleetingly at the past or look to a future glory intuited rather than fully known from his present horizon. He begins where he left off in the *Spiritual Canticle*, with the highest degree of perfection attainable in this life, transformation in God, called also spiritual marriage.

Within this state love can become more ardent, and the wood more incandescent and inflamed. In other words, the love is "deeper in quality and more perfect within this very state of transformation." What this means is that there is greater likelihood for habitual union to become actual, for the fire to burst into flame. The activity of the Holy Spirit is now more powerful, the experiences are on the borderline between faith and eternal glory. In different modes the stanzas concentrate on the same realities. Thus as he interprets his poem for us, John explains how there are two different aspects of union with God and the total union experienced in the substance and faculties of the soul may be either habitual or actual. The actual union, always a passing phenomenon, never becomes permanent on this earth. The habitual union of love is compatible with everyday life, less intense in form. Here John is speaking of those moments in which God's special self-communication is more alive and intense. He refers to these symbolically as living flames, delightful wounds, splendors from the lamps of fire, and awakenings of the Beloved.

The dominant theme is the wonderful work of God in his Trinitarian Being, illumining and delighting and absorbing the soul in the embrace of love. And John here describes and gives witness to this mystical experience taking place in his deepest center, in the profound caverns of his being. This is a new country to which he brings us. Now he speaks more of glorification than of purification. His absorption is not in some undetermined absolute, but in communion with the Father, the Son, and the Holy Spirit. The heightened periods of sublime union are like glimpses of glory offered to the spirit. It is as though the Holy Spirit were summoning a person to the next life by the "immense glory he marvelously and with gentle affection places before its eyes." This is made possible by a "highly illumined faith," the veil being now so thin that it no longer cloaks the light with darkness but allows it to begin to seep through. This soul finds as well a remarkable new delight in all of creation, for it now knows creatures in God. Absorbed in God, enlivened by his loving presence and communication, it receives a foretaste of eternal life. At the time of these glorious encounters, the soul comes within a step of departing from earth.

John senses that people may either think he is exaggerating or not believe him at all; in fact, what he says seems to him as far short of the reality as a painting is from the living object. He notes in such human skepticism a failure to understand who God really is, that the Lord delights in being with the children of this earth. Why should we marvel that he wants to be so prodigal in giving? John points out that lovers love and do good to others in the measure of their own nature and properties. Because God is liberal, the reasoning continues, he loves and favors and does good to us liberally. But perhaps Ana de Peñalosa was herself able to share something of the very realities John was describing. Those who are cleansed and enkindled with love are in the position to taste and relish this language of God; others without this preparation may find the words uninteresting, bitter, or incredible.

As with the *Spiritual Canticle*, two redactions have come down to us and are referred to as *Flame A* and *Flame B*. But the likeness to the *Canticle* stops there, for the differences between the two versions of the *Flame* are not notable. Without any change in the sequence of the stanzas, the modifications in the second redaction, *Flame B*, consist only of some clarifying insertions and some more detailed doctrinal explanations. Most probably John introduced these variations into the text while at La Peñuela in the last months of his life, August-September 1591. A witness who lived with him at La Peñuela told of how in the early morning John used to withdraw into the garden for prayer and remain there until, coaxed by the heat of the sun, he returned to his monastery cell where he spent his time writing on certain stanzas of poetry. By this date all his other works, including the *Canticle*, had reached their final stage. Moreover John brought a copy of the work with him to Ubeda. He gave it as a gift in gratitude to Ambrosio de Villareal, the doctor who had cared for him there. What must have been the doctor's thoughts as he read of "how much God exalts the soul that pleases him"?

The work may be divided this way:

Stanza 1
The nature and work of the flame (1-26).
> In the deepest center.
> A flame that previously purged.
The desire for glory (27-36).
> The veils of separation.
> The death of love.

Stanza 2
The work of the three divine Persons in the soul's substance (1-22).
> The blazing, wounding fire of the Holy Spirit.
> The powerful, bounteous hand of the Father.
> The delicate, delightful touch of the Word.
The hundredfold reward (23-36).

Stanza 3
The splendors produced by the lamps of fire (1-76).
> The work of both the soul and the Holy Spirit.
> The deep capacities of the caverns of the soul.
> Cautions against three blind guides.
> Blindness caused by the appetites.
The soul's gift to God (77-84).

Stanza 4
Awakening of the Word; knowledge of creation in him (1-13).
The secret indwelling of God in the soul's substance (14-16).
Participation in the breathing of the Holy Spirit (17).

We have translated the second redaction, or *Flame B,* and have followed the *Codex of Sevilla,* consulting as well the *Codex of Baeza* and the *Codex of Toledo,* which is a copy of the first redaction.

THE LIVING FLAME OF LOVE

Jesus Mary Joseph

A commentary on the stanzas that treat of a very intimate and elevated union and transformation of the soul in God, written at the request of Doña Ana de Peñalosa[1] by the author of the stanzas.

Prologue

1. I have felt somewhat reluctant, very noble and devout lady, to explain these four stanzas as you asked. Since they deal with matters so interior and spiritual, for which words are usually lacking—in that the spiritual surpasses sense—I find it difficult to say something of their content; also, one speaks badly of the intimate depths of the spirit if one does not do so with a deeply recollected soul. Because of my want of such recollection, I have deferred this commentary until now, a period in which the Lord seems to have uncovered some knowledge and bestowed some fervor. This must be the result of your holy desire; perhaps, since I have composed the stanzas for you, His Majesty wants me to explain them for you. I have been encouraged in knowing certainly that through my own ability I shall say nothing worthwhile, especially in matters so sublime and vital, and thus only the faults and mistakes of this commentary will be mine. Submitting it to the judgment and better opinion of our Holy Mother the Roman Catholic Church, by whose rule no one errs, finding my support in Sacred Scripture, and knowing the reader understands that everything I say is as far from the reality as is a painting from the living object represented, I will venture to declare what I know.

2. There is no reason to marvel at God's granting such sublime and strange gifts to souls he decides to favor. If we consider that he is God and that he bestows them as God, with infinite love and goodness, it does not

---

1. A Segovian, Doña Ana del Mercado y Peñalosa was left a widow in 1579. She lived in Granada and housed the discalced Carmelite nuns for seven months when they were in the process of making a foundation in that city. The prioress of the nuns was Ana de Jesús, for whom the *Spiritual Canticle* had been written. In 1582, John of the Cross began directing Doña Ana. They continued to correspond after he returned to Segovia.

seem unreasonable. For he declared that the Father, the Son, and the Holy Spirit would take up their abode in those who love him by making them live the life of God and dwell in the Father, the Son, and the Holy Spirit [Jn. 14:23], as the soul points out in these stanzas.

3. Although in the stanzas we have already commented on,[1] we speak of the highest degree of perfection one can reach in this life (transformation in God), these stanzas treat of a love deeper in quality and more perfect within this very state of transformation. Even though it is true that what these and the other stanzas describe is all one state of transformation, and as such one cannot pass beyond it; yet, with time and practice, love can grow deeper in quality, as I say, and become more ardent. We have an example of this in the activity of fire: Although the fire has penetrated the wood, transformed it, and united it with itself, yet as this fire grows hotter and continues to burn, so the wood becomes much more incandescent and inflamed, even to the point of flaring up and shooting out flames from itself.

4. It should be understood that the soul now speaking has reached this enkindled degree, and is so inwardly transformed in the fire of love and elevated by it that it is not merely united to this fire but produces within it a living flame. The soul feels this and speaks of it thus in these stanzas with intimate and delicate sweetness of love, burning in love's flame, and stressing in these stanzas some of the effects of this love.

In this commentary I will use the method I have used before: First I will quote all the stanzas together; then, after recording each stanza separately, I will present a brief explanation of it; finally I will quote each verse and comment upon it.

Stanzas the Soul Recites in Intimate Union With God.

1. O living flame of love
that tenderly wounds my soul
in its deepest center! Since
now you are not oppressive,
now consummate! if it be your will:
tear through the veil of this sweet encounter!

---

1. It seems that Ana de Peñalosa received a manuscript that contained the *Spiritual Canticle* together with this commentary.

2. O sweet cautery,
O delightful wound!
O gentle hand! O delicate touch
that tastes of eternal life
and pays every debt!
In killing you changed death to life.

3. O lamps of fire!
in whose splendors
the deep caverns of feeling,
once obscure and blind,
now give forth, so rarely, so exquisitely,
both warmth and light to their Beloved.

4. How gently and lovingly
you wake in my heart,
where in secret you dwell alone;
and in your sweet breathing,
filled with good and glory,
how tenderly you swell my heart with love.

The composition of these lyric lines is like those that in Boscán are given a religious meaning and that go:

La soledad siguiendo.
llorando mi fortuna,
me voy por los caminos que se ofrecen, and so on.

In these stanzas there are six lines; the fourth rhymes with the first, the fifth with the second, and the sixth with the third.[2]

---

2. These lines are not actually from Boscán but from Garcilaso. The compositions of these two poets were joined, and a "Boscán" was the popular term for the work containing the poems of both. Sebastián de Córdoba gave the verse a religious meaning in his *Las Obras de Boscán y Garcilaso trasladas en materias cristianas y religiosas,* Granada, 1575. The remaining three lines from the stanzas quoted by John are:

mis ansias proponiendo
a la que es sola una,
por quien los bienes en el alma crecen.

Walking in solitude,/ Weeping my lot,/I take the roads that come,/Telling my urgent longings/ to my only one,/through whom the blessings of my soul increase.

STANZA 1

O living flame of love
that tenderly wounds my soul
in its deepest center! Since
now you are not oppressive,
now consummate! if it be your will:
tear through the veil of this sweet encounter!

Commentary

1. The soul now feels that it is all inflamed in the divine union, its palate is all bathed in glory and love, that in the intimate part of its substance it is flooded with no less than rivers of glory, abounding in delights, and from its depths flow rivers of living water [Jn. 7:38], which the Son of God declared will rise up in such souls. It seems, because it is so forcefully transformed in God, so sublimely possessed by him, and arrayed with such rich gifts and virtues, that it is singularly close to beatitude—so close that only a thin veil separates it.

And the soul sees that every time the delicate flame of love, burning within, assails it, it does so as though glorifying it with gentle and powerful glory. Such is the glory this flame of love imparts that each time it absorbs and attacks, it seems that it is about to give eternal life and tear the veil of mortal life, that very little is lacking, and that because of this lack the soul does not receive eternal glory completely. With ardent desire the soul tells the flame, the Holy Spirit, to tear the veil of mortal life now by that sweet encounter in which he truly communicates entirely what he is seemingly about to give each time he encounters it, that is, complete and perfect glory. And thus it says:

O living flame of love

2. To lay stress on the sentiment and esteem with which it speaks in these four stanzas, the soul uses in all of them the exclamations, "O" and "how," which indicate an affectionate emphasis. Each time they are uttered they reveal more about the interior than the tongue expresses. "O" serves to express intense desire and to use persuasion in petitioning. The soul uses this expression for both reasons in this stanza because it intimates and stresses its tremendous desire, persuading love to loose it.

3. This flame of love is the Spirit of its Bridegroom, who is the Holy Spirit. The soul feels him within itself not only as a fire that has consumed and transformed it but as a fire that burns and flares within it, as I mentioned. And that flame, every time it flares up, bathes the soul in glory and refreshes it with the quality of divine life.

Such is the activity of the Holy Spirit in the soul transformed in love: The interior acts he produces shoot up flames, for they are acts of inflamed love, in which the will of the soul united with that flame, made one with it, loves most sublimely. Thus these acts of love are most precious; one of them is more meritorious and valuable than all the deeds a person may have performed in the whole of life without this transformation, however great they may have been. The same difference lying between a habit and an act lies between the transformation in love and the flame of love. It is like the difference between the wood on fire and the flame leaping up from it, for the flame is the effect of the fire present there.

4. We can compare the soul in its ordinary condition in this state of transformation of love to the log of wood that is ever immersed in fire, and the acts of this soul to the flame that blazes up from the fire of love. The more intense the fire of union, the more vehemently does this fire burst into flames. The acts of the will are united to this flame and ascend, carried away and absorbed in the flame of the Holy Spirit, just as the angel mounted to God in the flame of Manoah's sacrifice [Jgs. 13:20].

Thus in this state the soul cannot make acts because the Holy Spirit makes them all and moves it toward them. As a result all the acts of the soul are divine, since both the movement to these acts and their execution stem from God.[1]

It seems to such persons that every time this flame shoots up, making them love with delight and divine quality, it is giving them eternal life, since it raises them up to the activity of God in God.

5. This is the language and these the words God speaks in souls that are purged, cleansed, and all enkindled; as David exclaimed: *Your word is exceedingly enkindled* [Ps. 119:139]; and the prophet: *Are not my words, perchance, like a fire?* [Jer. 23:29]. As God himself says through St. John, these words are spirit and life [Jn. 6:63]. These words are perceived by souls who have ears to hear them, those souls, as I say, that are cleansed and enamored. Those who do not have a sound palate, but seek other tastes, cannot taste the spirit and life of God's words; his words, rather, are distasteful to them.

Hence the loftier were the words of the Son of God, the more tasteless they were to the impure, as happened when he preached the sovereign and loving doctrine of the Holy Eucharist, for many turned away [Jn. 6:60-61, 66].

---

1. In this respect, John speaks of "our Lady, the most glorious Virgin" as the supreme example; cf. A. 3. 2. 8-10.

6. Those who do not relish this language God speaks within them must not think on this account that others do not taste it. St. Peter tasted it in his soul when he said to Christ: *Lord, where shall we go? You have the words of eternal life* [Jn. 6:68]. And the Samaritan woman forgot the water and the water jar for the sweetness of God's words [Jn. 4:28].

Since this soul is so close to God that it is transformed into a flame of love in which the Father, the Son, and the Holy Spirit are communicated to it, how can it be thought incredible that it enjoy a foretaste of eternal life? Yet it does not enjoy eternal life perfectly since the conditions of this life do not allow it. But the delight that the flaring of the Holy Spirit generates in the soul is so sublime that it makes it know that which savors of eternal life. Thus it refers to this flame as living, not because the flame is not always living but because of this effect; it makes the soul live in God spiritually and experience the life of God in the manner David mentions: *My heart and my flesh rejoiced in the living God* [Ps. 84:2]. David did not refer to God as living because of a necessity to do so, for God is always living, but in order to manifest that the spirit and the senses, transformed in God, enjoy him in a living way, which is to taste the living God—that is, God's life, eternal life. Nor did David call him the living God other than because he enjoyed him in a living way, although not perfectly, but as though by a glimpse of eternal life. Thus in this flame the soul experiences God so vividly and tastes him with such delight and sweetness that it exclaims: O living flame of love!
                     that tenderly wounds my soul

7. That is, that with your ardor tenderly touches me. Since this flame is a flame of divine life, it wounds the soul with the tenderness of God's life, and it wounds and stirs it so deeply as to make it dissolve in love. What the bride affirmed in the Song of Songs is fulfilled in the soul. She was so moved that her soul melted, and so she says: *As soon as he spoke my soul melted* [Sg. 5:6]. For God's speech is the effect he produces in the soul.

8. But how can one claim that the flame wounds the soul, since there is nothing left in it to wound now that it is all cauterized with the fire of love? It is something splendid that since love is never idle, but in continual motion, it is always emitting flames everywhere like a blazing fire, and since its duty is to wound in order to cause love and delight, and it is present in this soul as a living flame, it dispatches its wounds like most tender flares of delicate love. Joyfully and festively it practices the arts and games of love, as though in the palace of its nuptials, as Ahasuerus did with his bride Esther [Est. 2:16-18]. God shows his graces there, manifests his riches and the glory of his grandeur that in this soul might be fulfilled what he asserted in Proverbs: *I was delighted every day, playing before him all the time, playing in the world. And my delights were to be with the children of the*

earth [Prv. 8:30-31], that is, by bestowing delights on them. Hence these wounds (his games) are flames of tender touches; arising from the fire of love, which is not idle, they suddenly touch the soul. These, it says, occur inwardly and wound the soul.

in its deepest center!

9. This feast takes place in the substance of the soul where neither the center of the senses nor the devil can reach. Therefore, the more interior it is, the more secure, substantial, and delightful, because the more interior it is, the purer it is. And the greater the purity, the more abundantly, frequently, and generously God communicates himself. Thus the delight and joy of the soul is so much more intense because God is the doer of all without the soul's doing anything. Since the soul cannot do any work of its own save through the means and aid of the corporeal senses, from which in this event it is very free and far removed, its sole occupation now is to receive from God, who alone can move the soul and do his work in its depths. Thus all the movements of this soul are divine. Although they belong to it, they belong to it because God works them in it and with it, for it wills and consents to them.[2] Since by saying that the flame wounds in its deepest center the soul indicates that it has other, less profound centers, we ought to explain what is meant by these words.

10. First it should be known that the soul, insofar as it is a spirit, does not possess in its being high and low, deeper or less deep, as do quantitative bodies. Since it has no parts, there is no difference as to inward and outward; it is all one kind and does not have degrees of quantitative depth. It cannot receive greater illumination in one part than in another like physical bodies, but all of it is illumined equally in a degree of greater or lesser intensity, like air that is illumined or not illumined according to degrees.

11. The deepest center of an object we take to signify the farthest point attainable by that object's being and power and force of operation and movement. So fire or a rock have the natural power and motion necessary to reach their center, but they cannot pass beyond it. They can fail to reach and rest in this center if a powerful contrary movement impedes them.

Accordingly, we assert that when a rock is in the ground it is, after a fashion, in its center, even though it is not in its deepest center, for it is within the sphere of its center, activity, and movement; yet we do not assert that it has reached its deepest center, which is the middle of the

---

2. In this stanza and generally throughout *Flame* the term "substance of the soul" stands for the deepest and most intimate part of one's being.

earth. Thus the rock always possesses the power, strength, and inclination to go deeper and reach the ultimate and deepest center; and this it would do if the hindrance were removed. When once it arrives and no longer has any power or inclination toward further movement, we declare that it is in its deepest center.

12. The soul's center is God. When it has reached God with all the capacity of its being and the strength of its operation and inclination, it will have attained its final and deepest center in God, it will know, love, and enjoy God with all its might. When it has not reached this point (as happens in this mortal life, in which the soul cannot reach God with all its strength, even though in its center—which is God through grace and his self-communication to it), it still has movement and strength for advancing further and is not satisfied. Although it is in its center, it is not yet in its deepest center, for it can go deeper in God.

13. It is noteworthy, then, that love is the inclination, strength, and power for the soul in making its way to God, for love unites it with God. The more degrees of love it has, the more deeply it enters into God and centers itself in him. We can say that there are as many centers in God possible to the soul, each one deeper than the other, as there are degrees of love of God possible to it. A stronger love is a more unitive love, and we can understand in this manner the many mansions the Son of God declared were in his Father's house [Jn. 14:2].

Hence, for the soul to be in its center—which is God, as we have said—it is sufficient for it to possess one degree of love, for by one degree alone it is united with him through grace. Should it have two degrees, it becomes united and concentrated in God in another, deeper center. Should it reach three, it centers itself in a third. But once it has attained the final degree, God's love has arrived at wounding the soul in its ultimate and deepest center, which is to illuminate and transform it in its whole being, power, and strength, and according to its capacity, until it appears to be God.

When light shines on a clean and pure crystal, we find that the more intense the degree of light, the more light the crystal has concentrated within it and the brighter it becomes; it can become so brilliant from the abundance of light received that it seems to be all light. And then the crystal is undistinguishable from the light, since it is illumined according to its full capacity, which is to appear to be light.

14. When the soul asserts that the flame of love wounds it in its deepest center, it means that insofar as this flame reaches its substance, power, and strength, the Holy Spirit assails and wounds it. It does not make such an assertion to indicate that this wounding is as essential and integral as

in the beatific vision of the next life. Even though a soul attains to as lofty a state of perfection in this mortal life as that which we are discussing, it neither can nor does reach the perfect state of glory, although perhaps in a passing way God might grant it some similar favor. Yet the soul says this in order to manifest the fullness and abundance of delight and glory it feels in this kind of communication from the Holy Spirit. This delight is so much more intense and tender the stronger and more substantially the soul is transformed and concentrated in God. Since this center is the furthest attainable in the present life—although not as perfectly attainable as in the next—the soul refers to it as the deepest center.

Even though the soul can perhaps possess in this life a habit of charity as perfect as in the next, yet the operation and fruition of charity in this life will not be so perfect, even though the operation and fruition of love increase to such a degree in this state that there is great resemblance to the beatific state. The similarity is such that the soul dares to affirm only what it would dare affirm about the next life, that is: in the deepest center of my soul.

15. Since these rare experiences (which are what we ascribe to the soul in this state) are more remarkable than credible, I do not doubt that some persons, not understanding them through their own knowledge or knowing of them through experience, will either fail to believe them or consider the account an exaggeration; or they will think these experiences less than what they really are.

Yet I reply to all these persons that the Father of lights [Jas. 1:17], who is not closefisted but diffuses himself abundantly as the sun does its rays, without being a respecter of persons [Acts 10:34], wherever there is room—always showing himself gladly along the highways and byways—does not hesitate or consider it of little import to find his delights with the children of the earth at a common table in the world [Prv. 8:31].

It should not be held as incredible in a soul now examined, purged, and tried in the fire of tribulations, trials, and many kinds of temptations, and found faithful in love, that the promise of the Son of God be fulfilled, the promise that the Most Blessed Trinity will come and dwell in anyone who loves him [Jn. 14:23]. The Blessed Trinity inhabits the soul by divinely illumining its intellect with the wisdom of the Son, delighting its will in the Holy Spirit, and absorbing it powerfully and mightily in the unfathomed embrace of the Father's sweetness.

16. If he acts thus in some souls, as it is true he does, it should be believed that this soul we are speaking of will not be left behind in regard to receiving these favors from God. For what we are explaining about the activity of the Holy Spirit within it is something far greater than what occurs in the communication and transformation of love. This latter

resembles glowing embers; the former is similar to embers that are not merely glowing but have become so hot that they shoot forth a living flame.[3]

And thus these two kinds of union (union of love alone, and union with an inflaming of love) are somehow comparable to the fire of God which, Isaiah says, is in Zion, and to his furnace which is in Jerusalem [Is. 31:9]. The one signifies the Church Militant, in which the fire of charity is not enkindled to an extreme; the other signifies the vision of peace, which is the Church Triumphant,[4] where this fire is like a furnace blazing in the perfection of love. Although, as we said,[5] the soul has not attained such great perfection as is present in this vision of peace, yet, in comparison with the other common union, this union resembles a blazing furnace in which there is a vision much more peaceful and glorious and tender, just as the flame is clearer and more resplendent than the burning coal.

17. The soul, feeling that this living flame of love is vividly communicating to it every good, since this divine love carries all things with it, exclaims: "O living flame of love that tenderly wounds my soul." This is like saying: O enkindled love, with your loving movements you are pleasantly glorifying me according to the greater capacity and strength of my soul, bestowing divine knowledge according to all the ability and capacity of my intellect, communicating love according to the greater power of my will, and rejoicing the substance of my soul with the torrent of your delight, your divine contact and substantial union, in harmony with the greater purity of my substance and the capacity and breath of my memory! And this is what happens, in an indescribable way, at the time this flame of love rises up within the soul.

Since the soul is completely purged in its substance and faculties (memory, intellect, and will), the divine substance, which because of its purity touches everywhere profoundly, subtly, and sublimely, as the Wise Man says [Wis. 7:23-24], absorbs the soul in itself with its divine flame. And in that immersion of the soul in wisdom, the Holy Spirit sets in motion the glorious flickerings of his flame. Since the flame is so gentle the soul adds:

> Since now you are not oppressive,

---

3. As in nos. 3-4, he distinguishes between the state of union or transformation (glowing embers) and the acts of union (living flames). This distinction is in accord with that made in A. 2. 5, where he explains the nature of union and distinguishes between habitual union and actual union.

4. John probably has in mind the hymn from first Vespers of the Dedication of a Church: *Coelestis urbs Jerusalem, beata pacis visio* (Heavenly city Jerusalem, blessed vision of peace).

5. In no. 14.

18. This means: since you no longer afflict or distress or weary me as you did before. It should be recalled that when the soul was in the state of spiritual purgation, which was at the time of the beginning of contemplation, this flame of God was not so friendly and gentle toward it as now in this state of union. In order to explain this we will have to delay somewhat.[6]

19. Before the divine fire is introduced into the substance of the soul and united with it through perfect and complete purgation and purity, its flame, which is the Holy Spirit, wounds the soul by destroying and consuming the imperfections of its bad habits. And this is the work of the Holy Spirit, in which he disposes it for divine union and transformation in God through love.

The very fire of love that afterward is united with the soul, glorifying it, is what previously assailed it by purging it, just as the fire that penetrates a log of wood is the same that first makes an assault on the wood, wounding it with the flame, drying it out, and stripping it of its unsightly qualities until it is so disposed that it can be penetrated and transformed into the fire.

Spiritual writers call this activity the purgative way. In it a person suffers great deprivation and feels heavy afflictions in the spirit that ordinarily overflow into the senses, for this flame is extremely oppressive.

In this preparatory purgation the flame is not bright for a person but dark. If it does shed some light, the only reason is so the soul may see its miseries and defects. It is not gentle but afflictive. Even though it sometimes imparts the warmth of love, it does so with torment and pain. And it is not delightful, but dry. Although sometimes out of his goodness God accords some delight in order to strengthen and encourage it, the soul suffers for this before and afterward with another trial.

Neither is the flame refreshing and peaceful, but it is consuming and contentious, making a person faint and suffer with self-knowledge. Thus it is not glorious for the soul, but rather makes it feel wretched and distressed in the spiritual light of self-knowledge that it bestows. As Jeremiah declares, God sends fire into its bones and instructs it [Lam. 1:13]; and as David also asserts, he tries it with fire [Ps. 17:3].

20. At this stage persons suffer from sharp trials in the intellect, severe dryness and distress in the will, and from the burdensome knowledge of their own miseries in the memory, for their spiritual eye gives them a very clear picture of themselves. In the substance of the soul they suffer aban-

---

6. As John has done before, he turns to look back at what the soul has undergone in order to reach this high state. He thus begins a digression on what was the central subject of the *Dark Night*, that is, purification.

donment, supreme poverty, dryness, cold, and sometimes heat. They find relief in nothing, nor does any thought console them, nor can they even raise the heart to God, so oppressed are they by this flame. This purgation resembles what Job said God did to him: *You have changed to being cruel toward me* [Jb. 30:21]. For when the soul suffers all these things jointly, it truly seems that God has become displeased with it and cruel.

21. A person's sufferings at this time cannot be exaggerated; they are but little less than the sufferings of purgatory. I do not know how to explain the severity of this oppression and the intensity of the suffering felt in it, save by what Jeremiah says of it in these words: *I am the man that sees my poverty in the rod of his indignation. He has led me and brought me into darkness and not into light. Only against me he has turned and turned again his hand. He has made my skin and my flesh old, and he has broken my bones. He has surrounded me and compassed me with gall and labor. He has set me in dark places as those who are dead forever. He has built around me that I might not get out. He made my fetters heavy. And besides this when I have cried out and prayed, he has shut out my prayer. He shut up my ways with square rocks and turned my steps and paths upside down* [Lam. 3:1-9]. Jeremiah laments all this and goes on to say much more.[7]

Since in this fashion God mediates and heals the soul of its many infirmities, bringing it to health, it must necessarily suffer from this purge and cure according to its sickness. For here Tobias is placing the heart on the coals to release and drive out every kind of demon [Tb. 6:8]. All the soul's infirmities are brought to light; they are set before its eyes to be felt and healed.

22. Now with the light and heat of the divine fire, it sees and feels those weaknesses and miseries that previously resided within it, hidden and unfelt, just as the dampness of the log of wood was unknown until the fire applied to it made it sweat and smoke and sputter. And this is what the flame does to the imperfect soul.

For (O wonderful thing!) contraries rise up at this time against contraries—those of the soul against those of God that assail it. And as the philosophers say: One contrary when close to the other makes it more manifest.[8] They war within the soul, striving to expel one another in order to reign. That is: The virtues and properties of God, extremely perfect, war against the habits and properties of the soul, extremely imperfect; and the soul suffers these two contraries within itself.

When this flame shines on the soul, since its light is excessively

---

7. In N. 2. 7. 2, John illustrates the suffering with this same text from the Lamentations, but includes the "much more" by continuing on to verse 20.
8. Cf. A. 1. 4. 2, and note 1; also A. 3. 6. 1, and note 1.

brilliant, it shines within the darknesses of the soul, which are also excessive. Persons then feel their natural and vicious darknesses that are contrary to the supernatural light; and they fail to experience the supernatural light because they do not have it within themselves as they do their darknesses—and the darknesses do not comprehend the light [Jn 1:5]. They feel these darknesses inasmuch as the light shines on them, for it is impossible to perceive one's darknesses without the divine light focusing on them. Once they are driven out a soul is illumined and, being transformed, beholds the light within itself, since its spiritual eye was cleansed and fortified by the divine light. A tremendous light causes total darkness in a weak and impure eye, for if a sensible object is too intense it deprives its relative faculty. And thus this flame was oppressive to the intellectual eye.

23. This flame of itself is extremely loving, and the will of itself is excessively dry and hard. When the flame tenderly and lovingly assails the will, hardness is felt beside the tenderness, and dryness beside the love. The will does not feel the love and tenderness of the flame since, because of its contrary hardness and dryness, it is unprepared for this until the love and tenderness of God expel the dryness and hardness and reign within it. Accordingly, this flame was oppressive to the will, making it feel and suffer its own hardness and dryness.

Because this flame is immense and far-reaching, and the will is narrow and restricted, the will feels its confinement and narrowness in the measure that the flame attacks it. It feels this until the flame, penetrating within it, enlarges, widens, and makes it capable of receiving the flame itself.

Because this flame is savory and sweet, and the will possesses a spiritual palate disturbed by the humors of inordinate affections, the flame is unpleasant and bitter to it; and the will cannot taste the sweet food of God's love. And in this fashion it feels distress and distastefulness beside so ample and delightful a flame. The will does not experience the savor of the flame because it does not feel this flame within itself; it only feels what it does have within itself—its own misery.

And finally, because this flame contains immense riches and delights and the soul of itself is extraordinarily poor, without any goods or satisfaction, the soul knows and feels clearly beside this goodness and these riches and delights its own misery, poverty, and evil. For evil cannot comprehend goodness, nor poverty riches, and so on, until this flame purifies a soul completely and by this transformation enriches, glorifies, and delights it.

This flame previously oppressed the soul in an indescribable way, since contraries were battling contraries: God, who is all perfect, against all the imperfections of the soul. God does this so, by transforming the soul into himself, he might soften, pacify, and illumine it, as does fire when it penetrates the log of wood.

24. Not many people undergo so strong a purgation, only those whom God wishes to elevate to the highest degree of union. For he prepares individuals by a purification more or less severe in accordance with the degree to which he wishes to raise them, and also according to their impurity and imperfection.[9]

This suffering resembles that of purgatory. Just as the spirits suffer purgation there so as to be able to see God through clear vision in the next life, souls in their own way suffer purgation here on earth so as to be able to be transformed in him through love in this life.

25. In *The Dark Night of The Ascent of Mount Carmel* we dealt with the intensity of this purgation,[10] how it is greater and how less, and when it is in the intellect, when in the will, how it is in the memory, when and how it is also in the soul's substance, and also when it involves the whole soul. We discussed, too, the purgation of the sensory part, and how it can be discerned when the purgation is of the sensory part and when of the spiritual part, and the time or stage along the spiritual road in which each begins. Since we have already explained all of this, and such is not our aim here, I will not go into it again.

Let it suffice to know that the very God who desires to enter within the soul through the union and transformation of love is he who first assails and purges it with the light and heat of his divine flame, just as the fire that penetrates the log of wood is the same that first prepares it for this, as we said.[11] Hence the very flame that is now gentle, since it has entered within the soul, is what was formerly oppressive, assailing it from without.

26. Such is the meaning of the present verse, "Now you are not oppressive." It is in sum like saying: Not only now are you no longer dark as you were before, but you are the divine light of my intellect by which I can look at you; and you not only have ceased making me faint in my weakness, but are rather the strength of my will by which I can love and enjoy you, being wholly converted into divine love; and you are no longer heavy and constraining to the substance of my soul but rather its glory and delight and amplitude, for the words of the divine Song of Songs can be spoken of me: *Who is this that comes up from the desert, flowing with delights,*

---

9. Within the general call to union or perfection there are degrees or levels of union; cf. A. 2. 5. 9-11; N. 2. 7. 3;
10. The reference is to his work *The Dark Night,* the subject matter of which he promised to treat, for example, in the prologue and chapter 1 of the *Ascent.*
11. In no. 19.

leaning upon her Beloved, diffusing love everywhere? [Sg. 8:5]. Since this is true,

now consummate! if it be your will:

27. That is, consummate the spiritual marriage with me perfectly by means of the beatific vision. This is the soul's petition. It is true that in this high state it is as conformed to the will of God and satisfied as it is transformed in love; it wants nothing for itself, nor dares ask for anything, but everything is for its Beloved, since as St. Paul says, charity seeks not things for itself [1 Cor. 13:5], but for the Beloved. Nonetheless, its sigh is as great as what it lacks for the perfect possession of the adoption of the children of God [Rom. 8:23]; for it still lives in hope, in which one cannot fail to feel emptiness. When the soul's glory is consummated, its appetite will come to rest. However intimate may be a person's union with God, there will never be satisfaction and rest until God's glory appears [Ps. 17:15], especially since the savor and sweetness of that glory is now experienced. This experience is so intense that if God had not favored the flesh by fortifying the sensory part with his right hand, as he did Moses in the rock, enabling him to behold the divine glory without dying [Ex. 33:22], nature would be torn apart and death would ensue, since the lower part is unequipped to suffer so much and such a sublime fire of glory.

28. Affliction, then, does not accompany this desire and petition, for the soul is no longer capable of such affliction; but with a gentle and delightful desire it seeks this in the conformity of both spirit and sense to God's will. As a result it says in this verse, "Now consummate! if it be your will," for its will and appetite are so united with God that it considers the fulfillment of God's will to be its glory.

Yet the sudden flashes of glory and love that appear vaguely in these touches at the door of entry into the soul, and are unable to fit into it because of the narrowness of the earthly house, are so sublime that it would rather be a sign of little love not to try to enter into that perfection and completion of love.

Moreover, a soul is conscious that in the vigor of the Bridegroom's delightful communication the Holy Spirit rouses and invites it by the immense glory he marvelously and with gentle affection places before its eyes, telling it what he told the bride in the Song of Songs. The bride thus refers to this: *Behold what my Spouse is saying to me: Arise and make haste, my love, my dove, my beautiful one, and come; for winter is now passed, and the rains are over and gone, and the flowers have appeared in our land; the fig tree has put forth her fruits; the vines in flower have given their fragrance. Arise, my love, my fair one, and come; my dove in the clefts of the rock, in the hollow of the wall, show me your face, let your voice sound in my ears, because your voice is sweet and your face beautiful* [Sg. 2:10-14]. The soul in a sublime experience of glory feels and understands most distinctly all these things that the Holy Spirit, desiring to introduce it into that glory, shows it in this gentle and tender blaze. Consequently, the soul thus roused answers: "Now consummate! if it be your will." It makes the two requests of the Bridegroom that he taught us in the Gospel: *Adveniat regnum tuum; fiat voluntas tua* [Mt. 6:10].[12] It is like saying: "Now consummate" giving me this kingdom, "if it be your will," according to your will. And that this may be true:

tear through the veil of this sweet encounter!

29. The veil is what impedes so singular an event. It is easy to reach God when all the impediments are removed and the veils that separate the soul from union with him are torn. We can say there are three veils that constitute a hindrance to this union with God and must be torn if the union is to be effected and possessed perfectly by the soul; that is: the temporal veil, comprising all creatures; the natural, embodying the purely natural inclinations and operations; and the sensitive, which consists only of the union of the soul with the body, that is, the sensitive and animal life of which St. Paul speaks: *We know that if this our earthly house is dissolved, we have a building of God in heaven* [2 Cor. 5:1].

The first two veils must necessarily be torn in order to obtain this union with God in which all the things of the world are renounced, all the natural appetites and affections mortified, and the natural operations of the soul divinized.

All of this was accomplished, and these veils were torn by means of the oppressive encounters of this flame. Through the spiritual purgation we referred to above, the soul tears these two veils completely and is united with God as it here is; only the third veil of this sensitive life remains to be torn. As a result it mentions a veil and not veils, since there is only this one to tear. Because the veil is now so tenuous, thin, and spiritualized through this union with God, the flame is not harsh in its encounter as it was with the other two, but savory and sweet. The soul hence calls it a "sweet encounter"; the sweeter and more savory, the more it seems about to tear through the veil of mortal life.

30. It should be known that the natural death of persons who have reached this state is far different in its cause and mode from the death of others, even though it is similar in natural circumstances. If the death of other people is caused by sickness or old age, the death of these persons

---

12. "Thy kingdom come; thy will be done." John mentions these two petitions of the Our Father from the perspective of this lofty union. In A. 3. 44. 4, he comments on the Lord's prayer as containing seven petitions that include "all our spiritual and temporal needs."

is not so induced, in spite of their being sick or old; their soul is not wrested from them unless by some impetus and encounter of love far more sublime than previous ones; of greater power, and more valiant, since it tears through this veil and carries off the jewel, which is the soul.

The death of such persons is very gentle and very sweet, sweeter and more gentle than was their whole spiritual life on earth. For they die with the most sublime impulses and delightful encounters of love, resembling the swan whose song is much sweeter at the moment of death. Accordingly, David affirmed that the death of the saints is precious in the sight of the Lord [Ps. 116:15]. The soul's riches gather together here, and its rivers of love move on to enter the sea, for these rivers, because they are blocked, become so vast that they themselves resemble seas. The just one's first treasures, and last, are heaped together as company for the departure and going off to the kingdom, while praises are heard from the ends of the earth, which, as Isaiah says, are the glory of the just one [Is. 24:16].

31. The soul, then, conscious of the abundance of its enrichment, at the time of these glorious encounters feels to be almost at the point of departing for complete and perfect possession of its kingdom, for it knows that it is pure, rich, full of virtues, and prepared for such a kingdom. God permits it in this state to see its beauty, and he entrusts to it the gifts and virtues he has bestowed; for everything is converted into love and praises, and it has no touch of presumption or vanity since it no longer bears the leaven of imperfection that corrupts the mass [1 Cor. 5:6; Gal. 5:9]. Since it is aware that nothing is wanting other than to tear the weak veil of this natural life, in which it feels the entanglement, hindrance, and captivity of its freedom, and since it desires to be dissolved and to be with Christ [Phil. 1:23], it laments that a life so weak and base impedes another so mighty and sublime, and asks that the veil be torn, saying: "Tear through the veil of this sweet encounter!"

32. There are three reasons for the term "veil": first, because of the union between the spirit and the flesh; second, because this union separates the soul from God; third, because a veil is not so thick and opaque that a brilliant light cannot shine through it; and in this state the bond seems to be so tenuous a veil, since it is now very spiritual, thin, and luminous, that it does not prevent the divinity from vaguely appearing through it. Since the soul perceives the power of the other life, it is conscious of the weakness of this one and that the veil is of delicate fabric, as thin as a spider's web; in David's words: *Our years shall be considered as the spider* [Ps. 90:9]. And this life is even much less in the eyes of persons thus exalted, for, since they have God's view of things, they regard them as God does, in whose sight, as David also declares, *a thousand years are as*

yesterday, which is past [Ps. 89:4], and according to Isaiah, *all nations are as though they were not* [Is. 40:17]. These things carry the same weight in the soul's view: All things are nothing to it, and it is nothing in its own eyes; God alone is its all.[13]

33. The reason it begs that the veil be torn and not cut or destroyed is noteworthy, for there does not seem to be much difference. We can offer four reasons.

First, we use this term for the sake of speaking more appropriately, since tearing is more proper to this encounter than cutting or destroying.

Second, because love is the friend of the power of love and of the strong and impetuous touch, exercised more in tearing than in cutting and destroying.

Third, because love desires the act to be very brief and quick. The strength and power of the act is commensurate with its brevity and spirituality, for virtue when united is stronger than when scattered. And love is introduced as form is introduced into matter; it is done in an instant, and until then there is no act but only the dispositions toward it. Spiritual acts are produced instantaneously in the soul because God infuses them. But those the soul makes of itself can better be referred to as dispositive acts by means of successive desires and affections, which only become perfect acts of love or contemplation, as I say, when God sometimes forms and perfects them very quickly in the spirit. As a result the Wise Man affirmed that the end of prayer is better than the beginning [Eccl. 7:9], and it is commonly quoted that the short prayer pierces the heavens.[14] A person already disposed can make many acts in a short time, acts far more intense than can be made in a long time by someone undisposed; and, by being so fully disposed, such a person usually remains for a long time in an act of love or contemplation. With one who is not disposed, all is spent in preparing the spirit, and even then the fire usually holds back without entering the wood, either because of excessive dampness of the wood or lack of sufficient heat to dispose it, or for both reasons. But in the prepared soul the act of love enters immediately, for at each touch the spark catches fire in the dry tinder, and thus the enamored soul desires the brevity of tearing more than the delay involved in cutting or destroying.

The fourth reason is that the veil of this life is done away with more quickly; cutting or destroying requires greater care since one must wait for the object to be prepared or ready, or for some other reason; whereas

---

13. One recalls at this height the teaching of the *Ascent* about the all and the nothing; cf. A. 1., the sketch of the Mount, and chapter 13.

14. This saying has its source in the biblical text of Ecclus. 35:17: "The prayer of the humble pierces the clouds." Cf. A. 2. 14. 11.

if one tears it there is no waiting, it seems to me, for this readiness or for anything of the sort.

34. The enamored soul desires this tearing so it may suffer no delay by waiting for its life to be destroyed naturally, or cut off at such and such a time. Both the force of love and the disposition the soul sees in itself make it desire and beg that the veil of life be torn immediately by a supernatural encounter and impetus of love.

A person having reached this stage knows full well that it is characteristic of God to take to himself, before their time, souls that love him ardently, perfecting them in a short while by means of that love, which in any event they would have gained at their own pace. This is what the Wise Man said: *He pleased God and was loved; and living among sinners he was translated and carried away lest evil should change his understanding or affection deceive his soul. Perfected in a short time, he fulfilled a long time. Because his soul was pleasing to God, he therefore made haste to take him out of the midst,* and so on [Wis. 4:10-11, 13-14]. These words are the words of the Wise Man in which it will be seen how rightly and adequately the soul uses the expression "tear through," for the Holy Spirit uses the words "carry away" and "make haste," which indicate something apart from all delay. God's making haste signifies the haste by which he perfected in a short time the love of the just one, and "carry away" refers to a premature death.

It is vital for individuals to make acts of love in this life so that in being perfected in a short time they may not be detained long, either here on earth or in the next life, before seeing God.[15]

35. Let us see now why it calls this inner assault of the Spirit an encounter rather than something else. The reason is that when the soul feels in God an infinite longing, as we said, for the ending of its life and this wish goes unfulfilled since the time of its perfection has not arrived, it is aware that he produces these divine and glorious assaults in the manner of encounters so as to perfect it and raise it out of the flesh. Since their purpose is to purify it and draw it out of the flesh, they are indeed encounters, by which he ever penetrates and deifies the substance of the soul, absorbing it above all being into his own being.

---

15. Nos. 30, 33, and 34 of this stanza were much read by St. Thérèse of Lisieux. Marking off passages on the death of love, she indicated, and then even spoke of, her own intense desires to die in this way. But she also reminded those around her that "our Lord died on the Cross in agony." According to witnesses she did die of love, saying, "Oh, I love Him! My God!...I love You!" But this moment was preceded by an agony, her "trial of faith" that lasted 18 months, and her severe physical sufferings. See *St. Thérèse of Lisieux: Her Last Conversations,* translated by John Clarke, O.C.D. (Washington, D.C.: ICS Publications, 1977) pp. 245-247.

And the cause of this absorption is that he vigorously encountered and transported it in the Holy Spirit, whose communications are impetuous when they are fervent, as is this encounter. Because the soul tastes God in a living way in this encounter, it calls it sweet; not because many other touches and encounters received in this state are not sweet but because of its eminence over all others. God grants this, as we said, in order soon to loose and glorify it. Whereon it acquires the courage to entreat: "Tear through the veil," and so on.

36. To sum up the entire stanza now, it is like saying: O flame of the Holy Spirit that so intimately and tenderly pierces the substance of my soul and cauterizes it with your glorious ardor! Previously my requests did not reach your ears, when, in the anxieties and weariness of love in which my sense and my spirit suffered because of considerable weakness, impurity, and lack of strong love, I was praying that you loose me and bring me to yourself because my soul longed for you, and impatient love did not allow me to be so conformed to the conditions of this life in which you desired me still to live. The previous impulses of love were not enough, because they did not have sufficient quality for the attainment of my desire; now I am so fortified in love that not only do my sense and spirit no longer faint in you, but my heart and my flesh, reinforced in you, rejoice in the living God [Ps. 84:2], with great conformity between the sensory and spiritual parts. What you desire me to ask for, I ask for; and what you do not desire, I do not desire, nor can I, nor does it even enter my mind to desire it. My petitions are now more valuable and estimable in your sight, since they come from you, and you move me to make them, and I make them in the delight and joy of the Holy Spirit, *my judgment now issuing from your countenance* [Ps. 17:2], that is, when you esteem and hear my prayer. Tear, then, the thin veil of this life and do not let old age cut it naturally, that from now on I may love you with the plenitude and fullness my soul desires forever and ever.

STANZA 2

> O sweet cautery,
> O delightful wound!
> O gentle hand! O delicate touch
> that tastes of eternal life
> and pays every debt!
> in killing you changed death to life.

Commentary

1. In this stanza the soul proclaims how the three Persons of the Most

Blessed Trinity, the Father, the Son, and the Holy Spirit, are the ones who effect this divine work of union in it. Thus the hand, the cautery, and the touch are in substance the same. The soul applies these terms to the Persons of the Trinity because of the effect each of the Persons produces. The cautery is the Holy Spirit, the hand is the Father, and the touch is the Son. The soul here magnifies the Father, the Son, and the Holy Spirit, stressing the three admirable favors and blessings they produce in it, having changed its death to life, transforming it in the Trinity.

The first is the delightful wound. This it attributes to the Holy Spirit, and hence calls him a sweet cautery.

The second is the taste of eternal life. This it attributes to the Son, and thus calls him a delicate touch.

The third is transformation, a gift by which all debts are fully paid. This it attributes to the Father and hence calls him a gentle hand.

Although it names the three according to the properties of their effects, it speaks only to one, saying "You changed death to life," because all of them work together; and accordingly it attributes everything to one, and everything to all. The verse is:

O sweet cautery,

2. This cautery, as we mentioned, is the Holy Spirit. For as Moses declares in Deuteronomy, *Our Lord God is a consuming fire* [Dt. 4:24], that is, a fire of love that, being of infinite power, can inestimably consume and transform into itself the soul it touches. Yet he burns each soul according to its preparation. He will burn one more, another less, and this he does insofar as he desires, and how and when he desires.[1] When he wills to touch somewhat vehemently, the soul's burning reaches such a high degree of love that it seems to surpass that of all the fires of the world, for he is an infinite fire of love. As a result, in this union the soul calls the Holy Spirit a cautery. Since in a cautery the fire is more intense and fierce and produces a more singular effect than it does in other combustibles, the soul calls the act of this union a cautery in comparison with other acts of union, for it is the outcome of a fire so much more aflame than all other fires. Because the soul in this case is entirely transformed by the divine flame, it not only feels a cautery, but has become a cautery of blazing fire.

3. It is a wonderful thing and worth relating that, since this fire of God is so mighty it would consume a thousand worlds more easily than the fire of this earth would burn up a straw, it does not consume and destroy the soul in which it so burns. And it does not afflict it; rather, commensurate with the strength of the love, it divinizes and delights it, burning gently within it.

---

1. Cf. F. 1. 24, and note 11.

And this is so on account of the purity and perfection with which the spirit burns in the Holy Spirit. Similarly, as told in the Acts of the Apostles, this fire came mightily and enkindled the disciples [Acts 2:2-3], who, as St. Gregory affirms, burned interiorly and gently with love.[2] This is the Church's meaning when, as regards the same subject, she says: *Fire came from heaven, not burning but shining bright; not devouring but illumining.*[3] Since God's purpose in granting these communications is to exalt the soul, he does not weary and restrict it but enlarges and delights it; he does not blacken it and convert it to ashes as fire does to coal, but he brightens and enriches it. Hence it calls him a sweet cautery.

4. The happy soul that by great fortune reaches this cautery knows all things, tastes all things, does all it wishes, and prospers; no one prevails before it and nothing touches it. This is the soul of which the Apostle speaks: *The spiritual person judges all things and is judged by no one* [1 Cor. 2:15]. And again: *The spirit searches out all things, even the deep things of God* [1 Cor. 2:10]. This is love's trait: to scrutinize all the good things of the Beloved.

5. Oh, the great glory of you who have merited this supreme fire! It is certain that, although it does not consume you—for it has infinite force to consume and annihilate you—it does overwhelmingly consume you in glory. Do not wonder that God brings some souls to this high peak. The sun is distinguished by some of its marvelous effects; as the Holy Spirit says, it burns the mountains (that is, the saints) in three ways [Ecclus. 43:4].

Since this cautery is sweet, then, how delighted will be the soul touched by it! The soul desiring to speak of it does not do so, but keeps the esteem in its heart and only expresses exclamation vocally through the use of "O," saying: "O sweet cautery!"

O delightful wound!

6. Having addressed the cautery, the soul now speaks to the wound caused by the cautery. The cautery was sweet, and the wound must logically conform to the cautery. Thus the wound issuing from a sweet cautery is a delightful wound. Since the cautery is a cautery of love, the wound is a wound of sweet love and is both delightful and sweet.

7. To understand the nature of this wound, which is addressed by the soul, it should be known that the cautery of material fire always leaves a

---

2. See *Homilia 30 in Evangelium,* in Migne, PL 76. 1220. Cf. N. 2. 20. 4; C. 14-15. 10.

3. In the *Roman Breviary,* Thursday within the Octave of Pentecost, First Response at Matins.

wound where it is applied. And it possesses this property: If applied to a wound not made by fire, it converts it into a wound caused by fire. Whether a soul is wounded by other wounds of miseries and sins or whether it is healthy, this cautery of love immediately effects a wound of love in the one it touches, and those wounds deriving from other causes become wounds of love.

Yet there is a difference between this loving cautery and the cautery produced by material fire. The wound left by material fire is only curable by other medicines, whereas the wound effected by the cautery of love is incurable through medicine; for the very cautery that causes it, cures it, and by curing it, causes it. As often as the cautery of love touches the wound of love, it causes a deeper wound of love, and thus the more it wounds, the more it cures and heals. The more wounded the lover, the healthier the lover is, and the cure caused by love is to wound and inflict wound upon wound, to such an extent that the entire soul is dissolved into a wound of love. And now all cauterized and made one wound of love, it is completely healthy in love, for it is transformed in love.

This is what is understood by the wound of which the soul (all wounded and all healthy) speaks. Even though the soul is all wounded and all healthy, the cautery of love does not fail to fulfill its task, which is to touch and wound with love. Being wholly delightful and completely sound, the wound brings delight, just as a good doctor usually does. As a result the soul says: "O delightful wound!"

Oh, then, wound, so much more delightful as the fire of love that causes it is higher and more sublime! The Holy Spirit produces it only for the sake of giving delight, and since his will to delight the soul is great, this wound will be great, for it will be extremely delightful.

8. O happy wound, wrought by one who knows only how to heal! O fortunate and choicest wound; you were made only for delight, and the quality of your affliction is delight and gratification for the wounded soul! You are great, O delightful wound, because he who caused you is great! And your delight is great because the fire of love is infinite and makes you delightful according to your capacity and greatness. O, then, delightful wound, so much more sublimely delightful the more the cautery touched the intimate center of the substance of the soul, burning all that was burnable in order to give delight to all that could be delighted!

It is understandable that this cautery and this wound are of the highest degree possible in this state. For there are many other ways God cauterizes the soul that are unlike this one and fail to reach such a degree. For this cautery is a touch only of divinity in the soul, without any intellectual or imaginative form or figure.

9. There is another way of cauterizing the soul; through an intellectual

form it usually comes about in a very sublime manner. It will happen that while the soul is inflamed with the love of God, although not with a love of as deep a quality as we mentioned—yet it is fitting that it be so for what I want to say—it will feel that a seraph is assailing it by means of an arrow or dart that is all afire with love. And the seraph pierces and cauterizes this soul that like a red-hot coal, or better a flame, is already enkindled. And then in this cauterization, when the soul is transpierced with that dart, the flame gushes forth fiercely and with a sudden ascent, like the fire in a furnace or an oven when someone uses a poker or bellows to stir and excite it. And being wounded by this fiery dart, the soul feels the wound with unsurpassable delight. Besides being fully stirred in great sweetness by the blowing or impetuous motion of the seraph, in which it feels in its intense ardor to be dissolving in love, it is aware of the delicate wound and the herb (which serves as a keen temper to the dart) as though it were a sharp point in the substance of the spirit, in the heart of the pierced soul.[4]

10. Who can fittingly speak of this intimate point of the wound, which seems to make its mark in the middle of the heart of the spirit, there where the soul experiences the excellence of the delight? The soul feels that the point is like a tiny mustard seed, very much alive and enkindled, sending into its surroundings a living and enkindled fire of love. The fire issuing from the substance and power of that living point, which contains the substance and power of the herb, is felt to be subtly diffused through all the spiritual and substantial veins of the soul in the measure of the soul's power and strength. The soul feels its ardor strengthen and increase and its love become so refined in this ardor that seemingly there flow seas of loving fire within it, reaching to the heights and depths of the earthly and heavenly spheres, imbuing all with love. It seems to it that the entire universe is a sea of love in which it is engulfed, for conscious of the living point or center of love within itself, it is unable to catch sight of the boundaries of this love.

11. There is nothing else to say about the soul's enjoyment here except that it realizes how appropriately the kingdom of heaven was compared in the Gospel to a grain of mustard seed that, by reason of its intense heat, grows into a large tree, despite its being so small [Mt. 13:31-32]. For the soul beholds itself converted into the immense fire of love that emanates from that enkindled point at the heart of the spirit.

---

4. In discussing this particular grace of the transpiercing of the soul, John explains its possible forms, its nature, and its effects. St. Teresa describes her experiences of this grace in her *Life* 29. 13-14, although they included an imaginative vision of the angel and she thought the angel, which appeared to be all afire, belonged to the cherubim. Her director Domingo Báñez, O.P., noted in the manuscript that the angel would seem to be from the seraphim instead.

12. Few persons have reached these heights. Some have, however, especially those whose virtue and spirit were to be diffused among their children. With respect to the first fruits of the spirit, God accords to founders wealth and value commensurate with the greater or lesser following they will have in their doctrine and spirituality.[5]

13. Let us return to the work of that seraph, for he truly inflicts a sore, and wounds inwardly in the spirit. Thus, if God sometimes permits an effect to extend to the bodily senses in the fashion in which it existed interiorly, the wound and sore appear outwardly, as happened when the seraph wounded St. Francis. When his soul was wounded with love by the five wounds, their effect extended to the body, and these wounds were impressed on the body, which was wounded just as his soul was wounded with love.[6]

God usually does not bestow a favor on the body without bestowing it first and principally on the soul. Thus the greater the delight and strength of love the wound produces in the soul, so much greater is that produced by the wound outside on the body, and when there is an increase in one there is an increase in the other. This so happens because these souls are purified and established in God, and what is a cause of pain and torment to their corruptible flesh is sweet and delectable to their strong and healthy spirit. It is, then, a wonderful thing, experiencing the pain augmented with the delectable.

Job, with his wounds, clearly beheld this marvel when he said to God: *Returning to me, you torment me wondrously* [Jb. 10:16]. This is an unspeakable marvel and worthy of the abundance and sweetness God has hidden for them that fear him [Ps. 31:19]: to give one enjoyment of as much savor and sweetness as there is experience of pain and torment.

Nevertheless, when the wound is made only in the soul without being communicated outwardly, the delight can be more intense and sublime. Since the flesh bridles the spirit, when the goods of the spirit are communicated also to the flesh, the flesh pulls the reins, pulls back at the mouth of this swift horse of the spirit, and restrains its wild impetuosity; for if the spirit makes use of its power the reins will break. Yet until the reins are broken the flesh does not fail to oppress the spirit's freedom, as the Wise Man asserts: *The corruptible body is a load on the soul, and the earthly dwelling oppresses the spiritual mind which of itself comprehends many things* [Wis. 9:15].

---

5. John himself, and other founders, experienced mystically the Gospel parable of the mustard seed. Here, too, St. Teresa must have come especially to his mind as he speaks of founders and their followers in doctrine and spirituality.

6. St. Francis of Assisi received the marks of the wounds on his hands, feet, and side on Mount La Verna in October 1224. See St. Bonaventure, *The Life of St. Francis,* Classics of Western Spirituality (New York: Paulist Press, 1978), ch. 13.

14. I say this in order to make it clear that the one who would go to God relying on natural ability and reasoning will not be very spiritual. There are some who think that by pure force and the activity of the senses, which of itself is lowly and no more than natural, they can reach the strength and height of the supernatural spirit. One does not attain to this peak without surpassing and leaving aside the activity of the senses.

Yet it is sometimes quite different when an effect of the spirit overflows into the senses. When this is true, the effect in the senses proceeds from an abundance of spirit, as in the event of the wounds that proceed from the inner strength and appear outwardly. This happened with St. Paul, whose immense compassion for the sufferings of Christ redounded in the body, as he explains to the Galatians: *I bear the wounds of the Lord Jesus in my body* [Gal. 6:17].

15. What we have expounded concerning the cautery and the wound is sufficient. If the picture we have painted of them is true, what, do you think, will be the hand that produces this cautery, and what the touch? The soul reveals this in the subsequent verse more through interjection than by explanation, saying:

O gentle hand! O delicate touch

16. This hand is, as we said,[7] the merciful and omnipotent Father. We should understand that, since it is as generous and bountiful as it is powerful and rich, it gives, when opened to favor the soul, rich and powerful presents. For this reason the soul calls it a gentle hand. It is like saying: O hand, you are as gentle to my soul, which you touch by resting gently, as you would be powerful enough to submerge the entire world if you rested somewhat heavily, for by your look alone the earth trembles [Ps. 104:32], the nations melt and faint, and the mountains crumble! [Hb. 3:6]. Oh, then again, great hand, by touching Job a little bit roughly, you were as hard and rigorous with him [Jb. 19:21] as you are friendly and gentle with me; how much more lovingly, graciously, and gently do you permanently touch my soul! You cause death, and you give life, and no one flees from your hand [Dt. 32:39].

For you, O divine life, never kill unless to give life, never wound unless to heal. When you chastise, your touch is gentle, but it is enough to destroy the world. When you give delight you rest very firmly, and thus the delight of your sweetness is immeasurable. You have wounded me in order to cure me, O divine hand, and you have put to death in me what made me lifeless, what deprived me of God's life in which I now see myself live. You granted this with the liberality of your generous grace, which you used in contacting me with the touch of the splendor of your glory and

---

7. In no. 1.

the figure of your substance [Heb. 1:3], which is your only begotten Son, through whom, he being your substance, you touch mightily from one end to the other [Wis. 8:1]. And your only begotten Son, O merciful hand of the Father, is the delicate touch by which you touched me with the force of your cautery and wounded me.

17. O you, then, delicate touch, the Word, the Son of God, through the delicacy of your divine being, you subtly penetrate the substance of my soul and, lightly touching it all, absorb it entirely in yourself in divine modes of delights and sweetnesses unheard of in the land of Canaan and never before seen in Teman [Bar. 3:22]! O, then, very delicate, exceedingly delicate touch of the Word, so much more delicate for me insofar as, after overthrowing the mountains and smashing the rocks to pieces on Mount Horeb with the shadow of might and power that went before you, you gave the prophet the sweetest and strongest experience of yourself in the gentle breeze [1 Kgs. 19:11-12]! O gentle breeze, since you are a delicate and mild breeze, tell us: How do you, the Word, the Son of God, touch mildly and gently, since you are so awesome and mighty?

Oh, happy is the soul that you, being terrible and strong, gently and lightly touch! Proclaim this to the world! But you are unwilling to proclaim this to the world because it does not know of a mild breeze, and will not experience you, for it can neither receive nor see you [Jn. 14:17]. But they, O my God and my life, will see and experience your mild touch who withdraw from the world and become mild, bringing the mild into harmony with the mild, thus enabling themselves to experience and enjoy you. The more you dwell permanently hidden within them, the more gently you touch them, for the substance of their soul is now refined, cleansed, and purified, withdrawn from every creature and every touch and trace of creature. As a result you hide them in the secret of your face, which is the Word, from human disturbance [Ps. 31:20].

18. O, then again, repeatedly delicate touch, so much stronger and mightier the more you are delicate, since you detach and withdraw the soul from all the other touches of created things by the might of your delicacy, and reserve it for and unite it to yourself alone, so mild an effect do you leave in the soul, that every other touch of all things both high and low seems coarse and spurious. It displeases the soul to look at these things, and to deal with them is a heavy pain and torment to it.

19. It should be known that the breadth and capacity of an object corresponds to its refinement, and the more diffuse and communicative it is, the more it is subtle and delicate. The Word is immensely subtle and delicate, for he is the touch that comes into contact with the soul. The soul is the vessel having breadth and capacity because of its remarkable

purity and refinement in this state.

O, then, delicate touch, the more abundantly you pervade my soul, the more substance you have and the greater purity my soul has!

20. It should also be known that the more subtle and delicate the touch, the more delight and gratification it communicates there where it touches; and the less volume, because the Word who grants it is alien to every mode and manner, and free from all the volume of form, figure, and accident that usually encircles and imposes boundaries or limits to the substance. This touch we are discussing is indescribable insofar as it is substantial, that is, from the divine substance.

Finally, then, O Word, indescribably delicate touch, produced in the soul only by your most simple being that, since it is infinite, is infinitely delicate and hence touches so subtly, lovingly, eminently, and delicately,
                   that tastes of eternal life

21. Although that which the soul tastes in this touch of God is not perfect, it does in fact have a certain savor of eternal life, as was mentioned.[8] And this is not incredible if we believe, as we should, that this is a touch of substances, that is, of the substance of God in the substance of the soul. Many saints have attained to this substantial touch during their lives on earth.

The delicateness of delight felt in this contact is inexpressible. I would desire not to speak of it so as to avoid giving the impression that it is no more than what I describe. There is no way to catch in words the sublime things of God that take place in these souls. The appropriate language for the persons receiving these favors is that they understand them, experience them within themselves, enjoy them, and be silent. One is conscious in this state that these things are in a certain way like the white pebble that St. John said would be given to the one who conquers: and on that pebble a new name written, which no one knows but the one who receives it [Rv. 2:17]. Thus one can only say, and truthfully, "that tastes of eternal life."

Although one does not have perfect fruition in this life as in glory, this touch, nevertheless, since it is a touch, tastes of eternal life. As a result the soul tastes here all the things of God, since God communicates to it fortitude, wisdom, love, beauty, grace, goodness, and so on. Because God is all these things, a person enjoys them in only one touch of God, and the soul rejoices within its faculties and within its substance.

22. Sometimes the unction of the Holy Spirit overflows into the body and all the sensory substance, all the members and bones and marrow rejoice, not in so slight a fashion as is customary, but with the feeling of

---

8. In nos. 13-16.

great delight and glory, even in the outermost joints of the hands and feet. The body experiences so much glory in that of the soul that in its own way it magnifies God, feeling in its bones something similar to what David declares: *All my bones shall say: God, who is like to you?* [Ps. 35:10]. And because everything that can be said of this unction is less than what it is, it is sufficient to say in reference to both the bodily and the spiritual experience, "that tastes of eternal life."

and pays every debt!

23. The soul affirms this because in the taste of eternal life, which it here enjoys, it feels the reward for the trials it passed through in order to reach this state. It feels not only that it has been compensated and satisfied justly but that it has been rewarded exceedingly. It thoroughly understands the truth of the promise made by the Bridegroom in the Gospel that he would repay a hundredfold [Mt. 19:29]. It has endured no tribulation or penance or trial to which there does not correspond a hundredfold of consolation and delight in this life; and it can truly say: "and pays every debt."

24. To know the nature of these debts for which the soul feels compensated here, it should be noted that ordinarily no one can reach this high state and kingdom of espousal without first undergoing many tribulations and trials. As is said in the Acts of the Apostles, *It is necessary to undergo many tribulations to enter the kingdom of heaven* [Acts 14:22]. In this state these tribulations are ended; the soul being purified suffers no more.

25. The trials that those who are to reach this state suffer are threefold: trials, discomforts, fears, and temptations from the world; and these in many ways: temptations, aridities, and afflictions in the senses; and tribulations, darknesses, distress, abandonment, temptations, and other trials in the spirit. In this way a soul is purified in its sensory and spiritual parts, as we mentioned in discussing the fourth verse of the first stanza.

The reason these trials are necessary in order to reach this state is that this highest union cannot be wrought in a soul that is not fortified by trials and temptations, and purified by tribulations, darknesses, and distress, just as a superior quality liqueur is poured only into a sturdy flask that is prepared and purified. By these trials the sensory part of the soul is purified and strengthened, and the spiritual part is refined, purged, and disposed. Since unpurified souls must undergo the sufferings of fire in the next life to attain union with God in glory, so in this life they must undergo the fire of these sufferings to reach the union of perfection. This fire acts on some more vigorously than on others, and on some for a longer time than on others, according to the degree of union to which God wishes to raise them, and according to what they must be purged of.[9]

26. Through these trials in which God places the spirit and the senses, the soul in bitterness acquires virtues, strength, and perfection, for virtue is made perfect in weakness [2 Cor. 12:9] and refined through the endurance of suffering. Iron cannot serve for the artificer's plan, or be adapted to it without fire and the hammer; as Jeremiah says of the fire that gave him knowledge: *You have sent fire into my bones and have instructed me* [Lam. 1:13]. And Jeremiah also says of the hammer: *You have chastised me, Lord, and I was instructed* [Jer. 31:18]. Hence Ecclesiasticus says: *What can anyone know who is not tried? And the one that has no experience knows little* [Ecclus. 34:9-10].

27. And here it ought to be pointed out why so few reach this high state of perfect union with God. It should be known that the reason is not that God wishes only a few of these spirits to be so elevated; he would rather want all to be perfect, but he finds few vessels that will endure so lofty and sublime a work. Since he tries them in little things and finds them so weak that they immediately flee from work, unwilling to be subject to the least discomfort and mortification, it follows that not finding them strong and faithful in that little [Mt. 25:21, 23], in which he favored them by beginning to hew and polish them, he realizes that they will be much less strong in these greater trials. As a result he proceeds no further in purifying them and raising them from the dust of the earth through the toil of mortification. They are in need of greater constancy and fortitude than they showed.

There are many who desire to advance and persistently beseech God to bring them to this state of perfection. Yet when God wills to conduct them through the initial trials and mortifications, as is necessary, they are unwilling to suffer them and they shun them, flee from the narrow road of life [Mt. 7:14] and seek the broad road of their own consolation, which is that of their own perdition [Mt. 7:13]; thus they do not allow God to begin to grant their petition. They are like useless containers, for although they desire to reach the state of the perfect they do not want to be guided by the path of trials that leads to it. They hardly even begin to walk along this road by submitting to what is least, that is, to ordinary sufferings.[10]

---

9. Cf. F. 1. 24 and note 11. In a number of places throughout his writings John compares this purification to purgatory; cf., e.g., A. 1. 4. 3; N. 2. 6. 6; 10. 5; 20. 5; F. 1. 21, 24.

10. Here John gives his answer, thus far partially avoided, to the question of why only a few reach this union with God, the goal of life. The vessel must be a strong one in order to hold a full measure of God's self-communication. God wants to give more; humans tend to balk at the strengthening process. The strengthening comes not through the trials in themselves but through the growth of the theological virtues.

We can answer them with Jeremiah's words: *If you have grown weary running with footmen, how will you contend with horses? And if you have had quiet in the land of peace, what will you do in the swelling of the Jordan?* [Jer. 12:5]. This is like saying: If by the common trials (on foot) that form part of human life, it seemed to you that you were running because there were so many, and you took such short steps, how will you keep up with the horse's stride, which signifies more than ordinary trials for which human strength and speed is not enough? And if you have not wanted to forego the peace and pleasure of your earth, which is your sensuality, or contradict it in anything or stir up a war, I do not know how you will desire to enter the impetuous waters of spiritual tribulations and trials that are deeper.

28. O souls who in spiritual matters desire to walk in security and consolation! If you but knew how much it behooves you to suffer in order to reach this security and consolation, and how without suffering you cannot attain to your desire but rather turn back, in no way would you look for comfort either from God or from creatures. You would instead carry the cross and, placed on it, desire to drink the pure gall and vinegar. You would consider it good fortune that, dying to this world and to yourselves, you would live to God in the delights of the spirit, and patiently and faithfully suffering exterior trials, which are small, you would merit that God fix his eyes on you and purge you more profoundly through deeper spiritual trials in order to give you more interior blessings.[11]

Those to whom God grants so signal a favor as to tempt them more interiorly must have performed many services for him, have had admirable patience and constancy for his sake, and in their life and works have been very acceptable to him. For he tries them in this way so as to make them advance in gifts and merits, as he did with holy Tobit to whom St. Raphael said: *Since you were acceptable to God, he favored you by sending you temptation that he might try you more in order to exalt you more* [Tb. 12:13]. After that temptation, *all the rest of his life was in joy,* as Sacred Scripture says [Tb. 14:4]. We also see in the life of holy Job that once God accepted his works in the sight of the good and evil spirits, he immediately favored him by sending those great trials so that subsequently he could extol him much more. And this he did, multiplying his goods, both spiritual and temporal [Jb. 1-2; 42:10, 12].

29. God acts similarly with those he wishes to lead on by means of what is most beneficial for them. He allows them to be tempted in order to elevate them as high as possible, that is, to union with divine wisdom,

---

11. These are nothing but the exigencies of following Christ and sharing in the mystery of his cross; cf. A. 2. 7 where John enlarges on this theme.

which, as David says, *is silver examined in the fire, tried in the earth*—that is, of our flesh—*and purged seven times,* which is all the purgation possible [Ps. 12:6]. There is no reason to be detained any longer in order to describe the nature of each of these seven purgations required to attain wisdom, or how the seven degrees of love correspond to them.[12] To the soul this wisdom is still like the silver of which David speaks, however great may be the union; but in the other life it will be like gold to it.

30. People, then, should live with great patience and constancy in all the tribulations and trials God places on them, whether they be exterior or interior, spiritual or bodily, great or small, and they should accept them all as from God's hand as a good remedy and not flee from them, for they bring health. In this matter let them take the counsel of the Wise Man: *If the spirit of him who has power descends upon you, do not abandon your place* (the place and site of your probation, which is the trial he sends you), *for the cure will make great sins cease* [Eccl. 10:4]; that is, it will cut of the roots of your sins and imperfections—your evil habits. The combat of trials, distress, and temptations deadens the evil and imperfect habits of the soul and purifies and strengthens it. People should hold in esteem the interior and exterior trials God sends them, realizing that there are few who merit to be brought to perfection through suffering and to undergo trials for the sake of so high a state.

31. Returning to our explanation,[13] the soul knows in this state that everything has ended well and that now *sicut tenebrae ejus ita et lumen ejus* [Ps. 139:12],[14] and that, as it was a sharer of tribulations, it is now a sharer of consolations and of the kingdom [2 Cor. 1:7]. For God repays the interior and exterior trials very well with divine goods for the soul and body, so there is not a trial that does not have a corresponding and considerable reward. It proclaims this by saying with full satisfaction: "and pays every debt." It thanks God in this verse for having withdrawn it from trials, as David also did in his psalm: *What great tribulations you have shown me, many and difficult, and you have freed me from them all, and have brought me back again from the abyss of the earth. You have multiplied your magnificence and turning to me you have comforted me* [Ps. 71:20-21].

Before attaining to this state, the soul was like Mordecai who sat at the gates of the palace, wept in the square of Susan over the danger of his life, wore sackcloth, and was unwilling to receive a garment from Queen Esther [Est. 4:1-2, 4] because he had not obtained any reward for the services he had rendered the king or for his fidelity in defending the

---

12. Cf. C. 26. 3.

13. Ending the digression begun in no. 24, John returns to his explanation of the verse, summing up in this number what was said in no. 23.

14. "As is its darkness, so is its light."

king's honor and life [Est. 6:3]. One day, just as with Mordecai, the soul
is repaid for all its trials and services [Est. 6:10-11], and not only made to
enter the palace and stand, clothed in royal garments, before the king,
but also accorded the royal crown, scepter, and throne, and possession
of the royal ring, so it might do anything it likes and omit anything it does
not like in the kingdom of its Bridegroom [Est. 8: 1-2, 15]. Those who are
in this state obtain everything they desire. Thus they are not merely paid,
but even the Judeans, their enemies, the inordinate appetites, are dead,
for these were eliminating the spiritual life in which it now lives through
its faculties and appetites. Hence it subsequently says:

in killing you changed death to life.

32. For death is nothing else than the privation of life, because when
life comes no vestige of death remains. Spiritually speaking, there are two
kinds of life:

One is beatific, consisting in the vision of God, which must be attained
by natural death, as St. Paul says: *We know that if this our clay house is
dissolved, we have a dwelling place of God in heaven* [2 Cor. 5:1].

The other is the perfect spiritual life, the possession of God through
union of love. This is acquired through complete mortification of all the
vices and appetites and of one's own nature. Until this is achieved one
cannot reach the perfection of the spiritual life of union with God, as the
Apostle also declares in these words: *If you live according to the flesh you shall
die; yet if with the spirit you mortify the deeds of the flesh you shall live* [Rom. 8:13].

33. Let it be known that what the soul calls death is all that goes to make
up the old self: the entire engagement of the faculties (memory, intellect,
and will) in the things of the world, and the indulgence of the appetites
in the pleasures of creatures. All this is the activity of the old life, which
is the death of the new spiritual life. The soul is unable to live perfectly
in this new life if the old self does not die completely. The Apostle warns:
*Take off the old self and put on the new self who according to God is created in
justice and holiness* [Eph. 4:22-24]. In this new life that the soul lives when
it has arrived at the perfect union with God here being discussed, all the
inclinations and activity of the appetites and faculties—of their own the
operation of death and the privation of the spiritual life—become divine.

34. Since every living being lives by its operations, as the philosophers
say, and the soul's operations are in God though its union with him, it
lives the life of God.[15] Thus it changed its death to life, its animal life to
spiritual life.

The intellect, which before this union understood naturally by the
vigor of its natural light by means of the natural senses, is now moved and

---

15. Cf. Aristotle, *On the soul* 2. 13; Aquinas, *Summa theologiae* 1. 18. 2-4; 2-2. 23. 2.

informed by another higher principle of supernatural divine light, and the senses are bypassed. Accordingly, the intellect becomes divine, because through its union with God's intellect both become one.

And the will, which previously loved in a base and deadly way with only its natural affection, is now changed into the life of divine love, for it loves in a lofty way with divine affection, moved by the strength of the Holy Spirit in which it now lives the life of love. By means of this union God's will and the soul's will are now one.

And the memory, which by itself perceived only the figures and phantasms of creatures, is changed through this union so as to have in its mind the eternal years mentioned by David [Ps. 77:5].

And the natural appetite that only had the ability and strength to relish creatures (which causes death), is changed now so that its taste and savor are divine, and it is moved and satisfied by another principle: the delight of God, in which it is more alive. And because it is united with him, it is no longer anything else than the appetite of God.

Finally all the movements, operations, and inclinations the soul had previously from the principle and strength of its natural life are now in this union dead to what they formerly were, changed into divine movements, and alive to God. For the soul, like a true daughter of God, is moved in all by the Spirit of God, as St. Paul teaches in saying that those who are moved by the Spirit of God are children of God himself [Rom. 8:14].[16]

Accordingly, the intellect of this soul is God's intellect; its will is God's will; its memory is the memory of God; and its delight is God's delight; and although the substance of this soul is not the substance of God, since it cannot undergo a substantial conversion into him, it has become God through participation in God, being united to and absorbed in him, as it is in this state. Such a union is wrought in this perfect state of the spiritual life, yet not as perfectly as in the next life. Consequently the soul is dead to all it was in itself, which was death to it, and alive to what God is in himself. Speaking of itself, the soul declares in this verse: "In killing you changed death to life."[17]

The soul can well repeat the words of St. Paul: *I live, now not I, but Christ lives in me* [Gal. 2:20]. The death of this soul is changed to the life of God. We can also apply the words of the Apostle *absorpta est mors in victoria* [1 Cor. 15:54],[18] as well as those the prophet Hosea speaks in the person of God: *O death, I will be your death* [Hos. 13:14]. In other words: Since I am life, being the death of death, death will be absorbed in life.

---

16. Cf. A. 3. 2. 7-16; there John identifies the "children of God" with those who are transformed in God and united to him, and explains how they are habitually moved by God and not by themselves in their operations.

17. Cf. C. 26. 5-10, 13-18; 36. 5.

18. "Death is swallowed up in victory."

35. The soul, then, is absorbed in divine life, withdrawn from its natural appetites and from all that is secular and temporal; it is brought into the king's cellars where it rejoices in its Beloved, remembering his breasts more than wine, saying: *Although I am dark I am beautiful, daughters of Jerusalem* [Sg. 1:4-5], for my natural black color was changed into the beauty of the heavenly king.

36. In this state of life so perfect, the soul always walks in festivity, inwardly and outwardly, and it frequently bears on its spiritual tongue a new song of great jubilation in God, a song always new, enfolded in a gladness and love arising from the knowledge the soul has of its happy state. Sometimes it walks in joy and fruition, expressing in its spirit those words of Job: *My glory will ever be renewed, and I shall multiply my days as a palm tree* [Jb. 29:20,18]. This is equivalent to declaring that God himself, always remaining the same, renews all things. As the Wise Man states: *Being ever one in my glory, I will ever renew my glory* [Wis. 7:27], that is, I will not let it grow old as it was before. And I will multiply my days as the palm tree, that is, raise my merits heavenward as the palm tree lifts its branches.

The merits of a person in this state are usually remarkable in number and quality, and ordinarily such a soul also sings in its spirit all that David proclaims in the psalm that begins: *Exaltabo te, Domine, quoniam suscepisti me,*[19] and especially in the last two lines: *Convertisti planctum meum in gaudium mihi,* and so on; *conscidisti saccum meum, et circumdedisti me laetitia,*[20] to the end that my glory may sing to you and I may not regret; my Lord, God, I will praise you forever [Ps. 30:1,11-12].

There is no need to be amazed that the soul so frequently walks amid this joy, jubilance, fruition, and praise of God. Besides the knowledge it has of the favors received, it feels in this state that God is so solicitous in regaling it with precious, delicate, and enhancing words, and in extolling it by various favors, that he has no one else in the world to favor nor anything else to do, that everything is for the soul alone. With this feeling it proclaims like the bride in the Song of Songs: *Dilectus meus mihi et ego illi* [Sg. 2:16].[21]

---

19. "I will extol you, O Lord, for you have upheld me."
20. "You have turned for me my mourning into joy; you have cut my sackcloth and surrounded me with gladness."
21. "My Beloved belongs to me and I to him."

STANZA 3

O lamps of fire!
in whose splendors
the deep caverns of feeling,
once obscure and blind,
now give forth, so rarely, so exquisitely,
both warmth and light to their Beloved.

Commentary

1. May God be pleased to help me here, for I certainly need his help to explain the deep meaning of this stanza. Readers of this commentary should be attentive for, if they have no experience, it will perhaps seem somewhat obscure and prolix; but if they do have experience, it will perhaps seem clear and pleasant to read.

In this stanza the soul exalts and thanks its Bridegroom for the admirable favors it receives from its union with him. It states that by means of this union it receives abundant and lofty knowledge of God, which is all loving and communicates light and love to its faculties and feeling. These who were once obscure and blind can now receive illumination and the warmth of love, as they do, so as to be able to give forth light and love to the one who illumined them and filled them with love. True lovers are only content when they employ all they are in themselves, all they are worth, have, and receive, in the beloved; and the greater all this is, the more satisfaction they receive in giving it. The soul rejoices on this account because, from the splendors and love it receives, it can shine brightly in the presence of its Bridegroom and give him love. The verse follows:

O lamps of fire!

2. First of all it should be known that lamps possess two properties: They transmit light and give off warmth.

To understand the nature of these lamps and how they shine and burn within the soul, it ought to be known that God in his unique and simple being is all the power and grandeur of his attributes. He is almighty, wise, and good; and he is merciful, just, powerful, loving, and so on; and he is the other infinite attributes and powers of which we have no knowledge. Since he is all of this in his simple being, the soul views distinctly in him, when he is united with it and deigns to disclose this knowledge, all these powers and grandeurs, that is: omnipotence, wisdom, goodness, mercy, and so on. Since each of these attributes is the very being of God in his one and only suppositum, which is the Father, the Son, and the Holy Spirit, and since each one is God himself, who is infinite light or divine fire, we deduce that the soul, like God, gives forth light and warmth through each of these innumerable attributes. Each of these attributes is a lamp that enlightens the soul and gives off the warmth of love.

3. Insofar as the soul receives the knowledge of these attributes in only one act of this union, God himself is for it many lamps together. They illumine and impart warmth to it individually, for it has clear knowledge of each, and through this knowledge is inflamed in love. By means of all the lamps the soul loves each individually, inflamed by each one and by all together because all these attributes are one being, as we said. All these lamps are one lamp, which according to its powers and attributes shines and burns like many lamps. Hence the soul in one act of knowledge of these lamps loves through each one and, in so doing, loves through them all together, bearing in that act the quality of love for each one and from each one, and from all together and for all together.

The splendor of this lamp of God's being, insofar as he is omnipotent, imparts light to the soul and the warmth of love of him according to his omnipotence. God is then to the soul a lamp of omnipotence that shines and bestows all knowledge in respect to this attribute. And the splendor of this lamp of God's being insofar as he is wisdom grants the soul light and the warmth of the love of God according to his wisdom. God is then a lamp of wisdom to it. And the splendor of this lamp insofar as he is goodness imparts to the soul light and the warmth of love according to his goodness. God is then a lamp of goodness to it.

He is also to the soul a lamp of justice, fortitude, and mercy, and of all the other attributes that are represented to it together in God. The light communicated to it from all these attributes together is enveloped in the warmth of love of God by which it loves him because he is all these things. In this communication and manifestation of himself to the soul, which in my opinion is the greatest possible in this life, he is to it innumerable lamps giving forth knowledge and love of himself.

4. Moses beheld these lamps on Mount Sinai where, when God passed by, he prostrated himself on the ground and began to call out and enumerate some of them: *Emperor, Lord, God, merciful, clement, patient, of much compassion, true, who keeps mercy unto thousands, who takes away iniquities and sins, no one is of himself innocent before you* [Ex. 34:6-8]. In this passage it is clear that the greatest attributes and powers that Moses knew there in God were those of God's omnipotence, dominion, deity, mercy, justice, truth, and righteousness; this was the highest knowledge of God. Because love was communicated to him in accord with the knowledge, the delight of love and the fruition he enjoyed there were most sublime.

5. It is noteworthy that the delight received by the soul in the rapture

of love, communicated by the fire of the light of these lamps, is wonderful and immense, for it is as abundant as it would be if it came from many lamps. Each lamp burns in love, and the warmth from each furthers the warmth of the other, and the flame of one, the flame of the other, just as the light of one sheds light on the other, because through each attribute the other is known. Thus all of them are one light and one fire, and each of them is one light and one fire.

Immensely absorbed in delicate flames, subtly wounded with love through each of them, and more wounded by all of them together, more alive in the love of the life of God, the soul perceives clearly that this love is proper to eternal life. Eternal life is the aggregation of all goods,[1] and the soul somehow experiences this here and fully understands the truth of the Bridegroom's assertion in the Song of Songs, that the lamps of love are lamps of fire and of flames [Sg. 8:6]. *You are beautiful in your steps and shoes, prince's daughter* [Sg. 7:1]. Who can relate the magnificence and rareness of your delight and majesty in the admirable splendor and love of your lamps?

6. Sacred Scripture recounts that in times long past one of these lamps went by Abraham and caused him a dark and terrible horror, for the lamp was from the rigorous justice that was to be exercised later on the Canaanites [Gn. 15:12-17]. All these lamps of the knowledge of God illumine you in a friendly and loving way, O enriched soul; how much light and happiness of love will they beget in you, much more than the darkness and horror one lamp produced in Abraham! How remarkable, how advantageous, and how multifaceted will be your delight; in all and from all you receive fruition and love, since God communicates himself to your faculties according to his attributes and powers!

When individuals love and do good to others, they love and do good to them in the measure of their own nature and properties. Thus your Bridegroom, dwelling within you, grants you favors according to his nature. Since he is omnipotent, he omnipotently loves and does good to you; since he is wise, you feel that he loves and does good to you with wisdom; since he is infinitely good, you feel that he loves you with goodness; since he is holy, you feel that with holiness he loves and favors you; since he is just, you feel that in justice he loves and favors you; since he is merciful, mild, and clement, you feel his mercy, mildness, and clemency; since he is a strong, sublime, and delicate being, you feel that his love for you is strong, sublime, and delicate; since he is pure and undefiled, you feel that he loves you in a pure and undefiled way; since he is truth, you feel that he loves you in truthfulness; since he is liberal, you feel that he liberally loves and favors you, without any personal profit,

---

1. This definition is from Boethius, *The Consolation of Philosophy* 3. 2.

only in order to do good to you; since he is the virtue of supreme humility, he loves you with supreme humility and esteem and makes you his equal, gladly revealing himself to you in these ways of knowledge, in this his countenance filled with graces, and telling you in this his union, not without great rejoicing: "I am yours and for you and delighted to be what I am so as to be yours and give myself to you."

7. Who, then, will be able to express your experience, O happy soul, since you know that you are so loved and with such esteem exalted? Your belly, which is your will, is like the bride's, similar to a bundle of wheat, covered and surrounded with lilies [Sg. 7:2]. For while you are enjoying together the grains of the bread of life, the lilies, or virtues, surrounding you provide you with delight. These are the king's daughters mentioned by David, who will delight you with myrrh, aloes, and other aromatic spices [Ps. 45:8-9]; for the knowledge of his graces and virtues, which the Beloved communicates to you, are his daughters. You so overflow with these and are so engulfed in them that you are likewise the well of living waters that flow impetuously from Mount Lebanon [Sg. 4:15], that is, from God.

You were made wonderfully joyful according to the whole harmonious composite of your soul and even your body, converted completely into a paradise divinely irrigated, so the psalmist's affirmation might also be fulfilled in you: *The impetus of the river makes the city of God joyful* [Ps. 46:4].

8. O marvelous thing, that the soul at this time is flooded with divine waters, abounding in them like a plentiful fount overflowing on all sides! Although it is true that this communication under discussion is the light and fire from these lamps of God, yet this fire here is so gentle that, being an immense fire, it is like the waters of life that satisfy the thirst of the spirit with the impetus the spirit desires. Hence these lamps of fire are living waters of the spirit like those that descended on the Apostles [Acts 2:3]; although they were lamps of fire they were clear and pure waters as well. The prophet Ezekiel referred to them in this fashion when he prophesied the coming of the Holy Spirit: *I will pour out upon you,* God says there, *clean waters and will put my spirit in the midst of you* [Ez. 36:25-27]. Although it is fire, it is also water. For this fire is represented by the fire of the sacrifice that Jeremiah hid in the cistern: While it was hidden it was water, and when they drew it out for the sacrifice it was fire [2 Mac. 1:19-23].

Thus the spirit of God, insofar as it is hidden in the veins of the soul, is like soft refreshing water that satisfies the thirst of the spirit; insofar as it is exercised in the sacrifice of loving God, it is like living flames of fire. These flames of fire are the lamps of the act of love and of flames that we ascribed above to the Bridegroom according to the Song of Songs: *Your lamps are lamps of fire and of flames* [Sg. 8:6]. The soul calls them flames here because it not only tastes them like water within itself, but also makes them active, like flames, in the love of God. Since in the communication of the spirit of these lamps, the soul is inflamed and placed in the activity of love, in the act of love, it calls them lamps rather than waters, saying: "O lamps of fire!"

All that can be said of this stanza is less than the reality, for the transformation of the soul in God is indescribable. Everything can be expressed in this statement: The soul becomes God from God through participation in him and in his attributes, which it terms the "lamps of fire."

in whose splendors

9. To understand what these splendors of the lamps are and how the soul is resplendent in them, it should be known that they are the loving knowledge that the lamps of God's attributes give forth from themselves to the soul. United with them in its faculties, the soul is also resplendent like them, transformed in loving splendors.

This illumination from the splendors, in which the soul shines brightly with the warmth of love, is not like that produced by material lamps that through their flames shed light round about them, but like the illumination that is within the very flames, for the soul is within these splendors. As a result it says, "in whose splendors," that is, within the splendors; and it does not merely mean "within" but, as we pointed out, it means transformed in them. The soul is like the air within the flame, enkindled and transformed in the flame, for the flame is nothing but enkindled air. The movements and splendors of the flame are not from the air alone or from the fire of which the flame is composed, but from both air and fire. And the fire causes the air, which it has enkindled, to produce these same movements and splendors.

10. We can consequently understand how the soul with its faculties is illumined within the splendors of God. The movements of these divine flames, which are the flickering and flaring up we have mentioned,[2] are not produced by the soul alone that is transformed in the flames of the Holy Spirit, nor does the Holy Spirit produce them alone, but they are the work of both the soul and him since he moves it in the manner that fire moves the enkindled air. Thus these movements of both God and the soul are not only splendors, but also glorifications of the soul.

These flames and their activity are the happy festivals and games that the Holy Spirit inspires in the soul, as we said in the commentary on verse 2 of the first stanza. It seems in these that he is always wanting to bestow eternal life and transport it completely to perfect glory by bringing it into

2. In 1. 3-4, 8.

himself. All the gifts, first and last, great and small, that God grants to the soul, he always grants in order to lead it to eternal life. In the same way, the flame flickers and flares together with the enkindled air in order to bring the air with itself to the center of its sphere, and it produces all these movements in order to persist in bringing the air nearer itself. As the flame does not carry the air away, because the air is in its own sphere, so too, although these movements of the Holy Spirit are most efficacious in absorbing the soul in sublime glory, they do not do so completely until the time comes for it to depart from the sphere of the air of this carnal life and enter into the center of the spirit of the perfect life in Christ.

11. Let it be known that these motions are motions of the soul more than of God, for God does not move. These glimpses of glory given to the soul are in God stable, perfect, continuous, and constantly serene. Afterward this will also be true of the soul. There will be no change as to more or less and no intrusion of these movements; it will see distinctly how, although here below God seemingly moved within it, he does not in himself move, just as fire does not move when in its center; and it will see how it experienced this movement and flaring of the flame because it was not perfect in glory.

12. By what was said and what we shall now say it will be more plainly understood how excellent the splendors of these lamps are, for by another name they are called "overshadowings." To understand this expression, it should be known that an overshadowing is the equivalent of casting a shadow; and casting a shadow is similar to protecting, favoring, and granting graces. For when a person is covered by a shadow, it is a sign that someone else is nearby to protect and favor. As a result the Angel Gabriel called the conception of the Son of God, that favor granted to the Virgin Mary, an overshadowing of the Holy Spirit: *The Holy Spirit will come upon you and the power of the Most High will overshadow you* [Lk. 1:35]

13. For a clear understanding of the nature of this casting of the shadow of God or these overshadowings of great splendor, which is all the same, it should be observed that everything has and makes a shadow according to its size and its properties. If an object is opaque and dark, it makes a dark shadow; if it is transparent and delicate its shadow is transparent and delicate. Thus the shadow of a dark object amounts to another darkness in the measure of the darkness of the object, and the shadow of something bright amounts to something else that is bright according to the brightness of the object.

14. Since the virtues and attributes of God are enkindled and resplen-

dent lamps, they cannot but touch the soul by their shadows, since, as we said, they are so close to it. These shadows must also be enkindled and resplendent in the measure of the splendor of the lamps that make them, and thus they will be splendors. As a result the shadow that the lamp of God's beauty casts over the soul will be another beauty according to the measure and property of God's beauty; and the shadow that fortitude casts over it will amount to another fortitude commensurate with God's; and the shadow of God's wisdom on it will be another wisdom corresponding to God's wisdom; and so on with the other lamps. To express it better: We have the very wisdom and the very beauty and the very fortitude of God in shadow, because the soul here cannot comprehend God perfectly. Since the shadow is so formed by God's size and properties that it is God himself in shadow, the soul knows well the excellence of God.

15. What, then, will be the shadows of the grandeurs of his virtues and attributes that the Holy Spirit casts on the soul? For he is so close to it that his shadows not only touch but unite it with these grandeurs in their shadows and splendors, so that it understands and enjoys God according to his property and measure in each of the shadows. For it understands and enjoys the divine power in the shadow of omnipotence; and it understands and enjoys the divine wisdom in the shadow of divine wisdom; and it understands and enjoys the infinite goodness in the shadow of infinite goodness that surrounds it, and so on. Finally, it enjoys God's glory in the shadow of his glory. All this occurs in the clear and enkindled shadows of those clear and enkindled lamps. And these lamps are within the one lamp of the undivided and simple being of God, which is actually resplendent in all these ways.[3]

16. Oh, then, what will be the soul's experience in the knowledge and communication of the figure that Ezekiel beheld in the animal with four faces and in the wheel with four wheels [Ez. 1:5, 15]? He saw how it resembled lamps and burning coal [Ez. 1:13]; and he beheld the wheel, which is God's wisdom, full of eyes within and without, which represent the divine knowledge and the splendors of its powers [Ez. 1:18]; and he heard in his spirit the sound it made in passing, which was like the sound

---

3. The scholastics spoke of knowing God by way of negation and by way of eminence. Here the mystical understanding resembles the knowing of God by way of eminence in which everything that can be considered a perfection pure and simple, without trace of imperfection, is attributed to God in an eminent degree. But God is not a collection of parts; in him all attributes are his being and not simply attached to it as with humans. For an example of mystical understanding resembling the way of negation, cf. C. 7. 9.

of a multitude, an army, which signifies God's countless grandeurs, which the soul knows distinctly here through the sound of his passing by it only once [Ez. 1:24]; and finally the prophet enjoyed that sound of the beating of its wings, which he asserted was like the sound of many waters and of the most high God, meaning here the force of the divine waters [Ez. 1:24]. These waters assail the soul by the fluttering of the Holy Spirit in the flame of love, gladdening it so it enjoys God's glory in likeness and shadow. For this prophet also said that the vision of that animal and wheel was a likeness of the Lord's glory [Ez. 1:28].

Who can express how elevated this happy soul feels here, how exalted, how much admired in holy beauty? Conscious of being so abundantly assailed by the waters of these divine splendors, it realizes that the eternal Father has generously granted it the upper and lower watery land, as did Achsah's father in response to her sigh [Jos. 15:17-19]. For these waters irrigate both the soul and the body, that is, the higher and lower parts of the soul.

17. O wonderful excellence of God! Since the lamps of the divine attributes are one simple being and are enjoyed only in him, they are seen and enjoyed distinctly, each one as enkindled as the other and each substantially the other. O abyss of delights! You are so much more abundant the more your riches are concentrated in the infinite unity and simplicity of your unique being, where one attribute is so known and enjoyed as not to hinder the perfect knowledge and enjoyment of the other; rather, each grace and virtue within you is a light for each of your other grandeurs. By your purity, O divine Wisdom, many things are beheld in you through one. For you are the deposit of the Father's treasures, the splendor of the eternal light, the unspotted mirror and image of his goodness [Wis. 7:26], in whose splendors

the deep caverns of feeling,

18. These caverns are the soul's faculties: memory, intellect, and will. They are as deep as the boundless goods of which they are capable since anything less than the infinite fails to fill them. From what they suffer when they are empty, we can gain some knowledge of their enjoyment and delight when they are filled with God, since one contrary sheds light on the other.

In the first place, it is noteworthy that when these caverns of the faculties are not emptied, purged, and cleansed of every affection for creatures, they do not feel the vast emptiness of their deep capacity. Any little thing that adheres to them in this life is sufficient to so burden and bewitch them that they do not perceive the harm or note the lack of their immense goods, or know their own capacity.

It is an amazing thing that the least of these goods is enough so to encumber these faculties, capable of infinite goods, that they cannot receive these infinite goods until they are completely empty, as we shall see. Yet when these caverns are empty and pure, the thirst, hunger, and yearning of the spiritual feeling is intolerable. Since these caverns have deep stomachs, they suffer profoundly; for the food they lack, which as I say is God, is also profound.

And this feeling that is so intense commonly occurs toward the end of the illumination and purification, just before the attainment of union, where a person is then satisfied. Since the spiritual appetite is emptied and purged of every creature and affection for creatures, and since it has lost its natural quality and is adapted to the divine, and since its void is disposed and the divine is not communicated to it in union with God, the pain of this void and the thirst are worse than death, especially when a divine ray appears vaguely as though through some crevices and is not communicated to the soul. These are the ones who suffer with impatient love, for they cannot remain long without either receiving or dying.[4]

19. In regard to the first cavern—the intellect—its void is a thirst for God. This thirst is so intense when the intellect is disposed that David compares it to the thirst of the hart. Such thirst, they say, is so vehement that David could find none greater for his comparison: *As the hart pants for the fountain of waters, so does my soul long for you, O God* [Ps. 42:2]. This thirst is for the waters of God's wisdom, the object of the intellect.

20. The second cavern is the will, and its void is a hunger for God so intense that it makes the soul faint, as David also affirms: *My soul longs and faints for the courts of the Lord* [Ps. 84:2]. This hunger is for the perfection of love after which the soul aims.

21. The third cavern is the memory, and its void is a yearning and melting away of the soul for the possession of God, as Jeremiah notes: *Memoria memor ero et tabescet in me anima mea,* that is: *With the memory I will be mindful and will remember him often, and my soul will melt within me. Thinking these things over in my heart I shall live in the hope of God* [Lam. 3:20-21].

22. The capacity of these caverns is deep because the object of this capacity, namely God, is profound and infinite. Thus in a certain fashion their capacity is infinite, their thirst is infinite, their hunger is also deep and infinite, and their languishing and suffering are infinite death.

---

4. This situation is characteristic of the purification experienced in the dark night of the spirit within the stage of spiritual betrothal as explained in *The Dark Night* and *The Spiritual Canticle.*

Although the suffering is not as intense as is the suffering of the next life, yet the soul is a living image of that infinite privation, since it is in a certain way disposed to receive its plenitude. This suffering, however, is of another quality because it lies within the recesses of the will's love; and love is not what alleviates the pain, since the greater the love, so much more impatient are such persons for the possession of God, for whom they hope at times with intense longing.

23. Yet—may the Lord help me—since it is true that when the soul desires God fully, it then possesses him whom it loves, as St. Gregory affirms in commenting on St. John,[5] how does it suffer for want of what it already possesses? In the desire that St. Peter says the angels have for the vision of the Son of God [1 Pt. 1:12] there is no pain or anxiety because they already possess him. Thus it seems that the more the soul desires God the more it possesses him, and the possession of God delights and satisfies it. Similarly the angels, in satisfying their desire, delight in possession, for their spirit is ever being filled by the object of their desire without the disgust of being satiated. Since there is no disgust, they are always desiring; and they do not suffer, for they have possession. As a result it seems that the greater the soul's desire, the greater will be its satisfaction and delight rather than its suffering and pain.

24. In this matter it is worth noting the difference between the possession of God through grace in itself and the possession of him through union, for one lies in loving and the other lies also in communicating. The difference resembles that between betrothal and marriage.

In betrothal there is only a mutual agreement and willingness between the two, and the bridegroom graciously gives jewels and ornaments to his betrothed. But in marriage there is also a communication and union between the persons. Although the bridegroom sometimes visits the bride in the betrothal and brings her presents, as we said, there is no union of persons, nor does this fall within the scope of betrothal.

Likewise, when the soul has reached such purity in itself and its faculties that the will is very pure and purged of other alien satisfactions and appetites in the inferior and superior parts, and has rendered its "yes" to God concerning all of this, since now God's will and the soul's are one through their own free consent, then the soul has attained possession of God insofar as this is possible by way of the will and grace. And this means that in the "yes" of the soul, God has given the true and complete "yes" of his grace.

---

5. *Homilia 30 in Evangelium,* in Migne, PL 76 1220.

25. This is a high state of spiritual betrothal between the soul and the Word, in which the Bridegroom favors it and frequently pays it loving visits wherein it receives wonderful delight. Yet these delights are not comparable to those of marriage, for these are preparations for the union of marriage. Although it is true that this betrothal occurs in the soul that is greatly purified of every affection for creatures—for the spiritual betrothal is not wrought until this comes to pass—the soul still needs other positive preparations from God. It needs his visits and gifts by which he purifies, beautifies, and refines it further so it might be suitably prepared for so lofty a union.

This preparation takes time, for some more than for others, since God carries out this work according to the mode of the soul.[6] This is typified in those young maidens chosen by King Ahasuerus. Although he had already brought them out of their countries and the house of their fathers, they had still to wait a year, even in the palace, before approaching the king's bed. For half of the year they were prepared by means of certain ointments of myrrh and other spices, and for the remaining half by other, more precious ointments. After this they went to the king's bed [Est. 2:3, 12].

26. During this time of the betrothal and expectation of marriage and the anointings of the Holy Spirit, when the ointments preparatory for union with God are more sublime, the anxieties of the caverns of the soul are usually extreme and delicate. Since these ointments are a more proximate preparation for union with God (for they are more closely related to God and consequently lure the soul and make it relish him more delicately), the desire for him becomes more refined and profound—and the desire for God is the preparation for union with him.

27. Oh, what an excellent place this is to advise souls on whom God bestows these delicate unctions to watch what they are doing, and into whose hands they are committing themselves, that they might not turn back! This does not pertain to our subject, yet the compassion and grief that come to my heart on seeing souls fall back (not only by hindering the anointings so there can be no progress from them but even by losing their effects) is so great that I do not think it improper here to advise them about what they should do to avoid such harm. Even though we may be somewhat detained before returning to our subject, for I plan to return to it soon, this will all help toward understanding the property of these caverns. Since this advice is very necessary, not only for all those who

---

6. This basic principle is spelled out in A. 2. 17. 1-8; cf. also C. 23.

advance so prosperously but also for all others who seek their Beloved, I want to speak of it.[7]

28. In the first place it should be known that if anyone is seeking God, the Beloved is seeking that person much more. And if a soul directs to God its loving desires, which are as fragrant to him as the pillar of smoke rising from the aromatic spices of myrrh and incense [Sg. 3:6], God sends it the fragrance of his ointments by which he draws it and makes it run after him [Sg. 1:3], and these are his divine inspirations and touches. As often as these inspirations and touches are his, they are always bound and regulated by the perfection of his law and of faith. It is by means of this perfection that a person must always draw closer to him. Thus it should be understood that the desire for himself that God grants in all his favors of unguents and fragrant anointings is a preparation for other more precious and delicate ointments, made more according to the quality of God, until the soul is so delicately and purely prepared that it merits union with him and substantial transformation in all its faculties.

29. The soul, then, should advert that God is the principal agent in this matter. He acts as guide of the blind, leading it by the hand to the place it knows not how to reach (to supernatural things of which neither its intellect nor will nor memory can know the nature). It should use all its principal care in watching so as not to place any obstacle in the way of God, its guide on this road ordained for it by him according to the perfection of his law and of the faith, as we said.

It can cause this obstacle by allowing itself to be led by another blind guide. There are three blind guides who can draw it off the road: the spiritual director, the devil, and the soul itself. So the soul may understand how this happens, we will briefly discuss each of these blind guides.

30. As regards the first, it is very important that individuals, desiring to advance in recollection and perfection, take care into whose hands they entrust themselves, for the disciple will become like the master, and as is the father so will be the son. Let them realize that for this journey,

---

7. With this digression (nos. 27-67) within this present one on the difference between spiritual betrothal and spiritual marriage, John speaks once more (cf. A. 2. 12-15; N. 1. 8-11) of the transition from meditation to contemplation and of the development of contemplation. This section is divided into four parts: God is the principal agent (nos. 28-29); the spiritual director may be a help or a hindrance (nos. 30-62); the devil seeks to disturb the recollection (nos. 63-65); the soul may be its own disturbance (nos. 66-67). The main focus is on spiritual directors, John inveighing against those who do not respect God's ways or the freedom of souls to follow them.

especially its most sublime parts (and even for the intermediate parts), they will hardly find a guide accomplished as to all their needs, for besides being learned and discreet, a director should have experience. Although the foundation for guiding a soul to spirit is knowledge and discretion, directors will not succeed in leading the soul onward in it when God bestows it, nor will they even understand it if they have no experience of what true and pure spirit is.

31. As a result, many spiritual masters cause great harm to a number of souls; not understanding the ways and properties of the spirit, they ordinarily make souls lose the unction of these delicate ointments with which the Holy Spirit anoints and prepares them for himself, and they instruct them in other inferior ways, serviceable only to beginners, which they themselves have used or read of somewhere. Knowing no more than what pertains to beginners—and please God they would even know this much—they do not wish to permit souls to pass beyond these beginnings and these discursive and imaginative ways (even though God may desire to lead them on). Thus they do not let them go beyond their natural capacity, but through their natural capacity souls cannot make much progress.

32. For a better understanding of this beginner's stage, it should be known that the practice of beginners is to meditate and make acts and discursive reflection with the imagination. Individuals in this state should be given matter for meditation and discursive reflection, and they should by themselves make interior acts and profit in spiritual things from the delight and satisfaction of the senses. For by being fed with the relish of spiritual things, the appetite is torn away from sensual things and weakened in regard to the things of the world.

But when the appetite has been fed somewhat and has become in a certain fashion accustomed to spiritual things and acquired some fortitude and constancy, God begins to wean the soul, as they say, and place it in the state of contemplation. This occurs in some persons after a very short time, especially with religious; in denying the things of the world more quickly, they accommodate their senses and appetites to God and pass on to the spirit in their activity, God thus working in them. This happens when the soul's discursive acts and meditations cease, as well as its initial sensible satisfaction and fervor, and it is unable to practice discursive meditation as before or find any support for the senses. The sensory part is left in dryness because its riches are transferred to the spirit, which does not pertain to the senses.

Since the soul cannot function naturally except by means of the senses, it is God who in this state is the agent; the soul is the receiver. The soul conducts itself only as the receiver and as one in whom something is being done; God is the giver and the one who works in it, by according spiritual goods in contemplation (which is knowledge and love together, that is, loving knowledge), without the soul's natural acts and discursive reflections, for it can no longer engage in these acts as before.

33. Hence persons at this time should be guided in a manner entirely contrary to the former. If, prior to this, directors suggested matter for meditation and these individuals meditated, now this matter should instead be withheld and they should not meditate. For, as I say, they are unable to do so even though they may want to; and were they to try they would be distracted instead of recollected. If previously they sought satisfaction, love, and devotion, and found it, now they should neither desire nor seek it; for not only do they fail to procure it through their own diligence but, on the contrary, they procure dryness. Through the activity they desire to carry on with the senses, they divert themselves from the peaceful and quiet good secretly being given to their spirit. In losing one good they do not gain the other, for these goods are no longer accorded through the senses as before.

Therefore directors should not impose meditation on persons in this state, nor should they oblige them to make acts or strive for satisfaction and fervor. Such activity would place an obstacle in the path of the principal agent who, as I say, is God, who secretly and quietly inserts in the soul loving wisdom and knowledge, without specified acts; although sometimes he makes specific ones in the soul for a certain length of time. Thus individuals also should proceed only with a loving attention to God, without making specific acts. They should conduct themselves passively, as we have said, without efforts of their own but with the simple, loving awareness, as when opening one's eyes with loving attention.

34. Since God, then, as the giver communes with individuals through a simple, loving knowledge, they also, as the receivers, commune with God through a simple and loving knowledge or attention, so knowledge is thus joined with knowledge and love with love. The receiver should act according to the mode of what is received, and not otherwise, in order to receive and keep it in the way it is given. For as the philosophers say: Whatever is received is received according to the mode of the receiver.[8]

It is obvious that if persons do not lay aside their natural active mode, they will not receive that good except in a natural mode; thus they will not receive it, but will remain only with their natural act. For the supernatural does not fit into the natural mode, nor does it have anything to do with it. If individuals should, then, desire to act on their own through an attitude different from the passive loving attention we mentioned, in

8. See N. 1. 4. 2 and note.

which they would remain very passive and tranquil without making any act unless God would unite himself with them in some act, they would utterly hinder the goods God communicates supernaturally to them in the loving knowledge. This loving knowledge is communicated in the beginning through the exercise of interior purgation, in which the individual suffers, as we said, and afterward in the delight of love.[9]

If as I say—and it is true—this loving knowledge is received passively in the soul according to the supernatural mode of God, and not according to the natural mode of the soul, individuals, if they want to receive it, should be very annihilated in their natural operations, unhampered, idle, quiet, peaceful, and serene, according to the mode of God. The more the air is cleansed of vapors and the quieter and more simple it is, the more the sun illumines and warms it. A person should not bear attachment to anything, neither to the practice of meditation nor to any savor, whether sensory or spiritual, nor to any other apprehensions. Individuals should be very free and annihilated regarding all things, because any thought or discursive reflection or satisfaction on which they may want to lean would impede and disquiet them and make noise in the profound silence of their senses and their spirit, which they possess for the sake of this deep and delicate listening. God speaks to the heart in this solitude, which he mentioned in Hosea [Hos. 2:14], in supreme peace and tranquility while the soul listens, like David, to what the Lord God speaks to it [Ps. 85:8], for he speaks this peace in this solitude.

35. When it happens, therefore, that souls are conscious in this manner of being placed in solitude and in the state of listening, they should even forget the practice of loving attentiveness I mentioned so as to remain free for what the Lord then desires of them. They should make use of that loving awareness only when they do not feel themselves placed in this solitude or inner idleness or oblivion or spiritual listening. So they may recognize it, it always comes to pass with a certain peace and calm and inward absorption.

36. Once individuals have begun to enter this simple and idle state of contemplation that comes about when they can no longer meditate, they should not at any time or season engage in meditations or look for support in spiritual savor or satisfaction, but stand upright on their own feet with their spirit completely detached from everything, as Habakkuk declared he was obliged to do in order to hear what God spoke to him: *I will stand on my watch and fix my foot upon my fortress, and I will contemplate what is said to me* [Hb. 2:1]. This is like saying: I will raise my mind above

---

9. In 1. 18-26; 2. 24-30. In this number we see how John, for the most part, equates the natural with the active and the supernatural with the passive.

all activity and knowledge belonging to my senses and what they can retain, leaving all below, and will fix the foot of the fortress (my faculties), not allowing these faculties to advance a step as regards their own operation that they may receive through contemplation what God communicates to me; for we have already asserted that pure contemplation lies in receiving.

37. It is impossible for this highest wisdom and language of God, which is contemplation, to be received in anything less than a spirit that is silent and detached from discursive knowledge and gratification. Isaiah speaks of it in these words: *Whom will he teach knowledge and whom will God make understand the hearing?* And Isaiah replies: *Those that are weaned from the milk* (that is from satisfaction) *and drawn away from the breasts* (from particular knowledge and apprehensions) [Is. 28:9].

38. Wipe away, O spiritual soul, the dust, hairs, and stains, and cleanse your eye; and the bright sun will illumine you, and you will see clearly. Pacify the soul, draw it out, and liberate it from the yoke and slavery of its own weak operation, which is the captivity of Egypt (amounting to not much more than gathering straws for baking bricks) [Ex. 5:7-19]. And, O spiritual master, guide it to the land of promise flowing with milk and honey [Ex. 3:8, 17]. Behold that for this holy liberty and idleness of the children of God, God calls the soul to the desert, where it journeys festively clothed and adorned with gold and silver jewels, since it has now left Egypt and been despoiled of its riches, which is the sensory part [Ex. 32:2-3]. Not only this, but the Egyptians are drowned in the sea of contemplation [Ex. 14:27-28], where the Egyptian of sense, not finding a foothold or some support, drowns and thereby frees the child of God, which is the spirit that has emerged from the narrow limits and slavery of the operation of the senses, from its little understanding, its base feeling, and its poor way of loving and being satisfied, that God may give it the sweet manna. Although this manna has all these tastes and savors [Wis. 16:20] with which you desire the soul to be occupied through its own labor, nonetheless, since it is so delicate it melts in one's mouth, it will not be tasted if mingled with some other taste or some other thing.

When a soul approaches this state, strive that it become detached from all satisfaction, relish, pleasure, and spiritual meditations, and do not disquiet it with cares and solicitude about heavenly things or, still less, earthly things. Bring it to as complete a withdrawal and solitude as possible, for the more solitude it obtains and the nearer it approaches this idle tranquility the more abundantly will the spirit of divine wisdom be infused into its soul. This wisdom is loving, tranquil, solitary, peaceful, mild, and an inebriator of the spirit, by which the soul feels tenderly and gently wounded and carried away, without knowing by whom or from where or how. The reason is that this wisdom is communicated without the soul's own activity.

39. And a little of this that God works in the soul in this holy idleness and solitude is an inestimable good, a good much greater at times than a soul or its director can imagine. And although one is not always so clearly conscious of it, it will in due time shed its light. The least that a person can manage to feel is a withdrawal and an estrangement as to all things, sometimes more than at other times, accompanied by an inclination toward solitude and a weariness with all creatures and with the world, in the gentle breathing of love and life in the spirit. Everything not included in this estrangement becomes distasteful, for, as they say, once the spirit has tasted, all flesh becomes bitter.[10]

40. Yet the blessings this silent communication and contemplation impress on the soul, without its then experiencing them, are inestimable, as I say. They are most hidden unctions of the Holy Spirit and hence most delicate; they secretly fill the soul with spiritual riches, gifts, and graces. Since it is God who grants them, he does so in no other manner than as God.

41. Because of the refined quality and purity of these delicate and sublime anointings and shadings of the Holy Spirit, neither the soul nor its director understands them; only he who bestows them in order to be more pleased with the soul comprehends them. Individuals can with the greatest ease disturb and hinder these anointings by no more than the least act they may desire of their memory, intellect, or will; or by making use of their senses, appetite, and knowledge, or their own satisfaction and pleasure. This is all seriously harmful and a great sorrow and pity.

42. Oh, it is a serious and regrettable situation that even though this interfering with these holy unctions seems to cause hardly any damage at all, the harm done is greater and worthy of deeper sorrow and compassion then the harm done in the disturbance and ruin of many other ordinary souls who are not in the position to receive such sublime adornment and shadings! Were a portrait of extremely delicate workmanship touched over with dull and harsh colors by an unpolished hand, the destruction would be worse, more noticeable, and a greater pity than if many other portraits of less artistry were effaced. Who will succeed in repairing that delicate painting of the Holy Spirit once it is marred by a coarse hand?

---

10. Cf. C. 16. 5 and note.

43. Although this damage is beyond anything imaginable, it is so common and frequent that scarcely any spiritual director will be found who does not cause it in souls God is beginning to recollect in this manner of contemplation. How often is God anointing a contemplative soul with some very delicate unguent of loving knowledge, serene, peaceful, solitary, and far withdrawn from the senses and what is imaginable, as a result of which it cannot meditate or reflect on anything, or enjoy anything heavenly or earthly (since God has engaged it in that lonely idleness and given it the inclination to solitude), when a spiritual director will happen along who, like a blacksmith, knows no more than how to hammer and pound with the faculties. Since hammering with the faculties is this director's only teaching, and he knows no more than how to meditate, he will say: "Come, now, lay aside these rest periods, which amount to idleness and a waste of time; take and meditate and make interior acts, for it is necessary that you do your part; this other method is the way of illusions[11] and typical of fools."

44. Thus, not understanding the stages of prayer or the ways of the spirit, these directors are not aware that those acts they say the soul should make, and the discursive reflection they want it to practice, have already been accomplished. The soul has already reached the negation and silence of the senses and of meditation, and has come to the way of the spirit that is contemplation. In contemplation the activity of the senses and of discursive reflection terminates, and God alone is the agent who then speaks secretly to the solitary and silent soul. These directors fail to observe that if they want to make souls who in this fashion have attained to spirit still walk the path of the senses, they will cause them to turn back and become distracted. If those who have reached the end of their journey continue to walk in order to reach the end, they will necessarily move away from that end, besides doing something ridiculous.

Once individuals, through the activity of their faculties, have reached the quiet recollection that every spiritual person pursues, in which the functioning of these faculties ceases, it would not merely be useless for them to repeat the acts of these same faculties in order to reach this recollection, but it would be harmful, for in abandoning the recollection already possessed they would become distracted.

45. Since these spiritual masters do not understand recollection and spiritual solitude or its properties (in which solitude God applies these sublime unctions to the soul), they superpose or interpose anointings from a lower spiritual exercise, which is the soul's activity, as we said.

---

11. The Spanish word *alumbramientos* suggests an accusation of illusions typical of those of the alumbrados (a sect accused of illuminism or quietism).

There is as much difference between what the soul does itself and what it receives from God as there is between a human work and a divine work, between the natural and the supernatural. In one, God works supernaturally in the soul; in the other, only the soul works naturally. What is worse is that by the activity of their natural operations individuals lose inner solitude and recollection and, consequently, the sublime image God was painting within them. Thus all their efforts are like hammering the horseshoe instead of the nail; on the one hand they do harm, and on the other hand they receive no profit.

46. These directors should reflect that they themselves are not the chief agent, guide, and mover of souls in this matter, but the principal guide is the Holy Spirit, who is never neglectful of souls, and they themselves are instruments for directing these souls to perfection through faith and the law of God, according to the spirit given by God to each one.

Thus the whole concern of directors should not be to accommodate souls to their own method and condition, but they should observe the road along which God is leading one; if they do not recognize it, they should leave the soul alone and not bother it. And in harmony with the path and spirit along which God leads a soul, the spiritual director should strive to conduct it into greater solitude, tranquility, and freedom of spirit. He should give it latitude so that when God introduces it into this solitude it does not bind its corporeal or spiritual faculties to some particular object, interior or exterior, and does not become anxious or afflicted with the thought that nothing is being done. Even though the soul is not then doing anything, God is doing something in it.

Directors should strive to disencumber the soul and bring it into solitude and idleness so it may not be tied to any particular knowledge, earthly or heavenly, or to any covetousness for some satisfaction or pleasure, or to any other apprehension; and in such a way that it may be empty through the pure negation of every creature, and placed in spiritual poverty. This is what the soul must do of itself, as the Son of God counsels: *Whoever does not renounce all possessions cannot be my disciple* [Lk. 14:33]. This counsel refers not only to the renunciation according to the will of all corporeal and temporal things, but also to the dispossession of spiritual things, which includes spiritual poverty, to which the Son of God ascribes beatitude [Mt. 5:3].

When the soul frees itself of all things and attains to emptiness and dispossession concerning them, which is equivalent to what it can do of itself, it is impossible that God fail to do his part by communicating himself to it, at least silently and secretly. It is more impossible than it would be for the sun not to shine on clear and uncluttered ground. As the sun rises in the morning and shines on your house so that its light may enter if you open the shutters, so God, who in watching over Israel does not doze [Ps. 121:4] or, still less, sleep, will enter the soul that is empty, and fill it with divine goods.

47. God, like the sun, stands above souls ready to communicate himself. Let directors be content with disposing them for this according to evangelical perfection, which lies in nakedness and emptiness of sense and spirit; and let them not desire to go any further than this in building, since that function belongs only to the Father of lights from whom descends every good and perfect gift [Jas. 1:17]. *If the Lord,* as David says, *does not build the house, in vain do its builders labor* [Ps. 127:1]. And since he is the supernatural artificer, he will construct supernaturally in each soul the edifice he desires, if you, director, will prepare it by striving to annihilate it in its natural operations and affections, which have neither the ability nor strength to build the supernatural edifice. The natural operations and affections at this time impede rather than help. It is your duty to prepare the soul, and God's office, as the Wise Man says, is to direct its path [Prv. 16:9], that is, toward supernatural goods, through modes and ways understandable to neither you nor the soul.

Do not say, therefore: "The soul does not advance, because it is not doing anything."[12] For if it is true that it is not doing anything, I will prove to you that it is accomplishing a great deal by doing nothing. If the intellect empties itself of particular knowledge, natural or spiritual, it advances; and the freer it becomes of particular knowledge and acts of understanding, the further it advances in its journey toward the supreme, supernatural Good.

48. "Or," you will say, "it doesn't understand anything in particular, and thus will be unable to make progress." I reply that, quite the contrary, if it would have particular knowledge it would not advance. The reason is that God transcends the intellect and is incomprehensible and inaccessible to it. Hence while the intellect is understanding, it is not approaching God but withdrawing from him. It must withdraw from itself and from its knowledge so as to journey to God in faith, by believing and not understanding. In this way it reaches perfection, because it is joined to God by faith and not by any other means, and it reaches God more by not understanding than by understanding.

Do not be disturbed on this account; if the intellect does not turn back (which it would do if it were to desire to be occupied with particular knowledge and other discursive reflections), but desires to remain in idleness, it advances. It thereby empties itself of everything comprehensible to it, because none of that is God; as we have said, God does not fit

---

12. John here puts three possible objections in the mouth of the spiritual director.

in an occupied heart. In this matter of striving for perfection, not to turn back is to go forward; and the intellect goes forward by establishing itself more in faith. Thus it advances by darkening itself, for faith is darkness to the intellect. Since the intellect cannot understand the nature of God, it must journey in surrender to him rather than by understanding, and thus it advances by not understanding. For its own well-being, the intellect should be doing what you condemn; that is, it should avoid busying itself with particular knowledge, for it cannot reach God through this knowledge, which would rather hinder it in its advance toward him.

49. "Or," you will say, "when the intellect does not understand particular things, the will is idle and does not love (something that must always be avoided on the spiritual road), because the will can only love what the intellect understands." This is true, especially in the natural operations and acts of the soul in which the will does not love except what the intellect understands distinctly. But in the contemplation we are discussing (by which God infuses himself into the soul), particular knowledge as well as acts made by the soul are unnecessary. The reason for this is that God in one act is communicating light and love together, which is loving supernatural knowledge. We can assert that this knowledge is like light that transmits heat, for that light also enkindles love. This knowledge is general and dark to the intellect because it is contemplative knowledge, which is a ray of darkness for the intellect, as St. Dionysius teaches.[13]

Love is therefore present in the will in the manner that knowledge is present in the intellect. Just as this knowledge infused by God in the intellect is general and dark, devoid of particular understanding, the love in the will is also general, without any clarity arising from particular understanding. Since God is divine light and love in his communication of himself to the soul, he equally informs these two faculties (intellect and will) with knowledge and love. Since God is unintelligible in this life, knowledge of him is dark, as I say, and the love present in the will is fashioned after this knowledge.

Yet sometimes in this delicate communication God wounds and communicates himself to one faculty more than to the other; sometimes more knowledge is experienced than love, and at other times more love than knowledge; and likewise at times all knowledge is felt without any love, or all love without any knowledge.

This is why I say that when the soul makes natural acts with the intellect, it cannot love without understanding. But in the acts God produces and infuses in it, as he does in these souls, there is a difference; God can communicate to one faculty and not to the other. He can inflame the will with

---

13. See Pseudo-Dionysius, *The Mystical Theology* 1. 1.

a touch of the warmth of his love even though the intellect does not understand, just as a person can feel warmth from a fire without seeing it.[14]

50. The will often feels enkindled or tenderly moved or captivated without knowing how or understanding anything more particularly than before, since God is ordaining love in it; as the bride declares in the Song of Songs: *The king brought me into the wine cellar and set in order charity in me* [Sg. 2:4].

There is no reason to fear idleness of the will in this situation. If the will stops making acts of love on its own and, in regard to particular knowledge, God makes them in it, inebriating it secretly with infused love either by means of the knowledge of contemplation or without it, as we just said, these acts are much more delightful and meritorious than the acts the soul makes on its own, just as God, who moves it and infuses this love, is much better.

51. God infuses this love in the will when it is empty and detached from other particular, earthly or heavenly pleasures and affections. Take care, then, to empty the will of its affections and detach it from them. If it does not retrogress through the desire for some satisfaction or pleasure, it advances, even though it experiences nothing particular in God, by ascending above all things to him. Although it does not enjoy God very particularly and distinctly, nor love him in so clear an act, it does enjoy him obscurely and secretly in that general infusion more than it does all particular things, for it then sees clearly that nothing satisfies it as much as that solitary quietude. And it loves him above all lovable things, since it has rejected all the gratifications and pleasures of these things and they have become distasteful to it.

One, therefore, should not be disturbed, for the will makes progress if it cannot dwell on the satisfactions and pleasures of particular acts. For by not turning back in the embrace of something sensible, it goes forward to the inaccessible, which is God; and so it is no wonder if it does not feel him.

To journey to God, the will must walk in detachment from every pleasant thing, rather than in attachment to it. It thus carries out well the commandment of love, which is to love God above all things; this cannot be done without nakedness and emptiness concerning them all.

52. Neither should there be any fear because the memory is void of forms and figures. Since God is formless and figureless, the memory

---

14. For other texts on this relationship between knowledge and love on both the natural plane and the supernatural or mystical, cf. N. 2. 12. 7; C. 26. 8.

walks safely when empty of form and figure, and it draws closer to God. The more it leans on the imagination, the farther away it moves from God and the more serious is its danger; for in being what he is—unimaginable—God cannot be grasped by the imagination.

53. These spiritual masters, not understanding souls that tread the path of quiet and solitary contemplation, since they themselves have not reached it and do not know what it is to part with discursive meditation, think these souls are idle. They hinder them and hamper the peace of restful and quiet contemplation that God of his own was according them, by making them walk along the path of meditation and imaginative reflection, and perform interior acts. In doing this, these souls find great repugnance, dryness, and distraction; they want to remain in their holy idleness and quiet and peaceful recollection.

Since the senses find nothing to be attached to, take pleasure in, or do in this recollection, these directors also persuade souls to strive for satisfaction and feelings of fervor when they should be counseling the opposite. When these persons cannot accomplish this as before, because the time for such activity has passed and this is not their road, they grow doubly disquieted, thinking that they are lost. Their directors foster this belief in them, cause in them aridity of spirit, and deprive them of the precious anointings God was bestowing on them in solitude and tranquility. This causes serious harm, as I said; and these directors bring them grief and ruin, for on the one hand such persons lose ground, and on the other they suffer a useless affliction.

54. These directors do not know what spirit is. They do a great injury to God and show disrespect toward him by intruding with a rough hand where he is working. It cost God a great deal to bring these souls to this stage, and he highly values his work of having introduced them into this solitude and emptiness regarding their faculties and activity so that he might speak to their hearts, which is what he always desires. Since it is he who now reigns in the soul with an abundance of peace and calm, he takes the initiative himself by making the natural acts of the faculties fail, by which the soul laboring the whole night accomplished nothing [Lk. 5:5]; and he feeds the spirit without the activity of the senses because neither the sense nor its function is capable of spirit.

55. The extent to which God values this tranquility and sleep, or annihilation of sense, is clear in the entreaty, so notable and efficacious, that he made in the Song of Songs: *I adjure you, daughters of Jerusalem, by the roes and the harts of the fields, that you stir not up nor awaken my beloved until she please* [Sg. 3:5]. He hereby indicates how much he loves solitary sleep and forgetfulness, for he compares it to these animals that are so retiring

and withdrawn. Yet these spiritual directors do not want the soul to rest and remain quiet, but want it always to labor and work, so that consequently it does not allow room for God's work and through its own activity ruins and effaces what he is doing. Its activities are like the little foxes that destroy the flourishing vineyard of the soul [Sg. 2:15]. Thus the Lord complains through Isaiah: *You have devoured my vineyard* [Is. 3:14].

56. Perhaps in their zeal these directors err with good will because they do not know any better. Not for this reason, however, should they be excused for the counsels they give rashly, without first understanding the road and spirit a person may be following, and for rudely meddling in something they do not understand, instead of leaving the matter to one who does understand. It is no light matter or fault to cause a soul to lose inestimable goods and sometimes leave it in ruin through temerarious counsel.

Thus one who recklessly errs will not escape a punishment corresponding to the harm caused, for such a one is obliged to be certain, as is everyone in the performance of duties. The affairs of God must be handled with great tact and open eyes, especially in so vital and sublime a matter as is that of these souls, where there is at stake almost an infinite gain in being right and almost an infinite loss in being wrong.

57. Since, however, you insist that you have some excuse, although I do not see it, at least you cannot hold that they have an excuse who in guiding a soul never let it out of their hands on account of vain considerations of which they are aware.[15] Such directors will not escape punishment for these considerations. For it is certain that since that soul must always advance along the spiritual road on which God is always a help to it, it will have to change its style and mode of prayer and will need another doctrine more sublime than yours, and another spirituality. Not everyone knows all the happenings and stages of the spiritual journey, nor is everyone spiritually so perfect as to know every state of the interior life in which a person must be conducted and guided. At least directors should not think that they have all the requirements, or that God will not want to lead the soul further on.

Not everyone capable of hewing the wood knows how to carve the statue, nor does everyone able to carve know how to perfect and polish the work, nor do all who know how to polish it know how to paint it, nor do all who can paint it know how to put the finishing touches on it and bring the work to completion. One can do with the statue only what one

---

15. Though it is bad enough that some err out of ignorance, the matter becomes much worse with those who are prompted by egoism, jealousy, and so on; cf. A. 2. 18. 6.

knows how to do, and when craftsmen try to do more than they know how to do, the statue is ruined.

58. Let us see, then: If you are only a hewer, which lies in guiding the soul to contempt of the world and mortification of its appetites, or a good carver, which consists in introducing it to holy meditations, and know no more, how can you lead this soul to the ultimate perfection of delicate painting, which no longer requires hewing or carving or even relief work, but the work that God must do in it?

It is certain that if you always bind it to your teaching, which is ever of one kind, it will either backslide or fail to advance. What, I ask, will the statue look like if all you do is hammer and hew, which, in the case of the soul, is the active use of the faculties? When will the statue be complete? When or how will it be left for God to paint? Is it possible that all these functions are yours and that you are so perfect the soul will never need any other than you?

59. Granted that you may possess the requisites for the full direction of some soul (for perhaps it does not have the talent to make progress), it is impossible for you to have the qualities demanded for the guidance of all those you refuse to allow out of your hands. God leads each one along different paths so that hardly one spirit will be found like another in even half its method of procedure.[16] For who is there who would become, like St. Paul, all things to all so as to win them all [1 Cor. 9:22]? You tyrannize souls and deprive them of their freedom, and judge for yourself the breadth of the evangelical doctrine. Therefore you endeavor to hold on to your penitents. But what is worse, you may by chance learn that one of them has consulted another (for perhaps you were not the suitable one to consult, or that person was led by God to another so as to learn what you did not teach), and you treat that penitent—I am ashamed to say it—with the very jealous quarrelsomeness we find among married couples. And this is not jealousy for the glory of God, but a jealousy motivated by your own pride and presumption or some other imperfection, for you should not assume that in turning from you this person turned from God.

60. God becomes extremely indignant with such directors and in Ezekiel promises them chastisement: *You ate the milk of my flock and you covered yourself with their wool and did not feed my flock; I will seek my flock at your hand,* he says [Ez. 34:3, 10].

---

16. This observation is important also in the interpretation and application of John's own writings.

61. Spiritual masters, then, should give freedom to souls and encourage them in their desire to seek improvement. The director does not know the means by which God may wish to benefit a soul, especially if it is no longer satisfied with the director's teaching. This dissatisfaction is in fact a sign that the director is not helping it, either because God is making it advance by a road different from the one along which it is being led, or because the master has changed style. These masters should themselves counsel this change; all the rest stems from foolish pride and presumption, or some other ambition.

62. Let us leave aside our discussion of this attitude and speak of another more pestiferous trait of these directors or of other worse methods used by them. It will happen that God is anointing some souls with the unctions of holy desires and motives for renouncing the world, changing their way of life, and serving him, with contempt of the world (and God esteems this stage to which he has brought them, because worldly things do not please him), when these directors, by their human rationalizations or reflections singularly contrary to the doctrine of Christ and of his humility and contempt for all things, and by depending on their own interests or satisfactions, or out of fear where there is no reason to fear, either make matters difficult for these souls or cause them to delay, or even worse try to make them put the thought from their minds. With a spirit not too devout, with little of Christ's meekness, and fully clothed in worldliness, since they do not enter by the narrow gate of life, these directors do not let others enter either.

Our Lord threatens them through St. Luke: *Woe to you, for you have taken away the key of knowledge, and you neither enter yourselves nor do you allow others to enter* [Lk. 11:52].

These directors are indeed like barriers or obstacles at the gate of heaven, hindering those who seek their counsel from entering. They know that God has commanded them not only to allow and help souls enter but even to compel them to enter, when he says through St. Luke: *Make them enter that my house may be filled with guests* [Lk. 14:23]. But they, on the contrary, compel them to stay out.[17]

The director is thus a blind guide who can be an obstacle to the life of the soul, which is the Holy Spirit. We discover this to be the case with spiritual masters in the many ways we mentioned, in which some are aware of it and others are unaware. But neither will escape punishment; since this is their duty, they are obliged to be careful and understand what they are doing.

---

17. The use of the word "pestiferous" has led some to think that John has in mind those who oppose a call to the religious life, for St. Thomas Aquinas wrote a little work entitled "Against the Pestiferous Doctrine of Those Who Would Deter Young Men from Entering Religious Life."

63. The second blind guide who, we said,[18] was capable of thwarting the soul in this kind of recollection is the devil; being blind himself, he desires that the soul be blind too. When the soul is in the loftiest solitudes, receiving the infusion of the delicate unctions of the Holy Spirit insofar as it is alone, despoiled, and withdrawn from every creature and trace of creature, the devil, with great sadness and envy, seeing that the soul is not only enriched but flying along at such a pace that he cannot catch it in anything, strives to intrude in this withdrawal with some clouds of knowledge and sensible satisfaction. This knowledge and satisfaction he gives is sometimes good, so he may feed the soul more and make it revert to particular things and the work of the senses, and make it turn thus to this good knowledge and satisfaction, embrace it, and journey to God leaning upon it.

He consequently distracts it very easily and draws it out of that solitude and recollection in which, as we said, the Holy Spirit is bringing about those secret marvels. Since humans of themselves are inclined toward feeling and tasting, especially if they are seeking something and do not understand the road they are traveling, they easily grow attached to the knowledge and satisfaction provided by the devil and lose the solitude God was providing. Since the soul was doing nothing in that solitude and quiet of the faculties, it thinks that this way is better because it is now doing something. It is a great pity that, in not understanding itself and for the sake of eating a morsel of particular knowledge and satisfaction, the soul impedes God from feeding on it entirely, which God does in that solitude where he places it, since he absorbs it in himself by means of those solitary spiritual anointings.[19]

64. With little more than nothing, the devil causes the gravest harm. He makes the soul lose abundant riches by alluring it with a little bait—as one would lure a fish—out of the simple waters of the spirit, where it was engulfed and swallowed up in God without finding any bottom or foothold. And by this bait he provides it with a prop and drags it ashore so it might find the ground and go on foot, with great effort, rather than swim in the unctions of God, in the waters of Shiloh that flow in silence [Is. 8:6].

The devil considers this so important that it is worth noting that, since he accomplishes more through a little harm caused in these souls than by great damage effected in many others, as we have mentioned, there is hardly anyone walking this path on whom he does not bring serious harm and loss. This evil one establishes himself cautiously at the passageway from sense to spirit, deceiving souls and feeding the sensory part itself,

---

18. In no. 29.
19. With regard to God feeding on the soul, cf. C. 17. 10.

as we said, with sensible things. The soul does not think there is any loss in this; it thus fails to enter into the inner dwelling of the Bridegroom, and remains at the threshold to watch what is happening outside in the sensory part. The devil sees every high thing, says Job [Jb. 41:25], that is, every spiritual height of souls in order to combat them. If, by chance, some soul enters a sublime recollection in such fashion that the devil cannot distract it in the way we mentioned, he struggles through horrors, fears, bodily pains, or exterior sounds and noises to make it at least advert to sense and to draw it out thereby and divert it from the interior spirit, until being able to do no more he leaves it.

But it is so easy for him to thwart and block the riches of these precious souls that even though he values doing this more than he does ruining many other souls, he still does not esteem it highly because of the ease in which he accomplishes it and the little it costs him.

We can in this sense interpret God's words to Job about him: *He will absorb a river and not wonder and he trusts that the Jordan will run into his mouth,* which refers to the highest matters of perfection. *In his eyes as with a hook he will catch him and with awls pierce his nostrils* [Jb. 40:23-24], that is, he will divert the spirit with the points of the knowledge by which he is wounding it; for the air that rushes out of the recollected nostrils that are pierced is scattered in many parts. And further on he says: *The rays of the sun will be under him and gold will be strewn under him like mire* [Jb. 41:22], for the devil causes illumined souls to lose wonderful rays of divine knowledge and seizes and scatters the precious gold of the divine embellishments.[20]

65. Oh, then, souls, when God is according you such sovereign favors as to lead you by the state of solitude and recollection, withdrawing you from the labors of the senses, do not revert to the senses. Abandon your activity, for if this helped you to deny the world and yourselves when you were beginners, it is a serious obstacle now that God favors you by being himself the agent. God will feed you with heavenly refreshment since you do not apply your faculties to anything, or encumber them, but detach them from everything, which is all you yourself have to do (besides the simple loving attentiveness in the way I mentioned above,[21] that is, when you feel no aversion toward it). You should not use any force except to detach your soul and liberate it, so as not to alter its peace and tranquility.

66. The third blind guide is the soul that, by not understanding itself, disturbs and harms itself. Since it only knows how to act by means of the senses and discursive reflection, it thinks it is doing nothing when God

---

20. This interference from the devil is dealt with somewhat at length also in N. 2. 23.
21. In nos. 47-52.

introduces it into that emptiness and solitude where it is unable to use the faculties and make acts; as a result it strains to perform these acts. The soul, therefore, that was enjoying the idleness of spiritual peace and silence, in which God was secretly adorning it, is distracted and filled with dryness and displeasure.

It will happen that while God persists in keeping the soul in that silent quietude, it persists in its desire to act through its own efforts with the intellect and the imagination. It resembles a little boy who kicks and cries, wanting to walk when his mother wants to carry him; thus he neither allows his mother to make any headway nor makes any himself.[22] Or it resembles one who moves a painting back and forth while the artist is at work so either nothing is accomplished or the painting is damaged.

67. Individuals should take note that even though they do not seem to be making any progress in this quietude or doing anything, they are advancing much faster than if they were treading along on foot, for God is carrying them. Although they are walking at God's pace, they do not feel this pace. Even though they do no work with their faculties, they achieve much more than if they did, for God is the agent.

It is no wonder if they do not advert to this, for the senses do not attain to what God effects in the soul at this time; it is done in silence. As the Wise Man says: *The words of wisdom are heard in silence* [Eccl. 9:17].

A soul, then, should abandon itself into God's hands, and not into its own or those of the other two blind guides. Insofar as it abandons itself to God and does not apply its faculties to anything, it will advance securely.

68. Let us return now to the subject of these deep caverns of the faculties of the soul, in which, we said,[23] its suffering is usually intense when God is anointing and disposing it with the most sublime unctions of the Holy Spirit for union with himself.

These anointings are so subtle and delicate that, in penetrating the intimate substance of the soul's depths, they prepare it and give it such savor that the suffering and the fainting of desire in the tremendous void of these caverns is immense.

Hence, if the anointings that prepare these caverns of the soul for the union of the spiritual marriage with God are so sublime, what will be the possession of knowledge, love, and glory of the intellect, will, and

---

22. John uses the image of the mother with her child, representing God's grace, in two ways to mark a transition in the spiritual life. In one case the mother makes her child walk on its own (N. 1. 1. 2; 12. 1); in the other, she carries her child against its wishes (A. prol. 3; F. 3. 66).

23. He ends the digression that began with no. 29.

memory in this union with God? Certainly the satisfaction, fullness, and delight of these caverns will then correspond to their former hunger and thirst. And the exquisite quality of both the soul's possession and the fruition of its feeling[24] will be in conformity with the delicacy of the preparations.

69. By the "feeling" of the soul, the verse refers to the power and strength the substance of the soul has for feeling and enjoying the objects of the spiritual faculties; through these faculties a person tastes the wisdom and love and communication of God.[25] The soul here calls these three faculties (memory, intellect, and will) "the deep caverns of feeling" because through them and in them it deeply experiences and enjoys the grandeurs of God's wisdom and excellence. It very appropriately calls them the deep caverns of feeling because, since it feels that the deep knowledge and splendors of the lamps of fire fit into them, it knows that its capacity and recesses correspond to the particular things it receives from the knowledge, savor, joy, delight, and so on, of God. All these things are received and seated in this feeling of the soul which, as I say, is its power and capacity for experiencing, possessing, and tasting them all. And the caverns of the faculties administer them to it, just as the bodily senses go to assist the common sense of the phantasy with the forms of their objects, and this common sense becomes the receptacle and archives of these forms.[26] Hence this common sense, or feeling, of the soul, which has become the receptacle or archives of God's grandeurs, is illumined and enriched according to what it attains of this high and enlightened possession.

                         once obscure and blind,

70. That is, before God enlightened and illumined it. To understand this it should be known that there are two reasons the sense of sight loses its power of vision: either because of obscurity or because of blindness.

God is the light and the object of the soul. When this light does not illumine it, the soul dwells in obscurity even though it may have very excellent vision. When it is in sin or occupies its appetites with other things, then it is blind; and even though God's light may shine on it, because it is blind it does not see its obscureness, which is its ignorance. Before God illumined it by means of this transformation, it was in obscurity and ignorant of so many of God's goods, as the Wise Man says he was before wisdom enlightened him: *He shed light on my ignorance* [Ecclus. 51:26].

---

24. The term "feeling" in the sense of "the deep caverns of feeling," refers to the intimate substance or depth.
25. Regarding the symbolic language of the "spiritual senses," cf. A. 2. 23. 2-3.
26. Cf. A. 2. 12. 3 and note 1; 16. 2.

71. Spiritually speaking, it is one thing to be in obscurity and another to be in darkness. To be in darkness, as we said, is to be blind in sin. Yet one can be in obscurity without being in sin, and this doubly: regarding the natural, by not having light or knowledge about certain natural things; and regarding the supernatural, by not having light or knowledge of supernatural things. The soul says here that before reaching this precious union its feeling was in obscurity concerning both.

Until the Lord said, *fiat lux*[27] [Gn. 1:3], darkness was over the face of the abyss of the caverns of the soul's feeling [Gn. 1:2]. The more unfathomable and deep-caverned is the feeling, the more profound are its chasms and its darknesses regarding the supernatural, when God who is its light does not illumine it.

Thus it is impossible for it to lift its eyes to the divine light, or even think of doing so, for in never having seen it, it knows not what it is. Accordingly, it will be unable to desire this light; it will rather desire darkness because it knows what darkness is, and will go from darkness to darkness, guided by that darkness. One darkness cannot but lead to another. As David says: *The day overflows into the day and the night teaches knowledge to the night* [Ps. 19:2]. Thus *one abyss calls to the other abyss* [Ps. 42:7], that is: An abyss of light summons another abyss of light, and an abyss of darkness calls to another abyss of darkness, each like evoking its like and communicating itself to it.

The light of grace that God had previously accorded this soul (by which he had illumined the eye of the abyss of its spirit, opened its eye to the divine light, and made it pleasing to himself) called to another abyss of grace, which is this divine transformation of the soul in God. In this transformation the eye of the soul's feeling is so illumined and agreeable to God that we can say God's light and that of the soul are one. The natural light of the soul is united with the supernatural light of God so that only the supernatural light is shining; just as the light God created was united to the light of the sun and now only the sun shines even though the other light is not lacking [Gn. 1:14-18].

72. Also, it was blind insofar as it was enjoying something else. The blindness of the rational and superior feeling is the appetite that, like a cataract and cloud, interferes with and hangs over the eye of reason so things present cannot be seen. Insofar as the appetite proposed some satisfaction, the feeling was blind to the grandeurs of the divine riches and beauty on the other side of the cataract. Just as something in front of the eye, no matter how small, is sufficient to obstruct its vision of things before it, no matter how large, so a small appetite and idle act of the soul

---

27. "Let there be light."

is enough to impede all these divine grandeurs that stand behind the soul's appetites and gratifications.

73. Oh, who can tell how impossible it is for a person with appetites to judge the things of God as they are! If there is to be success in judging the things of God, the appetites and satisfactions must be totally rejected, and these things of God must be weighed apart from them. For otherwise one will infallibly come to consider the things of God as not of God, and the things that are not of God as of God.

Since that cataract and cloud shrouds the eye of judgment, only the cataract is seen, sometimes of one color, sometimes another, according to the way the cataract appears to the eye. People judge that the cataract is God because, as I say, they see only the cataract that covers the faculty, and God cannot be grasped by the senses. Consequently the appetite and sensory gratifications impede the knowledge of high things. The Wise Man indicates this clearly with these words: *The deceitfulness of vanity obscures good things, and the inconstancy of concupiscence overturns the innocent mind* [Wis. 4:12], that is, good judgment.

74. Those who are not so spiritual as to be purged of appetites and satisfactions, but still keep in themselves something of the animal self, believe that things most vile and base to the spirit (those closest to the senses, according to which they are still living) are highly important; and those that are loftier and more precious to the spirit (those further withdrawn from the senses) are considered to be of little value and are not esteemed by them. They will even regard them sometimes as foolishness, as St. Paul clearly indicates: *The animal self does not perceive the things of God; they are foolishness to it and it cannot understand them* [1 Cor. 2:14]. By the animal self he means here the person who still lives with natural appetites and gratifications. Even though some satisfaction overflows from the spirit into the senses, that person has no more than natural appetites who desires to become attached to it. It matters little that the object or cause is supernatural, if the appetite arises naturally and finds its roots and strength in nature. It does not thus cease being a natural appetite, for it has the very substance and nature it would have were it to deal with a natural object or cause.

75. You will say to me: "Well, it therefore follows that when the soul desires God, it does not desire him supernaturally, and thus its desire will be unmeritorious before God."

I reply that it is true that the soul's desire for God is not always supernatural, but only when God infuses it and himself gives the strength for it. This is far different from the natural desire, and until God infuses the desire there is very little or no merit. Thus when you of your own power have the desire for God, your desire amounts to no more than a natural appetite; neither will it be anything more until God informs it supernaturally. When you of yourself become attached to spiritual things and bound to their savoriness, you exercise your natural appetite and thus you put cataracts before your eyes and become an animal self. You are then able neither to understand nor judge the spiritual self, which is above every natural feeling and appetite.

If you have any further doubts, I know not what to say, except that you reread this and perhaps you will understand. For the substance of the truth has been said, and this is not the place to enlarge on it.

76. This feeling, then, of the soul that was once obscure, without this divine light and blind through its appetites and affections, has now together with the deep caverns of its faculties become not only bright and clear, but like a resplendent light.

> now give forth, so rarely, so exquisitely,
> both warmth and light to their Beloved.

77. When these caverns of the faculties are so wonderfully and marvelously pervaded with the admirable splendors of those lamps that are burning within, they give forth to God in God with loving glory, besides their surrender to him, these very splendors they have received. Inclined in God toward God, having become enkindled lamps within the splendors of the divine lamps, they render the Beloved the same light and heat they receive. In the very manner they receive it, they return it to the one who gave it, and with the same exquisite beauty; just as the window when the sun shines on it, for it then too reflects the splendors. Yet the soul reflects the divine light in a more excellent way because of the active intervention of its will.

78. "So rarely, so exquisitely," means: in a way rare or foreign to every common thought, every exaggeration, and every mode and manner.

Corresponding to the exquisite quality with which the intellect receives divine wisdom, being made one with God's intellect, is the quality with which the soul gives this wisdom, for it cannot give it save according to the mode in which it was given.

And corresponding to the exquisite quality by which the will is united to goodness is the quality by which the soul gives in God the same goodness to God, for it only receives it in order to give it.

And, no more nor less, according to the exquisite quality by which it knows in the grandeur of God, being united to it, the soul shines and diffuses the warmth of love.

And according to the exquisite quality of the divine attributes (fortitude, beauty, justice, and so on) that the Beloved communicates, is the quality with which the soul's feeling gives joyfully to him the very light and heat it receives from him. Having been made one with God, the soul is somehow God through participation. Although it is not God as perfectly as it will be in the next life, it is like the shadow of God.[28]

Being the shadow of God through this substantial transformation, it performs in this measure in God and through God what he through himself does in it. For the will of the two is one will, and thus God's operation and the soul's are one. Since God gives himself with a free and gracious will, so too the soul (possessing a will more generous and free the more it is united with God) gives to God, God himself in God; and this is a true and complete gift of the soul to God.

It is conscious there that God is indeed its own and that it possesses him by inheritance, with the right of ownership, as his adopted child through the grace of his gift of himself. Having him for its own, it can give him and communicate him to whomever it wishes. Thus it gives him to its Beloved, who is the very God who gave himself to it. By this donation it repays God for all it owes him, since it willingly gives as much as it receives from him.

79. Because the soul in this gift to God offers him the Holy Spirit, with voluntary surrender, as something of its own (so that God loves himself in the Holy Spirit as he deserves), it enjoys inestimable delight and fruition, seeing that it gives God something of its own that is suited to him according to his infinite being. It is true that the soul cannot give God again to himself, since in himself he is ever himself. Nevertheless it does this truly and perfectly, giving all that was given it by him in order to repay love, which is to give as much as is given. And God, who could not be considered paid with anything less, is considered paid with that gift of the soul; and he accepts it gratefully as something it gives him of its own. In this very gift he loves it anew; and in this re-surrender of God to the soul, the soul also loves as though again.

A reciprocal love is thus actually formed between God and the soul, like the marriage union and surrender, in which the goods of both (the divine essence that each possesses freely by reason of the voluntary surrender between them) are possessed by both together. They say to each other what the Son of God spoke to the Father through St. John: *Omnia mea tua sunt et tua mea sunt et clarificatus sum in eis* (All my goods are yours and yours are mine, and I am glorified in them) [Jn. 17:10]. In the next life this will continue uninterrupted in perfect fruition, but in this state of union it occurs, although not as perfectly as in the next, when God produces in the soul this act of transformation.

Clearly the soul can give this gift, even though the gift has greater entity than the soul's own being and capacity; for those who own many

---

28. Again in this section, especially in nos. 82-85, he draws from *De Beatitudine;* cf. C. 38. 4 and note.

nations and kingdoms, which have more entity than they do as individuals, can give them to whomever they will.

80. This is the soul's deep satisfaction and happiness: To see that it gives God more than it is worth in itself, the very divine light and divine heat that are given to it. It does this in heaven by means of the light of glory and in this life by means of a highly illumined faith. Accordingly, "the deep caverns of feeling now give forth, so rarely, so exquisitely, both warmth and light to the Beloved."

It says "both warmth and light," because the communication of the Father and the Son and the Holy Spirit in the soul is combined; they are the light and fire of love in it.

81. Yet we should note briefly the refinement with which the soul makes this surrender. In this respect it should be known that, since it enjoys a certain image of fruition caused by the union of the intellect and affection with God, and is delighted and obliged by this inestimable favor, it makes this surrender of God and of itself to God in marvelous ways. With regard to love, the soul's presence before God is of rare and exquisite excellence, and so too in regard to this vestige of fruition, and also in regard to praise and to gratitude.

82. Concerning the first, there are chiefly three exquisite qualities of love. The first is that the soul here loves God, not through itself but through him. This is a remarkable quality, for the soul loves through the Holy Spirit, as the Father and the Son love each other, according to what the Son himself declares through St. John: *That the love with which you have loved me be in them and I in them* [Jn. 17:26].

The second exquisite quality is to love God in God, for in this union the soul is ardently absorbed in love of God, and God in great ardor surrenders himself to the soul.

The third exquisite quality of love is to love him on account of who he is. The soul does not love him only because he is generous, good, glorious, and so on, to it; but with greater intensity it loves him because he is all this in himself essentially.

83. In regard to this image of fruition, it has three other exquisite qualities that are precious and principal ones. The first is that it enjoys God, for it enjoys him by means of himself. Since it unites its intellect to the omnipotence, wisdom, goodness, and so on, although not clearly as it will in the next life, it delights in all these attributes, which are understood distinctly, as we mentioned above.[29] The second exquisite

29. See nos. 15-17.

quality of this joy is that the soul delights with order in God alone, without any intermingling of creature. The third delight is that it enjoys him only on account of who he is without any admixture of its own pleasure.

84. There are three exquisite qualities in the praise the soul renders God in this union. The first is that it praises him as its duty, for it sees that God created it for his own praise, as he asserts through Isaiah: *This people I have formed for myself; it will sing my praises* [Is. 43:21]. The second exquisite quality of praise is that the soul praises God for the goods it receives and the delight it has in praising. The third exquisite quality is that it praises God for what he is in himself. Even though the soul would experience no delight, it would praise him because of who he is.

85. As for gratitude, it has three other exquisite qualities. The first is gratefulness for the natural and spiritual goods and blessings it has received. The second is the intense delight it has in praising God, for it is absorbed with extreme ardor in this praise. The third is praise only because of what God is, which is a much stronger and more delightful praise.

STANZA 4

How gently and lovingly
you wake in my heart,
where in secret you dwell alone;
and in your sweet breathing,
filled with good and glory,
how tenderly you swell my heart with love.

Commentary

1. The soul here addresses its Bridegroom with deep love, esteeming him and thanking him for two admirable effects sometimes produced by him through this union, noting also the manner in which each is wrought, as well as another effect that overflows in it from this union.

2. The first effect is an awakening of God in the soul, brought about in gentleness and love. The second is the breathing of God within it, and this is brought about through the good and glory communicated to it in this breathing. And what overflows in it is its being tenderly and delicately inspired with love.

3. And thus it is as though the soul were to say: How gentle and loving (that is, extremely loving and gentle) is your awakening, O Bridegroom

Word, in the center and depth of my soul, which is its pure and intimate substance, in which secretly and silently, as its only lord, you dwell alone, not only as in your house, nor only as in your bed, but also as in my own heart, intimately and closely united to it. And how delicately you captivate me and arouse my affections toward you in the sweet breathing you produce in this awakening, a breathing delightful to me and full of good and glory. The soul uses this comparison because its experience here is similar to that of one who on awakening breathes deeply. The verses follow:

> How gently and lovingly
> you wake in my heart,

4. There are many kinds of awakening that God effects in the soul, so many that we would never finish explaining them all. Yet this awakening of the Son of God that the soul wishes to refer to here is one of the most elevated and beneficial. For this awakening is a movement of the Word in the substance of the soul, containing such grandeur, dominion, glory, and intimate sweetness that it seems to the soul that all the balsams and fragrant spices and flowers of the world are commingled, stirred, and shaken so as to yield their sweet odor, and all the kingdoms and dominions of the world and all the powers and virtues of heaven are moved; not only this, but it also seems that all the virtues and substances and perfections and graces of every created thing glow and make the same movement all at once.

Since, as St. John says, all things in him are life [Jn. 1:3-4], and in him they live and are and move, as the Apostle declares [Acts 17:28], it follows that when, within the soul, this great Emperor moves (whose principality, as Isaiah says, he bears on his shoulders [Is. 9:6]—which consists of the three spheres, celestial, terrestrial, and infernal [Phil. 2:10], and the things contained in them—upholding them all, as St. Paul says [Heb. 1:3], with the word of his power), all things seem to move in unison.

This happens in the same manner as when at the movement of the earth all material things in it move as though they were nothing. So it is when this Prince moves, who himself carries his court, instead of his court carrying him.[1]

5. Even this comparison is most inadequate; for in this awakening they not only seem to move, but they all likewise disclose the beauties of their

---

1. It seems John accepted the Copernican theory. In the first edition of his works (1618), the editor changed the text to read "if the earth were to move, all natural things in it would move." The University of Salamanca, where John studied, was the first to accept and teach the Copernican system. By the time the first edition appeared, Copernicus' work was on the Index of Forbidden Books.

being, power, loveliness, and graces, and the root of their duration and life. For the soul is conscious of how all creatures, earthly and heavenly, have their life, duration, and strength in him, and it clearly realizes what he says in the Book of Proverbs: *By me kings reign and princes rule and the mighty exercise justice and understand it* [Prv. 8:15-16]. Although it is indeed aware that these things are distinct from God, insofar as they have created being, nonetheless what it understands of God, by his being all these things with infinite eminence, is such that it knows these things better in God's being than in themselves.

And here lies the remarkable delight of this awakening: The soul knows creatures through God and not God through creatures. This amounts to knowing the effects through their cause and not the cause through its effects. The latter is knowledge *a posteriori,* and the former is essential knowledge.[2]

6. How this movement takes place in the soul, since God is immovable, is a wonderful thing, for it seems to the soul that God indeed moves; yet he does not really move. For since it is the soul that is renewed and moved by God so it might behold this supernatural sight, and since divine life and the being and harmony of every creature in that life, with its movements in God, is revealed to it with such newness, it seems to the soul that it is God who moves and the cause assumes the name of the effect it produces. According to this effect, we can assert that God moves, as the Wise Man says: *For wisdom is more movable than all movable things* [Wis. 7:24]. And this is not because she moves but because she is the principle and root of all movement. *Remaining in herself the same,* as he goes on to say, *she renews all things* [Wis. 7:27]. Thus what he wishes to say in this passage is that wisdom is more active than all active things. We then ought to say that in this movement it is the soul that is moved and awakened from the sleep of natural vision to supernatural vision. Hence it very adequately uses the term "awakening."

7. Yet God always acts in this way—as the soul is able to see—moving, governing, bestowing being, power, graces, and gifts on all creatures, bearing them all in himself by his power, presence, and substance. And the soul sees what God is in himself and what he is in his creatures in only one view, just as one who in opening the door of a palace beholds in one act the eminence of the person who dwells inside together with what that sovereign is doing.

Therefore what I understand about how God effects this awakening and view given to the soul (which is in him substantially as is every

---

2. This *a posteriori* knowledge is the equivalent of knowing the back of God; cf. C. 19. 4; 37. 4.

creature) is that he removes some of the many veils and curtains hanging in front of it so that it might get a glimmer of him as he is. And then that countenance of his, full of graces, becomes partially and vaguely discernible, for not all the veils are removed. Because all things are moving by his power, what he is doing is evident as well, so he seems to move in them and they in him with continual movement. Hence it seems to the soul that, in being itself moved and awakened, it was God who moved and awakened.

8. Such is the lowliness of our condition in this life; for we think others are like ourselves and we judge others according to what we ourselves are, since our judgment arises from within us and not outside us. Thus the thief thinks others also steal; and the lustful think others are lustful too; and the malicious think others also bear malice, their judgment stemming from their own malice; and the good think well of others, for their judgment flows from the goodness of their own thoughts; and to those who are careless and asleep, it seems that others are too.

Hence it is that when we are careless and asleep in God's presence, it seems to us it is God who is asleep and neglectful of us, as is seen in psalm 43 where David calls to him: *Arise, Lord, why do you sleep? Arise* [Ps. 44:23]. He attributed to God what is characteristic of humans, for since they are the ones who are fallen and asleep, he tells God to arise and awaken; although *he who watches over Israel never sleeps* [Ps. 121:4].

9. Yet, since everything in human beings comes from God, and they of themselves can do nothing good [Jas. 1:17], it is rightly asserted that our awakening is an awakening of God and our rising is God's rising. It is as though David were to say: Let us arise and be awakened twice, because we are doubly asleep and fallen. Since the soul was in a sleep from which it could never awaken itself, and only God could open its eyes and cause this awakening, it very appropriately calls this an awakening of God, saying: "You wake in my heart."

Awaken and enlighten us, my Lord, so we might know and love the blessings that you ever propose to us, and we might understand that you have moved to bestow favors on us and have remembered us.

10. What a person knows and experiences of God in this awakening is entirely beyond words. Since this awakening is the communication of God's excellence to the substance of the soul, which is its heart referred to in the verse, an immense, powerful voice sounds in it, the voice of a multitude of excellences, of thousands of virtues in God, infinite in number.[3] The soul is established in them, terribly and solidly set in array

---

3. For more on this voice of power, cf. C. 14-15. 9-11.

in them like an army [Sg. 6:4], and made gentle and charming with all the gentleness and charm of creatures.

11. Yet a doubt will arise: How can a soul endure so forcible a communication in the weakness of the flesh? For in point of fact it does not have the capacity and strength to undergo so much without dying. Merely at the sight of King Ahasuerus clothed in royal garments and resplendent with gold and precious stones, seated awesomely on his throne, Queen Esther feared so much that she fainted. She confesses there that she fainted because of the fear his great glory caused her, for he appeared like an angel and his countenance was full of graces [Est. 15:9-17]. When glory does not glorify, it weighs heavily on the one who beholds it. But what greater reason does the soul have for fainting in this awakening; it does not see an angel but God, his countenance filled with the graces of all creatures, awesome in power and glory, and with the voice of a multitude of excellences. Job says of this communication: *When we have heard scarcely a drop of his voice, who will be able to endure the greatness of his thunder?* [Jb. 26:14]. And in another place he declares: *I do not desire that he commune and deal with me with much strength lest he overwhelm me by the weight of his grandeur* [Jb. 23:6].

12. There are two reasons a person does not faint or become afraid in this awakening that is so powerful and glorious.

First, the soul that is in this state of perfection, in which the lower part is highly purged and in conformity with the spirit, does not feel the pain and detriment commonly experienced by souls unpurged in their spirit and senses and undisposed to receive spiritual communications. Yet this is insufficient to prevent the suffering of some detriment in the presence of such grandeur and glory. Even though what is of nature may be very pure, this communication would nevertheless overwhelm it by exceeding it, as would an object that causes intense physical sensation overwhelm its respective faculty. The passage of Job we referred to has this meaning.

The second reason is the important one; it is what the soul mentions in the first verse, that is, that he shows himself gently. As God shows the soul grandeur and glory in order to exalt and favor it, he aids it so no detriment is done, fortifying what is natural and unveiling his grandeur gently and with love, without using the natural, so that a person does not know whether this happens in the body or out of it [2 Cor. 12:2]. He who with his right hand fortified Moses, so his glory could be seen by him, can do this very easily [Ex. 33:22].

Thus the soul experiences in him as much gentleness and love as it does power and dominion and grandeur, for everything in God is one. The delight is strong; and the protection is strong in gentleness and love so the soul might endure the strong delight, and instead of fainting stand

powerful and strong. If Esther fainted, it was because the king did not at
first show himself to her favorably, but, as it says there, disclosed with
burning eyes the furor of his heart [Est. 15:7]. Yet she came to herself
after he favored her, held out his scepter and touched her with it, and
embraced her and told her that he was her brother and not to fear [Est.
15:8-12].

13. The soul no longer fears, since from henceforth the King of heaven
acts in a friendly way toward it, as its brother and equal. In revealing his
powerful strength and his good love to it in gentleness and not in furor,
he communicates strength and love to it from his heart, going out to it
from his throne, which is the soul itself, like the Bridegroom from his
bridal chamber [Ps. 19:5], where he was hidden and turned toward it,
touching it with his scepter and embracing it as a brother. There we find
the royal garments and their fragrance, which are God's admirable
virtues; there, the splendor of gold, which is charity; there, the glittering
of the precious stones of knowledge of the higher and lower substances;
there, the face of the Word, full of graces, which shines on the queen,
which is the soul, and clothes it in such fashion that, transformed in these
attributes of the heavenly King, it is aware of having become a queen, and
that what David says of the queen in the Psalm can indeed be said of it:
The queen stood at the right in garments of gold and surrounded with variety [Ps.
45:9]. Since all this occurs in the intimate substance of the soul, it adds:
                    where in secret you dwell alone;

14. The soul says he dwells in its heart in secret because this sweet
embrace is wrought in the depths of its substance.

It should be known that God dwells secretly in all souls and is hidden
in their substance, for otherwise they would not last. Yet there is a
difference, a great difference, in his dwelling in them. In some souls he
dwells alone, and in others he does not dwell alone. Abiding in some he
is pleased; and in others, he is displeased. He lives in some as though in
his own house, commanding and ruling everything; and in others as
though a stranger in a strange house, where they do not permit him to
give orders or do anything.

It is in the soul in which less of its own appetites and pleasures dwell
where he dwells more alone, more pleased, and more as though in his
own house, ruling and governing it. And he dwells more in secret, the
more he dwells alone. Thus in this soul in which neither any appetite nor
other images or forms nor any affections for created things dwell, the
Beloved dwells secretly with an embrace so much closer, more intimate
and interior, the purer and more alone the soul is to everything other
than God. His dwelling is in secret, then, because the devil cannot reach
the area of this embrace, nor can the human intellect understand how it
occurs.

Yet it is not secret to the soul itself that has attained this perfection, for within itself it has the experience of this intimate embrace. It does not, however, always experience these awakenings; for when the Beloved produces them, it seems to the soul that he is awakening in its heart, where before he remained as though asleep. Although it was experiencing and enjoying him, this took place as with a loved one who is asleep, for knowledge and love are not communicated mutually while one is still asleep.

15. Oh, how happy is this soul, which ever experiences God resting and reposing within it! Oh, how fitting it is for it to withdraw from things, flee from business matters, and live in immense tranquility, so that it may not, even with the slightest speck of dust or noise, disturb or trouble its heart where the Beloved dwells.

He is usually there, in this embrace with his bride, as though asleep in the substance of the soul. And it is very well aware of him and ordinarily enjoys him. Were he always awake within it, communicating knowledge and love, it would already be in glory. For if, when he does waken, scarcely opening his eyes, he has such an effect on the soul, what would things be like were he ordinarily in it fully awake?

16. Although he is not displeased with other souls that have not reached this union, for after all they are in the state of grace, yet insofar as they are not well disposed his dwelling is secret to them, even though he does dwell in them. They do not experience him ordinarily, except when he grants them some delightful awakening. But such an awakening is not of this kind and high quality, nor is it comparable to these or as secret to the intellect and the devil, which are still able to understand something through the movements of the senses. For the senses are not fully annihilated until the soul reaches this union, and they still have some activity and movements concerning the spiritual, since they are not yet totally spiritual.

But in this awakening of the Bridegroom in the perfect soul, everything that occurs and is caused is perfect, for he is the cause of it all. And in that awakening, which is as though one were to waken and breathe, the soul feels a strange delight in the breathing of the Holy Spirit in God, in which it is sovereignly glorified and taken with love. Hence it says in the subsequent verses:

> and in your sweet breathing,
> filled with good and glory,
> how tenderly you swell my heart with love!

17. I do not desire to speak of this spiration, filled for the soul with good and glory and delicate love of God, for I am aware of being incapable of doing so; and were I to try, it might seem less than it is. It is a spiration that God produces in the soul, in which, by that awakening of lofty knowledge of the Godhead, he breathes the Holy Spirit in it in the same proportion as its knowledge and understanding of him, absorbing it most profoundly in the Holy Spirit, rousing its love with a divine exquisite quality and delicacy according to what it beholds in him. Since the breathing is filled with good and glory, the Holy Spirit, through this breathing, filled the soul with good and glory in which he enkindled it in love of himself, indescribably and incomprehensibly, in the depths of God, to whom be honor and glory forever and ever. Amen.

Special Counsels

INTRODUCTION TO
THE PRECAUTIONS

John of the Cross wrote the *Precautions* for the nuns in Beas while he lived at El Calvario (1578-79), after he had escaped from prison in Toledo. These warnings represented some of the fruits of his years as spiritual director in Avila. The nuns, in turn, made copies and sent them to other houses. From the adaptations in gender that appear in some manuscripts, it seems that the friars, too, must have laid hands on the material and made copies for themselves.

The work is brief, with much doctrine condensed into a small amount of space. Written for nuns influenced personally by St. Teresa, the lean statements spoke to women who were ardent in their embrace of the spiritual journey. They wanted to reach poverty of spirit, union with God, and "the peaceful comfort of the Holy Spirit" in a short time. Love has little use for delay. The objective, then, is to overcome any obstacles interfering with rapid progress. People less passionate about their goals have other alternatives. The aspiration to avoid any stumbling blocks accounts for the negative tone of the work.

The condensed character and particular objective of this writing, then, require a reading in the doctrinal light of John's other works. In these he describes in detail how union with God comes about not through the observance of precautions but by adapting to God's communication through the theological life of faith, hope, and love. The precautions take any value they may have from their ability to promote this adaptation.

Christian spirituality, rooted in Scripture, spoke commonly of three spiritual enemies: the world, the flesh, and the devil. Within this tradition, John finds the structure for his work: three precautions against each of the three enemies. Building from this framework, he formulates the kind of behavior one must adopt as a precaution with respect to particular areas of life; he describes the harm and dangers that arise from not observing the specific precaution; and extols the advantages and benefits that follow from practicing it. If overlapping occurs in the presentation of the material it is because, as the friar himself points out, vanquishing one enemy means vanquishing the others also, and weakening one means weakening the others as well.

The text editors prefer is the autograph copy made by Alonso de la Madre de Dios conserved in the National Library of Madrid.

THE PRECAUTIONS

Instruction and precautions necessary for anyone desiring to be a true religious and reach perfection.

1. The soul must practice the following instructions if it wishes to attain in a short time holy recollection and spiritual silence, nakedness, and poverty of spirit, where one enjoys the peaceful comfort of the Holy Spirit, reaches union with God, is freed of all the obstacles incurred from the creatures of this world, defended against the wiles and deceits of the devil, and liberated from one's own self.

2. It should be noted, then, that all the harm the soul receives is born of its enemies, mentioned above: the world, the devil, and the flesh. The world is the enemy least difficult to conquer; the devil is the hardest to understand; but the flesh is the most tenacious, and its attacks continue as long as the old self lasts.

3. To gain complete mastery over any of these three enemies, one must vanquish all three of them; and in the weakening of one, the other two are weakened also. When all three are overpowered, no further war remains for the soul.

Against the World

4. To free yourself from the harm the world can do you, you should practice three precautions.

The first precaution

5. The first is that you should have an equal love for and an equal forgetfulness of all persons, whether relatives or not, and withdraw your heart from relatives as much as from others, and in some ways even more for fear that flesh and blood might be quickened by the natural love that is ever alive among kin, and must always be mortified for the sake of spiritual perfection.

6. Regard all as strangers, and you will fulfill your duty toward them better than by giving them the affection you owe God. Do not love one person more than another, for you will err;[1] the person who loves God

---

1. Though this seems inhuman and contradictory to the way John behaved toward his own mother and brother, the tone finds its roots in the Gospel (Lk. 14:26). Love must not be based on temporal goods, such as blood, status, or titles (A. 3. 18-20); nor on natural goods: beauty, intelligence, and so on (A. 3. 21-23).

more is the one more worthy of love, and you do not know who this is. But forgetting everyone alike, as is necessary for holy recollection, you will free yourself from this error of loving one person more or less than another.

Do not think about others, neither good things nor bad. Flee them inasmuch as possible. And if you do not observe this practice, you will not know how to be a religious, nor will you be able to reach holy recollection or deliver yourself from imperfections. And if you should wish to allow yourself some freedom in this matter, the devil will deceive you in one way or another, or you will deceive yourself under some guise of good or evil.

In doing what we said, you will have security, for in no other way will you be capable of freeing yourself from the imperfections and harm derived from creatures.

The second precaution

7. The second precaution against the world concerns temporal goods. To free yourself truly of the harm stemming from this kind of good and to moderate the excess of your appetite, you should abhor all manner of possessions and not allow yourself to worry about these goods, neither for food, nor for clothing, nor for any other created thing, nor for tomorrow, and direct this care to something higher—to seeking the kingdom of God (seeking not to fail God); and the rest, as His Majesty says, will be added unto us [Mt. 6:33], for he who looks after the beasts will not be forgetful of you. By this practice you will attain silence and peace in the senses.

The third precaution

8. The third precaution is very necessary so you may know how to guard yourself in the community against all harm that may arise in regard to the religious. Many, by not observing it, not only have lost the peace and good of their souls but have fallen and ordinarily continue to fall into many evils and sins.

It is that you very carefully guard yourself against thinking about what happens in the community, and even more against speaking of it, of anything in the past or present concerning a particular religious: nothing about his or her character or conduct or deeds no matter how serious any of this seems. Do not say anything under the color of zeal or of correcting a wrong, unless at the proper time to whomever by right you ought to tell. Never be scandalized or astonished at anything you happen to see or learn of, endeavoring to preserve your soul in forgetfulness of all that.

9. For, should you desire to pay heed to things, many will seem wrong, even were you to live among angels, because of your not understanding

the substance of them. Take Lot's wife as an example: Because she was troubled at the destruction of the Sodomites and turned her head to watch what was happening, God punished her by converting her into a pillar of salt [Gn. 19:26]. You are thus to understand God's will: that even were you to live among devils you should not turn the head of your thoughts to their affairs, but forget these things entirely and strive to keep your soul occupied purely and entirely in God, and not let the thought of this thing or that hinder you from so doing.

And to achieve this, be convinced that in monasteries and communities there is never a lack of stumbling blocks, since there is never a lack of devils who seek to overthrow the saints; God permits this in order to prove and try religious.

And if you do not guard yourself, acting as though you were not in the house, you will not know how to be a religious no matter how much you do, nor will you attain holy denudation and recollection or free yourself of the harm arising from these thoughts. If you are not cautious in this manner, no matter how good your intention and zeal, the devil will catch you in one way or another. And you are already fully captive when you allow yourself distractions of this sort.

Recall what the Apostle St. James asserts: *If anyone thinks he is religious, not restraining the tongue, that one's religion is vain* [Jas. 1:26]. This applies as much to the interior as to the exterior tongue.

Against the Devil

10. The one who aspires to perfection should use three precautions to be delivered from the devil, one's second enemy. It should be noted that among the many wiles of the devil for deceiving spiritual persons, the most common is deceiving them under the appearance of good rather than of evil, for the devil already knows that they will scarcely choose a recognized evil. Thus you should always be suspicious of what appears good, especially when not obliged by obedience. To do the right thing, and be safe in such a matter, you ought to take the proper counsel.

The first precaution

11. Let, then, the first precaution be that, without the command of obedience, you never take upon yourself any work—apart from the obligations of your state—however good and full of charity it may seem, whether for yourself or for anyone else inside or outside the house. By such a practice you will win merit and security, avoid possession, and flee from harm and evils unknown to you, for God will one day demand an account. If you do not observe this precaution in little things as well as big, you will be unable to avoid the devil's deceiving you to a small or great degree, no matter how right you think you are.

Even if your negligence amounts to no more than not being governed by obedience in all things, you culpably err, since God wants obedience more than sacrifice [1 Sm. 15:22]. The actions of religious are not their own, but belong to obedience, and if you withdraw them from obedience, you will have to count them as lost.

The second precaution

12. Let the second precaution be that you always look on the superior as though on God, no matter who he happens to be, for he takes God's place. And note that the devil, humility's enemy, is a great and crafty meddler in this area. Much profit and gain come from considering the superior in this light, but serious loss and harm lie in not doing so. Watch, therefore, with singular care that you not dwell on your superior's character, mode of behavior, ability, or any other methods of procedure, for you will so harm yourself as to change your obedience from divine to human, being motivated only by the visible traits of the superior, and not by the invisible God whom you serve through him.

Your obedience is vain and all the more fruitless in the measure that you allow the superior's unpleasant character to annoy you or his good and pleasing manners to make you happy. For I tell you that by inducing religious to consider these modes of conduct, the devil has ruined a vast number of them in their journey toward perfection. Their acts of obedience are worth little in God's sight, since they allow these considerations to interfere with obedience.

If you do not strive, with respect to your personal feelings, to be unconcerned about whether this one or another be superior, you will by no means be a spiritual person, nor will you keep your vows well.[2]

The third precaution

13. The third precaution, directly against the devil, is that you ever seek with all your heart to humble yourself in word and in deed, rejoicing in the good of others as if it were your own, desiring that they be given precedence over you in all things; and this you should do wholeheartedly. You will thereby overcome evil with good [Rom. 12:21], banish the devil, and possess a happy heart. Try to practice this more with those who least attract you. Realize that if you do not train yourself in this way, you will

---

2. The relationship between the superior and others in the community must be grounded in faith. As for superiors, according to Eliseo de los Mártires, John warned in his oral teaching against boorishness and cruelty on their part and the consequent effect of promoting pusillanimity in subjects and a fear of expressing one's opinion in community meetings lest the superior be offended.

not attain real charity or make any progress in it.

And ever prefer to be taught by all rather than desire to teach even the least of all.

Against Oneself and the Shrewdness of Sensuality

14. The other three precautions to be practiced in the wish to conquer one's own self and sensuality, the third enemy.

The first precaution

15. The first precaution is to understand that you have come to the monastery so that all may fashion you and try you. Thus, to free yourself from the imperfections and disturbances that can be engendered by the mannerisms and attitudes of the religious and draw profit from every occurrence, you should think that all in the community are artisans—as indeed they are—present there in order to prove you; that some will fashion you with words, others by deeds, and others with thoughts against you; and that in all this you must be submissive as is the statue to the craftsman who molds it, to the artist who paints it, and to the gilder who embellishes it.

If you fail to observe this precaution, you will not know how to overcome your sensuality and feelings, nor will you get along well in the community with the religious or attain holy peace or free yourself from many stumbling blocks and evils.

The second precaution

16. The second precaution is that you should never give up your works because of a want of satisfaction and delight in them, if they are fitting for the service of God. Neither should you carry out these works merely because of the satisfaction or delight they accord you, but you should do them just as you would the disagreeable ones. Otherwise it will be impossible for you to gain constancy and conquer your weakness.

The third precaution

17. The third precaution is that the interior person should never set eyes on the pleasant feelings found in spiritual exercises, becoming attached to them and carrying out these practices only for the sake of this satisfaction. Nor should such a person run from the bitterness that may be found in them, but rather seek the arduous and distasteful and embrace it. By this practice, sensuality is held in check; without this practice you will never lose self-love or gain the love of God.

INTRODUCTION TO THE
COUNSELS TO A RELIGIOUS

These *Counsels* written for a friar are similar in content and tone to the previous precautions. This fact suggests they were composed about the same time. If they differ from the *Precautions* in any way it is mainly in their not adhering to the fixed structure of that work.

The copy that editors find most reliable was made from an ancient manuscript that had been conserved by the Carmelite nuns in Bujalance. Appearing in the manuscript after these *Counsels* are the *Degrees of Perfection,* which editors often placed among John's *Sayings.* The tendency now is to leave them here since they seem destined for the same friar.

COUNSELS TO A RELIGIOUS
ON HOW TO REACH PERFECTION

Jesus Mariae filius

1. Your holy Charity[1] with few words asked me for a great deal. An answer would require much time and paper. Seeing, then, that I lack both of these, I will try to be concise and jot down only certain points and counsels that in sum will contain much, so that whoever observes them perfectly will attain a high degree of perfection.

The one who wishes to be a true religious and fulfill the promises of the profession that was made to God, advance in virtue, and enjoy the consolations and the delight of the Holy Spirit, will be unable to do so without trying to practice with the greatest diligence the four following counsels concerning resignation, mortification, the practice of virtue, and bodily and spiritual solitude.

2. In order to practice the first counsel, concerning resignation, you should live in the monastery as though no one else were in it. And thus you should never, by word or by thought, meddle in things that happen in the community, nor with individuals in it, desiring not to notice their good or bad qualities or their conduct. And in order to preserve your tranquility of soul, even if the whole world crumbles you should not desire to advert to these things or interfere, remembering Lot's wife who

---

1. "Your holy Charity" or "your Charity" was the form of addressing those friars who were not priests; "your Reverence" was the form used for priests.

was changed into hard stone because she turned her head to look at those who in the midst of much clamor and noise were perishing [Gn. 19:26].

You should practice this with great fortitude, for you will thereby free yourself from many sins and imperfections and guard the tranquility and quietude of your soul with much profit before God and others.

Ponder this often, because it is so important that, for not observing it, many religious not only failed to improve through their other works of virtue and religious observance, but ever slipped back from bad to worse.

3. To practice the second counsel, which concerns mortification, and profit by it, you should engrave this truth on your heart. And it is that you have not come to the monastery for any other reason than to be worked and tried in virtue; you are like the stone that must be chiseled and fashioned before being set in the building.

Thus you should understand that those who are in the monastery are craftsmen placed there by God to mortify you by working and chiseling at you. Some will chisel with words, telling you what you would rather not hear; others by deed, doing against you what you would rather not endure; others by their temperament, being in their person and in their actions a bother and annoyance to you; and others by their thoughts, neither esteeming nor feeling love for you.

You ought to suffer these mortifications and annoyances with inner patience, being silent for love of God and understanding that you did not enter the religious life for any other reason than for others to work you in this way, and so you become worthy of heaven. If this was not your reason for entering the religious state, you should not have done so, but should have remained in the world to seek your comfort, honor, reputation, and ease.

4. The second counsel is wholly necessary for religious so they may fulfill the obligations of their state and find genuine humility, inward quietude, and joy in the Holy Spirit. If you do not practice this, you will know neither how to be a religious nor even why you came to the religious life. Neither will you know how to seek Christ (but only yourself), or find peace of soul, or avoid sinning and often feeling troubled.

Trials will never be lacking in religious life, nor does God want them to be. Since he brings souls there to be proved and purified, like gold, with hammer and the fire [Ecclus. 2:5], it is fitting that they encounter trials and temptations from human beings and from devils, and the fire of anguish and affliction.[2]

---

2. The expressions resemble those used in John's treatment of the passive purification of the spirit (cf. F. 2. 25-26) and suggest that a frequent and efficacious form of passive purification is wrought through the charity practiced in community life.

The religious must undergo these trials and should endeavor to bear them patiently and in conformity to God's will, and not so sustain them that instead of being approved by God in this affliction he be reproved for not having wanted to carry the cross of Christ in patience.

Since many religious do not understand that they have entered religious life to carry Christ's cross, they do not get along well with others. At the time of reckoning they will find themselves greatly confused and frustrated.

5. To practice the third counsel, which concerns the practice of virtue, you should be constant in your religious observance and in obedience without any concern for the world, but only for God. In order to achieve this and avoid being deceived, you should never set your eyes on the satisfaction or dissatisfaction of the work at hand as a motive for doing it or failing to do it, but on doing it for God. Thus you must undertake all things, agreeable or disagreeable, for the sole purpose of pleasing God through them.

6. To do this with fortitude and constancy and acquire the virtues quickly, you should take care always to be inclined to the difficult more than to the easy, to the rugged more than to the soft, to the hard and distasteful in a work more than to its delightful and pleasant aspects; and do not go about choosing what is less a cross, for the cross is a light burden [Mt. 11:30]. The heavier a burden is, the lighter it becomes when borne for Christ.

You should try, too, by taking the lowest place always, that in things bringing comfort to your brothers in religion they be preferred to you. This you should do wholeheartedly, for it is the way to becoming greater in spiritual things, as God tells us in his Gospel: *Qui se humiliaverit exaltabitur*[3] [Mt. 23:12].

7. To practice the fourth counsel, which concerns solitude, you should deem everything in the world as finished. Thus, when (for not being able to avoid it) you have to deal with some matter, do so in as detached a way as you would if it did not exist.

8. Pay no heed to the things out in the world, for God has already withdrawn and released you from them. Do not handle any business yourself that you can do through a third person. It is very fitting for you to desire to see no one and that no one see you.

And note carefully that if God will ask a strict account from all the faithful of every idle word, how much more will he ask it of religious who

---

3. "Whoever humbles himself will be exalted."

have consecrated all their life and works to him. And God will demand all of this on the day of reckoning.

9. I do not mean here that you fail to fulfill the duties of your state with all necessary and possible care, and any others that obedience commands, but that you execute your tasks in such a way that no fault is committed; for neither God nor obedience wants you to commit a fault.

You should consequently strive to be incessant in prayer, and in the midst of your corporal practices do not abandon it. Whether you eat, or drink, or speak, or converse with lay people, or do anything else, you should always do so with desire for God and with your heart fixed on him. This is very necessary for inner solitude, which demands that the soul dismiss any thought that is not directed to God. And in forgetfulness of all the things that are and happen in this short and miserable life, do not desire to know anything in any way except how better to serve God and keep the observance of your institute.

10. If your Charity observes these four counsels with care, you will reach perfection in a very short time. These counsels are so interdependent that if you are lacking in one of them, you will begin to lose the profit and gain you have from practicing the others.

DEGREES OF PERFECTION

1. Do not commit a sin for all there is in the world, or any deliberate venial sin, or any known imperfection.

2. Endeavor to remain always in the presence of God, either real, imaginative, or unitive insofar as is permitted by your works.

3. Neither do anything nor say any notable word that Christ would not have done or said were he in the state I am, as old as I, and with the same kind of health.

4. Strive for the greater honor and glory of God in all things.

5. Do not omit mental prayer for any occupation, for it is the sustenance of your soul.

6. Do not omit examination of conscience because of any of your occupations, and for every fault do some penance.

7. Be deeply sorry for any time that is lost or that passes without your loving God.

8. In all things, both high and low, let God be your goal, for in no other way will you grow in merit and perfection.

9. Never give up prayer, and should you find dryness and difficulty, persevere in it for this very reason. God often desires to see what love your soul has, and love is not tried by ease and satisfaction.

10. In heaven and on earth, always the lowest and last place and office.

11. Never interfere in what you are not ordered to do, or be obstinate about anything, even though you may be right. And if, as the saying goes, they give you an inch, do not take a mile. Some deceive themselves in such matters and think they have an obligation to do that which—if they reflect upon it well—in no way obliges them.

12. Pay no attention to the affairs of others, whether they be good or bad, for besides the danger of sin, this is a cause of distractions and lack of spirit.

13. Strive always to confess your sins with a deep knowledge of your own wretchedness and with clarity and purity.

14. Even though your obligations and duties are difficult and disagreeable to you, you should not become dismayed, for this will not always be so. And God, who proves the soul by a precept under the guise of a trial [Ps.94:20], will after a time accord it the experience of blessing and gain.

15. Remember always that everything that happens to you, whether prosperous or adverse, comes from God, so that you become neither puffed up in prosperity nor discouraged in adversity.

16. Remember always that you came here for no other reason than to be a saint; thus let nothing reign in your soul that does not lead you to sanctity.

17. Always be more disposed toward giving to others than giving to yourself, and thus you will not be envious of or selfish toward your neighbor. This is to be understood from the viewpoint of perfection, for God is angered with those who do not give precedence to his good pleasure over that of humans.

Soli Deo honor et gloria.

INTRODUCTION TO THE
CENSURE AND OPINION

At the time Nicolás Doria was vicar general he asked John of the Cross to examine an account written by a discalced Carmelite nun and give his opinion about her spirit. We do not know who this nun was or the community to which she belonged, but we know that other learned men had judged her favorably. Discerning five defects in the nun's report on her experiences, John gives a negative evaluation of her spirit in this written opinion for his vicar general.

CENSURE AND OPINION

[On the spirit and procedure in prayer of a discalced Carmelite
nun, given by St. John of the Cross
Segovia, 1588-91]

In the affective manner with which this soul proceeds there appear to be five defects manifesting a lack of the good spirit.

First, it seems she bears within herself a great fondness for possessing things, whereas the good spirit is always very detached in its appetites.

Second, she is too secure in her spirit and has little fear of being inwardly mistaken. Where this fear is absent, the spirit of God is never present to preserve the soul from harm, as the Wise Man says [Prv. 15:27].

Third, it seems she has the desire to persuade others that her experiences are good and manifold. Persons of a genuine spirit do not desire to do this, but, on the contrary, desire that their experiences be considered of little value and despised, and this they do themselves.

Fourth—and this is the main fault—the effects of humility are not manifest in her attitude. When favors are genuine, as she says here that hers are, they are ordinarily never communicated to a soul without first undoing and annihilating it in the inner abasement of humility. And if these favors had produced this effect in her, she would not have failed to say something about it here, and even a great deal. For the first thing the soul esteems and is eager to speak of are the effects of humility, which, certainly, are so strong that they cannot be disguised. For although they may not be so noticeable in all the apprehensions of God, still, these apprehensions that she here calls union are never present without them: *Quoniam antequam exaltetur anima, humiliatur* [Prv. 18:12][1] and, *Bonum mihi quia humiliasti me* [Ps. 119:71].[2]

---

1. "Before the soul is exalted, it is humbled."
2. "It is good for me that you have humbled me."

730

Fifth, her style and language don't seem to come from the spirit she claims, for the good spirit itself teaches a simpler style, one without the affectation or exaggeration she uses. And all this about what she said to God and God said to her seems to be nonsense.

I would advise that they should not command or allow her to write anything about this, and her confessor should not show willingness to hear of it, other than to hold it in little esteem and contradict it. Let them try her in the practice of sheer virtue, especially in self-contempt, humility, and obedience; and by the sound of the metal when tapped the quality of soul caused by so many favors will show itself. And the tests must be good ones, for there is no devil that will not suffer something for his honor.

The Letters

INTRODUCTION TO
THE LETTERS

The number of St. John of the Cross's letters, or letter fragments, thus far discovered is unfortunately small. One would have hoped for many more than 33. The date on the earliest is as late as 1581. One reason for the scarcity is that during the investigation against John in the final year of his life many of his disciples burned his letters, as well as other little works, out of fear that calumnies would be spread against both him and themselves. But even at that, we have no letters to his mother, who died in 1580, or to his brother of whom he was so fond. None of his words to Teresa, who did not save letters once she had answered them, has remained; nor of hers to him. But even as his letters were being destroyed and he was on his death bed, John continued generously, with the help of his secretary, to carry on correspondence.

One recipient of his letters, a Carmelite nun in Toledo, testified that a letter from him had the same effect as hearing him speak. Revealing John as warm, compassionate, and deep, his correspondence served mostly for the purpose of spiritual direction. It provides examples of the application of his teaching to the particular needs of individuals. The general content of the letters is unmistakably his: live in the poverty of faith, hope, and love because to receive the embraces of God you must be empty of desire for earthly and heavenly satisfaction.

The places where extant autographs are conserved will be mentioned in the footnotes. Manuscript copies of the other letters, with some exceptions that will also be pointed out, are conserved in the National Library of Madrid.

Letter 1

[To Catalina de Jesús, discalced Carmelite
Baeza, July 6, 1581]

Jesus be in your soul, my daughter Catalina.[1]

Although I don't know where you are, I want to write these lines trusting that our Madre[2] will send them on to you if you are not with her. And if it is so—that you are not with her—be consoled with the thought that you are not as abandoned and alone as I am down here. For after that whale swallowed me up and vomited me out on this alien port, I have never merited to see her again or the saints up there.[3] God has done well, for, after all, abandonment is a steel file and the endurance of darkness leads to great light. May it please God that we do not walk in darkness!

Oh, how many things I should like to say! But I am writing this very much in the dark as to whether you will receive it or not. So, I'll stop here without finishing.

Commend me to God. I do not want to say any more about matters down here, for I have no desire to do so.

From Baeza, July 6, 1581.

Your servant in Christ,

Fray John of the Cross

Address: for Sister Catalina de Jesús, discalced Carmelite, wherever she may be.

Letter 2

[To María de Soto, in Baeza
Granada, March 1582][4]

Jesus be in your soul, my daughter in Christ.

I received your letter, which was an act of charity toward me, and I

---

1. Catalina de Jesús made her religious profession in Valladolid (1572). In 1580 she was transferred to the foundation in Palencia and in 1582, accompanied St. Teresa on the new foundation in Burgos. She later transferred to Soria, where she died in 1599. John helped her when she suffered from interior trials.
2. He is alluding to St. Teresa to whom he also wrote, including this letter along with hers.
3. The biblical allusion is to Jonah 2:1-2; through it John refers to his imprisonment in Toledo and his subsequent transfer to Andalusia.
4. The autograph is conserved by the discalced Carmelite nuns in Gmunden, Austria.

would very much like to comply with what you ask of me in it and thereby please you and your sisters.[5] But since God ordains things differently from what we may have in mind, we must conform ourselves to his will.

They have made me prior of this house in Granada; and it is a place very apt for the service of God. His Majesty does everything for the best. Would that you with your sisters lived here so that I could then in some way make you happy. I trust in God that he will give you great happiness.

Be careful that you do not stop going to confession; and tell the same to your sisters. May you all recommend me to God, for I will never forget to do so for you.

Don't fail to have recourse to Father Fray Juan,[6] however tired he may be. Remain with God, and may His Majesty give you his Holy Spirit.

From Los Santos Mártires in Granada, March 1582

Your servant in Christ

Fray John of the Cross

Letter 3

[To Madre Ana de San Alberto, prioress of Caravaca[7]
Granada, 1582]

...since you say nothing to me, I tell you not to be foolish and not to walk with fears that intimidate your soul. Return to God what he has given you and gives you each day. It seems you want to measure God by the measure of your own capacity, but it will not be so. Prepare yourself, for God desires to grant you a great favor.

---

5. María de Soto lived as a beata; one of her sisters was named Ana. They had belonged to a circle of people John directed in Baeza, but in January, 1582, he was elected prior of the community in Granada.

6. Probably Fray Juan de Santa Ana, to whom John writes in Letter 32.

7. Ana de San Alberto was born in Malagón and entered the monastery founded there by St. Teresa. Teresa brought her with her on the foundations in Beas and Sevilla. From Sevilla she sent her to make the foundation in Caravaca. Madre Ana was prioress there for 15 consecutive years and died in 1624. About January, 1580, Teresa wrote to her: "I will arrange for Padre Fray John of the Cross to go down there. Deal with him as though he were myself. Let the Sisters speak frankly with him about their souls. Let them find comfort in him, for he is a soul to whom God communicates his spirit." In her *Foundations,* 27. 8, Teresa writes of Ana de San Alberto: "I arranged for someone to be prioress who I trusted would fulfill the office very well, for she is better than I."

Letter 4

[To the same Ana de San Alberto
Granada, 1582]

...How long, daughter, do you think you will be carried in the arms of others? Now I desire to see you so greatly despoiled of and detached from creatures that all hell would not be enough to disturb you. What tears are these, so trifling, that you are shedding these days? How much good time do you think you have lost with these scruples? Should you desire to let me know of your trials, go to that Spotless Mirror of the Eternal Father [Wis. 7:26], that is, His Son, for there I see your soul every day, and doubtless you will be consoled and not find it necessary to beg at the doors of poor people.

Letter 5

[To Madre Ana de San Alberto, prioress of Caravaca
Sevilla, June 1586][8]

Jesus be in your soul.

At the time I left Granada for the foundation in Córdoba, I wrote to you in haste. And afterward, while in Córdoba, I received your letters and those of the gentlemen who were going to Madrid and who must have thought they would meet me while I was at the meeting of definitors. But you know this meeting never took place because we were waiting for the completion of these foundations and visitations. The Lord gives us so much to do these days that we can hardly keep up with it all. The foundation for the friars in Córdoba was completed with greater applause and solemnity throughout the entire city than was ever given there to any other religious order. All the clergy and confraternities of Córdoba gathered, and the Most Blessed Sacrament was brought with great solemnity from the Cathedral. All the streets were beautifully decorated, and the people acted as though it were the feast of Corpus Christi. This took place on the Sunday after Ascension Thursday. The Bishop came and preached, praising us highly. The house is situated in the best district of the city, in the neighborhood of the Cathedral.

I am now in Sevilla for the transference of our nuns, who have bought some very fine houses. Although the houses cost around 14,000 ducats,

---

8. A photocopy of the lost autograph was published in *Biblioteca Mística Carmelitana*, vol. 13.

they are worth more than 20,000. The nuns are now settled in them, and on the feast of St. Barnabas, the Cardinal will reserve the Most Blessed Sacrament with great solemnity. I intend to leave another monastery of friars here before departing, so there will then be two monasteries of friars here in Sevilla. Between now and the feast of St. John I shall depart for Ecija, where with God's help, we shall make another foundation, then to Málaga, and from there to the definitory meeting.

Would that I had the commission for this foundation as I have had for the others and could avoid these many delays. But I hope in God that it will be accomplished, and in the meeting I will do all I can. Tell this to these gentlemen to whom I am writing.

I am sorry you did not immediately sign the deed regarding the matter with the Fathers of the Society, for from what I observe they are not people who keep to their word. Thus I think they will not only deviate partly but, if the matter is deferred and if it is expedient for them, they will turn back completely. Hence take careful note of what I say: Without mentioning anything to them or to anyone, discuss with Señor Gonzalo Muñoz the purchase of the other house in that other locale, and sign the deed. For since they see that they have you by the hook, they are in no hurry. It matters little if afterward it be known that we bought only with the intention of being freed from our annoyance. Thus they will agree without so much breaking of heads, and we will even oblige them to agree to whatever we desire. Tell this to only a few, and do it, for sometimes you cannot surmount one ruse without using another.[9]

I should like you to send me the small book of the Canticles of the Bride, for surely by now Sister Francisca de la Madre de Dios is finished copying them.[10]

This definitory meeting is being greatly delayed, and I am sorry on account of my desire that Doña Catalina enter, for I want to give...[11]

From Seville, June, 1586.

Dear Daughter in Christ.

Your Servant

Fray John of the Cross

Be sure to give my heartiest greetings to Señor Gonzalo Muñoz. I am not writing to His Honor because I do not want to tire him and because Your Reverence can tell him what I have said here.

---

9. "For reasons of charity" this paragraph was suppressed in past editions and manuscript copies.

10. He is alluding to the *Spiritual Canticle*.

11. Catalina de Otálora was one of the lady foundresses of the monastery in Caravaca. Teresa speaks of her in *Foundations*, ch. 27. Here the rest of the autograph (about 15 lines) is torn off. What follows comes from other sources.

Letter 6

[To a discalced Carmelite nun[12]
en route from Granada to Madrid, August 1586]

...Daughter, those who are strong soldiers God will try in dryness and emptiness concerning all things so they might be victorious in battle, for they know how to drink water from their hands while standing—not bending over to the ground. They are like the soldiers of Gideon who conquered through the dry clay jars that had lighted candles within [Jgs. 7:5-7, 16-23]. The jars signify the dryness of sense; and within, the good and enkindled spirit.

Letter 7

[To the discalced Carmelite nuns of Beas
Málaga, November 18, 1586][13]

Jesus be in your souls, my daughters.

Do you think that, since you see me so silent, I have lost sight of you and have ceased considering how with great ease you can become saints and walk in the joy of your beloved Bridegroom with great delight and sure protection? I am coming to Beas, and you will see how I have not forgotten. And we shall see the riches gained in pure love and in the paths of eternal life and the beautiful steps you are making in Christ, whose brides are his delight and crown. It is unworthy of the crown that it roll along the ground, for it should be taken in the hands of the angels and seraphim and placed with reverence and esteem on the head of its Lord.

When the heart walks along the ground among base things, the crown rolls and is kicked by every base thing. But when a person attains to a lofty heart, as David says, then God is exalted [Ps. 64:7-8] with the crown of his bride's lofty heart, with which they crowned him on the day of the joy of his heart [Sg. 3:11], that day in which his delights were to be with the children of the earth [Prv. 8:31]. These waters of inward delights do not spring from the earth. One must open toward heaven the mouth of desire, empty of all other fullness, that thus it may not be reduced or restricted by some mouthful of another pleasure, but truly empty and open toward him who says: *Open your mouth wide and I will fill it* [Ps. 81:11].

Accordingly, those who seek satisfaction in something no longer keep themselves empty that God might fill them with his ineffable delight. And

---

12. Probably María del Nacimiento, subprioress in Madrid.
13. A copy is conserved in the parish museum of Pastrana.

thus just as they go to God so do they return, for their hands are encumbered and cannot receive what God is giving. May God deliver us from these evil obstacles that hinder such sweet and delightful freedom.

Serve God, my beloved daughters in Christ, following in his footsteps of mortification, in utter patience, in total silence, and with every desire to suffer, becoming executioners of your own satisfactions, mortifying yourselves, if perhaps something remains that must die and something still impedes the inner resurrection of the Spirit who dwells within your souls. Amen.

From Málaga, November 18, 1586

Your servant,

Fray John of the Cross

Letter 8

[To the discalced Carmelite nuns of Beas
Granada, November 22, 1587]

Jesus and Mary be in your souls, my daughters in Christ.

Your letter was a great comfort to me. May Our Lord repay you. My failure to write was not due to any unwillingness, for indeed I desire your great good, but to my belief that enough has already been said and written for doing what is important; and that what is wanting, if anything is wanting, is not writing or speaking—rather these usually superabound—but silence and work. Furthermore, speaking distracts one, while silence and work recollects and strengthens the spirit. Once individuals know what has been told them for their benefit, they no longer need to hear or speak, but to put it into practice, silently and carefully and in humility and charity and contempt of self. They must not then go in search of new things that serve only to satisfy the appetite outwardly—although they are not able to satisfy it—and leave the spirit weak and empty without interior virtue. Hence it follows that neither the former nor the latter is of profit. We can compare this situation to one who eats before digesting what was previously eaten; for since the natural heart is divided between the two portions, it has not the strength to convert everything into substance, and one becomes sick.

It is very necessary, my daughters, to hide the spirit from the devil and from our senses, for if we do not, without realizing it we shall find ourselves very backward and far from the virtues of Christ. Afterward we shall awaken only to find our labor and work done in the wrong way, and thinking that we were carrying a lighted lamp, we shall discover that it has gone out [Mt. 25:7-8]. Because by blowing, in our opinion to keep it lighted, we perhaps did more to extinguish it. I say, then, so this might not happen and the spirit be preserved, that there is no better remedy than to suffer, to do, and to be silent, and to close the senses through the inclination toward and practice of solitude and forgetfulness of all creatures and happenings, even though the whole world crumbles. Never, whether in adversity or in prosperity, cease to quiet your heart with deepest love, so as to suffer whatever comes along. For perfection is so singularly important and the delight of the spirit is so high-priced that all of this is hardly enough to obtain it. It is impossible to advance without doing and suffering virtuously, all enveloped in silence.

Keep this in mind, daughters: the soul that is quick to turn to speaking and conversing is slow to turn to God. For when it is turned toward God, it is then strongly and inwardly drawn toward silence and flight from all conversation. For God desires a soul to rejoice with him more than with any other person, however advanced and helpful the person may be.

I commend myself to your prayers; and be assured that although my charity is little, it is so directed toward you that I do not forget those whom I owe so much in the Lord. May he be with us all. Amen.

From Granada, November 22, 1587.

Fray John of the Cross

Our greatest need is to be silent before this great God with the appetite and with the tongue, for the only language he hears is the silent language of love.

Address: To Ana de Jesús[14] and the other discalced Carmelite Sisters of the Convent of Beas.

Letter 9

[To Madre Leonor Bautista,[15] discalced Carmelite in Beas
Granada, February 8, 1588][16]

Jesus be in Your Reverence.

Do not think, daughter in Christ, that I have ceased to grieve for you in your trials and for the others who share in them. Yet, in remembering that since God called you to live an apostolic life, which is a life of contempt, he is leading you along its road, I am consoled. After all, God

---

14. This is not Ana de Jesús (Lobera) for whom he wrote the *Spiritual Canticle;* this Ana was born near Madrid and made profession in Beas in 1585.

15. Leonor Bautista (Albacete) was born in Alcaraz and made profession in Beas in 1578. She later went on the foundation to Valencia, where she died in 1604.

16. A photocopy of the autograph appears in *Autógrafos del Místico Doctor San Juan de la Cruz* by Gerardo de San Juan la Cruz.

wishes religious to be religious—in such a way that they be done with all and that all be done with them. For it is God himself who wishes to be their riches, comfort, and delightful glory. God has granted Your Reverence a great favor, because truly forgetful of all things you will be able to enjoy his good in solitude, and for love of him have no care that they do to you what they will, since you do not belong to yourself but to God.[17]

Let me know if your departure for Madrid is certain and if Mother Prioress is coming, and give my best regards to my daughters Magdalena and Ana and to all the others, for I have no time to write them.

From Granada, February 8, 1588

Fray John of the Cross

Letter 10

[To Padre Ambrosio Mariano,[18] discalced Carmelite, prior in Madrid
Segovia, November 9, 1588][19]

Jesus be in Your Reverence.

Because of the many foundations, the need for religious, as Your Reverence knows, is very great. Thus Your Reverence must be patient, for Fray Miguel has to go to await Father Provincial in Pastrana and then finish the foundation of that monastery in Molina.[20]

Also, the fathers thought it would be expedient to give Your Reverence a subprior at once. And so they have given you Father Fray Angel, thinking that he will get along well with his prior, something that is most desirable in a monastery.[21] Your Reverence may give his patent letter to each one. You should be careful that no priest or other religious interfere with the novices, for as Your Reverence knows there is nothing more

---

17. He is alluding to the end of her term as prioress.
18. Ambrosio Azzaro (Mariano de San Benito) (1510-1594) was born in Italy. A student of law and theology, he was a theologian at the Council of Trent, but also a versatile engineer enlisted by Philip II for a project on the Guadalquivir River in Spain. He later left all to become a hermit, and then through the influence of St. Teresa entered the discalced Carmelites, making profession in 1570; see *Foundations* 17. 6-15.
19. The autograph is conserved by the discalced Carmelite nuns at San José in Avila.
20. Fray Miguel, who had recently finished his office of prior in Segovia, was at the time subprior in Madrid. The foundation in Molina never materialized.
21. The fathers are the other members of the council. John is presiding in the absence of the Vicar General. This Fray Angel seems to be Angel de San Gabriel of whom St. Teresa complains in *Foundations* 23. 9.

harmful than that the novices pass through many hands and others be disturbing them. Since he has so many novices, it is right to help and assist Father Fray Angel and even give him the authority of subprior (which he has now been given) so he might receive more respect in the house.

It seems now there was not much need for Father Fray Miguel here and he can better serve the order elsewhere.

There is nothing new concerning Father Gracián, except that Father Fray Antonio is already here.[22]

From Segovia, November 9, 1588.

Fray John of the Cross[23]

Letter 11

[To Doña Juana de Pedraza,[24] in Granada
Segovia, January 28, 1589][25]

Jesus be in your soul.

A few days ago I wrote to you through Father Fray Juan[26] in answer to your last letter, which, as was your hope, I prized. I have answered you in that letter, since I believe I have received all your letters. And I have felt your grief, afflictions, and loneliness. These, in silence, ever tell me so much that the pen cannot declare it. They are all comparable to knocks and rappings at the door of your soul so it might love more, for they cause more prayer and spiritual sighs to God that he might fulfill the soul's petition. I have already told you there is no reason to become disturbed over those little things, but do what they have ordered you to do; and when they impede it, be obedient and let me know of it, for God will provide what is best. God watches over the affairs of those who truly love him without their worrying about them.

In what concerns the soul, it is safest not to lean on anything or desire anything. A soul should find its support wholly and entirely in its director,

---

22. Father Jerónimo Gracián (1545-1614) was the son of one of Philip II's secretaries and worked closely with St. Teresa in the establishment of the discalced friars and nuns; see her glowing account of him in *Foundations* 23. Antonio de Heredia (1510-1601) was the Carmelite, along with John of the Cross, to join Teresa in inaugurating her way of life for the friars; see *Foundations* 13-14. He was present at the deaths of both Teresa and John of the Cross.

23. On the autograph, the secretary adds: P. fr. Gregorio de S. Angelo kisses the hands of Your Reverence.

24. Little is known of this devout penitent of John's in Granada.

25. The autograph is conserved by the discalced Carmelite friars in Concesa, Italy.

26. He seems to be referring to Juan Evangelista (1562-1638) who was his faithful disciple, friend, and confessor. From Juan Evangelista we have our best extant copy of the *Ascent of Mount Carmel*.

for not to do so would amount to no longer wanting a director. And when one director is sufficient and suitable, all the others are useless or a hindrance. Let not the soul be attached to anything, for since prayer is not wanting, God will take care of its possessions; they belong to no other owner, nor should they. I see this with myself: The more that things are mine, the more I set my heart and soul and care on them. The loved object becomes one with the lover, and so does God with the one who loves him. Hence one cannot forget the loved object without forgetting one's own soul; and even one's own soul is forgotten for the loved object, because one lives in the loved object more than in oneself.

O great God of love, and Lord! How many riches do you place in the soul that neither loves nor is satisfied save in you alone, for you give yourself to it and become one with it through love. And consequently you give for its enjoyment and love what it most desires in you and what brings it most profit. But because it behooves us not to go without the cross, just as our Beloved did not go without it, even to the death of love, God ordains our sufferings that we may love what we most desire, make greater sacrifices, and be worth more. But everything is brief, for it lasts only until the knife is raised; and then Isaac remains alive with the promise of a multiplied offspring [Gn. 22:1-18].

Patience is necessary in this poverty, my daughter; it is helpful in truly departing from our land and entering into life so as to enjoy everything completely, which is a privation of life.

Now I do not know when I shall leave. I am well, although my soul lags far behind. Commend me to God, and, when you can, give your letters to Fray Juan or to the nuns more often—and it would be better if they were not so short.

From Segovia, January 28, 1589.

Fray John of the Cross

Letter 12

[To a young lady from Narros del Castillo (Avila),[27] aspirant to the discalced Carmelites.
Segovia, February 1589(?)][28]

Jesus be in your soul.

The messenger, arriving at a time when I was unable to answer, continued his journey, and now on his return is here awaiting my reply.

---

27. This young lady, whom John had known when confessor at the monastery of the Incarnation in Avila, entered the community in Arenas, which later moved to Guadalajara. She took the name Ana de la Cruz.
28. The autograph is conserved by the discalced Carmelite nuns in Alcalá de Henares.

May God ever give you, my daughter, his holy grace so that in all things you may employ yourself entirely in his holy love and service, as is your obligation, since this is why he created and redeemed you.

A great deal could be said about the three points you raised, more than my lack of time and paper now permits. But I will speak to you of another three that you will find a help.

In regard to sins, which God so abhors that they obliged him to die: You should, in order to weep truly over them and avoid falling into them, have as little to do with people as possible, flee from them and never speak more than is necessary in each case. For conversing with people more than entirely necessary was never good for anyone, however holy. And together with this you should keep the law of God with great punctuality and love.

With regard to the Lord's passion: You should endeavor to treat your body with a discreet rigor, strive after self-contempt and mortification, and renounce the desire to do your own will or seek your own satisfaction, since that was the cause of his passion and death. And in all you do let it be with your mother's counsel.

In regard to the third point, which is glory: To have the right idea of glory and to love it, you should consider all the riches of the world and its delights as mud and vanity and weariness, as they truly are, and do not esteem anything, however signal and precious, except being in God's grace. All that is best here below is ugly and bitter when compared to those eternal goods for which we were created. And however brief the ugliness and bitterness, it will last forever in the soul that esteems it.

I have not forgotten your business matter, but nothing more can be done now, although I have a great desire to do so. Entrust this earnestly to God and take our Lady and St. Joseph as your advocates in it.

Give my best regards to your mother and let this letter be for her too. Will you both pray for me and ask your friends also to do so out of charity.

May God grant you his Spirit.

From Segovia, February.

> Fray John of the Cross

Letter 13

[To a discalced Carmelite friar
Segovia, April 14, 1589(?)]

May the peace of Jesus Christ, my son, be always in your soul.

I received Your Reverence's letter in which you told me of the great desires our Lord gives you to occupy your will in him alone by loving him above all things, and in which you asked for some counsels to help you do this.

I am happy God has given you such holy desires, and I shall be much happier if you carry them out. In order to do so, you should observe how all pleasures, joys, and attachments are ever caused in the soul by means of the desire and will for things that appear good, suitable, and delightful, being in that soul's opinion satisfying and precious. And accordingly the appetite of the will moves toward these things, hopes for them, rejoices in their possession, fears their loss, and grieves on losing them. And thus, according to its attachments and joy in things, the soul is disturbed and restless.

In order to annihilate and mortify these attachments to pleasures in all that is not God, Your Reverence ought to note that every particular thing in which the will can rejoice is sweet and delightful, since it is in one's opinion satisfying; and nothing delightful and sweet in which one can rejoice is God. For, since God is not apprehensible to the faculties, he cannot be the object of the appetites and satisfactions of the will. Since the soul cannot enjoy God essentially in this life, all the sweetness and delight it tastes, however sublime, cannot be God. Likewise, any particular satisfaction and desire of the will derives from its knowledge of such and such an object.

Since the will has never tasted God as he is or known him through some gratification of the appetite, and consequently does not know what God is like, it cannot know what the pleasure of God is; nor can its being, appetite, and satisfaction know how to desire God, for he transcends all its capacity. Thus it is obvious that none of all those particular things in which it can rejoice is God. In order to be united with him, the will must consequently be emptied of and detached from all disordered appetite and satisfaction with respect to every particular thing in which it can rejoice, whether earthly or heavenly, temporal or spiritual, so that purged and cleansed of all inordinate satisfactions, joys, and appetites it might be wholly occupied in loving God with its affections.

For if in any way the will can comprehend God and be united with him, it is through love and not through any gratification of the appetite. And since the delight, sweetness, and satisfaction that can come to the will is not love, none of the delightful feelings can be an adequate means for union of the will with God; it is the operation of the will that is the proportionate means for this union. The will's operation is quite distinct from the will's feeling: By its operation, which is love, the will is united with God and terminates in him, and not by the feeling and gratification of its appetite that remains in the soul and goes no further. The feelings only serve as stimulants to love, if the will desires to pass beyond them; and they serve for no more. Thus the delightful feelings do not of themselves lead the soul to God, but rather cause it to become attached to delightful feelings. But the operation of the will, which is the love of God, concentrates the affection, joy, pleasure, satisfaction, and love of the soul only on God, leaving aside all things and loving him above them all.

Hence if persons are moved to the love of God without dependence on the sweetness they feel, they leave aside this sweetness and center their love on God whom they cannot feel. Were they to love the sweetness and satisfaction, pausing and being detained in it, making an end and goal of the means, the work of the will would consequently be faulty. Since God is incomprehensible and inaccessible, the will, if it is to center its activity of love on him, must not set itself on what it can touch and apprehend with the appetite, but on what is incomprehensible and inaccessible to the appetite. Loving in this way, a soul loves truly and certainly according to the demands of faith; also in emptiness and darkness concerning its feelings, going beyond all the feelings it may experience in understanding its concepts. Thus it believes and loves above everything it can understand.

Hence they would be very foolish who would think that God is failing them because of their lack of spiritual sweetness and delight, or would rejoice, thinking they possess God because of the presence of this sweetness. And they would be more foolish if they were to go in search of this sweetness in God and rejoice and be detained in it. With such an attitude they would no longer be seeking God with their wills grounded in the emptiness of faith and charity, but they would be seeking spiritual satisfaction and sweetness, which are creatures, by following after their own pleasure and appetite. And thus they would no longer be loving God purely, above all things, which means centering all the strength of one's will on him. In being bound and attached to that creature by means of the appetite, the will does not rise above it to God, who is inaccessible. It is impossible for the will to reach the sweetness and delight of the divine union and receive and feel the sweet and loving embraces of God without the nakedness and void of its appetite with respect to every particular satisfaction, earthly and heavenly. This is what David meant when he said: *Dilata os tuum et implebo illud* [Ps. 81:10].[29]

It is worth knowing, then, that the appetite is the mouth of the will. It is opened wide when it is not encumbered or occupied with any mouthful of pleasure. When the appetite is centered on something, it becomes narrow by this very fact, since outside of God everything is narrow. That the soul have success in journeying to God and being joined to him, it must have the mouth of its will opened only to God himself, empty and dispossessed of every morsel of appetite, so God may fill it with his love and sweetness; and it must remain with this hunger and thirst for God alone, without desiring to be satisfied by any other thing, since here below it cannot enjoy God as he is in himself. And what is enjoyable—if there is a desire for it, as I say—impedes this union. Isaiah taught this

---

29. "Open wide your mouth and I will fill it."

when he said: *All you who thirst, come to the waters* [Is. 55:1]. He invites to the abundance of the divine waters of union with God only those who thirst for God alone and who have no money, that is, appetites.

It is very important and fitting for Your Reverence, if you desire to possess profound peace in your soul and attain perfection, that you surrender your whole will to God so that it may thus be united with him and that you do not let it be occupied with the vile and base things of earth.

May His Majesty make you as spiritual and holy as I desire you to be.

From Segovia, April 14,

Fray John of the Cross

Letter 14

[To Madre María de Jesús,[30] discalced Carmelite, prioress of Córdoba
Segovia, June 7, 1589][31]

Jesus be in Your Reverence and make you as holy and poor in spirit as you desire, and may His Majesty also grant this to me.

Enclosed is the permission for the four novices. See that they be good servants of God.

Now I want to answer all your questions briefly, for I have little time. I discussed them first with the fathers here because Our Father[32] is down there. May God bring him back to us safely.

1. The discipline of rods is no longer in use, even though the Office may be from the ferial day. This practice expired with the Carmelite rite, for with that rite this occurred only at certain times and there were few ferial days.[33]

2. Second, give neither to all—nor to anyone in particular—general permission to take the discipline three times a week as a recompense for this or anything else. In individual cases, as is the custom, you can make the decision. Keep to the common practice.

3. They should not ordinarily arise earlier in the morning than the

---

30. María de Jesús (Sandoval y Godínez) (1549-1604) was one of the young women of whom Teresa speaks in her *Foundations,* 22. She made profession in Beas, where she first met John. In 1589 she went as prioress to Córdoba.
31. The autograph is conserved by the discalced Carmelite nuns in Brussels.
32. The fathers are the members of the council, and "Our Father" is the title used in referring to the Vicar General, Nicolás Doria, who was in Andalusia at the time.
33. In the meeting of 1586, of which he speaks in Letter 5, the discalced Carmelites changed from the Jerusalem rite (observed in the Carmelite order) to the Roman rite. John was not in favor of the change, but adapted to it.

Constitutions prescribe—that is, the community.

4. Permissions expire when the major superior goes out of office. And so now as a result I am again sending you permission to allow the confessor, doctor, barber-surgeon, and laborers to enter the cloister in case of necessity.

5. Since you now have many empty places, we can discuss your question concerning Sister Aldonza when what you say is necessary. Give her my regards and commend me to God. Abide with him. I cannot write at greater length.

From Segovia, June 7, 1589

Fray John of the Cross

Letter 15

[To Madre Leonor de San Gabriel,[34] discalced Carmelite in
Córdoba
Segovia, July 8, 1589]

Jesus be in your soul, my daughter in Christ.

Thank you for your letter. And I thank God for having desired to use you in this foundation, since His Majesty has done this in order to bring you greater profit. The more he wants to give, the more he makes us desire—even to the point of leaving us empty in order to fill us with goods. You will be repaid for the goods (the love of your sisters) that you leave behind in Sevilla. Since the immense blessings of God can only enter and fit into an empty and solitary heart, the Lord wants you to be alone. For he truly loves you with the desire of being himself all your company. And Your Reverence will have to strive carefully to be content only with his companionship, so you might discover in it every happiness. Even though the soul may be in heaven, it will not be happy if it does not conform its will to this. And we will be unhappy with God, even though he is always present with us, if our heart is not alone, but attached to something else.

I truly believe the nuns in Sevilla will feel lonely without Your Reverence. But perhaps you have done all you could there and God desires you to be of use in the new place, for the foundation will be an important one. Endeavor to be of genuine help to your Mother Prioress,[35] with great conformity and love in all things; although I clearly see that I do not have to make this recommendation, for since you are older and more experi-

---

34. Leonor de San Gabriel made profession in Malagón. She accompanied St. Teresa on the foundations in Beas and Sevilla. She went on the foundation in Córdoba in 1589.

35. Madre María de Jesús to whom the previous letter was addressed.

enced, you already know what usually happens in these foundations. This was why we chose Your Reverence. Were it simply a matter of nuns, there are so many in the region that there is hardly room for them all.

Best regards to Sister María de la Visitación, and thank Sister Juana de San Gabriel for her greetings. May God give Your Reverence his Spirit.

From Segovia, July 8, 1589

Fray John of the Cross

Letter 16

[To Madre María de Jesús, discalced Carmelite,
prioress in Córdoba
Segovia, July 18, 1589]

Jesus be in your soul.

You have the obligation of responding to the Lord in accordance with the acclaim with which you were received in Córdoba, for I was certainly consoled in reading the account. It was ordained by God that you enter such poor houses and in such heat so that you could give some edification and let them know what you profess, which is the naked Christ, so those who are inclined to join you may know with what spirit they ought to come.

Enclosed are all the permissions. Be very careful about whom you receive in the beginning, for those who come after will look to them. See to it that they preserve the spirit of poverty and contempt for all things, with the desire to be content with God alone. If they don't, be assured that they will fall into a thousand spiritual and temporal necessities. And keep in mind that they will neither have nor feel any more needs than those to which they desire to submit their hearts. For the poor in spirit are happier and more constant in the midst of want because they have placed their all in nothingness, and in all things they thus find freedom of heart. O happy nothingness, and happy hiding place of the heart! For the heart has such power that it subjects all things to itself; this it does by desiring to be subject to nothing and losing all care so as to burn more in love.

My greetings in the Lord to all the sisters. Tell them that since our Lord has chosen them as foundation stones, they should consider what kind they ought to be, for the others must rest on the stronger ones. May they profit by this initial spirit that God gives in these beginnings so as to take up once again the way of perfection in all humility and detachment, interior and exterior, not with a childish spirit but with a robust will. Let them follow the path of mortification and penance, desiring that this Christ cost them something, and not be like those who seek their comfort and consolation either in God or outside him; but let them seek suffering, both in God and outside him, for love of him, in silence and hope and loving remembrance. Tell this to Gabriela and to her companions from Málaga, for I am writing to the others. May God give you his Spirit. Amen.

From Segovia, July 18, 1589

Fray John of the Cross

Father Fray Antonio and the other fathers send their regards. Give my greetings to Father Prior of Guadalcázar.

Address: For Madre María de Jesús, prioress of the monastery of Santa Ana de Córdoba, of the discalced Carmelites.

Letter 17

[To Magdalena del Espíritu Santo,[36] discalced Carmelite in Córdoba
Segovia, July 28, 1589]

Jesus be in your soul, my daughter in Christ.

I am happy to see the good resolutions shown in your letter. I praise God who provides in all things, for you will truly have need of these resolutions at the beginning of the foundation because of the heat, crowded quarters, poverty, and work that is everywhere; there will be so much of all this that you will not notice whether you suffer or not. Reflect that in these beginnings God does not want sluggish or cowardly souls, nor still less those who love themselves. And to avoid this, His Majesty helps more at these times so with a little diligence they can advance in every virtue. And it has been fortunate for you and a sign from God in that he has passed by others and chosen you. However much it costs you to leave everything behind, it shouldn't matter, because soon you would have had to leave it anyhow. To possess God in all, you should possess nothing in all. For how can the heart that belongs to one belong completely to the other?

Tell the same to Sister Juana, and commend me to God. May he be in your soul. Amen.

From Segovia, July 28, 1589

Fray John of the Cross

---

36. Magdalena del Espíritu Santo (d. 1640) made profession in Beas and went on the foundation to Córdoba in 1589, where she died. John drew a sketch of Mount Carmel and the path leading to its summit for her; a copy of this is extant. See his *Sketch of the Mount* at the beginning of the *Ascent*.

Letter 18

[To Padre Nicolás de Jesús (Doria),[37] vicar general
of the discalced Carmelites
Segovia, September 21, 1589]

Jesus and Mary be with Your Reverence.

We were very glad to know that Your Reverence arrived in good health
and that everything is so well there, and that the nuncio is well too. I hope
that God will look after his family; the religious here are in good health
and well united. I will try to carry out quickly what you ordered, although
the floods have not yet arrived.

Regarding the reception of aspirants in Genoa without their having
studied the humanities, the fathers[38] say that this does not matter if the
aspirants understand enough Latin to comply with the decrees of the
Council[39] (that they know how to construct sentences well) and that, if
with this alone they may be ordained there, they can be admitted. But the
fathers think that, if the Ordinaries there are not content with this, it
would seem that these aspirants do not have the sufficient knowledge
demanded by the Council and it would be burdensome to have to bring
them here to ordain or teach them. And, to tell the truth, they would not
want many Italians to come here.

The letters will be sent to Father Fray Nicolás[40] as Your Reverence says.
May our Lord watch over you as he sees is necessary.

From Segovia, September 21, 1589

Fray John of the Cross

---

37. Nicolás de Jesús (Doria) (1539-1594). St. Teresa speaks of him in her
Foundations, 30. Born in Genoa, he came to Spain as a banker and settled in
Sevilla. Renouncing his career, he entered the discalced Carmelites. In 1585, he
was elected provincial, and in 1588 became Vicar General for the Discalced. In
1593, he attended the general chapter in Cremona in which the separation of the
two branches of Carmelites was approved. He then received the title of General
for the Discalced, but died in the following year.
38. Doria had made a foundation for the discalced Carmelites in Genoa in 1584;
the fathers are the members of his council.
39. The Council of Trent (1545-1563).
40. Nicolás de San Juan (de Mena), who was at the time the order's procurator.

Letter 19

[To Doña Juana de Pedraza, in Granada
Segovia, October 12, 1589][41]

Jesus be in your soul and thanks to him that he has enabled me not to forget the poor, as you say, or be idle, as you say. For it greatly vexes me to think you believe what you say; this would be very bad after so many kindnesses on your part when I least deserved them. That's all I need now is to forget you! Look, how could this be so in the case of one who is in my soul as you are?

Since you walk in these darknesses and voids of spiritual poverty, you think that everyone and everything is failing you. It is no wonder that in this it also seems God is failing you. But nothing is failing you, neither do you have to discuss anything, nor is there anything to discuss, nor do you know this, nor will you find it, because all of these are doubts without basis. Those who desire nothing else than God walk not in darkness, however poor and dark they are in their own sight. And those who walk not presumptuously, or according to their own satisfactions, whether from God or from creatures, nor do their own will in anything, have nothing to stumble over or discuss with anyone. You are making good progress. Do not worry, but be glad! Who are you that you should guide yourself? Wouldn't that end up fine!

You were never better off than now because you were never so humble or so submissive, or considered yourself and all worldly things to be so small; nor did you know that you were so evil or God was so good, nor did you serve God so purely and so disinterestedly as now, nor do you follow after the imperfections of your own will and interests as perhaps you were accustomed to do. What is it you desire? What kind of life or method of procedure do you paint for yourself in this life? What do you think serving God involves other than avoiding evil, keeping his commandments, and being occupied with the things of God as best we can? When this is had, what need is there of other apprehensions or other lights and satisfactions from this source or that? In these there is hardly ever a lack of stumbling blocks and dangers for the soul, which by its understanding and appetites is deceived and charmed; and its own faculties cause it to err. And thus God does one a great favor when he darkens the faculties and impoverishes the soul in such a way that one cannot err with these. And if one does not err in this, what need is there in order to be right other than to walk along the level road of the law of God and of the Church, and live only in dark and true faith and certain hope and complete charity, expecting all our blessings in heaven, living here below like

---

41. The autograph is conserved by the discalced Carmelite nuns in Valladolid.

pilgrims, the poor, the exiled, orphans, the thirsty, without a road and without anything, hoping for everything in heaven?

Rejoice and trust in God, for he has given you signs that you can very well do so, and in fact you must do so. If you do not, it will not be surprising if he becomes angry at seeing you walk so foolishly when he is leading you by a road most suitable for you and has brought you to so safe a place. Desire no other path than this and adjust your soul to it (for it is a good one) and receive Communion as usual. Go to confession when you have something definite; you don't have to discuss these things with anyone. Should you have some problem, write to me about it. Write soon, and more frequently, for you can do so in care of Doña Ana when you are unable to do so through the nuns.[42]

I have been somewhat ill. Now I am well, but Fray Juan Evangelista is sick. Commend him and me also to God, my daughter in the Lord.

From Segovia, October 12, 1589

Fray John of the Cross

Address: To Doña Juana de Pedraza, in the house of the archdeacon of Granada, in front of the College of the Abbots.

Letter 20

[To a discalced Carmelite nun suffering from scruples
Shortly before Pentecost, 1590][43]

Jesus, Mary.

In these days try to keep interiorly occupied with a desire for the coming of the Holy Spirit and on the feast and afterward with his continual presence. Let your care and esteem for this be so great that nothing else will matter to you or receive your attention, whether it may concern some affliction or some other disturbing memories. And if there be faults in the house during these days, pass over them for love of the Holy Spirit and of what you owe to the peace and quietude of the soul in which he is pleased to dwell.

If you could put an end to your scruples, I think it would be better for your quietude of soul not to confess during these days. But when you do confess, you should do so in this manner:

In regard to thoughts and imaginings (whether they concern judgments, or other inordinate objects or representations, or any other

---

42. He is referring to Doña Ana de Peñalosa for whom he wrote the *Living Flame of Love*.

43. The autograph is conserved by the discalced Carmelite nuns of Santa Ana y San José in Madrid.

motions) that occur without being desired or accepted or deliberately adverted to: Do not confess them or pay attention to them or worry about them. It is better to forget them no matter how much they afflict the soul. At most you can mention in general any omission or remissness as regards the purity and perfection you ought to have in the interior faculties: memory, intellect, and will.

In regard to words: Confess any want of caution in speaking with truthfulness and rectitude, out of necessity, and with purity of intention.

In regard to deeds: Confess any lack of the proper and only motive—God alone without any other concern.

By such a confession you can be content and need not tell any other particular thing, however much it may battle against you. Receive Communion on Pentecost in addition to those days on which you usually receive.

When something distasteful or unpleasant comes your way, remember Christ crucified and be silent.

Live in faith and hope, even though you are in darkness, because it is in these darknesses that God protects the soul.

Cast your care on God, for he watches over you and will not forget you. Do not think that he leaves you alone; that would be an affront to him.

Read, pray, rejoice in God, both your good and your salvation. May he grant you this good and this salvation and conserve it all until the day of eternity. Amen. Amen.

Fray John of the Cross

Letter 21

[To Madre María de Jesús, discalced Carmelite,
prioress of Córdoba
Madrid, June 20, 1590][44]

Jesus be in your soul, my daughter in Christ.

The reason for my not having written during all this time is due more to my having been in such an out-of-the-way place, as is Segovia, than because of a lack of desire. My will to write remains ever the same, and I hope in God this will continue to be so. I have been sorry about your troubles.

I would desire that you not be so solicitous for the temporal things of the house because God will gradually forget you and you will come to a state of great spiritual and temporal need; for it is our anxiety that creates our needs. Cast your care on the Lord, daughter, and he will sustain you

---

44. The autograph is conserved by the discalced Carmelite nuns in Córdoba.

[Ps. 55:22], for he who gives, and wants to give, the highest cannot fail to give the least. Be careful that you do not lack the desire to be poor and in want; for if you do, at that very hour devotion will fail you and you will gradually weaken in the practice of virtue. If previously you desired poverty, now that you are superior you ought to desire and love it much more. You ought to govern and provide the house with virtues and ardent desires for heaven rather than with worries and plans about temporal and earthly things. The Lord tells us not to be thinking about food or clothing or tomorrow [Mt. 6:31-34].

What you should do is endeavor to keep yourself and the nuns most perfectly and religiously united with God, in forgetfulness of all creatures and of any concern about them, wholly one with God, and happy with him alone; for I assure you all the rest. I find it difficult to believe that the houses will help you out any longer,[45] since you are in so good a locality and receiving nuns from such well-to-do families. However, if I see some chance anywhere of helping you, I will not fail to do what I can.

I desire to send great comfort to Mother Subprioress. I hope in the Lord you will extend it to her, encouraging her to bear her pilgrimage and exile for love of him. Enclosed is a letter for her. To my daughters Magdalena, San Gabriel, and María de San Pablo, María de la Visitación, San Francisco and all, many greetings in our Good.[46] May he be ever in your spirit, my daughter. Amen.

From Madrid, June 20, 1590

Fray John of the Cross

Letter 22

[To Madre Leonor de San Gabriel, discalced Carmelite,
in Córdoba
Madrid, June or July, 1590(?)][47]

Jesus be in your soul, my daughter in Christ.

In reading your letter I felt sorry for you in your affliction, and I grieve over it because of the harm it can do your spirit and even your health. But you ought to know that I don't think you should be as afflicted as you are. For I do not see in Our Father any kind of dissatisfaction with you or even

---

45. He is probably referring to financial help given by the communities from which the nuns in Córdoba came.

46. They were all nuns of the community well known by John; some he refers to by their first name, and others by their religious title.

47. This autograph, in bad condition, is in possession of the discalced Carmelite nuns of Sanlúcar la Mayor in Sevilla.

any recollection of such a thing. And even if he may have had some, now with your repentance it would be lessened. And if he should still show some displeasure, I will take care to speak well of the matter. Do not be troubled or pay any attention to this, for you have no reason to. I certainly believe it is a temptation the devil brings to your mind so that what should be employed in God is taken up with this.

Be courageous, my daughter, and give yourself greatly to prayer, forgetting this thing and that, for after all we have no other good or security or comfort than this, for after having left all for God, it is right that we not long for support or comfort in anything but him, and it is still a great mercy...[48]

Address: To Madre Leonor de San Gabriel, subprioress of the discalced Carmelite nuns in Córdoba.

Letter 23

[To a person under his direction
Of uncertain date][49]

You have seen, daughter, how good it is not to have money, which only troubles us and is stolen from us, and for the treasures of the soul to be hidden and at peace so we cannot even know of or see them ourselves, for there is no worse thief than the one inside the house.

God deliver us from ourselves. May he give us what pleases him and never show it to us until he wishes to do so. And, after all, the one who stores up treasures out of love, stores them up for another. It is good that God guards and enjoys them, since they are all for him; and that we neither see them nor enjoy them so as not to deprive God of the joy he finds in the humility and the nakedness of our heart and in our contempt of worldly things for love of him.

It is a very manifest treasure and it gives great joy to see that the soul continues to please God openly, paying no attention to the foolish ones of the world who know not how to keep anything for the next life.

The Masses will be said, and I shall go willingly unless they notify me to the contrary. May God keep you.

Fray John of the Cross

---

48. The autograph of this letter has been so damaged that the contents cannot be completely deciphered.
49. A copy is contained in the manuscript Tardonense-Granadino, Montserrat.

Letter 24

[To Padre Luis de San Angelo,[50] in Andalusia
Segovia, 1589-1590 ?]

...If at any time someone, whether superior or anyone else, should try to persuade you of a lax teaching, even though it be confirmed by miracles, do not believe or embrace it; rather, greater penance and greater detachment from all things. And do not seek Christ without the cross.

Fray John of the Cross

Letter 25

[To Madre Ana de Jesús,[51] in Segovia
Madrid, July 6, 1591][52]

Jesus be in your soul.

Thank you very much for your letter; this puts me under greater obligation than before. If things did not turn out as you desired, you ought rather to be consoled and thank God profusely. Since His Majesty has so arranged matters, it is what most suits everyone. All that remains for us is to accept it willingly so that, since we believe he has arranged this, we may show it by our actions. Things that do not please us seem to be evil and harmful, however good and fitting they may be. And it is obvious that this is not evil or harmful, neither for me nor for anyone. It is in my favor since, being freed and relieved from the care of souls, I can, if I want and with God's help, enjoy peace, solitude, and the delightful fruit of forgetfulness of self and of all things. It is also good for others that I be separated from them, for thus they will be freed of the faults they would have committed on account of my misery.

What I ask of you, daughter, are your prayers to the Lord that whatever happens he may continue to grant me this favor. I still fear they will make me go to Segovia and not leave me so free from all things, although I will do what I can to free myself from this too. But if this cannot be, Madre Ana de Jesús will not be left without my direction, as she fears, and thus she

---

50. Luis de San Angelo received the habit from John in Granada in 1583, having had him for a confessor in Baeza. He at times accompanied John on his journeys.
51. Ana de Jesús (Jimena), a widow, made her profession in Segovia in 1575. St. Teresa speaks of her in her *Foundations*, 21.
52. A photocopy of the autograph may be found in the *Biblioteca Mística Carmelitana*, vol. 13.

will not die of this sorrow that the opportunity, in her opinion, of being very holy has come to an end. But whether leaving or staying, wherever or however things may come to pass, I will neither forget nor neglect you, as you say, because truly I desire your good forever.

Now, until God gives us this good in heaven, pass the time in the virtues of mortification and patience, desiring to resemble somewhat in suffering this great God of ours, humbled and crucified. This life is not good if it is not an imitation of his life. May His Majesty preserve you and augment his love in you as his holy beloved. Amen.

From Madrid, July 6, 1591

Fray John of the Cross

Address: To Madre Ana de Jesús, discalced Carmelite in Segovia

Letter 26

[To Madre María de la Encarnación,[53]
discalced Carmelite in Segovia
July 6, 1591][54]

...Do not let what is happening to me, daughter, cause you any grief, for it does not cause me any. What greatly grieves me is that the one who is not at fault is blamed. Men do not do these things, but God, who knows what is suitable for us and arranges things for our good. Think nothing else but that God ordains all, and where there is no love, put love, and you will draw out love...

Letter 27

[To Madre María de la Encarnación,
discalced Carmelite in Segovia
Segovia, July (?) 1591][55]

Jesus be in your soul, my daughter in Christ.

I thank you for sending for me so openly and with such determination because as a result my perplexity will not give me cause for delay. So, I will

---

53. María de la Encarnación (Jimena) was the daughter of Madre Ana de Jesús (Jimena). Both mother and daughter made their profession on the same day, July 2, 1575. María was prioress at the time this letter was written.
54. A fragment preserved by Jerónimo de San José in his *Historia*.
55. The autograph is conserved by the discalced Carmelite nuns of Antignano-Livorno, Italy.

certainly come tomorrow even though the weather may not be nice and I may not be feeling so well. Thus, I shall say no more than that I feel sorry for the sisters who are sick and that I am pleased with Your Reverence's good courage. May our Lord bring you to dwell in him so that the foolish things, which are ever arising, will make no impression on you.

Fray John of the Cross

Address: To the Mother Prioress

Letter 28

[To Doña Ana del Mercado y Peñalosa,[56] in Granada
La Peñuela, August 19, 1591]

Jesus be in your soul.

Although I have sent a letter by way of Baeza concerning the outcome of my journey, I am happy that these two servants of Señor Don Francisco are passing because of the opportunity it affords of sending these lines, which I am more certain will reach you.

I mentioned in the other letter how I desire to remain in this desert of La Peñuela, where I arrived about nine days ago and which is about six leagues north of Baeza. I like it very much, glory to God, and I am well. The vastness of the desert is a great help to the soul and body, although the soul fares very poorly. The Lord must be desiring that it have its spiritual desert. Well and good if it be for his service; His Majesty already knows what we are of ourselves. I don't know how long this will last, for Father Fray Antonio de Jesús threatens from Baeza that he will not leave me here for long. Be that as it may, for in the meanwhile I am well off without knowing anything, and the life of the desert is admirable.

This morning we have already returned from gathering our chickpeas, and so the mornings go by. On another day we shall thresh them. It is nice to handle these mute creatures, better than being badly handled by living ones. God grant that I may stay here. Pray for this, my daughter. But even though I am so happy here, I would not fail to come should you desire.

Take care of your soul and do not confess scruples or first movements or imaginings in which the soul does not desire to be detained. Look after your health, and do not fail to pray when you can.

I already mentioned in the other letter, though this one will reach you first, that you can write to me by way of Baeza since they have mail service

---

56. Ana de Peñalosa is the one for whom John wrote *The Living Flame of Love*.

there. You can address the letters to the Discalced Fathers in Baeza; I have notified them to send the letters on to me.

Regards to Señor Don Luis and to my daughter, Doña Inés.

May God give you his Spirit as I desire. Amen.

From La Peñuela, August 19, 1591

Fray John of the Cross

Letter 29

[To a woman under his direction[57] La Peñuela, August 22, 1591]

May God grant us the right intention in all these things and that we might not consent knowingly to sin; for in this way, even though the battery of temptation be great and of many kinds, one will walk safely and everything will be converted into a crown.

Give my greetings to your sister; and to Isabel de Soria my best regards in the Lord, and tell her that I marveled that she is not in Jaén, since there is a monastery there.

The Lord be in your soul, my daughter in Christ.

From La Peñuela, August 22, 1591

Fray John of the Cross

Letter 30

[To Madre Ana de San Alberto, discalced Carmelite in Caravaca La Peñuela, August-September 1591]

...You already know, daughter, the trials they are now suffering. God permits it to try his elect. In silence and in hope shall our strength be [Is. 30:15]. May God keep you and make you holy. Commend me to God.

---

57. This was probably one of the Soto sisters, Ana or María, who were friends of Isabel de Soria (mentioned later in the letter) and belonged to a group of persons directed by John in Baeza.

Letter 31

[To Doña Ana del Mercado y Peñalosa
La Peñuela, September 21, 1591][58]

Jesus be in your soul, my daughter in Christ.

I received here in La Peñuela the packet of letters the servant brought me. I greatly appreciate your concern. Tomorrow I am going to Ubeda for the cure of a slight bout of fever. Since it has been returning each day now for more than a week and does not leave me, it seems I shall need the help of medicine. Yet I plan to return here immediately, for I am indeed very happy in this holy solitude. And thus in regard to what you said about being careful not to accompany Padre Fray Antonio, be sure that in this matter and in all else that may require it, I shall be as cautious as possible.

I am very happy to know that Señor Don Luis[59] is now a priest of the Lord. May he be so for many years and may His Majesty fulfill the desires of his soul. Oh, how blessed a state this is for leaving aside cares and speedily enriching the soul! Congratulate him for me. I dare not ask him that he might some day remember me at the sacrifice of the Mass, and I as a debtor will ever remember him. Even though I am forgetful, I will not be able to forget him, since he is so close to his sister whom I always remember.

Greetings in the Lord to my daughter Doña Inés.[60] And may both of you pray God to prepare me that he may bring me to himself. I cannot think of any more to write now and I am also closing on account of the fever, for I would like to write at greater length.

From La Peñuela, September 21, 1591

Fray John of the Cross

You say nothing about the lawsuit, whether it is being tried or still to come up.

---

58. The autograph is conserved by the discalced Carmelite nuns in Salamanca.
59. Doña Ana's brother.
60. Doña Ana's niece. Later, in 1597, both Doña Ana and her niece received permission from Rome to live in a monastery of discalced Carmelite nuns and wear a religious habit.

Letter 32

[To Padre Juan de Santa Ana,[61] discalced Carmelite in Málaga
Ubeda, October-November, 1591][62]

...Son, do not let this grieve you, for they cannot take the habit from me save for being incorrigible or disobedient. I am very ready to amend all I may have done wrong and obey in whatever penance they may give me.

Letter 33

[To a discalced Carmelite nun in Segovia[63]
Ubeda, October-November 1591]

...Have a great love for those who contradict and fail to love you, for in this way love is begotten in a heart that has no love. God so acts with us, for he loves us that we might love by means of the very love he bears toward us.

---

61. Juan de Santa Ana was at El Calvario when John went there after escaping from prison, and was his companion on a number of journeys.
62. This fragment is conserved by José de Jesús María (Quiroga) in his *Historia.*
63. This person's identity is unknown.

Glossary
and
Indices

GLOSSARY OF TERMS

The purpose of this glossary is to present briefly the thought that lies behind many of John of the Cross's important words. Under each entry the meanings are explained, and further clarifications made, with John's own style, doctrine, and explanations in mind. No attempt was made to be exhaustive, neither in the import of the words nor in the references provided as mere examples. Further information may be gathered by consulting the index.

ANNIHILATION. 1. In the metaphysical sense: the termination of existence (A. 2. 5. 3).
2. In the moral, spiritual sense: the emptiness or poverty of spirit that disposes one for a greater infusion of faith, hope, and love (A. 2. 7. 8; 24. 8).

APPETITES. Generally: inordinate affective desires in which the will participates; that is, willful desires not rightly ordered to a moral or spiritual good. Thus the term is generally used in a more restricted way than might be expected (A. 1. 11. 1-3). Especially when habitual, they both impede union with God and weary, torment, darken, defile, and weaken the soul (A. 1. 6. 1; 11. 3; 12. 2-6).

APPREHENSIONS. Denote the activity and content of perception. Are distinct; sensory or spiritual; natural or supernatural. Used frequently in chapters dealing with the intellect and memory, they are contradistinguished from contemplation, which is a general, obscure knowledge given in faith (A. 2. 10. 1-4).

BEGINNERS. Representing those in the first stage of the spiritual life, they experience conversion and begin to respond to the divine call. As long as they are aware of responding to this call, they advance on their journey. Not responding, not going forward, is to go backward; but one may have only the feeling of going backward. Find motivation for denying their appetites mainly through meditation on the life of Christ (using discourse and the imagination) and through the satisfaction coming from love and consolation in the sensory part of the soul (A. 1. 12. 6; 14. 2; A. 2. 12. 5; N. 1. 1. 2-3; 8).

CHURCH. The bride and body of Christ; participates in the beauty of the Bridegroom (C. 30. 7; 36. 5). In all that regards faith and the Christian life, we must be guided by the law of Christ, who is human, and that of his

Church; for example, in regard to the articles of faith, in the use of images, and in the use of ceremonies (A. 2. 22. 7, 11; 27. 4; A. 3. 35. 3; 44. 3). God grants special graces to members of the Church for the benefit of others (A. 3. 31. 7). Pure love is the best service that one can render in the Church (C. 29. 3).

COMMUNICATION. God's communication is the loving knowledge of himself that he shares with humans (A. 2. 5. 4; 15. 2). He begins by giving it through elements that are palpable and accommodated to sense, and thus only in "morsels" (A. 2. 17. 3-5). The more spiritual a communication becomes, the more abundant it is and the less comprehensible to the senses (A. 2. 14. 8).

CONTEMPLATION. The communication of God untied to the senses, or the particular, received passively by the spirit in an attitude of faith and love, of general loving attention (A. 2. 14. 2; 15. 5; 29. 6; F. 3. 40). Also called mystical theology (A. 2. 8. 6; N. 2. 5. 1). May be referred to as infused because the soul receives it passively, just as one receives sunlight by doing no more than opening the shutters (N. 1. 10. 6; F. 3. 34, 46). Takes away the satisfaction associated with discursive prayer (N. 1. 9. 8). In accordance with its functions or effects, the adjectives purgative, illuminative, and unitive are used; the prevalence of some effects over others is what determines the use of these adjectives (N. 2. 7. 4; 23. 14). Its signs are: an inability to practice discursive meditation; a disinclination to fix the imagination on other things; the desire to remain alone in loving awareness of God without particular considerations; or in this latter case, when the contemplation is purgative, a solicitous and painful care about serving God and not turning back despite feelings of aversion or dryness in the things of God (A. 2. 13-15; N. 1. 9; F. 3. 27-67).

DETACHMENT. The equivalent of poverty of spirit, refers to a freedom from the appetites so the heart may be surrendered entirely to God in the union of faith, hope, and love (A. 1. 11. 8; A. 2. 4. 4-6; A. 3. 20. 4).

DRYNESS. A lack of satisfaction and savor in one's prayer and spiritual practices (N. 1. 8. 3). As an effect of God's communication, purifies and is discernible as purgative through the solicitude of love that accompanies it in various degrees of intensity (N. 1. 9. 3-4).

ENEMIES OF THE SOUL. 1. The world, the devil, and the flesh are the three enemies that war against the soul trying to prevent its progress on the spiritual journey (N. 2. 21. 3). The means of defending oneself against these enemies are the theological virtues: hope in struggling against the world, faith in combating the devil, and love in gaining dominion over the flesh (N. 2. 21).

2. The world represents such things as the favor of others, friends, reputation, importance, wealth, delights, and comforts (C. 3. 6).

3. The devil, usually placed second in the group, is a spiritual being that personifies evil and disguises himself as an angel of light, as good (A. 2.

11. 7; A. 3. 37. 1). In his attacks he is more difficult to understand because of his deceit and cunning (N. 2. 21. 4; Pr. 2, 20, 12).

4. The flesh is the most tenacious in the group and represents the sensory appetites and natural affections that covet against the spirit (C. 3. 10; Pr. 2).

FAITH. 1. The theological virtue that brings together, from the objective viewpoint, Christ, who is God's full revelation of himself, and, from the subjective viewpoint, the soul insofar as it adheres and responds (A. 2. 22. 3-7; C. 12. 5-6). Involves paradox: the light, the truths of God, are clouded in darkness (A. 2. 3. 4-6).

2. As subjective or personal, denotes an attitude of fidelity to the divine person, the Word, which involves the whole of one's life. Demands the exclusion of every purely human or natural criterion; excludes every support outside itself. Detached from such supports, one must be guided only by the reality that faith communicates. But this reality surpasses earthly understanding, and thus the articles of faith are dark to the intellect (A. 2. 4. 1-7; 9. 1). Insofar as faith involves the whole person, it is a living faith and moves lovingly toward God whom the articles hide, and away from reliance on particular knowledge, on supernatural visions and revelations (A. 1. 2. 3; A. 2. 8. 5-6).

3. The dark light of faith enters the soul imperceptibly insofar as one adapts to its demands (A. 2. 24. 8-9). At the end of the journey in faithfulness, the soul finds itself completely illumined, in a "highly illumined faith," and contemplates God through what becomes but a thin veil, a veil that disappears with the beatific vision (F. 3. 80; 1. 32).

FATHER (ETERNAL). Where the Son of God is hidden. The Son is his only delight and place of rest (C. 1. 3). The Son prays that where he is those whom the Father has given him will also be; there are many mansions in the Father's house (C. 39. 5; F. 1. 13). Delights to be with the children of the earth (F. 1. 15). Gentle and bountiful, he gives his Son, the splendor of his glory, as his gift to souls (F. 2. 16).

FORM. 1. Also referred to by terms such as: figure, image, species, or accident (A. 3. 13. 4). As sensory, the particular representation of some thing produced in the phantasy or imagination through which one comes to knowledge (A. 2. 8. 3); as intelligible, the object of the intellect, the particular idea (A. 2. 14. 8, 10). In contemplation one receives communications and knowledge without these forms (N. 2. 17. 3; C. 16. 10-11; F. 2. 20).

2. The nature of a thing as distinguished from matter (A. 1. 6. 2).

GIFTS. A generic designation for God's graces and favors (N. 2. 9. 9; C. 14. 2).

GLORY. Seeing God clearly and loving him; knowing the mysteries of Christ (C. 38. 5; 37. 1). The constant aspiration of the soul roused by the Holy Spirit in the state of transformation. Death is the condition for entering into it, that glory of which only a faint resemblance may be experienced in this life (F. 1. 27-28).

GOD. The central reality of the soul and of the whole world, designated also by the threefold personal name: Father, Son, and Holy Spirit (C. 1. 1; 6; F. 2. 1). Both one and three, he has his own intimate life of love and communion (A. 2. 9. 1; C. 39. 4-5). His attributes are modes of his being and self-communication (F. 3. 2-4). Is both transcendent and immanent (A. 2. 8. 3-7; 5. 3-4; C. 1. 6-12). Reveals himself and his plan for his creatures fully in Jesus Christ (A. 2. 22. 3-7). Divinizes humans, and they become God through participation (C. 22. 3-5).

HOLY SPIRIT. The third person of the blessed Trinity, the love between the Father and the Son (C. 30. 3). The inspirer of Sacred Scripture (C. pro. 1). The principal agent of sanctification (F. 3. 46). Moves and illumines the intellect (A. 2. 29. 6). Prepares one for union and brings it about (C. 20. 2; 22. 2). Teaches the bride how to love as she is loved. In the state of union the soul loves with the strength of God himself through the Holy Spirit who is given to her (C. 38. 3-4).

HOPE. 1. One of the three theological virtues, which, in its more specific function, unites the memory with God and empties it of all possessions (A. 2. 6. 1-3). To live in pure theological hope one must turn to God in loving affection, away from distinct ideas, forms, and images when they arise, in emptiness of everything rememberable. The more the memory gives up the possession of things, the more hope it has, and the more hope it has the greater will be its union with God (A. 3. 15. 1). No harm comes to this hope, though, from use of the memory in the fulfillment of one's obligations (A. 3. 15. 1). Hope also implies a "moaning" in that it keeps glory in mind and longs for the full possession of it (C. 1. 14). 2. Also, one of the four passions of the soul (A. 3. 16. 2-5).

IMAGINATION. A human power or faculty belonging to the interior sensory part of the soul and often used, without differentiation, together with the term phantasy. The power of forming material images, put to use naturally through meditation. Does not have the capacity to reach God, nor does it serve proximately as a means to union (A. 2. 12. 2-4). Must be quieted in order to enter the way of the spirit (A. 2. 14. 1; N. 1. 10. 2-6).

IMPERFECTIONS. From the viewpoint of their object, the diminutive is used: "small attachments," "little satisfactions." The problem lies not in the object but in the subject; that is, one's attachment interferes with the dynamism of love and spiritual progress. Habitual imperfections, when known, recognized, and voluntary, impede one from reaching the freedom of union (A. 1. 11. 3-4). Souls may have many also with regard to their spiritual practices and works (N. 1. 1. 2-3). Some are more to the surface; others, more deeply rooted in the spirit and less perceptible (N. 2. 2. 1). The dark night purges the soul of its habitual imperfections (N. 2. 5. 1). In the spiritual marriage, all the bride's words, thoughts, and works are of God and directed toward him without any of the former imperfections (C. 28. 7). Even after reaching this union one may fall into imperfections, but without advertence, or knowledge, or control. Of these semivoluntary imperfections it is written that the just one falls seven times a day (A. 1. 11. 3).

INTELLECT. A spiritual power or faculty for knowing, which in its ordinary functioning receives help from the external and internal senses (A. 2. 8. 4-5). The active intellect abstracts the immaterial or universal form, or species, from the sensible form provided by the interior senses and impresses it on the passive intellect. Understanding comes about through this interdependence (A. 2. 8. 4-5; C. 39. 12). No material or created thing serves the intellect as a proximate means to union with God. Only by means of faith is the intellect united with God (A. 2. 8. 1-5; 9. 1). The intellect may receive communications passively in ways different from its ordinary functioning (A. 2. 10). Mystical knowledge is given to the passive intellect (C. 39. 12).

INTERDEPENDENCE. The sense and the spirit, the senses and the intellect in the knowing process, and the cognitive and affective capacities interact and are interdependent (N. 2. 1. 1; C. 18. 7; 13. 4; F. 3. 49). The appetites increase and diminish jointly; the vices increase with the increase of any one (A. 1. 12. 5). The passions are conditioned by one another (A. 3. 16. 5). The spiritual faculties are purified separately and simultaneously (A. 3. 1. 1). The virtues grow and are perfected in the exercise of any one of them (A. 1. 12. 5).

JESUS CHRIST. God the infinite, transcendent Creator, having left some trace of who he is in creation, becomes human in Jesus Christ and reveals himself fully (C. 5. 1; A. 2. 22. 3-7). Many titles express the various aspects of this mystery; he is the Word, Master, Way, and Example; or the Beloved, Brother, Companion, and Savior. These may be reduced to Revealer and Bridegroom (A. 1. 13. 3-4; 14. 2-3; A. 2. 7; 22. 5; C. 1. 1-2; 12. 2-3). As Revealer, he makes known God the Father in that he is the word, image, wisdom, and beauty of the Father (A. 2. 22. 5; C. 5. 1-4). As Bridegroom, he is the principal lover, choosing, dignifying, and giving us gifts (C. 31. 2; 32. 4-5; 19. 6; F. 3. 24-26). The redemption and liberation of the soul is the work of Christ the Revealer and Bridegroom. Like the good shepherd, he searches for, pardons, and brings his bride back (C. 23. 1-3; 22. 1). Through the cross, he shows us the way to union and gives us the example; through it he also gives us his grace and the pledge of union (A. 2. 7. 11; C. 23. 1-6). His communication of love is the Holy Spirit (C. 39. 2-3). Thus Christ is the All (A. 2. 22. 4). In him, the one God has revealed his Trinitarian mystery, and given and done all (A. 2. 22. 5-7; C. 37).

LOVE. 1. Used most frequently in referring to the theological virtue of charity. From this perspective, is associated with the will. As such, has primacy over all other human activities (A. 3. 16. 1). It is the property of love to make the lover equal to the loved one (A. 1. 5. 1; C. 28. 1). Since what God most wants is to exalt his bride by making her his equal, he is pleased only with love (C. 28. 1). Imposes the discipline of emptying oneself for God of all inordinate attachments, of all that is not God (A. 2. 5. 7). Finds satisfaction in nothing less than God (C. 1. 14).

2. Love of neighbor increases with love of God (A. 23. 1; N. 1. 4. 7). The appetites destroy both (A. 1. 10. 4).

3. Self-love is the seeking of one's own satisfaction in preference to God (A. 2. 7. 5, 12). One overcomes it only by embracing what is difficult (Pr. 17).

MEDITATION. A discursive activity proper to beginners and built on images formed in the imagination and phantasy (A. 2. 12. 2). Serving as a remote means to union by habituating the spirit to spiritual things through the use of the senses, it empties the imagination of profane images (N. 1. 8. 3; A. 2. 12. 2-5; 13. 1). Its purpose is to acquire some knowledge and love of God (A. 2. 14. 2). Helpful for learning how to follow and imitate Christ (A. 1. 13. 3). As the acts of knowledge and love of God increase, a habit of knowing and loving God is begotten in the meditator, and the activity of meditation simplifies into a loving attention (A. 2. 14. 2). In the simplification of meditation, one begins to perceive the three signs and pass to contemplation (A. 2. 13; N. 1. 9).

MEMORY. 1. One of the three spiritual faculties of the soul, it represents a power to recall and relive what is past (A. 2. 6. 1; A. 3. 14. 2). The seat of theological hope; hope both empties it of its finite possessions and unites it with God (A. 2. 6. 1, 3).

2. The sense memory is an interior sense faculty, along with the imagination and phantasy, the archives or receptacle of all intelligible images (A. 2. 16. 2; C. 18. 7).

MORTIFICATION. A radical attitude, a putting to death of all inordinate appetites within oneself (and all actions deriving from them). One cannot find God without mortifying evil within oneself; this gets to the root of the practice of all virtues. This death is embraced out of love for Jesus Christ and patterned after his death (A. 2. 7. 5-12; A. 1. 13. 3-7).

MYSTICAL. An adjective meaning secret or hidden that at times accompanies the words "knowledge," "wisdom," and "theology." Used in this way, it is another term for contemplation (A. 2. 8. 6; N. 2. 5. 1).

NATURAL. Referring to human nature, may denote the basic human condition, the disordered state caused by sin, or the incapacity of humans to take the initiative in all that regards the order of grace (C. 3. 10; 23. 2-6; 33. 1-6; F. 3. 74). Or it may refer to the fundamental makeup and activity of the human person, which grace does not destroy but perfects (C. 8. 3; A. 3. 2. 7-8).

NIGHT. 1. In comparing contemplation to natural night, different aspects might so become the focus that the night is "dark," "tranquil," or "serene" (N. 2. 5. 1-2; C. 15. 22; 39. 12).

2. Expresses the privation of satisfaction and activity consequent on one's communion with God, who is both near and transcendent (A. 1. 2). Insofar as it refers to a privation of satisfaction or to the darkening light of faith, it has different stages and characteristics: active and passive; of the senses and of the spirit; the beginning (or twilight), the middle (or midnight), the end (or the first hints of dawn) (A. 1. 1; 2). One must pass through the dark night in order to reach union with God (A 1. 1. 1; N. 1. 7. 5). The dark night par excellence is the passive night of the spirit; the causes of its darkness and affliction are human misery and the abundance of divine light (N. 2. 3. 1; N. 2. 5. 2; F. 1. 18, 26).

NOTHING (NADA). 1. A privation of all reality (A. 1. 6. 4).

2. A reality lacking meaning and value (A. 1. 13. 11-12; F. 1. 32).

3. The reverse side (poverty of spirit, emptiness) of the theological virtues (A. 2. 6. 1; C. 34. 5-6; F. 3. 46).

4. In contemplation, "doing nothing" is a spiritual attitude of receptivity (A. 2. 12. 7-8; N. 1. 10. 1-6; F. 3. 47).

5. It may also be used as the personification of the creature when placed autonomously in opposition to God who is the "All" (A. 1. 4. 3).

PASSIONS. Also called emotions, belong, with the appetites, to the human affective (or appetitive) part (A. 3. 16. 2). The eleven classic passions defined by Aristotle can be reduced to four principal ones: joy, hope, fear, and sorrow (A. 3. 16. 6). In them, interlinked in their activity, lies one's strength. When unbridled, become the source of all vices and imperfections; when properly regulated, give rise to all the virtues (A. 3. 16. 2-5). In divine union, are alive but so transformed that God alone is their rule (C. 28. 3-5).

PERFECT. Those who have passed through the nights of purification and have reached perfection, or the full union of spiritual marriage, in which one lives only for the service of the Bridegroom and has no other manner or style than the exercise of love (A. 1. 1. 1-3; N. 2. 24; C. 28).

PHANTASY. An interior sense faculty, along with the imagination and the sense memory, that receives sense images, naturally or supernaturally, contains them within itself, and in turn presents them to the intellect (A. 2. 16. 2; 12. 3).

POVERTY (OF SPIRIT). A detachment from particular knowledge, earthly and heavenly, and from satisfaction and pleasure. The reality indicated by other expressions such as purity of heart, emptiness (void), night, nothing (nada), detachment, and nakedness (denudation) (A. 2. 24. 8-9; F. 3. 46). The negative aspect of the theological virtues, which bring it about (A. 2. 6. 1; 7. 5). Those who have attained it are blessed; only they find complete satisfaction of heart (C. 1. 14; N. 2. 8. 5).

PRAYER. Communion with God, requiring a will that is with him and a mind set on him (A. 3. 36. 1; C. 1. 13). Its aims should be what is more pleasing to God (A. 3. 44. 1-2). Objects and places should be means to help one pray in the living temple, which is interior recollection (A. 3. 40. 1). All the prayers of the Church are reducible to the Our Father (A. 3. 44. 4). May be meditative or contemplative (A. 2. 12; 14). In union, it becomes wholly the exercise of love (C. 28. 9).

PROFICIENTS. Persons who are in the second of the three stages of the spiritual journey, or the illuminative way. Their prayer is contemplative (N. 1. 1. 1). May experience imaginative visions and ecstasies (A. 2. 16. 3; N. 2. 1. 1; 2. 3; C. 13. 6). Suffer from physical, psychological, and moral limitations (N. 2. 1. 2; 5. 6); from aridity, darkness, and longings of love (N. 2. 5. 2; 6. 4; 11. 7). May know deep quiet, peace, and love in God's presence (N. 2. 17. 3-6; F. 3. 49-54). Bring to prayer no other support than faith, hope, and love (S. 119).

PURIFICATION. The process by which one eliminates, through the theological virtues, all that is contrary to receiving into one's own life the fullness of God's life (A. 2. 6. 1-7). Both a disposition for and an effect of union (N. 2. 10; F. 1. 22-23). From the perspective of the source of a privation, it may be either active or passive (A. 1. 13. 1). The expression purgative way is applied to beginners (C. theme. 2); but the work of purification is brought to completion especially through the passive spiritual suffering of the dark night, which belongs to the illuminative way (N. 1. 14. 1; N. 2. 3). The entire spiritual journey, however, is purifying, comprising God's communication and the human person's efforts to respond (A. 1. 2. 1).

SENSE. In the plural (senses), refers to the bodily faculties or powers that have corporeal things as their objects (A. 2. 17. 4). The exterior senses are: sight, hearing, smell, taste, and touch (A. 1. 3. 2). The interior senses that are mentioned include the phantasy, imagination, and sense memory (A. 1. 12. C. 18. 7). The sense, or sensory part, designates all the faculties taken together (interior and exterior), or the whole person under the rule of the values perceived by them (C. 18. 7-8). It comes into play both in the natural and supernatural realm. God cannot be grasped by the senses (F. 3. 73-74). They are not capable of spiritual things (A. 2. 11. 2). As a part of the soul, the lower, inferior, or exterior part (C. 18. 7).

SOUL. Frequently used in referring to the whole person (a soul or souls) with an emphasis on the spiritual dimension (A. 1. 1. 1-3; C. 19. 2). A beautiful image of God, where God dwells (A. 1. 9. 1; F. 4. 14). Comprises two main parts: sense and spirit; but the emphasis placed on the purification of these two parts does not seek to establish a dichotomy in the human being (N. 2. 3. 1-2; C. 13. 3-6). In its operations it has a cognitive and an affective, or appetitive, dimension (C. 28. 3-5). Its deep center or depth may refer either to its substance or to the limit to which the active or receptive capacity of the individual can reach (F. 1. 9-13; 4. 4). In accommodation to the bridal symbolism, is the bride; Christ, the Bride-groom (C. 22. 1).

SPIRIT. 1. The higher, superior, or interior part of the soul in contradistinction to the sensory part (A. 3. 26. 4). In it reside the three faculties of intellect, memory, and will (C. 18. 4-8; A. 2. 6. 1, 6). Is the part that communes with God (A. 3. 26. 4).

2. It may also refer to what is most profound about something, its substance or truth (A. 2. 19. 5); the loving knowledge or participation in the Holy Spirit (F. 3. 8, 54). Pure spirit refers to what has no ties to the material (N. 2. 17. 4; F. 3. 30).

3. The Holy Spirit (C. 13. 4).

SPIRITUAL BETROTHAL. 1. Also called spiritual espousal, it is a symbolic term for an elevated degree of union that takes place in the illuminative way (C. theme. 2; 14. 2). In it there is a fluctuating between the feeling of God's nearness, the sweetness of his communication, and the experience both of his absence and of other painful trials of purification by which the sensory part is gradually accommodated to the spirit (C. 13. 1-2; 15. 30). The coming to completion of the espousal brought about by Christ through the cross and baptism (C. 23. 5-6).

2. Sometimes used to refer to a full union of love, like the spiritual marriage (N. 2. 24. 3; C. 27. 8).

SPIRITUAL DIRECTOR. Also called spiritual father, master, or guide, the one freely chosen as a guide on the spiritual journey (F. 3. 30). Directors can do much harm if they do not know God's ways of leading souls from the lowest and most exterior to the highest and most interior (F. 3. 44). Should have learning, discretion, and experience (F. 3. 30). They must reflect that the principal guide is the Holy Spirit and they are instruments for leading souls according to the spirit God gives each one (F. 3. 46).

SPIRITUAL MARRIAGE. A symbolic expression with roots in the Bible designating full union with God or transformation in God, the highest state attainable in this life (C. 12. 8). A mutual, total surrender of love between the soul and God (C. 22. 3). This union is permanent in the substance. In frequent actual unions, God communicates his secrets and love to the soul in a direct manner (C. 26. 11; F. 4. 14-15). She corresponds fully, able to love as much as she is loved (that is, with all her being), affectively and effectively (through works of service) (C. 38. 3; 36. 4; 28. 1). Being so united with Christ she enters into and shares the intimate life of the Blessed Trinity (C. 39. 3; F. 2. 1).

SPIRITUAL SENSES. Capacities of the spirit analogous to those of the senses; receive spiritual visions, locutions, and feelings (fragrances, tastes, and touches) (A. 2. 23; C. 14. 9-18).

STAGES. States, degrees, or ways of spiritual growth or development. The main classifications are: beginners, proficients, and perfect; or purgative, illuminative, and unitive ways (C. theme, 1-2; 22. 3; N. 1. 1. 1; N. 2. 1;). Having only a relative value, these classifications help to explain the doctrine in a structured way (A. 2. 17. 4; N. 2. 18. 3). God's ways are many, and he leads souls along different paths so one spirit will rarely be found like another in even half its method of procedure, though there will always be similarities (F. 3. 46, 59-61).

SUBSTANCE. 1. In general, that which is most inward, deep, and authentic in God, persons, and things (A. 2. 6. 7; A. 3. 29. 2). Used in contradistinction both to the accidents (species, images) of knowledge and to the faculties (A. 3. 13. 4). The substance of the soul is a deep, secret region that escapes ordinary psychological observation (F. 4. 14-16). 2. The essence of an existing being (A. 2. 24. 5; F. 2. 34).

SUPERNATURAL. In general, that which is above the natural (A. 2. 4. 2). May refer to the realm of the mystery of God, of Christ, his grace and gifts of sanctification (A. 2. 5. 3-5). May apply to the manner or way in which God communicates his graces either to the senses or to the spirit, that is, in a way beyond one's natural powers (A. 2. 10). May refer to the being of a person in grace (A. 2. 5. 4). May designate an infused activity, one experienced passively (F. 3. 75). May also refer to apprehensions experienced passively but without God as their source (A. 2. 16. 4).

THEOLOGICAL VIRTUES. Faith, hope and love (charity); working interdependently and being the likeness of God, they are the means that bridge the infinite distance between God and his creatures. Thus the only proper and proximate means to union with him (A. 2. 6. 1; 24. 8). Primarily passive, forms of God's self-communication: transcendent truth, generous love, possession of himself (C. 12. 1-8; A. 2. 6. 1-5). As modes by which God is already communicating himself, are more than mere preparations for a later communion (N. 2. 4. 1-2). Capable of using all kinds of means and at the same time of making them relative, urge one, in their dynamics, toward immediate union with God, a union that is personal and reflects God's transcendence (A. 3. 15. 1-2).

TOUCHES. Communications from God perceived passively by the spirit in ways analogous to the sense experience of touch (A. 2. 23. 1-3; 32. 2-3). Imply immediacy and intimacy in the communication and may be granted either to the substance of the soul or to the intellect or the will (C. 14. 12-16; A. 2. 26. 3-10; 32. 2).

TRANSFORMATION. A term for union, implies a change in form by which a soul receives a new form, God's likeness in its being and activity, while remaining different from God in its nature (A. 2. 5. 4). It is the human person who is transformed in God, and not vice versa (A. 2. 5. 5). The life of one transformed is Christ's life (C. 12. 8).

UNION. 1. Natural union is that by which God is present to creatures preserving them in being. 2. Supernatural union is the goal of the spiritual journey, a union of likeness brought about through love (A. 2. 5. 3). In it all the cognitive-affective activity bears a full likeness to God's activity, or life, with nothing repugnant to it (F. 2. 34; A. 2. 5. 3-4). This complete elevation and transformation of a person's activity is wrought by means of the theological virtues; one is then habitually moved by the Holy Spirit (A. 2. 6. 1; A. 3. 2. 8-10). The actual unions of the faculties (intense, lively moments of fire and love) are transitory (F. 1. 3-4; C. 26. 11). The habitual union of the faculties (a more subdued state) is permanent, as is also the actual union in the substance (A. 2. 5. 2; F. 4. 14-15). In order to reach this permanent union in the substance and the faculties one must pass through the nights (A. 1. 1. 1-3; A. 3. 2. 14).

VIRTUE. 1. A capacity or power (C. 6. 1; F. 4. 4).

2. A good operative habit; as a "moral good" producing salutary work, it merits esteem (A. 3. 27. 1-3). But the Christian must transcend the merely human value of virtue, and measure its worth by the love of God with which it is informed (A. 3. 27. 4). Destroys vices; virtues grow together; are acquired and strengthened through trial and adversity in the following of Christ (A. 1. 12. 5-6; A. 2. 7. 8). Experienced as graces, gifts, or favors received, they adorn the soul and make it beautiful (C. 17. 5-8). The work of both God and the soul, the work of love (C. 24. 3, 6; 30. 6). In beginners, virtues are weak and imperfect; in proficients, they are strong and solid; in the perfect they are heroic (N. 1. 1. 1-3; 13. 5; C. 20. 3).

WILL. A spiritual faculty of the soul that moves and governs the other two faculties and the entire cognitive-affective activity (A. 3. 16. 1). Emptied, purified, and united with God through love (A. 2. 6. 1, 4). Christian self-denial is a work of the will (A. 2. 7. 6). The will's operation is distinct from its feelings; by its operation, which is love, the will is united with God and terminates in him, not by delightful feelings (L. 13).

WISDOM. The loving knowledge of God both in himself and in the salvific order; the antithesis of the wisdom of the world (C. 26. 13-17; 37. 1-3). In Christ lie hidden all the treasures of the divine wisdom (C. 37. 4). Is simple, secret, incomprehensible, ineffable (N. 2. 17. 3-4); never given without love (N. 2. 12. 2). Received through love, silence, and mortification (S. 109).

GENERAL INDEX

hensions, 239; free of, 456; not a, 288; of creatures, 169, 653; of spiritual directors, 116, 695, 698, 745; to faith, 183; to freedom, 450, 654; to God's anointings, 684, 689; to the soul, 117, 142-43, 178, 209, 311, 333, 336, 428, 508; to union with God, 142, 168, 189, 239, 252, 273, 279, 283, 288, 311, 429, 653-54

Holy Spirit, 89, 94, 115, 128, 217, 220, 256-78 passim, 309, 436, 444, 470, 516, 523, 543-75 passim, 591, 597, 617, 619, 622-23, 627, 656-726 passim, 741; flame of love, 641-43, 645-53, 657; fruits of, 391; reborn in, 164; soul's principal guide, 691; unctions of, 665, 683, 685, 689, 699, 701; worthy temple of, 308 See also **Spirit (of God), Trinity.**

Honey, 87, 246, 565, 583, 613, 688

Honor, 89, 296, 319; devil's, 731; of God, 92, 148, 219, 221, 292, 294, 303, 317-18, 334, 338, 345, 506, 525, 728-29; of the soul, 261, 603-4; worldly, 606, 726

Hope, 94, 225, 275, 280, 301, 317, 365, 380, 410, 415, 421, 443, 450, 480, 483, 507, 602, 652, 682, 752, 754, 756, 762; act of, 280; and memory, 166-67, 268, 274, 279, 283-85, 290-91, 448-49; calmed in dark night, 392; passion of, 149, 226, 292-94, 392, 553-56, 580, 585; signified by color green, 446-48; virtue of, 166-67, 243, 267, 282, 291, 329, 409, 446, 489. See also **Virtues (theological).**

Horror(s), 450, 532-33, 540, 675; devil disturbs soul with, 451, 453, 540, 555, 700; of the night, 393, 429-30

House, 118-19, 123, 152-55, 297, 360-61, 392, 400, 428-30, 434, 454-55, 491, 540, 559, 574, 604, 608, 652-53, 691-92, 698, 709, 713, 722, 738-39, 755-58; Father's, 526, 645

Human respect, 88, 90, 319, 585, 590, 598

Humanity of Christ, 186, 529, 616, 618

Humility, 88, 93, 96-97, 151, 172, 181, 183, 208, 210-11, 215, 234-66 passim, 280-82, 289, 308, 312, 322, 362-65, 370-73, 380, 385, 388-89, 394, 439, 444, 484, 491, 493, 528, 581, 676, 723, 726, 730-31, 741, 751, 754, 758; least act of, 282; of Christ, 216, 698; of God, 581

Humor(s), 91, 164, 190, 368-69, 377-80, 417, 650

Hundredfold, 303, 314, 666

Hunger, 131-34; for God, 93, 420, 427, 443, 498, 506, 681, 702, 748

Idleness, 188, 193, 196, 199, 379, 381-82,

505, 588, 687-95, 701

Idolatry, 300

Ignorance, 122, 125, 127, 136-37, 204, 232, 333-34, 336, 344, 384, 386, 401, 422, 438, 533, 577-78, 613; soul does not see its, 702

Illumination(s), 298, 423; in the dark night, 158-59, 358, 413, 417, 427; of the soul, 135, 156, 164-65, 198, 242, 249, 258, 268, 271, 387, 408, 422-23, 436, 438, 505-3, 509, 534, 557, 601, 627, 644, 646, 650, 673, 677, 681, 702-3

Illuminative Way, 392, 477, 522 See also **Proficients.**

Image(s), 129, 139, 157-58, 175-206 passim, 239, 242-43, 253, 269-91 passim, 319, 331-41, 365-66, 393, 436-37, 533, 541, 548, 609, 626, 682, 713; devil produces, 538-39; God's, 87, 135, 138, 496-97, 510, 514-15, 517-18, 534, 623, 680, 691; of fruition, 532, 707

Imagination, 160-61, 166, 175-206 passim, 239, 254, 269, 283-85, 309, 312, 330, 335, 380-81, 393, 395, 430, 437, 492, 538-39, 548, 553, 660, 685, 695, 701; gate of the soul, 200; God not grasped by, 309-10, 695k; wanderings of, 193, 553

Imitation, of Christ, 85, 148, 172, 259, 481, 728, 760

Impatience, 370, 391; impatient love, 427, 501, 505, 657, 681-82

Impediment(s), 124, 131, 135-36, 179, 182, 199, 204, 239, 243-44, 251, 266, 276-77, 286, 291, 314, 340, 348, 361, 382, 426, 547, 553, 562, 692, 699, 704; to union, 142-43, 161, 239, 243-44, 273, 280, 283, 653-54, 748

Imperfection(s), 94, 96, 118, 140, 144-46, 154, 164, 211, 273-76, 306, 310, 325, 333, 337, 5513, 551-52, 554, 573, 580, 582, 594, 648-50, 697, 721, 724, 726, 728, 754; divine touch removes, 247; habitual, 94, 143, 163, 396-97, 401, 578, 585-86, 669; hinder, 203, 208-9; inadvertent, 142; natural, 553, 567, 580; of beginners, 148, 361-77, 384-86; of pride, 388; of proficients, 396-435 passim; purged, 389-94, 625, 651; source of, 293; spirit of, 117, 150, 154

Impurity, 86, 257, 274, 276-77, 308, 312, 314, 367-69, 401-3, 408, 431-32, 563, 642, 650-51, 657

Inclination(s), 89-90, 149, 170, 190, 212, 233, 242-43, 250, 338, 340, 342, 365, 429, 431, 493, 539, 585, 699; become divine, 670-71; natural, 212, 337, 343, 485, 653;

SCRIPTURAL INDEX